ANNOTATED

CONSTITUTION

OF THE

UNITED STATES

BY

A. J. BAKER

OF THE IOWA BAR

CHICAGO

CALLAGHAN AND COMPANY

1891

STATE JOURNAL PRINTING COMPANY,
PRINTERS AND STEREOTYPERS,
MADISON, WIS.

PREFACE.

The purpose of this edition of the Constitution of the United States is to furnish to the bar of the Nation a complete digest of the decisions of the Supreme Court of the United States, wherein is called in question any of the provisions of the Constitution, arranged under the headings of the several articles, sections and clauses upon which the decisions are predicated, thereby making a complete and ready reference to the case, and giving the exact point decided in each case, so as to save the labor of searching through numerous and long opinions to find the exact question desired.

Persons unfamiliar with litigation would naturally and ordinarily suppose that after more than a century of judicial history these constitutional questions would all be settled and determined, so that they would rarely arise in litigated cases Experience teaches a different lesson; and the facts are that never during the history of the Nation were there so many grave constitutional questions brought before the courts as during the last decade; and they are still arising, and will continue to arise under our increasing wealth and commerce.

The multiplication of corporations in the conduct of all lines of business, and the diversity of operations attending them, the extending and consolidating of the numerous lines of railroad, and the transportation of freight and passengers interstate thereon; the privileges and exemptions granted by states and municipalities to corporate bodies, and the questions of contractual obligations arising therein, the questions growing out of the late civil war and the reconstruction of the states in rebellion, together with the three last amendments, are some of the causes which have brought and will continue to bring these great fundamental questions before the courts.

The compiler therefore places this annotated copy of the Constitution before the profession, with the confident belief that it will be a means of lightening to a great extent the labor of an already overworked profession.

A. J. BAKER.

DES MOINES IOWA,
July, 1891

TABLE OF CASES.

[The black figures refer to paragraphs, the other figures are to pages]

Abbott, Hanger v. (6 Wall 535), **14,** 51

Ableman v. Booth (21 How 506), **10,** 3, **79,** 146, **12,** 172, **5,** 160

Achison v Huddleson (12 How 293), **30,** 175, **25,** 100

Adams v. Palmer (51 Me. 480), **17,** 167.

Adams v. Crittenden (106 U S 576) **23, 26,** 139

Adams v Nashville (95 U S 19), **15,** 173

Ætna Ins Co., Warren Mfg Co v. (3 Paine, 501), **22,** 154, **18,** 159

Ah Fong, In re (3 Sawyer, 144), **35,** 215

Aikin, Ouachita Packet Co v. (121 U S 444), **4,** 104

Alabama, Boyd v (94 U.S 645), **203,** 92

Alabama, Smith v. (124 U S 465), **168,** 40.

Alabama, Nashville & C R R v (128 U S. 96), **133,** 36, **53,** 218.

Alabama, Pace v (106 U. S 583), **79,** 222.

Alabama, Western Union Tel Co v (132 U S 472), **94, 95,** 31

Alabama v Georgia (23 How 505), **17,** 138

Aldermen, Austin v. (7 Wall. 694), **6,** 229

Alexander, Downham v. (10 Wall 173), **57,** 28

Alexander's, Mrs, Cotton (2 Wall 417), **9,** 231, **15,** 51.

Allen v B & O. R. R Co (114 U. S 311), **13,** 203, **224,** 95.

Alling, Sherlock v (93 U S. 99), **101,** 32; **120,** 34; **124,** 35

Almy v. California (24 How 169), **4,** **5,** 103

American Ins Co v. Canter (1 Pet. 511), **16,** 51, **18,** 165; **9, 13,** 166, **5, 6,** 120, **23, 29,** 124

American Transportation Co, Moore v (24 How 1), **149,** 38

Ames v Kansas (11 U. S. 449). **2,** 136, **11,** 137

Amoskeag Mfg Co, Head v (113 U S 9), **95,** 224.

Amy v Barkholder (11 Wall 136), **85,** 131

Amy, Galena v. (5 Wall 705), **175,** 88

Amy v Shelby Taxing Dist. (114 U S 387), **184,** 89

Anderson v Dunn (6 Wheat 204), **1,** 11, **4,** 12, **1,** 46; **1, 2,** 56

Anderson, McMillen v. (95 U S 37), **59,** 219, **43,** 216, **44,** 217.

Anderson v Terry (95 U S 628), **50,** 69

Anderson v. Terry (95 U S. 634), **52,** 70

Anderson v United States (10 Biss 283), **8,** 228

Anderson v Van Brocken (117 U S. 151), **12,** 196

Andover Jenkins v. (103 Mass. 94), **18,** 197

Angell, United States v. (11 Fed. Rep. 34), **15,** 17

Angelo De Giacoma, *In re* (12 Blatch. 101), **19,** 65

Ankrim, *In re* (3 McLean, 285), **4,** 14.

Antoni v Greenhow (107 U S 769), **225, 226,** 96, **81,** 73.

Appeal Tax Court, Bonaparte v (104 U S 592), **20,** 154.

Appeal Tax Court, Gordon v. (3 How 133), **126,** 80

Arjona, United States v. (120 U S 479), **2,** 46, **4,** 49

Arkansas, Beers v (20 How 527), **81,** 78, **21,** 204, **23,** 205.

Arkansas, Curran v (15 How 309) **6,** 64, **11,** 64, **82,** 74, **217,** 95, **32,** 207

Arkansas, Bank of Washington v. (20 How. 530), **4,** 201

Arkansas Cattle Co. v. Mann (130 U S 69) **20,** 193

Armstrong v Treas of Athens (16 Pet. 281), **96,** 133, **155,** 85

Armstrong v. United States (13 Wall 154), **15,** 114, **23,** 115

Armas, New Orleans v. (9 Pet 224), **4,** 121

Arnold v United States (9 Cranch 119), **4,** 14

Arredondo, United States v (6 Pet 736), **88,** 74

Arrowsmith v Harmoning (118 U. S 194), **70,** 221

Asher v. Texas (128 U S 129), **91,** 30

Aspinwall v Commissioners (22 How 364), **89,** 75

Assessors, Van Allen v. (3 Wall. 537) **6, 7,** 18

Atchison, etc R. R. v. Kansas Pac R R (112 U S 414), **21,** 139

Athens Armory, United States v (7 Pet 160), **20,** 114

Atlantic & Gulf R R. v. Georgia (98 U. S 359), **162,** 86

Augusta, Home Ins Co v (93 U. S. 116), **46,** 142, **154,** 85

Augusta, Williams v (4 Ga. 509), **7,** 148

Austin v Aldermen (7 Wall 694), **6,** 229

Austin, Low v (13 Wall 229), **13,** 104, **1,** 202.

Avegno v. Schmidt (113 U. S. 293), **2,** 151.

Ayers, In re (123 U. S 500), **7, 8,** 202, **12,** 203, **17,** 204; **23,** 205, **28,** 206, **226,** 96, **81,** 73.

Babcock v Weston (1 Gall. 168), **19,** 45

Bacon v. Howard (20 How. 22), **31,** 198.

Bacon, Otis v. (7 Cranch, 589), **3,** 112

Badger, United States v (16 Fed Rep. 116), **1,** 4.

Bailey, United States v (1 McLean, 234), **1,** 20; **138,** 86

Bailey, Electors v. (Cl. & H 411), **2,** 5

Bailey v Maguire (22 Wall 215), **135,** 81.

Bailey v Milner (1 Abb (U S) 261), **15,** 65.

Bain, Ex parte (121 U S 1), **39,** 187

Bainbridge, United States v (1 Mason, 71), **2,** 52, **3,** 53

Baiz, In re (135 U. S 403), **11,** 116, **20,** 123

Baldwin v Bank of Newberry (1 Wall 239), **17,** 45

Baldwin v Hale (1 Wall 223), **14,** 44, **17, 19,** 45, **43,** 199

Baldwin, Railroad Co v (103 U S 426), **14,** 167

Baldwin v Franks (120 U S 678), **22,** 174, **14,** 212, **7,** 229.

Baldwin, Newberry v (117 U S. 201), **18,** 45

Baldwin v. Payne (6 How 301) **105,** 77

Baldwin v. Stark (107 U. S. 463), **52,** 143

Baldwin St Jo & Den. R R. v. (103 U. S 426), **32,** 174

Baliff v. Tipping (2 Cranch, 406), **115,** 135

Ball, Kimmish v (129 U. S. 217), **170,** 40, **13,** 158

Ballon Gassies v. (6 Pet. 761), **1,** 56, **10,** 44.

Baltimore, Barron v. (7 Pet. 243), **1**, 59, **1**, 194, **52**, 189, **1**, 182

Baltimore, Guy v. (100 U. S. 434), **72**, 28

Baltimore & Susquehannah R. R. Co. v. Nesbit (10 How. 395), **87**, 74.

B. & O. R. R. Co., Allen v. (114 U. S. 311), **13**, 203

B. & O. R. R. Co., Cully v. (1 Hughes, 536), **17**, 212

B. & O. R. R. Co. v. Harris (12 Wall. 65), **61**, 128, **46**, **47**, 200.

B. & O. R. R. Co., Marshall v. (16 How. 314), **56**, **58**, **61**, 128

B. & O. R. R. v. Maryland (20 Wall. 643), **40**, 141, **44**, 142

B. & O. R. R., Maryland v. (3 How. 534), **90**, 75

Bank of Augusta v. Earle (13 Pet. 519), **53**, 127; **18**, 159

Bank of Alabama, Darrington v. (13 How. 12), **32**, 207, **6**, 64

Bank of Alabama v. Dalton (9 How. 522), **21**, 154.

Bank v. Buckingham's Ex'r (5 How. 317), **55**, 144

Bank of Columbia v. Okely (4 Wheat. 235), **14**, 193

Bank of Commerce v. New York (2 Black. 620), **1**, 170, **5**, 171, **4**, 57

Bank of Kentucky, Briscoe v. (11 Pet. 324), **32**, 207, **2**, 63, **4**, **7**, **8**, **11**, 64

Bank of Veazie, Fenno v. (8 Wall. 533), **3**, 6

Bank, Osborn v. (9 Wheat. 738), **4**, 57, **2**, 121; **11**, 202

Bank v. Supervisors (7 Wall. 26), **5**, 18

Bank of Washington v. Arkansas (20 How. 530), **4**, 201.

Bank v. Knoop (16 How. 369), **5**, 201, **69**, 130

Bank v. Skelly (1 Black, 436), **5**, 201; **39**, 141

Bank v. Debolt (18 How. 380), **5**, 201, **69**, 130

Bank v. Horn (17 How. 157), **78**, 131.

Bank of Hamilton v. Dudley (2 Pet. 492), **12**, 192

Bank v. Smith (6 Wheat. 131), **14**, 15, **221**, 95

Bank, Briscoe v. (11 Pet. 257), **1**, 16

Bank, Breithaupt v. (1 Pet. 238), **52**, 127.

Bank, Sample v. (1 Woods, 523), **52**, 70

Bank v. Sharp (6 How. 301–327), **39**, 68, **105**, 77

Bank v. McVeigh (98 U. S. 332), **238**, 98.

Bank Tax Cases (3 Wall. 573), **14**, 196

Bank of United States v. Deveaux (5 Cranch, 61), **50**, **53**, 127

Bank of United States v. Planters' Bank (9 Wheat. 907), **31**, 206

Bank of United States v. Halstead (10 Wheat. 51), **92**, 132.

Barber, Minnesota v. (136 U. S. 314), **20**, 105.

Barbier v. Connolly (113 U. S. 27), **67**, 221, **90**, 224, **38**, 325

Barbour v. Barton (104 U. S. 126), **2**, 191

Barclay, St. Luke's Hospital v. (3 Blatch. 268), **2**, 136; **11**, 137

Barkholder, Amy v. (11 Wall. 136), **85**, 131.

Barnard, Clark v. (108 U. S. 436), **19**, 204.

Barney, Gardner v. (6 Wall. 499), **1**, 14.

Barney v. Haskins (15 Pet. 457), **52**, 70

Barney v. McCreary (Cl. & H. 176) **1**, 8

Barrett v. Holmes (102 U. S. 651) **49**, 69

Barron v. Mayor of Baltimore (7 Pet. 243), **1**, 59, **5**, 2, **1**, 182, **1**, 194, **52**, 189

Barron v. Burnside (121 U. S. 126), **20**, **21**, 159, **68**, 129

Barry, Gunn v. (15 Wall. 610), **191**, 91.

Bartemeyer v Iowa (18 Wall 129), 22, 213, 26, 214
Barton v. Barbour (104 U S 126), 2, 191.
Barton, Florentine v (2 Wall. 216), 82, 74.
Bas v Tingy (4 Dall. 37), 3, 5, 50; 9, 11, 12, 51.
Bates v Clark (95 U S 204), 9, 202
Bazadone, Clarke v. (1 Cranch, 212), 24, 139
Beason, Davis v. (133 U S. 333), 5, 179
Beaty v Lessee of Knowler (4 Pet. 165) 88, 79
Beckwith, Minneapolis R'y Co. v (129 U S 26), 64, 220, 89, 229
Beckwith, Mt. Pleasant v (100 U S. 514), 231, 97
Bedford, Parsons v. (3 Pet. 433), 1, 2, 191.
Bedley, Green v (8 Wheat. 1), 14, 206
Beebe, Hallett v. (13 How 25), 10, 166
Beer Co. v. Massachusetts (97 U S 25), 198, 91, 26, 214; 26, 198
Beers v. Arkansas (20 How. 527), 81, 73, 21, 204, 23, 205
Beers v Houghton (9 Pet. 359), 44, 69 178, 88.
Beers, Wabash & Erie Canal Co v (2 Black, 448), 216, 95.
Beidelman, Dow v (125 U S 680). 58, 219, 91, 224.
Bell's Gap R. R. Co v Pennsylvania (134 U S. 232), 86, 223.
Benedict, Williams v (8 How 107), 78, 131
Benner v Porter (9 How 235), 6, 120, 9, 166
Bennett, Denny v. (128 U. S 489), 19, 45, 82, 74
Bergen, In re (2 Hughes, 517), 92, 224.
Berthold v McDonald (22 How 334), 36, 141.
Bethell v. Demaret (10 Wall. 537), 64, 144, 84, 147, 28, 234.
Bevans, United States v (3 Wheat. 336), 27, 28, 124, 2, 53.
Biddle, Greene v (8 Wheat. 1), 82, 74, 178, 88, 212, 94
Bigelow v Forrest (9 Wall. 339) 23, 115, 2, 151.
Bigelow v N. J R. R. Co (Book 16, L. C. Ed. U S. Sup Ct. Rep 799), 50, 25
Billings, Providence Bank v. (4 Pet 415), 88, 74, 120, 79, 142, 82 150, 84.
Binghamton Bridge, Chenango Bridge v (3 Wall 51), 116, 79.
Bird v Commonwealth (12 Mass. 442). 120, 79
Bissell v City of Jeffersonville (24 How 287), 215, 94
Black Bird Creek Marsh Willson v (2 Pet 245), 17, 21, 63, 27, 102, 32
Blaine, Stewart v (1 MacArthur, 453), 2, 11
Blake, Loughborough v. (5 Wheat 317). 1, 6, 1, 7, 16, 9, 55
Blake, Winona & C R. R. Co v (94 U S 180), 102, 32, 161, 39
Blanchard v Sprague (2 Story, 164, S. C 3 Sumn 535), 3, 48
Bland v Humphries (2 How 9), 81, 131
Bledsoe's Case (Cl & H 869), 1, 7
Bloomer v Stolley (5 McLean, 165) 36, 68
Blount v Walker (134 U S 607), 34, 156
Blount v. Windley (95 U S 173), 109, 78
Board of Comm'rs, Mitchell v. (91 U S. 206). 5, 18
Board of Liquidation, Durkee v. (103 U S 646), 193, 91
Board of Liquidation, Guaranty Co v. (105 U S 622), 240, 99
Board of Liquidation v McComb (92 U. S 531), 13, 203.
Board of Pub Works v. Columbia College (17 Wall. 521), 27, 155

Board of Wardens v Cooley (12 How 299), **14, 17**, **5, 13**, 20, **43**, 21, **63**, 27, **102**, 32, **16**, 107
Board of Works, Cooper v (14 C B (N S) 180), **44**, 217.
Boardman, Hope Ins. Co v. (5 Cranch, 57), **49**, 127
Bocock, Dugger v (104 U S. 596), **238**, 98
Bogart, *In re* (2 Sawy 396), clause 11, 53 **55**, 189
Boggs v Mining Co. (3 Wall. 304), **82**, 147
Bollman, Ex parte (4 Cranch, 75) **74, 78**, 146, **4, 17**, 149; **1**, 180, **10**, 60, **11**, 61
Bonaparte v Appeal Tax Court (104 U S 592), **20**, 154.
Boom Co v Patterson (98 U S 403), **59**, 219
Booth, Ableman v (21 How 506), **10**, 3, **79**, 146, **5**, 160, **12**, 172.
Booth, United States v (21 How 506) **33, 34, 35**, 234, **6**, 60, **5**, 160
Borden, Luther v (7 How 48), **2**, 112, **9**, 60, **1, 2, 3**, 168, **5**, 181, **45**, 200, **4**, 229
Boreme, Little v (2 Cranch, 170), **3**, 112
Borer v. Chapman (119 U. S 587) **15**, 151
Borger, United States v. (19 Blatchf 250), **4**, 148
Börs v Preston (111 U. S 252), **2**, 136, **11**, 137
Boston Steamship Co, Butler v (130 U. S 527), **37**, 235
Bosworth, Ill Cent R. R v (133 U S 92) **1, 4**, 151
Botiller v. Dominguez (130 U. S 238), **23**, 174
Boutwell, United States v (17 Wall 604), **13**, 203.
Bowerbank, Hodgson & Thompson v (5 Cranch, 303), **118**, 135
Bowman v C. & N W R y Co (125 U S 465), **101**, 32, **130**, 36
Boyce v Tabb (18 Wall. 546), **8**, 209.
Boyd Ex parte (105 U S 647) **93**, 132
Boyd v Alabama (99 U S 645), **203**, 92
Boyd v. United States (116 U S 616), **4**, 181, **40**, 187
Boyer v Boyer (113 U. S 689), **17, 19**, 173
Boyle v Zacharie (2 Pet. 635), **14**, 11; **19**, 15, **45**, 69
Boynton v Ball (121 U S 457), **10**, 153
Bradley v Illinois (4 Wall 459) **2**, 16; **6**, 18
Bradwell v State (16 Wall 130), **6**, 157, **27**, 214
Brailsford, Georgia v (2 Dall 401), **2**, 201.
Branch, Charleston v (15 Wall. 470), **10**, 195, **15**, 196
Branch v Charleston (92 U S 697), note, p. 87.
Branch Tomlinson v (15 Wall 460), **10**, 195, **15, 16**, 196, **150**, 84, note, p 87
Branch Bank of Mobile, Crawford v. (7 How 279), **64**, 71
Brashear v Mason (6 How 92), **5**, 136
Breedlove, Gwinn v (2 How 29) **6**, 46
Breedlove v Nicolet (7 Pet 413), **117**, 135
Breithaupt v Bank (1 Pet. 238), **52**, 127
Breitting, United States v (20 How 252), **76**, 130
Bridge Proprietors v Hoboken Land & Imp Co (1 Wall 116) **96**, 133, **60**, 141, **113, 114**, 78
Bridge Co v United States (105 U S 491), **3**, 164
Bridge Co, Cardwell v (113 U. S 205). **126**, 35
Brig Martha Washington (1 Cliff 463), **16**, 202, **101**, 32
Briscoe v Bank of Kentucky (11 Pet. 256) **1**, 46. **2**, 63, **4, 7, 8, 11**, 64, **32**, 207.

Britton v Nat. Bank (105 U. S 322), **18**, 137
Broadnax v Suydam (14 Pet 67), **14**, 44, **17**, 45 **75**, 130, **77**, 131.
Broadwell, Lewis v (3 McLean, 569), **52**, 70
Broderick v. Magraw (8 Wall 639), **3**, 46
Bronson v Kinzie (1 How 311) **41**, 68, **72**, 72, **178**, 88, **58**, **59**, 70
Bronson v Kimpton (8 Wall. 444), **12**, 153
Bronson v Rhodes (4 Wall. 229), **12**, 153
Brown, Wm., Ex parte (5 Cranch 554), **3**, 53.
Brown, Lathrop v (1 Woods, 474), **62**, 71.
Brown v Atwell (92 U S 327) **47**, 142.
Brown v Colorado (106 U S. 95), **241**, 99 **70**, 145
Brown v. Houston (114 U S 622), **80**, 28 29, **10**, 103; **12**, 104; **126**, 35, **135**, 36
Brown v. Maryland (12 Wheat. 455), **1**, 1, **103**, 32. **173**, 41 **13**, **17**, 104, **1**, **3**, 202, **5**, 171.
Brown v United States (8 Cranch, 153), **21**, 52
Brown v. Huger (21 How 305), **9**, 202
Browne, Lomai v (92 U S 187), **23**, 52
Broughton v Pensacola (93 U S 266), **231**, 97
Bruffy, Williams v (96 U S 176), **233**, 98
Brumagen, Chew v (13 Wall 497) **13**, 153
Buck v Colbath (4 Wall 334), **97**, 133
Buckingham's Ex'r v Bank (5 How 317), **55**, 144
Buckley, Withers v. (20 How 92), **3**, 164 **1**, 182, **1**, 194, **52**, 143
Buel v Van Ness (8 Wheat. 312), **23**, **26**, 139.
Buffington v Day (11 Wall 113), **11**, 17
Bugbee, Howard v (24 How 461), **60**, 71, **73**, 72
Bull Calder v (3 Dall 386) **18**, 65, **24**, 66, **32**, 67. **37**, 68, **13**, 114, **38**, 199 **97**, 225
Bull v. Boynton (121 U. S 457), **10**, 153
Burgess, United States v (3 McCrary 278), **34**, 186
Burgess, Pace v. (92 U. S 372), **7**, **8**, 62, **5**, 203
Burgess Turpin v (117 U. S 504), **8**, 62.
Burke v Gaines (19 How 328), **9**, 122.
Burlington Larned v (4 Wall 275) **186**, 90.
Burlington, Mitchell v. (4 Wall 270), **186**, 90
Burr, United States v (4 Cranch, 470) **9**, 149, **19**, 150
Burrage, Unity v (103 U S 447), **5**, 229
Burroughs, Marsh v (1 Woods, 463), **61**, 71.
Burrows Nudd v (91 U S 426). **89**, 132.
Burton, Koshkonong v (104 U. S 668), **51**, 70
Bush v Kentucky (107 U S 110) **78**, 222
Butchers' Union v Crescent City etc Co (111 U. S 746) **200**, 92
Butler v Hopper (1 Wash C C 499), **10**, 163 **1**, 59
Butler v. Horwitz (7 Wall 258), **12**, 153
Butler v. Boston Steamship Co (130 U S 527), **37**, 235
Butler v. Pennsylvania (10 How. 402), **17**, 167 **206**, **209**, 93
Byrne v. Missouri (8 Pet. 40) **3**, 63
Cairo & Fulton R R. v Hecht (95 U S 168) **42**, 68
Cæsar Griffin's Case (Chase's Decisions, 364), **1**, 227

Calder v Bull (3 Dall 386–398), **13,** 114, **18,** 65; **24,** 66; **32,** 67, **37,** 68, **38,** 119 **97,** 225
Calef, Hawthorne v (2 Wall 10), **82,** 74 **219,** 95
California v Pac R R. Co. (127 U S 1), **90,** 30, **172,** 41, **40,** 176
California, Almy v (24 How 169), **4,** **5,** 103
California, McCall v (136 U S 104), **176,** 42
Callan v Wilson (127 U S 540), **7,** 148 · **9,** 190
Campbell v Clundin (Peters, C. C 484), **14,** **44** 45
Campbell, McKay v. (2 Sawyer, 129), **6,** 228.
Campbell v. Holt (115 U. S. 620), **71,** 221.
Canal Co, Gilfillan v (109 U. S 401), **242,** 99
Canal Co Pumpelly v (13 Wall. 166), **1,** 182; **17,** 184
Canal Co Rundle v (14 How 80) **214,** 94
Cannon v. New Orleans (20 Wall 577), **5,** 105, **7,** **8,** 106
Canter American Ins Co v (1 Pet. 511), **5,** 115, **5,** **6,** 120, **16,** 51, **23,** **29,** 124, **1,** **2,** 165, **9,** **13,** 16
Cardwell v. Bridge Co (113 U S 205), **126,** 35
Carlisle v. United States (16 Wall. 147) **17,** 114, **28,** **29,** 151.
Carlisle, Respublica v (1 Dall 35), **8,** 149
Carpenter v Commonwealth (17 How 493), **20,** 114.
Carpenter v Pennsylvania (17 How 463), **18,** 65, **30,** 67, **37,** 68.
Carskaddon, Pierce v (16 Wall 234), **16,** **19,** 65
Carter, Ryan v (93 U S 78), **12,** 158
Cary v. Devlin (B 23, L C Pub Co Ed U S Sup Ct. Rep 510), **82,** 147
Case of State Freight Tax (15 Wall 232), **60,** 26, **64,** 27.
Case v Terrell (11 Wall 199), **44,** 126
C & A R R Co v Wiggins Ferry Co (119 U S. 615), **16,** 151
Cassidy, People v. (19 N Y 46), **6,** 229
Case of Jno P Stockton, of N J (Senate Journal, Dec 4, 1865 January 30, 1866, March 26, 1866), **1,** 1-7
Catlettsburg Cincinnati & C. Packet Co v (105 U S 559), **147,** 37, **5,** 105
C, B & Q R. R. Co v Iowa (94 U S 155), **56,** 218
City of Alton v Sturtevants (3 McLean, 393), **2,** 47
Chaffin v Taylor (114 U. S 309), **224,** 95 **226,** 96
Chambers, Kennett v. (14 How 38), **25,** 205
Chapman, Borer v. (119 U. S. 587), **15,** 154
Chapman v Douglas Co (107 U S 318), **79,** 73.
Charles River Bridge v Warren Bridge (11 Pet. 645), **12,** 183
Charles River Bridge v Warren Bridge (11 Pet. 420), **84,** **85,** 74.
Charleston, Branch v (92 U S 677), note, p 87
Charleston Weston v. (2 Pet 449) **4,** 59.
Charleston, Murray v (96 U S 432) **136,** 81, **1,** 202
Charleston v Branch (15 Wall 470) **10,** 195, **15,** 196
Charleston, Weston v. (2 Pet. 444), **46,** 142
Chase v. Curtis (113 U. S 452), **10,** 158
Chase, Samuel, Associate Justice United States Supreme Court November 30, 1804, March 1 1805 **7,** 8
Chenango Bridge v Binghamton Bridge (3 Wall 51), **116,** 79
Cherokee Nation v. Georgia (5 Pet. 1), **121,** 135.

Cherokee Nation v. Railway Co (135 U. S 641), **5**, 182, **16**, 184

Cherokee Nation v Southern Kansas R'y Co (135 U S 641), **145**, 37.

Chester v Pennsylvania (134 U. S 240), **82**, 223

Chew v. Brumagen (13 Wall. 497), **13**, 153

Chicago & C R. R Co v Guffey (122 U S 561), **171**, 88

Chicago, Ducat v. (10 Wall. 410), **18**, **19**, 159

Chicago Elevator Co, Johnson v (119 U S 388), 1, 59, **41**, 126

Chicago v. Escanaba Transportation Co (107 U S 678), **28**, 22

Chicago Life Ins Co v Needles (113 U S 574), **201**, 92, **83**, 223

Chicago, M. & St. P R. R. v. Minnesota (134 U. S 418), **122**, 80 **55**, 418

Chicago v Sheldon (9 Wall 50), **188**, 90, **21**, 233.

Chicago, Transportation Co v (99 U S 635), **13**, 183

Chicago, United States v. (7 How 185), **9**, 183.

Chinese Exclusion Cases (130 U. S 581), **1**, **2**, 3, **98**, **99**, 133, **44**, 236

Chirac v. Chirac (2 Wheat. 269), **3**, 43, **7**, 44

Chisholm v Georgia (2 Dall 419) **48**, 127 **1**, 201

Chisholm v Georgia (2 Dall 475). 1, **1**, **6**, 2

Chouteau, Gibson v (13 Wall 92), **11**, 166.

Christ Church v Philadelphia (24 How 300). **120**, 79, **141**, 82.

Christmas v Russell (5 Wall. 291), **52**, 70, **9**, 153, **19**, 154

Church v Kelsey (121 U. S 282), **252**, 100, **74**, 221.

Chy Lung v Freeman (92 U S 275), **70**, 27, **75**, 28, **66**, 220

Cincinnati, etc Packet Co v Catlettsburg (105 U. S 559), **5**, 105

Cincinnati, Fox v (104 U. S. 783), **237**, 98

Cissel v. McDonald (16 Blatch. 150), **12**, 57

Cisna, United States v (1 McLean, 259), **137**, 36, **142**, 37

Citizens' Bank v West Tennessee Bank (13 Wall 432), **64**, 114

Citizens' Gas Lt. Co, Louisville Gas Co v (115 U S 683), **246**, 100

City of Charleston, Weston v (2 Pet. 449), **1**, 17, **12**, 19

City of Jeffersonville, Bissell v (24 How 287), **215**, 94

City of Richmond, Richmond, Fredericksburg & Pot. Ry. Co. v. (96 U S 521), **60**, 219

Civil Rights Cases (109 U. S. 3), **3**, 227, **1**, 208, **5**, 211

Clafflin v. Houseman (93 U. S. 130), **19**, 232

Clark, Mitchell v (110 U S 633), **41**, 187, **53**, 70, **284**, 100

Clark, Reith v (97 U S 454), **140**, 82

Clark v Dick (1 Dill 8), **23**, 66

Clark, Ex parte (100 U S 399), **1**, 4 **77**, 146

Clark Warring v. (5 How 441), **3**, 191, **31**, 125

Clark, Town of Pawlet v (9 Cranch, 296), **111**, 135

Clark, Bates v. (95 U. S 204), **9**, 202

Clark v Barnard (108 U S 436), **19**, 204

Clarke v Bazadone (1 Cranch, 212), **24**, 139

Claudius, Campbell v. (Peters, C. C 484), 14, 44, 45

Clay County v. Society for Savings (104 U S 579), **194**, 91

Clayton v Utah (132 U S. 632), **19**, 168

Clinton v Englebrecht (13 Wall. 434), **6**, 120

C., M & St P R R Co. v United States (104 U S 687), **27**, 233

C. & N W. R. R. Co, Peik v (94 U S 164), **57**, 218, **159**, 30; **162**, 39.

C. & N. W. R'y Co., Bowman v. (125 U. S. 465), **101,** 32, **130,** 36
C. & N. W. R. R. v. Fuller (17 Wall. 560), **155,** 38
C. & N. W. R'y Co. v. Whitton (13 Wall. 270), **62, 64,** 120
C. & N. W. R. R. Co. v. United States (104 U. S. 680), **27,** 233.
Coe v. Town of Erol (116 U. S. 517), **11,** 103, **100,** 31
Cohens v. Virginia (6 Wheat. 264), **7, 8,** 2, **2,** 7, **1,** 46, **7,** 55; **2,** 136; **11,** 137, **13,** 138, **11, 12,** 172, **2, 3,** 201, **44,** 236
Cohen, McElmoyle v. (13 Pet. 312), **3,** 152.
Coite, Society for Savings v. (6 Wall. 594), **4,** 18, **12, 16,** 19, **3,** 195
Colbath, Buck v. (4 Wall. 334), **97,** 133
Cole v. Cunningham (133 U. S. 107), **25,** 155, **33,** 156
Collet v. Collet (2 Dall. 294), **1,** 43, **6,** 44.
Colorado, Brown v. (106 U. S. 95), **241,** 94, **70,** 145.
Colson v. Lewis (2 Wheat. 377), **112,** 135.
Columbia College, Board of Pub. Works v. (17 Wall. 521), **27,** 155
Commissioners of Erie Co., Dobbins v. (16 Pet. 435), **35,** 141; **6,** 62.
Commissioners, Worthy v. (9 Wall. 611), **62,** 144
Commissioners of Taxes v. People (104 U. S. 466), **7,** 103.
Commissioners, Aspinwall v. (22 How. 364), **89,** 75
Commissioners, New York v. (4 Wall. 244), **6,** 18
Commissioners of Taxes v. New York (2 Wall. 200), **2,** 17; **10,** 18.
Commissioners of Taxes v. New York (2 Black, 620), **2,** 17; **10,** 18, **12,** 19.
Commissioners v. Lucas (93 U. S. 108), **179,** 89
Commissioners, Memphis & Charleston R. R. v. (112 U. S. 609), **173,** 88
Commissioners of Taxes, People v. (4 Wall. 244), **14,** 196
Commonwealth, Carpenter v. (17 How. 493), **20,** 114
Commonwealth v. McGuire (3 Wall. 385), **46,** 142
Commonwealth, Prigg v. (16 Pet. 539), **4,** 56, **9,** 57, **53,** 89
Commonwealth v. Shaver (3 W. & S. 338), **32,** 186.
Commonwealth v. Peirear (5 Wall. 475), **1,** 194, **21,** 197, **30,** 198
Commonwealth, Twitchell v. (7 Wall. 321), **1,** 194
Commonwealth v. National Bank (9 Wall. 353) **36,** 176
Commonwealth v. Bird (12 Mass. 442), **120,** 79
Compagnie Gen. Transatlantique, People v. (107 U. S. 59), **76,** 28; **2,** 59 **19,** 104
Comstock, Ins. Co. v. (16 Wall. 258), **2,** 191
C. & O. R. R. Co. v. Miller (114 U. S. 176), **173,** 88.
Confederate Note Case (19 Wall. 556), **24,** 233
Confiscation Cases (2 Wall. 92), **4,** 151, **22,** 114.
Congdon v. Goodman (2 Black, 574), **59,** 144.
Conlin, State v. (27 Vt. 318), **7,** 148
Connecticut, New York v. (4 Dall. 3), **18,** 138.
Connor v. Elliott (18 How. 591), **4,** 157, **15,** 212
Connoly, Barbier v. (113 U. S. 27) **38,** 235, **4,** 160; **67,** 221; **90,** 224
Continental Ins. Co., Doyle v. (94 U. S. 535), **66, 68,** 129, **18,** 159
Conway v. Taylor (1 Black, 603), **36,** 199
Cook v. Moffat (5 How. 295), **45,** 69, **10,** 172
Cook v. Pennsylvania (97 U. S. 566), **66,** 27, **6,** 103
Cooley v. Board of Wardens (12 How. 299), **14,** 17, **5, 13,** 20; **43,** 24, **63,** 27, **102,** 32, **2,** 62, **16,** 107.

Coolidge, United States v (1 Wheat 415), **6**, 148, note, 120
Coombs, United States v (12 Pet 72), **38**, 23, 24, **103**, 32; **4**, 57
Cooper v Board of Works (14 C. B. (N S) 180), **44**, 217.
Cooper, Nashville v (6 Wall. 247), **16**, 58
Coppell v. Hall (7 Wall. 557), **14**, 51.
Coppersmith, United States v (4 Fed Rep 198), **36**, 187.
Corbins, Mulligan v (7 Wall. 487), **222**, 95
Corfield v. Coryell (4 Wash. 371), **3**, 20, **31**, 23, **15**, 158.
Cornell, United States v (2 Mason, 66), **4**, **5**, **8**, 55
Cornise v Cornise (54 Penn St. 255), **17**, 167
Corson v. Maryland (120 U. S 502), **69**, 27, **84**, 29
Coryell, Corfield v (4 Wash 381), **3**, 20, **31**, 23, **15**, 158
County of Lincoln v Luning (133 U. S 529), **26**, 205.
Cousin v Labatut (19 How. 202), **9**, 122.
Cowles, Mercer Co v (7 Wall. 118), **83**, 131.
Covell v Heyman (111 U S 176), **97**, 133
Covington Drawbridge v. Shepherd (20 How 227), **57**, **59**, 128.
Coxe v. McClenachan (3 Dall. 478), **1**, **3**, 13
Cox, St. Clair v. (106 U. S. 350), **26**, 155
Coy, In re (127 U. S. 731), **7**, 60, **42**, 176
Craig v. Missouri (4 Pet. 410), **3**, 63, **10**, 64, **13**, 65
Crane v. Meginnis (1 Gill & J 463), **17**, 167
Crandall v Nevada (6 Wall 42), **64**, 27 **102**, 32, **35**, 156, **30**, 215
Crawford, Gittings v (Taney's Dec 1), **2**, 136; **11**, 137.
Crawford v Branch Bank of Mobile (7 How 279), **64**, 71.
Crenshaw v United States (134 U S 99), **207**, 93
Crescent City, etc Co v Butchers' Union (111 U S 746), **200**, 92
C, R I. & P. Ry v Glinn (114 U S 542), **4**, 55
Crittenden, Adams v (106 U S 576), **23**, **26**, 139
Crones, Gordon v. (47 N. Y 608), **6**, 229
Cross v Harrison (16 How 164), **10**, 113; **18**, 167
Cross v. North Carolina (132 U S 131), **76**, 222
Crosley, United States v (7 Cranch, 115), **4**, 55
Crowninshield, Sturgis v (4 Wheat. 122), **14**, 44, **24**, 45, **40**, 68, **178**, 88, **220**, 95 **445**, 236
Crowell v Randell (10 Pet. 368), **96**, 133, **27**, 139, **30**, 140
Crowley, Soo Hing v (113 U. S. 703), **66**, 220, **67**, 221, **20**, 224, **38**, 235
Cruikshank, United States v (92 U S 542) **4**, 56, **2**, 112, **1**, **8**, 179; **9**, 180, **6**, 190, **1**, 194, **51**, 200, **1**, 210, **80**, 222, **3**, 227, **3**, 228
Cully v B & O R R Co. (1 Hughes, 536), **17**, 212
Cumming, United States v (130 U. S 452), **36**, 234
Cumming v Missouri (4 Wall. 277), **16**, **19**, 65, **20**, **22**, 66, **68**, 221
Cunningham v Hall (1 Cliff 45), **37**, 126.
Cunningham, Cole v (133 U. S. 107), **25**, 155, **33**, 156
Cunningham v Macon R. R. (109 U S 446), **6**, **9**, 202, **13**, 203, **27**, 206
Curran v Arkansas (15 How 304), **32**, 207, **11**, 64, **82**, 74, **213**, 95
Curtis, *Ex parte* (106 U S 371), **11**, 58.
Curtis, Chase v (113 U S 452), **10**, 153.

Curtis, United States v. (4 Mason, 232), 5, 148.
Cuyahoga Co., Palmer v (3 McLean, 226), 41, 24.

Daggs, Ewell v. (108 U. S. 143), 67, 71.
Dale v Governor (3 Stewart, 387), 120, 79
Dalton, Bank of Alabama v (9 How 522), 21, 154.
Dana, In re (7 Bene 1), 7, 148
Daniels v. Leamey (102 U. S 415), 50, 143
Darlington v. Jackson Co (101 U S 688), 187, 90
Darrington v. Bank of Alabama (13 How 12), 32, 207; 6, 64.
Darst, Duncan v (1 How. 301), 20, 45
Dartmouth College v. Woodward (4 Wheat 518), 102, 77, 17, 167
Davenport Bank v Davenport (123 U. S 83) 12, 231
Davenport, Foster v. (21 How. 244), 49, 25.
Davenport v Sinnot (22 How 227), 49, 25, 101, 32, 1, 170, 5, 171
Davidson v New Orleans (96 U S 97), 21, 185, 1, 194, 38, 216, 44, 217, 59, 219
Davis v Gray (16 Wall 203), 5, 201
Davis, Wood v (18 How. 467), 79, 131
Davis v. Packard (7 Pet. 276), 19, 123
Davis v. Tennessee (100 U. S 257), 8, 57, 5, 121, 90, 91, 132 2, 170.
Davis v Beason (133 U. S. 333), 5, 179. 5, 190.
Davis, United States v. (5 Mason, 364). 4, 55
Dawson, United States v. (15 How. 467), 3, 190
Day, Buffington v. (11 Wall. 113), 11, 17
Day v Micou (18 Wall 156), 23, 115
Dearing, Farmers', etc National Bank v (91 U S 29), 13, 172
Debolt, Mechanics' Bank v (18 How 380), 115, 79, 129, 8, 69, 130, 5, 201 102, 131.
Debolt, Ohio Life & Trust Co v. (16 How 432), 186, 90
De Cuir, Hall v. (95 U. S. 498), 101, 32, 124, 35, 163, 39
Defrees, Tyler v (11 Wall. 331), 1, 49, 15, 51
Delaware, Neal v. (103 U S. 370), 66, 220, 78, 222, 7, 228 44, 217
Delmas v. Merchants' Mut. Ins Co (14 Wall. 661), 192, 91, 41, 142; 84, 147.
Demaret, Bethell v (10 Wall 537), 64, 144; 84, 147, 28, 234
Dennis, Vicksburg R. R v. (116 U S. 665), 150, 84, 157, 85
Dennison, Kentucky v (24 How. 66), 10, 137, 1, 2, 160.
Denny v. Bennett (128 U S. 489), 19, 45; 45, 69, 82, 74.
Dent v West Virginia (129 U S 114), 52, 218, 68, 221
De Treville v Smalls (98 U. S. 517), 26, 185
Deveaux, Bank of United States v (5 Cranch, 61), 50, 53, 127
Dewing v. Perdicaries (96 U S. 193), 233, 98.
De Witt, United States v. (9 Wall 41), 107, 33.
De Young, League v. (11 How. 185), 234, 98
Dibble, New York v. (21 How. 366), 34, 199.
Dick, Clark v (1 Dill 8), 23, 66.
Diggs & Keith v. Wolcott (4 Cranch, 179), 13, 122
Dillin v Hamilton (21 Wall 73), 19, 52
District of Columbia, Metropolitan R. R v. (132 U S 1), 13, 56
District Court of Plymouth Co., Eilenbecker v (134 U S 31), 8, 148; 1, 182, 2, 189, 1, 194, 25, 214 69, 221
Ditson v Ditson (4 R. I 87), 17, 167.

Dix, West River Bridge Co v. (6 How 507), 3, 182, 11, 183, 204, 93
Dobbins v. Commissioners of Erie Co (16 Pet. 435), 2, 16; 34, 141; 38, 176, 6, 62, 6, 171.
Dodge v Woolsey (18 How 331), 115, 79, 129, 81, 178, 88, 14, 122 69, 130, 102, 134, 41, 176
Dominick v. Sayer (3 Sandf 355), 178, 88
Dooley v Smith (13 Wall 603), 4, 46, 15, 51.
Douglas Co., Chapman v (107 U. S 348), 79, 73, 187, 90
Dow v Johnson (100 U. S 158), 7, 231.
Dow v Beidelman (125 U S 680), 58, 219, 91, 224.
Dowley, Waite v (94 U. S 527), 7, 171; 14, 173
Downham v Alexander (10 Wall 173), 57, 26.
Doyle v Ins. Co (94 U. S. 535), 12, 20. 66, 68, 129, 18, 159, 39, 199.
Drehman v. Stifle (8 Wall. 595), 17, 65; 23, 66
Drew, Trigg v (10 How 224), 107, 77
Drew, Paup v (10 How. 218) 107, 77
Dubuque, Gelpcke v. (1 Wall 175), 186, 90
Dubuque, etc R R v Richmond (19 Wall 584), 156, 39
Ducat v Chicago (10 Wall 410), 18, 19, 159
Dudley Bank of Hamilton v (2 Pet. 492), 12, 192
Dugger v Bocock (104 U S 596), 238, 98
Dumphy v Kleinsmith (11 Wall 610), 12, 166
Duncan v The Francis Wright (105 U. S. 381), 25, 139.
Duncan v Darst (1 How 301), 20, 45
Dunn Home Life Ins Co v (19 Wall 214), 17, 193
Dunn, Anderson v (6 Wheat. 204) 1, 11, 4, 12, 1, 46, 1, 2, 56
Dupasseur v Rochereau (21 Wall 130), 49, 143
Durant, Supervisors v. (9 Wall 415), 87, 132
Durkee v Board of Liquidation (103 U S 646), 193, 91
Durousseau v. United States (6 Cranch, 307), 22, 139
Duryee, Mills v (7 Cranch, 481), 4, 152
Dynes v Hoover (20 How 65), clause 14, 53.

Earle, Bank of Augusta v (13 Pet. 519), 53, 127, 18, 159.
East Hartford v Hartford Bridge Co (10 How 511) 108, 78.
East St. Louis, Wiggins Ferry Co v. (107 U S 365), 82, 29, 153, 84, 37, 199
Easton, Hodges v. (106 U S. 408), 9, 192
Easton, Lehigh Water Co v. (121 U S 338), 252, 100
Eaton, Evans v (3 Wheat. 454), 2, 48.
Ebbinghaus, Kilhan v. (110 U S 568), 7, 192.
Edge v Robinson (112 U. S 580), 78, 28.
Edmunds, Sands v. (116 U S 585), 224, 95
Edsall, Norris v (1 Wall, Jr. 189), 3, 13
Edwards v Elliott (21 Wall. 532), 37, 38, 126, 60, 144, 1, 189, 11, 192, 1, 194
Edwards' Case (Cl. & H 92), 1, 6
Edwards v Kearzey (96 U. S 610), 58, 70, 76, 73.
Effinger v Kennedy, (115 U S. 556), 25, 233
Eichelberger, Schofield v (7 Pet. 586), 14, 51.
Eilenbecker v Dist. Court of Plymouth Co. (134 U. S. 31), 69, 221, 8, 146, 1, 182, 2, 189, 25, 114, 1, 194.

Electors v Bailey (Cl & H. 411), **2**, 5
Elk v. Wilkins (112 U. S 94), **12**, 212.
Eliason, United States v (16 Pet. 291), **4**, 113.
Elliott, Connor v (18 How 591), **15**, 212, **4**, 157
Elliott, Edwards v (21 Wall 542), **51**, 143, **60**, 144, **37**, **38**, 120, **1**, 189, **11**, 192, **1**, 194
Elliott v Wiltz (107 U S 711), **22**, 205
Ellzey, Hepburn v. (2 Cranch, 445), **74**, 130
Emory v Greenough (3 Dall. 369), **19**, 45.
Emporia v Volmer (12 Kansas, 622), **7**, 148,
Englebrecht, Clinton v (13 Wall. 434), **6**, 120
Enquist, Morewood v (23 How. 491), **37**, 126
Erie Ry. v Pennsylvania (21 Wall 492), **148**, **151**, 84, **38**, 176
Erol, Coe v (116 U S 517), **100**, 31.
Escanaba Transportation Co. v. Chicago (107 U S 678), **28**, 22.
Evans v Eaton (3 Wheat. 454), **2**, 48.
Ewell v Daggs (108 U. S. 144), **67**, 71
Ewing, Noel v (9 Ind. 37), **17**, 167
Ewing, Gantly's Lessee v. (3 How. 707), **72**, 72
Exchange Bank, Hills v (105 U S. 319), **18**, 173.

Fairchilds, United States v. (1 Abb (U S) 74), **4**, 57
Fanning v Gregoire (8 How. 490), **37**, 199
Fargo v Michigan (121 U. S. 230) **7**, 20; **85**, 29; **94**, 31
Farmers' Bank v Smith (6 Wheat 131), **17**, 45
Farmers' Nat Bank v Dearing (91 U S 29), **13**, 172
Farney v Towle (1 Black, 351), **61**, 144
Farrington v Tennessee (95 U. S. 679), **137**, 82, **213**, 94
Farrand, Matter of (1 Abb. (U. S.) 140), **4**, 53
Fellows v Blacksmith (19 How 366), **21**, 173
Fenno, Veazie Bank v. (8 Wall. 533), **5**, 46, **24**, 61
Ferreira, United States v. (13 How 40), **13**, 58
Ferry Co v Pennsylvania (114 U. S 196), **79**, 28.
Field, Ex parte (5 Blatch. 63), **15**, 61
Field, United States v. (16 Fed. Rep. 778), **36**, 187
First Municipality, Permoli v (3 How 589), **3**, 179, **40**, 235
First Nat Bank of Louisville v Kentucky (9 Wall 353), **3**, **6**, 18, **13**, 19
Fisher v United States (2 Cranch, 358), **2**, 56, **4**, 57
Fisk v Police Jury (116 U. S 131), **210**, 93.
Fitzhugh, Propeller Gennesee Chief v (12 How 443) **33**, **35**, 125
Fitzhugh, Transportation Co v (1 Black, 574), **32**, 125
Fitzgerald v Green (134 U S 377), clause 2, 110
Flemming v Page (9 How 603), **1**, 164, **16**, 51 **9**, 60, **5**, 113.
Fletcher v Peck (6 Cranch, 87–137), **25**, 66, **32**, 67; **97**, 76, **178**, 88
Florida v. Georgia (17 How. 478), **17**, 138
Florentine v Boston (2 Wall 216), **82**, 76
Foley, Porter v. (24 How 415), **58**, 144
Foote v Pike Co (101 U S 688). **187**, 90
Forrest, Bigelow v (9 Wall 359) **2**, 151, **23**, 115
Forsyth, Kelsey v (21 How 85), **94**, 133, **9**, 166, **11**, 231
Foster v Davenport (22 How 244), **49**, 25

Foster & Elam v. Nelson (2 Pet 314), **2**, 115
Foster v. Kansas (112 U. S 205), **99**, 225
Foster, Springer v (2 Story, 383), **19**, 45
Fowler v Miller (3 Dall 411), **18**, 138
Fowler v Lindsey (3 Dall 411), **18**, 138.
Fox v State of Ohio (5 How 433), **151**, 38, **2**, 180 **3**, 181, **1**, 179; **52**, 189, **11**, 192, **1**, 194; **1**, 46 **3**, **5**, 47
Fox v Cincinnati (104 U S 783), **237**, 98
Franklin Co, Stines v. (14 Wall 15), **66**, 145 **82**, 76
Franks, Baldwin v. (120 U. S 678), **22**, 174, **7**, 229, **1**, 210, **14**, 212
Freeborn v Smith (2 Wall 175), **82**, 74; **97**, 225
Freeland v. Williams (131 U S 405), **96**, **97**, 225
Freeland v Williams (21 Wall 203), **259**, **260**, 100, **69**, 72
Freeman, Chy Lung v (92 U S 275), **66**, 220. **70**, 27, **75**, 28
Freeman v Howe (24 How 450). **97**, 133
French, Lafayette Ins Co. v. (18 How 404), **8**, 153, **24**, 155, **18**, 159, **58**, 128
Frisbie v Whitney (9 Wall. 187), **261**, 102.
Fritton, Mays v. (B 21, L C Pub Co Ed U S Sup Ct. Rep 127) **43**, 142
Fritts v Palmer (132 U. S 282), **171**, 41
Ft Leavenworth v. Lowe (114 U. S 525) **4**, 55
Fuller, C & N W R R v. (17 Wall 560) **155**, 38
Fulton v McAfee (16 Pet 149), **9**, 122
Furgeson Tucker v (22 Wall 257), **144**, 83.
Furman v Nichol (8 Wall 44), **38**, 111, **60**, 141, **117**, 97, **140**, 82.
Gage, Howe Machine Co v (100 U S 676), **73**, 28
Gaillard, South Carolina v (101 U S 433), **120**, 79
Gaines, Memphis & Charleston R R v (97 U S 697), **149**, **152**, 84.
Gaines, Burk v (19 How 328) **9**, 122
Galena v Amy (5 Wall 705), **175**, 88
Gantly's Lessees v. Ewing (3 How. 707), **72**, 72
Gardner, United States v. (10 Pet. 618) **1**, 46
Garland, Ex parte (4 Wall 333), **19**, 65 **20**, **28**, 66, **3**, 179; **68**, 22; **24**, 115, **4**, 151
Garnett, Merriwether v (102 U S 472), **96**, 76, **179**, 88
Garrison v New York City (21 Wall 203) **259**, **260**, 101, **94**, 76
Garza, Neilson v (2 Woods, 287), **19**, 104
Gassies v Ballon (6 Pet. 761), **1**, 156; **10**, 44
Geissler, Ex parte (9 Biss. 492), **1**, 4
Gelpcke v. Dubuque (1 Wall 175), **186**, 90
Gelston v Hoyt (3 Wheat 246), **7**, 122 **3**, 118
Geoffry v Riggs (133 U S. 258), **20**, 173.
Georgia, Atlantic & Gulf R. R v (98 U S 359), **162**, 86.
Georgia, Worcester v (6 Pet 515), **6**, 2, **140**, 37 **1**, 165
Georgia, Florida v (17 How. 478), **17**, 138
Georgia Alabama v (23 How 505) **17**, 138
Georgia, Chisholm v (2 Dall 475) **1**, **3**, 1, **6**, 2 **1**, 201, **48**, 127, **121**, 135
Georgia v Stanton (6 Wall 50), **17**, 123.
Georgia South Carolina v (93 U S 4), **27**, 22
Georgia v Brailsford (2 Dall. 401), **2**, 201.

Gibbons v. Ogden (9 Wheat. 1), **1**, 19; **6**, **10**, 20, **36**, 23, **101**, **103**, 32, **10**, **13**, 230, **1**, 170, **5**, 171; **11**, **3**, **2**, 202, **173**, 41

Gibbons v. United States (8 Wall 269), **36**, 234

Gibson v. Chouteau (13 Wall 92), **11**, 166

Gilfillan v. Canal Co (109 U. S 401), **242**, 99

Gilman v. Philadelphia (3 Wall 713), **24**, 21, 22, **102**, **103**, 32, **114**, **115**, 34, **153**, 38

Gilman v. Lockwood (4 Wall 409), **21**, 45

Girard v. Philadelphia (7 Wall. 1), **231**, 97.

Gittings v. Crawford (Taney's Dec 1), **2**, 136, **11**, 137.

Given v. Wright (117 U S 648), **124**, 80

Gloucester Ferry Co v. Pennsylvania (114 U. S 196), **127**, 35, **148**, 38.

Glover, Huse v. (119 U S 543), **32**, **23**; **1**, **4**, 105.

Golden v. Prince (3 Wash C. C. 313), **4**, 43

Goldman, United States v. (3 Woods, 187), **1**, **4**

Gomila Rio Grande R R Co v. (132 U S 478), **97**, 133.

Good v. Martin (95 U S 90), **6**, 120

Goodtitle v. Kibbe (9 How 471) **10**, 166

Gordon v. Crones (47 N Y 608), **6**, 229.

Gordon v. Appeal Tax Court (3 How 133), **126**, 80

Gordon, Congdon v. (2 Black, 574), **59**, 144

Governor, Dale v. (3 Stewart, 387), **120**, 79

Governor of Ga v. Madrazo (1 Pet 123), **29**, 206

Graham, Salomans v. (15 Wall. 208), **65**, 145

Graham, Strader v. (10 How 82) **10**, 163, **5**, 164, **52**, 143.

Gray, Davis v. (16 Wall 203), **5**, 201

Great Falls Mfg Co, United States v. (112 U S. 645), **15**, 184

Greathouse, United States v. (2 Abb. (U S) 364), **2**, 148, **16**, 149, **25**, 150

Green, In re (134 U. S 377), **1**, **2**, 208.

Green, Fitzgerald v. (134 U. S 377), clause 2, 110

Green v. Van Buskirk (7 Wall 139), **11**, 153

Green v. Sarmiento (3 Wash. C C 17), **29**, 155

Green v. Bedley (8 Wheat. 1), **14**, 206, **178**, 88 **212**, 94

Greene v. Biddle (8 Wheat 1), **82**, 74

Greene Co, State ex rel. Att'y-Gen'l v. (54 Mo 540) note, p 87

Greenhow, Poindexter v. (114 U. S 270), **9**, 64 **10**, 202, **224**, 95

Greenhow Antoni v. (107 U S 769) **81**, 73, **225**, 96

Greenhow, Antoni v. (107 U S 672) **226**, 96

Greenhow, Moore v. (114 U. S 338), **225**, 96

Greenhow, Hartman v. (102 U S. 672) **224**, 95, **226**, 96

Greenhow, White v. (114 U S 307), **224**, 95

Greenman, Juliard v. (110 U S. 421), **18**, 19, **1**, 63

Greenough, Emory v. (3 Dall 369), **19**, 45.

Greenwood v. Union Ft. Ry Co (105 U S 13), **229**, 97

Gregoire, Fanning v. (8 How 490), **37**, 199

Greneaux Prevost v. (19 How 1), **43**, 176

Griffin v. Thompson (2 How 244), **6**, 46

Grima, Mayer v. (8 How 490), **35**, 199

Grisar v. McDowell (6 Wall 363) **9**, 202

Griswold, Hepburn v. (8 Wall 603), **5**, 230, **17**, 19, **7**, 55. **2**, 46.

Gross v United States Mortgage Co (108 U S 477), **93**, 224
Groves v Slaughter (15 Pet 504), **101**, 32
Grush, United States v (3 Mason, 290), **7**, 49
Guaranty Co v Board of Liquidation (105 U S 622), **240**, 99
Guffey, Chicago, etc R R v (122 U S 561), **171**, 88
Guild v Frontin (18 How 135), **94**, 133
Gunn v. Barry (15 Wall 610), **191**, 91
Gut v Minnesota (9 Wall 35), **35**, 68, **41**, 199
Guthrie, United States v (17 How 284), **15**, 128
Guy v Baltimore (100 U. S 434), **72**, 28
Gwin v Breedlove (2 How 29), **6**, 46
Gyer s Lessees v Irwin (4 Dall 107), **1**, 13

Habeas Corpus Cases (100 U. S 371), **2**, 10 · **12**, 116.
Haile, Mason v (12 Wheat 370), **43**, 69 **178**, 88
Hagar v Reclamation Dist. No 108 (111 U S 701), **39**, 176; **24**, 198; **37**, 216
Hagan, Pollard v (3 How. 212), **19**, 21 **1**, 64, **2**, **3**, **4**, 164 **10**, 166; **9**, 172, **15**, 204
Hale Baldwin v. (1 Wall 228), **14**, **17**, **19**, 45 **43**, 199
Hall, Coppell v (7 Wall 557), **14**, 51.
Hall Cunningham v (1 Cliff 45), **37**, 126
Hall, United States v (98 U S 343) **15**, 58
Hall v Wisconsin (103 U. S. 5), **228**, 97
Hall v De Cuir (95 U S 498), **101**, 32, **163**, 39, **124**, 35
Hallett v Beebe (13 How 25), **10**, 166
Halstead, Bank of United States v. (10 Wheat 51), **92**, 132
Hamblen Co R R. Co. v (102 U S 273), **173**, 88
Hamersley, R R. Co v (104 U S 239), 98
Hamilton Mfg Co v Massachusetts (6 Wall. 632), **3**, 195, **2**, 202, **12**, **16**, 19
Hamilton v Dillin (21 Wall. 73), **19**, 52
Hamilton v Vicksburg, S & P R R. Co (119 U S 280), **152**, 38
Hamilton, United States v. (3 Dall. 17), **78**, 146
Hampton v McConnell (3 Wheat 234), **5**, 152
Hanauer v Woodruff (15 Wall 448), **24**, 233
Hanger v Abbott (6 Wall 535), **14**, 51
Hans Nielsen, Ex parte (131 U. S 176) **8**, 60, **41**, 235
Hans v Louisiana (134 U. S. 1), **20**, 204
Happersett, Miner v (21 Wall. 162), **21**, 159, **19**, 213, **1**, 227
Hardin, Leisey v (135 U S 108), **9**, 103; **12**, 104, **1**, 202, **177**, 42. **101**, **103**, 32. **134**, **135a**, 36
Harmony, Mitchell v (13 How 115), **109**, 134, **20**, 184, **9**, 202
Harmoning, Arrowsmith v (118 U. S. 194), **70**, 221
Harris, United States v (106 U S 629), **5**, **6**, 209, **1**, 210, **7**, 229, **5**, 57; **37**, 68, **18**, 65, **16**, 158, **3**, 227, **4**, 228 **2**, 229.
Harris, Mut Life Ins Co v (97 U S 331), **14**, 153.
Harris, B & O R. R Co v (12 Wall 65). **61**, 128, **46**, **47**, 200
Harris, United States v (1 Abb (U S) 110) **20**, 114.
Harrison v Cross (16 How. 164), **18**, 167 **10**, 113
Hart White v (13 Wall. 646), **74**, 72, **15**, 168
Hartford Bridge Co East Hartford v (10 How 511) **108**, 78
Hartman v Greenhow (102 U. S. 672), **224**, 95 **226**, 96

Harvey v Tyler (2 Wall 328), **59**, 219
Haskell, Sevier v (14 Wall 12), **46**, 142, **83**, 147, **66**, 145
Haskell, United States v. (4 Wash. C C 402), **46**, 188
Hatch, People v. (33 Ill. 9), **2**, 118.
Hatch, Willamette Bridge Co v (125 U S. 1), **33**, **34**, **35**, 23
Haughton, Beers v (9 Pet 350), **44**, 69; **178**, 88
Hawkins v Barney (5 Pet. 457), **52**, 70
Hawthorne v. Calef (2 Wall. 10), **82**, 74; **219**, 95
Hayburn's Case (2 Dall 410; 1 Lawyer's Co-operative Ed. 436), **1**, 121
Hays v Missouri (120 U S 68), **82**, 223
Hays v Steamship Co. (17 How 596), **55**, 26.
Hayward McCracken v. (2 How 608), **59**, 70 **72**, 72
Head v Amoskeag Mfg Co. (113 U. S. 9), **95**, 221
Head Money Cases (18 Fed. Rep 135), **5**, 62
Head Money Cases (112 U. S 580), **23**, 174
Hebard, Ex parte (4 Dill. 384), **5**, 55.
Hecht, Cairo & Fulton R. R. v. (95 U. S 168), **42**, 68, **65**, 71
Henden, Ins. Co. v. (92 U. S 286), **238**, 98
Henderson v. Mayor of N Y (92 U S 259), **70**, 27, **75**, 28, **101**, **105**, 32, **66**, 220, **118**, **119**, 34
Hennen, Ex parte (13 Pet. 259), **8**, 116
Hennick, Stoutenburgh v. (129 U. S 141), **2**, 54, **93**, 30
Henry, Red Rock v. (106 U S 596), **230**, 97
Henshaw, Hortsman v. (11 How 177), **6**, 152
Hepburn v. Griswold (8 Wall. 603), **17**, 19, **2**, 46, **7**, 50; **6**, 230, **74**, 130.
Herman v Phalen (14 How 79), **234**, 98
Herrick v Minn & St. L. R. R. (127 U S 210), **54**, 218.
Heyman, Covell v. (111 U S. 176), **97**, 133
Hickman, Rex v (1 Moody, 34), **32**, 186
Hicke v Starke (1 Pet 94), **33**, 140.
Hill, Maynard v (125 U S 190), **17**, 167
Hill v United States (9 How 386), **43**, 126
Hills v Exchange Bank (105 U S 319), **18**, 173
Hilton v Merritt (110 U. S 97), **28**, 186.
Hilton Ware v (3 Dall 199), **18**, 232
Hine v Trevor (4 Wall 555) **35**, 125
Hinkley v Marean (3 Mason, 88), **19**, 45
Hinson v Scott (8 Wall. 148), **1**, 202, **9**, 103.
Hoagland, Wurts v (114 U S [illegible] **48**, 217
Hobbs and Johnson, Ex parte (1 Woods, 537), **32**, 215
Hoboken L. & T Co, Bridge Proprietors v (1 Wall 116), **96**, 133, **113**, **114**, 78, **60**, **144**.
Hoboken Land, etc Co Murray v (18 How 272), **21**, **22**, **26**, **27**, 185; **7**, 181
Hodges v Easton (106 U. S 408), **9**, 192.
Hodgsons & Thompson v Bowerbank (5 Cranch, 303), **118**, 135
Hoffman, People ex rel The Banks v (7 Wall. 16), **11**, 18
Hoge's Case (Cl. & H 135) **3**, 7
Holden v. Joy (17 Wall 211), **3**, 115.
Holliday, United States v (3 Wall 407), **136**, 36, **143**, **144**, 37
Hollingsworth v. Virginia (3 Dall. 378), **2**, 201.
Holmes, Barrett v (102 U S 651), **49**, 69
Holmes v Jennison (14 Pet 540), **13**, 117, **13**, **14**, 162.

Holmes v. Sevier (B. 20, L. C Pub Co Ed. U S Sup Ct R. 877) **66,** 145, **83,** 147.
Holmes, United States v (5 Wheat 412) **1,** 49
Holt, Compbell v. (115 U. S. 620), **71,** 221
Holton, Thompson v. (6 McLean, 386), **158,** 85
Holyoke Water Power Co v Lyman (15 Wall 500), **166,** 86
Home of the Friendless v Rouse (8 Wall 430), **130,** 81; **6,** 195
Home Ins Co v. Augusta (93 U. S. 116), **154,** 85; **46,** 142
Home Life Ins. Co. v. Dunn (19 Wall. 214) **17,** 193.
Home Ins Co v Morse (20 Wall 445), **65, 66, 68,** 129
Home Ins Co. v New York (134 U. S 594), **15,** 19, **87,** 224.
Home Ins. Co v New York (119 U S. 129), **75,** 222
Hook, Payne v. (7 Wall. 425), **97,** 133, **106,** 134
Hope Ins Co v Boardman (5 Cranch, 57), **49,** 127
Hopkins, Yick Wo v. (118 U. S. 356), **66,** 220.
Hopper, Butler v (1 Wash. C. C. 499), **1,** 59, **10,** 163
Horn, Bank v. (17 How. 157), **78,** 131
Hornbuckle v Toombs (18 Wall. 648), **6,** 120
Horst, Indianapolis, etc R. R Co. v (93 U S 291), **89,** 132
Hortsman v Henshaw (11 How 177), **6,** 152
Horwitz, Butler v. (7 Wall 258), **12,** 153
Hotchkiss, Kirtland v (100 U S 491), **258,** 101
Houston, Brown v. (114 U S 622), **80,** 28, 29
Houston v Moore (5 Wheat. 1-34), **5,** 151.
Houseman, Clafflin v (93 U S 130), **19,** 232.
Hoven, Dynes v. (10 How 65), clause 14, 53.
Howard, Bacon v (20 How. 22), **31,** 198
Howard v. Bugbee (24 How 461), **60,** 71
Howe, Freeman v. (24 How 450), **97,** 133.
Howe Machine Co v Gage (100 U S. 676), **73,** 28
Howland, United States v (4 Wheat. 103), **107, 108,** 134.
Hoyt, Gelston v. (3 Wheat 246). **7,** 122
Hoyt v. Shelden (1 Black, 521), **61,** 144.
Huber v Reily (53 Penn. St. 115), **3,** 4.
Huber, Milne v. (3 McLean, 217), **36,** 68
Huddleson, Achison v (12 How 293), **30,** 175, **251,** 100
Hudson & Goodwin, United States v (7 Cranch, 32), **8,** 120 **6,** 148
Huger, Brown v (21 How 305), **9,** 202
Huling v Kaw Valley R y (130 U S 559), **59,** 219.
Humes, Mo Pac R. R Co v (115 U. S 512), **61,** 219, **90,** 224.
Humphrey v Pegues (16 Wall. 244), **133,** 81; **10,** 195
Humphries, Bland v. (2 How 9), **81,** 131
Hunt v. Hunt (Book 24, L. Co-operative Ed. U S Sup. Ct. Rep 1109), **235,** 98, **262,** 102
Hunter's Lessees, Martin v (1 Wheat 304), **1,** 1, **2, 7,** 15, **1,** 46; **46,** 142, **2,** 170, **50,** 200
Hurtado v California (110 U. S. 516), **77,** 222
Huse v Glover (119 U S 543), **32,** 23; **4,** 105
Husen, Railroad v (95 U. S. 465), **101, 105,** 32; **158,** 39
Huston, Brown v. (114 U S 622), **126,** 35; **135,** 36, **10,** 103; **12,** 104

Huston v. Moore (5 Wheat. 1), **4, 43, 7, 44, 3, 53, 5, 54, 118,** 79, **7,** 163
Hyde v. Stone (20 How. 170), **75,** 130, **97,** 133
Hylton v. United States (3 Dall 171), **1,** 6; **1, 4,** 61
Hylton, Ware v (3 Dall 199), **6,** 2; **1,** 6, **1, 2,** 115

Illinois, Bradley v (4 Wall 459), **6,** 18
Illinois Cent R R. v Bosworth (133 U S 92), **1, 4,** 151
Illinois, Ker v. (119 U S 436), **94,** 224
Illinois, Munn v (94 U S 113), **22,** 197; **124,** 35, **104,** 225. **157,** 39, **162,** 39, **56,** 218
Illinois, Presser v (116 U S 252), **1,** 194, **20,** 213; **73,** 221, **5, 7,** 229
Illinois, Spies v (123 U S. 131), **38,** 187, **4,** 190, **1,** 194
Illinois, Wabash R'y v (118 U S 587), **162,** 39
Indiana Vincennes University v (14 How 268), **111,** 78.
Indianapolis, etc R. R. v Horst (93 U. S. 291), **89,** 132.
Insurance Co v Comstock (16 Wall 258), **2,** 191
Insurance Co, Delmas v. (14 Wall 666), **238,** 98.
Insurance Co, Delmas v (14 Wall 661), **41,** 142, **84,** 147.
Insurance Co, Doyle v (94 U S 535), **12,** 20
Insurance Co v Henden (92 U S 286), **238,** 98.
Insurance Co., Mauran v. (6 Wall 1), **9,** 231
Insurance Co v Massachusetts (10 Wall 566), **8,** 20, **18,** 159.
Insurance Co. v New Orleans (1 Woods, 85), **7,** 211.
Insurance Co, Stark v (7 Cranch, 420), **12,** 44.
Insurance Co, United States v (29 Wall 99), **30,** 234.
Insurance Co, Stockdale v (100 U S 323), **10,** 58.
Iowa, Bartemeyer v. (18 Wall. 129), **22,** 213, **26,** 214.
Iowa, C, B & Q R. R. Co v (94 U S 155), **56, 57,** 218.
Iowa, Missouri v (7 How 660), **17,** 138
Iowa R. R. Contracting Co, Ochiltree v (21 Wall 249), **93,** 75, 76
Iowa, Railroad Co v (94 U S 155), **124,** 35, **160, 162,** 39
Inman Steamship Co. v Tinker (94 U S 238), **2,** 105
Irwin, Gyer's Lessees v (4 Dall. 107), **1,** 13

Jackson, Ex parte (96 U S 727), **4, 5,** 48.
Jackson, In re (14 Blatch 245), **4,** 47, 48.
Jackson, In Matter of (96 U. S 727), **7,** 179, **2,** 181
Jackson v Lamphire (3 Pet. 280), **82,** 70 **70,** 72, **88,** 74, **52,** 143.
Jackson v Twentyman (2 Pet 136), **119,** 135
Jackson, Quincy v (113 U S. 322), **183,** 89.
Jackson, Railway Co v (7 Wall 262), **31,** 234.
Jackson, Wilcox v. (16 Pet. 498), **9,** 202.
Jaehne v New York (128 U. S 189), **34,** 67.
Jecker v Montgomery (13 How. 498), **13,** 113.
Jecker v. Montgomery (18 How 110), **14,** 51
Jefferson Branch Bank v Skelly (1 Black, 436), **39,** 141; **123,** 80 **245,** 100
Jenkins v Andover (103 Mass. 96), **18,** 197
Jennison, Holmes v (14 Pet. 540), **13, 14,** 162, **13,** 117
Jersey City, Provident Inst. v (13 U S 506), **45,** 217
Jessup, Tomlinson v (15 Wall. 454), **150,** 84, **166,** 86, **10,** 195.

Johnson Andrew, Trial, p. 8
Johnson v Chicago Elevator Co (119 U S 388), **41**, 126, **1**, 54
Johnson, Dow v (100 U S. 158), **7**, 231.
Johnson & Graham's Lessees v. McIntosh (8 Wheat. 543), **14**, 232
Johnson, Mississippi v (4 Wall. 475), **19**, 114, **12**, 122, **5**, 118
Johnson, Norwich & C R. R. v (15 Wall. 195), **4**, 46.
Johnson, Riggs v (6 Wall. 176), **97**, 133, **103**, 134.
Johnson, Riggs v. (6 Wall. 166), **17**, 58
Johnson R. R. Co v. (15 Wall. 195), **15**, 51.
Johnson v Vandyke (6 McLean, 441), **36**, 68.
Joliffe, Pacific S. S Co v. (2 Wall 450), **44**, **46**, 24
Jolly v Terre Haute Draw-bridge Co. (6 McLean, 237), **42**, 24
Jolly, Union Bank v. (18 How. 503), **75**, 130
Jones v Robbins (8 Gray, 329), **7**, 148
Jones, Scott v (5 How. 343), **6**, 137; **4**, 168.
Jones, United States v. (3 Wash. C C 209), **6**, 49
Jones United States v (109 U. S. 513), **7**, 183.
Jones v Van Zandt (5 How 215), **9**, 163
Joseph Smith, Ex parte (3 McLean, 121), **11**, 162
Jose Ferreira dos Santos, Case of (2 Brock C C 493), **5**, 49
Joy Holden v. (17 Wall 211), **3**, 115
Julian v Greenman (110 U. S 421), **18**, 19. **1**, 63
Jumel, Louisiana v (107 U. S 711), **14**, 203, **22**, 205
Justice, Mahon v (127 U S 700), **7**, 161.

Kagama v United States (118 U S 375), **16**, 167
Kahn, Stewart v (11 Wall. 493), **17**, 51.
Kaine, In re (14 How 103). **1**, 230
Kalbfleisch, Wade v (58 N Y. 282), **17**, 167.
Kansas, Ames v (111 U. S. 449), **2**, 136, **11**, 137
Kansas, Foster v. (112 U. S. 205), **99**, 225
Kansas, Mugler v (123 U S 623). **23**, 214
Kansas Pacific R. R v Atchison, etc. R R (112 U S 414). **21**, 139
Kansas Pacific R. R. Co, Republican River Bridge Co. v (92 U S. 315), **48**, 143
Kaw Valley R y, Huling v. (130 U S 559), **59**, 219
Keach, Traver v (15 Wall 68), **238**, 98.
Kearzey, Edwards v. (96 U. S. 610), **58**, 70, **76**, 73
Kearney, Ex parte (7 Wheat. 38), **78**, 146
Keeler, In Matter of (Hemp 306) **9**, 110
Keen, United States v (1 McLean, 429), **47**, 188
Keith v Clark (97 U S 454) **140**, 82.
Kelly v Pittsburg (104 U S 78), **1**, 194, **41**, 216.
Kelsey v Forsyth (21 How 85). **94**, 133
Kelsey, Church v. (121 U S 282), **74**, 221, **253**, 100
Kemmler, In re (136 U S 436), **1**, 194, **21**, 213
Kendall v United States (12 Pet 524), **1**, 108, **7**, 110, **42**, 126
Kendall v Stokes (3 How 87), **13**, 203
Kennett v Chambers (14 How 38), **25**, 205.
Kennedy, Effinger v. (115 U S 556), **25**, 233
Kennard v. Louisiana (92 U S 480), **81**, 147, **33**, 215.
Kennebec & P R. R v Port. & Kennebec R. R. (14 Wall 23), **66**, 145
Kentucky, Bush v. (107 U S 110), **78**, 222

Kentucky v. Dennison (24 How 66), 10, 137, 1, 2, 160.
Kentucky, First Nat Bank v (9 Wall 353), 3, 6, 18, 13, 19
Kentucky, Patterson v (97 U S 501), 33, 175, 25, 198
Kentucky R R Tax Cases (115 U S 321), 44, 210, 81, 223
Keokuk v Keokuk, etc. Packet Co (95 U. S. 80), 3, 5, 105, 57, 229
Keokuk, etc Packet Co, Keokuk v (95 U S. 80), 3, 5, 105, 5, 7, 229
Keokuk, United States v (6 Wall 514), 44, 177
Ker v. Illinois (119 U. S. 436), 94, 224
Keys v United States (109 U. S 336), 9, 116
Kibbe, Goodtitle v. (9 How. 471), 10, 166
Kidd v Pearson (128 U. S. 1), 25, 214, 169, 40.
Kilbourn v Thompson (103 U S. 168), 1, 10; 3, 11, 15, 232
Kilbourn Mfg Co, Woodman v (1 Abb U S 158, S. C 1 Biss. 546), 5, 164.
Killian v. Ebbinghaus (110 U. S. 568), 7, 192
Kimball, Mobile v. (102 U. S. 691), 1, 19, 20; 32, 28, 51, 26
Kimmish v Ball (129 U S 217), 170, 40, 13, 158.
Kimpton, Bronson v (8 Wall. 444), 12, 153
King, Wilmington, etc R. R Co v (91 U S. 3), 24, 233, 75, 72; 238, 98
Kinzie, Bronson v. (1 How 319), 41, 68, 72, 72, 58, 59, 70, 178, 88
Kirk v Lynd (106 U S. 315), 8, 50
Kirtland v Hotchkiss (101 U S 419), 258, 101
Klein, In re (1 How 279), 14, 44, 22, 23, 45
Klein, United States v (13 Wall. 128), 8, 113, 21, 114, 24, 115.
Kleinsmith, Dumphy v (11 Wall 610), 12, 166
Klinger v Missouri (13 Wall. 257), 40, 141
Knevals v Van Wyck (104 U S 360), 14, 167
Knoop, Piqua Bank v. (16 How 369), 5, 201, 69, 130, 115, 79; 129, 81, 178, 88
Knote v United States (95 U. S. 149), 4, 151.
Knowler s Lessee, Beaty v. (4 Pet. 165), 88, 74
Knox v. Lee (12 Wall 457), 12, 3.
Kohl v United States (91 U S 367), 18, 59, 10, 183
Kohn, Stewart v (11 Wall 493), 39, 235, 7, 57
Koshkonong v Burton (104 U S 668), 51, 70.
Kreiger, Randall v (23 Wall 137), 95, 76
Kring v Missouri (107 U. S. 221), 32, 33, 67

Labatut, Cousin v (19 How 202), 9, 122
Lafayette Ins. Co v French (18 How 404) 58, 128, 8, 153; 24, 155, 18, 159
Laird, Stewart v (1 Cranch, 299), 1, 119.
Lamar v Browne (92 U S 187), 23, 52
Lamphire, Jackson v (3 Pet. 280), 52, 70, 70, 72; 88, 74 53, 143
Lane County v. Oregon (7 Wall 71), 4, 195
Lange, Ex parte (18 Wall 163), 8, 60, 29, 186, 42, 187, 51, 88, 42, 235
Langford v United States (101 U S. 341), 23, 233
Lanman s Case (Cl & H). 2, 7
Larned v Burlington (4 Wall 275), 186, 90.
Lathrop v Brown (1 Woods, 471), 62, 71
Lavender Yonley v (21 Wall. 276), 97, 133, 32, 190.

La Vengance, United States v. (3 Dall. 297), **2**, 191.
Law v Austin (13 Wall. 29), **1**, 202
Lawler v. Walker (14 How. 149), **55**, 144.
League v De Young (11 How. 185), **234**, 98
Lee County v. United States (7 Wall. 175), **9**, 137, **22**, 233
Lee County, Thompson v (3 Wall. 327), **186**, 90
Lee, Knox v (12 Wall. 457), **12**, 3.
Lee, United States v. (106 U S. 196), **45**, 127.
Legal Tender Cases (12 Wall 457), **8**, 15, **4**, 46, **15**, 51, **4**, 56.
Lehigh Water Co. v Easton (121 U S 338), **252**, 100
Leisey v Hardin (135 U S 100), **101**, **103**, 32; **134**, **135a**, 36, **9**, 103, **12**, 104, **177**, 42, **1**, 202.
Leland, Wilkinson v (2 Pet 658), **12**, 183
Leloup v Port of Mobile (127 U. S. 640), **94**, **96**, **97**, **98**, 31.
Lenox, Mitchell v (14 Pet. 49), **2**, 152.
Lent, People v. (2 Wheel. C. C. 548), **6**, 55
Lessee of Fleeger, Poole v (11 Pet. 185), **12**, 106
Leszynsky, In re (16 Blatch. 9), **43**, 187
Letson, Louisville, etc R. R. Co v (2 How 550), **30**, 206.
Letson, Railroad Co v (2 How 497), **54**, **61**, 128
Lewis v Broadwell (3 McLean, 569), **52**, 70
Lewis, Colson v. (2 Wheat 377), **112**, 135
Lewis, Missouri v (101 U S 22), **81**, **84**, 223
Lewis, Seibert v. (122 U. S 284) **80**, 73
Lewis Westervelt v (2 McLean, 511), **30**, 155
License Cases (5 How. 585), **34**, 175, **4**, 43; **7**, 44.
License Cases (4 Wall 462), **4**, 16.
License Tax Cases (5 Wall. 477), **1**, 6
License Tax Cases (5 Wall. 462), **10**, 17, **63**, 27, **106**, **107**, 33, **28**, **29**, 198.
Lindsey, Fowler v. (3 Dall 411), **18**, 138
Lionberger v Rouse (9 Wall. 468), **6**, **9**, 18, **13**, **14**, 19.
Lithographic Co v Sarony (111 U S 53), **1**, 48.
Little v Barreme (2 Cranch, 170), **3**, 112
Live Stock Assoc. v Crescent City, etc Co (1 Abb (U S) 398), **16**, 212
Livingston's Lessees v Moore (7 Pet 469), **15**, 193, **1**, 194
Loughborough v Blake (5 Wheat. 317), **9**, 55, **1**, 6 **1**, **7**, 16
Lobrano v Nelligan (9 Wall 295), **92**, 75.
Locke v. New Orleans (4 Wall 172), **26**, 66
Lockwood, Gilman v. (4 Wall. 409) **21**, 45
Loney, Thomas v (134 U S 372), **2**, 10.
Lord v Steamship Co. (102 U. S 541), **39**, 24, **112**, 3.
Lord, The Mayor v (9 Wall 409), **86**, 131
Lott, Hinson v (8 Wall 148), **9**, 103, **1**, 202
Louisville Gas Co v Citizens' Gas Lt. Co. (115 U S 683), **246**, 100
Louisville & N R R. Co. v Woodson (134 U S 614), **88**, 224
Louisville, etc R. R Co v Letson (2 How 550), **30**, 206
Louisville & N. O. R. R. v Mississippi (133 U S. 587), **178**, 42
Louisville R. R Co v. Palmes (109 U S 257), **245**, **247**, 100
Louisiana, Hans v (134 U S 1), **20**, 204
Louisiana v Jumel (107 U S 711), **14**, 203, **22**, 205

Louisiana, Kennard v. (92 U S 480), **81**, 147, **38**, 215
Louisiana, Morgan Steamship Co. v. (118 U S. 455), **4**, 105, **1**, 59, **173**, 88, **10**, 54
Louisiana v Mayor of New Orleans (109 U S 285), **182**, 89, **10**, 153, **260**, 101, **50**, 217
Louisiana, Nathan v (8 How 73) **53**, **54**, **56**, 26
Louisiana, New Hampshire v (108 U S 76), **47**, 127, **24**, 205, **18**, 138.
Louisiana v New Orleans (102 U S. 203), **38**, 68
Louisiana, New York v (108 U S 76), **47**, 127, **18**, 138, **24**, 205
Louisiana v Police Jury (111 U. S 716), **68**, 72, **78**, 73, **182**, 89, **10**, 153
Louisiana v Pilsbury (105 U S 278), **55**, 70; **190**, 98
Louisiana Sugar Co, New Orleans Water Works Co v (125 U S. 18–32), **185**, 90, **233**, 98, **248**, 100, **64**, 144, **71**, 145
Louisiana v Steele (134 U. S 230), **18**, 204
Louisiana Lt Co, N O Gas Lt Co v (115 U. S 650), **197**, 91; **202**, 92
Louisiana, Williams v. (103 U. S. 637), **193**, 91.
Low v. Austin (12 Wall 220), **13**, 106
Lowe, Ft. Leavenworth v. (114 U S 525), **4**, 55
Lucas, Comm rs v (93 U. S. 108), **179**, 89
Luning, County of Lincoln v. (133 U S. 529), **26**, 205
Luther v Borden (7 How 43), **2**, 112, **9**, 60, **2**, **4**, 53; **5**, 181, **16**, 123; **1**, **2**, **3**, 168, **26**, 205, **45**, 200, **4**, 229, **17**, 232.
L. R R Co, R., F & P R. R. Co. v (13 How 71), **110**, 78, **205**, 93
Lyman, Holyoke Water Power Co v (15 Wall 500), **166**, 86.
Lynd, Kirk v (106 U. S 315), **8**, 50
Lyng v Michigan (135 U S 161), **177**, 12
Maberry, Slocum v (2 Wheat. 1), **7**, 122
Mackey, Mo Pac R. R v (127 U S 205) **54**, 218
Macomb Board of Liquidation v (92 U S 531), **13**, 203
Macon R. R., Cunningham v (109 U S 446), **6**, **9**, 202, **13**, 203, **27**, 206
Madison, Marbury v (1 Cranch, 137), **3**, 109, **6**, **7**, 16, **78**, 146, **3**, 136, **12**, 172, **13**, 203
Madrazo, Governor of Ga v (1 Pet. 123), **29**, 206
Mager v Grima (8 How 490), **35**, 199
Magraw, Ballard v. (8 Wall 639) **3**, 46
Maguire, Trask v (18 Wall 391), **145**, 83
Maguire v Maguire (7 Dana, 181), **17**, 167
Maguire, North Mo. R R. v. (20 Wall 46), **7**, 195. **147**, 83.
Maguire, Pacific R R Co v. (20 Wall. 36), **134**, 81, **150**, 84, **10**, 195
Maguire, Bailey v (22 Wall. 215), **135**, 81
Mahew v Thatcher (6 Wheat 129), **13**, 192
Mahon v Justice (127 U S 700), **7**, 161.
Mahoning Comm rs, Newton v (100 U S 548), **236**, 98
Manistee Riv Imp Co, Sands v (123 U S 288), **257**, 101; **65**, 220, **32**, 23
Mann, Arkansas Cattle Co v. (130 U S 69), **20**, 193
Marbury v. Madison (1 Cranch, 137), **3**, 109; **6**, **7**, 116, **78**, 146 **3**, 136, **2**, 172, **13**, 203
Marean, Hinkley v (3 Mason, 88) **19**, 45
Marigold, United States v (9 How. 560) **151**, 38, **1**, 46, **3**, **4**, 47, **2**, 56, **4**, 57

Marks, United States v (2 Abb (U S) 541), **4**, 57
Marsh v Burrows (1 Woods, 463), **61**, 71 **73**, 72
Marshall v B & O R R Co (16 How 314) **56**, **58**, **61**, 128
Marshall, Renner v (1 Wheat. 215), **13**, 192
Marshall, Turney v (1 Cong El Cas 167), **3**, 5
Marston, Palmer v (14 Wall 10), **64**, 144 **66**, 145
Martin In Matter of (2 Paine, 284), **5**, 192
Martin v Waddell (16 Pet. 410), **2**, 230
Martin, Good v (95 U S 90), **6**, 120
Martin v Hunter s Lessees (1 Wheat 304), **1**, 1, **2**, **7**, 15, **1**, 46, **1**, **4**, 53, **9**, 60 **12**, 61, **1**, 112; **27**, **28**, 139, **3**, 168, **2**, 170, **50**, 200.
Maryland, Ward v (12 Wall 418), **5**, 157 **69**, 27
Maryland Phila, Wil & Balt R R v (10 How 376), **16**, 196, **127**, 8; note, p 87
Maryland, Smith v (18 How 71), **11**, 20, **1**, 194
Maryland, Turner v. (107 U. S. 38), **15**, 104
Maryland v. B & O R R. (3 How 534) **90**, 75
Maryland, B & O R. R. Co v (20 Wall 643), **40**, 141, **44**, 142
Maryland Corson v (120 U. S 502), **84**, 24.
Maryland, W & B Turnpike Co v (3 Wall 210), **218**, 95
Maryland, McCulloch v (4 Wheat. 316), **3**, **1**, **9**, 3, **4**, **5**, 15, **8**, 16; **1**, **2**, **3**, **4**, 56, **12**, **19**, 220, **20**, 59, **6**, 57, **48**, 200, **1**, 170, **12**, 172
Maryland, Brown v (12 Wheat 455), **1**, 1, **103**, 32; **173**, 41, **13**, **17**, 104, **5**, 171, **1**, 202 **3**, 203
Mason v Ship Blaireau (2 Cranch, 240), **115**, 135
Mason, Brasheai v. (6 How 92), **5**, 136.
Mason, Messenger v (10 Wall 507), **60**, **63**, 144
Mason v Haile (12 Wheat. 373), **178**, 88, **43**, 69
Massachusetts, Pervear v (5 Wall. 475), **14**, 104
Massachusetts, McGuire v (3 Wall 387), **34**, 175
Massachusetts, Beer Co v (97 U S 25), **196**, 91, **26**, 198, **26**, 214, **9**, 230
Massachusetts, Western Union Tel. Co v (125 U S 530) **89**, 30; **35**, 175
Massachusetts, Provident Inst v (6 Wall 611), **3**, **6**, 18. **16**, 19; **3**, 195.
Massachusetts, Ins Co v (10 Wall 566), **8**, 20; **18**, 159
Massachusetts, Hamilton Mfg Co v (6 Wall 632) **12**, **16**, 19, **3**, 195, **2**, 202
Massachusetts, Rhode Island v (12 Pet. 657), **11**, 3 **12**, 106, **46**, 127, **17**, 138
Mathis, McGee v (4 Wall 143), **139**, 82, **255**, 100
Matthews v Rae (3 Cranch, C C 699), **4**, 43.
Matthews v. McStea (20 Wall 646), **45**, 142.
Matthews v Zane (7 Wheat 164), **3**, 14, **110**, 134 · **46**, 142 **8**, 122
Matthewson, Satterlee v (6 Pet 380), **83**, **84**, 74, **95**, 76, **260**, 101, **97**, 225
Maurran v Ins Co (6 Wall 1), **9**, 231
Maurice, United States v. (2 Brock 109), **10**, 3, **4**, 57
Maxwell v Stewart (21 Wall 71, 22 Wall 77), **8**, 192
Maxwell, United States v (2 Dill. 275), **32**, **33**, 186
Mayhew v Thatcher (6 Wheat. 129), **1**, 152
Maynard v Hill (125 U S 190), **17**, 167
Mayor of Balt., Barron v (7 Pet. 243), **5**, 2, **52**, 189, **1**, 182.

Mayor of N Y. v Miln (11 Pet. 102), **173**, 41.

Mayor of N Y, Miller v. (109 U S. 385), **29**, 22

Mayor of New Orleans, Louisiana v (109 U S 285), **182**, 89, **265**, 101, **10**, 153; **50**, 217

Mayor of Memphis Murdock v (20 Wall 590), **31**, 40

Mayor, Garrison v (21 Wall. 196), **94**, 76

Mayor, Henderson v (92 U S 259), **70**, 27 **75**, 28, **101**, **105**, 32, **118**, **119**, 34, **66**, 220

Mays v Fritton (B 21, L C Pub Co Ed U S Sup Ct. Rep 127), **43**, 142

M & C. R R Co v Tennessee (101 U S 337) **63**, 71

McAfee, Fulton v. (16 Pet. 149), **9**, 122

McCall v California (136 U. S. 109), **176**, 42

McCall v McDowell (Deady, 233, S C 1 Abb (U S) 212), **8**, **110**, **13**, **14**, 61

McClung v Silliman (6 Wheat. 598), **13**, 232

McClenachan, Coxe v. (3 Dall. 478), **1**, **3**, 13

McClung, Meigs v (9 Cranch, 11), **9**, 202

McCluny v Silliman (2 Wheat. 369), **4**, 136

McConnell, Hampton v. (3 Wheat. 234), **5**, 152

McCracken v Hayward (2 How 608), **59**, 70, **72**, 72; **178**, 88

McCready v Virginia (94 U S 391), **7**, 157 **3**, 164

McCoy v Washington Co (3 Wall. Jr 381) **12**, 65

McCreary, Barney v (Cl & H 176), **1**, 8

McCulloch v. Maryland (4 Wheat 316), **3**, 1, **9**, 3, **4**, **5**, 15, **8**, 16, **12**, 19, **2**, 20, **1**, **2**, **3**, **4**, 56, **6**, 57; **20**, 59; **1**, 170 **12**, 172, **48**, 200

McDonald, Berthold v. (22 How 334), **36**, 141.

McDonald, Cissel v (16 Blatch 150), **12**, 55

McDowell, Grisar v. (6 Wall 363), **9**, 202

McDowell, McCall v (Deady, 233; S C 1 Abb (U S) 212), **8**, **111**, **13**, **14**, 61

McDonald v Smalley (1 Pet 620), **82**, 131.

McElmoyle v Cohen (13 Pet 312), **3**, 152

McElrath v United States (102 U S. 426), **19**, 193

McFaddon, The Exchange v (7 Cranch 116), **16**, 17

McGuire v Commonwealth (3 Wall. 385), **46**, 142

McGuire v Massachusetts (3 Wall. 387), **34**, 175

McGee v. Mathis (4 Wall. 143), **139**, 82, **255**, 100

McGoon v Scales (9 Wall. 23) **33**, 199

McGahey v Virginia (135 U S 662), **226**, 96, **7**, 202

McGear v Woodruff (4 Vroom, 213), **7**, 148

McGlinn, C, R I. & P R'y Co v. (114 U. S. 542), **4**, 55.

McIntosh, Johnson & Graham's Lessee v. (8 Wheat. 543), **14**, 232

McIntire v Wood (7 Cranch, 504), **13**, 232

McKay v Campbell (2 Sawyer 129), **6**, 228

McKinley, Sherry v (99 U S 496), **26**, 185

McMillan v McNeill (4 Wheat 209), **100**, 77

McMahon, Palmer v (133 U S 660) **47**, 217

McMillen v Anderson (95 U S 37), **43**, 216, **44**, 217; **59**, 219

McMillan v McNeill (4 Wheat 209), **14**, 44, **19**, 45, **100**, 77.

McNamee v. Wilson (102 U S 572), **47**, 25.

McNeil, Ex parte (13 Wall 236), **46**, 24, **102**, 32
McNeill, McMillan v (4 Wheat 209) **14**, 44, 45, **19**, 45 **100**, 77
McQuerry, Miller v (5 McLean, 469), **10**, 168 **5**, 192
McStea, Matthews v (20 Wall 646), **45**, 142
McVeigh, Bank v. (98 U S 322), **238**, 98
Meador, In Matter of (1 Abb (U. S) 317), **6**, 181
Mead, Spaulding v. (Cl & H 16), 3, 11
Mechanics' Bank v Debolt (18 How. 380), **115**, 79, **129**, 81, **69**, 130, 5, 201 **102**, 134
Mechanics Bank v Thomas (18 How 384), **115**, 79, **129**, 81
Medberry v Ohio (24 How 413), **58**, 144
Medley, Ex parte (134 U S 160), **32**, 67.
Meginnis Crane v (1 Gill & J 463), **17**, 167
Meigs v McClung (9 Cranch, 11), **9**, 202
Memphis & Charleston R. R v Commissioners (112 U S 609), **173**, 88
Memphis & Charleston R R v Gaines (97 U S 697), **149**, **152**, 81
Memphis Gas Light Co. v Shelby Co (109 U S 398), **151**, 84
Memphis, Murdock v (20 Wall. 590), **44**, 142.
Memphis v United States (97 U. S 293), **65**, 71
Mercer s Case (Cl & H 44), **1**, 6.
Mercer, Watson v (8 Pet 88), **97**, 225, **143**, 32, **29**, 67
Mercer, Watson v (8 Pet 110), **18**, 65, **31**, 67, **37**, 68, **13**, 114, **95**, 76
Mercer Co v Cowles (7 Wall 118), **83**, 131
Merchants Nat Bk, Tappan v (19 Wall 490), **13**, 196
Merchants' Mut Ins Co, Delmas v (14 Wall 661), **192**, 91
Merchant, Spencer v (125 U S 345), **10**, 122, **46**, 217
Merritt, Hilton v (110 U S. 97), **28**, 186
Merriwether v Garrett (102 U. S. 472), **96**, 76, **179**, 88
Merryman, John, Ex parte (Taney, 246), **11**, **12**, 61
Messenger v Mason (10 Wall 507), **60**, **63**, 144.
Metropolitan R. R v Dist of Columbia (132 U. S 1), **13**, 56
Meyer v Muscatine (1 Wall 384), **186**, 90
Michigan, Walling v (116 U S 446), **81**, 29, **105**, 32
Michigan, Fargo v (121 U. S 230), **7**, 20 **85**, 29, **94**, 31
Michigan, Lyng v (135 U S 161), **177**, 42
Micou, Day v (18 Wall 156), **23**, 115
Miller v United States (11 Wall 268), **26**, 185, **10**, 191, **15**, 51.
Miller Fowler v (3 Dall. 411), **18**, 138
Miller, Pennsylvania v (132 U. S 75), **12**, 230 **168**, 87.
Miller, C & O R R v. (114 U S. 176), **173**, 88
Miller v McQuerry (5 McLean, 469), **10**, 163, **5**, 192
Miller v. State (15 Wall 478), **166**, **167**, 86.
Miller v Mayor of N Y (109 U S 385), **29**, 22
Milligan, Ex parte (4 Wall 114), **1**, 59 **12**, **13**, 61, **18**, 52 **1**, 147, **8**, 181, **7**, 190
Mills v Duryee (7 Cranch, 481), **4**, 152
Miln, New York v (11 Pet 155), **103**, 32, **173**, 41
Milne v Huber (3 McLean, 217), **36**, 68
Milner, Bailey v (1 Abb (U. S) 261) **15**, 65
Milnor v New Jersey R R (Book 16, L. C Ed U S Sup Ct. Rep 799), **50**, 25

Minor v. Happersett (21 Wall. 162), **21,** 159, **9,** 211, **19,** 213, **1,** 227.
Mining Co. v. Boggs (3 Wall. 304), **82,** 147
Minn. & St. L. R R. v. Herrick (127 U. S. 210), **54,** 218
Minneapolis R'y Co. v. Beckwith (129 U. S. 26), **64,** 220, **89,** 224
Minnesota, Chic., Mil. & St. P. R. R. Co. v. (134 U. S. 418), **122,** 80, **55,** 418
Minnesota, Gut v. (9 Wall. 35), **35,** 68; **41,** 199
Minnesota v. Barber (136 U. S. 313), **175,** 42, **20,** 105.
Minot v. Phila., Wil. & Balt. R. R. Co. (The Delaware R. R. Tax), (48 Wall. 206), **15,** 196
Mississippi, Moore v. (21 Wall. 636), **67,** 145
Mississippi v. Johnson (4 Wall. 475), **19,** 114, **5,** 118; **12,** 122
Mississippi, L. & N. O. R. R. v. (133 U. S. 587), **178,** 42
Mississippi, Stone v. (101 U. S. 814), **199,** 92 **118,** 79
Missouri v. Hays (120 U. S. 68), **82,** 223
Missouri v. Lewis (101 U. S. 22), **81,** **84,** 223
Missouri, Welton v. (91 U. S. 275), **4,** 20 **65,** **68,** 27, **71,** 28, **81,** 29 **101,** 32.
Missouri, Cummings v. (4 Wall. 277), **16,** **19,** 65, **20,** **22,** 66, **68,** 221
Missouri, Craig v. (4 Pet. 410), **3,** 63, **10,** 64, **13,** 65
Missouri, Byrne v. (8 Pet. 40), **3,** 63
Missouri, Kring v. (107 U. S. 221) **32,** **33,** 67
Missouri, Klinger v. (13 Wall. 257), **40,** 141
Missouri v. Kentucky (11 Wall. 395), **17,** 138
Missouri v. Iowa (7 How. 660), **17,** 138.
Missouri Pac. R. R. v. Humes (115 U. S. 572), **61,** 219, **90,** 224
Missouri Pac. R. R. v. Mackey (127 U. S. 205), **54,** 218
M. & M. R. R. Co. v. Rock (4 Wall. 177), **37,** 141
Mitchell v. Clark (110 U. S. 633), **41,** 187, **284,** 100, **53,** 70.
Mitchell v. Harmony (13 How. 115), **109,** 134, **20,** 184, **9,** 202
Mitchell v. Board of Com'rs (91 U. S. 206), **5,** 18.
Mitchell v. Lenox (14 Pet. 49), **2,** 152.
Mitchell v. Burlington (4 Wall. 270), **186,** 90
Mitchell, United States v. (2 Dall. 348), **1,** 148.
Mobile, Osborne v. (16 Wall. 479), **62,** 26, 27, **63,** 27, **10,** 195
Mobile v. Kimball (102 U. S. 691), **1,** 19, 20, **32,** 23, **51,** 26, **135,** 36
Mobile, Waring v. (8 Wall. 110), **13,** **14,** 104
Moffat, Cook v. (5 How. 295) **45,** 69, **10,** 172
Montgomery, Jecker v. (18 How. 110) **14,** 51, **13,** 113
Montgomery v. Hernandez (12 Wheat. 129) **33,** 110
Montalet v. Murray (4 Cranch, 46), **116,** 135
Moore v. Mississippi (21 Wall. 636), **67,** 145
Moore, Livingstone's Lessees v. (7 Pet. 469), **15,** 193, **1,** 194.
Moore v. People (14 How. 3), **53,** 189, **27,** 198
Moore, Veazie v. (14 How. 568), **21,** 21
Moore v. American Transportation Co. (24 How. 1), **149,** 38
Moore, Houston v. (5 Wheat. 1), **4,** 43 **3,** 53, **5,** 151, **7,** 163
Moore v. Greenhow (114 U. S. 338), **225,** 96
Moran v. New Orleans (112 U. S. 69), **77,** 28.
Morewood v. Enquist (23 How. 491), **37,** 126

Morgan v Parham (16 Wall. 471), **61**, 26
Morgan, Peete v (19 Wall 581), **7**, 106
Morgan Steamship Co v. Louisiana (118 U S 455), **1**, 59, **165**, 40; **172**, **173**, 88 **41**, 105
Mormon Church v United States (136 U. S. 1), **3**, **4**, 165, **7**, 166
Morrill v Wisconsin (Book 23, L. C. Pub Co. Ed. U S Sup. Ct Rep 1009), **71**, 28; **164**, 40.
Morris v New Orleans (105 U. S. 600), **181**, 89.
Morris, Winn v. (3 How 3), **56**, 144
Morris v. United States (Morris' Cotton), (8 Wall. 507), **18**, 193
Morris, United States v (1 Curtis 23), **47**, 188
Morrison v Springer (15 Iowa, 345), **3**, 4
Morse Home Ins Co v (20 Wall 445), **65**, **66**, **68**, 129
Morton, Taylor v (2 Curtis, 454), **99**, 133 **23**, 174
Mott, Martin v (12 Wheat. 19), **1**, 112, **1**, **4**, 53, **1**, 117, **9**, 60, **12**, 61 **3**, 168.
Moultrie Co. v. Savings Bank (92 U S 631), **195**, 91
Mt Pleasant v Beckwith (100 U S. 514), **231**, 97
Mugler v. Kansas (123 U S 623), **23**, 214
Mulligan v Corbins (7 Wall. 487), **222**, 95
Munford, United States v (16 Fed Rep 223), **1**, 4, **10**, 228
Munn v Illinois (94 U S 113), **124**, 35; **157**, **162**, 39; **1**, 59, **22**, 197, **56**, 218; **104**, 225
Murdock v Memphis (20 Wall 590), **44**, 142; **31**, 140
Murray, Montalet v. (4 Cranch, 46), **116**, 135
Murray, Justice v (9 Wall 274), **16**, 193, **1**, 194
Murray v Ramsey (114 U. S. 15), **5**, **6**, 165
Murray v Charleston (96 U S. 432), **136**, 81, **1**, 202
Murray, Hoboken Land Co v (18 How 272), **7**, 181, **21**, **22**, **26**, **27**, 185
Muscatine, Meyer v. (1 Wall 384), **186**, 90
Mut. Benefit Ins Co v. Tisdale (91 U S 238), **12**, 44
Mutual Life Ins Co v. Harris (97 U S 331), **14**, 153

Nagle, Wright v. (101 U S 794), **245**, 100.
Nagle, in re (135 U S 1), **3**, 171, **7**, 118.
Nashville v. Cooper (6 Wall 247), **16**, 58.
Nashville, Adams v. (95 U S 19), **15**, 173
Nashville & Chattanooga R Co v. Alabama (128 U S 96), **133**, 36; **53**, 218
Nathan v Louisiana (8 How 73), **53**, **54**, **56**, 26
National Bank, Britton v. (105 U S. 322), **18**, 173
National Bank v. Commonwealth (9 Wall 353), **36**, 176
National Bank, Tappan v (19 Wall. 490), **6**, **8**, 18
National Bank v. Yankton County (101 U S 129) **4**, 165, **15**, 167
Neal v Delaware (103 U S 370), **66**, 220, **78**, 222, **7**, 228, **4**, 217
Needles, Chicago Life Ins Co v (113 U S 574), **83**, 228 **205**, 92
Neil, Moore & Co v. Ohio (3 How 720) **1**, 47
Neilson v. Garza (2 Woods, 287), **19**, 104
Neff, Pennoyer v. (95 U. S. 714), **59**, 219
Nelligan, Lobrano v. (9 Wall 295), **92**, 75
Nesbit, Baltimore & Susquehanna R R Co v (10 How 395), **87**, 74
Nevada, Crandall v (6 Wall 42), **64**, 27, **102**, 32, **2**, 156, **30**, 215.

Neves v Scott (13 How. 268), **107**, 134
Nevin, Walston v (128 U S 578), **49**, 217.
Newberry, Baldwin v (117 U S 201), **18**, 45.
New Hampshire v Louisiana (108 U S 76), **47**, 127, **18**, 138, **24**, 205
New Hampshire, Prince v (5 How. 504), **135**, 36
New Jersey v Yard (95 U. S 104), **167**, 87
New Jersey v Wilson (7 Cranch, 164), **124**, 80, **155**, 85, **178**, 88
New Jersey v New York (5 Pet 284), **12**, 137, **17**, 138
New Jersey, Bigelow v (Book 16, L. C Ed. U S Sup. Ct. Rep. 799), **50**, 25.
New Jersey, Milnor v. (Book 16, L. C Ed U S Sup Ct Rep 799), **50**, 25.
New Orleans, Davidson v. (96 U S 97) **21**, 185, **1**, 194, **38**, 216; **59**, 219.
New Orleans v N Y. Steamship Co (20 Wall 387), **10**, 231
New Orleans, Cannon v (20 Wall 577), **5**, 105, **7**, **8**, 106
New Orleans, Louisiana v (109 U. S. 285), **10**, 153, **50**, 217
New Orleans, Louisiana v (102 U S 203) **38**, 68
New Orleans v Moran (112 U. S 69), **77**, 28
New Orleans v Morris (105 U. S. 600) **181**, 89
New Orleans, Wolf v (103 U S. 358), **180**, 89, **176**, 88
New Orleans, Locke v. (4 Wall 172), **26**, 66
New Orleans v Armas (9 Pet. 224), **4**, 121
New Orleans v Houston (119 U S 265), **118**, 79
New Orleans, United States v. (103 U S 358), **227**, 96
New Orleans v Winter (1 Wheat 91), **72**, 130
New Orleans Gaslight Co. v. Louisiana Light Co (115 U S 650), **197**, 91, **202**, 92
New Orleans Water-works v La. Sugar Works (125 U. S. 31), **233**, 98, **248**, 100, **64**, 144, **71**, 151.
New Orleans Water-works, St Tammany Water-works v (120 U S 64), **119**, 79
New Orleans Water-works Co v Rivers (115 U S 674), **202**, 92
New Orleans Water-works v Louisiana Sugar Co (125 U S 18), **185**, 90
New Orleans Water-works Co v St. Tammany Water-works Co. (14 Fed Rep 194), **14**, 184
Newport, etc Bridge Co. v. United States (105 U S 470), **6**, 183.
Newton's Case (Cl. & H 47), **1**, **6**
Newton v Mahoning Comm'rs (100 U S 548), **236**, 98
New York, Starin v. (115 U S 248), **6**, 121.
New York v Louisiana (108 U S 76), **47**, 127, **18**, 138, **24**, 205
New York, New Jersey v (5 Pet. 284), **12**, 137 **17**, 138
New York v. Connecticut (4 Dall 3), **18**, 138
New York v. Comm'rs (4 Wall 244), **6**, 18
New York v Commissioners of Taxes (2 Wall 200), **2**, 17, **10**, 18, **12**, 19
New York v Comm'rs of Taxes (2 Black, 620), **2**, 17, 18, **12**, 19
New York, Phila Fire Ass'n v (119 U S 110), **63**, 220
New York v Joehne (128 U S. 189) **34**, 67
New York v Dibble (21 How 366), **34**, 199
New York v Miln (11 Pet 155), **103**, 32
New York, Bank of Commerce v (2 Black, 620), **1**, 170. **5**, 171
New York Home Ins. Co v (131 U S 599), **15**, 19, **75**, 222, **87**, 224.

New York City, Garrison v (21 Wall. 203), **259, 260,** 100
New York Steamship Co, New Orleans v (20 Wall. 387), **10,** 231
Nichol Furman v (8 Wall 44), **38,** 141, **60,** 144, **117,** 79
Nicholson, Osborn v (13 Wall. 654), **7,** 204, **74,** 72.
Nicolet Breedlove v (7 Pet. 413), **117,** 135
Noel v Ewing (9 Ind 37), **17,** 167.
Nones v Edsall (1 Wall Jr 189), **3,** 13.
Norfolk & W R R v Benna (136 U S 114), **176,** 42
Norris, Williams v (12 Wheat 117), **32,** 140, **46,** 142.
North Carolina, Cross v (132 U S. 131) **76,** 222.
North Carolina v Temple (134 U S 22) **18,** 204
North Mo R R v Maguire (20 Wall 46). **7,** 195 **147,** 83
Northrup, Vaughn v (15 Pet. 2), **78,** 131
Northwestern University v People (99 U S 309). **138.** 82.
Northwestern Union Packet Co v St Louis (100 U S 423), **3,** 101.
Norton v Shelby Co (118 U S 425), **26,** 233
Norwich, etc R. R. v. Johnson (15 Wall. 195), **4,** 46
Norwood's Lessees Owings v. (5 Cranch, 344), **11,** 122
Nudd v Burrows (91 U S 426), **89,** 132.

Ochiltree v Iowa R. R. Contracting Co (21 Wall. 249), **93,** 75, 76
Ogden v Saunders (12 Wheat. 213), **45,** 69, **178,** 88, **4,** 43, **14,** 41, **15,** 45
Ogden Gibbons v (9 Wheat. 187), **11,** 3, **10, 13,** 230, **1,** 19, **6, 10,** 20, **36,** 23, **101, 103,** 32, **2,** 202, **1,** 170, **5,** 171, **173,** 41
Ohio, Medberry v (24 How. 413), **58,** 144
Ohio v Neil, Moore & Co. (3 How. 720) **1,** 47
Ohio, Shields v. (95 U. S. 319), **169,** 87
Ohio, Fox v. (5 How. 410), **1,** 46, **3, 5,** 47; **1,** 179; **2,** 180, **3,** 181, **52,** 189, **2,** 189; **11,** 192.
Ohio Life Trust Co v. Debolt (16 How 432), **186,** 90, **5,** 201
Ohio & Miss R. R Co v Wheeler (1 Black, 286), **60, 61,** 128; **46,** 200
Okely, Bank of Columbia v. (4 Wheat. 235), **14,** 193.
Olcott v Supervisors (16 Wall 689), **18,** 197, **4,** 182
Oregon, Dane County v (7 Wall 71), **4,** 195
Ortega, United States v (11 Wheat. 467), **21,** 123
Osborn v. U S. Bank (9 Wheat 738), **2,** 16, **13,** 44, **4,** 57, **2,** 121, **11,** 202
Osborn v Nicholson (13 Wall. 654), **7,** 209, **74,** 72
Osborne v Mobile (16 Wall 479), **62,** 26, 27; **63,** 27; **10,** 195
Otis v Bacon (7 Cranch, 589), 3, 112
Ouachita Packet Co. v Aiken (121 U S 444), **4,** 105
Owings v Norwood's Lessees (5 Cranch, 344), **11,** 122.
Owings v. Speed (5 Wheat. 420), **10,** 77

Pace v Alabama (106 U S 583), **79,** 222
Pace v. Burgess (92 U. S. 372), **7, 8,** 62, **5,** 203.
Pacific Ins. Co v Soule (7 Wall. 433), **2,** 6, **4,** 61
Pacific R R v Maguire (20 Wall. 36), **10,** 195, **134,** 81 **150,** 84
Pacific R R. California v (127 U S 1), **172,** 41, **90,** 30; **40,** 176
Pacific R R v. Thompson (9 Wall. 579), **4,** 57
Pacific M S. S Co. v. Joliffe (2 Wall. 450), **44, 46,** 24

Packard, Davis v. (7 Pet. 276), **19,** 123
Packet Company v. Catlettsburg (105 U. S. 559), **147,** 37
Packet Co. v. Keokuk (95 U. S. 80), **5,** 7, 229
Packet Co. v. St. Louis (100 U. S. 428) **5,** 105
Page, Fleming v. (9 How. 603), **9,** 60, **5,** 113, **16,** 51, **1,** 164
Palmer v. Marston (14 Wall. 10) **64,** 144
Palmer v. McMahon (133 U. S. 660) **47,** 217
Palmer v. Cuyahoga Co. (3 McLean, 226), **41,** 24
Palmer, Fritts v. (132 U. S. 282), **171,** 41
Palmer, Louisville, etc. R. R. Co. v. (109 U. S. 257), **245, 247,** 100
Palmer, United States v. (3 Wheat. 610), **3,** 118, **8,** 231
Pargoud v. United States (13 Wall. 156), **15,** 114, **23,** 115
Parham, Woodruff v. (8 Wall. 123), **12,** 104, **8,** 113, **1,** 202, **8,** 203.
Parham, Morgan v. (16 Wall. 471), **61,** 26
Parker v. United States (1 Pet. 293), **11,** 113
Parkersburg, Transportation Co. v. (107 U. S. 691), **4,** 105
Parkinson v. United States (121 U. S. 281), **30,** 186
Parsons v. Bedford (3 Pet. 433), **1, 2,** 191
Passenger Cases (7 How. 283), **52,** 26, **107,** 33, **3,** 62; **4,** 43; **101, 103,** 32.
Patterson, Boom Co. v. (98 U. S. 403), **59,** 219
Patterson v. Kentucky (97 U. S. 501), **25,** 198, **33,** 175
Paul v. Virginia (8 Wall. 168), **9, 12,** 20, **21,** 139, **3,** 156, **18,** 159
Paup v. Drew (10 How. 218), **107,** 77
Payne, Baldwin v. (6 How. 301), **105,** 77
Payne v. Hook (7 Wall. 425) **97,** 133; **106,** 134
Peal v. Phillips (14 How. 368), **78,** 131
Pearson v. Yewdall (95 U. S. 294), **11,** 192; **1,** 194, **34,** 215
Pearson, Kidd v. (128 U. S. 1), **25,** 214, **169,** 40
Pease, Starr v. (8 Conn. 541), **17,** 167
Peck, Fletcher v. (6 Cranch 87, 137), **25,** 66, **32,** 67, **97,** 76, **178,** 88
Peete v. Morgan (19 Wall. 581) **6,** 106.
Pegues, Humphrey v. (16 Wall. 244), **133,** 81, **10,** 195
Pelican Ins. Co., Wisconsin v. (127 U. S. 265) **8,** 137, **14, 19,** 138, **10,** 153
Pembina Mining Co. v. Pennsylvania (125 U. S. 181) **88,** 30, **64,** 220.
Pendleton, Western Union Tel. Co. v. (122 U. S. 347), **22,** 197, **166, 167,** 40
Pennie v. Reis (132 U. S. 464), **208,** 93, **211,** 94
Penniman's Case (103 U. S. 714), **44,** 69, **5,** 229
Penniston, U. P. R'y Co. v. (18 Wall. 5), **45,** 177, **8,** 195
Pennoyer v. Neff (95 U. S. 714) **59,** 219
Pennsylvania, Prigg v. (16 Pet. 539), **1,** 229, **1, 5, 8,** 163
Pennsylvania, Chester v. (134 U. S. 240) **82,** 223
Pennsylvania, Norfolk, etc. R. R. v. (136 U. S. 114), **176,** 42
Pennsylvania College Cases (13 Wall. 190), **163,** 86
Pennsylvania, Pembina Mining Co. v. (125 U. S. 181), **64,** 220, **88,** 30
Pennsylvania v. Miller (132 U. S. 75), **12,** 230, **168,** 87
Pennsylvania, Powell v. (127 U. S. 678) **4,** 211
Pennsylvania, Bell's Gap R. R. Co. v. (134 U. S. 232), **86,** 223
Pennsylvania, Phila. Steamship Co. v. (122 U. S. 326), **86,** 29; **87,** 30, **94,** 31.

Pennsylvania v Carpenter (17 How 463) **18**, 65, **30**, 67, **37**, 68
Pennsylvania, Butler v (10 How 402), **17**, 167 **206**, **209**, 93
Pennsylvania, Twitchell v. (7 Wall 321), **2**, 189.
Pennsylvania, Cook v (97 U S 566), **66**, 27 **6**, 103
Pennsylvania v Wheeling Bridge Co. (18 How 421), **20**, **22**, 21, 1, 162, **150**, 38; **15**, **16**, 138, **21**, 139, **7**, 137
Pennsylvania, Erie R y Co v (21 Wall 492), **148**, **151**, 84
Pennsylvania, Gloster Ferry Co v (114 U S. 196), **79**, 28, **127**, 35, **148**, 38
Pensacola Broughton v (93 U S 266), **231**, 96
Pensacola Tel Co v Western Union Tel Co (96 U. S 1), **4**, 47, **110**, **111**, 33.
People v Whipple (9 Cow 707), **32**, 186
People Moore v (14 How. 13), **53**, 189, **27**, 198
People v Salem (20 Mich 452), **18**, 197
People v Hatch (33 Ill 9), **2**, 118
People v Lent (2 Wheel. C. C. 548), **6**, 55
People v Cassidy (49 N Y 46) **6**, 229
People v Comm'rs of Taxes (4 Wall. 244) **14**, 196
People v. Compagnie Gen Transatlantique (107 U S. 59-62), **3**, 59, **76**, 28
People, Northwestern University v (99 U S 309), **138**, 82
People v Weaver (100 U S 539), **16**, **18**, 173
People ex rel v Com'rs Taxes (104 U S 466) **7**, 103
People ex rel The Banks v. Hoffman (7 Wall 16), **11**, 18
Perdicaries, Dewing v (96 U S. 193), **233**, 98
Pereles v Watertown (6 Biss. 79), **54**, 70
Perez. United States v (9 Wheat. 579). **45**, 188
Permoli v First Municipality (3 How 588), **40**, 235, **3**, 179
Perveat v Commonwealth (5 Wall 475), **1**, 194 **21**, 197, **30**, 198, **5**, 16, **14**, 104
Peters, United States v (5 Cranch, 115), **30**, 206
Petit, United States v. (114 U S 429) **31**, 108
Phalen, Herman v. (14 How 79), **234**, 98
Phalen v Virginia (8 How. 163), **91**, 75
Philadelphia Gilman v. (3 Wall 713), **24**, 21, 22, **102**, **103**, 32, **114**, **115**, 34
Philadelphia, Girard v (7 Wall 1), **231**, 97
Philadelphia, Christ Church v (24 How 300), **120**, 79, **141**, 82
Philadelphia, Union Passenger R y v. (101 U S 528), **160**, 86
Philadelphia Wil & Balt R R Co, Minot v. (18 Wall 206) **15**, 196
Philadelphia & Wil R R v Maryland (10 How 376), **127**, 80, **16**, 196, note, p 87
Philadelphia Fire Asso v New York (119 U S 110), **63**, 220
Philadelphia Steamship Co v Pennsylvania (122 U S 326), **86**, 29, **87**, 30, **94**, 31; **128**, **129**, 35.
Phipps Peale v (14 How 368), **80**, 131.
Pickard v Pullman Southern Car Co (117 U S 34), **83**, 29
Pickering, John, U S District Judge March 3, 1803, March 12, 1803 **7**, 8
Piek v C & N W R. R. Co (94 U S 164) **57**, 218 **159**, **162**, 39
Pierce v New Hampshire (5 How 504), **135a**, 36
Pierce v Carskaddon (16 Wall 234), **16**, **19**, 65
Pike Co Douglass v (101 U S 677), **187**, 90

Pike Co, Foote v (101 U S 688), **187**, 90
Pilsbury, Louisiana v. (105 U S 278), **55**, 70
Piqua Bank v Knoop (16 How 369), **178**, 88, **102**, 134, **69**, 130, **115**, 79
Pitot, Sere & Lavalde v (6 Cranch, 332), **16**, 51 **73**, 130, **1**, 165
Pittsburg, Kelly v (104 U S 78), **1**, 194, **42**, 216
Planters' Bank v Sharp (6 How 327), **178**, 88
Planters Bank, Bank of United States v (9 Wheat. 907), **31**, 206
Poindexter v Greenhow (114 U S 270), **9**, 64, **10**, 202
Police Jury, Louisiana v (111 U S 716), **68**, 72, **78**, 73, **182**, 89 **210**, 93, **10**, 153.
Pollard v Hagan (3 How 212), **19**, 21, **1**, 54, **2**, **3**, **4**, 164, **10**, 166, **9**, 172, **3**, 230
Palmer v. Marston (14 Wall 10), **66**, 145
Poole v Lessee of Fleeger (11 Pet 185), **12**, 106
Portland & Kennebec R R, Kennebec & Portland R R. v. (14 Wall 23), **66**, 145
Port of Mobile, Leolup v (127 U S 640), **94**, **96**, **97**, **98**, 31
Port of Mobile v Watson (116 U S. 289), **232**, 97
Porter, Benner v. (9 How 235), **9**, 166
Porter v Foley (24 How. 415), **58**, 144
Porter, Benner (9 How. 235), **6**, 120
Portwardens, Steamship Co v. (6 Wall. 31), **46**, 24
Postmaster Genl v Early (12 Wheat 136), **3**, 121
Pound v Turck (95 U S 462), **102**, 32, **125**, 35
Powell v. Pennsylvania (127 U S 678), **4**, 211.
Presbury, Willard v (14 Wall. 676), **3**, 54, **11**, 55
Presser v Illinois (116 U S 252), **2**, 180, **20**, 213, **73**, 221, **1**, 194
Preston, Bors v (111 U S 252), **2**, 136, **11**, 137
Prevost v Greneaux (19 How. 1), **43**, 170
Prigg v Pennsylvania (16 Pet 539), **1**, 229, **53**, 189, **4**, 56, **9**, 57, **1**, **5**, **8**, 163
Prize Cases (2 Black, 635), **12**, 113; **4**, 118, **2**, **4**, 50, **15**, 51
Propeller Genessee Chief v Fitzhugh (12 How 443), **33**, **35**, 125
Providence Bank v Billings (4 Pet 514), **120**, 79, **142**, 82, **150**, 84, **88**, 74.
Provident Inst v Jersey City (113 U S 506) **45**, 217
Provident Inst v. Mass (6 Wall 611), **3**, **6**, 18, **16**, 19, **3**, 195
Pryor, United States v (3 Wash 234), **22**, 150
Pullman Southern Car Co Pickard v (117 U. S 34), **83**, 29
Pullman Southern Car Co, Tennessee v (117 U S 51), **83**, 29
Pumpelly v. Canal Co. (13 Wall 166), **1**, 182; **17**, 184
Putnam Pittsburg, etc R R Co v (118 U S. 545), **89**, 132

Quincy v Jackson (113 U S 332), **183**, 89
Quincy Von Hoffman v (4 Wall 535) **174**, **177**, 88, **46**, **47**, 69, **57**, 70, **213**, 94, **189**, 90

Rae, Matthews v (3 Cranch, C C 699), **4**, 43
Railroad Co. v Penn State Tax on Foreign Held Bonds (15 Wall. 300), **19**, 197
Railroad Co v Tennessee (101 U S 337), **23**, 205, **81**, 73
Railroad Co, Stone v (116 U S 347), **121**, 79
Railroad Co v Baldwin (103 U S. 426), **14**, 167
Railroad Co v Reid (13 Wall. 264), **13**, 181.

Railroad Co v Rock (4 Wall. 80), **61**, 144

Railroad Co. v Letson (2 How 497), **54**, **61**, 128

Railroad Co, Secombe v (3 Wall. 108), **59**, 219

Railroad Co v. Richmond (19 Wall 584), **37**, 23.

Railroad Co v Hamblen Co (102 U S 273), **173**, 88

Railroad Co v Hamersley (104 U. S 1), **239**, 98

Railroad Co v King (91 U S 3), **238**, 98

Railroad Co, Allen v (114 U. S. 311), **224**, 95

Railroad Co, Piek v. (94 U. S. 178), **102**, 32

Railroad Co v. Johnson (15 Wall 195), **15**, 51

Railroad Co. v. Hecht (95 U S. 168), **65**, 71

Railroad Co v Husen (95 U S 465), **101**, **105**, 32; **158**, 39

Railroad Co v. Iowa (99 U. S 155), **124**, 35 **160**, **162**, 39.

Railroad Companies v. Schuette (103 U. S 108), **6**, 229

Railroad Companies v. Richmond (15 Wall. 3), **42**, 142.

Railroad Commission Cases (116 U. S 307), **42**, 199; **121**, 79

Railway Co., Cherokee Nation v. (135 U S 641), **5**, 182

Railway Co. v Renwick (102 U. S. 180), **37**, 176

Railway Co. v. Jackson (7 Wall. 262), **31**, 234

Ralls Co v. United States (105 U. S. 733), **196**, 91.

Ramsey, Murray v. (114 U S. 15), **5**, **6**, 165.

Randall v. Kreiger (23 Wall 137), **95**, 76

Randell Crowell v. (10 Pet. 368), **96**, 133, **27**, 139, **30**, 140

Rathbone, United States v. (2 Paine. 578), **6**, 192

Rauscher, United States v (119 U S. 407), **24**, 174.

Ravord, United States v. (2 Dall. 297), **1**, 136; **11**, 137

Reclamation Dist No. 108, Hagar v (111 U S 701), **24**, 198, **37**, 211, **29**, 219, **39**, 176.

Red Rock v. Henry (106 U. S 596), **230**, 97

Rees v Watertown (19 Wall. 107), **9**, 137

Reese, United States v. (92 U. S. 214) **7**, 229; **9**, 57, **5**, 10.

Reeves, Virginia v (100 U S. 313), **3**, 227, **1**, 210, **29**, 214

Reggel, Ex parte (114 U S 642), **6**, 160

Reid, Railroad Co. v. (13 Wall 264), **131**, 81

Reilly, Roberts v. (116 U S 80), **8**, 161

Reily, United States v (5 Blatch. 204), **48**, 188

Reis, Pennie v (132 U. S 464), **208**, 93, **211**, 94

Renner v Marshall (1 Wheat. 215), **13**, 192.

Republican River Bridge Co v Kansas Pac R R. Co (92 U S 315), **48**, 143.

Respublica v Roberts (1 Dall 39), **18**, 150

Respublica v. Carlisle (1 Dall 35), **8**, 149

Rew, Scholey v. (23 Wall 331), **4**, **6**, **13**, 17

Rex v Hickman (1 Moody, 34), **32**, 186

Reynolds v United States (98 U S 145), **7**, 120, **4**, 179

R F & P. R. R Co v L. R. R. Co (13 How 71), **110**, 78, **205**, 93

Rhode Island v Massachusetts (12 Pet 657), **11**, 3, **9**, 230, **46**, 127, **12**, 106, **17**, 138

Rhodes, Bronson v (4 Wall. 229), **12**, 153

Richard's Case (Cl. & H. 16) **3,** 11
Richardson, In re (2 Story, 571), **2,** 14
Richmond, Fredericksburg & Pot. R'y Co v Richmond (96 U. S. 521), **60,** 219
Richmond, Railroad Companies v. (15 Wall 3) **42,** 142
Richmond Dubuque etc R. R. v (19 Wall 584) **37,** 23; **156,** 39
Rhodes, United States v (1 Abb (U S) 78), **4,** 43, **1,** 53, **4,** 115, **1,** 168, **5,** 209.
Ried, Webster v (11 How 437), **10,** 192
Riggs v. Johnson (6 Wall. 176), **97,** 133, **103,** 134, **17,** 58
Riggs, Geoffrey v (133 U S 258), **20,** 173
Rinker, Tiernan v (102 U S 123), **67,** 27.
Rio Grande R R Co. v. Gomila (132 U S 478), **97,** 133.
Rivers, N O Water-works Co v (115 U S 674), **202,** 92
Rives, Virginia v (100 U S 313), **100,** 225.
Robb v Connolly (111 U S 624), **4,** 160.
Robbins, Jones v (8 Gray, 329), **7,** 148
Robbins v. Shelby Taxing Dist (120 U S 489), **69,** 27, **84,** 29, **105,** 32, **135,** 36; **129,** 35
Roberts v Reilly (116 U. S 80), **8,** 161
Roberts, Respublica v (1 Dall 39), **18,** 150
Robertson, Whitney v. (124 U S 190), **23,** 174; **29,** 175
Robinson, Edye v. (12 U. S. 580), **78,** 28
Rochereau, Dupasseur v. (21 Wall. 130), **49,** 143
Rock, M & M R. R. v. (4 Wall. 177), **37,** 141, **61,** 144
Rockhold v. Rockhold (92 U S 480), **81,** 147, **238,** 98
Ross v Doe (1 Pet. 655), **34,** 141.
Rouse Lionberger v (9 Wall. 468), **6, 9,** 18, **13, 14,** 19
Rouse, Home of the Friendless v. (8 Wall 430), **130,** 81; **6,** 195
Rouse, Washington University v (8 Wall 439), **130,** 81.
Royall v. Virginia (121 U S 102), **226,** 96
Royall v. Virginia (116 U S 572), **224,** 95, **226,** 96
Royall, Ex parte (117 U S 241), **76,** 146
Ruddle v Canal Co (14 How 80), **214,** 94
Russell, United States v (13 Wall 623), **19,** 184
Russell, Christmas v. (5 Wall 290), **9,** 153. **19,** 154, **52,** 70.
Ryan v Carter (93 U S 78), **12,** 158
Salem, People v (20 Mich 452), **18,** 197
Sales, McGoon v. (9 Wall 23) **33,** 199
Salmon, Stewart v (94 U S 435), **238,** 98
Salomons v Graham (15 Wall. 208), **65,** 145.
Sampeyreac v. United States (7 Pet. 222), **97,** 225
Samples v. Bank (1 Woods, 523) **52,** 70.
Sampson, Wiswall v (14 How. 52), **78,** 131.
Sandford, Scott v (19 How 393), **2,** **3,** 1, **13,** 3, **2,** 4, **4, 5,** 48, **16,** 51, **2,** 59, **2,** 163, **5,** 164; **13,** 166.
Sands v Manistee Riv Imp Co. (123 U S 288), **32,** 23, **65,** 220
Sands v Edmunds (116 U. S. 585), **224,** 95, **226,** 96
Santa Clara Co v South. Pac. R. R Co (118 U. S 394), **62, 64,** 220
Sarmiento, Green v. (3 Wash. C. C. 17), **29,** 155
Sarony, Lithographic Co v (111 U. S. 53), **1,** 48
Satterlee v Matthewson (2 Pet. 380), **97,** 225, **260,** 101.
Saunders, Ogden v (12 Wheat. 277), **14,** 44, **15,** 45, **178,** 88; **45,** 69, **4,** 48.

Sauvinet Walker v (92 U. S 90), **11,** 92, **1,** 194
Savin Ex parte (131 U S 267), **18,** 123
Savings Bank, Moultrie v. (92 U S 631), **195,** 91
Savings & Loan Assoc v Topeka (20 Wall 655), **12,** 196, **17, 18,** 197
Sayer, Dominick v (3 Sandf. 555), **178,** 88
Schaffer v. Scuddy (10 How 16) **113,** 135
Schiff Shields v. (124 U S. 351), **2,** 151
Schmidt, Avegno v (113 U. S. 293), **2,** 151
Schofield v Eichelberger (7 Pet. 586), **14,** 51
Scholey v Rew (23 Wall 331), **4,** 6, **13,** 17
Schottler, Spring Valley Water Co. v. (110 U S 347), **161,** 86
Schurz, United States v (102 U S 378) **13,** 203.
Schutte Railroad Companies v (103 U S 108) **6,** 229
Scotland County v Thomas (94 U. S. 682) **16,** 196, note to p 87.
Scott, Neves v. (13 How 268) **107,** 134
Scott v Jones (3 How 343), **6,** 137, **4,** 168.
Scott v Sandford (19 How 393), **2,** 1; **13,** 3, **2,** 4, **2,** 163 **5,** 164, **13,** 166, **4, 5,** 43; **8, 9,** 44, **16,** 51, **2,** 59, **70,** 130
Scuddy, Schaffer v. (10 How 16), **113,** 135
Seacombe v Railroad Co (23 Wall 108), **59,** 219
Seaman Talbott v (1 Cranch, 28), **3,** 50 **9,** 51
Searight v Stokes (3 How 151), **1,** 47.
Seibert v Lewis (122 U S 281), **80,** 73.
Semmes v United States (91 U S 21), **4,** 151.
Sere & Laralde v Pitot (6 Cranch, 332), **16,** 51, **73,** 130, **1,** 165
Sevier v. Haskell (14 Wall 12), **46,** 142, **66,** 145, **83,** 117.
Sevier, Holmes v (B 20, L C Pub Co. Ed U S. Sup. Ct. R. 877), **66,** 145.
Sewing Machine Companies (18 Wall. 553), **2,** 119
Sharp, Planters Bank v (6 How 327), **178,** 88, **39,** 68, **105,** 77
Shelby Taxing Dist., Robbins v (120 U S 429) **69,** 27, **84,** 29, **105,** 32, **129,** 35
Shelby Taxing Dist., Amy v (114 U S 387), **184,** 89
Shelby County, Norton v (118 U S. 425), **26,** 233
Sheldon, Hoyt v. (1 Black, 521), **61,** 144
Sheldon, Chicago v (9 Wall 50), **21,** 233, **188,** 90.
Sheldon v. Sill (8 How 441) **80,** 131.
Shepherd Covington Draw Bridge v (20 How 227), **57, 59,** 128
Shepard, United States v (1 Abb (U S) 431) **32, 33,** 186
Sherman v Smith (1 Black, 587), **159,** 86
Sherry v McKinley (99 U S 496), **26,** 185
Shields v. Schiff (124 U S 351), **2,** 151
Shields v. Thomas (18 How. 253), **2,** **4,** 191
Shields v. Ohio (95 U S 319), **169,** 87.
Ship v Blaneau (2 Cranch, 210), **115,** 135
Shoemaker, United States v (2 McLean, 114), **49,** 188
Siebold Ex parte (100 U S 371), **77,** 146, **1,** 4 **41,** 235, **3,** 171, **8,** 60, **77,** 146
Sill, Sheldon v (8 How 441), **80,** 131
Silliman, McCluny v (2 Wheat 369), **4,** 136, **13,** 232
Singer United States v (15 Wall 111), **12,** 17
Sinot v. Davenport (22 How 227), **49,** 25, **101,** 32, **5,** 17, **1,** 170.

Skelly, Jefferson Branch Bank v (1 Black, 436) **39**, 141, **123**, 80, **5**, 201, **245**, 100
Slaughter House Cases (16 Wall 36), **2**, 209, **3**, 210, **6**, **8**, 211, **18**, 213, **30**, **31**, 215, **101**, 32, **14**, **15**, 158.
Slocum v Maberry (2 Wheat 1), **7**, 122
Smalley, McDonald v (1 Pet 620), **85**, 131
Smalls, De Treville v. (98 U S 517), **26**, 185
Smith, Thorington v (8 Wall 1), **24**, 233; **238**, 98
Smith v Alabama (124 U S. 465), **168**, 40
Smith, United States v. (5 Wheat 153), **3**, 49
Smith, Dooley v. (13 Wall 604), **4**, 46, **15**, 51
Smith, Freborn v (2 Wall. 175), **82**, 74
Smith Farmers' Bank v (6 Wheat. 131), **221**, 95, **14**, 45, **17**, 45
Smith, White's Bank v. (7 Wall 646), **16**, 20, 21.
Smith v Maryland (18 How 71), **11**, 20; **1**, 194.
Sneed, Tennessee v. (96 U. S 69), **48**, 69, **65**, 71
Snow, In re (120 U S. 274), **44**, 188.
Society for Propagation of Gospel v. Town of New Haven (8 Wheat 464), **27**, 174
Society for Savings v Coite (6 Wall 594), **4**, 18, **12**, **16**, 19, **104**, 91, **3**, 195
Sohn v. Waterson (17 Wall 596), **52**, 70
Soo Hing v Crowley (113 U S 703) **66**, 220, **67**, 221 **90**, 224, **38**, 235
Soule, Pac Ins. Co v. (7 Wall 433), **2**, 6, **4**, 61
Southard, Wyman v (10 Wheat 22), **21**, 59, **99**, 132
Southern, Hagood v. (117 U. S 53), **15**, 204.
Southern Kansas R'y Cherokee Nation v (135 U S 641), **145**, 37
South Carolina v Gaillard (101 U S. 433), **120**, 79
South Carolina v. Georgia (93 U. S. 4), **27**, 22
South Pac R y Co, Santa Clara Co v (118 U S 399), **62**, **64**, 220
Sparhawk v. Sparhawk (116 Mass. 315), **17**, 167
Spaulding v. Mead (Cl & H 16), **3**, 11
Speed, Owings v (5 Wheat. 420), **101**, 77.
Spencer v Merchant (125 U S. 345), **10**, 122, **46**, 217
Spies v Illinois (123 U S. 131), **122**, 136, **38**, 187
Spragins v. Houghton (3 Ill. 395), **3**, 4
Spragins v Thompson (118 U S 90), **48**, 25, **8**, 229
Spratt v Spratt (4 Pet. 393) **12**, 44
Spring Valley Water Co v Schottler (110 U S 347), **161**, 86
Springer v Foster (2 Story, 383), **19**, 45.
Springer v United States (102 U S. 586), **25**, **26**, 185. **2**, **3**, 61
Stanley, Albany Co v (105 U S 306), **18**, 173
Stanley, Supervisors v (105 U S 305), **6**, 229
Stanley v Supervisors (121 U. S 535), **8**, 171
Starin v New York (115 U S 248), **6**, 121
Stark, Baldwin v (107 U S 463) **52**, 143
Stark v Ins Co (7 Cranch, 420), **12**, 44
Starr v Pease (8 Conn 541) **17**, 167
State, Bradwell v (16 Wall 130), **27**, 214, **6**, 157
State v Cohn (27 Vt 318) **7**, 148
State ex rel Att'y Gen l v Greene Co (54 Mo 540), note p 87
State Tax on Foreign Held Bonds (15 Wall. 300), **223**, 95.

State Tax on Railroad Gross Receipts (15 Wall 284), **129**, 85, **20**, 197, **58**, **59**, 26, **129**, 85
State Freight Tax Cases (15 Wall 232), **6**, 229, **116**, 31, **129**, 35
State, Miller v (15 Wall. 478), **166**, **167**, 86.
State (Minn), Gut v (9 Wall. 35), **41**, 199
State of Ohio, Fox v (5 How 433), **151**, 38.
State Railroad Tax Cases (92 U. S 575), **44**, 217
State, Turnpike Co v (3 Wall. 210), **15**, 84, **16**, 104, **2**, 105, **8**, **9**, 106, **2**, 202
State v Fry (4 Mo 120), **17**, 167
St Clair v Cox (106 U. S 350), **26**, 155
St. Tammany Water-works Co., New Orleans Water-works Co v. (14 Fed Rep 194), **14**, 184
St. Tammany Water-works v New Orleans Water-works (120 U S 64), **119**, 79.
Steamship Co., Hays v. (17 How. 596), **55**, 26
Steamship Co, Lord v. (102 U. S 541), **39**, 24, **112**, 83.
Steamship Co. v Tugman (106 U S 118), **63**, 129
Steamship Co v Port Wardens (6 Wall 31), **46**, 24.
Steele, Louisiana v. (134 U. S. 230), **18**, 204
Stewart v Blaine (1 MacArthur, 453), **2**, 11
Stewart v Salmon (94 U S 435), **238**, 98
Stewart v Kohn (11 Wall 493). **17**, 51 · **7**, 57, **39**, 235
Stewart, Maxwell v (21 Wall 71, 22 Wall 77), **8**, 192
Stifle, Dichman v (8 Wall 595), **17**, 65, **23**, 66
Stines v Franklin Co (14 Wall 15), **66**, 145
St Luke's Hospital v Barclay (3 Blatch 265) **2**, 136, **11**, 137.
St. Jo & Denver R. R. v Baldwin (103 U S 426), **32**, 175
St. Louis, Northwestern Union Packet Co v (100 U. S 223), **3**, 105
St. Louis, Packet Co v (100 U. S. 423), **5**, 105
St. Louis, etc. R'y v Vickers (122 U S 360) **89**, 132
St. Louis v Wiggins Ferry Co. (11 Wall 423), **11**, 195; **17**, 158, **21**, 130.
Stockdale v Insurance Co (20 Wall. 323) **10**, 58
Stokes, Kendall v. (3 How 87), **13**, 203
Stokes, Searight v. (3 How 151), **1**, 47
Stolley, Bloomer v. (5 McLean, 165), **36**, 68
Stone, Hyde v. (20 How 170), **97**, 133, **75**, 130
Stone v. Mississippi (101 U S 814), **199**, 92, **118**, 79
Stone v Railroad Co (116 U. S 347), **121**, 79.
Stone v. Wisconsin (94 U S 181), 3, 229, **43**, 236
Stoutenburgh v Hennick (129 U. S 141), **2**, 54, **93**, 30.
Strader v. Graham (10 How. 82), **52**, 143, **10**, 163, **5**, 164.
Strauder v West Virginia (100 U S. 303), **103**, 225; **9**, 57, **91**, 132, **2**, 210, **29**, 214
Strong v United States (9 Wall 788), **10**, 116
Stuart v. Laird (1 Cranch, 299), **1**, 119
Sturgis v. Crowninshield (4 Wheat 122), **45**, 236, **40**, 68, **43**, 44, **24**, 45, **43**, **44**, 69; **99**, 77, **220**, 95, **178**, 88.
Sturtevants v City of Alton (3 McLean, 393), **2**, 47.
Sugg v Thornton (132 U S 524), **100**, 133, **51**, 218, **72**, 221.
Supervisors v. Durant (9 Wall 415), **87**, 132.
Supervisors, Bank v. (7 Wall. 26), **5**, 18.

Supervisors, Olcott v (16 Wall 689), **18**, 197, **4**, 182
Supervisors v Stanley (105 U S 305), **6**, 229, **18**, 173.
Supervisors, Stanley v. (121 U S 535), **8**, 171
Supervisors, Williams v (122 U S 159), **8, 171**
Suydam v Broadnax (14 Pet 67), **14**, 44, 45, **17**, 45, **75**, 130; **77**, 131
Suydam v Williamson (24 How 433), **2**, 48

Tabb, Boyce v (18 Wall 546), **8**, 209
Tainter, Taylor v (16 Wall 366), **3**, 160, **12**, 162
Talbott v Seaman (1 Cranch, 28), **3**, 50, **9**, 51
Tappan v Merchants' Nat. Bank (19 Wall 490), **13**, 196, **6, 8**, 18
Tarble's Case (13 Wall. 397), **1**, 52, **4**, 53, **6**, 60, **4**, 171, **5**, 160.
Tax Com'rs v Bank of Commerce (2 Black. 620), **4**, 57
Taylor Chaffin v. (114 U. S. 309). **224**, 95 **226**, 96
Taylor, Conway v (1 Black, 603), **36**, 199.
Taylor v. Morton (2 Curtis, 454), **99**, 133, **23**, 174
Taylor v Tainter (16 Wall. 366), **3**, 160, **12**, 162.
Taylor, Terrett v. (9 Cranch, 43), **178**, 88.
Taylor v Thomas (22 Wall. 479), **29**, 234
Taylor v Walker (5 How 64), **69**, 145
Taylor, Willard v (8 Wall. 557), **3**, 46; **4**, 231
Tearney, Daniels v (102 U S 415), **50**, 148
Telegraph Co v Texas (105 U S 460) **94, 99**, 31, **113**, 33.
Temple, North Carolina v. (134 U S 22), **18**, 204.
Tennessee v Davis (100 U. S 257), **5**, 121, **8**, 57, **2**, 170; **90, 91**, 132
Tennessee, Farrington v (95 U S 679), **137**, 82, **213**, 94
Tennessee, M. C R R Co v (101 U S 337), **63**, 71
Tennessee v Pullman Southern Car Co (117 U S 51), **83**, 29
Tennessee, Railroad Co v (101 U S 337), **81**, 73; **23**, 205
Tennessee v Sneed (96 U S 69), **48**, 69, **65**, 71
Terrell, Case v (11 Wall 199), **44**, 126
Terre Haute Draw-bridge Co, Jolly v. (6 McLean, 237), **42**, 24
Terry v Anderson (95 U S 628), **50**, 69, **66**, 71.
Terry v Anderson (95 U S 634), **52**, 70.
Terry, Ex parte (128 U S 289), **18**, 123
Terrett v Taylor (9 Cranch, 43), **178**, 88
Texas, Asher v (128 U S. 129), **91**, 30
Texas, Telegraph Co. v (105 U. S. 460), **94, 99**, 31, **113**, 33
Texas v White (7 Wall. 700), **32**, 234, **1**, 168, **9**, 157
Thatcher, Mayhew v. (6 Wheat. 129), **1**, 152
The Acorn (2 Abb (U. S) 443), **12**, 44
The Barque Chusan (2 Story, 455), **15**, 20; **101**, 32
The Belfast (7 Wall 644), **38**, 126
The Belgenland (114 U. S 355), **39**, 126.
The Brig Wilson (1 Brock. 423), **14**, 20, **18**, 21
The Cherokee Tobacco (11 Wall 616), **23**, 174
The Clinton Bridge (10 Wall 454), **154**, 38
The Confiscation Cases (20 Wall 109), **4**, 113
The Daniel Ball (10 Wall 557) **1**, 19, 20 **107**, 33
The Delaware Tax (18 Wall. 206), **146**, 83

The Divina Pastora (4 Wheat. 52), **3**, 118
The Exchange v McFaddon (7 Cranch, 116), **16**, 17, **2**, 53
The Eliza (4 Dall 37), **9**, **11**, **12**
The Francis Hatch (13 Am L. Reg 289), **10**, 110
The Francis Wright, Duncan v. (105 U S 381), **25**, 139
The Jefferson (20 How 400), **37**, 126
The Justices v Murray (9 Wall 274), **16**, 193, **1**, 194.
The Junction R R Co, Works v (5 McLean, 246), **40**, 24
The General Smith (4 Wheat 438), **26**, 124
The Grapeshot (9 Wall 129), **14**, 113
The Kansas Indians (5 Wall 757), **25**, 174
The Louisa (2 Sawy 57) **10**, 110
The Lottawanna (21 Wall 558), **117**, 34, **36**, 126
The Mayor v Lord (9 Wall 409), **86**, 131
The Montello (11 Wall 411) **26**, 22.
The Moses Taylor (4 Wall 411), **38**, 126, **95**, 133
The Neustra Senora de la Caridad (4 Wheat 497), **3**, 118
The Neustra Senora del Regala (108 U. S 92), **20**, 223
The Orpheus, Young v (2 Cliff 35), **37**, 126
The Prize Cases (2 Black, 636), **9**, 231
The Richmond (9 Cranch, 102), **94**, 224.
The Rapid (1 Gall 295, S C 8 Cranch, 155), **14**, 51
The Schooner Harriett (1 Story, 259) **7**, 49
The Santissima Trinidad (7 Wheat. 305), **9**, 60
The Sarah (8 Wheat 391) **18**, 193
The Ship Sapphire (11 Wall 164) **120**, 135
The William Bagley (5 Wall 377), **14**, 51
Thatcher, Mahew v. (6 Wheat 129), **13**, 192
Thomas Kilbourn v (103 U S 168), **1**, 10, **3**, 11, **15**, 232
Thomas v Loney (134 U S 372), **2**, 10
Thomas, Mechanics' Bank v (18 How 384), **115**, 79, **129**, 81, **69**, 130.
Thomas, Scotland Co v (94 U S 682), **16**, 196
Thomas Shields v (18 How 253) **2**, **4**, 191
Thomas, Taylor v (22 Wall 479), **29**, 234
Thomas, Yazoo & Miss Val R y v (132 U. S 174) **125**, 80, **150**, 84, **156**, 85, **101**, 134
Thomasson, United States v. (4 Biss 340), **23**, 115
Thompson, Giffin v (2 How 244), **6**, 46
Thompson v Holton (6 McLean 386), **158**, 85.
Thompson v Lee Co (3 Wall 327), **186**, 90
Thompson v Pacific R. R (9 Wall 579) **4**, 57
Thompson, Sprague v (118 U S 90), **48**, 25, **8**, 229
Thompson United States v (93 U S 586), **68**, 145
Thompson v Whitman (18 Wall 457), **7**, 153, **28**, 155
Thomson v U P R y Co (9 Wall 579), **45**, 177, **2**, 194
Thornton, Sugg v (132 U S 524), **100**, 133, **51**, 218, **72**, 221
Thorington v Smith (8 Wall. 1) **24**, 233; **238**, 98
Three hundred Fifty-six Bales of Cotton (1 Pet. 511), **1**, 48, **6**, 50
Tied v. R R Co. (94 U. S 178), **102**, 32
Tiernan v Rinker (102 U S 123), **67**, 27
Tierney, United States v (1 Bond, 571), **5**, 55
Tinder, Inman Steamship Co v (94 U S 238), **2**, 105
Tingy, Bas v (4 Dall 37), **3**, **5**, 50; **9**, **11**, **12**, 51.

Tipping, Bailiff v (2 Cranch, 406), **115**, 135
Tisdale, Mut Benefit Ins Co v (91 U S 238), **12, 44**
Tomlinson v Branch (15 Wall 460), **150**, 84, note, p 87, **10**, 195, **15, 16**, 196
Tomlinson v Jessup (15 Wall 454), **150**, 84, **166**, 86, **10**, 195.
Toombs, Hornbuckle v (18 Wall. 648), **6**, 120
Topeka Sav & Loan Assoc v (20 Wall 655), **12**, 196, **17, 18**, 197.
Totten v United States (92 U. S. 105), **7**, 113
Towle, Forney v (1 Black, 351), **61**, 144
Town of Erroi, Coe v. (116 U. S. 517), **11**, 103
Town of New Haven v Society for Propagation of Gospel (8 Wheat 464), **27**, 174
Town of Pawlet v Clark (9 Cranch, 296), **111**, 135
Tracy v Swartwout (10 Pet 80), **3**, 112
Trade-mark Cases (100 U S 82), **5, 7**, 229
Transportation Co v Chicago (99 U S 635), **13**, 183
Transportation Co v. Fitzhugh (1 Black 574), **32**, 125
Transportation Co. v Parkersburg (107 U S 691), **4**, 105.
Trapnall Woodruff v (10 How 190), **7, 11**, 64, **106**, 77
Trask v Maguire (18 Wall. 391), **145**, 83
Traver v Reach (15 Wall 68), **238**, 98
Travers, United States v (2 Wheel. C C. 490), **4**, 55
Treasurer of Athens Co Armstrong v (16 Pet 281), **96**, 133, **155**, 85
Trevor, Hine v. (4 Wall 555) **35, 38**, 125
Trigg v Drew (10 How 224), **107**, 77
Trumbull's Case (1 Cong El Cas 167), **3**, 5, **1**, 8
Tucker v. Furgeson (22 Wall 527), **144**, 83
Tugman, Steamship Co. v. (106 U S 118), **63**, 129
Turck, Pound v. (95 U. S 462), **102**, 32, **125**, 35
Turner, Ex parte (Chase's Decisions, 364) **2**, 227, S C (1 Abb (U S) 88), **5**, 228
Turner In Matter of (1 Abb (U S) 84), **3, 4**, 209.
Turney v Marshall (1 Cong. El Cas. 167), **3**, 5 **1**, 8
Turner v Maryland (107 U. S. 38), **15**, 104
Turnpike Co v State (3 Wall. 210), **150**, 84
Turpin v Burgess (117 U. S 504), **8**, 62
Twentyman Jackson v (2 Pet 136), **119**, 135
Twitchell v Commonwealth (7 Wall 321), **1**, 194
Twitchell v Penn (7 Wall 321), **2**, 189
Tyler v Defrees (11 Wall 331), **1**, 49, **15**, 51, **26**, 185
Tyler v Harvey (2 Wall 328), **59**, 219.

Union Bank v. Jolly (18 How 503), **75**, 130.
Union Passenger R y v Philadelphia (101 U S 528), **160**, 86
Union Freight R'y, Greenwood v (105 U S 13), **229**, 97
U P R R v Penniston (18 Wall 5), **8**, 195, **45**, 177
Union Pac R R. Co v. United States (99 U S 700). **24**, 185, **14**, 58
Union Pacific R y Co, Thompson v (9 Wall 579). **45**, 177 **2**, 191
United States v Amsden (10 Biss 283). **8**, 228
United States v Angell (11 Fed Rep. 34). **15**, 17
United States v Anthony (11 Blatch 204) **18, 19**, 213
United States Armstrong v (13 Wall. 154) **15**, 114, **23**, 115

United States, Arnold v. (9 Cranch 119), **4**, 14
United States v Arredondo (6 Pet 736), **88**, 74
United States v Arjona (120 U S. 479), **4**, 49, **2**, 46
United States v. Cisna (1 McLean, 259), **137**, 36 **142**, 37.
United States v Athens Armory (7 Pet. 160) **20**, 114
United States v Bader, 16 Fed. Rep 116). **1**, 4.
United States v Bailey (1 McLean, 234), **138**, 36, **1**, 19, 20.
United States v Bainbridge (1 Mason 71), **2**, 52
United States Bank, Osborne v. (9 Wheat. 738), **12**, 19 **13**, 41
United States, Bridge Co v (105 U S 491) **3**, 164.
United States v Bevans (3 Wheat. 336), **2**, 53, **27**, **28**, 124
United States v Boutwell (17 Wall. 604), **13**, 203
United States v Booth (21 How. 506) **33**, **34**, **35**, 234, **6**, 60; **5**, 160
United States v Breitling (20 How 252), **76**, 130
United States, Brown v (8 Cranch, 153), **21**, 52
United States, Boyd v (116 U S 616), **4**, 181, **40**, 187
United States v. Burr (4 Cranch, 470), **9**, 149 **19**, 150
United States v Burger (19 Blackf. 256), **4**, 118
United States v Burgess (3 McCrary, 278), **34**, 186
United States v Cruikshank **4**, 56, **18**, 179, **9**, 180, **12**, 180, **6**, 190, **1**, 194 **51**, 200, **5**, 209 **1**, 210, **80**, 222 **3**, 227, **3**, 228 **2**, 112
United States v Coolidge (1 Wheat. 415), note p 120, **6**, 148
United States, Carlisle v (16 Wall 147) **17**, 114. **28**, **29**, 151
United States, Crenshaw v (134 U. S 99), **207**, 93.
United States v Curtis (4 Mason, 232), **5**, 148
United States v Cumming (130 U. S. 452) **36**, 234
United States v Chicago (7 How. 185) **9**, 183
United States, C & N W R. R. Co. v (104 U S 680) **27**, 233
United States C, M & St P R R. Co v (104 U S 687), **27**, 233.
United States v Coppersmith (4 Fed Rep 198), **36**, 187
United States v Crosby (7 Cranch, 115), **4**, 55
United States v. Coombs (12 Pet 72), **38**, 23, 24, **103**, 32 **4**, 57.
United States v Cornell (2 Mason, 66), **4**, **5**, **8**, 55
United States v Davis (5 Mason, 364), **4**, 55
United States v Dewitt (9 Wall. 41), **107**, 33
United States v. Dawson (15 How. 467), **3**, 190
United States, Durousseau v (6 Cranch, 307) **22**, 139
United States v Eliason (16 Pet. 291), **4**, 112.
United States v Fisher (2 Cranch, 358), **2**, 56, **4**, 57
United States, Forsythe v (9 How 571), **11**, 231, **9**, 166
United States v Ferreira (13 How. 40), **13**, 58
United States v Fairchilds (1 Abb. (U S) 74), **4**, 57
United States v Field (16 Fed. Rep 778) **36**, 187
United States v Forty-three Gallons of Whisky (93 U S 188), **109**, 33
United States v Grush (5 Mason, 290), **7**, 49
United States v Goldman (3 Woods, 187), **1**, 1
United States, Gibbons v (8 Wall. 269) **36**, 234
United States v Great Falls Mfg Co (112 U. S. 645), **15**, 184.

United States v. Guthrie (17 How 284), **15**, 123
United States v. Gardner (10 Pet 618), **1**, 46
United States v. Greathouse (2 Abb (U S) 364), **2**, 148, **16**, 119, **25**, 150
United States v. Harris (106 U S 629), **5**, **6**, 209, **1**, 210, **7**, 229, **37**, 68, **5**, 57, **4**, 228, **2**, 229, **16**, 158
United States v. Holliday (3 Wall 407), **136**, 36, **143**, **144**, 37.
United States, Hylton v. (3 Dall 171), **1**, 6, **1**, **4**, 61.
United States v. Haskell (4 Wash C. C 402), **46**, 188
United States v. Hall (98 U S. 343), **15**, 58
United States v. Hudson & Goodwin (7 Cranch, 32), **6**, 120
United States v. Howland (4 Wheat 108), **107**, **108**, 139
United States v. Hamilton (3 Dall 17), **78**, 146.
United States v. Harris (1 Abb (U S) 110), **20**, 114.
United States v. Holmes (5 Wheat 412), **1**, 49
United States v. Hudson (7 Cranch 32), **6**, 148
United States v. Ins Co (29 Wall 99), **30**, 234
United States v. Jones (109 U S 513), **7**, 183
United States v. Jones (3 Wash C C 209), **6**, 49
United States v. Keen (1 McLean, 429), **47**, 188
United States Kohl v (91 U S 367), **10**, 183, **18**, 59.
United States Kendall v (12 Pet 524), **1**, 108, **7**, 110, **42**, 126
United States v Klein (13 Wall 128) **8**, 113, **21**, 114, **24**, 115
United States, Kagama v (118 U S 375) **16**, 167
United States, Knote v (95 U S. 149), **4**, 151.
United States v. Keokuk (6 Wall 514), **44**, 177
United States, Keys v (109 U S 336), **9**, 116
United States, Langford v (101 U S 341), **23**, 233
United States v. Lee (106 U S 196), **45**, 127, **2**, 182, **6**, 202, **14**, 213
United States, Lee County v (7 Wall 175), **9**, 137, **22**, 233
United States v. Singer (15 Wall 111), **12**, 17.
United States v La Vengeance (3 Dall 297), **2**, 101
United States v. Mumford (16 Fed. Rep 223), **1**, 4, **10**, 228
United States v. Marks (2 Abb (U. S) 541), **4**, 57
United States, Miller v (11 Wall 268), **26**, 185; **10**, 91, **15**, 57
United States v Maurice (2 Brock. 109), **10**, 3, **4**, 57
United States, Memphis v (97 U S. 293), **65**, 70
United States Mortgage Co, Gross v. (108 U S 477), **93**, 224
United States v Maxwell (2 Dill 275), **32**, **33**, 186
United States, Mormon Church v. (136 U S 1), **3**, **4**, 165, **7**, 166
United States v Mitchell (2 Dall 348), **1**, 148.
United States, McElrath v (102 U. S. 426), **19**, 193
United States v Morris (1 Curtis, 23), **47**, 188.
United States, Morris v (Morris Cotton) (8 Wall 507) **18**, 193
United States v Marigold (9 How 560) **1**, 46, **3**, **4**, 47 **2**, 56, **15**, 138, **4**, 57
United States v New Orleans (102 U S 358), **176**, 88 **227**, 96
United States, Hill v (9 How 386), **43**, 126
United States v Ortega (11 Wheat. 467) **21**, 123
United States v Petit (114 U S 429), **31**, 108

United States v Petit (11 Fed Rep. 58), **36**, 187
United States, Pargoud v (13 Wall. 156), **15**, 114, **23**, 115
United States v. Pryor (3 Wash 234), **22**, 150
United States v. Perez (9 Wheat. 579), **45**, 188.
United States v Peters (5 Cranch, 115) **30**, 206
United States v Palmer (3 Wheat. 610), **6**, 49 **8**, 231, **3**, 118
United States, Parker v (1 Pet. 293), **11**, 113
United States Parkinson v (121 U. S 281), **30**, 186
United States v Reese (92 U S 214) **5**, 10, **9**, 57 **7**, 229
United States v Rauscher (119 U. S. 407), **24**, 174
United States v Riley (5 Blatch 204), **48**, 188
United States v Ravara (2 Dall 297), **1**, 136. **11**, 137
United States v Rathbone (2 Paine, 578) **6**, 192
United States, Reynolds v (98 U. S 145), **7**, 125· **4**, 179, **5**, 190.
United States v Russell (13 Wall 623), **19**, 181
United States, Springer v (102 U. S 586), **2**, **3**, 61, **25**, **26**, 185
United States v Shepard (1 Abb (U S) 431), **32**, **33**, 186
United States v Smith (5 Wheat. 153), **3**, **6**, 49
United States v Schurz (102 U S 378) **13**, 203
United States, Strong v. (9 Wall. 788), **10**, 116
United States, Semmes v. (91 U S 21), **4**, 151
United States, Sampeyreac v. (7 Pet 222), **97**, 225.
United States v Shoemaker (2 McLean, 114), **49**, 188
United States v. Tierney (1 Bond, 571) **5**, 55.
United States v Thomasson (4 Biss 340), **23**, 115
United States v Travers (2 Wheel. C. C 490), **4**, 55
United States v Thompson (98 U S 586), **68**, 145
United States v. Tappan (11 Wheat 419), **3**, 16
United States v Ralls Co (105 U S 733), **196**, 91
United States v Railroad Co (17 Wall 322), **179**, 89
United States, Reynolds v (98 U S 145), **4**, 179, **5**, 190
United States v Rhodes (1 Abb (U S) 28), **4**, 43; **1**, 53, **4**, 115, **5**, 209, **6**, 171
United States Union Pac. R R Co v (99 U S 700) **24**, 185, **14**, 58
United States v Union Pac R'y Co (98 U S 549), **3**, **4**, 119
United States v Van Buskirk (15 Wall 123), **12**, 17
United States v Vigol (2 Dall 346) **1**, 148
United States v Villato (2 Dall 370), **27**, 150, **4**, 43.
United States v Wilson (7 Pet. 150) **18**, **20**, 114, **18**, 65, **37**, 68, **54**, 189
United States v. Wilson (8 Wheat 253) **16**, 45
United States v Wiltberger (5 Wheat. 76), **40**, 120 **2**, 49.
United States v Wynn (3 McCrary 266) **35**, 186
United States v Weise (2 Wall Jr 72) **4**, 55
United States v Williams (4 Cranch, C C. 393), **10**, 55
United States v Waddell (112 U. S. 76) **12**, 58
United States v Williams (1 Paine, 261), **4**, 14
United States v Yates (6 Fed. Rep. 861), **36**, 187
Unity v Burrage (103 U. S 447), **5**, 229.

Utah, Clayton v (132 U. S 632), **19,** 168

Vallandigham, Ex parte (1 Wall 243), **75,** 146
Vance v Vance (108 U S 514) **56,** 70.
Van Allen v. Assessors (3 Wall 573), **6, 7,** 18. **6,** 15, **2,** 16
Van Buskirk, Green v (7 Wall 139) **11,** 153
Van Buskirk v United States (15 Wall 123), **12,** 17
Van Brocken v. Anderson (117 U S 151) **12,** 196
Van Ness Buel v (8 Wheat 312), **23, 26,** 139
Van Riswick, Wallach v (92 U S 202), **2, 3,** 151, **23,** 115
Van Slyke v Wisconsin (Book 20, L C P Co Ed Sup. Ct. Rep 240), **6,** 18
Van Wyck v Knevals (106 U S 360) **14,** 167
Van Zandt, Jones v. (5 How 215) **9,** 163
Varienne Von Glahn v (1 Dill 515), **19,** 45
Vaughn v Williams (3 McLean, 530), **10,** 163
Vaughn v Northrup (15 Pet. 2), **78,** 131
Veazie v Moor (14 How 568) **22,** 21
Veazie v Bank of Fenno (8 Wall 533), **3,** 6; **5,** 46, **2, 4,** 61
Vickers, St. Louis R y Co v (122 U S 360), **89,** 132
Vicksburg R R v Dennis (116 U S 665), **150,** 84. **157,** 85
Vicksburg v Tobin (100 U S 430), **3,** 105
Vicksburg, etc R. R v Putnam (118 U S 545), **79,** 131
Vicksburg, etc. R. R., Hamilton v (119 U S 280), **152,** 38
Vigol, United States v (2 Wall 346), **1,** 148.
Village of Middleton, Ex parte (82 N Y 196), **6,** 229.

Villato, United States v (2 Dall 372) **4,** 43, **27,** 152
Vincennes University v Indiana (14 How 268), **111,** 78
Virginia McCready v (94 U S 391) **7,** 157 **3,** 164.
Virginia, Paul v (8 Wall 168) **9, 12,** 20, **3,** 150, **21,** 139, **18,** 159
Virginia, Cohens v. (6 Wheat. 264), **7, 8,** 2 **2,** 7, **1,** 46, **7,** 55 **2,** 136 **11,** 137. **13,** 138, **11, 12,** 172 **3,** 201. **44,** 236
Virginia v Reeves (100 U S 313), **3,** 227; **100,** 225, **1,** 210. **29,** 211
Virginia, Webber v (103 U S 344), **33,** 175 **164,** 40.
Virginia v West Virginia (11 Wall 39) **15,** 107 **16, 17,** 138
Virginia, Phalen v (8 How 163) **91,** 75
Virginia, Royall v (116 U S 572) **224,** 95
Virginia, Royall v (121 U S 102) **226,** 96
Virginia, McGahey v (135 U S. 662) **7,** 202 **226,** 96
Virginia Ex parte (100 U S 339) **66,** 220 **98,** 225
Virginia Hollingsworth v (3 Dall 378) **2,** 201
Virginia Coupon Cases (114 U S 269) **226,** 96
Volmer Emporia v (12 Kansas 622), **7,** 148
Von Glahn v Varienne (1 Dill 515) **19,** 45, **174, 177,** 88
Von Hoffman v Quincy (4 Wall 535), **46, 47,** 69, **57,** 70, **213,** 94 **189,** 90.

Wabash R y Co v Illinois (118 U S 587), **162,** 39
Wabash & Erie Canal Co v Beers (2 Black. 448) **216,** 95
W & B Turnpike Co v Maryland (3 Wall 210). **218,** 95
Waddell, United States v (112 U S 76), **12,** 58.

Waddell, Martin v (16 Pet. 410), **2,** 230
Waite v Dowley (94 U S. 527), **7,** 171, **14,** 173
Waite v. Kalbfleisch (58 N Y 282), **17,** 167
Walker, Blount v (134 U S 607), **34,** 156
Walker, Lawler v (14 How 149), **55,** 144
Walker v Taylor (5 How 64), **69,** 145
Walker v Sauvinet (92 U S 90), **11,** 192, **1,** 194
Walker v Whitehead (16 Wall 314), **82,** 74
Wall Ex parte (107 U. S 265) **4,** 148 **37,** 187 **21,** 185
Walling v Michigan (116 U S 446) **81,** 29, **105,** 32
Wallach v Van Riswick (92 U S. 202), **2, 3,** 151 **23,** 115
Walston v Nevin (128 U S 578), **49,** 217
Ware v Hylton (2 Dall 272), **1, 2,** 115. **18,** 232, **6,** 21 **1,** 6
Warren Bridge, Charles River Bridge v (11 Pet 420) **84, 85,** 71, **12,** 188
Warren Mfg Co v Ætna Ins Co (2 Paine, 501), **22,** 154; **18,** 159
Waring v Mobile (8 Wall. 110), **13, 14,** 104
Warring v Clark (5 How 441), **31,** 125, **3,** 191.
Washington, McCoy v (3 Wall Jr. 381), **12,** 65
Washington University v. Rouse (8 Wall 439) **130,** 81
Watertown, Rees v (19 Wall 107), **9,** 137
Watertown, Pereles v (6 Biss 79) **54,** 70
Waterson, Sohn v (17 Wall 596) **52,** 70.
Watkins, Ex parte (7 Pet. 568), **78,** 146, **4,** 60, **2,** 194.
Watson v Mercer (8 Pet 110) **18,** 65, **29, 30,** 67, **37,** 68, **20,** 114, **97,** 225; **142,** 87.
Watson v Tarpley (18 How. 517), **179,** 42, **79,** 131.
Watson, Port of Mobile v (116 U. S. 287), **232,** 97
Waul v Maryland (12 Wall 418), **69,** 27, **5,** 157
Weaver, People v (100 U S 539), **16, 18,** 173.
Webber v Virginia (103 U S 344), **33,** 175, **164,** 40
Webster v Reid (11 How. 437), **10,** 192
Weise, United States v (2 Wall Jr. 72), **4,** 55.
Wells, Ex parte (8 How 307), **9,** 113.
Welton v Missouri (91 U S 275), **4,** 20 **68,** 27, **71,** 28· **81,** 29, **101,** 32
West Tennessee Bank v. Citizens' Bank (13 Wall. 432), **64,** 144
Westervelt v. Lewis (2 McLean, 511), **30,** 155
Weston v. Charleston (2 Pet. 449), **46,** 142, **2,** 16, **4,** 57 **1,** 17
Weston, Babcock v (1 Gall 168), **19,** 45
West River Bridge v Dix (6 How. 507), **204,** 93, **3,** 182, **11,** 183
Western Union Tel Co v Massachusetts (125 U S 530), **35,** 175, **89,** 30.
Western Union Tel Co v Pendleton (122 U S 347), **166, 167,** 40, **22,** 197
Western Union Tel. Co, Pensacola Tel Co v (96 U. S 1), **110, 111,** 33, **4,** 17
Western Union Tel Co v Alabama (132 U. S 472), **94, 95,** 31
West Virginia, Strauder v (100 U. S. 303) **2,** 210, **29,** 214; **91,** 132, **9,** 57 **101,** 225
West Virginia, Dent v (129 U S 114), **68,** 221, **52,** 218.
West Virginia, Virginia v (11 Wall 39), **15,** 107, **16, 17,** 138.
Wheeler, O & M R R Co v (1 Black, 286), **60, 61,** 128, **46,** 200.

Wheeling Bridge Co., Pennsylvania v. (18 How. 421), **20, 22,** 21, **1,** 62, **7,** 137, **15, 16,** 138, **21,** 139, **31,** 175, **150,** 38.
Wheeling, P. & C. Trans. Co. v. (99 U. S. 273), **10,** 106
Whipple, People v. (9 Cow. 707), **32,** 186
White v. Hart (13 Wall. 646), **1, 5,** 168, **74,** 72
White, Texas v. (7 Wall. 700), **32,** 234, **9,** 157; **1,** 168.
White v. Wright (22 How. 19), **57,** 144.
White v. Greenhow (114 U. S. 307), **224,** 95
White's Bank v. Smith (7 Wall. 646) **16,** 20, 21
Whitehead, Walker v. (16 Wall. 314), **82,** 74.
Whitman, Thompson v. (18 Wall. 457), **7,** 153, **28,** 155.
Whitney, Frisbee v. (9 Wall. 187). **261,** 102
Whitney v. Robertson (124 U. S. 190), **23,** 174, **29,** 175.
Whitton, C. & N. W. R'y Co. v. (13 Wall. 270), **62, 64,** 129
Wickelhausen v. Willett (10 Abb. Pr. 164), **2,** 11
Wiggins Ferry Co., C. & A. R. R. Co. v. (119 U. S. 615), **16,** 154
Wiggins Ferry Co., St. Louis v. (11 Wall. 423), **11,** 195, **17,** 158 **21,** 139
Wiggins Ferry Co. v. East St. Louis (107 U. S. 365), **37,** 199, **82,** 29, 153, **84**
Wilcox v. Jackson (16 Pet. 498), **9,** 202
Wilkins, Elk v. (112 U. S. 94), **12,** 212
Wilkinson v. Leland (2 Pet. 658), **12,** 183
Willamette Iron Bridge Co. v. Hatch (125 U. S. 1), **33, 34, 35,** 23
Willard v. Taylor (8 Wall. 557), **4,** 230, **3,** 46
Willard v. Presbury (14 Wall. 676), **3,** 54; **11,** 55
William Blount's Trial, December 17, 1797, to January 15, 1799, **7,** 8
Williams v. Louisiana (103 U. S. 637), **193,** 91
Williams v. Bruffy (96 U. S. 176), **233,** 98.
Williams, United States v. (4 Cranch, C. C. 393) **10,** 55
Williams, Freeland v. (21 Wall. 203), **259, 260,** 100 **96, 97,** 225 **69,** 72
Williams v. Benedict (8 How. 107), **78,** 131, **114,** 135
Williams v. Augusta (4 Ga. 509), **7,** 148
Williams v. Norris (12 Wheat. 117), **46,** 142, **32,** 140
Williams, Vaughn v. (3 McLean, 530), **10,** 163
Williams v. Supervisors (122 U. S. 159), **8,** 171
Wilmington, etc. R. R. v. King (91 U. S. 3), **75,** 72, **24,** 233
Wilson, Ex parte (114 U. S. 417), **31,** 186
Wilson, United States v. (7 Pet. 150), **18, 20,** 114, **54,** 187, **18,** 65, **16,** 45
Wilson v. Black Bird Creek Marsh Co. (2 Pet. 245), **17,** 21, **63,** 27; **102,** 82
Wilson v. McNamee (102 U. S. 572), **47,** 25
Wilson, New Jersey v. (7 Cranch, 164), **124,** 80, **155,** 85
Wilson v. Callan (127 U. S. 40), **9,** 190, **7,** 148
Wiltberger, United States v. (5 Wheat. 76), **40,** 120, **2,** 19
Wiltz, Elliott v. (107 U. S. 711), **22,** 205
Windley, Blount v. (95 U. S. 173), **109,** 78.
Winona, etc. R. R. v. Blade (94 U. S. 180), **161,** 39, **102,** 32
Winter, N. O. v. (1 Wheat. 91), **72,** 130
Wisconsin, Stone v. (94 U. S. 181), **3,** 229, **43,** 236.

Wisconsin, Van Slyke v. (Book 20, L. C P Co Ed Sup Ct. Rep 240), **6,** 18
Wisconsin, Morrill v (Book 23 L C Pub Co Ed U. S Sup Ct. Rep. 1009), **71,** 28, **164,** 40
Wisconsin, Hall v. (103 U S 5), **228,** 97
Wisconsin v. Pelican Ins. Co (127 U S 265), **8,** 137; **14,** 19, **10,** 153; **18,** 155
Wiswall v Sampson (14 How 52), **78,** 131.
Withers v Buckley (20 How. 92), **3,** 164 **1,** 182; **52,** 143 **1,** 194
Wolcott, Diggs & Keith v (4 Cranch, 179), **13,** 122.
Wolf v New Orleans (103 U S 358), **180,** 89
Wolsey, Dodge v (18 How. 331) **115,** 79, **129,** 8, **178,** 88; **5,** 201, **14,** 122; **64,** 130, **102,** 134; **11,** **14,** 176.
Wood McIntire v. (7 Cranch, 504), **13,** 232
Wood v Davis (18 How. 467) **79,** 131
Woodruff, McGear v. (4 Vroom, 213), **7,** 148
Woodruff Hanauer v (15 Wall. 448), **24,** 233
Woodruff v Parham (8 Wall 123), **12,** 104, **8,** 103, **1,** 202
Woodruff v Trapnall (10 How 190), **7,** **11,** 64, **140,** 82, **106,** 77.
Woodman v Kilbourn Mfg Co (1 Abb (U S.) 158, S. C. 1 Biss. 546), **5,** 164
Woodson, Louisville & N R R Co v (134 U S 614) **88,** 224
Woodward, Dartmouth College v (4 Wheat 518), **102,** 77, **17,** 167
Worcester v. Georgia (6 Pet. 515), **6,** 2, **140,** 37
Works v The Junction R. R. Co. (5 McLean 426), **40,** 24
Worthy v Comrs (9 Wall. 611), **62,** 144
Wright v. Nagle (101 U. S 794), **245,** 100
Wright, Given v (117 U S 648), **124,** 80
Wurts v. Hoagland (114 U S 606), **48,** 217
Wyman v. Southard (10 Wheat 1), **92,** 132

Yankton County, National Bank v (101 U. S 129), **4,** 165 **15,** 167
Yarborough Ex parte (110 U S 651), **1,** 10
Yard, New Jersey v (95 U. S 104), **169,** 87 **178,** 88
Yates, United States v (6 Fed Rep. 861), **36,** 187.
Yazoo Valley R'y Co v Thomas (132 U. S. 174), **125,** 80 **150,** 84, **156,** 85, **101,** 134
Yewdall, Pearson v. (95 U S 294) **11,** 192, **1,** 194, **34,** 215
Yick Wo v. Hopkins (118 U S 356), **66,** 220
Yonley v. Lavender (21 Wall 276), **97,** 133 **32,** 199
Yosemite Valley Case (15 Wall 77), **261,** 102
Young v The Orphans (2 Cliff. 35), **37,** 126

Zacharie, Boyle v (2 Pet. 635), **14,** 44 **19,** 45; **45,** 69
Zane Matthews v. (7 Wheat. 164) **3,** 11, **8,** 122, **110,** 134, **46,** 142

DECLARATION OF INDEPENDENCE.

IN CONGRESS, JULY 4, 1776.

THE UNANIMOUS DECLARATION OF THE THIRTEEN UNITED STATES OF AMERICA.

When, in the course of human events, it becomes necessary for one people to dissolve the political bands which have connected them with another, and to assume among the powers of the earth, the separate and equal station to which the laws of nature and of nature's God entitle them, a decent respect to the opinions of mankind requires that they should declare the causes which impel them to the separation

We hold these truths to be self-evident: that all men are created equal, that they are endowed by their Creator with certain unalienable rights, that among these are life, liberty, and the pursuit of happiness. That, to secure these rights, governments are instituted among them, deriving their just powers from the consent of the governed, that whenever any form of government becomes destructive of these ends it is the right of the people to alter or abolish it, and to institute a new government, laying its foundation on such principles, and organizing its powers in such form as to them shall seem most likely to effect their safety and happiness Prudence, indeed, will dictate, that governments long established should not be changed for light and transient causes; and accordingly all experience hath shown, that mankind are more disposed to suffer, while evils are sufferable, than to right themselves by abolishing the forms to which they are accustomed But when a long train of abuses and usurpations, pursuing invariably the same object, evinces a design to reduce them under absolute despotism, it is their right, it is their duty to throw off such government, and to provide new guards for their future security. Such has been the patient sufferance of these colonies, and such is now the necessity which constrains them to alter their former system of government. The history of the present king of Great Britain is a history of repeated injuries and usurpations, all having in direct object the establishment of an absolute tyranny over these states. To prove this, let facts be submitted to a candid world

He has refused his assent to laws the most wholesome and necessary for the public good

He has forbidden his governors to pass laws of immediate and pressing importance, unless suspended in their operation till his assent should be obtained, and, when so suspended, he has utterly neglected to attend to them

He has refused to pass other laws for the accommodation of large districts of people, unless those people would relinquish the right of representation in the legislature — a right inestimable to them, and formidable to tyrants only.

He has called together legislative bodies, at places unusual, uncomfortable, and distant from the repository of their public records, for the sole purpose of fatiguing them into compliance with his measures.

He has dissolved representative houses repeatedly, for opposing, with manly firmness, his invasions on the rights of the people.

He has refused for a long time after such dissolutions, to cause others to be elected; whereby the legislative powers, incapable of annihilation, have returned to the people at large, for their exercise; the state remaining, in the meantime, exposed to all the dangers of invasion from without, and convulsions within

He has endeavored to prevent the population of these states; for that purpose obstructing the laws for naturalization of foreigners, refusing to pass others, to encourage their migration hither, and raising the conditions of new appropriations of lands.

He has obstructed the administration of justice, by refusing his assent to laws for establishing judiciary powers.

He has made judges dependent on his will alone, for the

tenure of their offices, and the amount and payment of their salaries.

He has erected a multitude of new offices, and sent hither swarms of officers to harass our people and eat out their substance.

He has kept among us, in times of peace, standing armies, without the consent of our legislatures

He has affected to render the military independent of, and superior to, the civil power.

He has combined with others, to subject us to a jurisdiction, foreign to our constitution, and unacknowledged by our laws, giving his assent to their acts of pretended legislation

For quartering large bodies of armed troops among us:

For protecting them by a mock trial, from punishment for any murders which they should commit on the inhabitants of these states

For cutting off our trade with all parts of the world:

For imposing taxes on us, without our consent.

For depriving us, in many cases, of the benefits of trial by jury.

For transporting us beyond seas, to be tried for pretended offences:

For abolishing the free system of English laws in a neighboring province, establishing therein an arbitrary government, and enlarging its boundaries, so as to render it at once an example and fit instrument for introducing the same absolute rule into these colonies

For taking away our charters, abolishing our most valuable laws, and altering fundamentally the forms of our governments:

For suspending our own legislatures, and declaring themselves invested with power to legislate for us in all cases whatsoever.

He has abdicated government here, by declaring us out of his protection, and waging war against us.

He has plundered our seas, ravaged our coasts, burnt our towns, and destroyed the lives of our people.

He is, at this time, transporting large armies of foreign mercenaries to complete the works of death, desolation, and tyranny, already begun, with circumstances of cruelty and perfidy, scarcely paralleled in the most barbarous ages, and totally unworthy the head of a civilized nation.

He has constrained our fellow-citizens, taken captive on the high seas, to bear arms against their country, to become the executioners of their friends and brethren, or to fall themselves by their hands.

He has excited domestic insurrections amongst us, and has endeavored to bring on the inhabitants of our frontiers, the merciless Indian savages, whose known rule of warfare is an undistinguished destruction of all ages, sexes and conditions.

In every stage of these oppressions we have petitioned for redress, in the most humble terms, our repeated petitions have been answered only by repeated injury. A prince, whose character is thus marked by every act which may define a tyrant, is unfit to be the ruler of a free people.

Nor have we been wanting in attentions to our British brethren We have warned them, from time to time, of attempts, by their legislature, to extend an unwarrantable jurisdiction over us We have reminded them of the circumstances of our emigration and settlement here We have appealed to their native justice and magnanimity, and we have conjured them, by the ties of our common kindred, to disavow these usurpations, which would inevitably interrupt our connexions and correspondence. They, too, have been deaf to the voice of justice, and of consanguinity We must, therefore, acquiesce in the necessity which denounces our separation, and hold them, as we hold the rest of mankind, enemies in war, in peace friends

We, therefore, the representatives of the United States of America, in general congress assembled, appealing to the Supreme Judge of the world, for the rectitude of our intentions, do, in the name and by the authority of the good people of these colonies, solemnly publish and declare, that these united colonies are, and of right ought to be, free and independent states, that they are absolved from all allegiance to the British crown, and that all political connexion between them and the state of Great Britain, is, and ought to be totally dissolved, and that as free and independent states, they have full power to levy war, conclude peace, contract alliances, establish commerce, and do all other acts and things, which independent states may of right do And for the support of this declaration, with a firm reliance on the protection of Divine Providence, we mutually pledge to each other, our lives, our fortunes, and our sacred honor

JOHN HANCOCK

New Hampshire — Josiah Bartlett, William Whipple, Matthew Thornton

Massachusetts Bay — Samuel Adams, John Adams, Robert Treat Paine, Elbridge Gerry.

Rhode Island, &c — Stephen Hopkins, William Ellery.

Connecticut.— Roger Sherman, Samuel Huntington, William Williams, Oliver Wolcott

New York — William Floyd, Philip Livingston, Francis Lewis, Lewis Morris

New Jersey — Richard Stockton, John Witherspoon, Francis Hopkinson, John Hart, Abraham Clark

Pennsylvania — Robert Morris, Benjamin Rush, Benjamin Franklin, John Morton, George Clymer, James Smith, George Taylor, James Wilson, George Ross

Delaware — Cæsar Rodney, George Read, Thomas M'Kean.

Maryland — Samuel Chase, William Paca, Thomas Stone, Charles Carroll of Carrollton.

Virginia — George Wythe, Richard Henry Lee, Thomas Jefferson, Benjamin Harrison, Thomas Nelson, Jun, Francis Lightfoot Lee, Carter Braxton.

North Carolina — William Hooper, Joseph Hewes, John Penn

South Carolina — Edward Rutledge, Thomas Hayward, Jun, Thomas Lynch, Jun, Arthur Middleton

Georgia.— Button Gwinnett, Lyman Hall, George Walton.

ARTICLES OF CONFEDERATION.

ARTICLES *of Confederation and Perpetual Union between the States of New Hampshire, Massachusetts Bay Rhode Island and Providence Plantations, Connecticut, New York, New Jersey, Pennsylvania, Delaware, Maryland, Virginia, North Carolina, South Carolina, and Georgia.*

ARTICLE I. The style of this Confederacy shall be, "The United States of America"

ART. II. Each State retains its sovereignty, freedom, and independence, and every power, jurisdiction, and right, which is not by this Confederation expressly delegated to the United States in Congress assembled

ART III The said States hereby severally enter into a firm league of friendship with each other, for their common defense, the security of their liberties, and their mutual and general welfare, binding themselves to assist each other against all force offered to, or attacks made upon them, or any of them, on account of religion, sovereignty, trade, or any other pretense whatever

ART IV. The better to secure and perpetuate mutual friendship and intercourse among the people of the different States in this Union, the free inhabitants of each of these States, paupers, vagabonds, and fugitives from justice excepted, shall be entitled to all privileges and immunities of free citizens in the several States; and the people of each State shall have free ingress and egress to and from any other State, and shall enjoy therein all the privileges of trade and commerce subject to the same duties, impositions, and restrictions as the inhabitants thereof respectively; provided that such restrictions shall not extend so far as to prevent the removal of property imported into any State to any other State of which the owner is an inhabitant, provided also that no imposition, duties, or restriction shall be laid by any State on the property of the United States or either of them If any person guilty of, or charged with, treason, felony, or other high misdemeanor in any State shall flee from justice and be found in any of the United States, he shall, upon demand of the governor or executive power of the State from which he fled, be delivered up and removed to the State having jurisdiction of his offense. Full faith and credit shall be given in each of these States to the records, acts, and judicial proceedings of the courts and magistrates of every other State

Art V. For the more convenient management of the general interests of the United States, delegates shall be annually appointed in such manner as the Legislature of each State shall direct, to meet in Congress on the first Monday in November in every year, with a power reserved to each State to recall its delegates or any of them, at any time within the year, and to send others in their stead for the remainder of the year No State shall be represented in Congress by less than two, nor by more than seven members; and no person shall be capable of being a delegate for more than three years in any term of six years; nor shall any person, being a delegate, be capable of holding any office under the United States for which he or another for his benefit, receives any salary, fees, or emolument of any kind Each State shall maintain its own delegates in any meeting of the States and while they act as members of the Committee of the States In determining questions in the United States in Congress assembled, each State shall have one vote. Freedom of speech and debate in Congress shall not be impeached or questioned in any court or place out of Congress; and the members of Congress shall be protected in their persons from arrests and imprisonment during the time of their going to and from, and attendance on, Congress, except for treason, felony or breach of the peace

Art VI. No State, without the consent of the United States, in Congress assembled, shall send any embassy to, or receive any embassy from, or enter into any conference, agreement, alliance, or treaty with any king, prince, or state, nor shall any person holding any office of profit or trust under the United States, or any of them, accept of any present, emolument, office, or title of any kind whatever from any king, prince, or foreign state, nor shall the United States, in Congress assembled, or any of them, grant any title of nobility

No two or more States shall enter into any treaty, confederation, or alliance whatever between them, without the consent of the United States, in Congress assembled, specifying accurately the purposes for which the same is to be entered into, and how long it shall continue

No State shall lay any imposts or duties which may interfere with any stipulations in treaties entered into by the United States, in Congress assembled, with any king, prince, or state, in pursuance of any treaties already proposed by Congress to the courts of France and Spain.

No vessels of war shall be kept up in time of peace by any State, except such number only as shall be deemed necessary by the United States, in Congress assembled, for the defense of such State or its trade, nor shall any body of forces be kept up by any State in time of peace, except such number only as, in the judgment of the United States, in Congress assembled, shall be deemed requisite to garrison the forts necessary for the defense of such State; but every State shall always keep up a well-regulated and disciplined militia, sufficiently armed and accoutred, and shall provide and constantly have ready for use in public stores a due number of field-pieces and tents, and a proper quantity of arms, ammunition, and camp equipage.

No State shall engage in any war without the consent of the United States, in Congress assembled, unless such State be actually invaded by enemies, or shall have received certain advice of a resolution being formed by some nation of Indians to invade such State, and the danger is so imminent as not to admit of a delay till the United States, in Congress assembled, can be consulted, nor shall any State grant commissions to any ships or vessels of war, nor letters of marque or reprisal, except it be after a declaration of war by the United States, in Congress assembled, and then only against the kingdom or state, and the subjects thereof, against which war has been so declared, and under such regulations as shall be established by the United States, in Congress assembled, unless such State be infested by pirates, in which case vessels of war may be fitted out for that occasion, and kept so long as the danger shall continue, or until the United States, in Congress assembled, shall determine otherwise.

ART. VII. When land forces are raised by any State for the common defense, all officers of or under the rank of Colonel shall be appointed by the Legislature of each State respectively by whom such forces shall be raised, or in such manner as such State shall direct, and all vacancies shall be filled up by the State which first made the appointment.

ART. VIII. All charges of war, and all other expenses that shall be incurred for the common defense, or general welfare, and allowed by the United States, in Congress assembled, shall be defrayed out of a common treasury, which shall be supplied by the several States in proportion to the value of all land within each State, granted to, or surveyed for, any person, as such land and the buildings and improvements thereon shall be estimated, according to such mode as the United States, in Congress assembled, shall, from time to time, direct and appoint. The taxes for paying that proportion shall be laid and levied by the authority and direction of the Legislatures of the several States, within the time agreed upon by the United States, in Congress assembled.

ART. IX. The United States, in Congress assembled, shall have the sole and exclusive right and power of determining on peace and war, except in the cases mentioned in the sixth Article, of sending and receiving ambassadors, entering into treaties and alliances, provided that no treaty of commerce shall be made, whereby the legislative power of the respective States shall be restrained from imposing such imposts and duties on foreigners as their own people are subjected to, or from prohibiting the exportation or importation of any species of goods or commodities whatever, of establishing rules for deciding, in all cases, what captures on land and water shall be legal, and in what manner prizes taken by land or naval forces in the service of the United States shall be divided or appropriated, of granting letters of marque and reprisal in times of peace, appointing courts for the trial of piracies and felonies committed on the high seas, and establishing courts for receiving and determining finally appeals in all cases of captures, provided that no member of Congress shall be appointed a judge of any of the said courts.

The United States, in Congress assembled, shall also be the last resort on appeal in all disputes and differences now subsisting, or that hereafter may arise between two or more States concerning boundary, jurisdiction, or any other cause whatever, which authority shall always be exercised in the manner following. Whenever the legislative or executive authority, or lawful agent of any State in controversy with another, shall present a petition to Congress, stating the matter in question, and praying for a hearing, notice thereof shall be given by order of Congress to the legislative or executive authority of the other State in controversy, and a day assigned for the appearance of the parties by their lawful agents, who shall then be directed to appoint, by joint consent, commissioners or judges to constitute a court for hearing and determining the matter in question, but if they cannot agree, Congress shall name three persons out of each of the United States, and from the list of such persons each party shall alternately strike out one, the petitioners beginning, until the number shall be reduced to thirteen; and from that number not less than seven nor more than nine names, as Congress shall direct, shall, in the presence of Congress, be drawn out by lot; and the persons whose names shall be so drawn, or any five of them, shall be commissioners or judges, to hear and finally determine the controversy, so always as a major part of the judges who shall hear the cause shall agree in the determination; and if either party shall neglect to attend at the day appointed, without showing reasons which Congress shall judge sufficient, or being present, shall refuse to strike, the Congress shall proceed to nominate three persons out of each State, and the secretary of Congress shall strike in behalf of such party absent or refusing; and the judgment and sentence of the court, to be appointed in the manner before prescribed, shall be final and conclusive, and if any of the parties shall refuse to submit to the authority of such court, or to appear or defend their claim or cause, the court shall nevertheless proceed to pronounce sentence or judgment, which shall in like manner be final and decisive, the judgment or sentence and other proceedings being in either case transmitted to Congress, and lodged among the acts of Congress for the security of the parties concerned; provided, that every commissioner, before he sits in judgment, shall take an oath, to be administered by one of the judges of the supreme or superior court of the State where the cause shall be tried, "well and truly to hear and determine the matter in question, according to the best of his judgment, without favor, affection, or hope of reward" Provided, also, that no State shall be deprived of territory for the benefit of the United States.

All controversies concerning the private right of soil claimed under different grants of two or more States, whose jurisdictions, as they may respect such lands, and the States which passed such grants are adjusted the said grants or either of them being at the same time claimed to have originated antecedent to such settlement of jurisdiction, shall, on the petition of either party to the Congress of the United States, be finally determined, as near as may be, in the same manner as is before prescribed for deciding disputes respecting territorial jurisdiction between different States.

The United States in Congress assembled, shall also have the sole and exclusive right and power of regulating the alloy and value of coin struck by their own authority, or by that of the respective States, fixing the standard of weights and measures throughout the United States regulating the trade and managing all affairs with the Indians, not members of any of the States, provided that the legislative right of any State, within its own limits, be not infringed or violated, establishing and regulating post-offices from one State to another, throughout all the United States and exacting such postage on the papers passing through the same as may be requisite to defray the expenses of the said office, appointing all officers of the land forces in the service of the United States, excepting regimental officers; appointing all the officers of the naval forces, and commissioning all officers whatever in the service of the United States, making rules for the government and regulation of the said land and naval forces, and directing their operations

The United States, in Congress assembled, shall have authority to appoint a committee, to sit in the recess of Congress, to be denominated "A Committee of the States," and to consist of one delegate from each State, and to appoint such other committees and civil officers as may be necessary for managing the general affairs of the United States under their direction; to appoint one of their number to preside; provided that no person shall be allowed to serve in the office of president more than one year in any term of three years; to ascertain the necessary sums of money to be raised for the service of the United States, and to appropriate and apply the same for defraying the public expenses, to borrow money or emit bills on the credit of the United States, transmitting every half year to the respective States an account of the sums of money so borrowed or emitted; to build and equip a navy, to agree upon the number of land forces, and to make requisitions from each State for its quota, in proportion to the number of white inhabitants in such State, which requisition shall be binding, and thereupon the Legislature of each State shall appoint the regimental officers, raise the men, and clothe, arm, and equip them in a soldier-like manner, at the expense of the United States, and the officers and men so clothed, armed, and equipped shall march to the place appointed, and within the time agreed on by the United States, in Congress assembled, but if the United States, in Congress assembled, shall, on consideration of circumstances, judge proper that any State should not raise men, or should raise a smaller number than its quota, and that any other State should raise a greater number of men than the quota thereof, such extra number shall be raised, officered, clothed, armed, and equipped in the same manner as the quota of such State, unless the Legislature of such State shall judge that such extra number can not be safely spared out of the same, in which case they shall raise, officer, clothe, arm, and equip as many of such extra number as they judge can be safely spared, and the officers and men so clothed, armed, and equipped shall march to the place appointed, and within the time agreed on by the United States, in Congress assembled.

The United States, in Congress assembled, shall never engage in a war, nor grant letters of marque and reprisal in time of peace, nor enter into any treaties or alliances, nor coin money, nor regulate the value thereof, nor ascertain the sums and expenses necessary for the defense and welfare of the United States, or any of them, nor emit bills, nor borrow money on the credit of the United States, nor appropriate money, nor agree upon the number of vessels of war to be built or purchased, or the number of land or sea forces to be raised, nor appoint a commander-in-chief of the army or navy, unless nine States assent to the same, nor shall a question on any other point, except for adjourning from day to day, be determined, unless by the votes of a majority of the United States, in Congress assembled.

The Congress of the United States shall have power to adjourn to any time within the year, and to any place within the United States, so that no period of adjournment be for a longer duration than the space of six months, and shall publish the journal of their proceedings monthly, except such parts thereof relating to treaties, alliances, or military operations as in their judgment require secrecy, and the yeas and nays of the delegates of each State, on any question, shall be entered on the journal when it is desired by any delegate, and the delegates of a State, or any of them, at his or their request, shall be furnished with a transcript of the said journal except such parts as are above excepted, to lay before the Legislatures of the several States

ART X The Committee of the States, or any nine of them, shall be authorized to execute, in the recess of Congress, such of the powers of Congress as the United States, in Congress assembled, by the consent of nine States, shall, from time to time, think expedient to vest them with; provided that no power be delegated to the said Committee, for the exercise of which, by the Articles of Confederation, the voice of nine States in the Congress of the United States assembled is requisite

ART XI Canada, acceding to this Confederation, and joining in the measures of the United States shall be admitted into, and entitled to all the advantages of this Union, but no other colony shall be admitted into the same, unless such admission be agreed to by nine States

ART XII. All bills of credit emitted, moneys borrowed, and debts contracted by or under the authority of Congress, before the assembling of the United States, in pursuance of the present Confederation, shall be deemed and considered as a charge against the United States, for payment and satisfaction whereof the said United States and the public faith are hereby solemnly pledged.

ART XIII Every State shall abide by the determinations of the United States in Congress assembled on all questions which by this Confederation are submitted to them And the Articles of this Confederation shall be inviolably observed by every State, and the Union shall be perpetual, nor shall any alteration at any time hereafter be made in any of them unless such alteration be agreed to in a Congress of the United States, and be afterwards confirmed by the Legislatures of every State

AND WHEREAS it hath pleased the great Governor of the world to incline the hearts of the Legislatures we respectively represent in Congress to approve of, and to authorize us to ratify, the said Articles of Confederation and perpetual Union, know ye, that we, the undersigned delegates, by virtue of the power and authority to us given for that purpose, do, by these presents in the name and in behalf of our respective constituents, fully and entirely ratify and confirm each and every of the said Articles of Confederation and perpetual Union and all and singular the matters and things therein contained. And we do further solemnly plight and engage the faith of our respective constituents, that they shall abide by the determinations of the United States, in Congress assembled, on all questions which by the said Confederation are submitted to them, and that the Articles thereof shall be inviolably observed by the States we respectively represent, and that the Union shall be perpetual. In witness whereof, we have hereunto set our hands in Congress. Done at Philadelphia, in the State of Pennsylvania, the ninth day of July, in the year of our Lord 1778, and in the third year of the Independence of America.

CONSTITUTION

OF THE

UNITED STATES OF AMERICA.

PREAMBLE

We the people of the United States, in order to form a more perfect union, establish justice, insure domestic tranquillity, provide for the common defense, promote the general welfare, and secure the blessings of liberty to ourselves and our posterity, do ordain and establish this Constitution for the United States of America.

ARTICLE I

LEGISLATIVE DEPARTMENT.

Section I.

CONGRESS IN GENERAL

All legislative powers herein granted shall be vested in a Congress of the United States, which shall consist of a Senate and House of Representatives.

Section II.

HOUSE OF REPRESENTATIVES.

1 The House of Representatives shall be composed of members chosen every second year by the people of the several States, and the electors in each State shall have the qualifications requisite for electors of the most numerous branch of the State Legislature.

2 No person shall be a representative who shall not have attained to the age of twenty-five years, and been seven years a citizen of the United States, and who shall not, when elected, be an inhabitant of that State in which he shall be chosen

3. Representatives and direct taxes shall be apportioned among the several States which may be included within this Union, according to their respective numbers, which shall be determined by adding to the whole number of free persons, including those bound to service for a term of years, and excluding Indians not taxed, three-fifths of all other persons. The actual enumeration shall be made within three years after the first meeting of the Congress of the United States, and within every subsequent term of ten years, in such manner as they shall by law direct. The number of representatives shall not exceed one for every thirty thousand, but each State shall have at least one representative, and until such enumeration shall be made, the State of New Hampshire shall be entitled to choose three, Massachusetts eight, Rhode Island and Providence Plantations one, Connecticut five, New York six, New Jersey four, Pennsylvania eight, Delaware one, Maryland six, Virginia ten, North Carolina five, South Carolina five, and Georgia three.

4. When vacancies happen in the representation from any State, the executive authority thereof shall issue writs of election to fill such vacancies.

5. The House of Representatives shall choose their speaker and other officers, and shall have the sole power of impeachment.

SECTION III.

SENATE.

1. The Senate of the United States shall be composed of two senators from each State, chosen by the Legislature thereof for six years, and each senator shall have one vote.

2. Immediately after they shall be assembled in consequence of the first election, they shall be divided, as equally as may be, into three classes. The seats of the senators of the first class shall be vacated at the expiration of the second year, of the second class at the expiration of the fourth year, and of the third class at the expiration of the sixth year, so that one-third may be chosen every second year, and if vacancies happen, by resignation or otherwise, during the recess of the Legislature of any State, the executive thereof may make temporary appointments until the next meeting of the Legislature, which shall then fill such vacancies.

3 No person shall be a senator who shall not have attained to the age of thirty years, and been nine years a citizen of the United States, and who shall not, when elected, be an inhabitant of that State for which he shall be chosen.

4. The Vice-President of the United States shall be President of the Senate, but shall have no vote, unless they be equally divided

5 The Senate shall choose their officers and also a president *pro tempore*, in the absence of the Vice-President, or when he shall exercise the office of President of the United States

6. The Senate shall have the sole power to try all impeachments. When sitting for that purpose, they shall be on oath or affirmation When the President of the United States is tried, the chief justice shall preside, and no person shall be convicted without the concurrence of two-thirds of the members present

7 Judgment in case of impeachment shall not extend farther than to removal from office, and disqualification to hold and enjoy any office of honor, trust, or profit under the United States, but the party convicted shall, nevertheless, be liable and subject to indictment, trial, judgment, and punishment according to law.

Section IV.

BOTH HOUSES.

1 The times, places, and manner of holding elections for senators and representatives shall be prescribed in each State by the Legislature thereof, but the Congress may at any time, by law, make or alter such regulations, except as to the place of choosing senators

2 The Congress shall assemble at least once in every year, and such meeting shall be on the first Monday in December, unless they shall by law appoint a different day.

Section V

THE HOUSES SEPARATELY

1 Each house shall be the judge of the elections, returns, and qualifications of its own members, and a majority of each shall constitute a quorum to do business, but a smaller num-

ber may adjourn from day to day, and may be authorized to compel the attendance of absent members, in such manner and under such penalties as each house may provide

2 Each house may determine the rules of its proceedings, punish its members for disorderly behavior, and, with the concurrence of two-thirds, expel a member

3 Each house shall keep a journal of its proceedings, and from time to time publish the same, excepting such parts as may in their judgment require secrecy, and the yeas and nays of the members of either house, on any question, shall, at the desire of one-fifth of those present, be entered on the journal.

4 Neither house during the session of Congress shall, without the consent of the other, adjourn for more than three days nor to any other place than that in which the two houses shall be sitting.

Section VI.

DISABILITIES OF MEMBERS.

1 The senators and representatives shall receive a compensation for their services to be ascertained by law and paid out of the treasury of the United States. They shall in all cases, except treason, felony, and breach of the peace, be privileged from arrest during their attendance at the session of their respective houses, and in going to or returning from the same, and for any speech or debate in either house, they shall not be questioned in any other place.

2 No senator or representative shall, during the time for which he was elected, be appointed to any civil office under the authority of the United States, which shall have been created, or the emoluments whereof shall have been increased, during such time and no person holding any office under the United States shall be a member of either house during his continuance in office

Section VII

MODE OF PASSING LAWS

1 All bills for raising revenue shall originate in the House of Representatives but the Senate may propose or concur with amendments, as on other bills.

2 Every bill which shall have passed the House of Representatives and the Senate shall, before it become a law, be presented to the President of the United States, if he approve,

he shall sign it, but if not, he shall return it, with his objections, to that house in which it shall have originated, who shall enter the objections at large on their journal, and proceed to reconsider it. If, after such reconsideration, two-thirds of that house shall agree to pass the bill, it shall be sent, together with the objections to the other house, by which it shall likewise be reconsidered, and if approved by two-thirds of that house, it shall become a law. But in all such cases the votes of both houses shall be determined by yeas and nays, and the names of the persons voting for and against the bill shall be entered on the journal of each house respectively. If any bill shall not be returned by the President within ten days (Sundays excepted) after it shall have been presented to him, the same shall be a law in like manner as if he had signed it, unless the Congress by their adjournment prevent its return, in which case it shall not be a law.

3. Every order, resolution, or vote to which the concurrence of the Senate and House of Representatives may be necessary (except on a question of adjournment) shall be presented to the President of the United States; and before the same shall take effect, shall be approved by him, or, being disapproved by him, shall be repassed by two-thirds of the Senate and House of Representatives, according to the rules and limitations prescribed in the case of a bill.

Section VIII.

POWERS GRANTED TO CONGRESS.

The Congress shall have power:

1. To lay and collect taxes, duties, imposts, and excises to pay the debts and provide for the common defense and general welfare of the United States; but all duties, imposts, and excises shall be uniform throughout the United States;

2. To borrow money on the credit of the United States;

3. To regulate commerce with foreign nations, and among the several States, and with the Indian tribes;

4. To establish a uniform rule of naturalization, and uniform laws on the subject of bankruptcies, throughout the United States;

5. To coin money, regulate the value thereof and of foreign coin, and fix the standard of weights and measures;

6. To provide for the punishment of counterfeiting the securities and current coin of the United States;

7. To establish post-offices and post-roads;

8. To promote the progress of science and useful arts, by securing for limited times to authors and inventors the exclusive right to their respective writings and discoveries;

9. To constitute tribunals inferior to the Supreme Court;

10. To define and punish felonies committed on the high seas, and offenses against the law of nations;

11. To declare war, grant letters of marque and reprisal, and make rules concerning captures on land and water;

12. To raise and support armies, but no appropriation of money to that use shall be for a longer term than two years;

13. To provide and maintain a navy;

14. To make rules for the government and regulation of the land and naval forces;

15. To provide for calling forth the militia to execute the laws of the Union, suppress insurrections, and repel invasions;

16. To provide for organizing, arming, and disciplining the militia, and for governing such part of them as may be employed in the service of the United States, reserving to the States respectively the appointment of the officers, and the authority of training the militia according to the discipline prescribed by Congress;

17. To exercise exclusive legislation, in all cases whatsoever, over such district (not exceeding ten miles square) as may, by cession of particular States and the acceptance of Congress, become the seat of government of the United States, and to exercise like authority over all places purchased, by the consent of the Legislature of the State, in which the same shall be, for the erection of forts, magazines, arsenals, dock-yards, and all other needful buildings; and

18. To make all laws which shall be necessary and proper for carrying into execution the foregoing powers, and all other powers vested by this Constitution in the government of the United States, or in any department or office thereof.

SECTION IX.

POWERS DENIED TO THE UNITED STATES.

1. The migration or importation of such persons as any of the States now existing shall think proper to admit shall

not be prohibited by the Congress prior to the year one thousand eight hundred and eight, but a tax or duty may be imposed on such importation, not exceeding ten dollars for each person

2 The privilege of the writ of *habeas corpus* shall not be suspended unless when, in case of rebellion or invasion, the public safety may require it.

3 No bill of attainder, or *ex post facto* law, shall be passed.

4 No capitation or other direct tax shall be laid, unless in proportion to the census or enumeration herein before directed to be taken

5 No tax or duty shall be laid on articles exported from any State

6 No preference shall be given by any regulation of commerce or revenue to the ports of one State over those of another nor shall vessels bound to or from one State be obliged to enter, clear, or pay duties in another

7 No money shall be drawn from the treasury but in consequence of appropriations made by law, and a regular statement and account of the receipts and expenditures of all public money shall be published from time to time.

8 No title of nobility shall be granted by the United States; and no person holding any office of profit or trust under them shall, without the consent of the Congress, accept of any present, emolument, office, or title of any kind whatever, from any king, prince, or foreign state.

SECTION X.

POWERS DENIED TO THE STATES

1 No State shall enter into any treaty, alliance, or confederation, grant letters of marque and reprisal, coin money, emit bills of credit, make anything but gold and silver coin a tender in payment of debts, pass any bill of attainder, *ex post facto* law, or law impairing the obligation of contracts or grant any title of nobility

2 No State shall, without the consent of Congress, lay any imposts or duties on imports or exports, except what may be absolutely necessary for executing its inspection laws, and the net produce of all duties and imposts laid by any State on

imports or exports shall be for the use of the treasury of the United States, and all such laws shall be subject to the revision and control of the Congress

3 No State shall, without the consent of Congress, lay any duty of tonnage, keep troops or ships of war in time of peace, enter into any agreement or compact with another State or with a foreign power, or engage in war unless actually invaded, or in such imminent danger as will not admit of delays.

ARTICLE II.

EXECUTIVE DEPARTMENT.

SECTION I.

PRESIDENT AND VICE-PRESIDENT.

1 The executive power shall be vested in a President of the United States of America He shall hold his office during the term of four years, and, together with the Vice-President, chosen for the same term, be elected as follows —

2 Each State shall appoint, in such manner as the Legislature thereof may direct, a number of electors, equal to the whole number of senators and representatives to which the State may be entitled in the Congress, but no senator or representative, or person holding an office of trust or profit under the United States, shall be appointed an elector.

3. [The electors shall meet in their respective States, and vote by ballot for two persons, of whom one at least shall not be an inhabitant of the same State with themselves. And they shall make a list of all the persons voted for, and of the number of votes for each; which list they shall sign and certify, and transmit, sealed, to the seat of the government of the United States, directed to the President of the Senate The President of the Senate shall, in the presence of the Senate and House of Representatives, open all the certificates, and the votes shall then be counted. The person having the greatest number of votes shall be the President, if such number be a majority of the whole number of electors appointed; and if there be more than one who have such majority, and have an equal number of votes, then the House of Representatives shall immediately choose by ballot one of them for President, and if no person have a majority, then, from the five highest on

the list, the said House shall in like manner choose the President. But in choosing the President, the votes shall be taken by States, the representation from each State having one vote, a quorum for this purpose shall consist of a member or members from two-thirds of the States, and a majority of all the States shall be necessary to a choice In every case, after the choice of the President, the person having the greatest number of votes of the electors shall be the Vice-President. But if there should remain two or more who have equal votes, the Senate shall choose from them by ballot the Vice-President][1]

4 The Congress may determine the time of choosing the electors, and the day on which they shall give their votes, which day shall be the same throughout the United States

5 No person except a natural-born citizen, or a citizen of the United States at the time of the adoption of this Constitution, shall be eligible to the office of President, neither shall any person be eligible to that office who shall not have attained to the age of thirty-five years, and been fourteen years a resident within the United States

6. In case of the removal of the President from office, or of his death, resignation, or inability to discharge the powers and duties of the said office, the same shall devolve on the Vice-President; and the Congress may by law provide for the case of removal, death, resignation, or inability, both of the President and Vice-President, declaring what officer shall then act as President; and such officer shall act accordingly, until the disability be removed or a President shall be elected

7. The President shall, at stated times, receive for his services a compensation, which shall neither be increased nor diminished during the period for which he shall have been elected, and he shall not receive within that period any other emolument from the United States, or any of them

8. Before he enter on the execution of his office, he shall take the following oath or affirmation —

"I do solemnly swear (or affirm) that I will faithfully execute the office of President of the United States, and will, to the best of my ability, preserve, protect, and defend the Constitution of the United States"

[1] Altered by the XIIth Amendment.

Section II.

POWERS OF THE PRESIDENT.

1 The President shall be commander-in-chief of the army and navy of the United States, and of the militia of the several States when called into the actual service of the United States; he may require the opinion in writing of the principal officer in each of the executive departments upon any subject relating to the duties of their respective offices, and he shall have power to grant reprieves and pardons for offenses against the United States, except in cases of impeachment

2 He shall have power, by and with the advice and consent of the Senate, to make treaties, provided two-thirds of the senators present concur, and he shall nominate, and by and with the advice and consent of the Senate, shall appoint ambassadors, other public ministers and consuls, judges of the Supreme Court, and all other officers of the United States, whose appointments are not herein otherwise provided for and which shall be established by law, but the Congress may by law vest the appointment of such inferior officers as they think proper in the President alone, in the courts of law, or in the heads of departments

3 The President shall have power to fill up all vacancies that may happen during the recess of the Senate, by granting commissions, which shall expire at the end of their next session.

Section III.

DUTIES OF THE PRESIDENT.

He shall, from time to time, give to the Congress information of the state of the Union, and recommend to their consideration such measures as he shall judge necessary and expedient, he may, on extraordinary occasions, convene both houses, or either of them, and in case of disagreement between them, with respect to the time of adjournment, he may adjourn them to such time as he shall think proper, he shall receive ambassadors and other public ministers, he shall take care that the laws be faithfully executed, and shall commission all the officers of the United States.

Section IV.

IMPEACHMENT OF THE PRESIDENT

The President, Vice-President, and all civil officers of the United States shall be removed from office on impeachment for and conviction of treason, bribery, or other high crimes and misdemeanors.

ARTICLE III

JUDICIAL DEPARTMENT

Section I.

UNITED STATES COURTS

The judicial power of the United States shall be vested in one Supreme Court, and in such inferior courts as Congress may from time to time ordain and establish The judges, both of the supreme and inferior courts, shall hold their offices during good behavior, and shall, at stated times, receive for their services a compensation, which shall not be diminished during their continuance in office.

Section II.

JURISDICTION OF THE UNITED STATES COURTS.

1 The judicial power shall extend to all cases in law and equity arising under this Constitution, the laws of the United States, and treaties made or which shall be made, under their authority, to all cases affecting ambassadors, other public ministers, and consuls, to all cases of admiralty and maritime jurisdiction, to controversies to which the United States shall be a party, to controversies between two or more States, between a State and citizens of another State, between citizens of different States, between citizens of the same State claiming lands under grants of different States, and between a State, or the citizens thereof, and foreign states, citizens, or subjects [1]

2 In all cases affecting ambassadors, other public ministers, and consuls, and those in which a State shall be party, the Supreme Court shall have original jurisdiction In all the other cases before mentioned, the Supreme Court shall have

[1] Altered by XIth Amendment.

appellate jurisdiction, both as to law and fact, with such exceptions and under such regulations as the Congress shall make.

3 The trial of all crimes, except in cases of impeachment, shall be by jury, and such trial shall be held in the State where the said crimes shall have been committed, but when not committed within any State, the trial shall be at such place or places as the Congress may by law have directed.

Section III.

TREASON.

1. Treason against the United States shall consist only in levying war against them, or in adhering to their enemies, giving them aid and comfort. No person shall be convicted of treason unless on the testimony of two witnesses to the same overt act, or on confession in open court

2 The Congress shall have power to declare the punishment of treason, but no attainder of treason shall work corruption of blood, or forfeiture, except during the life of the person attainted.

ARTICLE IV.

THE STATES AND THE FEDERAL GOVERNMENT.

Section I.

STATE RECORDS.

Full faith and credit shall be given in each State to the public acts, records, and judicial proceedings of every other State. And the Congress may, by general laws, prescribe the manner in which such acts, records, and proceedings shall be proved, and the effect thereof.

Section II.

PRIVILEGES OF CITIZENS, ETC

1. The citizens of each State shall be entitled to all privileges and immunities of citizens in the several States.

2 A person charged in any State with treason, felony, or other crime, who shall flee from justice and be found in another State, shall, on demand of the executive authority of the State from which he fled, be delivered up, to be removed to the State having jurisdiction of the crime.

3. No person held to service or labor in one State, under the laws thereof, escaping into another, shall, in consequence of any law or regulation therein, be discharged from such service or labor, but shall be delivered up on claim of the party to whom such service or labor may be due

Section III.

NEW STATES AND TERRITORIES.

1 New States may be admitted by the Congress into this Union; but no new State shall be formed or erected within the jurisdiction of any other State, nor any State be formed by the junction of two or more States, or parts of States, without the consent of the Legislatures of the States concerned, as well as of the Congress

2. The Congress shall have power to dispose of, and make all needful rules and regulations respecting, the territory or other property belonging to the United States, and nothing in this Constitution shall be so construed as to prejudice any claims of the United States or of any particular State.

Section IV.

GUARANTEE TO THE STATES.

The United States shall guarantee to every State in this Union a republican form of government, and shall protect each of them against invasion, and, on application of the Legislature, or of the executive (when the Legislature cannot be convened), against domestic violence.

ARTICLE V

POWER OF AMENDMENT.

The Congress, whenever two-thirds of both houses shall deem it necessary, shall propose amendments to this Constitution, or, on the application of the Legislatures of two-thirds of the several States, shall call a convention for proposing amendments, which, in either case, shall be valid to all intents and purposes as part of this Constitution, when ratified by the Legislatures of three-fourths of the several States, or by conventions in three-fourths thereof, as the one or the other mode of ratification may be proposed by Congress, provided that no amendment which may be made prior to the year one thousand eight hundred and eight shall in any manner affect the first and fourth clauses in the ninth section of the first Article. and that no State, without its consent, shall be deprived of its equal suffrage in the Senate.

ARTICLE VI

PUBLIC DEBT, SUPREMACY OF THE CONSTITUTION, OATH OF OFFICE, RELIGIOUS TEST

1 All debts contracted and engagements entered into before the adoption of this Constitution shall be as valid against the United States under this Constitution as under the Confederation.

2 This Constitution, and the laws of the United States which shall be made in pursuance thereof, and all treaties made, or which shall be made, under the authority of the United States, shall be the supreme law of the land, and the judges in every State shall be bound thereby, anything in the Constitution or laws of any State to the contrary notwithstanding

3. The senators and representatives before mentioned, and the members of the several State Legislatures, and all executive and judicial officers, both of the United States and of the several States. shall be bound by oath or affirmation to support this Constitution, but no religious test shall ever be required as a qualification to any office or public trust under the United States

ARTICLE VII.

RATIFICATION OF THE CONSTITUTION

The ratifications of the Conventions of nine States shall be sufficient for the establishment of this Constitution between the States so ratifying the same

Done in Convention, by the unanimous consent of the States present, the seventeenth day of September, in the year of our Lord one thousand seven hundred and eighty-seven, and of the Independence of the United States of America the twelfth.

AMENDMENTS TO THE CONSTITUTION.

ARTICLE I

Congress shall make no law respecting an establishment of religion, or prohibiting the free exercise thereof; or abridging the freedom of speech, or of the press, or the right of the people peaceably to assemble, and to petition the government for a redress of grievances

ARTICLE II

A well regulated militia being necessary to the security of a free state, the right of the people to keep and bear arms shall not be infringed.

ARTICLE III

No soldier shall, in time of peace, be quartered in any house, without the consent of the owner, nor in time of war, but in a manner to be prescribed by law.

ARTICLE IV.

The right of the people to be secure in their persons, houses, papers, and effects, against unreasonable searches and seizures shall not be violated, and no warrants shall issue but upon probable cause, supported by oath or affirmation, and particularly describing the place to be searched, and the persons or things to be seized

ARTICLE V

No person shall be held to answer for a capital, or otherwise infamous crime, unless on a presentment or indictment of a grand jury, except in cases arising in the land or naval forces. or in the militia when in active service in time of war or public danger; nor shall any person be subject for the same offense to be twice put in jeopardy of life or limb, nor shall be compelled, in any criminal case, to be a witness against himself, nor be deprived of life, liberty, or property, without due process of law; nor shall private property be taken for public use without just compensation

ARTICLE VI.

In all criminal prosecutions, the accused shall enjoy the right to a speedy and public trial, by an impartial jury of the

State and district wherein the crime shall have been committed, which district shall have been previously ascertained by law, and to be informed of the nature and cause of the accusation, to be confronted with the witnesses against him, to have compulsory process for obtaining witnesses in his favor, and to have the assistance of counsel for his defense

ARTICLE VII.

In suits at common law, where the value in controversy shall exceed twenty dollars, the right of trial by jury shall be preserved, and no fact tried by a jury shall be otherwise re-examined in any court of the United States than according to the rules of the common law

ARTICLE VIII.

Excessive bail shall not be required, nor excessive fines imposed, nor cruel and unusual punishment inflicted.

ARTICLE IX.

The enumeration in the Constitution of certain rights shall not be construed to deny or disparage others retained by the people.

ARTICLE X.

The powers not granted to the United States by the Constitution, nor prohibited by it to the States, are reserved to the States respectively or to the people

ARTICLE XI.[1]

The judicial power of the United States shall not be construed to extend to any suit in law or equity, commenced or prosecuted against one of the United States by citizens of another State, or by citizens or subjects of any foreign State

ARTICLE XII[2]

1 The electors shall meet in their respective States, and vote by ballot for President and Vice-President, one of whom,

[1] Proposed by Congress March 5, 1794, and declared in force January 8, 1798

[2] Proposed by Congress December 12, 1803, and declared in force September 25, 1804.

at least, shall not be an inhabitant of the same State with themselves: they shall name in their ballots the person voted for as President, and in distinct ballots the person voted for as Vice-President, and they shall make distinct lists of all persons voted for as President, and of all persons voted for as Vice-President, and of the number of votes for each, which lists they shall sign and certify, and transmit sealed to the seat of government of the United States, directed to the President of the Senate, the President of the Senate shall, in the presence of the Senate and House of Representatives, open all the certificates, and the votes shall then be counted, the person having the greatest number of votes for President shall be the President, if such number be a majority of the whole number of electors appointed, and if no person have such majority, then from the persons having the highest numbers, not exceeding three, on the list of those voted for as President, the House of Representatives shall choose immediately by ballot the President But in choosing the President, the votes shall be taken by States, the representation from each State having one vote, a quorum for this purpose shall consist of a member or members from two-thirds of the States, and a majority of all the States shall be necessary to a choice. And if the House of Representatives shall not choose a President, whenever the right of choice shall devolve upon them, before the fourth day of March next following, then the Vice-President shall act as President, as in the case of death or other constitutional disability of the President

2. The person having the greatest number of votes as Vice-President shall be the Vice-President, if such number be a majority of the whole number of electors appointed, and if no person have a majority, then from the two highest numbers on the list the Senate shall choose the Vice-President; a quorum for the purpose shall consist of two-thirds of the whole number of senators, and a majority of the whole number shall be necessary to a choice.

3 But no person constitutionally ineligible to the office of President shall be eligible to that of Vice-President of the United States.

ARTICLE XIII.[1]

1 Neither slavery nor involuntary servitude, except as a punishment for crime whereof the party shall have been duly convicted, shall exist within the United States, or any place subject to their jurisdiction.

2 Congress shall have power to enforce this article by appropriate legislation

ARTICLE XIV[2]

1 All persons born or naturalized in the United States, and subject to the jurisdiction thereof, are citizens of the United States and of the State wherein they reside. No State shall make or enforce any law which shall abridge the privileges or immunities of citizens of the United States, nor shall any State deprive any person of life, liberty, or property, without due process of law, nor deny to any person within its jurisdiction the equal protection of the laws.

2 Representatives shall be apportioned among the several States according to their respective numbers, counting the whole number of persons in each State, excluding Indians not taxed. But when the right to vote at any election for the choice of electors for President and Vice-President of the United States, representatives in Congress, the executive and judicial officers of a State, or the members of the Legislature thereof, is denied to any of the male members of such State, being twenty-one years of age, and citizens of the United States, or in any way abridged, except for participation in rebellion or other crime, the basis of representation therein shall be reduced in the proportion which the number of such male citizens shall bear to the whole number of male citizens twenty-one years of age in such State.

3 No person shall be a senator or representative in Congress, or elector of President or Vice-President, or hold any office, civil or military, under the United States, or under any State, who, having previously taken an oath, as a member of Congress, or as an officer of the United States, or as a member

[1] Proposed by Congress February 1, 1865, and declared in force December 18 1865

[2] Proposed by Congress June 16, 1866, and declared in force July 28, 1868.

of any State Legislature, or as an executive or judicial officer of any State, to support the Constitution of the United States, shall have engaged in insurrection or rebellion against the same, or given aid and comfort to the enemies thereof. But Congress may, by a vote of two-thirds of each House, remove such disability

4 The validity of the public debt of the United States, authorized by law, including debts incurred for payment of pensions and bounties for services in suppressing insurrection or rebellion, shall not be questioned. But neither the United States nor any State shall assume or pay any debt or obligation incurred in aid of insurrection or rebellion against the United States, or any claim for the loss or emancipation of any slave, but all such debts, obligations, and claims shall be held illegal and void.

5 The Congress shall have power to enforce by appropriate legislation the provisions of this article

ARTICLE XV[1]

1 The right of citizens of the United States to vote shall not be denied or abridged by the United States or any State on account of race, color, or previous condition of servitude

2 The Congress shall have power to enforce by appropriate legislation the provisions of this article

[1] Proposed by Congress February 26, 1869, and declared in force March 30, 1870

CONSTITUTION

OF THE

UNITED STATES OF AMERICA.

PREAMBLE.

We the people of the United States, in order to form a more perfect union, establish justice, insure domestic tranquillity, provide for the common defense, promote the general welfare, and secure the blessings of liberty to ourselves and our posterity, do ordain and establish this Constitution for the United States of America

1. **We the people** —The constitution of the United States was ordained and established, not by the states in their sovereign capacity, but emphatically, as the preamble declares, by "the people of the United States" It was competent for the people to invest the general government with all the powers which they might deem proper and necessary; to extend or restrain these powers according to their own good pleasure, and to give them a paramount and supreme authority Martin v. Hunter's Lessees, 1 Wheat. 304-324, Chisholm v Georgia, 2 Dall 419, Brown v Maryland, 12 Wheat 455

2. Negroes or persons of African descent, whether free or slave, were not designed to be included either in the term "we the 'people,' or "citizens of the United States" Dred Scott v Sandford, 19 How 393, 404 407.

3. The government of the Union is emphatically and truly a government of the people. In form and substance it emanates from them Its powers are granted by them and are to be exercised directly by them and for their benefit McColloch v Maryland, 4 Wheat 316

4 'People of the United States" and 'citizens' are synonymous terms and mean the same thing They both describe the political body who, according to our republican institutions, form the sovereignty and who hold the power and conduct the government through their representatives They are what we call the "sovereign people," and every citizen is one of this people and a constituent member of the sovereignty Dred Scott v. Sandford, 19 How 393.

5. The constitution of the United States was ordained and established by the people of the United States for themselves, for their own government, and not for the government of individual states. Barron v. Mayor, etc of Baltimore, 7 Pet. 243

6 The constitution of the United States was not formed by the people of the United States nor by the states, but by a combined power exercised by the people through their delegates, limited in their sanctions to the respective states Had the constitution emanated from the people, and the states had been referred to merely as convenient districts by which the public expression could be ascertained, the popular vote throughout the Union would have been the only rule for its adoption. The vote of the people, however, was limited to the respective states in which they resided So there was an expression of popular suffrage and state sanction most happily united in its adoption Mr Justice McLean in Worcester v Georgia, 6 Pet. 515-569 To same effect see Ware v. Hylton, 3 Dall. 199, Chisholm v. Georgia, 2 Dall. 419

7 **Of the United States and for the United States** — This means the national government, "The Government of the United States" Cohens v Virginia, 6 Wheat, 264

8. "The American states as well as the American people have believed a close and firm union to be essential to their liberty and to their happiness They have been taught by experience that this Union cannot exist without a government of the whole, and they have been taught by the same experience that this government would be a mere shadow that must disappoint all hopes, unless invested with large portions of that sovereignty which belongs to independent states Under the influence of this opinion, and thus instructed by experience, the American people, in the conventions of their respective states, adopted the present constitution If it could be doubted, whether, from its nature, it were not supreme in all cases where it is empowered to act, that doubt would be removed by the declaration that 'this constitution, and the laws of the United States which shall be made in pursuance thereof, and all treaties made, or which shall be made, under the authorities of the United States, shall be the supreme law of the land, and the judges in every state shall be bound thereby, anything in the constitution or laws of any state to the contrary notwithstanding' This is the authoritative language of the AMERICAN PEOPLE, and, if the gentlemen please, of the AMERICAN STATES. It marks, with lines too strong to be mistaken, the characteristic distinction between the government of the Union and those of the states The general government, though limited as to its objects, is supreme with respect to those objects. This principle is a part of the constitution and if there be those who deny its necessity, none can deny its authority To this *supreme government* ample powers are confided, and if it was possible to doubt the great purposes for which they are so confided, the people of the United States have declared that they are 'given in order to form a more perfect Union, establish justice, insure domestic tranquility provide for common defense, promote the general welfare, and secure the blessings of liberty to themselves and their posterity.' With ample powers confided to this *supreme government*, for these interesting purposes, are connected many express and important limitations of the sovereignty of the

states which are made for the same purposes." Cohens v Virginia, 6 Wheat. 264–381

9 **The general government — One of the people.** — "The government of the Union is a government of the people In form and in substance it emanates from them. Its powers are granted by them, and are to be exercised directly on them, and for their benefit.' Per Marshall, C J. McCulloch v Maryland, 4 Wheat. 316

10 **Corporate powers.** — The United States is a government, and so possesses corporate powers, and may sue in its corporate name, and may by its consent be sued United States v Maurice, 2 Brock 109; Ableman v Booth, 21 How. 506

11 **Not a league.** — The United States is a government, and the constitution is the supreme law of the land, and the laws enacted and treaties made in compliance therewith can be enforced by its own authority over all persons and on all subjects-matter within its jurisdiction It is not a league, but a government. Rhode Island v Massachusetts, 12 Pet. 657–729, Gibbons v Ogden, 9 Wheat. 187. It went into operation on Wednesday, March 4, 1789. Owings v. Speed, 5 Wheat. 420.

12. The United States is not only a government, but it is a national government, and the only government in this country that has the character of nationality It is invested with power over all the foreign relations of the country war, peace, and negotiations and intercourse with other nations, all which are forbidden to the state governments It has power to suppress insurrections as well as repel invasions, and to organize, arm, discipline, and call into service the militia of the whole country The president is charged with the duty and invested with the power, to take care that the laws be faithfully executed The judiciary has jurisdiction to decide controversies between the states, and between their respective citizens as well as questions of national concern, and the government is clothed with power to guaranty to every state a republican form of government, and to protect each of them against invasion and domestic violence Knox v Lee, 12 Wall. 457–555; The Chinese Exclusion Case, 130 U. S. 581–603.

13 The new government was not a mere change of dynasty It was a new political body. A new nation in the family of nations. Dred Scott v. Sandford, 19 How 397.

ARTICLE I.

LEGISLATIVE DEPARTMENT.

Section I.

CONGRESS IN GENERAL.

All legislative powers herein granted shall be vested in a Congress of the United States, which shall consist of a Senate and House of Representatives.

Section II.

HOUSE OF REPRESENTATIVES.

1. The House of Representatives shall be composed of members chosen every second year by the people of the several States, and the electors in each State shall have the qualifications requisite for electors of the most numerous branch of the State Legislature.

1 Under this clause the qualified electors of the state who are qualified under the laws of the state to vote for representatives in the state legislature, have the right to vote for members of congress, and the congress has power by law to protect such persons in that right. United States v Goldman, 3 Woods, 187, United States v Bader, 16 Fed Rep 116; United States v Munford, 16 Fed Rep 223, Ex parte Geissler, 9 Biss. 492, Ex parte Siebold, 100 U.S. 371, Ex parte Clarke, 100 U S 399, United States v Gale, 109 U S. 65

2. **"Electors of the most numerous branch of the legislature."** These are not necessarily uniform in the different states In some states aliens who have declared their intention to become citizens may vote for representatives to the state legislature, and so are qualified under this clause to vote for representatives in congress "Electors" are not necessarily citizens The state may confer upon aliens the right to vote within the state, but it cannot make them citizens of the United States. Dred Scott v Sandford, 19 How. 404–411

3 Each state has the exclusive power to regulate the right of suffrage and to determine who shall have the right to vote therein Huber v Reily, 53 Penn. St. 115, Morrison v Springer, 15 Iowa, 345, Spragins v Houghton, 3 Ill. 395

Note — The fifteenth amendment qualifies this right to the extent that no distinction shall be made on account of race, color or previous condition of servitude, but no further.

2 No person shall be a representative who shall not have attained to the age of twenty-five years, and been seven years a citizen of the United States, and who shall not, when elected, be an inhabitant of that State in which he shall be chosen.

1 **Inhabitant of that state in which he shall be chosen.**—The word "inhabitant" as here used is not synonymous with "resident." The latter word was in the original draft of the constitution and gave place to the word "inhabitant." Mr McCrary speaking of this says "It would seem that the framers of the constitution were impressed with a deep sense of the importance of an actual *bona fide* residence of the representative among the constituency — a residence in the sense of actual living among them and commingling with them" McCrary on Elections, § 289

2. An inhabitant of a state within the meaning of this clause is one who in good faith is a member of the state and subject to its jurisdiction and to the requirements of its laws, and entitled to all the privileges and advantages conferred thereby. Electors v. Bailey, Cl. & H 411

3 **Qualification of representatives** —The constitution having fixed the qualification of members no additional qualification can be added by the states Barney v McCreery, Cl & H. 176, Turney v Marshall, 1 Cong El. Cas 167, Trumbull's Case, id 618

4 The constitution of Illinois (1848) provided as follows: "The judges of the supreme and circuit courts shall not be eligible to any other office of public trust or profit in this state *or the United States* during the term for which they shall be elected, nor for one year thereafter" The house of representatives of the United States held this provision of the constitution of Illinois void in so far as it applied to persons elected members of the said house. Turney v Marshall, *supra*, Trumbull's Case, *supra*

3 Representatives and direct taxes shall be apportioned among the several States which may be included within this Union, according to their respective numbers, which shall be determined by adding to the whole number of free persons, including those bound to service for a term of years, and excluding Indians not taxed, three-fifths of all other persons. The actual enumeration shall be made within three years after the first meeting of the Congress of the United States, and within every subsequent term of ten years, in such manner as they shall by law direct The number of representatives shall not exceed one for every thirty thousand, but each State shall have at least one representative, and until such enumeration shall be made, the State of New Hampshire shall be entitled to choose three, Massachusetts eight, Rhode Island and Providence Plantations one, Connecticut five, New York six, New Jersey four, Pennsylvania eight, Delaware one, Mary-

land six, Virginia ten, North Carolina five, South Carolina five, and Georgia three.

1. **Direct taxes** — There are five kinds of taxes, viz.: Duties, imposts, excises, capitation tax and direct taxes on lands The three first named are required to be uniform The two last named are laid by the rule of apportionment as required by this clause. Hylton v United States, 3 Dall. 171; License Tax Cases, 5 Wall. 462. Direct taxes are a capitation or poll tax or tax on land. Hylton v. United States, 3 Dall. 171. This may be imposed on the District of Columbia or on the territories. Loughborough v. Blake, 5 Wheat. 317.

2 **Income tax** — The ninth section of the internal revenue act, July 13, 1866, is to be construed to require that the difference between coined money and legal tender currency shall be added to the return of a person's income when made in coined money, and that he shall pay tax or duty on the amount thus increased. Such tax is not a direct tax, but a duty or excise, and is obligatory Pacific Ins. Co v. Soule, 7 Wall 433.

3. **Bank circulation.**— Direct taxes are limited to taxes on land and appurtenances and taxes on polls or capitation tax. The power to tax without apportionment extends to all other objects. So a tax on bank circulation is not a direct tax. Veazie Bank v Fenno, 8 Wall 533

4. **Succession tax** is not a direct tax. It is an impost or excise tax and valid Scholey v. Rew, 23 Wall. 331.

4 When vacancies happen in the representation from any State, the executive authority thereof shall issue writs of election to fill such vacancies.

1. **Vacancies in house of representatives, how filled** — The governor of a state may receive the resignation of a member of the house of representatives of the United States and cause a new election to be held to fill the vacancy without waiting to be notified of the vacancy by the house. Mercer's Case, Cl. & Hall, 44, Edwards' Case, id 92

2. Yell of Arkansas, accepted a commission as colonel of volunteers from Arkansas during the Mexican war He did not resign his seat as a member in congress from that state. The governor treated the seat as vacant and ordered an election to fill it. Newton was elected and the house seated him, and he served out Yell's unexpired term. The acceptance of any office under the United States by a member of congress after election to congress operates as a forfeiture of his seat. Van Ness' Case, Cl. & Hall, 122

3. When the legislature of a state has failed to "prescribe the times, places and manner" of holding elections as required by this clause, the governor may, in case of a vacancy, designate in his writ of election the time and place when and where such election will be held. A reasonable time should be allowed for the promulgation of the notice Hoge's Case, Cl & Hall, 135.

5 The House of Representatives shall choose their speaker and other officers, and shall have the sole power of impeachment.

Section III.

SENATE.

1. The Senate of the United States shall be composed of two senators from each State, chosen by the Legislature thereof for six years, and each senator shall have one vote

1. A plurality of the votes cast by a legislature in choosing a senator will not elect. Case of Jno. P Stockton of N J, Senate Journal, Dec. 4, 1865; January 30, 1866, March 26, 1866

2. "In case a majority of the states should refuse to elect senators the government would necessarily come to an end." Cohens v. Virginia, 6 Wheat. 624.

2. Immediately after they shall be assembled in consequence of the first election, they shall be divided, as equally as may be, into three classes The seats of the senators of the first class shall be vacated at the expiration of the second year, of the second class at the expiration of the fourth year, and of the third class at the expiration of the sixth year, so that one-third may be chosen every second year; and if vacancies happen, by resignation or otherwise, during the recess of the Legislature of any State, the executive thereof may make temporary appointments until the next meeting of the Legislature, which shall then fill such vacancies.

1. **Vacancies** — The seat of a senator is vacated by a resignation addressed to the governor of his state. It does not depend upon notice of acceptance. Bledsoe's Case, Cl. & Hall, 869.

2. The governor of a state cannot appoint a senator to fill an expected vacancy during the recess of the legislature. Lanman's Case, Cl. & Hall, 871.

3. **Classification.**—The classification is settled by lot when the senators first appear from the new states, in the mode adopted in the first classification, so as to prevent two vacancies occurring in the same state at the same time. Journal Senate, May 15, 1789, 25th and 26th Edition, 1820.

3. No person shall be a senator who shall not have attained to the age of thirty years, and been nine years a citizen of the United States, and who shall not, when elected, be an inhabitant of the State for which he shall be chosen

1 The constitution having fixed the qualification, states cannot add to the requirements thus fixed. Barney v McCreery, Cl. & H 176; Turney v. Marshall, 1 Cong. Election Cases, 167, Trumbull's Case, id. 618

4. The Vice-President of the United States shall be President of the Senate, but shall have no vote, unless they be equally divided

5. The Senate shall choose their officers, and also a president *pro tempore*, in the absence of the Vice-President, or when he shall exercise the office of President of the United States.

6. The Senate shall have the sole power to try all impeachments When sitting for that purpose, they shall be on oath or affirmation When the President of the United States is tried, the chief justice shall preside, and no person shall be convicted without the concurrence of two-thirds of the members present

7. Judgment in case of impeachment shall not extend further than to removal from office, and disqualification to hold and enjoy any office of honor, trust, or profit under the United States, but the party convicted shall, nevertheless, be liable and subject to indictment, trial, judgment, and punishment according to law.

For the doctrine of impeachment and the rules governing trials thereof, reference is made to

William Blount's Trial, December 17, 1798, to January 15, 1799

John Pickering, United States District Judge, March 8, 1803, March 12, 1803

Samuel Chase, Associate Justice United States Supreme Court, November 30, 1804, March 1, 1805 (See Appendix 3d Vol Legislative Journal Senate)

James H Peck, United States District Judge, May 11, 1830, May 25, 1830, and from December 13, 1830, to January 31, 1831. (See Appendix Legislative Journal of Senate, 1830, 1831.)

Andrew Johnson, President of the United States, February 26, 1868

1. **Impeachment — Evidence — Question on admission of.**— In the trial of Andrew Johnson, president of the United States, upon impeachment, Mr Chief Justice Chase presiding Upon objection to evidence offered by the managers, the chief justice decided as follows

"The chief justice states to the senate that, in his judgment, it is his duty to decide upon questions of evidence in the first instance, and that, if any senator desires that the question shall then be submitted to the senate, it is his duty to submit it. So far as he is aware that has been the usual course of practice in trials of persons in the house of lords and in the senate of the United States."

Again the chief justice stated his ruling in the following language·

"The chief justice will state the rule which he conceives to be applicable once more In this body he is presiding officer He is so in virtue of his high office under the constitution. He is chief justice of the United States, and, therefore when the president of the United States is tried by the senate, it is his duty to preside in that body, and, as he understands, he is therefore the president of the senate sitting as a court of impeachment. The rule of the senate which applies to this question is the seventh rule, which declares 'that the presiding officer may in the first instance submit to the senate without a division all questions of evidence and incidental questions.' He is not required by that rule to so submit those questions in the first instance, but, for the dispatch of business, as is usual in the supreme court, he expresses his opinion in the first instance If the senate, who constitute the court, or any member of it, desires the opinion of the senate to be taken, it is his duty then to ask for the opinion of the court" And the chief justice thinks this appeal to the court cannot be made by a manager of the impeachment, but must be by the action of the court or a member of it. Trial of Andrew Johnson, vol. 1, pp 175, 176.

The senate, having retired for consultation, adopted the following rule upon the subject, being an amendment to rule 7 of the senate:

"The presiding officer of the senate shall direct all necessary preparations in the senate chamber, and the presiding officer of the *trial* shall direct all the forms of proceeding while the senate are sitting for the purpose of trying an impeachment, and all forms during the trial not otherwise provided for And the presiding officer of the *trial* may rule on all questions of evidence and incidental questions, which ruling shall stand as the judgment of the senate unless some member of the senate shall ask that a formal vote be taken thereon, in which case it shall be submitted to the senate for decision, or he may, at his option, in the first instance submit any such question to a vote of the members of the senate" Trial of Andrew Johnson, vol 1, p. 186

Section IV.

BOTH HOUSES.

1 The times, places, and manner of holding elections for senators and representatives shall be prescribed in each State by the Legislature thereof, but the Congress may at any time, by law, make or alter such regulations, except as to the place of choosing senators

2 The Congress shall assemble at least once in every year, and such meeting shall be on the first Monday in December, unless they shall by law appoint a different day.

1. Implied powers — Protection of voters — The implied power of congress is as much a part of the constitution as any of the expressed powers. And under this implied power congress may provide by law for the protection of voters at election of representatives, and may affix punishments for hindering or intimidating or maltreating voters intending to vote at such election. And thus when at the same time and place state officers are also elected. Sections 5508 and 5520, Revised Statutes, held valid. Ex parte Yarbrough, 110 U. S 651.

2. The provision in the laws relating to election of representatives in congress which authorizes the deputy marshals to keep the peace at such election is constitutional Habeas Corpus Cases, 100 U. S 371, 399.

3. Congress had power to pass sections 5515 and 5522, Revised Statutes, fixing penalties for violation of election laws, and for interfering with supervisors of election of representatives to congress, as provided in sections 2016, 2017, 2021, 2022, title XXVI, Revised Statutes, and said laws are constitutional Habeas Corpus Cases, 100 U S. 371, 399, 404, 422

4. Same.—In making regulations congress need not assume entire and exclusive control It has a supervisory power over the subject, and may either make entirely new regulations, or it may supplement or modify the regulations made by the states Id

5 Rights and immunities created by or dependent upon the constitution can be protected by congress The form and manner of such protection lies with the congress to determine. United States v. Reese, 92 U. S. 214.

Section V.

THE HOUSES SEPARATELY.

1 Each house shall be the judge of the elections, returns, and qualifications of its own members, and a majority of each shall constitute a quorum to do business; but a smaller number may adjourn from day to day, and may be authorized to compel the attendance of absent members, in such manner and under such penalties as each house may provide.

1. Inquiry as to qualification of members—In determining qualification each house has the right to examine witnesses and require the production of papers and may punish witnesses for contumacy. Kilbourn v. Thompson, 103 U S. 168

2 Testimony taken before a notary public or other officer designated by congress to take depositions in cases of contested election of members, and with the single object of being returned to and considered by the house of representatives, when exercising the judicial powers vested in it by the constitution of judging of the qualifications of its members, stands upon the same ground as testimony taken before any judge or officer of the United States, and perjury in giving such testimony is punishable in the courts of the United States only In re Loney, 134 U S 372, citing United States v. Bailey, 9 Pet. 238

3. Each house shall be the judge of the election, return and qualification of its own members—The returns from the state authorities, showing or declaring that a certain person has been elected representative or senator in congress, are *prima facie* evidence of qualification only. Spaulding v. Mead, Cl & Hall, 157 (see pp. 16, 18, 29, 30, 41, id), Reed v. Cosden, id 353 And the refusal of the executive of the state to grant a certificate does not prejudice the right of one entitled to a seat. Richards' Case, Cl & Hall, 95.

2. Each house may determine the rules of its proceedings, punish its members for disorderly behavior, and, with the concurrence of two-thirds, expel a member.

3. Each house shall keep a journal of its proceedings, and from time to time publish the same, excepting such parts as may in their judgment require secrecy, and the yeas and nays of the members of either house, on any question, shall, at the desire of one-fifth of those present, be entered on the journal.

4 Neither house during the session of Congress shall, without the consent of the other, adjourn for more than three days, nor to any other place than that in which the two houses shall be sitting.

1. **Contempt — House may punish others than its own members.** The house of representatives of the United States has power to cause the arrest of and to try and punish persons other than its members for contempt committed in its presence when in session The warrant of the house, signed by the speaker and clerk thereof, is authority to the sergeant-at-arms and justifies an arrest for such contempt anywhere within the United States Anderson v Dunn, 6 Wheat 204

2. **Must terminate with adjournment.**—Although the legislative power continues perpetual, the legislative body ceases to exist the moment of its adjournment or periodical dissolution. It follows that imprisonment for contempt must terminate with that adjournment. Id See, also. Stewart v. Blaine, 1 MacArthur, 453, Wickelhausen v Willett, 10 Abb Pr 164

3. **Parliament of Great Britain — Powers to punish for contempt not analogous.**—The right of either house of congress to punish for contempts cannot be inferred from analogy arising from the jurisdiction to so punish as exercised by the parliament of Great Britain That body has always exercised the powers of a high court of judicature as well as that of legislation. When the lords, bishops, knights and burgesses met as one body they were called the high court of parliament. Upon the separation into two houses the respective houses retained each some of their judicial character, the house of lords retaining the right of reviewing upon appeal the decisions of the courts of Westminster Hall And jointly, and until within a recent period, they retained the power of passing bills of attainder, which are but in fact judicial declarations of punishment for crime. It is upon this idea that the two houses of parliament have retained this power to punish as for contempts The right, therefore, of the house of congress to punish the citizen for a contempt of its authority or breach of its privileges can derive no support from the precedents and practices of the houses of the English parliament. Kilbourn v. Thompson 103 U S 168.

4 **Right to punish for contempt exists at common law** — The constitution says nothing of contempts or punishment therefor The houses of congress, however, may punish for contempt other persons than its members This right exists at common law, and may be exercised by the houses of congress upon the same principles that courts of law act in protecting themselves from insult and contempts. Without this right of self-protection they could not discharge their high and important duties Bolton v. Martin, 1 Dall 296, Anderson v Dunn, 6 Wheat 204, Nugent's Case, 1 Am. L. J. 139 Sam Houston's Case, 11th vol Benton's Debates, pp 644–658.

5 **Right to examine witnesses and punish for contumacy** — Each house of congress is the judge of the election and qualification of its own members In trying a contested election case the body would have the right to examine witnesses, and require the production of papers, and it may be that a witness would be subject to punishment by that body when so acting, the same as he would if the case were pending before a court of judicature The same would be true as to the senate when trying a case of impeachment. But no person can be punished for contumacy as a witness before either house unless his testimony is required in a matter into which the house has jurisdiction to inquire, and neither body possesses the general power of making inquiry into the private affairs of the citizen Kilbourn v. Thompson 103 U S 168

6 **Disorderly conduct of members** — The punishment for this may, in a proper case, extend to imprisonment. Id.

7 **Compel attendance of members.**— So also under this clause it may extend to imprisonment. Id

8 **The house of representatives is not the final judge** of its own power and privileges in cases in which the rights and liberties of the citizen are concerned The legality of its action in such cases may be determined by the federal supreme court. Id

9 **Expulsion of members** — Either house may expel a member for any misdemeanor, and it is not essential that there be a statutory penalty attached to such misdemeanor It may exercise this right whenever in the judgment of two-thirds of the members the conduct of a member is such as to unfit him for parliamentary duty. Blount's Case, 1 Story's Const § 838, Smith's Case, 1 Hall's L J 459; Brooks' Case for Assault on Hon Chas. Sumner in the Senate Chamber, Case of Jesse D Bright, Senate Jour March 1, 1861.

Section VI.

PRIVILEGES AND DISABILITIES OF MEMBERS.

1. The senators and representatives shall receive a compensation for their services, to be ascertained by law and paid out of the treasury of the United States They shall in all cases, except treason, felony, and breach of the peace, be privileged from arrest during their attendance at the session of their respective houses, and in going to or returning from the same;

and for any speech or debate in either house, they shall not be questioned in any other place.

2 No senator or representative shall, during the time for which he was elected, be appointed to any civil office under the authority of the United States, which shall have been created, or the emoluments whereof shall have been increased, during such time, and no person holding any office under the United States shall be a member of either house during his continuance in office

1 **Privilege from arrest.**— This is an undoubted privilege which can be pleaded in bar of any suit or prosecution other than treason, felony and breach of the peace But to be available must be pleaded at the proper time or it will be forever waived. Courts will not take judicial notice of the privilege. Gyer's Lessees v. Irwin, 4 Dall. 107, Coxe v McClenachan, 3 Dall. 478

2. The privilege is personal and does not extend to servants or to property levied on 4 Jefferson's Manual, § 3

3. Attendance upon congress as a member of that body does not confer such "privilege" as to entitle a party to have a postponement of his suit as a *matter of right*, though the court may grant a postponement, under particular circumstances, in its discretion and upon terms. The language in Gyer's Lessees v Irwin, *supra*, held *dictum*. Nones v Edsall, 1 Wall Jr. 189.

4. Mr Jefferson says this privilege commences from date of election and before a member takes his seat and is sworn (in going to and returning from the same) Jefferson's Manual, § 3 See, also, Story's Const. § 864.

5. One who goes to Washington duly commissioned to represent a state or district in congress has this privilege, and if it is afterward decided by congress that he is not entitled to his seat, he is protected until he reaches home upon his return *Provided* he goes within a reasonable time. Dunton v Halstead, 2 Penn L. J. Rep. 450

See as to exemption from service of process, Juneau Bank v. McSpedan, 5 Biss 64, Miner v Markham, 28 Fed. Rep 387.

Section VII.

MODE OF PASSING LAWS.

1. All bills for raising revenue shall originate in the House of Representatives, but the Senate may propose or concur with amendments, as on other bills.

2 Every bill which shall have passed the House of Representatives and the Senate shall, before it become a law, be presented to the President of the United States, if he approve, he shall sign it, but if not, he shall return it, with his objections,

to that house in which it shall have originated, who shall enter the objections at large on their journal, and proceed to reconsider it. If, after such reconsideration, two-thirds of that house shall agree to pass the bill, it shall be sent, together with the objections, to the other house, by which it shall likewise be reconsidered, and if approved by two-thirds of that house, it shall become a law. But in all such cases the votes of both houses shall be determined by yeas and nays, and the names of the persons voting for and against the bill shall be entered on the journal of each house respectively. If any bill shall not be returned by the President within ten days (Sundays excepted) after it shall have been presented to him, the same shall be a law in like manner as if he had signed it, unless the Congress by their adjournment prevent its return, in which case it shall not be a law.

3. Every order, resolution, or vote to which the concurrence of the Senate and House of Representatives may be necessary (except on a question of adjournment) shall be presented to the President of the United States, and before the same shall take effect, shall be approved by him, or, being disapproved by him, shall be repassed by two-thirds of the Senate and House of Representatives, according to the rules and limitations prescribed in the case of a bill.

1. **Becomes a law, when.**—The bill becomes a law upon the date of its approval by the president. The constitution does not require the president to affix the date to his signature of approval, nor does any act of congress require him to do so. When a question arises as to when a statute took effect, the court may resort to any source of information, unless the positive law has enacted a different rule. Gardner v. Barney, 6 Wall. 499.

2. The act however, may provide by its terms the exact time at which it shall take effect. In re Richardson, 2 Story, 571.

3. When no time is fixed at which it shall commence, the statute takes effect from its date. Matthews v. Zane, 7 Wheat. 164.

4. No fraction of a day is computed in the taking effect of the statute, except in cases where substantial justice may be otherwise defeated. Arnold v. United States, 9 Cranch, 119; In re Ankrim, 3 McLean, 285; In re Richardson, 2 Story, 571; United States v. Williams, 1 Paine, 261.

Section VIII.

POWERS GRANTED TO CONGRESS.

The Congress shall have power:

1. **Right of people to grant.**—It was competent for the people to invest the general government with all the powers they might deem proper and necessary, to extend or restrain these powers according to their own good pleasure, and to give them a paramount and supreme authority. Martin v. Hunter's Lessee, 1 Wheat. 304.

2. **Extent of powers granted.**—The government can claim no powers not granted to it by the constitution, and the powers actually granted must be such as are expressly given, or given by necessary implication. The instrument is to have a reasonable construction according to the import of its terms, and where a power is expressly given in general terms it is not to be restrained to particular cases unless the construction grow out of the context or by necessary implication. Id.

3. The constitution deals in general language. It did not suit the purpose of the people in framing it to provide for minute specifications of its powers or to declare the means by which those powers should be carried into execution. Id.

4. **Classification of powers.**—The powers granted may be classed as enumerated and non-enumerated, or express and implied. Martin v. Hunter's Lessees, 1 Wheat. 304; McCulloch v. Maryland, 4 id. 405; Legal Tender Cases, 12 Wall. 457.

5. **Implied powers.**—There is no phrase in the constitution which, like the articles of confederation, excludes incidental or implied powers. These, therefore, when necessary to carry into effect the enumerated powers, are as much within the provision of the constitution as if they were expressly declared. McCulloch v. Maryland, 4 Wheat. 316. See "Implied powers," art. I, sec. IV, par. 1.

6. Congress cannot confer upon a state the exercise of powers which by the constitution have been exclusively vested in congress. Van Allen v. Assessors (Bank Tax Cases), 3 Wall. 573.

7. **Construing power—Rules for.**—The words are to be taken in their natural and obvious sense, and not in a sense unreasonably restricted or enlarged. Martin v. Hunter's Lessees, 1 Wheat. 304-326.

8. The objects for which the powers were granted must be kept in view. This is a universal rule of construction, applied alike to statutes, wills, contracts and constitutions. It is impossible to know what the non-enumerated powers are, and what is their nature and extent, without considering the purpose they were intended to subserve. These purposes were left to the discretion of congress, subject only to the restrictions that they be not prohibited, and be necessary and proper for carrying into execution the enumerated powers. Legal Tender Cases, 12 Wall. 457.

9. It is not indispensable to the existence of any power claimed for the federal government that it can be found specified in words in the constitution, or clearly and directly traceable to some one of the specified powers. Its existence may be deduced from more than one of the substantive powers expressly defined, or from them all combined. It is allowable to group

together any number of them and infer from them all, that the power claimed has been conferred Powers not expressly conferred may be implied from restrictive clauses, as in the case of suspension of *habeas corpus*. Id.

1. To lay and collect taxes, duties, imposts, and excises, to pay the debts and provide for the common defense and general welfare of the United States, but all duties, imposts, and excises shall be uniform throughout the United States.

1. **Taxation — To lay and collect taxes — Extent of power.**— The power of the congress to lay taxes is co-extensive with the territory of the United States Loughborough v Blake, 5 Wheat 317.

2. **Not exclusive.**— It is not exclusive, however The states possess the power of laying taxes within their several jurisdictions, subject to the restriction that they cannot tax the instruments employed by the United States in carrying on the national government Van Allen v Assessors, 3 Wall 585, Bradley v. People, 4 Wall 462, McCulloch v Maryland, 4 Wheat 327 Osborn v Bank of United States, 9 Wheat. 738; Weston v City of Charleston, 2 Pet 449, Dobbins v Commissioners of Erie Co, 16 Pet. 435

3. **Duties — Imposts.**— These are practically synonymous, and mean a tax levied on any kind of goods or articles imported from a foreign country Hylton v United States, 3 Dall 171, United States v Tappan, 11 Wheat 419

4. **Excise.**— This is an inland tax laid on products and commodities, and is usually imposed on the manufacturer It is sometimes confounded with license but is not synonymous A tax, however, upon a license is an excise tax License Cases, 5 Wall 462

5 An excise tax levied by congress on a license to manufacture and sell intoxicating liquors is no bar to a prosecution under state laws prohibiting such manufacture and sale within the state License Cases, 5 Wall 462. Pervear v Commonwealth 5 Wall 475

6 **State banks, tax on** — Section 3413 of Revised Statutes, which lays a tax on state banks and bankers or banking associations, held valid Merchants Nat Bank v United States, 101 U S 1

7 **District of Columbia — Direct tax on.**— The power of congress to levy and collect taxes, duties, imposts and excises is co-extensive with the territory of the United States It has therefore power to impose a direct tax on the District of Columbia in proportion to the census directed to be taken by the constitution Loughborough v Blake, 5 Wheat 317

8. **Limitation on powers of states to tax** — The state governments have no right to tax any of the constitutional means employed by the government of the United States to execute its constitutional powers Nor have they power by taxation or otherwise to retard or burden, or in any manner control, the operation of the constitutional laws of congress McCulloch v. Maryland, 4 Wheat 316

9. **Internal revenue act** — The license internal revenue act of congress is constitutional, and not against public policy. So the law of congress imposing a tax on sale of lottery tickets and making the non-payment thereof

an indictable offense is valid, although such selling is prohibited by state law License Tax Cases, 5 Wall 462

10. Limitation of power.—The power given in the constitution to congress to tax is limited only in two ways 1st. Direct tax must be imposed by the rule of apportionment. 2d It cannot tax exports License Tax Cases, 5 Wall 462

11. Salaries of state officers —Congress cannot, under the constitution, levy a tax on the salary of a judicial officer of a state. Buffington v Day, 11 Wall 113

12 On distilled spirits —The act of congress of July 20, 1868, imposing a tax on distilled spirits, is not subject to any constitutional objection It is in the nature of an excise, and the only limitation on the power of congress in the imposition of taxes of this character is that they shall be 'uniform throughout the United States.' United States v. Singer, 15 Wall. 111, Same v Van Buskirk, 15 Wall. 123.

13. Succession tax —The act imposing the succession tax is valid. It is neither a tax on land nor a capitation tax, although it is made a lien on the land to enforce its collection. Scholey v Rew, 23 Wall 331.

14 State law regulating pilotage —A law of Pennsylvania providing that vessels neglecting or refusing to take a pilot shall forfeit a certain sum for the use of the society for the relief of distressed and decayed pilots is not repugnant to this clause, for the reason that the charge is neither a duty, impost, or excise Neither is it repugnant thereto because of not being uniform throughout the United States. Being neither of the prohibited impositions named in this clause, it is not required that it shall have such uniformity Cooley v. Board of Wardens, 12 How 299

15. In the exercise of this power congress may raise money in any way not forbidden by the constitution, and as a means thereto it may tax employments. United States v. Angell, 11 Fed Rep 34.

16 May exclude aliens —The government of the United States, through the action of its legislative department, can exclude aliens from its territory Jurisdiction over its own territory to that extent is an incident of every independent nation. It is a part of its independence, and one method whereby it is enabled to maintain its independence from control of another power 'The jurisdiction of the nation within its own territory is necessarily exclusive and absolute, and is susceptible of no limitation not imposed by itself Any restriction upon it, deriving validity from an external source, would imply a diminution of its sovereignty to the extent of the restriction, and an investment of that sovereignty to the same extent in that power which could impose such restrictions' Chief Justice Marshall in The Exchange v McFaddon, 7 Cranch, 116, 136, cited and approved in The Chinese Exclusion Case, 130 U S 581-604.

2 To borrow money on the credit of the United States

1 Taxation of government securities —A tax imposed by a state or under its authority on stock issued for loans made to the United States is unconstitutional. Weston v City of Charleston 2 Pet 449

2 United States stocks as capital of state banks —The stock of the United States which constitutes the whole or a part of the capital stock of a state bank is not subject to state taxation. To so tax the stocks of the government is regarded as a tax upon the exercise of the powers conferred upon congress by this clause of the constitution If such power was recognized in the states it might be carried to such extent as to, in effect, destroy this power in congress People of New York v Comm'rs of Taxes, 2 Wall 200; Same v Same 2 Black, 620, Same v. Same, id 635.

3 **Same** — Securities of the United States are exempt from state taxation, and such immunity extends to the capital stock of a corporation if made up of such public funds Provident Inst. v Massachusetts, 6 Wall. 611, First Nat Bank of Louisville v Kentucky, 9 id 353.

4. **Franchises not exempt** — The franchises of a corporation, however, are not so exempt, although the corporation has made investments in such securities Society for Savings v. Coite, 6 Wall 594.

5 **United States notes** are exempt from taxation by or under state or municipal authority. Mitchell v. Board of County Commissioners, 91 U. S. 206, Bank v Supervisors, 7 Wall. 26

6. **Shares in national banks** — A state may tax shares of stockholders in national banks Van Slyke v Wisconsin, Bagnall v Wisconsin, Book 20, L. C. P. Co's Ed of U S. Sup. Court Rep, 240, Lionberger v Rouse, 9 Wall. 468, First Nat. Bank of Louisville v Kentucky, 9 Wall 353, Provident Inst. v. Massachusetts, 6 id 611, Van Allen v. Assessors (Bank Tax Cases), 3 id. 573, New York v Com'rs of Taxes, 4 id 244, Bradley v. Illinois, id. 459; Tappan v National Bank, 19 id. 490.

7 **Same.**— The states have power to tax the shares of national banks in the hands of stockholders, whose capital is wholly invested in the stock and bonds of the United States The state tax under the banking act of congress involves no question as to the pledged faith of the government The tax is the condition of the new rights and privileges conferred upon these associations And congress has so legislated in respect to them as to leave such shares subject to state taxation. Van Allen v Assessors (Bank Tax Cases), 3 Wall 573

8 **Same — Conditions on which may be taxed.**— This right of taxation is subject, however to the conditions, viz. That the taxes shall be imposed, by and under state authority, at the place where such bank is located, and not elsewhere, and shall not be at a greater rate than is assessed upon other moneyed capital in the hands of the individual citizen of such state, nor exceed the rate imposed upon the shares of any of the banks organized under the authority of the state where such association is located Id, Bradley v Illinois, 4 Wall. 459

9 The bank, instead of the individual shareholders, may be required to pay such tax. Lionberger v Rouse, 9 Wall 468.

10. **Federal stock is not subject to the general taxing power of a state** — The tax on the stock is regarded as a tax on the power of the government to borrow money on the credit of the United States." It makes no difference that the tax is on the aggregate of the tax-payer's property, and the stock is not taxed by name People v Commissioners of N Y City, 2 Black, 620, People v Commissioners, 2 Wall 200

11. **United States bonds or certificates of indebtedness** issued by the general government directly to creditors are subject to taxation by the states People ex rel. The Banks v Hoffman, 7 Wall. 16

12. United States securities are not subject to taxation by states Society for Savings v. Coite, 6 Wall 594; Hamilton Manuf Co v Massachusetts, 6 Wall 632; New York v Commrs of Taxes, 2 Black, 620; Same v. Same, id. 635; Same v Same, 2 Wall 200, Weston v Charleston, 2 Pet. 449; McCulloch v Maryland, 4 Wheat. 316, Osborne v. United States Bank, 9 Wheat. 738.

13 **Bank capital in government bonds** — Where the capital of a bank is invested in government bonds it cannot be taxed by the states But the shares of stock may be taxed as such in hands of stockholders And *held* that the revenue law of Kentucky which imposes a tax on bank stock, and requires the officers of the bank to pay the tax so levied on the shares of stock, is a tax on the stockholders and not on the capital of the bank, and is valid. First Nat. Bank v. Kentucky, 9 Wall. 353 To the same effect is Lionberger v Rouse, 9 Wall 468

14. **And further.**— Congress in imposing conditions on the power of the state to tax banks had reference alone to banks of circulation Lionberger v Rouse, 9 Wall 468

15. A tax upon the bonds of the United States is a tax upon the power of congress to borrow money, and such tax, when imposed by a state of the Union, is invalid The fact, however, that a corporation has invested its capital partly in United States bonds does not prevent the state from laying a tax upon the corporate franchises or business of such corporation Home Ins. Co of N. Y v. People of State of N Y, 134 U S 594.

16 No constitutional objection lies in the way of a legislative body prescribing any mode of measurement to determine the amount it will charge for the privilege it bestows Id See, also, Society for Savings v Coite, 6 Wall. 594, and Provident Institution v Massachusetts, 6 Wall. 611, Hamilton Manuf Co. v Massachusetts, 6 Wall. 632

17 **Legal tender acts.**—The legal tender acts are constitutional as applied both to contracts entered into before and after their passage Hepburn v Griswold, 8 Wall. 603, in so far as it conflicts with this doctrine, is overruled Legal Tender Cases, 12 Wall. 457.

18. Under the power to borrow money on the credit of the United States, and to issue circulating notes for the money borrowed, the authority of congress to define the quality and force of these notes as currency is as broad as the like power over metallic currency under the power to coin money and regulate the value thereof Under the two powers, taken together congress is authorized to establish a national currency, either in coin or in paper, and to make that currency lawful money for all purposes, as regards the national government or individuals, and this whether in time of war or peace. Juilliard v Greenman, 110 U. S. 421.

3. To regulate commerce with foreign nations, and among the several States, and with the Indian tribes.

1 **Commerce — What constitutes — Traffic.**— Commerce is traffic. But it is also something more, it is intercourse It describes the commercial intercourse between nations and parts of nations, in all its branches. It comprehends navigation. Gibbons v Ogden, 9 Wheat. 1; United States v

Bailey, 1 McLean, 234; The Daniel Ball, 10 Wall 557, Mobile v. Kimball, 102 U. S 691

2 **Sale** is the object of importation, and is an essential ingredient of commerce Brown v Maryland, 12 Wheat. 419, Leisy v Hardin, 135 U S 100

3. **Intercourse** — Commerce means nothing more than intercourse among nations and the several states for the purpose of trade, be the object of the trade what it may Corfield v Coryell 4 Wash 371–378

4 **Includes manufactures and growth** — It includes the products of the several states — as well that which is the product and manufacture as that which is the growth thereof Welton v State of Missouri, 91 U S 275

5. It extends to the persons who conduct it as well as to the instruments used. Cooley v Board of Wardens, 12 How. 299–316

6. **Commerce among the states is commerce with the states.**— It commences in one state and terminates in another, and may pass through one or many states in its operation Gibbons v Ogden, 9 Wheat. 1.

7. **Freights carried** from points without a state to points within that state, or from points within the state to points without, is as much commerce among the several states, in so far as such state is concerned, as is freight taken up at points without such state and carried across it to points in other states. Fargo v. Michigan, 121 U S 230

8. **Insurance not commerce** — The business of insurance is not commerce, and a corporation of one state doing insurance in another is not engaged in commerce among the states Insurance Co v Massachusetts, 10 Wall 566

9. Issuing a policy of insurance is not a transaction of commerce, and so is not subject to congressional regulation Paul v. Virginia, 8 Wall. 168, Insurance Co v Morse 20 Wall. 450

10. **Regulation — Definition** — To regulate commerce is to prescribe the rule by which it is to be governed. Gibbons v Ogden, 9 Wheat. 1

11. **What is not a regulation** — A state law which prohibits the dredging for oysters with a scoop or drag, or any instrument other than tongs or rakes, within the limits of the state, and forfeiting to the state the vessel so engaged, is not a regulation of commerce, and is valid. Smith v. Maryland, 18 How 71

12. **Same** — A law of a state which requires insurance companies of other states to file bond and security, etc., before issuing policies in such state, is not a regulation of commerce, and is constitutional. Paul v. Virginia, 8 Wall 168, Doyle v Insurance Co, 94 U S. 535

13 **Includes navigation** — The power to regulate includes the regulation of navigation, which comprehends the power to prescribe rules in conformity with which navigation must be carried on. Cooley v Board of Wardens, 12 How 299, 315, 316.

14. The vessels, as well as the articles they bring, are subject to regulation The Brig Wilson v United States, 1 Brock 423, 431.

15. It includes the power to regulate navigation with foreign nations and among the states, and is an exclusive power in congress, which may be exercised with or without positive regulations The Barque Chusan, 2 Story, 455.

16. A bill providing for the recording of mortgage, hypothecation or conveyance of any vessel is a regulation of commerce and within the powers

of congress White's Bank v Smith, 7 Wall 646, Blanchard v Brig Martha Washington, 1 Cliff 463

17. Navigable waters — Black Bird creek was a small creek or marsh in Delaware in which the tide ebbed and flowed, and which was at times navigated by small craft. A corporation, "The Black Bird Creek Marsh Company," was authorized by the legislature of Delaware to construct a dam across the creek, and did so *Held*, in a suit wherein the question was raised, that the law was not repugnant to the constitution in that it regulated commerce, especially in view of the fact that congress had not enacted any legislation upon the subject with which the act of Delaware came in conflict. Willson v Black Bird Creek Marsh Co, 2 Pet. 245.

18 The power of controlling navigation is incidental to the power to regulate commerce, which the constitution confers upon congress; and, consequently, the power of congress over the vessel is co-extensive with that over the cargo The Brig Wilson v. United States, 1 Brock 423

19. The declaration in the compact entered into when Alabama was admitted as a state "that all navigable waters within the said state shall forever remain public highways, free to the citizens of said state and of the United States, without any tax, duty, impost or toll therefor imposed by said state," is nothing more than a regulation of commerce, to that extent, among the several states It conveys no more rights over the navigable waters of Alabama than the United States possesses over the same character of waters in the several states Pollard v Hagan, 3 How 212.

20. The supreme court of the United States, by decree thereof declared a bridge across the River Ohio an obstruction to navigation and directed its removal Afterwards congress by an act declared the bridge to be a lawful structure, "anything in the laws of the United States to the contrary notwithstanding" *Held*, that while congress cannot annul a judgment of court upon private rights of parties, it can so annul a judgment founded on the unlawful interference with the enjoyment of a public right, which is subject to congressional regulation In this case it is an exercise of the power to regulate commerce. Pennsylvania v Wheeling, etc. Bridge Co, 18 How. 421.

21. The act above referred to is not in conflict with the clause that "no preference shall be given to the ports of one state over those of another" Id.

22 The Penobscot river is wholly within the state of Maine The lower eight miles is crossed by several dams, and is not navigable. Above that there is imperfect navigation. *Held*, that a law of the state providing for the improvement of this upper navigation and granting exclusive privileges thereto to the company improving the same, is not in conflict with this clause of the constitution Veazie v Moor, 14 How 568.

23. The River Ohio is a navigable stream, and as such is subject to the commercial powers of congress which have been exercised over it, and if a bridge is so erected across it as to obstruct navigation it is a nuisance and an act of the legislature of Virginia authorizing its construction would afford no justification to the bridge company. Pennsylvania v Wheeling Bridge Co, 13 How 518.

24 The power in congress to regulate commerce comprehends the control for that purpose of all the navigable waters of the United States which are accessible from a state other than that in which they lie And it is for congress to determine when its full powers will be brought into activity and as to the regulations it will provide Gilman v Philadelphia, 3 Wall. 713.

25 The Ohio river is a navigable stream, and congress has the paramount power to regulate bridges over said stream which affect the navigation thereof This power of congress over interstate commerce is free from state interference. Newport & Cin Bridge Co v United States, 105 U. S. 470

26 If a river is not of itself a highway for commerce with other states or foreign countries, or does not form such highway by its connection with other waters, and is only navigable between different places within the state, then it is not a navigable water of the United States, and the act of congress for the enrollment and license of vessels does not apply And the fact that the steamer was employed in transporting products of Wisconsin destined for other states, and in transporting the products of other states brought into Wisconsin, and destined to different places within its limits, does not affect the question under consideration, for congress has not prescribed any regulations governing such commerce, except so far as it is conducted in vessels on the navigable waters of the United States. The Daniel Ball, 10 Wall. 557, referred to and distinguished. The Montello, 11 Wall. 411.

27 The compact between South Carolina and Georgia made in 1787, prior to the ratification of the constitution, whereby the northern branch of the Savannah river was fixed as a boundary line, with the agreement that it should be forever free to the citizens of both states, and exempt from hindrance, etc, attempted by one state against the citizens of the other, has no effect upon this provision of the constitution subsequently adopted Congress has the same power over that river as over any of the other navigable waters of the nation. The right to regulate commerce includes the right to regulate navigation, and hence to regulate and improve navigable waters and ports thereon, and it may for that purpose close to navigation one of several channels in a navigable stream. South Carolina v Georgia, 93 U S 4

28. The Chicago river and its branches, notwithstanding the fact of its being wholly within the state of Illinois, must be deemed navigable waters of the United States, over which congress under this clause may exercise control to the extent necessary to preserve and improve the free navigation thereof But in the absence of congressional legislation the courts will not interfere with reasonable state regulations over that river within the limits of the city of Chicago. Escanaba Transportation Co v Chicago, 107 U S. 678

29. Navigation being a branch of commerce, congress has the control of all navigable rivers between the states, or connecting with the ocean, so as to preserve and protect free navigation. As a corollary of this, congress has the paramount right to conclusively determine what shall be deemed, so far as commerce is concerned, an obstruction thereto Miller v Mayor of N. Y, 109 U S 385

30 A bridge constructed in accordance with the legislation of both the state and federal governments must be deemed a lawful structure, and it cannot thereafter be treated as a public nuisance nor be subject to complaint before the courts. By "navigable waters of the United States" are meant

such as are navigable in fact, and which by themselves, or their connections with other waters, form a continuous channel for commerce with other nations or among the states. Id.

31. Commerce is intercourse and includes all the means by which it can be carried on, including free navigation of the waters of the several states. Corfield v. Coryell, 4 Wash 371, 378

32 Streams entirely within a state.— Where a river is wholly within the limits of a state it (the state) can authorize any improvement which in its judgment will enhance its value as a means of transportation from one part of the state to another The internal commerce of a state — that is, commerce which is wholly confined within its limits — is as much under its control as foreign or interstate commerce is under the control of the general government Citing and approving County of Mobile v Kimball, 102 U. S 691, and Huse v Glover, 119 U. S. 543 Sands v Manistee Riv Imp Co, 123 U S 288

33. Until congress acts respecting navigable streams entirely within a state, the state has plenary powers, but congress is not concluded by anything that the state, or individuals by its authority or acquiescence, may have done, from assuming entire control, and abating any erections that may have been made, and preventing any other from being made, except in conformity with such regulations as it may impose Willamette Iron Bridge Co v. Hatch, 125 U. S 1

34. The provision in the act of congress admitting Oregon, that the navigable waters of the state "shall be common highways and forever free as well to the inhabitants of said state as to all other citizens of the United States, without any tax, duty, impost or toll therefor," refers to political regulations hampering the freedom of commerce and not to natural obstructions. Id

35. The act of congress appropriating money for the improvement of navigation of Willamette river, a stream wholly within the state of Oregon, was no assumption of police power Nor did congress, by conferring the privilege of a port of entry on Portland, come in conflict with the police power of the state exercised in bridging a navigable stream of the state at that point Id.

36 The acts of the legislature of New York granting Robert R Livingston and Robert Fulton the exclusive navigation of all the waters within that state, with boats moved by fire or steam, for a term of years, are repugnant to this clause of the constitution of the United States Gibbons v Ogden, 9 Wheat. 1

37. Congress may authorize the erection of railroad bridges across navigable waters for the purpose of preventing trammels to commerce among the states. Railroad Co v Richmond, 19 Wall 584

38. Navigation.— Under this clause congress possesses the power to punish offenses of the sort enumerated in the ninth section of the act of 1825 The power to regulate commerce includes the power to regulate navigation, as connected with commerce both foreign and interstate It does not stop at the boundary line of the state nor is it confined to acts done on the waters, or in the necessary course of the navigation thereof It extends to acts done on land which interfere, obstruct or prevent the due exercise of the power to regulate commerce and navigation both foreign and among the states Any offense which thus interferes with, obstructs, or prevents such commerce and navigation, though done on land, may be punished by congress, under the general authority to make all laws necessary and proper to execute its delegated constitutional powers United States v Coombs, 12 Pet. 72.

39. Navigation on the high seas is necessarily national in its character and is clearly a matter of national concern and must be subject to national government. Therefore congress has power to regulate the liability of owners of vessels navigating the high seas, but engaged only in transporting goods and passengers between ports and places in the same state. Lord v. Steamship Co, 102 U S 541.

40. The right to cross a navigable water by a railroad bridge must be given by the sovereign power by a special or general act. Under the power to regulate commerce, congress has power to prevent the obstruction of any navigable river which is a means of commerce between any two or more states The exercise of this great public right is not incompatible with the enjoyment of local rights The public right consists in an unobstructed use of a navigable water connecting two or more states The local right is to cross such water The general commercial right is paramount to the state authority. Works v The Junction R. R., 5 McLean, 426

41. No state can obstruct a navigable stream which extends to other states or is connected with a river or lake which falls into the sea States may improve the navigation. Palmer v Commissioners of Cuyahoga Co 3 McLean, 226

42. A steamboat, enrolled and licensed under act of congress, is entitled to the protection of the general government while engaged in carrying on commerce between different states, and her owners have a right to use the navigable streams of the country, free from all material obstructions to navigation Jolly v. Terre Haute Draw-bridge Co, 6 McLean, 237

43 Pilotage —The grant of power to congress to regulate commerce does not prohibit the states from legislating upon the subject of pilotage. Upon some of the subjects included in the power to regulate commerce there should be a uniform rule Upon others there may be different rules in different localities In the former the power of congress is exclusive. In the other it is not. Cooley v. Board of Wardens, 12 How 299

44. The power to regulate commerce as conferred on congress does not exclude the exercise of authority by the states to regulate pilots. Pacific M. S S Co v Joliffe, 2 Wall. 450

45 Pilot regulations are regulations of commerce. State pilotage laws are constitutional and valid, but are subject to the power of congress over the matter Ex parte McNiel, 13 Wall 236

46 A statute of Louisiana authorizing the master and wardens of the port of New Orleans to demand and receive, in addition to other fees, the sum of five cents whether called upon to perform any service or not, for every vessel arriving in port, is in violation of this clause (The difference between this law and the law in regard to pilots, as expounded in Steamship Co v Joliffe, 2 Wall. 450, is stated and commented on) Steamship Co v Port-wardens, 6 Wall. 31.

47. The pilot laws of New York are not in conflict with this clause. Wilson v McNamee, 102 U S 572

48 Section 4235, Revised Statutes of the United States, enacts that "Until further provision is made by congress, all pilots in the bays, inlets, rivers, harbors and ports of the United States shall continue to be regulated in conformity with the existing laws of the states respectively wherein such pilots may be, or with such laws as the states may respectively enact for the purpose." Section 4237 of same statutes provides that "No regulations or provisions shall be adopted by any state which shall make any discrimination in the rate of pilotage or half-pilotage between vessels sailing between the ports of one state, and vessels sailing between the ports of different states, or any discrimination against vessels propelled in whole or in part by steam, or against national vessels of the United States, all existing regulations or provisions making any such discrimination are annulled and abrogated" Section 1512 of the code of Georgia provides that "Any person, master or commander of a ship or vessel bearing toward any of the ports or harbors of this state, except coasters in this state and between the ports of this state and those of South Carolina, . . and of Florida who refuses to receive a pilot on board, shall be liable, on his arrival in such port in this state, to pay the first pilot who may have offered his services outside the bar, and exhibited his license as a pilot, if demanded by the master, the full rates of pilotage established by law for such vessels ' *Held* (1) Under the constitution congress has paramount authority over legislation regulating commerce and navigation (2) That the provisions of section 1512 of the code of Georgia are annulled and abrogated by the provisions of section 4237 of the Revised Statutes (3) A vessel of another state licensed as a coastwise steam vessel may employ its own pilot for the harbors of Georgia when such pilot is licensed under the laws of the United States, and under the provisions of sections 4401 and 4444, Revised Statutes such vessel cannot be required to take a pilot licensed under the laws of Georgia, anything in the laws of that state to the contrary notwithstanding Spraigue v Thompson, 118 U. S 90

49 **Supremacy of congress over.**—The whole commercial marine of the country is placed by the constitution under the regulation of congress, and all laws of congress on that subject, whether in relation to foreign or coastwise trade, are supreme, and where a state law contravenes such federal laws it must give way, and this without regard to the source of power whence the state legislature derived its enactment. Sinnot v. Davenport, 22 How 227, Foster v Davenport, id 244

50. Congress has exclusive power to regulate commerce, but this has never been construed to include the means whereby commerce is carried on within a state It has never attempted to regulate canals, turnpikes, bridges and railroads. The establishment of postoffices and post-roads does not affect or control the absolute power of the state over its highways and bridges The police power to make bridges is as absolutely vested in a state as is the commercial power vested in congress Milnor v New Jersey R R Bigelow v Same, Milnor v Newark Plank-road, decided by Grier, J, in Circuit Court of United States, district of New Jersey, and affirmed by divided court. See Book 16, Lawyers' Co-operative ed. United States Supreme Court Reports, p. 799.

51 This clause authorizes congress to prescribe the conditions upon which commerce in all its forms shall be conducted between our citizens and the citizens or subjects of other countries, and between the citizens of the several states, and to adopt measures to promote its growth and insure its safety Commerce embraces navigation; and the improvements of the harbors and bays along our coasts, and of navigable rivers within the states connecting with such bays and coasts, falls within the power. But subjects of local nature, and intended only as aids to commerce, and which are best provided by special regulations, may be exercised by the states without conflicting with the commercial powers of congress. Mobile County v Kimball, 102 U S 691

52. **Taxation.**—A law of a state imposing a tax upon passengers arriving in the ports of such state from a foreign country is a regulation of commerce and void Passenger Cases, 7 How. 283.

53. A tax imposed by a state on money or exchange brokers doing business in the state is not unconstitutional Nathan v Louisiana, 8 How 73.

54. **Same**—Foreign bills of exchange are instruments of commerce So also are products of agriculture or manufactures, and over these the taxing power is undoubted until they become separated from the general mass of property by becoming exports Id.

55. A state has no right to levy a tax on a vessel engaged in commerce and which plies between the ports of different states where such vessel is registered, as required by the laws of congress, in a port of another state. The vessel is subject to taxation only in the port of register. That is its *situs* A law of another state, therefore, which assumes to levy a tax on such vessel is void as a regulation of commerce. Hays v Steamship Company, 17 How 596

56 A state has the right to tax its own citizens for the prosecution of any particular business or profession within the state. Nathan v Louisiana, 8 How 73

57. Special license tax imposed by a city as a privilege of selling beer in casks manufactured in the same state is not obnoxious to the constitution. Downham v Alexandria, 10 Wall. 173

58 **Interstate commerce, regulation of.**—A tax levied on the gross receipts of a railroad company is not a tax on interstate transportation, and is not in conflict with this clause of the constitution. State Tax on Railway Gross Receipts, 15 Wall. 282, 284

59 Nor is it an impost or duty on imposts. Id.

60. A tax on freight transported from state to state is a regulation of interstate commerce, and when levied by a state, is void so far as it applies to articles carried through the state, or to articles taken up outside and carried into the state, or to articles taken up within the state to be carried to points without. Case of State Freight Tax, 15 Wall 232

61. A tax upon a vessel by a state other than that in which it has its home port and *situs*, when such vessel is lawfully engaged in interstate transportation over the navigable waters of the nation, is an interference with commerce not permitted to the states Morgan v Parham 16 Wall. 471.

62 An ordinance of a city which requires that every railroad company or express company transacting business in such city, and having a business extending beyond the limits of the state, should pay an annual license fee,

and imposing penalties for violation, is not repugnant to this clause of the constitution. Osborne v Mobile, 16 Wall., 479.

63. "Congress has never undertaken to exercise its power in any manner inconsistent with such municipal ordinance and there are several cases in which this court has asserted the right of the state to legislate in the absence of legislation by congress upon subjects over which the constitution has clothed that body with legislative authority" Citing License Cases, 5 How 504, Willson v Black Bird Creek M Co, 2 Pet 245, Cooley v Board of Wardens, 12 How 315 Chase, C J, in Osborne v Mobile, 16 Wall. 479

64 A stipulation in the charter of a railroad company that the company shall pay to the state a *bonus* or a portion of its earnings is not repugnant to this section and is different in principle from a tax on the movement or transportation of goods or persons from one state to another Within this limit, viz, that a state may not impose a tax on persons or property transported from one state to another, the power of a state to construct railroads or other highways and impose tolls and fares for transportation thereon, is unlimited and uncontrolled. Crandall v Nevada, 6 Wall. 42; Freight Tax Cases, 15 Wall 232, distinguished and affirmed. Railroad Co. v Maryland, 21 Wall. 456

65. A law of a state requiring a person engaged in peddling goods, wares and merchandise, not produced in the state, to take out a license and pay a tax thereon for the privilege of selling the same, where no such license or tax is required of persons selling similar articles which are the growth, produce or manufacture of the state, is in conflict with this section of the constitution. Welton v Missouri, 91 U S. 275

66. A tax on the amount of sales made by an auctioneer is a tax on the goods thus sold And if the tax thus laid is upon sales of imported goods sold in the original packages, and for the importer, it is a regulation of commerce, and such tax, if laid by a state or under authority of a state, is invalid. Cook v Pennsylvania, 97 U S. 566

67 A law of Texas entitled "An act regulating taxation" levied a tax on persons selling wine and beer manufactured out of the state, but exacted no such tax from those engaged in the sale of similar liquors manufactured within the state *Held,* that the law was unconstitutional. Tiernan v Rinker, 102 U. S 123.

68. The object of vesting this power in congress was to insure uniformity against discriminating state legislation. Welton v. Missouri, 91 U S. 275

69. The fact that congress has not legislated upon the subject of interstate commerce is equivalent to a declaration that it shall remain free and untrammeled. Id. And see, also, Ward v Maryland, 12 Wall. 418, Robbins v. Shelby Taxing Dist, 120 U S 489, Corson v Maryland, id 502.

70. In whatever language a statute may be framed, its purpose must be determined by its effect, and where it is apparent that the object of the statute is to compel the owners of vessels carrying passengers from foreign countries to the ports of a state of the Union to pay a tax on such passengers when landed, the effect is to tax commerce with a foreign nation, and so void Henderson v Mayor of New York, 92 U S 259, Chy Lung v Freeman, 92 U S 275

71. A statute of a state imposing a license-tax upon peddlers selling goods not grown or manufactured in the state is in conflict with this clause of the constitution Following and re-affirming Welton v. Missouri. Morrill v Wisconsin, Book 23, p. 1009, L C P Co Ed U S Sup Ct Rep

72 It must be regarded as settled that no state can, consistently with the federal constitution, impose upon the products of other states brought therein for sale or use, or upon the citizens thus engaged in the sale therein or the transportation thereto of the products of other states, more onerous public burdens or taxes than are imposed upon like products of its own territory Guy v Baltimore, 100 U S 434.

73 But a tax on peddlers of sewing machines applied alike to those manufactured in the state and those manufactured out of the state, is valid. Howe Machine Co. v Gage, 100 U S. 676.

74 A law of Maryland requiring all tobacco shipped out of the state in hogsheads to be inspected at a state warehouse and to pay storage and outage charges, examined, and held not to conflict with the commercial powers of congress Turner v. Maryland, 107 U S 38.

75 The statute of New York imposing a tax on passengers from foreign countries landing at the ports of that state, and holding the vessels liable for such tax, is unconstitutional. Henderson v Mayor, 92 U. S 259 Chy Lung v Freeman, 92 U S 275, cited and approved.

76. The constitutional disability is not removed by calling the law an inspection law to prevent the landing of criminals, paupers, lunatics, etc People v Compagnie Gen. Transatlantique, 107 U S 59.

77. An ordinance of New Orleans imposed a license tax upon ' every member of a firm or company, every agency or person or corporation owning and running tow-boats to and from the Gulf of Mexico, $500." *Held* to be a regulation of commerce and void Moran v New Orleans, 112 U S 69

78 An act of congress imposing upon the owners of steam sailing vessels a tax of fifty cents for every passenger brought from a foreign port, and who is not a citizen of this country, is a valid exercise of the power to regulate commerce as conferred by this section The right to make such regulation is exclusively in congress, and any such regulation when imposed by a state is invalid. Edye v Robertson, 112 U S. 580

79 Transportation implies the taking up of persons or property at some point and putting them down at another A tax upon such receiving and landing of passengers and freight is a tax upon their transportation, that is, a tax upon the commerce between the two states involved in such transportation And the character of this commerce between the states is not changed by the character of the means of transportation The power to regulate commerce among the states, as well as with foreign countries, vested in congress, is the power to prescribe the rules by which it shall be governed — that is, the conditions on which it shall be conducted to determine when it shall be free and when subject to duties or exactions Gloucester Ferry Co v. Pennsylvania, 114 U. S 196

80. The taxing of goods coming from other states, as such, or by reason of their so coming, is a discrimination against them, and is a regulation of interstate commerce inconsistent with that perfect freedom of trade which congress has seen fit should remain undisturbed But if after their arrival within the state — that being the place of their destination either for use or for trade — they are subjected to a general tax laid alike on all property, such taxation cannot be deemed a regulation of commerce. Brown v. Houston, 114 U. S. 622.

81. A state tax on persons engaged in selling liquors not manufactured in the state, when no such tax is imposed on persons selling such liquors when the same are manufactured in the state, is a discriminating tax and a regulation of commerce among the states, and therefore void. Affirming Welton v. Missouri, 91 U. S. 275. Walling v. Michigan, 116 U. S. 446.

82. The levying of a tax upon vessels or other water craft, or the exaction of a license fee by the state within which the property has its *situs*, is not a regulation of commerce within the meaning of this clause. When, therefore, a state grants to a city the right to license, tax and regulate ferries, the latter may impose a license tax on the keeping of ferries although their boats ply between landings lying in two different states. This is one of the immense mass of undelegated powers reserved to the states. Wiggins Ferry Co. v. East St. Louis, 107 U. S. 365.

83. A law of Tennessee imposed a tax of $50 per car upon each and every sleeping-car used by any railroad company within the state and not owned by such company, and declared such tax to be a privilege tax. And it was made unlawful for the railroad companies to use such cars unless such tax was paid. *Held*, that said act was a regulation of interstate commerce, in so far as it applied to sleeping-cars used upon trains which ran from points within the state to points without the state, or from points without to points within the state, or that ran through the state. Pickard v. Pullman Southern Car Co., 117 U. S. 34; Tennessee v. Pullman Southern Car Co., id. 51.

84. A statute of Tennessee providing that "all drummers and all persons not having a regular licensed house of business in the taxing district of Shelby county, etc., selling goods, etc., therein, shall be taxed from $10 to $25 per week," is, in so far as such law applies to firms doing business in another state whose agents take orders for goods in said taxing district, a regulation of commerce among the states, and void. Interstate commerce cannot be taxed by a state even though an equal tax be laid upon like domestic commerce. Non-action by congress in such cases is an expression of its will that the subject shall be left free from imposition or restriction. Robbins v. Shelby Taxing District, 120 U. S. 489; Corson v. Maryland, 120 U. S. 502.

85. While a state may tax the money actually in the state and which is earned in commerce transacted by the carrying trade between different states, after it has been so earned, in the same manner as it may tax other money or property within its limits, it cannot levy such tax upon the gross receipts of a railroad company for the carriage of freights or passengers interstate. Fargo v. Michigan, 121 U. S. 230.

86. A tax by a state upon a transportation company incorporated under its laws, which is levied directly upon the receipts derived by the company from its fares and freights for the transportation of persons and goods between different states, and between the states and foreign countries, and from the charter of its vessels, used for the same purpose, is an act regulating and taxing interstate and foreign commerce, and is unconstitutional. Phila. Steamship Co. v. Pennsylvania, 122 U. S. 326.

that commodity, or by that means of transportation shall be free Mobile County v Kimball 102 U S 691, Gibbons v Ogden, 9 Wheat. 1, Groves v Slaughter, 15 Pet 504; Passenger Cases, 7 How 283, Sherlock v Alling, 93 U S 99, Railroad Co v Husen, 95 U S 465, Hall v De Cuir, 95 U S 498, Sinnot v Davenport 22 How. 227, Henderson v Mayor of N Y., 92 U S. 259, Welton v. Missouri, 91 U. S 275, The Chusan, 2 Story, 455, Blanchard v. The Martha Washington, 1 Cliff 473, Bowman v C & N. W. R. R, 125 U S 465, Leisy v. Hardin 135 U S. 100

102 When not exclusive.—When the subjects of commerce are not national but local, and do not require a uniform rule of action, the powers of congress are not exclusive, and in such cases the states, in the exercise of their police powers, may, in the absence of congressional regulation, exercise local control over them Cooley v Board of Wardens, 12 How 299, Gilman v Philadelphia, 3 Wall. 713, Ex parte McNiel, 13 Wall. 240, Crandall v Nevada, 6 Wall 35, Pound v Turck, 95 U S 462; Willson v Black Bird Creek, 2 Pet 245 Peik v. Railroad Co, 94 U. S. 178, Winona, etc R R. Co. v Blake, 94 U S 180

103. Powers of congress supreme when exercised.—When, however, congress has legislated upon the subject its power is both supreme and exclusive and covers the whole subject Gilman v Philadelphia, 3 Wall. 713, New York v. Miln, 11 Pet. 155, United States v. Coombs, 12 Pet. 72; Gibbons v Ogden 9 Wheat 219, Brown v. Maryland, 12 Wheat 419, Passenger Cases, 7 How. 283

104. Definition of the power.—The power "to regulate commerce with foreign nations and among the several states and with the Indian tribes" is the power to prescribe the rule by which that commerce is to be governed, and is a power complete in itself, acknowledging no limitations other than those prescribed by the constitution It is co-extensive with the subject on which it acts, and cannot be stopped at the external boundary of a state but must enter its interior, and must be capable of authorizing the disposition of those articles which it produces, so that they may become mingled with the common mass of property within the territory entered. Leisy v Hardin, 135 U. S. 100–108

105 Police power of state, limit of—While, by virtue of its jurisdiction over persons and property within its limits, a state may provide for the security of the lives, limbs, health and comfort of persons and the protection of property so situated, yet a subject-matter which has been confided exclusively to congress by the constitution is not within the jurisdiction of the police power of the state unless placed there by congressional action Leisy v Hardin, 135 U S 100–108, citing Henderson v Mayor, 92 U S 259 Railroad Co v Husen, 95 U S 465, Walling v Michigan, 116 U. S 446, Robbins v Shelby Taxing District, 120 U S 489

106 Extent of power.—The grant of power to congress extends no further than to regulate commerce with foreign nations and among the several states. Every state, therefore, may regulate its own internal commerce according to its own judgment and views as as to the interest and well-being of its citizens. So the laws of the states of Massachusetts, Rhode Island and New Hampshire, imposing license on sale of intoxicating liquors, are held valid, notwithstanding in the case from Rhode Island the liquor was duly imported from France and purchased by the party indicted from the original importer, and in the case from New Hampshire the liquor sold was a barrel of American gin purchased in Boston and carried coastwise to New Hampshire and there sold in the same barrel License Cases, 5 How 504.

107. Congress has no power to regulate commerce or trade wholly within a state Hence a law of congress making it a misdemeanor to mix for sale naphtha and illuminating oils, or to sell petroleum below a fixed standard of temperature, is invalid except as applied to places within the United States, but without the limits of any state. United States v Dewitt, 9 Wall. 41, citing Passenger Cases, 7 How 283, License Tax Cases, 5 Wall 470

108 There is undoubtedly an internal commerce which is subject to the control of the states, while the power of congress is limited to commerce "among the several states." It is not the volume of commerce, however, that determines the jurisdiction of congress over the subject. However limited it may be, if it is commerce between states, congress has power to regulate it. It makes no difference that several different and independent agencies are employed in transporting the commodity, some acting entirely in one state, and some acting through two or more states. Whenever the commodity has begun to move as an article of trade from one state to another, commerce in that commodity between the states has commenced. Therefore, a vessel propelled by steam navigating a river confined wholly within one state, if it transports goods destined from within the state to points without, or from points without to points within the state, is subject to inspection and license under the laws of congress. The Daniel Ball, 10 Wall. 557.

109 Under this clause congress has power to exclude spirituous liquors from the "Indian country," as well as from territory which has ceased to be so by reason of its cession to the United States United States v Forty-three Gallons of Whiskey, 93 U. S 188

110 This power includes the right to control the electric telegraph as an instrument or agency of commerce. The act of July 24, 1866, "To aid in the construction of telegraph lines, etc.," is a legitimate regulation of commerce among the states, and amounts to a prohibition of state monopolies over telegraphing Pensacola Telegraph Co v. Western Union Telegraph Co 96 U. S 1

111 Same.—The act of Florida of December 11, 1866, declared in conflict with this clause and invalid. Id.

112 Congress has nothing to do with purely internal commerce of a state that is, with such commerce as is carried on between different parts of the same state, if its operations are confined exclusively to the jurisdiction and territory of the state and do not affect other nations or other states or Indian tribes. Lord v. Steamship Co, 102 U S 541

113. The rule that the regulation of commerce which is confined exclusively within the jurisdiction and territory of a state, and does not affect other nations or states or Indian tribes (that is to say, the purely internal commerce of a state), belongs exclusively to the state, is as well settled as that the regulation of commerce which does affect other nations or states or Indian tribes belongs to congress Telegraph Co v Texas 105 U S 460.

114 In relation to the exclusive power of congress, and when states may act.—Until the dormant powers of congress are exercised, that commodity, or by that means of transportation, shall be free Mobile County v. Kimball, 102 U S 691, Gibbons v Ogden, 9 Wheat. 1, Groves v Slaughter, 15 Pet 504, Passenger Cases, 7 How. 283, Sherlock v Alling, 93 U S. 99, Railroad Co v Husen, 95 U. S 465, Hall v De Cuir, 95 U S 498, Sinnot v Davenport 22 How 227, Henderson v. Mayor of N Y., 92 U S 259, Welton v Missouri, 91 U S 275, The Chusan, 2 Story, 455, Blanchard v. The Martha Washington, 1 Cliff 473, Bowman v. C & N. W. R. R, 125 U S 465, Leisy v. Hardin 135 U S. 100

102 **When not exclusive** — When the subjects of commerce are not national but local, and do not require a uniform rule of action, the powers of congress are not exclusive, and in such cases the states, in the exercise of their police powers, may, in the absence of congressional regulation, exercise local control over them Cooley v Board of Wardens, 12 How 299, Gilman v Philadelphia, 3 Wall 713, Ex parte McNiel, 13 Wall 240, Crandall v Nevada, 6 Wall. 35, Pound v Turck, 95 U S 462, Willson v Black Bird Creek, 2 Pet 245, Peik v Railroad Co., 94 U. S. 178, Winona, etc R R Co. v Blake, 94 U. S 180

103. **Powers of congress supreme when exercised.**— When, however, congress has legislated upon the subject its power is both supreme and exclusive and covers the whole subject. Gilman v Philadelphia, 3 Wall. 713, New York v Miln, 11 Pet 155, United States v. Coombs, 12 Pet 72, Gibbons v. Ogden, 9 Wheat. 219, Brown v Maryland, 12 Wheat. 419; Passenger Cases, 7 How 283

104. **Definition of the power.**— The power "to regulate commerce with foreign nations and among the several states and with the Indian tribes" is the power to prescribe the rule by which that commerce is to be governed, and is a power complete in itself, acknowledging no limitations other than those prescribed by the constitution. It is co-extensive with the subject on which it acts, and cannot be stopped at the external boundary of a state, but must enter its interior, and must be capable of authorizing the disposition of those articles which it produces, so that they may become mingled with the common mass of property within the territory entered. Leisy v Hardin, 135 U. S. 100–108.

105. **Police power of state, limit of.**— While, by virtue of its jurisdiction over persons and property within its limits, a state may provide for the security of the lives, limbs, health and comfort of persons and the protection of property so situated, yet a subject-matter which has been confided exclusively to congress by the constitution is not within the jurisdiction of the police power of the state unless placed there by congressional action Leisy v Hardin, 135 U S 100–108, citing Henderson v Mayor, 92 U S. 259, Railroad Co v Husen, 95 U S 465, Walling v Michigan, 116 U S 446, Robbins v Shelby Taxing District, 120 U S 489

106. **Extent of power** — The grant of power to congress extends no further than to regulate commerce with foreign nations and among the several states Every state, therefore, may regulate its own internal commerce according to its own judgment and views as as to the interest and well-being of its citizens So the laws of the states of Massachusetts, Rhode Island and New Hampshire, imposing license on sale of intoxicating liquors, are held valid notwithstanding in the case from Rhode Island the liquor was duly imported from France and purchased by the party indicted from the origi-

nal importer, and in the case from New Hampshire the liquor sold was a barrel of American gin purchased in Boston and carried coastwise to New Hampshire and there sold in the same barrel. License Cases, 5 How. 504.

107. Congress has no power to regulate commerce or trade wholly within a state Hence a law of congress making it a misdemeanor to mix for sale naphtha and illuminating oils, or to sell petroleum below a fixed standard of temperature, is invalid except as applied to places within the United States, but without the limits of any state United States v Dewitt, 9 Wall. 41, citing Passenger Cases, 7 How 283, License Tax Cases, 5 Wall 470

108 There is undoubtedly an internal commerce which is subject to the control of the states, while the power of congress is limited to commerce "among the several states." It is not the volume of commerce, however, that determines the jurisdiction of congress over the subject. However limited it may be, if it is commerce between states, congress has power to regulate it. It makes no difference that several different and independent agencies are employed in transporting the commodity, some acting entirely in one state, and some acting through two or more states Whenever the commodity has begun to move as an article of trade from one state to another, commerce in that commodity between the states has commenced. Therefore, a vessel propelled by steam navigating a river confined wholly within one state, if it transports goods destined from within the state to points without, or from points without to points within the state, is subject to inspection and license under the laws of congress. The Daniel Ball, 10 Wall 557.

109. Under this clause congress has power to exclude spirituous liquors from the "Indian country," as well as from territory which has ceased to be so by reason of its cession to the United States. United States v Forty-three Gallons of Whiskey, 93 U S 188

110. This power includes the right to control the electric telegraph as an instrument or agency of commerce The act of July 24, 1866, "To aid in the construction of telegraph lines, etc.," is a legitimate regulation of commerce among the states, and amounts to a prohibition of state monopolies over telegraphing. Pensacola Telegraph Co v. Western Union Telegraph Co, 96 U S 1.

111 Same —The act of Florida of December 11, 1866, declared in conflict with this clause and invalid Id

112. Congress has nothing to do with purely internal commerce of a state, that is, with such commerce as is carried on between different parts of the same state, if its operations are confined exclusively to the jurisdiction and territory of the state and do not affect other nations or other states or Indian tribes Lord v Steamship Co, 102 U S 541

113 The rule that the regulation of commerce which is confined exclusively within the jurisdiction and territory of a state, and does not affect other nations or states or Indian tribes (that is to say, the purely internal commerce of a state) belongs exclusively to the state, is as well settled as that the regulation of commerce which does affect other nations or states or Indian tribes belongs to congress Telegraph Co v. Texas, 105 U S 460.

114 **In relation to the exclusive power of congress, and when states may act** —Until the dormant powers of congress are exercised,

the reserved powers of the state are plenary, and their exercise in good faith cannot be reviewed by the supreme court of the United States. Gilman v Philadelphia, 3 Wall. 713.

115 The states may exercise concurrent powers with congress, or independent powers in all cases but the following three: 1. Where the power is lodged exclusively in congress by the federal constitution 2 Where it is given to the United States and prohibited to the states. 3 Where from the nature and subjects of the power it must necessarily be exercised by the federal government exclusively. The power to build bridges over navigable waters does not fall within either of these exceptions. Id.

116. Whenever the subject over which the power to regulate commerce is exercised is national in its nature, or admits of one uniform system or plan of regulation, it may be said to be of such a nature as to require congressional legislation, and in such case the power of regulation is exclusively in congress Transportation from one state to another is of this nature State Freight Tax Cases, 15 Wall. 232.

117 Congress under its power to regulate commerce, has authority to establish a lien on vessels of the United States in favor of material-men, uniform throughout the whole country In particular cases in which congress has not exercised the power of regulating commerce, and where the subject does not require the exclusive exercise of that power, the states, until congress acts, may continue to legislate *Hence*, a lien granted by state law to material-men who furnish necessaries to a vessel in its home port in such state is valid. The Lottawanna, 21 Wall. 558.

118 Though it be conceded that there is a class of legislation which may affect commerce both with foreign nations and between the states, in regard to which the laws of the states may be valid in the absence of action under the authority of congress on the same subjects, this can have no reference to matters which are in their nature national, or which admit of a uniform system or plan of regulation Henderson v. Mayor of New York, 92 U S. 259

119. Whenever the statute of a state invades the domain of legislation which belongs exclusively to congress, it is void, no matter under what class of powers it may fall, or how closely allied to powers conceded to belong to the states Id.

120. Until congress has made some regulation upon the subject of the liability of parties for marine torts resulting in death of the person injured, a state law giving to the representatives of such person a right of action where his death was caused by the wrongful act or omission of another, within the territorial limits of such state, is not void as an interference with this clause of the constitution Sherlock v Alling, 93 U S. 99

121. A statute which imposes no tax, prescribes no duty, nor places any burden on commerce, and in no respect interferes with any regulations for the navigation and use of vessels, but simply declares a general principle respecting liability of all persons within the state for torts resulting in the death of the party injured, and applicable alike to all persons, whether engaged in navigation or not, is not repugnant to this clause of the constitution Id.

122 In conferring upon congress the regulation of commerce, it was never intended to cut off the states from legislating on all subjects relating

to the health, life and safety of their citizens, though the legislation might indirectly affect the commerce of the country. Id.

123 Same.—While it is true that the commercial power conferred by the constitution is one without limitation, it may, nevertheless, be said generally that, until congress has legislated upon the subject, the legislation of a state, not directed against commerce or any of its regulations, but relating to the rights, duties and liabilities of citizens, and only indirectly and remotely affecting the operations of commerce, is of obligatory force upon citizens within its territorial jurisdiction, whether on land or water, or engaged in commerce, foreign or interstate, or in any other pursuit. Id

124. "Legislation may in a great variety of ways affect commerce and persons engaged in it without constituting a regulation of it within the meaning of the constitution." Sherlock v Alling, 93 U. S 99, State Tax on Gross Receipts, 15 Wall 284, Munn v Illinois, 94 U S. 113, Railroad Co v Iowa, 94 U. S 155, Hall v. De Cuir, 95 U. S. 485.

125 In the absence of legislation by congress upon the subject a state may authorize the construction of a dam across a navigable stream within the state Pound v Turck, 95 U S 459

126. A state legislature may, in the absence of a law of congress, authorize the construction of a bridge across a navigable river wholly within such state, such law being local in its nature and a mere aid to commerce When congress intervenes, however, its authority is supreme and its regulations exclusive. Cardwell v Bridge Co, 113 U S 205, Brown v. Houston, 114 U S 622

127. While with reference to some subjects of commerce which are local in their nature and limited in their sphere of operation, the states may prescribe regulations until congress intervenes and assumes control of them, yet when they are national in their character and require uniformity of regulation, affecting alike all of the states, the power of congress is exclusive; and with regard to such latter class the non-action of congress is a declaration that it shall remain free from burdens imposed by state legislation. Gloucester Ferry Co v. Pennsylvania, 114 U S 196

128. Foreign commerce has been fully regulated by congress, and any regulations imposed by the states upon that branch of commerce is a palpable interference Phila Steamship Co. v Pennsylvania, 122 U S 326

129 If congress has not made any express regulations with regard to interstate commerce, its inaction is equivalent to a declaration that it shall be free, in all cases where its power is exclusive, and its power is necessarily exclusive whenever the subject-matter is national in its character and properly admits of one uniform system See cases collected in Robbins v Shelby Taxing District, 120 U S 489 Interstate commerce carried on by ships on the sea is of a national character. Phila. Steamship Co v Pennsylvania, 122 U S. 326 State Freight Tax, 15 Wall 232, examined and approved; and State Tax on Railway Gross Receipts, 15 Wall. 284, criticised and questioned Id

130. The question whether the fact that congress has failed in any particular instance to provide by law a regulation of commerce among the states is conclusive of its intention that the subject shall be free from all positive regulation, or that until it positively interferes such commerce may be left to be freely dealt with by the respective states, is one that should still be considered in each case as it arises Bowman v. C. & N. W R y Co, 125 U S 465

131. A state cannot, for the purpose of protecting its people against the evils of intemperance, enact laws which regulate commerce between its people and those of other states of the Union, unless the consent of congress, express or implied, is first obtained Id

132 Whether the right of transportation of an article of commerce from one state to another includes by necessary implication the right of the consignee to sell it in unbroken packages at the place where the transportation terminates *quere*. Id

133. A state statute which requires locomotive engineers engaged in running locomotive engines on railroads which are operated in and through different states to be examined as to their power of distinguishing the colors of different color-signals used upon such railroads, and which requires the corporation whose trains are so operated to pay a fee for such examination, is not repugnant to this clause of the constitution until congress legislates upon the subject. Nashville & Chattanooga R. R v Alabama, 128 U. S 96

134 The power to regulate commerce among the states is a unit, but if particular subjects within its operation do not require the application of a general or uniform system, the states may legislate in regard to them with a view to local needs and circumstances until congress otherwise directs; the power, when thus exercised, however, is not identical in its extent with the power to regulate commerce among the states. . . . For cases enumerated falling within this power in the state, see Leisy v. Hardin, 135 U. S 108

135 When, however, the power is such as must necessarily be exercised by the general government and it remains silent, the only legitimate conclusion is that the general government intended that such power should not be affirmatively exercised by the state. Id , citing County of Mobile v Kimball, 102 U S. 691, Brown v Houston, 114 U S 622-631, Wabash, etc. R y v. Illinois, 118 U S 557, Robbins v Shelby Taxing District, 120 U S 489-493.

135a Case overruled —The authority of Pierce v. New Hampshire, 5 How 504-586, in so far as it rests on the view that the law of New Hampshire was valid because congress had made no regulation on the subject, is overruled Leisy v. Hardin, 135 U S 100-118.

136 Commerce with Indian tribes.—If commerce, traffic or intercourse is carried on with an Indian tribe or a member of such tribe, it is a subject of congressional regulation notwithstanding it is within the limits of a state Neither the constitution of a state nor a legislative act can withdraw Indians from the operation of an act of congress regulating such traffic United States v Holliday, Same v. Haas, 3 Wall 407

137. Traffic with Indian tribes may be prohibited or regulated by license under congressional enactments United States v Cisna, 1 McLean, 259

138 Congress have a right to select the means which have a direct relation to the object in the regulation of commerce with the Indians United States v Bailey, 1 McLean, 234

139 Under this clause congress cannot prescribe the punishment for crimes committed within the limits of Indian reservations lying wholly

within a state, and provide for trial of such crimes in the United States courts. Id

140 The act of Georgia legislature of December 22, 1830 entitled "An act to prevent the exercise of assumed and arbitrary power by all persons under pretext of authority from the Cherokee Indians," etc, is unconstitutional and void It interferes forcibly with the relations established between the United States and the Cherokee Indians, the regulation of which by the constitution is committed exclusively to congress It is hostile to the treaties made with the Indians and to the laws of congress enacted in relation thereto Worcester v Georgia 6 Pet. 515

141. The tribe constitutes a distinct community, and over them the laws of the state have no force Citizens of the state, without the assent of the tribe or in conformity to existing treaties, have no right to enter the community Id

142. The power of congress to regulate commerce with the Indians does not necessarily cease on their being included within the limits of a state But where the federal relations are not withdrawn from the Indians within a state by the concurrent acts of the federal and state governments, and the Indians occupy a territory of very limited extent, surrounded by white population, which necessarily have daily intercourse with the Indians, and it becomes impracticable to enforce the law, the federal jurisdiction must cease. United States v. Cisna, 1 McLean, 254

143. The act of February 12, 1862, making it a penal offense to sell ardent spirits to an Indian, is valid under the powers conferred by this section. This power extends to the regulation of commerce with the Indian tribes and with the individual members of such tribes, though the traffic and the Indian with whom it is carried on are wholly within the territorial limits of a state. No state can by either its constitution or by legislation withdraw the Indians within its limits from the operation of the laws of congress regulating trade with them, notwithstanding any rights it may confer on such Indians as electors or citizens United States v Holliday, 3 Wall 407.

144 Whether any particular class of Indians is still to be regarded as a tribe, or has ceased to hold the tribal relation, is primarily a question for the political departments of the government, and if they have decided it the supreme court will follow their lead. United States v. Holliday 3 Wall 407, The Kansas Indians, 5 Wall. 737

145. The act of congress of July 4, 1884 (23 Stat. 73, ch 179), granting a right of way through the Indian Territory to the Southern Kansas Railway Company for a railroad, telegraph and telephone line, is a valid exercise of the power of congress to regulate commerce among the states and with the Indian tribes Cherokee Nation v Southern Kansas R y Co, 135 U S 641

146. Commerce — Instrumentalities employed.— In the exercise of its power to regulate commerce congress may employ as instrumentalities therefor, corporations created by it or by the states Id

147. Wharfage.—A city or town on a navigable river may exact a reasonable compensation for the use of the wharf which it owns without infringing the constitutional provisions concerning tonnage taxes or regulations of commerce Packet Company v Catlettsburg, 105 U S 559

148 No foreign or interstate commerce can be carried on with the citizens of a state without a wharf or other place within its limits on which passengers and freight can be landed and received. The fact that such landing place is used in a state does not confer upon such state the right to tax the capital of the corporations engaged in such commerce, unless the same is within the jurisdiction of such state The only interference by a state with such commerce which is permissible is confined to port regulations and such measures as will insure safety and prevent confusion in landing and receiving freight and passengers Gloucester Ferry Co v Pennsylvania, 114 U S 196

149. Miscellaneous — State regulation of.— Commerce upon lakes lying within a state is not within congressional regulation The laws of congress (act March 3, 1851) apply only to vessels engaged in foreign or interstate commerce. The purely internal commerce and navigation of a state is exclusively under state regulation. Moore v American Transportation Co, 24 How 1

150. Compact between states.— The compact between Virginia and Kentucky cannot operate to abridge the powers of congress to regulate commerce among the several states, etc. Pennsylvania v. Wheeling & B. Bridge Co, 18 How. 421

151 Bringing counterfeit coin into the states — Congress may punish.— Congress has power to enact laws for the punishment of persons who may bring into the United States any counterfeit coin, and the federal courts to punish for circulating the same This is a legitimate exercise of the power to regulate commerce, and also of the power to coin money and determine the value thereof, and is not inconsistent with the doctrine of Fox v State of Ohio, 5 How 433. United States v. Marigold, 9 How 560.

152 Bridges — A state legislature may determine what the form and character of the railroad bridges crossing its navigable waters may be, and the height at which they shall be erected and of what materials constructed. Until congress intervenes the state's power in such cases is plenary Hamilton v. Vicksburg, Shreveport & Pacific R. R Co, 119 U S. 280

153 The power to authorize the building of bridges is not to be found in the federal constitution, it has not been taken from the states Gilman v. Philadelphia, 3 Wall. 713.

154 Pending a suit to have a bridge across the Mississippi river declared a nuisance, it was competent for congress, under the power conferred by this clause, to interfere and by an act legalize such bridge The Clinton Bridge, 10 Wall. 454.

155 Railroads required to fix rates and post same.— A state statute requiring railway companies operating railroads within the state to annually fix their rates for freight and passengers, and to cause printed copies thereof to be put up at all stations on the lines of the railroads and to remain posted during the year, is neither unreasonable nor unconstitutional It is a valid exercise of the police powers of the state C & N W R R. Co. v. Fuller, 17 Wall 560.

156 Railroad, contract with held not repugnant — A contract between a railroad company and an elevator company that the elevator company shall handle all the grain for through shipment over such railroad that passed through Dubuque at a stipulated price per bushel is not repugnant to this clause of the constitution, nor to the laws of congress regulating commerce in certain respects, approved June 15 and July 25, 1866. The power to regulate commerce among the several states was vested in congress in order to secure equality and freedom in commercial intercourse against discriminating state legislation, it was never intended that the power should be so exercised as to interfere with private contracts not designed at the time they were made to create impediments to such intercourse. Dubuque, etc R R. Co v Richmond, 19 Wall 584

157. Right of state over warehouse rates — It is no violation of the provisions of this clause of the constitution for a state to fix by law the maximum of charges that may be made by public warehouses and elevators for the storage of grain, even though such warehouses or elevators are engaged in receiving and storing and reshipping grain destined from one state to another Munn v Illinois, 94 U S 113

158. Texas cattle, transportation of.— A statute of Missouri which prohibited Mexican, Texas or Indian cattle from being driven or conveyed through the state between the 1st days of March and December of each year is in conflict with this clause Such statute is more than a quarantine law, which a state in the exercise of its police powers may enact. Railroad v. Husen, 95 U. S 465.

159. Railroads; right of state to fix rates for — A statute which fixes the maximum rates for fare and freight on a railroad which extends from one state to another is not repugnant to this clause of the constitution, although incidentally such regulation may reach beyond the limits of the state Peik v Northwestern R R., 94 U S. 164

NOTE — The last clause in this syllabus has been overruled by a majority of the court in Wabash R'y Co. v. Illinois, 118 U S 587.

160 Nor is a statute void which fixes the maximum rates of fare and freight on railroads for passage or shipment wholly within the state Railroad v Iowa, 94 U S 155

161 A railroad company whose charter does not exempt it from such control may be required by state legislation to convey when called upon for that purpose, and to charge no more than a reasonable compensation, which may be limited by statute. Winona & C. R R. Co v Blake, 94 U S 180

162 A statute of Illinois which enacts that if any railroad company within that state shall charge or receive for transporting passengers or freight, of the same class, the same or a greater sum for any distance than it does for a longer distance, shall be liable to a penalty for unjust discrimination, is, when applied to contracts for shipment beyond the state limits, a regulation of commerce among the states, and is so far void Cases of Munn v. Illinois, 94 U S. 113, C., B & Q R. R. Co v Iowa, id 155, Peik v C & N W R R. Co, id. 164, examined and explained, and in some parts overruled. Wabash R'y Co v Illinois, 118 U S 587

163 Regulating passage on steamboats.— State legislation which seeks to impose a direct burden upon interstate commerce, or to interfere directly with its freedom, encroaches upon the exclusive power of congress. The statute of Louisiana of February 23, 1869, so far as it applied to steamboats navigating the River Mississippi and passing from state to state thereon, was a regulation of commerce among the states and void Hall v De Cuir, 95 U S 485

164. Non-residents — Discrimination against.— An act of a state legislature which discriminates against non-resident merchants and manufacturers and in favor of those of the state is invalid Commerce among the states can only be free when there are no such discriminations Webber v Virginia, 103 U S 344, Morrill v. Wisconsin, Book 23, p 1009 Lawyers' C. P Co's Ed. Sup Ct Rep

165. Quarantine.— The laws of the states on the subject of quarantine, while they may in some of their rules amount to a regulation of commerce, though not so designed, belong to that class of laws which a state may enact until congress shall have interposed by legislation over the subject or shall have forbidden state laws in relation thereto Congress has not done this, but has adopted the state laws upon that subject (see ch 53, R S, and 20 Stat. at Large p 37) Morgan's Steamship Co v Louisiana, 118 U S 455

166. Telegraph messages, delivery of — Whatever authority a state may possess over the transmission and delivery of messages by telegraph companies within her limits, it does not extend to the delivery of messages in other states Therefore sections 4176, 4178, Revised Statutes of Indiana, 1881, in so far as regards messages sent from points within that state to points without the state, is an attempted regulation of interstate commerce, and are void. W. U. Tel Co v Pendleton, 122 U S 347

167. Objects of clause.— The object of vesting in congress the power to regulate commerce was to secure, with reference to its subjects uniform regulations, where such uniformity is practicable, against conflicting state legislation. W U Tel Co v Pendleton, 122 U S 347.

168. Railroad engineers, examination of — In reference to a statute of a state which provides that it shall be "unlawful for the engineer of any railroad train in this state to drive or operate or engineer any train of cars or engine upon the main line or road-bed of any railroad in this state which is used for the transportation of passengers or freight, without first undergoing an examination and obtaining a license as hereinafter provided," it was *held* that the statute was valid when applied to an engineer who ran trains on a through line between that state and another, and who did not at any time run or engineer a locomotive or train wholly from point to point within that state, that the statute was not in the nature of a regulation of commerce among the states when so applied. Smith v. Alabama, 124 U. S. 465

169 Alcohol, manufacture of.— The statutes of Iowa, as construed by the supreme court of that state, authorize the manufacture of alcohol within the state for the following purposes · 1st. For sale for mechanical purposes. 2d. For sale for medicinal purposes 3d For sale for culinary purposes 4th. For sale for sacramental purposes, and prohibits its manufacture within the state for any other purpose including the manufacture for purpose of exportation to and sale within other states and foreign countries *Held*, that the statute as thus construed is not repugnant to this clause of the constitution Kidd v Pearson, 128 U. S. 1, 19, 20

170 Texas cattle, possession of — Section 4059 of the code of Iowa, which provides that a person having in his possession within the state "Texas cattle" which have not been wintered north of the northern boundary of Missouri and Kansas shall be liable for any damages which may accrue from allowing them to run at large and thereby spread the disease known as 'Texas cattle fever,' is not in conflict with this clause of the constitution. Kimmish v Ball, 129 U S 217.

171 Foreign corporations, regulation of —The constitution of Colorado provides that no foreign corporation shall do business in that state without having a place of business and an agent on whom process can be served A statute of the state makes provision for filing by such corporation with the secretary of state of a certificate showing its place of business and designating such agent or agents, and also a copy of its charter, etc, and in case of failure to do so that each and every officer, agent and stockholder of the corporation should be jointly and severally personally liable on its contracts made while in default of compliance with such provision of law The act made further provision that no corporation, foreign or domestic, should purchase or hold real estate except as provided in the act no mode was pointed out whereby foreign corporations might acquire and hold real estate. A corporation of Wisconsin, which had not complied with the law, purchased real estate of G and took a warranty deed therefor After making this warranty deed to the corporation G. made a quitclaim deed to the same property to P., who was plaintiff below. F, defendant below, held under conveyance from the corporation *Held*, (1) that perhaps a reasonable interpretation of the statute was, that a foreign corporation should not purchase or hold real estate in Colorado until it should acquire, in the mode provided by the state laws, the right to transact business in the state, (2) that these constitutional and statutory provisions were valid so far as they did not directly affect foreign or interstate commerce The conveyance to the corporation was held valid under other provisions in the statute Fritts v Palmer, 132 U S 282

172 Power of congress to authorize railroads within states — Congress has authority, in the exercise of its power to regulate commerce among the states, to either construct, or authorize individuals or corporations to construct, railroads across the states and territories of the United States. California v. Pac. R R. Co, 127 U S 1

173. Police power — An act of the legislature of New York provided, *inter alia*, that the master of every vessel arriving in the port of New York from a foreign port, or from a port of any state of the Union other than the state of New York, should under penalties make a report in twenty-four hours after his landing, containing the name, age and last legal settlement of each passenger who shall have been on board such vessel during the voyage, etc. *Held*, not to be a regulation of commerce, but that it was a legitimate exercise of the state's police power, the law was intended to prevent the state from being burdened with an influx of foreigners, and to prevent them becoming paupers, etc Gibbons v Ogden, 9 Wheat. 203, and Brown v Maryland, 12 Wheat 419, are discussed and distinguished from the case at bar Mayor of New York v Miln, 11 Pet 102

174 Same.— The powers of a state are fully discussed by the court. Id.

175. Police laws — Inspection of cattle designed for meat — Minnesota law —The statute of Minnesota providing for inspection within the state of animals designed for meat, by its necessary operation practically excludes from the markets of that state all fresh beef, veal, mutton, lamb or pork, in whatever form, if taken from animals slaughtered in other states, notwithstanding the same may be sound and healthy The result is that it thus directly tends to restrict the slaughtering of animals whose meat is to be sold in Minnesota to those engaged in such business in that state. This discrimination is an incumbrance on commerce among the states, and is unconstitutional. It cannot be regarded as a rightful exertion of the police power of the state. A burden thus imposed is not to be sustained simply because the statute imposing it applies alike to the people of all the states, including the people of the state enacting it. Minnesota v. Barber, 136 U. S. 313

176. Agency for inducing passengers to take certain route — An agency for a line of railroad between Chicago and New York, established in San Francisco for the purpose of inducing passengers going from San Francisco to New York to take that line from Chicago, but not engaged in selling tickets for the route, or receiving or paying out money on account of it, is an agency engaged in interstate commerce, and a municipal license tax sought to be imposed upon such agency is unconstitutional. McCall v. California, 136 U S 104 To the same effect see Norfolk & W R R. v Pennsylvania, 136 U S. 114.

177. Interstate commerce in intoxicating liquors — Case stated. The statute of Iowa prohibiting the sale of intoxicating liquors, except for certain named purposes and under state regulations provided for therein, is, as applied to the sale by the importer in the original package in which it is imported, unbroken and unopened of such liquors, manufactured in and brought from another state, unconstitutional and void Leisy v Hardin, 135 U S 100, followed and applied to a license law in Lyng v. Michigan, 135 U S 161.

178 Accommodations for colored passengers.—The act of Mississippi of March 2, 1888, as construed by the supreme court of that state, applies only to commerce within the state Following this construction of the act, *held*, that it is not in violation of this section as a regulation of commerce among the several states The distinction between interstate and intrastate commerce examined and stated Louisville & N O R R Co. v. State of Mississippi, 133 U. S 587.

179 Commercial regulation.— "The general commercial law being circumscribed within no local limits, nor committed for its administration to any peculiar jurisdiction, and the constitution and laws of the United States having conferred upon the citizens of the several states and upon aliens the privilege of litigating and enforcing their rights acquired under and defined by that commercial law before the judicial tribunals of the United States, it must follow by regular consequence that any state law, the effect of which is to impair the rights thus secured, or to divest the federal courts of cognizance thereof, in their fullest acceptation under the commercial law, must be nugatory. The statute of Mississippi, so far as it may be understood to deny, or in any degree to impair, the right of a non-resident holder of a bill of exchange, immediately after presentment to, and refusal to accept by, the drawee, and after protest and notice, to resort forthwith to the courts of the United States by suit upon such bill, must be regarded as wholly without authority and inoperative The same want of authority may be affirmed of a provision in the statute which would seek to render the right to recover dependent upon a second presentment, notice and protest. A requisition like this would be a violation of the general commercial law, which a state would have no power to impose, and which the courts of the United States would be bound to disregard. Watson v Tarpley, 18 How. 517

4. To establish a uniform rule of naturalization, and uniform laws on the subject of bankruptcies, throughout the United States

1. **Naturalization.**—After the adoption of the constitution of the United States the states still individually enjoyed a concurrent authority upon the subject of naturalization But their individual authority cannot be so exercised as to contravene the rules established by the laws of congress The true reason for investing congress with the power to establish a uniform rule was to guard against a too narrow instead of a too liberal mode of conferring the rights of citizenship Collet v Collet, 2 Dall 294.

2 A state cannot exclude those citizens who have been adopted by the United States, but it can adopt citizens upon easier terms than those which congress may deem expedient to impose Id

3. "That the power of naturalization is exclusively in congress does not seem to be, and certainly ought not to be, controverted." Per Marshall, C. J, in Chirac v Chirac, 2 Wheat. 269

4. Commenting on this language in License Cases, Taney, C. J, says "In the case of Chirac v Chirac, which arose under the grant of power to establish a uniform rule of naturalization, when the court speak of the power of congress as exclusive they are evidently merely sanctioning the argument of counsel stated in the preceding sentence, which placed the invalidity of the naturalization under the law of Maryland, not solely upon the grant of power in the constitution, but insisted that the Maryland law was 'virtually repealed by the constitution of the United States and the act of naturalization enacted by congress' Undoubtedly it was so repealed, for the law of the United States covered every part of the Union, and there could not, therefore be a state law which did not come in conflict with it. And in this case it might well have been doubted whether the grant in the constitution itself did not abrogate the power of the states, inasmuch as the constitution also provided that the citizens of each state should be entitled to all the privileges and immunities of citizens in the several states, and it would seem to be hardly consistent with this provision to allow any one state, after the adoption of the constitution, to exercise a power which, if it operated at all, must operate beyond the territory of the state, and compel other states to acknowledge as citizens those whom it might not be willing to receive." License Cases, 5 How 585, cited and commented on in opinion of Mr Justice Woodbury, Passenger Cases, 7 How. 556 See, also, United States v Villato, 2 Dall 372; Houston v Moore, 5 Wheat. 1, Ogden v Saunders, 12 Wheat. 277, Scott v Sandford, 19 How. 393, United States v Rhodes, 1 Abb (U S) 78, Matthews v Rae, 3 Cranch, C C 699, Golden v Prince, 3 Wash C C 313

5. Since the adoption of the constitution of the United States no state can by any subsequent law make a foreigner a citizen of the United States. It may put a foreigner upon a footing with its own citizens as to all rights and privileges enjoyed by them within its dominion and under its laws But that will not make him a citizen of the United States nor entitle him to sue in its courts, nor to any of the privileges and immunities of a citizen in another state. Dred Scott v. Sandford, 19 How. 393.

6. An individual state still possesses concurrent authority with congress upon the subject of naturalization, but this authority cannot be so used as to contravene a rule established by the latter Collet v Collet, 2 Dall. 294

7. The power to naturalize is exclusively in the government of the United States Chirac v Chirac, 2 Wheat 259, Huston v Moore, 5 Wheat. 48, License Cases, 5 How 505, Passenger Cases, 7 How. 556

8 It can only be exercised in behalf of those born in a foreign country. An African born in the United States cannot be naturalized Dred Scott v Sandford, 19 How. 417.

9 A state cannot make a subject of a foreign government a citizen of the United States. Citizenship and the right to vote are neither identical nor inseparable Lanz v Randall, 4 Dill 425.

10 An alien who has been duly naturalized becomes thereby a citizen of the United States, and is a citizen of any state of the Union in which he may reside Gassies v Ballon, 6 Pet. 761

11 **Naturalization of Indians** — Indian tribes have always been treated and recognized as independent and foreign nations, notwithstanding the country they inhabit is incorporated into and forms a part of the territory of the United States Treaties are negotiated with them, and their alliance has been sought in wars. And they may, like the subjects of any other foreign government, be naturalized by authority of congress and become citizens of the United States Scott v Sandford, 19 How 393–404

12 **Evidence of naturalization.**—The judgment of a court of competent jurisdiction admitting an alien to citizenship is conclusive evidence that all the prerequisites thereto have been complied with Stark v Insurance Co, 7 Cranch, 420, Spratt v Spratt, 4 Pet. 393, Mutual Benefit Ins Co v Tisdale 91 U. S 238, The Acorn, 2 Abb (U S) 443

13 **Effect of naturalization.**—A naturalized citizen is made a citizen under the act of congress, but the act does not proceed to give, to regulate or to prescribe his capacities. He becomes a member of society, possessing all the rights of a native citizen, and standing, in the view of the constitution, on the footing of a native. The constitution does not authorize congress to enlarge or abridge those rights. The simple power of the national legislature is to prescribe a uniform rule of naturalization, and the exercise of this power exhausts it so far as respects the rights of the individual The constitution then takes him up, and, among other rights, extends to him the right to sue in the United States courts the same as a native might do He is distinguishable in nothing from a native citizen except in so far as the constitution makes the distinction Osborn v United States Bank, 9 Wheat 738–827.

14 **Bankruptcy** — Since the adoption of the constitution of the United States a state legislature may enact a valid law on the subject of bankruptcy 1st If there is no act of congress at the time in force establishing a uniform system of bankruptcy with which such state law conflicts 2d Provided such state law does not have the effect of impairing the obligation of contracts within the meaning of the United States constitution Sturges v. Crowninshield, 4 Wheat. 122, Ogden v Saunders, 12 Wheat. 213, Boyle v. Zacharie, 6 Pet. 635, In re Klein, 1 How 279, note, McMillan v McNeill, 4

Wheat 209, Baldwin v Hale, 1 Wall 228; Bank v Smith, 6 Wheat 131, Campbell v Claudius Peters, C C 481, Suydam v Broadnax, 14 Pet. 67

15 This section does not exclude the right of a state to legislate on the same subject, except when the power is actually exercised by congress and the state laws conflict therewith Ogden v Saunders, 12 Wheat. 213.

16 An insolvent debtor who has received a certificate of discharge from arrest and imprisonment under a state insolvent law is not thereby entitled to be discharged from imprisonment under an execution against his person at suit of the United States United States v Wilson, 8 Wheat. 253

17 Insolvent laws of one state cannot discharge the contracts of citizens of another state Baldwin v Hale, 1 Wall. 223, Farmers', etc. Bank v. Smith, 6 Wheat 131, Suydam v. Broadnax, 14 Pet. 67 And this although by the terms of the contract it is to be performed in the state enacting the bankrupt or insolvent law Baldwin v. Bank of Newbury, 1 Wall 234, Baldwin v. Hale, 1 Wall. 223

18 A state insolvent law is valid although enacted while a national bankrupt law is in force The enactment of such state statute during the life of the bankrupt act is merely tantamount to a provision that the former shall take effect upon the repeal of the latter. Tua v Carriere, 117 U S. 201.

19. State bankrupt laws have no extraterritorial effect and cannot operate upon non-residents of the state. Baldwin v Hale, 1 Wall 223, Von Glahn v Varienne, 1 Dill 515, Emory v Greenough, 3 Dall 369, McMillan v. McNeill, 4 Wheat. 209, Boyle v Zacharie, 6 Pet 635, Babcock v Weston, 1 Gall. 168, Hinkley v. Marean, 3 Mason, 88, Springer v Foster, 2 Story, 383 See Denny v Bennett, 128 U. S 489

20. A person in custody under a *capias ad satisfaciendum* issued under the authority of a circuit court of the United States cannot legally be discharged from imprisonment by a state officer acting under a state insolvent law. Duncan v Darst, 1 How. 301.

21. A discharge from bankruptcy under a state law is no bar in the courts of the United States or of another state to non-resident creditors Gilman v. Lockwood, 4 Wall 409.

22. Powers of congress over — The power of congress to enact bankrupt laws is not limited to the enactment of such laws as existed in England at and prior to the adoption of the constitution It may provide by law that the debtor may upon his own application be adjudged a bankrupt and require his creditors to prove up their claims in a specified time and share *pro rata* or be barred from future recovery In re Klein, 1 How 277, 278, 279, note, Silverman's Case, 2 Abb (U. S) 243.

23. Congress may by these laws relieve against debts contracted prior to the enactment of the law It is not limited by the provision which forbids states to enact laws impairing the obligation of contracts In re Klein, 1 How. 277, note, Carpenter v Commonwealth, 17 How. 463.

24 Insolvent laws distinguished.—Insolvent laws operate at the instance of an imprisoned debtor, bankrupt laws at the instance of a creditor. But a bankrupt law which authorizes a commission to issue at the instance of a debtor is not unconstitutional Sturges v Crowninshield, 4 Wheat. 123-194.

25. Bankruptcy — Uniformity.— Congress is not authorized merely to pass laws the operation of which shall be uniform, but to establish uniform laws on the subject throughout the United States This uniformity is incompatible with state legislation on that part of the subject to which the acts of congress may extend. Id

26. Action by congress optional —The power granted to congress over the subject may be exercised or declined, as the wisdom of that body shall decide. Id

5. To coin money, regulate the value thereof and of foreign coin, and fix the standard of weights and measures.

1. While there is no express grant of power to congress to declare what shall be a legal tender, the right to do so has been uniformly exercised and unquestioned since the organization of the government. This universal recognition is tantamount to a direct constitutional declaration, and the power can now be considered as settled Martin v. Hunter's Lessee, 1 Wheat. 304, Cohens v Virginia, 6 Wheat. 421; Briscoe v. Bank of K., 11 Pet. 257, Anderson v Dunn, 6 Wheat. 204.

2. Making bills of credit a legal tender is inconsistent with the spirit of the constitution and is in violation thereof. Hepburn v. Griswold, 8 Wall. 603.

3. The act of congress of February 25, 1862, making United States treasury notes legal tender, is, when applied to contracts in existence prior thereto, unconstitutional. Willard v Tayloe, 8 Wall. 557, Broderick v Magraw, 8 Wall 639.

4 The decisions in above cases are overruled and the acts of congress making United States treasury notes legal tender are held to be valid when applied to antecedent as well as to subsequent contracts Legal Tender Cases, 12 Wall 547, Dooley v. Smith, 13 Wall. 604, Norwich, etc. R. R. v. Johnson, 15 Wall 195

5. Congress has power by suitable legislation to restrain the circulation as money of any notes not issued by its own authority Veazie Bank v. Fenno, 8 Wall. 533.

6 A marshal who receives bank-notes in satisfaction of an execution must account to the plaintiff in execution in gold and silver; the constitution of the United States recognizing only gold and silver as legal tender. Gwin v Breedlove, 2 How 29, Griffin v Thompson, id. 244.

6 To provide for the punishment of counterfeiting the securities and current coin of the United States.

1. Congress may provide by law for punishing persons who bring into the country counterfeit money from foreign countries. United States v. Marigold, 9 How. 560, Fox v Ohio, 5 How. 435, United States v. Gardner, 10 Pet. 618.

2 Congress has power to provide by law for the punishment of the offense of counterfeiting notes of foreign banks or for having in possession a plate from which such counterfeit notes may be printed. United States v. Arjona, 120 U. S 479.

3. "The language of the constitution, by its proper signification, is limited to the facts or to the faculty in congress of coining and stamping the standard of value upon what the government creates or shall adopt, and of punishing the offense of producing a false representation of what may have been so created or adopted The imposture of passing a false coin creates, produces or alters nothing; it leaves the legal coin as it was — affects its intrinsic value in no wise whatsoever " Fox v. Ohio, 5 How 410–433 Compare with United States v. Marigold, 9 How 560

4. Under the power here given, as well as under the power to regulate commerce, congress has authority to enact laws providing for the punishment of persons who shall bring into the United States, with intent to pass the same, any false, forged or counterfeited coin, and also to punish persons for passing, altering, publishing or selling any such false, forged or counterfeited coin. United States v Marigold, 9 How 560

5 **Power of states.**— These clauses do not prevent a state from passing laws to punish the offense of circulating counterfeit coin of the United States The offenses of counterfeiting and of circulating counterfeit coin are essentially different in their character The former is an offense against the government which may affect individuals, the latter is a private wrong by which the government may be remotely, if at all, affected. Fox v. The State of Ohio, 5 How 410.

7. To establish post-offices and post-roads.

1. Under the act of congress ceding to Pennsylvania that part of the Cumberland road which is within the state, and the acts of Pennsylvania accepting the surrender, a carriage whenever it is carrying the mail must be held to be laden with the property of the United States within the true meaning of the compact, and consequently exempted from payment of tolls This does not apply to other property or to persons (other than such as are in the service of the United States) who may be traveling in it. Nor can the United States claim exemption for more carriages than are necessary to carry the mails. Searight v Stokes, 3 How 151 As germane to this same question see also Neil, Moore & Co. v. State of Ohio, 3 How. 720.

2. **Implied powers under.**— In carrying out this principal power, the mail operations of the United States are regulated. Postmasters are appointed and their duties prescribed, mail contracts are made and carriers of mail regulated, provisions are made for the punishment of depredations on the mail. These powers are incident to the main power. Sturtevants v City of Alton, 3 McLean, 393, United States v Rhodes, 1 Abb. (U S) 50.

3. The powers conferred are not confined to the instrumentalities in use when the constitution was adopted. Congress in its exercise should keep pace with the progress of the country and adapt the regulations to the development of time and circumstances The powers were conferred for the government of business for all time and under all circumstances. To this end congress may establish telegraph lines, and in this is not limited in its operation to such military and post-roads as are on the public domain. Pensacola Tel Co v Western Union Tel Co., 96 U S 1

4 The powers conferred embrace the regulation of the entire postal system of the country, and under it congress may designate what shall be carried in the mail and what shall be excluded. The law excluding circulars

of lotteries, gift concerts, etc, is a valid exercise of the power conferred Ex parte Jackson, 96 U S 727; In re Jackson, 14 Blatchf. 245

5 The power vested in congress by this clause, viz. "To establish post-offices and post-roads," embraces the regulation of the entire postal system of the country Under this provision congress has the authority to designate by law what shall be carried in the mail and what excluded This power, however, cannot be so enforced as to interfere with the liberty of the press Liberty of circulating is essential to that freedom When, therefore, any printed matter is by law excluded from the mail, its transportation by other means cannot be forbidden by congress. Ex parte Jackson, 96 U S 727

6. This embraces the regulations of the entire postal service of the country and confers on congress the power to declare what may, and what shall not, be transported in the mails But when any matter is excluded from the mails congress cannot forbid its transportation by other methods, so as to interfere with the freedom of the press This freedom includes the right to circulate Id

8 To promote the progress of science and useful arts, by securing for limited times to authors and inventors the exclusive right to their respective writings and discoveries.

1. Congress may provide for copyright on photographs as works of art and science, so far as they are representations of original intellectual conceptions of the author Lithographic Co. v Sarony, 111 U S 53

2 Whether congress can by act decide that a particular individual is the author or inventor of a certain writing or invention, so as to preclude judicial inquiry into such fact, *quere* Evans v Eaton, 3 Wheat 454

3. Congress has power to grant the extension of a patent which has been renewed under the act of 1836 Bloomer v Stolley, 5 McLean, 158 It is for congress to say when, for what length of time and under what circumstances a patent shall be granted It has power to pass an act which operates retrospectively to give a patent for an invention already in use Blanchard v. Sprague, 2 Story, 164, S C 3 Sumn 535

9 To constitute tribunals inferior to the Supreme Court

1. The courts of a territory are in a sense inferior tribunals created by congress In legislating for the territory congress exercises the combined powers of general and state governments American & Ocean Ins Co v Three Hundred and Fifty-six Bales of Cotton, 1 Pet. 511, 545

2 The power to establish federal courts, and to endow them with jurisdiction to determine controversies between certain parties, affords no pretext for abrogating any established law of property, or for removing any obligation of her citizens to submit to the rule of the local sovereign. Suydam v Williamson, 24 How. 433

10 To define and punish felonies committed on the high seas, and offenses against the law of nations

1 The courts of the United States have jurisdiction under this clause and the act of congress of April 30, 1790 chapter 36, if the offense of murder or

robbery be committed (1) on board a foreign vessel by a citizen of the United States, (2) on board a vessel of the United States by a foreigner, (3) by a citizen or foreigner on board a piratical vessel It makes no difference in such a case and under the same act whether the offense was committed on board a vessel or in the sea, as by throwing the deceased overboard and drowning him, or by shooting him when in the sea, although not thrown overboard United States v. Holmes, 5 Wheat. 412

2 No jurisdiction can be conferred by congress over felonies committed by the master of a vessel on a seaman while in the navigable rivers of a foreign nation The words "high seas" do not include such waters United States v Wiltberger, 5 Wheat. 76.

3 The act of March 3, 1819, chapter 76, section 5, referring to the law of nations for the definition of the crime of piracy, is a constitutional exercise of the power of congress to define and punish that crime Robbery or forcible depredation upon the sea, *animo furandi*, is piracy by the law of nations and by act of congress. United States v Smith, 5 Wheat. 153; Same v Pirates, id. 184.

4. Congress has power to provide by law for the punishment of the offense of counterfeiting notes of foreign banks, or for having in possession a plate from which such counterfeit notes may be printed It is an offense against the law of nations as defined in this section. United States v Arjona, 120 U S. 479

5. **Offense against all nations.**— Piracy is an offense against *all* nations — against the United States as well as others, and the constitution of the United States authorizes congress to define and punish piracy A person charged with piracy by a foreign nation will not be arrested and held by the courts of the United States, or by them be given up to the authorities of such foreign government. Case of Jose Ferreira dos Santos, 2 Brock. C C 493.

6. **Robbery on high seas,** or forcible depredation, *animo furandi*, is piracy by the law of nations and act of congress United States v Smith, 5 Wheat. 153, Same v Palmer, 3 Wheat. 610, Same v Jones, 3 Wash C. C. 209

7. **What are high seas.**— The sea embraces all tide-waters on the coast of our country and the bays thereof When once any boat or vessel is out of the limits of our ports or harbors, *extra fauces terræ, vel portus*, it is in legal as well as nautical sense at sea The Schooner Harriett, 1 Story, 259, United States v Grush, 5 Mason, 290.

11 To declare war, grant letters of marque and reprisal, and make rules concerning captures on land and water

1. **Power of congress — Suppression of rebellion.**— Congress has the same power to make war, levy taxes, etc, to suppress rebellion, as it has in case of war with foreign powers Tyler v. Defrees, 11 Wall 331

2. **Civil war exists, when** — A civil war is never proclaimed *eo nomine* Its actual existence is a fact in our history, of which courts are bound to take notice It may be said to exist whenever the regular course of justice is interrupted by armed resistance, so great as to overcome the local au-

4

thorities, or when the local authorities refuse to suppress it. Prize Cases, 2 Black, 667.

3 **Power exclusive in congress.**— The whole powers of war are vested in the congress, and it is to the acts of that body alone that resort can be had to guide inquiry as to whether or not at any time war was in existence The congress may authorize general hostilities, in which case the general laws of war would apply to questions affected thereby; or it may authorize partial hostilities, in which case the laws of war, so far as they apply to such situations will be in force. The doctrine of Bas v. Tingy, 4 Dall. 37, recognized. Talbot v. Seeman, 1 Cranch, 28.

4 Congress alone has the power to declare a foreign or national war. It cannot declare war against a state, or any number of states, by virtue of any clause in the constitution The constitution confers on the president the whole executive power He is bound to take care that the laws be faithfully executed. If war is tendered either by a foreign invasion or domestic insurrection the president is bound to accept the challenge without waiting for any special legislative authority. Prize Cases, 2 Black, 667.

5. **What constitutes war** — Every contention by force between two nations, in external matters under the authority of their respective governments, is not only war, but public war If it be declared in form, it is called solemn and of the perfect kind, because one whole nation is at war with another whole nation, and all the members of the nation declaring war are authorized to commit hostilities against all the members of the other, in every place and under every circumstance . . . But hostilities may subsist between two nations more confined in their nature and extent, being limited to places, persons and things, and be more properly termed imperfect war, because not solemn, and because those who are authorized to commit hostilities act under special authority and can go no further than to the extent of their commission Still, however, it is a public war, because it is an external condition of force between some of the members of the two nations, authorized by legitimate powers Bas v Tingy, 4 Dall 37

6. **Incidental power to acquire territory** —The constitution confers on government the power to declare war and make treaties Consequently the government possesses the power to acquire territory either by conquest or treaty. Insurance Companies v Three Hundred and Fifty-six Bales of Cotton, 1 Pet 511

7. **Legal tender.**—Making notes a legal tender is not an appropriate means for the execution of the power to declare or carry on war Hepburn v. Griswold, 8 Wall. 603.

8 **Condemnation of property.**— All private property used or intended to be used in aid of an insurrection, with the knowledge or consent of the owner, is by this clause made the lawful subject of capture and judicial condemnation, not to punish the owner for crime but to weaken the insurrection. The provisions of the act of August 6, 1861 (ch. 60, 12 Stat at Large, 319), was enacted in compliance with this provision, and a sale of real estate thereunder conveys the fee-simple to the purchaser The act of July 17, 1862 (ch 95, Stat. at Large 589), referred to and distinguished from that under consideration The object of the act of 1862 was to punish traitors by confiscating their property Kirk v Lynd, 106 U. S. 315, citing Miller v United States, 11 Wall. 308

9. Declaration of war, what is.—War may be declared as well by acts of hostility as by formal declaration Bas v. Tingy, "The Eliza," 4 Dall 37, Talbot v. Seeman, 1 Cranch, 1

10. Effect of—Does not confiscate enemy's property—A mere declaration of war does not confiscate enemy's property or debts due to an enemy, nor does it so vest the property or debts in the government as to support judicial proceedings for confiscation of the property or debts, without the expression of the will of the government through its proper department to that effect. Under the constitution this power is in congress alone Britton v Butler, 9 Blatch. 456.

11 Public war, what is.—Every contention by force, between two nations, in external matters under authority of their respective governments, is a public war Bas v. Tingy, "The Eliza," 4 Dall. 37, Talbot v. Seeman, 1 Cranch, 1.

12. Solemn war—If it be declared in form it is called solemn war, and is of the perfect kind; because one whole nation is at war with another whole nation. Bas v. Tingy, "The Eliza," 4 Dall. 37–40

13. Rights of members of nation declaring war.—All the members of the nation declaring war are authorized to commit hostilities against all the members of the other, in every place and under every circumstance. In this they act under general authority, and all the rights and consequences of war attach to their condition Id.

14. After a declaration of war an American citizen cannot lawfully send a vessel to the enemy's country to bring away his property. The Rapid, 1 Gall. 295; same case affirmed, 8 Cranch, 155; Scholefield v Eichelberger, 7 Pet 586, Jecker v Montgomery, 18 How 110, The William Bagaley 5 Wall. 377–405, Hanger v. Abbott, 6 Wall 535, Coppell v Hall, 7 Wall 557

15. Implied powers.—The power to declare war carries with it as an incident thereto and inseparable therefrom the right to prosecute the war by all the means known to and recognized by civilized nations This includes the power to confiscate the property of enemies, to provide funds for defraying expenses, and to this end to make and issue legal tender notes. Legal Tender Cases, 12 Wall. 457, Miller v. United States, 11 Wall 305 Tyler v Defrees, 11 Wall, 331; Prize Cases, 2 Black, 635, Alexander s Cotton, 2 Wall. 404, Dooley v. Smith, 13 Wall 604, Railroad Co v Johnson, 15 Wall. 195

16. It carries with it as an incident the right to acquire territory by conquest. But congress has no power to declare war for the purpose of such acquisition. Sere v Pitot, 6 Cranch, 332, American Ins Co v Canter, 1 Peters, 542, Fleming v Page, 9 How 603· Scott v. Sandford, 19 How. 611

17. It carries with it inherently the power to guard against the immediate renewal of the conflict, and to remedy the evils which have arisen from its rise and progress. The act of congress of June 11, 1864, entitled "An act in relation to limitation of actions in certain cases," when construed to be retrospective in its operation falls within this category Stewart v Kahn, 11 Wall. 493–507.

18 Under this clause congress has the power to provide by law for carrying on war. This necessarily extends to all legislation essential to the prosecution of war with vigor and success, except such as interferes with the command of the forces and the conduct of campaigns Ex parte Milligan. 4 Wall 2-139

19. The government of the United States has power to permit limited commercial intercourse with an enemy in times of war, and to impose such conditions thereon as it sees fit. This power is an incident to the power to declare war and to carry it on successfully. Hamilton v Dillin, 21 Wall 73 *Quere*, whether the president alone can exercise this power. Id.

20 The act of congress of July 13 1861, which interdicted commercial intercourse with states in insurrection but authorized the president to permit or license it in his discretion, for such time and by such persons as he might think conducive of the public interest, held valid Id

21 **Rules for captures on land and water** — This power extends to captures within the territorial limits of the United States as well as to captures outside such limits Brown v United States, 8 Cranch, 153.

22 These rights of capture can only be enforced after congress has acted upon the subject and by law authorized them Id.

23. The United States, in the enforcement of their constitutional rights against armed insurrection, have all the powers of a sovereign, and of the most favored belligerent, and as such may, by capture, enforce their authority. What shall be the subject of capture as against the enemy is always within the control of every belligerent. It is the duty of the military forces in the field to seize and hold that which is apparently so subject, leaving the owner to make good his claim as against the capture in the appropriate tribunal. In that regard they occupy the same position on land as on water Lamar v Browne 92 U. S 187

24. **Effect of capture.**— Unless restrained by governmental regulations, the capture of movable property on land changes the ownership of it without adjudication. Id.

25. **Liability of captors.**— Neither the captors, nor the special agent of the treasury to whom they delivered the captured property, is liable to the owner thereof in an action for anything done within the scope of their powers. Id.

12. To raise and support armies; but no appropriation of money to that use shall be for a longer term than two years.

1. The control of the general government over this subject is plenary and exclusive It determines without question from any state authority how the armies shall be raised, whether by voluntary enlistment or forced draft, the age at which the soldier shall be received, and the period of service, the compensation to be allowed, and to what service assigned It provides for the rules that shall govern the army, defines military offenses, and prescribes punishment, and no state can be permitted to interfere with the discharge of these national duties by *habeas corpus* or other proceedings. Tarble s Case, 13 Wall. 397

2. The constitution has delegated to congress the power to "raise and support armies" and "to provide and maintain a navy," and, independent of the express clause in the constitution, this must include the power "to make all laws which shall be necessary and proper for carrying into effect the foregoing powers." United States v. Bainbridge, 1 Mason, 71-79.

3. Congress has constitutional power to enlist minors in the navy or army without the consent of their parents. United States v. Bainbridge, 1 Mason, 71; Ex parte Wm. Brown, 5 Cranch, C. C. 554.

4. State courts cannot examine into the validity of enlistments in the army of the United States, or discharge persons so enlisted by *habeas corpus* for any cause. The jurisdiction of the United States courts in such cases is exclusive. Tarble's Case, 13 Wall. 397; Matter of Farrand, 1 Abb. (U. S.) 146.

13. To provide and maintain a navy.

1. This authorizes the government to buy or build any number of steam or other ships of war, to man, arm and otherwise prepare them for war, and to dispatch them to any accessible part of the globe. Under this power the naval academy has been established. United States v. Rhodes, 1 Abb. (U. S.) 28-50; Same v. Bevans, 3 Wheat. 336-390.

2. The jurisdiction of this government cannot extend to a foreign war vessel whose government is at peace with the United States, while the same is within our ports and demeans itself in a friendly manner. The Exchange v. McFaddon, 7 Cranch, 116.

14. To make rules for the government and regulation of the land and naval forces.

Congress has power to provide for the trial and punishment of military and naval offenders, in the manner practiced by civilized nations. Dynes v. Hoover, 20 How. 65; In re Bogart, 2 Sawyer, 396.

15. To provide for calling forth the militia to execute the laws of the Union, suppress insurrections, and repel invasions.

1. The law of congress passed in pursuance of this section confers on the president the power, and makes it his duty in case of insurrection, invasion, etc., to call out the militia. *Held*, that the authority to decide upon the exigencies contemplated in the constitution and the act of congress rests exclusively with the president. His decision is conclusive on all other persons. Martin v. Mott, 12 Wheat. 19.

2. The power here conferred is to be exercised when some sudden emergency renders it necessary in order to preserve the public peace and to insure to the states a republican form of government. Luther v. Borden, 7 How. 8.

3. An act of Pennsylvania providing that the officers and privates of the militia of that state neglecting or refusing to serve when called into service by the president shall be liable to penalties prescribed by congress, and providing for trial of such delinquents by state court-martial, etc., is not repugnant to the constitution of the United States. Houston v. Moore, 5 Wheat. 1.

4. Congress may delegate the power to call out the militia to the president, and may make his decision as to the necessity of such call final. Luther v. Borden, 7 How. 18; Martin v. Mott, 12 Wheat. 19.

5. In calling out the militia the president's orders may be given to the chief executive of the state or to any militia officer he may think proper Houston v Moore, 5 Wheat 1-15

6. Neglect or refusal to obey the order is an offense against the laws of the United States and subjects the offender to trial and punishment by court-martial. Id.

16. To provide for organizing, arming, and disciplining the militia, and for governing such part of them as may be employed in the service of the United States, reserving to the States respectively the appointment of the officers, and the authority of training the militia according to the discipline prescribed by Congress

The power of congress over the militia is limited but by two reservations in favor of the states, viz. the right of officering and that of training them When distributed by the states, under their own officers, the general government have the right if they choose to exercise it, of designating both the officers and privates who shall serve, and to call them forth and punish them for not coming. Houston v Moore, 5 Wheat. 1-86

17. To exercise exclusive legislation, in all cases whatsoever, over such district (not exceeding ten miles square) as may, by cession of particular States and the acceptance of Congress, become the seat of government of the United States, and to exercise like authority over all places purchased, by the consent of the Legislature of the State, in which the same shall be, for the erection of forts, magazines, arsenals, dock-yards, and other needful buildings, and

1. **Over District of Columbia.**—Within the District of Columbia, and the other places purchased and used for the purposes named in the constitution the national and municipal powers of government of every description are united in the government of the Union. And these are the only cases in which all the powers of government are so united. Pollard v Hagan, 3 How 212

2 Under this clause and the power conferred in it to exercise exclusive legislation over the seat of government, congress may constitute the District of Columbia a body corporate for municipal purposes, but can only authorize it to exercise municipal power. Stoutenburgh v Hennick, 129 U S 141

3 Congress may authorize Washington city to assess the expense of repairing streets against the adjacent proprietors of lots Willard v. Presbury, 14 Wall 676

4. **Government lands within a state.**—Where lands within a state are acquired by the government without the consent of the state, the possession of the United States, unless political jurisdiction be ceded to them in

some other way, is simply that of an ordinary proprietor The property in that case, unless used as a means to carry out the purposes of the government, is subject to the legislative authority of the state equally with the property of private persons. If, however, forts, arsenals or other public buildings are erected upon them for the uses of the general government, such buildings with their appurtenances as instrumentalities for the execution of its powers will be free from any such interference and jurisdiction of the state as would destroy or impair their effective use for the purposes designed Fort Leavenworth R. R. Co v Lowe, 114 U. S 525; C., R. I & P. R y v McGlinn, id. 542, United States v Crosby, 7 Cranch, 115, United States v. Cornell, 2 Mason, 66, United States v Davis, 5 Mason, 364, United States v Travers, 2 Wheel. C. C 490 Lands thus held, however, are not subject to taxation by the state or municipalities. United States v Weise, 2 Wall. Jr 72

5 **Ratification by state necessary for full control.**—The general government can only acquire control and jurisdiction over places within the limits of a state by ratification on part of the state Simple purchase is not sufficient. United States v Tierney, 1 Bond, 571, United States v Cornell, 2 Mason, 66, Ex parte Hebard, 4 Dill. 384.

6. **There must be acceptance by congress**—Neither will the assent of the state legislature be sufficient without the acceptance of the grant or cession by the general government. People v Lent, 2 Wheel. C C. 548

7. **In what character congress legislates.**—This power, like all others which are specified, is conferred on congress as the legislature of the Union In no other character can it be exercised In legislating for the district they necessarily preserve the character of the legislature of the Union It is in that character alone that the constitution confers on them this power of exclusive legislation Cohens v Virginia, 6 Wheat. 264-424.

8. **Exclusive legislation carries with it exclusive jurisdiction.** And where a murder is committed within a fort, so purchased with the consent of a state legislature, the circuit court has jurisdiction over the offense notwithstanding a reservation by the state, in the act of cession, that the state should execute within the fort the civil and criminal processes issuing under state authority. United States v Cornell, 2 Mason, 91

9 **Power of taxation in**—The power here conferred includes the power to tax, and congress may levy a direct tax on the District of Columbia in proportion to the census directed to be taken by the constitution Loughborough v Blake, 5 Wheat 317.

10. **Process of courts.**—Courts established under this authority for the District of Columbia may issue all processes necessary to carry their orders into effect, and such process may be executed within any state. United States v Williams, 4 Cranch, C. C. 393.

11. **Local municipal assessments.**—Under the power here conferred congress may authorize the municipal authorities of the city of Washington to provide for paving the streets of the city and to levy assessments on abutting property to pay for the same. Willard v Presbury, 14 Wall 676

12. **Citizenship.**—An inhabitant of the District of Columbia who there has his permanent abode is not a citizen of a state. Cissel v McDonald, 16 Blatch. 150.

13. **District of Columbia.**—The sovereign power of the District of Columbia is lodged in the government of the United States and not in the corporation of the District. But the District municipal corporation is a person and subject to suit as any other municipality, and cannot claim exemption from the provisions of a statute of limitations on the ground that it is a department of the government of the United States. Metropolitan R. R. Co v District of Columbia, 132 U. S. 1.

18 To make all laws which shall be necessary and proper for carrying into execution the foregoing powers, and all other powers vested by this Constitution in the government of the United States, or in any department or officer thereof

1. **Implied powers.**—There is not in the constitution a grant of powers which does not draw after it others not expressed or vital to their exercise, not substantive and independent, but auxiliary and subordinate The sole end and aim of our institutions is the safety and happiness of the citizen The science of government is the science of experiment, but the maxim which necessarily overrides all others is that the public functionaries must be at liberty to exercise the powers the people have intrusted to them That "the safety of the people is the supreme law" not only comports with, but is indispensable to, the exercise of those powers without which that safety cannot be guarded. Public necessity is the test of incidental powers where the end to be attained is legitimate and within the scope of the constitution Anderson v. Dunn, 6 Wheat 204, McCulloch v Maryland, 4 Wheat. 421

2. This clause of the constitution is a direct authority for the exercise of all necessary, incidental or implied powers to enable congress to carry out the great provisions of the constitution It is not a limitation upon its powers but an enlargement thereof. McCulloch v. Maryland, 4 Wheat. 316, Anderson v. Dunn, 6 Wheat. 204, United States v Fisher, 2 Cranch, 358, United States v Marigold, 9 How. 560.

3. **Implied powers not excluded.**—There is no phrase in the constitution, such as was in the articles of confederation, excluding incidental or implied powers Even the tenth amendment, which was framed for the purpose of quieting the excessive jealousies which had been excited, omits the word "expressly," as found in the articles of confederation, and declares only that the powers "not delegated to the United States nor prohibited to the states are reserved to the states or to the people," thus leaving the question whether the particular power which may become the subject of dispute has been delegated to the one government or prohibited to the other, to depend on a fair construction of the whole instrument. McCulloch v. Maryland, 4 Wheat. 316, 406

4. **Implied powers requisite to the nature of the constitution**—The nature of the constitution requires that only its great outlines should be marked, its important objects designated, and the minor ingredients which compose those objects be deduced from the nature of the objects themselves. It does not profess to enumerate the means by which the powers it confers may be executed McCulloch v Maryland, 4 Wheat 316, 407, 408; Prigg v Commonwealth, 16 Pet. 539, United States v. Cruikshank, 92 U. S. 542,

S. C. 1 Woods, 308; Legal Tender Cases, 12 Wall. 534, Thompson v Pac. R. R. Co, 9 Wall. 579, United States v Maurice, 2 Brock. 96, United States v Fisher, 2 Cranch, 358, Weston v. Charleston, 2 Pet. 449, Bank of Commerce v Tax Commissioners, 2 Black, 620, United States v Coombs, 12 Pet. 78, United States v Marigold, 9 How 560, United States v Fairchilds, 1 Abb (U S) 74, United States v Marks, 2 Abb (U S) 511, Osborn v Bank, 9 Wheat. 738

5 The following, from Story's Commentaries on Constitution, referred to and approved "Whenever a question arises concerning the constitutionality of a particular power, the first question is whether the power is expressed in the constitution If it be, the question is decided. If it be not expressed the next question is, is it properly an incident to an expressed power and necessary to its execution? If it be, then it may be exercised by congress. If not, congress cannot exercise it." United States v Harris, 106 U. S 629

6. "The sound construction of this clause must allow to the national legislature that discretion, with respect to the means by which the powers it confers are to be carried into execution, which will enable that body to perform the high duties assigned to it, in the manner most beneficial to the people. Let the end be legitimate, let it be within the scope of the constitution, and all the means which are appropriate, which are plainly adapted to that end, which are not prohibited, but consistent with the letter and spirit of the constitution, are constitutional." Marshall, C. J, in McCulloch v Maryland, 4 Wheat. 316–421

7 The act of congress approved June 11, 1864, respecting the statute of limitations where parties were beyond reach of service during the civil war, refers and applies as well to cases in the state courts as to cases in the federal courts and said act is constitutional and valid Stewart v Kahn, 11 Wall 493.

8 **Supremacy of general government.**— The United States is a government with authority extending over the whole territory of the Union, acting upon the states, and upon the people of the states While it is limited in the *number* of its powers, so far as its sovereignty extends it is supreme No state government can exclude it from the exercise of any authority conferred upon it by the constitution, obstruct its authorized officers against its will, or withhold from it, for a moment, the cognizance of any subject which the constitution has committed to it. Tennessee v. Davis, 100 U S 257

9. **Rights and immunities protected.**— A right or an immunity, whether created by the constitution or only guaranteed by it, even without any express delegation of power, may be protected by congress Prigg v. Comm., 16 Pet. 539, United States v. Reese, 92 U S 214 Rights and immunities created by or dependent upon the constitution of the United States can be protected by congress, and the form and manner of the protection may be such as congress in the legitimate exercise of its discretion shall provide. Strauder v. West Virginia, 100 U S. 303.

10. **Legislative construction and retrospective laws distinguished.**— In our system of government the law-making power is vested in congress and the power to construe the laws in the course of their admin-

istration between citizens in the courts. Congress cannot, under cover of giving a construction to an existing or an expired statute, invade private rights, with which it could not interfere by a new or affirmative statute. But where it can exercise a power by passing a new statute, which may be retroactive in its effect, the form of words which it uses to put this power in operation cannot be material if the purpose is clear and within the power. Held in this case that the act in question was a retrospective law designed to recast the internal revenue laws, and therefore not an invasion of the domain of the courts. Stockdale v Insurance Cos, 20 Wall. 323.

11. Necessity — Determination of belongs to congress.— Within the legitimate scope of this clause, congress is permitted to determine for itself what is necessary and what is proper Section 6, act of August 15, 1876, prohibiting officers or employees of the United States from requesting, giving to, receiving, etc., money for political purposes, is for the purpose of promoting efficiency and integrity in public service, and is constitutional. Ex parte Curtis, 106 U. S 371.

12. Homesteads on public lands — Protection of by law.— Section 5508, Revised Statutes, is constitutional, and may be invoked to protect settlers upon public lands from violence at the hands of persons conspiring to defeat them in the rights of homesteads or pre-emptions, or other valid public land claims. United States v. Waddell, 112 U S 76.

13. Indemnity under treaty — Congress may name commission to hear and determine — Where a treaty designated no tribunal in which persons claiming indemnity under it could be heard, it remained for congress to refer the claim to commissioners to be appointed to try them, such being the established practice of the government in such cases. Where a territorial district court was designated it acted, by its judge, as a commissioner and not as a court. His judgment was a mere award, subject to review by the secretary of the treasury, but not by the supreme court. United States v Ferreira, 13 How 40

14. Sinking fund.— That part of the act of May 7, 1878, which establishes in the treasury of the United States a sinking fund to pay the indebtedness of the Union Pacific Railroad Company is not unconstitutional. U. P. R. R Co. v United States, 99 U. S. 700.

15. Embezzlement of pension money by guardian — Punishment of — Congress may define and provide punishment for the crime of embezzlement by a guardian of his ward's United States pension money Such an act is warranted by the constitution. United States v. Hall, 98 U S 343.

16. Acts of war — Statute exempting from liability valid — The acts of March 3, 1863, and May 1, 1866, providing that for acts done by order of the president of the United States or secretary of war, or any military officer, the United States courts shall have jurisdiction, and that such orders shall be a defense in all courts for all concerned, and providing for removal from state to federal courts, is constitutional. Nashville v. Cooper, 6 Wall 247

17 Processes from federal court.— Congress possesses the uncontrolled power to legislate in respect to both the form and effect of executions and other final process to be issued by the federal courts. Riggs v. Johnson Co, 6 Wall. 166.

18. **Eminent domain.**—The right of eminent domain exists in the federal government, and may be exercised within the states, so far as is necessary to the enjoyment of the powers conferred upon it by the constitution And under acts of congress, March 2, 1872, and June 10, 1872, the United States, by exercise of this power, could acquire lands in Cincinnati for custom-house Kohl v. United States, 91 U S. 367.

19 The right of eminent domain exists in the general government, and may be exercised within the states when necessary to the execution of the powers conferred upon the government by the constitution Id.

20 Congress had power to "incorporate the subscribers to the Bank of the United States" McCulloch v. Maryland, 4 Wheat. 316

21. This confers on congress power to make laws for carrying into effect and execution all the judgments which the judicial department have authority to pronounce. Wayman v. Southard, 10 Wheat. at page 22

Section IX.

POWERS DENIED TO THE UNITED STATES

1. The migration or importation of such persons as any of the States now existing shall think proper to admit shall not be prohibited by the Congress prior to the year one thousand eight hundred and eight; but a tax or duty may be imposed on such importation, not exceeding ten dollars for each person

1. The several clauses of this section are intended as limitations upon the powers of congress, and in this respect affect the states in the regulation of their domestic affairs. Munn v Illinois, 94 U S. 113 Morgan v Louisiana, 118 U S 455, Johnson v Chicago Elevator Co, 119 id 388, Butler v Hopper, 1 Wash C C. 499, Barron v. Mayor of Baltimore, 7 Pet. 243

2. The provision of the first clause of this section relates solely to the suppression of the slave trade, and the words "such persons as any of the states now existing shall think proper to admit" refer to African slaves brought to the United States in the prosecution of the slave trade. Scott v. Sandford, 19 How. 393

3. There has never been any doubt that the first clause of this section refers only to persons of the African race The words "migration" and "importation" refer to the different conditions of the race as regards freedom and slavery When the free black man came he migrated when the slave came he was imported Free human beings are not articles of import. People v. Compagnie Gen. Transatlantique, 107 U S 59-62

2 The privilege of the writ of *habeas corpus* shall not be suspended unless when, in case of rebellion or invasion, the public safety may require it.

1. The suspension of the privilege of the writ of *habeas corpus* does not suspend the writ itself Ex parte Milligan, 4 Wall. 2.

2 In a state where the federal authority was always unopposed and its courts always open to hear and determine criminal accusations and redress grievances, no usage of war could sanction a military trial, for any offense whatever, of a citizen in civil life, in nowise connected with the military service Congress could grant no such power. Id.

3 Martial law cannot arise from a threatened invasion. The necessity must be actual and present; the invasion real, and such as effectually closes the courts and disposes of the civil administration. Id

4 The appellate jurisdiction of the supreme court exercisable by *habeas corpus* extends to a case of imprisonment under conviction and sentence by an inferior court of the United States, under and by virtue of an unconstitutional act of congress, whether there is jurisdiction to review such judgment by writ of error or not. Ex parte Siebold, 100 U S 371

5. No law of congress prescribes the cases in which the writ of *habeas corpus* shall issue, nor the power of the court over the party brought up by it The term used in the constitution is well understood, and the judiciary act authorizes all courts of the United States and the judges thereof to issue the writ "for the purpose of inquiring into the causes of commitment." Ex parte Watkins, 3 Pet. 193.

6. A state judge has no jurisdiction to issue a writ of *habeas corpus*, or to continue proceeding thereunder if issued, for the discharge of a person held under authority of the United States by an officer of that government, civil or military If the application discloses that the person is so held the state court should refuse the writ. If the application does not disclose such fact, but it is so disclosed by the return, then the court should abate the writ and proceed no farther. The courts of the United States alone possess the jurisdiction to determine upon the legality of any imprisonment or detention of a person held by the federal officers under claim of right. Tarble's Case, 13 Wall. 397, United States v. Booth, 21 How. 506.

7. The power of congress to pass a statute under which a prisoner is held in custody may be inquired into under a writ of *habeas corpus* as affecting the jurisdiction of the court. And if their want of power appears on the face of the record, whether in the indictment or elsewhere, the court which has authority to issue the writ is bound to release In re Coy, 127 U S 731

8. A party is entitled to a *habeas corpus* not merely where the court is without jurisdiction of the cause, but where there is no constitutional authority for the conviction of the accused. Ex parte Hans Nielsen. 131 U. S. 176, Ex parte Lange 18 Wall. 163, Ex parte Siebold, 100 U S 371

9. The writ of *habeas corpus* here referred to is the writ *ad subjiciendum* The Santissima Trinidad, 7 Wheat. 305, Martin v Mott, 12 Wheat 29, Luther v. Borden, 7 How 1, Fleming v Page, 9 How. 615.

10 The phrase *habeas corpus* is a generic term and includes every species of that writ. But when used singly, when we say "the writ of *habeas corpus*," without addition, we most generally mean the great writ *ad subjiciendum*. Ex parte Bollman, 4 Cranch, 75–95

11. Under the constitution congress is the only power which can authorize the suspension of the writ. The president can neither suspend it nor au-

thorize a military officer to do so. Ex parte John Merryman, Taney, 246, Ex parte Bollman, 4 Cranch, 75.

12. The power being given to congress to suspend the writ in cases of rebellion or invasion, that body is the exclusive judge as to whether such facts exist. Martin v. Mott, 12 Wheat. 19, Ex parte John Merryman, Taney, 246, Ex parte Milligan 4 Wall 114.

13. Congress need not suspend the writ by a direct enactment, but may confer the power to do so upon the president, when in his judgment the public safety requires it. Ex parte Milligan, 4 Wall 114; McCall v. McDowell, 1 Abb. (U. S) 212

14. And this power of congress extends so as to enable them to pass laws indemnifying or protecting officers against actions for arrest previously made. McCall v. McDowell, 1 Abb (U S.) 212

15. The orders of the war department issued August 8, 1862 — one being "to prevent the evasion of military duty, and for the suppression of disloyal practices," and the other "authorizing the arrest of persons discouraging enlistments" — were in violation of this clause, as well as of articles 4 and 5 of amendments Ex parte Field, 5 Blatch 63.

3. No bill of attainder, or *ex post facto* law, shall be passed.

While no language can be more general than is this clause, "yet the demonstration is complete that it applies solely to the government of the United States This provision, therefore, however comprehensive its language, contains no restriction on state legislation.' Chief Justice Marshall, in Barron v. Mayor, etc of Baltimore, 7 Pet. at 248 For definitions of "bill of attainder" and "*ex post facto* law," and the rules governing these clauses, see annotation to art. I, sec. X.

4 No capitation or other direct tax shall be laid, unless in proportion to the census or enumeration herein before directed to be taken.

5. No tax or duty shall be laid on articles exported from any State

1. A capitation tax is a direct tax. Hylton v. United States, 3 Dall. 171

2. Direct taxes are limited to taxes on land and appurtenances, and to capitation or poll tax; a tax on bank circulation is not a direct tax, and may be laid without apportionment as may all species of tax except direct tax. Springer v. United States, 102 U. S 586, Veazie Bank v. Fenno, 8 Wall 533

3. Direct taxes, within the meaning of this clause, are only capitation taxes as expressed therein, and taxes on real estate. Springer v United States, 102 U. S. 586

4 A tax on bank circulation is not a direct tax. Veazie Bank v. Fenno, 8 Wall 533. Nor is a tax on the business of insurance a direct tax Pac. Ins Co. v Soule, 7 Wall. 433. Nor a tax on carriages. Hylton v. United States, 3 Dall. 171.

5. A tax on an alien arriving from a foreign country is not a direct tax. Head-Money Cases, 18 Fed. Rep. 135

6. In our system of government there are limitations upon the sovereign right of taxation. There is a concurrent right of legislation in the states and the United States, except as both are restrained by the constitution of the United States. Both are restrained by express prohibition in the constitution, and the states by such as are reciprocally implied, when the exercise of the right by a state conflicts with the perfect execution of the sovereign power delegated to the United States. That occurs when taxation by a state acts upon the instruments and emoluments and persons which the United States may use and employ as necessary means to execute their sovereign power. Dobbins v. Commissioners of Erie Co., 16 Pet. 435.

7. **Duty on exports.**—The acts of congress of July 20, 1868, and June 6, 1872, so far as they relate to snuff and tobacco intended for exportation, do not impose a tax or duty on exports within the meaning of this clause. The stamp thereby required is simply a means for the prevention of fraud by separating and identifying the tobacco intended for exportation, thus relieving it from the taxation to which other tobacco was subjected. Pace v. Burgess, 92 U. S. 372.

8. The stamp act of July 20, 1868, requiring an exportation stamp to be placed on tobacco before it is removed from the manufactory, is not an export duty within the meaning of this clause of the constitution, and is valid. Pace v. Burgess, 92 U. S. 372; Turpin v. Burgess, 117 U. S. 504.

6. No preference shall be given by any regulation of commerce or revenue to the ports of one State over those of another, nor shall vessels bound to or from one State be obliged to enter, clear, or pay duties in another.

1. An act of congress which declared a bridge over the Ohio river at Wheeling, W. Va., to be a lawful structure, "anything in the laws of the United States to the contrary notwithstanding," does not conflict with the clause that prohibits congress from giving a preference, by any regulation of commerce or revenue, to the ports of one state over those of another. Pennsylvania v. Wheeling Bridge Co., 18 How. 421.

2. A law of Pennsylvania, providing that vessels neglecting or refusing to take a pilot shall forfeit a certain sum for the use of the society for the relief of distressed and decayed pilots, is not in conflict with the above. It neither gives preference to one port over another, nor does it require vessels bound to or from one state to enter, clear, or pay duties in another. Cooley v. Board of Wardens, 12 How. 299.

3. This clause is a limitation upon the powers of congress in the regulation of commerce, and intended to prevent what otherwise might have resulted in discrimination in favor of one state against others. Passenger Cases, 7 How. 283.

7. No money shall be drawn from the treasury but in consequence of appropriations made by law; and a regular state-

ment and account of the receipts and expenditures of all public money shall be published from time to time

8 No title of nobility shall be granted by the United States; and no person holding any office of profit or trust under them shall, without the consent of Congress, accept of any present, emolument, office, or title of any kind whatever. from any king, prince, or foreign state.

SECTION X.

POWERS DENIED TO THE STATES.

1. No State shall enter into any treaty, alliance, or confederation, grant letters of marque and reprisal, coin money, emit bills of credit, make anything but gold and silver coin a tender in payment of debts, pass any bill of attainder, *ex post facto* law, or law impairing the obligation of contracts; or grant any title of nobility.

1. **Powers of congress not denied.**—From this prohibition to the states it cannot be inferred that congress is denied either of those powers. Juilliard v. Greenman, 110 U S 421

2. **Bills of credit—Definition of.**—The definition of the term "bills of credit," as used in the constitution, if not impracticable, will be found a work of no small difficulty. In a mercantile sense they comprehend a great variety of evidences of debt, which circulate in a commercial country now usually known as bank-bills or bank-notes. Used in the sense in which bills of credit were issued by the colonies and states prior to the adoption of the constitution, it is a paper issued by a sovereign power containing a pledge of its faith, and designed to circulate as money. Briscoe v Bank of Kentucky, 11 Pet. 256.

3 In its enlarged sense, the term "bills of credit" may comprehend any instrument issued by a state engaging to pay money at a future date, thus including a certificate given for money borrowed. But the language of the constitution, and the mischief designed to be prevented, limit this meaning. *Held, also,* not to include contracts by which the state binds itself to pay money at a future day for services actually rendered, or for money borrowed. "To emit bills of credit" means to issue paper intended to circulate through the community for its ordinary purposes as money, which paper is redeemable at a future day. Craig v. Missouri, 4 Pet. 410 Revised and confirmed, Byrne v Missouri, 8 Pet. 40.

4. **Bills of credit, what are.**—To constitute a bill of credit within the constitution, it must be issued by a state, and designed to circulate as money It must be a paper which circulates on the credit of the state, and so received and used in the ordinary business of life. The individual or committee who issue it must have power to bind the state; they must act as

agents, and, of course, not incur any personal responsibility, nor impart as individuals any credit to the paper. These are leading characteristics of a bill of credit which a state is forbidden to issue. When these are not present, the paper cannot properly be denominated bills of credit issued by a state. Briscoe v Bank of Kentucky, 11 Pet. 257.

5 The state cannot, however, by any indirect means, emit bills which will have the effect of "bills of credit," although the requisites here mentioned may not be directly expressed in the act creating them Courts will look beyond the words to the effect of the statute. Id.

6. **Banking corporations** — The bills of a banking corporation which has corporate property are not bills of credit within the meaning of the constitution. This is true, even though the state which charters the bank is the only stockholder, and pledges its faith for the ultimate redemption of the bills Darrington v. Bank of Alabama 13 How. 12 Followed in Veazie Bank v. Fenno, 8 Wall. 553, and cited in Curran v Arkansas, 15 How. 309–318

7. A state cannot emit bills of credit, or, in other words, it cannot issue that description of paper to answer the purpose of money, which was denominated, before the adoption of the constitution, "bills of credit," *but* a state may grant *acts of incorporation* for the attainment of those objects which are essential to the interests of society; this power is incident to sovereignty, and there is no limitation on its exercise by the states in the federal constitution Briscoe v Bank of Kentucky, 11 Pet. 258, Woodruff v. Trapnall, 10 How. 190–205.

8. **Legal tender** — An act of the legislature of a state making the notes of such bank legal tender would be unconstitutional, but such act would not affect the constitutionality of the law establishing the bank. Briscoe v Bank of Kentucky, 11 Pet. 256.

9. **State bonds — Coupons receivable for taxes.** — The act of the legislature of Virginia by which it was provided that the coupons detached from the bonds of the state should be receivable in payment of taxes due to the state did not make such coupons "bills of credit" within the meaning of this clause, notwithstanding the said coupons did pass from hand to hand by delivery They were not intended to circulate as money for the ordinary purposes of society. Poindexter v. Greenhow, 114 U. S 270

10. The act of the Missouri legislature, approved June 21, 1821, entitled "An act for the establishment of loan offices," *held*, to authorize the emission of bills of credit and therefore void. Craig v Missouri, 4 Pet. 410.

11 **State bank notes receivable for state debts** — The state of Arkansas chartered a bank, the whole of the capital of which belonged to the state, and the president and directors of which were appointed by the general assembly A provision of the charter was "that the bills and notes of said institution shall be received in all payments of debts due to the state of Arkansas" *Held*, that the notes issued by the bank were not bills of credit. Citing and approving Briscoe v The Bank of the Commonwealth of Kentucky, 11 Pet 256 Woodruff v. Trapnall, 10 How 190–205 See, also, Curran v. Arkansas, 15 How 304

12. The constitution does not forbid states or counties from borrowing money and giving proper securities therefor, and such securities are not

bills of credit within the meaning of this provision. McCoy v. Washington Co, 3 Wall Jr 381

13. State credit must be substituted for money.— A certificate or bill cannot be considered a "bill of credit" within the meaning of the constitution of the United States to which the receiver must not give credit to the promise of the state. A bill which the state agrees to accept in payment of public dues when presented is not a bill of credit A bill which the state promises to redeem from the holder at a future day is There must be a substitution of the credit of the state for money This may be considered an essential ingredient. When this is wanting, whatever other designation may be given to the thing — whether it be called paper, money or a state bill — it cannot be called a bill of credit Craig v. Missouri, 4 Pet. 410

14 Need not be legal tender.— The emission of bills of credit and the enactment of tender laws are distinct operations which may be separately performed Both are forbidden Bills of credit when issued by a state are void, though not made legal tender. Id.

15. Confederate treasury notes — The securities known as "Confederate treasury notes," issued by the self-styled Confederate States during the civil war, were not bills of credit To come within the prohibition of this clause the bills must be issued by a state Bailey v. Milner, 1 Abb. (U S) 261.

16 Bill of attainder.— A bill of attainder is a legislative act which inflicts punishment without trial Cummings v Missouri, 4 Wall. 277, Pierce v Carskadon, 16 Wall. 234

17 Bill of attainder, as here used, is a generic term, and embraces both bills of attainder and bills of pains and penalties A provision in the constitution of Missouri, granting exemption from suit for acts done by military authority, is neither attainder nor a bill of pains and penalties. Nor does it impair the obligation of contracts, and is not an *ex post facto* law Drehman v Stifle, 8 Wall 595.

18. Sense in which term is used.— If the term "bill of attainder" had a well known meaning in that language and in that system of jurisprudence, which language and jurisprudence the people of the United States brought with them as colonists and established here, the conclusion is irresistible that the convention which framed the constitution had reference to that meaning when it employed the term, and that the people accepted it in that sense when they ratified the constitution United States v Harris, 1 Abb (U. S) 110–114, 115, Calder v Bull, 3 Dall 390; Watson v Mercer, 8 Pet. 110, Carpenter v. Pennsylvania, 17 How. 463; United States v Wilson 7 Pet. 150

19. Definition — A bill of attainder is a legislative act which inflicts punishment without a judicial trial If the punishment be less than death the act is termed a bill of pains and penalties. Within the meaning of the constitution bills of attainder include bills of pains and penalties. They are generally directed against individuals by name, but may be directed against a class, and may inflict punishment absolutely or conditionally Cummings v Missouri, 4 Wall 277, Ex parte Garland 4 Wall 333 Pierce v Carskadon, 16 Wall 234, In re Angelo De Giacoma, 12 Blatch 401

20. A clause in a state constitution which requires priests and clergymen to take and subscribe an oath, in order to be permitted to act in their profession, that they have not committed certain designated acts, some of which were at the time penal offenses and some of which acts were at the time innocent in themselves, constitutes a bill of attainder. Cummings v. Missouri, 4 Wall 277.

21. *Semble* as to oaths required by act of congress as a condition precedent to the right of an attorney at law to practice his profession in the courts of the United States. Ex parte Garland, 4 Wall. 333.

22. **Object of provision.** — This prohibition was intended to secure the rights of the citizen against deprivation for past conduct by legislative enactment under any form, however disguised. Cummings v. Missouri, 4 Wall 277.

23. Section 4 of the constitution of Missouri, adopted in 1865, which provides that no person shall be liable for acts done by him under and by virtue of military authority vested in him by the United States during the war of the rebellion, and permitting him to plead the section in defense to pending or subsequent actions based on such acts, is not a bill of attainder. Drehman v. Stifle, 8 Wall 595; Clark v. Dick, 1 Dill. 8.

24. **Ex post facto law — Definition.** — An *ex post facto* law, within the meaning of the constitution of the United States, is one which makes an act done before the passing of the law, which was innocent when done, criminal; or makes a crime greater than it was before committed; or inflicts a greater punishment than the law annexed to the crime when committed; or alters the legal rules of evidence, and receives less or different testimony than the law required at the commission of the offense in order to convict the offender. Such laws extend to criminal and not to civil cases. Calder v. Bull, 3 Dall 386.

25. An *ex post facto* law is one which renders an act punishable in a manner in which it was not punishable when it was committed. Fletcher v. Peck, 6 Cranch, 87–137.

26. *Ex post facto* laws are such only as impose or affect penalties or forfeitures; they do not include retrospective laws having any other operation. Locke v. New Orleans, 4 Wall. 172.

27. An *ex post facto* law is one which imposes a punishment for an act which was not punishable at the time it was committed, or imposes additional punishment to that then prescribed. Disqualification from office or from pursuit of an avocation is a punishment. The test oath of Missouri which prohibited any one from preaching, teaching, etc., and from holding office because of their participation in or sympathy with the rebellion, was both *attainder* and *ex post facto* law. Cummings v. Missouri, 4 Wall 277.

28. The act of congress prescribing the test oath that deponent had never voluntarily borne arms against the United States, etc., as a qualification of admission to the United States supreme court, falls within the inhibition on congress to pass bills of attainder. Ex parte Garland, 4 Wall. 333.

29. **Does not apply to civil proceedings.** — This provision does not apply to civil proceedings, and the supreme court of the United States cannot declare a law unconstitutional from the mere fact that it divests ante-

cedent vested rights of property. The constitution does not prohibit states from passing retrospective laws, but only *ex post facto* laws Watson v. Mercer, 8 Pet. 88.

30. A law which levied a succession tax, and was so worded as to be, and was so held to be, retrospective and to apply to estates in course of administration at the time the law was enacted, is not an *ex post facto* law. The term *ex post facto* relates to criminal laws only Carpenter v Pennsylvania, 17 How 456

31 *Ex post facto* laws relate to penal and criminal proceedings which impose punishments or forfeitures, and not to civil proceedings which affect private rights retrospectively Watson v Mercer, 8 Pet. 110

32 The act of Colorado, April 9, 1889, and which went into effect July 19, 1889, is as applied to the crime of murder committed on May 13, 1889, an *ex post facto* law and void The term *ex post facto* law as found in the constitution applies to criminal law alone. And any law which was passed after the commission of the offense for which the party is being tried is an *ex post facto* law when it inflicts a greater punishment than the law annexed to the crime at the time it was committed Citing Calder v Bull, 3 Dall. 386, Kring v. Missouri, 107 U S 221, Fletcher v. Peck, 6 Cranch, 87 Or which alters the situation of the accused to his disadvantage, and no one can be criminally punished in this country except according to a law prescribed for his government by the sovereign authority before the imputed offense was committed, or by some law passed afterwards by which the punishment is not increased A provision for solitary confinement pending the interval betwixt conviction and execution, and a provision keeping secret from the condemned the day of his execution, are increased punishments Ex parte Medley, 134 U. S. 160.

33. In 1875 K committed murder in the state of Missouri, and to an indictment for murder in the first degree pleaded (and his plea was accepted) guilty of murder in the second degree, and he was sentenced upon said plea to imprisonment for a term of years Upon appeal the conviction was reversed By the law in force when the crime was committed a conviction of murder in the second degree was an acquittal of the higher offense and precluded a conviction upon a new trial of any higher offense than was sustained by the former conviction. That law was changed so that a judgment for murder in the first degree could be rendered upon a new trial after conviction for the lesser crime *Held*, that as applied to K.'s case it was an *ex post facto law*. Kring v. Missouri, 107 U. S 221

34. A state statute which by its terms may be retrospective as well as prospective in its operation, and which provides as punishment for crime a penalty in excess of the penalty theretofore in force for a like crime, is, when applied to a crime committed prior to its enactment, *ex post facto* and void. But this does not render it void and inoperative when applied to crimes committed after it went into effect. Jaehne v New York, 128 U S 189.

35. What is not an ex post facto law.— A law of Connecticut setting aside a decree of a court of probate disproving a will of real estate, and granting a new hearing with liberty to appeal, after the right of appeal was barred by the statute, there previously being no law whereby a new hearing could be obtained, is not an *ex post facto* law. A statute of a state changing the place of trial to another county in the district, or to a different district from that in which the offense was committed or the indictment found is not an *ex post facto* law though enacted subsequent to the finding of the indictment Gut v Minnesota 9 Wall 35

36. **Retrospective laws** which do not impair the obligation of contracts or partake of the character of *ex post facto* laws are not forbidden by the constitution Milne v Huber, 3 McLean, 217, Bloomer v Stolley, 5 McLean, 165, Johnston v Vandyke, 6 McLean, 441

37. **Interpretation of language.**—It will be given the meaning which was applied to it by the language and jurisprudence which the colonists brought with them from the mother country and established here United States v Harris, 1 Abb (U. S.) 110, 114, 115, Calder v Bull, 3 Dall 390, Watson v Mercer, 8 Pet 110, Carpenter v. Pennsylvania, 17 How 463, United States v Wilson, 7 Pet. 160.

38. **"Or law impairing the obligation of contracts"—Definition.** The obligation of a contract in the constitutional sense is the means provided by law by which it can be enforced, by which the parties can be obliged to perform it. Whatever legislation lessens the efficacy of these means impairs the obligation If it tend to postpone or retard the enforcement, the obligation is to that extent weakened and the law is in conflict with the constitutional inhibition Louisiana v New Orleans, 102 U S 203

39 **Test, diminished value**—One of the tests that a contract has been impaired is that its value has, by legislation, been diminished It is not by the constitution to be impaired at all. This is not a question of degree or manner or cause but of encroaching in any respect on its obligation, dispensing with any part of its force Bank v. Sharp, 6 How. 327.

40 **Remedy, when change of does not impair contract.**—The distinction between the obligation of a contract and the remedy exists in the nature of things Without impairing the obligation, the remedy may be modified as the wisdom of the state may direct. Sturges v. Crowninshield, 4 Wheat. 122-201

41 A law, passed after the contract is made which merely changes the remedy would be liable to no constitutional objection A state may regulate at pleasure the mode of proceedings in its courts in relation to past contracts as well as future It may shorten the period of limitation It may make reasonable exemption laws And although a remedy may be more tardy and difficult, yet it will not follow that the law is unconstitutional. Whatever belongs merely to the remedy may be altered according to the will of the state, provided the alteration does not impair the obligation of the contract. But if that effect is produced, it is immaterial whether it is done by acting on the remedy or directly on the contract itself In either case it is prohibited by the constitution Bronson v Kinzie, 1 How 311

42 The legislative power as to change of remedy may be exercised when it does not affect injuriously rights which have been secured by the contract. Therefore, held, that a statute prescribing a mode of service upon a railroad company different from that provided for in its charter is not void because of impairment of the obligation of the contract. Cairo & Fulton R R. Co v Hecht, 95 U S 168. In delivering the opinion in the above cause Waite, C J, says "The regulations of the forms of administering justice

by the courts is an incident of sovereignty The surrender of this power is never to be presumed "

43 **As to imprisonment for debt** — Confinement of the debtor may be a punishment for not performing his contract, or may be allowed as a means of inducing him to perform it. But the state may refuse to inflict this punishment, or withhold the means and leave the contract in force Imprisonment is no part of the contract, and to release the prisoner does not impair its obligation. Sturges v. Crowninshield, 4 Wheat. 200, 201, Mason v Haile, 12 Wheat. 370

44. A law abolishing imprisonment for debt does not impair the obligation of contracts theretofore existing Sturges v. Crowninshield, 4 Wheat. 122 and Beers v Haughton, 9 Pet 359, cited and followed, and the general doctrine of the court declared to be, ' in modes of proceeding and of forms to enforce the contract the legislature has the control, and may enlarge, limit or alter them, provided it does not deny a remedy, or so embarrass it with conditions or restrictions as seriously to impair the value of the right." Penniman's Case, 103 U S 714.

45 **Discharge by bankruptcy.** — A bankrupt law of a state which discharges both the person of the debtor and his future acquisitions of property is not a "law impairing the obligation of contracts," so far as respects debts contracted after the passage of such law. But a certificate of discharge under such law cannot be pleaded against a citizen of another state, in the courts of the United States, or of any other state than that where the discharge was obtained Ogden v Saunders, 12 Wheat 213, adhered to. Boyle v Zacharie, 6 Pet. 348, S C. 6 Pet. 635, Cook v. Moffat, 5 How. 295. See Denny v Bennett, 128 U S 489

46. A statute providing that a previous contract of indebtment may be extinguished by process and discharge in bankruptcy would be void. Von Hoffman v Quincy, 4 Wall 535

47. **Form of remedy.**— It is competent for the state to change the form of the remedy, or to modify it otherwise as it may see fit, provided no substantial right secured by the contract is thereby impaired Von Hoffman v. Quincy, 4 Wall 535

48. **Mode of proceeding.**— "The rule seems to be that in modes of proceeding and of forms to enforce the contract the legislature has the control and may enlarge, limit or alter them, *provided* that it does not deny a remedy, or so embarrass it with restrictions and conditions as seriously to impair the value of the right" Mr Justice Hunt in Tennessee v Sneed, 96 U S 69

49. **Limitation on tax sales.**— The statute of Iowa limiting the time in which suits shall be brought for the recovery of lands sold for taxes does not conflict with this section Barrett v. Holmes, 102 U S. 651

50. **Limitations, statutes of** — A statute of limitation, when applied to existing contracts, is not invalid, provided a reasonable time is given, after the law takes effect, in which to commence an action, before the bar of the statute takes effect. Terry v. Anderson, 95 U S 628

51. A statute limiting the time in which suits shall be brought on causes of action in force prior to its passage to a shorter period than when the contract was made does not impair the obligation of the contracts on which

such causes of action are based, *provided* a reasonable time, taking all things into consideration. be given by the new law before such actions are barred. Koshkonong v Burton, 104 U. S 668.

52. Where a reasonable time must elapse after the enactment of a statute of limitations before the bar is complete, effect must be given to the statute even as against debts in existence at the time of its enactment. Lewis v. Broadwell, 3 McLean, 569; Jackson v. Lamphire, 3 Pet 280, Hawkins v Bainey, 5 Pet 457, Christmas v Russell, 5 Wall 290, Sohn v Waterson, 17 Wall 596, Samples v Bank, 1 Woods, 523, Terry v Anderson, 95 U S. 634.

53 A state statute of limitations which reduces materially the time of bringing actions, though passed after the contract on which suit is brought was made, is not void if a reasonable time is left for the enforcement of the contract by suit before the statute bars that right. Mitchell v Clark, 110 U. S 633.

54. Where municipal bonds had been issued to be negotiated in a foreign market, a statute of limitations passed thereafter, limiting the time to one year, *held* to be unreasonable and to impair the obligation of the contract. Pereles v Watertown, 6 Biss 79

55 The only ground on which a change of remedy existing when a contract was made is permissible without impairment of the contract is that a new and adequate and efficacious remedy be substituted for that which is superseded Louisiana v. Pilsbury, 105 U. S 278.

56. A constitution and statute of a state which provides that tacit mortgages shall cease to have effect against third persons unless recorded within a stated reasonable time does not impair the obligation of the contract in such cases even as to minors, it is in the nature of a statute of limitations. Vance v Vance, 108 U. S 514.

57 **Statute of frauds.**— A statute of frauds embracing a pre-existing contract, not before required to be in writing, would be void Von Hoffman v Quincy, 4 Wall 535–552

58 **Exemption law.**— A law exempting a reasonable amount of necessary property from sale on execution is valid even as to pre-existing debts, but where the amount so exempted is unreasonably large and the contract is thereby impaired, the law will be held invalid Mr. Justice Hunt in Edwards v. Kearzey, 96 U. S 610 Mr Justice Clifford, same case, p 608. The court, in this last case, adopts the language of Mr Chief Justice Taney in Bronson v Kinzie, 1 How, 311, where he says a state may, if it thinks proper, direct that the necessary implements of agriculture, or the tools of the mechanic, or articles of necessity in household furniture, shall, like wearing apparel, not be liable to execution on judgments. Regulations of this description have always been considered in every civilized community as properly belonging to the remedy, to be executed or not by every sovereignty according to its own views of policy and humanity

59 **Stay, appraisement and redemption laws** —A law, passed subsequent to the execution of a mortgage, which delays the extinguishment of the equitable estate of the mortgagor for twelve months after sale, and which prevents any sale unless the property brings two-thirds its appraised value, is invalid Bronson v Kinzie, 1 How 311, McCracken v. Hayward, 2 How 608

60 A statute of Alabama authorizing a redemption of mortgaged property in two years after the sale, under a decree by *bona fide* creditors of the mortgagor, is void as to sales made under a mortgage executed prior to the date of the enactment. Howard v. Bugbee, 24 How 461.

61. **Rules of evidence** — A provision in the constitution of Georgia of 1868, which so changes the rule of evidence as to throw the burden of proof on the plaintiff to show that bills sued on have never been used in aid of the rebellion, if only the defendant swears he has reason to believe they were so used, is unconstitutional Marsh v Burroughs, 1 Woods, 463

62. A statute of Georgia which required that in all suits brought for debts the court should be satisfied that the contract of indebtedness had been legally returned for taxes, and the taxes paid thereon before the plaintiff could recover on it, *held* unconstitutional as applied to debts contracted prior to the enactment. Lathrop v Brown, 1 Woods, 474

63. **Right of repeal** — Where a state has by law given its creditors a right to sue it in its own courts, such law does not form a contract between the state and them, and such right may at any time be withdrawn by repeal without the violation of any contract obligation If judgment were rendered against the state while such law were in force, the power of the court over the state would then end The courts are in such case powerless to enforce their judgment, and everything after the judgment would depend on the will of the state M & C R. R. Co. v. Tennessee, 101 U. S 337, S & N Ala. R R. v Alabama, 101 U. S. 832.

64. **Name in which suit must be brought.** — A statute of Alabama directing that notes executed to a bank shall be sued in the name of the cashier of such bank affects only the remedy, and as to notes executed before its enactment such law is valid Crawford v. Branch Bank of Mobile, 7 How. 279

65. **Form of action — Same.** — The legislature may change the forms of action or method of enforcing a contract at its discretion, provided it leaves a competent tribunal and adequate remedy for enforcing it. Id See, also, Railroad Co v Hecht, 95 U S. 168, Tennessee v Sneed, 96 U. S 69, Memphis v United States, 97 U. S 293.

66. **Same.** — A statutory liability is as much subject to remedial legislation as is a liability created by private contract, provided the remedy does not enter into and form a part of the obligation created by such statute Terry v. Anderson, 95 U S 628

67 **Usury laws — Act repealing** — A law repealing a usury law which is made retrospective so as to apply to debts already contracted at usurious rates of interest does not, as to such debts, impair the obligation of contract. Ewell v. Daggs, 108 U S 144

68. **Judgment, enforcement of — Inquiry whether sounding in contract or tort** — Where it was sought to enforce a judgment against a municipal corporation by *mandamus* to the taxing officers thereof, and where the constitution adopted subsequent to the rendition of such judgment limited the authority of the municipality in the levy of such tax it was proper for the court to inquire whether such judgment had been rendered in an action sounding in contract or tort. If the former, the constitutional limitation would be invalid as applied to the payment of such judg-

ment, if the latter, no such invalidity could be imputed to the provision. Louisiana v. Police Jury, 111 U. S. 716.

69. A judgment rendered in an action of tort is not a contract within the meaning of this clause of the constitution, and is not protected thereby. And the provision of the constitution of West Virginia that the property of a citizen shall not be sold on a judgment for an act done during the late civil war does not violate the obligation of a contract, where such judgment was founded on a tort committed as an act of public war. Freeland v. Williams, 131 U. S. 405.

70. **Recording acts.**—It is within the undoubted power of state legislatures to pass a recording act by which the elder grantee shall be postponed to a younger if the prior deed is not recorded within a limited time, and the power is the same whether the deed is dated before or after the recording act. It does not in any manner impair the obligation of a contract. Jackson v. Lamphire, 3 Pet. 280.

71. **Same.**—The same rule applies to limitation laws. Id.

72. **Remedy; laws affecting held void.**—A state law passed subsequently to the execution of a mortgage, which declares that the equitable estate of the mortgagor shall not be extinguished for twelve months after a sale under a decree in chancery, and which prevents *any* sale unless two-thirds of the amount of the valuation of the property as fixed by appraisers be bid therefor, impairs the obligation of a contract made prior to the passage of the statute, and as to such contracts is void. Bronson v. Kinzie, 1 How. 311; McCracken v. Hayward, 2 How. 608; Gantly's Lessee v. Ewing, 3 How. 707.

73. A state law authorizing redemption from sale under foreclosure of mortgage is, as applied to mortgages in existence prior to its passage, void under this section of the constitution. Affirming Bronson v. Kinzie, 1 How. 316. Howard v. Bugbee, 24 How. 461.

74. The clause in the constitution of Georgia of 1868 denying to the courts jurisdiction to try and give judgment for a debt where the consideration was the price of a slave or of the hire thereof is, as to such debts as were contracted prior to its adoption, founded on such consideration, void under this section. A contract can no more be impaired by a constitutional provision than by a legislative one. White v. Hart, 13 Wall. 646. See, also, Osborn v. Nicholson, 13 Wall. 654.

75. A statute of North Carolina provided that in civil actions "for debts contracted during the late war, in which the nature of the obligation is not set forth, nor the value of the property for which such debt was created is stated, it shall be admissible for either party to show on the trial, by affidavit or otherwise, what was the consideration of the contract, and that the jury, in making up their verdict, shall take into consideration and determine the value of said contract in present currency in the particular locality in which it is to be performed, and render their verdict accordingly." This statute, as construed by the court, allowed the jury to place their own judgment upon the value of the contract in suit, and did not require them to take the value stipulated by the parties. As thus construed, said law impairs the obligation of contracts, and is void. Wilmington & W. R. R. v. King, 91 U. S. 3.

76 "The remedy subsisting in a state when and where a contract is made and is to be performed is a part of its obligation, and any subsequent law of the state which so affects that remedy as substantially to impair and lessen the value of the contract is forbidden by the constitution, and is therefore void" Mr Justice Swayne in Edwards v Kearzey, 96 U S 607

77. "When an appropriate remedy exists for the enforcement of the contract at the time it was made the state legislature cannot deprive the party of such remedy, nor can the legislature append to the right such restrictions or conditions as to render its exercise ineffectual or unavailing" Mr Justice Clifford in same case, p 608

78. When a contract is made with a municipality upon the faith that taxes will be levied to provide for the payment thereof, a subsequent law limiting the power of taxation in such municipality so as to deprive the creditor of a speedy and efficacious remedy is void, as impairing the obligation of the contract. Louisiana v Police Jury, 111 U S 716

79 A statute of limitations which, when applied to an existing contract, takes away a right of action, by reason of the shortening of the period of limitation, is unconstitutional as applied to such existing contract Chapman v. Douglas Co Com'rs, 107 U S 348.

80. It is the settled law of the nation that the "remedy subsisting in a state when and where a contract is made and is to be performed is a part of the obligation of the contract, and a subsequent law of the state which substantially affects the remedy so as to lessen the value of the contract impairs its obligation" Therefore, held, that the law of Missouri (act of March 23, 1868) which authorized and directed the county court from time to time to levy and cause to be collected, *in the same manner as county taxes*, a special tax, to pay the interest and principal of bonds issued under the laws of the state by municipal corporations in aid of railroads, was a part of the contract inhering in such bonds, and a subsequent law which provided a different method of assessment and collection, less expeditious, is void as applied to such bonds Seibert v Lewis, 122 U. S 284.

81. "In the case of contracts between individuals, the remedies for their enforcement or breach, in existence at the time they were entered into, are a part of the agreement itself and constitute a substantial part of its obligation and that obligation cannot be impaired by subsequent legislation Thus not only the covenants and conditions of the contract are preserved but also the substance of the original remedies for its enforcement. It is different with contracts between individuals and a state In respect to these, by virtue of the eleventh amendment to the constitution, there being no remedy by suit against the state, the contract is substantially without sanction, except that which arises out of the honor and good faith of the state itself, and these are not subject to coercion Although the state may, at the inception of the contract, have consented, as one of its conditions, to subject itself to suit, it may subsequently withdraw that consent and resume its original immunity, without any violation of the obligation of its contract in the constitutional sense" Mr Justice Matthews in In re Ayers, 123 U. S 505 citing Beers v Arkansas, 20 How 527; Railroad Co v Tennessee, 101 U S 337. To the same effect see language of Mr Justice Matthews in separate opinion in Antoni v Greenhow, 107 U S 769, 788.

82. A statute of a state which provides that whenever the property of a debtor is seized by attachment or execution against him, he may make an assignment of all his property and estate not exempt by law, for the equal benefit of all his creditors who shall file releases of their debts and claims, and that his property shall be equitably distributed among such creditors, is as applied to debts existing prior to its enactment repugnant to this clause of the constitution, but is valid as to all contracts of indebtedness accruing after the enactment of the statute Denny v. Bennett, 128 U S 489. For further authority on change of remedy generally, see Hawthorne v Calef, 2 Wall 10, Walker v. Whitehead, 16 Wall. 314, Greene v Biddle, 8 Wheat. 1, Curran v. Arkansas, 15 How. 319, Freeborn v Smith, 2 Wall. 175, Florentine v Barton, 2 Wall 216

83 **Vested rights** — There is nothing in the constitution which forbids the legislature of a state to exercise judicial functions, nor which forbids it from divesting vested rights, provided its effect be not to impair the obligation of a contract Satterlee v. Matthewson, 2 Pet. 380

84 **Same.**— The strong expressions of the court upon this point in the case of Vanhorne's Lessees v Dorrance, and The Society for the Propagation of the Gospel v. Wheeler, were founded expressly on the constitution of the respective states in which those cases were tried. Id.

85 It is well settled by the decisions of this court that a state law may be retrospective in its character and may divest vested rights, and yet not violate the constitution of the United States, unless it also impairs the obligation of a contract. Taney, C J, in Charles River Bridge v Warren Bridge, 11 Pet. 420, citing Satterlee v Matthewson, 2 Pet. 413

86. **Bridge charter** — And held that the grant of a charter to a corporation to erect a bridge, and to pay to Harvard College £200 a year during a period of seventy years, there being no exclusive privilege given over the waters of the river in respect to bridges, etc., does not constitute a contract on the part of the state not to authorize other and competing bridges or free bridges, to be erected over such stream within the period of seventy years Charles River Bridge v. Warren Bridge, 11 Pet. 420

87 **Rehearing of cases** — The states have a right to direct the rehearing of cases decided in their own courts. The only limit on their power to pass retrospective laws is the restriction on them prohibiting the enactment of *ex post facto* laws, which are retrospective penal laws A law merely divesting antecedent vested rights, where there is no contract impaired, is not inconsistent with the constitution. Baltimore & Susquehanna R. R. Co. v Nesbit, 10 How 395

88 The following cases are cited as sustaining the decision, viz United States v Arredondo, 6 Pet. 736, Jackson v Lamphire, 3 Pet. 289, Beaty v Lessee of Knowler, 4 Pet 165, Providence Bank v Billings, 4 Pet. 514 See, also, constitutional views of Mr Justice Baldwin in Book 9, Lawyers' Co-operative Publishing Co's Edition of United States Supreme Court Reports, current page, 873

89 **Right of municipal corporations to subscribe to railroads.** By the acts incorporating the Ohio & Mississippi Railroad Company, and the amendments thereto, no such rights to county subscriptions to the stock thereof vested in the corporation as excluded the operation of the new con-

stitution of Indiana forbidding such subscriptions, and which new constitution took effect after such subscription had been voted and before it had been actually made and accepted by the corporation By such vote the corporation acquired no such rights to the subscription as would be protected by this clause of the constitution of the United States Aspinwall v Commissioners, 22 How 364

90. A statute of Maryland directed a subscription to be made to the Baltimore & Ohio Railroad Company, with the proviso, "That, if the said company shall not locate the said road in the manner provided for in this act, then and in that case they shall forfeit $1,000,000 to the state of Maryland for the use of Washington county" Thereafter another statute repealed so much of the prior act as required the road to be constructed by the route therein named, and remitted the penalty, directing also that any suit brought to recover the same be dismissed. *Held*, that the provision for the penalty was a measure of state policy which it had a right to change, and neither the commissioners nor the county or any citizen thereof acquired any separate or private interest under it which could be maintained in court. Being a penalty imposed by law, the legislature had the right to remit it. Maryland v B & O R. R Co, 3 How 534

91 Lottery.— A law of Virginia authorized a lottery for the benefit of a turnpike company Thereafter the legislature limited the time to which lotteries might exist in the state *Held*, that the first law was not a contract the obligations of which were impaired by the latter act, that it may be doubted whether it was a contract at all, if it was, the latter act could only be construed as a statute of limitations, which the states have the right to enact. Phalen v Virginia, 8 How 163.

92 Estates of minors — The state legislature has full power to determine the manner in which estates of minors within the state shall be preserved, and to alter and amend such laws at pleasure, and a statute amending the law in relation to security for the preservation of such property impairs no obligation of contract Lobrano v Nelligan, 9 Wall 295

93 Stockholders' corporate liability.— The constitution of the state of Missouri adopted in 1865 provided that stockholders in corporations should be individually liable for the debts of the corporation to an amount equal to their stock at par value and one hundred per cent. in addition thereto. An amendment to this constitution adopted in 1870 limited the personal liability of stockholders to the amount of the par value of their stock. *Held* by the state court, that those who subscribed for stock in a corporation while the constitution of 1865 was in force were and remained liable under said double liability clause of that constitution, and that such liability attached to and followed the stock into whose hands so ever the same passed (McClaren v Franciscus, 43 Mo. 452.) But that those who subscribed for and took original stock in such corporations after the amendment of 1870 repealing the double liability were liable only to the amount of the stock by them so subscribed, and that this limited liability applied to debts of the corporation contracted while the double liability clause of the constitution was in force. On error to the state court, *held*, by the federal supreme court, that the repeal of the constitutional liability of 1865 did not deprive the plaintiff of any of the rights secured to him when the contract was made, that they still exist against all the holders of stock in existence prior to the repeal, together with the remedy for their enforcement, and that the repeal of the double liability as to those who thereafter became stockholders did not impair the obligation of plaintiff's contract Ochiltree v. The Iowa R R Contracting Co, 21 Wall 249

94 **Widening a street** — An act of the legislature of New York passed in 1871, in relation to the widening and straightening of Broadway, in the city of New York, authorizing the supreme court to vacate an order made in 1870, confirming the report of commissioners of estimate and assessment respecting the property taken, from which order no appeal was allowable if error, mistake, irregularity or illegal acts appeared in the proceedings of the commissioners, or the assessments for benefits or the awards for damages, or either of them, had been unfair and unjust or inequitable or oppressive, as respects the city or anybody affected thereby, and to refer the matter back to new commissioners to amend or correct the report or to make a new assessment, is not unconstitutional as impairing the obligation of contracts or depriving a person of a vested right without due process of law. In the proceeding to condemn property for public use there is *nothing in the nature* of a contract between the owner and the state or the corporation which the state, in virtue of her right of eminent domain, authorizes to take the property, all that the constitution of the state or of the United States or justice requires in such cases being that a just compensation shall be made to the owner This being done, the property can be taken without the owner's consent. Garrison v Mayor, etc. of N Y, 21 Wall 196

95 **Judicial functions by legislature** — There is nothing in the constitution of the United States which prohibits the legislature of a state or a territory from exercising judicial functions, nor from passing an act which divests vested rights by law, provided its effect is not to impair the obligation of a contract Contracts are not impaired but confirmed by curative acts Randall v Kreiger, 23 Wall 137, citing Satterlee v Matthewson, 2 Pet. 380, Watson v. Mercer, 8 Pet 110

96. **Taxes in aid of corporation — Repeal of charter.** — Where taxes have been levied for the payment of existing bonds or subsisting debts of a municipal corporation, the charter of the corporation may be repealed by legislative action, and thus put an end to the tax without impairing the obligation of the contract which forms the basis of the indebtedness To this rule there are some exceptions, viz., where the tax provided is so connected with a contract as to form the inducement for its execution, courts will hold the law to be invalid as impairing the obligation of contracts Mr Justice Field in Meriwether v Garrett, 102 U S 472

97. **When cannot be divested — Not when contract exists.** — When a law is in its nature a contract, when absolute rights have vested under that contract, a repeal of the law cannot divest those rights Fletcher v Peck, 6 Cranch, 87

98. **Annulling conveyances.** — A law annulling conveyances is unconstitutional because it impairs the obligation of contracts within the meaning of the constitution Id

99. **Discharging debts** — An act of a state legislature which attempts to discharge a debtor from the payment of a debt is contrary to the consti-

tution of the United States, and is void. Sturges v Crowninshield, 4 Wheat. 122-200

100. And it makes no difference in the application of this principle whether the law was passed before or after the debt was contracted McMillan v McNeill, 4 Wheat 209

101 The constitution of the United States went into operation on the first Wednesday of March, 1789 An existing law of a state operating on vested rights and impairing the obligation of a contract was not affected by this provision of the constitution. Owings v Speed, 5 Wheat 420

102 Corporation — When charter a contract — Dartmouth College — The charter granted by the British crown to trustees of Dartmouth College is a contract and protected by the constitution. And an act of the legislature of New Hampshire altering the charter in a material point without the consent of the corporation is an act impairing the obligation of a contract, and is void Dartmouth College v. Woodward, 4 Wheat. 518

103. Consideration — The grant of corporate powers is for objects such as the government wishes to promote. They are deemed beneficial to the country, and this benefit constitutes the consideration Per Marshall, C J Id

104. Same — Acceptance of charter an implied contract.—"Upon the acceptance" (of the charter) "there is an implied contract on part of the grantees, in consideration of the charter, that they will perform the duties and exercise the authority conferred by it' Per Story, J Id

105 Legislative charter — Change of, impairs contract.— Where a state legislature chartered a bank, and among other powers it was authorized 'to receive money on deposit, pay away the same free of expenses, discount bills of exchange and notes, and to make loans," etc, and in the course of its business it discounted notes and bills, and thereafter by act of the legislature, it was made unlawful "for any bank to transfer by indorsement, or otherwise, any note," etc, *held,* that the last statute impaired the obligation of contracts made under authority of the former, and was invalid Bank v Sharp, and Baldwin v Payne, 6 How. 301

106 Where a state legislature enacted a bank charter, the whole capital of which belonged to the state, the president and directors of which were appointed by the state, and the bills of which were made receivable in all payments of debts due to the state, and thereafter repealed so much of the charter as made the said notes so receivable for state debts, *held* that as to notes issued prior to the said amendment the law was void under this section of the constitution Woodruff v Trapnall, 10 How. 190.

107 Exception — But where the state, as trustee for the benefit of a seminary, sold lands which by the terms of the sale were to be paid in specie, *held,* that as to such debts the bank-notes were not legal tender The fund belonged to the state only as trustee, and was not a debt due the state within the meaning of the charter. Paup v. Drew, 10 How 218, 224, Trigg v Drew, id 224

108 Ferry franchise to a town not a contract.—The grant of a franchise for a ferry made to a town, to continue during the pleasure of the legislature, forms no contract such as is protected by this section of the constitution. This would seem to be so even if the provision respecting the pleasure of the legislature was not incorporated in the grant. East Hartford v Hartford Bridge Co, 10 How 511

109 Judgment by bank — Authority to set off notes thereof against judgment.— A statute of North Carolina, passed after a bank obtained a judgment, which authorizes the defendant to set off against it the circulating notes of the bank procured after judgment, is, as between him and the bank, valid, and does not impair the obligation of the contract sued on or of the judgment Blount v Windley, 95 U S 173 But if the rights of the creditors of the bank, or any others interested in the judgment, were such that they would have a right to have the judgment paid in lawful money, the case would be different. Id.

110 Legislative reservation implied.— Where a charter was granted to a railroad company to construct a road from F. to R, and there was a provision therein that the legislature would not charter another line of road for thirty years, etc, between those places or any portion of the distance, the probable effect of which would be to diminish the number of *passengers* traveling between the one city and the other, *held*, that a charter or permission to another company to construct another road parallel to the first for a part of the distance was no impairment of the contract contained in the first act. There is an implied reservation to permit the construction of another railroad for all purposes save that of carrying *passengers* between the points on the first, and if the latter were to infringe on the rights of the former, there would be a remedy at law R. F & P. R R. Co v. L R. R Co., 13 How 71

111. Executory contract —A law of congress whereby a township of land was reserved to the use of a seminary in the territory of Indiana presupposes the formation of a corporation capable of taking such grant. And as soon as the corporation is *in esse* and the franchise and property become vested in it, it is as much an executed contract as if the corporation had been in existence at the time the reservation was made and the grant had been made directly to it. Trustees of Vincennes University v. Indiana, 14 How 268

112 Same.— The corporation formed under the law to take the grant is not a public corporation which the legislature may modify or abolish at pleasure And the incorporators, by accepting and exercising the corporate powers bestowed, acquired certain rights and made contracts which future legislation could not impair Id

113 Exclusive right to maintain a bridge.— A grant of authority to proprietors to erect a bridge and charge and receive tolls, with a provision in the act that no other bridge shall be built within certain distance thereof for a limited time, is, when accepted and acted on by such proprietors, a contract, and as such protected by the constitution. Bridge Proprietors v Hoboken L & I. Co, 1 Wall 116

114 Exclusive right in bridge charter held not to include railroad bridge — Where, in 1790, proprietors were granted the right to construct a bridge over a stream with the exclusive right to its use for ninety years, and a provision that during that time no other bridge should be erected, etc, *held*, that this will be construed to mean the ordinary traffic bridges in use at the time of the grant, and not to include a railroad bridge erected for that purpose only. Bridge Props. v. Hoboken L. & I Co, 1 Wall 116.

115. Charter of state bank held to include branches — The law of Ohio passed February 24, 1845, entitled "An act to incorporate the State Bank of Ohio and other banking companies," was a contract with all banks organized under such law Dodge v. Woolsey, 18 How. 331 Piqua Bank v. Knoop, 16 How 369, Mechanics Bank v Debolt, 18 How. 380, Mechanics' Bank v. Thomas, 18 How 381.

116 Right of one corporation conferred on another.— Charters to private corporations are contracts, and as such are protected by the constitution So where a legislature gave to one corporation at its creation all the rights and privileges of another previously existing corporation, a restriction in the former charter that no other bridge should be built within two miles is a part of the latter charter, and protected from legislative invasion Chenango Bridge Co. v. Binghamton Bridge Co, 3 Wall 51

117. Agreement in bank charter to accept its notes for taxes a contract.— A state may, in chartering a bank, agree to receive its notes in payment of taxes due the state, and, when accepted by the bank, this becomes a contract, and is within the protection of the constitution. Furman v. Nichol, 8 Wall 44.

118. Lottery charter a contract — Where the constitution of a state grants a privilege to a corporation to establish and maintain a lottery, such privilege is not subject to repeal by the legislature The ruling in Stone v Mississippi, 101 U S. 814, adhered to and distinguished from present case New Orleans v. Houston, 119 U. S 265

119. Exclusive right to streets in water company — The case of New Orleans Water-works v. Rivers, 115 U S 674, is affirmed upon a question of the right of the state to interfere with the contract of said company to furnish water to the city of New Orleans and, in part consideration therefor, to have the exclusive right of the streets and alleys in which to lay its mains. St. Tammany Water-works v New Orleans Water-works, 120 U S 64

120. Rights conferred subsequent to charter not a contract.— Where an act granting privileges to corporations is passed subsequently to the granting of the charter, and forms no part of the charter contract, the state is not restrained by contract obligation from changing such granted privilege South Carolina v Gaillard, 101 U S 433, Christ Church v Philadelphia, 24 How 300; Dale v. Governor, 3 Stewart, 387 Commonwealth v. Bird, 12 Mass 442, Providence Bank v Billings, 4 Pet 514

121 Right to fix rates by railroad not exclusive.— The fact that the charter of a railroad company contains a provision authorizing the board of directors to fix tariffs of fare and freight, and alter and change the same at pleasure, is not a contract on the part of the state that such rates of fare or freight shall not be subject to legislative control The state, notwithstanding such provision in the charter, is left free within the limits of its general authority to declare what shall be deemed reasonable rates. Railroad Commission Cases, 116 U S 307, Stone v Railroad Co, id 347

122 Provision authorizing railroad directors to fix rates not a contract, when.— A grant of power in the charter of a railroad company, to the directors, to make needful rules and regulations touching the rates of tolls and the manner of collecting them, is not a contract upon the part of the state that it will not at any time thereafter interfere to regulate such tolls And a statute otherwise valid which thereafter provides for the regulation of charges for freight and passengers on such railroad does not impair the obligation of any contract. Chicago, M. & St. P. R. R. Co v. State of Minnesota, 134 U. S. 418

123. **Exemption from taxation, when a contract.**—A state, when not prohibited by its constitution, may contract by legislation to release a particular thing, person or corporation from taxation, and a law thereafter taxing such thing, person or corporation in violation of such statutory contract is unconstitutional and void. Jefferson Branch Bank v Skelly, 1 Black, 436

124. A legislative act declaring that certain lands which should be purchased for the Indians should not thereafter be subject to any tax constituted a contract which could not be rescinded by a subsequent legislative act. New Jersey v Wilson, 7 Cranch, 164. The above case is reviewed and adhered to in Given v Wright 117 U S 648.

125 **Exemption in charter a contract.**—Where a provision is contained in the charter of a railroad company exempting it from taxation it is a contract, and an act of the legislature of the state attempting to subject such railroad to taxation is an act impairing the obligation of such contract. Yazoo & Miss. Val. Ry. Co. v. Thomas, 132 U S 174

126 **Exemption of franchise held not to exempt corporate property.**—The charter of a bank is a franchise which is not taxable as such if a price has been paid for it which the legislature accepts But the corporate property is separable from the franchise, and may be taxed unless there is a special agreement to the contrary. The legislature of Maryland, in 1821, continued the charters of several banks to 1845, upon condition that they would make a road and pay a school tax This exempted their franchise, but not their property, from taxation But the law went further and pledged the faith of the state that upon accepting these terms no further tax or burden should be imposed upon them during the continuance of their charters This was a contract relating to something beyond the franchise, and exempted the stock and stockholders as well as the franchise. Gordon v Appeal Tax Court, 3 How 133.

127 **Railroad corporations—Effect of consolidation on exemption.**—Where three railroad corporations existing under charters from three several states consolidated under authority of the three several states and formed one corporation, and the original corporation within one of the states was exempt from taxation, while those existing in the other states were not, *held*, that part of the railroad not exempted from taxation by its charter would still remain subject to taxation in the hands of the consolidated company just as it would have been in the hands of the original company Phila. & Wil R. R Co. v Maryland, 10 How. 376

128. That portion which was exempt before consolidation held to remain exempt under consolidation Id.

129 **Exemption of bank held to exempt stock.**—The law of Ohio passed February 24, 1845, entitled "An act to incorporate the State Bank of Ohio and other banking companies,' and under which the Commercial Branch Bank of Cleveland was incorporated was an agreement with the bank *quasi ex contractu*—and also an agreement separately with the share-

holders *quasi ex contractu* — that neither the banks, as such, nor the stockholders, as such, should be liable to any other tax larger than that which was to be levied under the sixtieth section of that act And the act of April 18, 1852, under which the bank was taxed by a different method, and in a greater sum, impaired the obligation of said contract and is void Dodge v. Woolsey, 18 How 331, Piqua Bank v Knoop, 16 How 369, Mechanics' Bank v. Debolt, 18 How 380, Mechanics' Bank v Thomas, 18 How 384

130. Charitable institution — Implied consideration.— A clause in the charter of a charitable institution that its property shall be exempt from taxation is a contract and protected by the constitution, and no named consideration is necessary to uphold it The objects for which the corporation was created by the legislature are to be beneficial to the community, and this benefit constitutes the consideration Home of the Friendless v Rouse, 8 Wall 430, Washington University v Rouse, 8 Wall 439.

131 Exemption of railroad company held to include rolling stock.— Where a state law in chartering a corporation provided that the *property* of the company should be exempt from taxation, a subsequent statute taxing the franchises and rolling stock impairs the obligation of contract. Railroad Co v Reid, 13 Wall. 264

132 Same — The franchise of a corporation is property, and a clause exempting the property of the company from taxation applies to the franchise as well as to other and tangible property Id

133 State has power to exempt — A state has power to exempt the property of a corporation from taxation, and such provision in the charter becomes a contract protected by the constitution. Humphrey v Pegues, 16 Wall. 244

134 State ordinance held invalid.— The act of December 25, 1852 (Mo Leg), whereby the Missouri Pacific Railroad and branch were exempted from taxation for a certain period after completion, was a contract which the state was not at liberty thereafter to impair And the ordinance of 1865, imposing a tax on said road before the expiration of the time limited in the act of 1852, is in violation of this section of the constitution Pacific R R. Co v Maguire, 20 Wall. 36

135. Exemption will not be implied.— An intention to surrender the power of taxation will not be imputed. The language of the act relied upon in support of such surrender must be such as leaves no other alternative Bailey v Maguire, 22 Wall 215

136. Taxing power — This provision is a limitation thereon by the state — A change of the expressed stipulations of a contract, or a relief of a debtor from strict and literal compliance with its requirements, can no more be effected by an exertion of the taxing power than it can be by the exertion of any other power of a state legislature The provision against impairing contract obligations is a limitation upon the taxing power as well as upon all legislation, whatever form it may assume Therefore an ordinance of a city directing that a tax be assessed upon its own stock, the amount thereof retained by the city by deducting it from the payments of interest upon such stock as it fell due to the holders, is a law impairing the obligation of a contract, and is void Murray v Charleston, 96 U S 432

137. A fixed tax in lieu of all others a contract —A charter of a bank which provides that a specific per cent. of tax shall be imposed "in lieu of all other taxes" is a contract, and a law imposing other taxes on the shares than those mentioned in the charter is void. Farrington v. Tennessee, 95 U S 679

138. As applied to state university.—An act of Illinois legislature of 1855, referring to the state university, provided' 'All property of whatever kind or description, belonging to or owned by said corporation, shall be forever free from taxation for any and all purposes" *Held*, that the provision constituted a contract, and that a subsequent act imposing a tax on all property of the corporation not in actual use for school purposes is in violation of this clause Northwestern University v. People, 99 U S. 309

139. Land scrip exemption a contract.—The act of general assembly of Arkansas of 1851, authorizing the issuance of transferable land scrip and its receipt in payment of swamp lands by locators, and providing that such scrip, or the lands located with it, should be exempt from taxation for ten years or until the swamp land was reclaimed, etc, was a contract between the state and the holder of such scrip or his assignees, and a subsequent statute subjecting such land to taxation contrary to the provisions of such contract is void McGee v Mathis, 4 Wall, 143

140. Bank charter provision that notes of bank are receivable for taxes is a contract — The twelfth section of the charter of the Bank of Tennessee, enacted in 1838, made the notes of the bank receivable for all taxes or other moneys due the state Section 6 of the schedule to the constitutional amendment of 1865 declared that all notes of the bank issued by it after the 6th of May, 1861,— that being the date when Tennessee seceded from the United States,— were null and void, and forbade the enactment of any laws for the redemption of such notes. *Held*, that the said amendment to the constitution of Tennessee was a law impairing the obligation of a contract and void Keith v Clark, 97 U S 454, citing Woodruff v. Trapnall, 10 How 190, Furman v Nichol, 8 Wall 44.

141. Consideration — Lack of, authorizes repeal of exemption. Where the property of a corporation in existence was exempted from taxation by spontaneous act of the legislature, and no concessions therefor were made or obligations assumed by the corporation, or no service or duty or remunerative condition imposed, the exemption was *privilegia favorabilia*, and was subject to repeal at the pleasure of the legislature, without impairing any obligation of contract Christ Church v Philadelphia, 24 How 300

142 Same — The act of the legislature of Rhode Island granting a charter to the Providence Bank contains no stipulation promising exemption from taxation *Held*, that a law passed subsequent to said charter, whereby said bank was taxed, did not impair any contract between the corporation and state, and was valid Providence Bank v Billings 4 Pet 514

143 A law of Pennsylvania held not to have the effect to impair the obligation of contracts Watson v Mercer, 8 Pet 88

144. Same.—A provision in a state law exempting railroad lands from taxation for local purposes for three years, *held* to be a gratuity, and not a contract, and that the same might be kept, changed or recalled at the pleasure of the state. Where a contract of exemption is claimed it will be rigidly scrutinized, and never be permitted to extend either in scope or duration beyond what the terms of concession clearly require. Tucker v. Ferguson, 22 Wall 527.

145. **Iron Mountain Railroad — Exemption of, held invalid.**— The St Louis & Iron Mountain Railroad Company by its original charter was exempt from all taxes, and there was no limit to such exemption. To aid in the construction of the road the state of Missouri indorsed the bonds of the company and acquired a statutory mortgage on the road, its property, franchises, etc. The company made default and the state foreclosed its lien, and at foreclosure sale became the purchaser of the property, franchise, etc., of the corporation. Subsequently the state sold the road and its property and franchises to individuals who became incorporated under a law of the state passed to enable them so to do and wherein it was enacted that the said purchasers, when so incorporated, should be possessed of all the franchises, privileges and immunities of the said St. Louis & Iron Mountain Railroad Company. The new constitution of the state in force prior to and at the time of the last sale prohibited the legislature from exempting any property from taxation other than as enumerated in the constitution. Railroad corporations or property was not in the excepted enumeration. *Held*, that the constitutional inhibition applied to the renewal of an exemption as well as to the creation of a new exemption, and that any attempt on part of the legislature to exempt the property, etc., of the St. Louis & Iron Mountain Railroad Company from taxation in the hands of the new purchasers or the corporation formed by them was void. Therefore the law providing for taxing the railroad did not impair the obligation of any contract. Trask v. Maguire, 18 Wall 391.

146. **Stipulated amount no contract.** — A provision in the charter of a railroad company that it shall pay annually into the state treasury a tax of one quarter of one per cent. on its capital stock does not amount to a contract that the state shall impose no additional tax. The Delaware Tax, 18 Wall 206.

147. The act of the legislature of Missouri providing for the completion of the North Missouri Railroad does not contain a contract of exemption from taxation. So the state ordinance of 1865 requiring said property to be taxed on its gross earnings is no violation of the provisions of this clause of the constitution. North Missouri R. R. Co. v. Maguire, 20 Wall 46.

148. **Construction — Language exempting must be explicit.** — As has been held many times by the supreme court, a state may make a valid contract that a corporation, or its property within its territory, shall be exempt from taxation, or shall be subjected to a limited specified tax. The court has, however, in the most emphatic terms, and on every occasion, declared that the language in which the surrender is made must be clear and unmistakable. The covenant or enactment must distinctly express that there shall be no further or other liability for taxation. A state cannot strip itself of this most essential power by doubtful words. Therefore, *held*, that where a provision is made in a state statute that after a railroad had been completed an accurate account of that portion of it situate in such state should be filed in the office of the auditor-general of the state, and thereafter

the company should annually pay into the state treasury the sum of $10,000, was not a contract that thereafter no greater tax should be imposed Erie R'y v Pennsylvania, 21 Wall. 492.

149. Railroad stock tax — Construction — Exemption never presumed — A perpetual exemption of the capital stock of a railroad company from taxation, with a clause that the "road with all its fixtures and appurtenances, including workshops, warehouses and vehicles of transportation, shall be exempt for a certain number of years, is equivalent to an express power to tax the said property after that time, and cannot be understood to mean that the perpetual exemption of the capital stock is equivalent to an exemption of the property purchased with or represented by the capital Exemptions from taxation are never presumed. On the contrary the presumptions are always against them. Memphis & Charleston R. R. Co v Gaines, 97 U S 697

150. Exemptions from taxation being in derogation of the sovereign authority and of common right are not to be extended beyond the express requirements of the language used, when most rigidly construed. Yazoo & Miss. Val R. R. v Thomas, 132 U S 174, Vicksburg, etc R R. v. Dennis, 116 U. S 665, Pacific R R. v Maguire, 20 Wall 42, Tomlinson v. Branch, 15 Wall. 460, Same v Jessup, id. 454, Providence Bank v. Billings, 4 Pet. 514; Charles River Bridge v Warren Bridge, 11 Pet. 420, Turnpike Co. v. State, 3 Wall. 210

151. The constitution of the United States does not profess in all cases to protect property from unjust or oppressive taxation by the states That is left to the state constitutions and state laws A contract not to tax certain property otherwise subject to taxation must be clearly expressed and will not be implied. The covenant or enactment must clearly express such intent A state cannot strip itself of this most essential power by doubtful words. It cannot by ambiguous terms be deprived of this highest attribute of sovereignty. Memphis Gas Lt. Co v Shelby Co, 109 U S 398, Erie R y Co. v Pennsylvania, 21 Wall. 492

152 Exemption held void for want of power in legislature — The property of the M & C R R. Co., under the provisions of the charter, would become taxable in 1877 The constitution adopted in 1870 requires that all property shall be taxed. *Held,* that a law of 1875, looking to an exemption of the property of the said railroad from taxes for years subsequent to 1877, was unauthorized, and void, even if founded on a consideration. M & C. R. R Co. v. Gaines, 97 U S 697.

153 Municipal tax — Exemption held not to include. — A clause in the charter of a ferry company that it should be subject to the same taxes as were then or might thereafter be imposed on other ferry companies in the state does not exempt such ferry from municipal tax by a city whose charter authorizes it to regulate, tax and license ferry-boats Wiggins Ferry Co v East St. Louis, 107 U S 365

154 Same —Where a state has authorized a foreign insurance company to transact business within the state, in conformity to the laws thereof, which laws imposed a tax of one per cent. on the gross earnings, and where the city in which the agency of such corporation was located, imposed by ordinance an additional tax for city purposes, *held,* that the ordinance imposing such tax was not void by reason of being in conflict with this clause of the constitution Home Ins Co v Augusta, 93 U S 116.

155. Exemption held not to pass to purchaser — Certain lands in Ohio were granted to the Ohio university at Athens By an act of the Ohio legislature of 1804, these lands were exempted from taxation In 1826 the legislature authorized all the lands then held by the university, and which were unincumbered by leases, etc, to be sold in fee-simple for the benefit of the university *Held*, that the lands sold under the provisions of this act of 1826, and not under the act of 1804, were not exempt from taxation by reason of the provisions of said act of 1804 Armstrong v Treasurer of Athens County, 16 Pet 281 The case of New Jersey v. Wilson, 7 Cranch, 164 adhered to and distinguished Id.

156. Case stated — When exemption begins and how long it runs — The charter of the Yazoo & Mississippi Valley Railroad Company contained the following provision in regard to taxation "It is hereby declared that said company, its stock, its railroads and appurtenances, and all its property in this state necessary or incident to the full exercise of all the powers herein granted,— not to include compresses and oil mills,— shall be exempt from taxation for a term of twenty years from the completion of said railroad to the Mississippi river, but not to extend beyond twenty-five years from the date of the approval of this act, and when the period of exemption herein prescribed shall have expired, the property of said railroad may be taxed at the same rate as other property in this state" *Held* When the Mississippi river was reached, then the period of exemption would begin, but how long it would continue would depend upon the length of time to elapse before the end of the twenty-five years from the approval of the charter." Yazoo R R. v Thomas, 132 U. S 174–188

157 Same — The charter of the Vicksburg, Shreveport & Pacific Railroad Company provided that "the capital stock of said company shall be exempt from taxation, and its road, fixtures, workshops, warehouses, vehicles of transportation and other appurtenances shall be exempt from taxation for ten years after the completion of said road within the limits of this state ' *Held*, that there was no exemption before completion Vicksburg, etc R. R. Co v. Dennis, 116 U. S 665

158. Lands purchased from United States, under statutory exemption, are protected by this clause — Under a compact with the United States, a law of Indiana was passed declaring that lands sold by the United States within the state should be exempt from tax for five years after sale In 1847 an act of congress declared that in all states which came into the Union prior to 1820 the restriction of taxation in such states should be annulled The act in Indiana, however, remained unrepealed until 1852. Prior to this repeal certain lands were sold, and after the repeal, but prior to the expiration of the five years, the lands were taxed *Held* that the repealing act as thus applied impaired the obligation of the contract of purchase. Thompson v Holton, 6 McLean, 386

159 Legislative reservation — Effect of, on contract — The thirty-second section of the New York banking law reserves to the legislature the right to alter or repeal the act. This gives the legislature the power to repeal an exemption from personal liability of stockholders contained in a bank charter. The law in force at the time the articles were adopted enter into and become a part of the charter, and all rights granted therein are subject to alteration or repeal the same as any other part of the general system. Sherman v Smith, 1 Black, 587.

160 A charter was granted to a street railway company and provided for a license of $30 per car for each car run by the company A subsequent statute fixed the license for such cars at $50 When the charter was granted the power to alter, amend, revoke, etc, was reserved by the state constitution. *Held*, that the law imposing the tax of $50 per car did not impair the obligation of a contract, and was valid. Union Passenger R'y Co v Philadelphia, 101 U. S. 528

161 Under a reservation in the constitution of a state that the legislature shall have the power to alter or repeal the charter of any corporation organized under the laws thereof, such corporations are from the moment of their creation subject to the legislative power of alteration, to the extent of absolute extinguishment of the corporate body, if deemed expedient. Spring Valley Water Co v Schottler, 110 U. S. 347.

162 The code of Georgia which went into force January 1, 1863, provided that private corporations were subject to be changed, modified or destroyed at will of the creator, etc. Prior to 1863 two railroad companies were chartered, with a limited exemption from taxation in each charter. Subsequent to 1863 these two companies consolidated under the provisions of an act authorizing it, approved April 18, 1863, and which conferred upon the consolidated company full corporate powers and continued to it the franchises, privileges and immunities of the constituent companies. *Held*, that the consolidation created a new corporation, that became subject to the provisions of the code in respect to amendment, etc, and that a subsequent act of the legislature taxing the property was not prohibited by this clause of the constitution. Atlantic & Gulf R. R. Co. v. Georgia, 98 U S 359

163 A statutory amendment to the charter of a corporation, when the same is accepted by the corporation by a vote, does not impair the obligation of contract. Pennsylvania College Cases, 13 Wall 190.

164 A provision in a charter to a corporation that it shall not be altered or amended except by legislative enactment is equivalent to an express provision reserving to the legislature the power of alteration or amendment at the pleasure of the legislature Id

165 The existence of a contract by the corporation with individuals or other corporations which may be affected by the change will not annul the reserved power of the legislature to amend the charter Id

166 Where the right to repeal, alter or amend articles of incorporation is reserved to the state, either in the constitution, or in a general law applicable to all corporations, or in legislative act of incorporation, the state may exercise the right so reserved without impairing the obligation of contract with such corporations Miller v The State, 15 Wall 478, Holyoke Water-power Co v Lyman, 15 Wall 500, Tomlinson v Jessup, 15 Wall. 454.

167. Where the constitution of a state declares that all laws granting charters to corporations shall be subject to alteration or repeal, the constitutional provision inheres in all such laws, and forms an inalienable legislative power The power thus limited cannot be bargained away by any act of

the legislature, because the power itself is beyond legislative control But where the limitation on such legislation is contained in a law declaring that all charters thereafter granted shall be so subjected, it does not limit the power of subsequent legislatures. It then becomes a question in every case of a contract made by the legislature, whether that body intended that the right to change or repeal it should inhere in it, or whether, like other contracts, it is perfect and not within the power of the legislature to impair its obligation. New Jersey v. Yard, 95 U. S 104

168. Neither the charter of the Pennsylvania Railroad Company contained in an act of the legislature of Pennsylvania, April 13, 1846, nor acts supplemental thereto, nor act of May 16, 1857, constituted a contract between the state and the company The company took its charter originally subject to the general law of the state, and subject to future constitutional and legislative provisions, there being no prior contract with it exempting it from liability to such future general legislation, in respect of the subject-matter involved Penn R. R Co v Miller, 132 U S 75.

169. **Obligation of contract — Consolidation of railroad corporations, effect of** — Under a law of Ohio providing for consolidation of railroad companies, *held*, that the effect of consolidation under the authority thereof was to destroy the constituent corporations, and to create a new corporation with such powers and liabilities as were imposed by the laws then in force, the same as if the old companies had never existed, and the same as if neither of them had ever enjoyed franchises conferred by prior laws So where the constitution in force at the date of such consolidation provided that "no special privileges or immunities shall ever be granted that may not be altered, revoked or repealed by the general assembly, it entered into the acts under which the consolidation was effected, and rendered the new corporation and its franchises subject to alteration and repeal. Shields v. Ohio, 95 U. S 319.

170. An act of the legislature prescribing the rate of fare applicable to such consolidated company was a legitimate exercise of such reserved power of alteration, and was valid. Id.

NOTE — Under certain laws it was held in the following cases that the consolidated company succeeded to the franchises, rights and immunities of the constituent corporations Philadelphia & Wil R R v Maryland, 10 How. 376, Tomlinson v Branch, 15 Wall 460, Scotland County v. Thomas, 94 U. S. 682, Branch v. Charleston, 92 U. S 677, State ex rel. Att'y-Gen l v. Greene County, 54 Mo 540

171. By the charter of the St. Jo & Iowa R. R. Co. granted by the legislature of Missouri in 1857 it was provided that "the stock of said company shall be exempt from all state and county taxes.' By an act of the legislature of Missouri, March 24, 1870 (see § 52, art. 2, ch 37, Wagner s Statutes of 1872), it is provided *inter alia* "that if a railroad corporation shall loan or sell its line of railroad to a corporation of another state such part of said railroad as is within that state shall be subject to taxation " The St. Jo & Iowa Railroad having sold its line of road, etc , to a corporation of another state which connected with it at the Iowa line, was by the courts of Missouri held to be subject to taxation under the provisions of the act of March

24, 1870 *Held*, that said act of March 24, 1870, did not impair any contract of the St. Jo & Iowa R. R Co with the state of Missouri Chicago, etc. R. R. Co v Guffey, 122 U. S. 561

172. Exemption not transferable — The sale of the property and franchises of a railroad company under decree of foreclosure or on execution for a money judgment does not transfer to the purchaser an immunity from taxation granted by the state in the charter of the corporation. Morgan v Louisiana, 93 U. S 217.

173. An immunity from taxation granted to a railroad corporation, although it may be a contract with the corporation to which it is granted, and as such protected by this clause, is not a franchise that passes with the sale of the railroad and franchise on foreclosure of a mortgage Affirming Morgan v. Louisiana, 93 U. S 217. Railroad Company v. Hamblen County, 103 U S 273, Memphis, etc. R R. v Railroad Com'rs, 112 U S 609, C & O. R. R Co v. Miller, 114 U S. 176

174. Municipal corporations—Law giving authority to incur debts a contract with creditors —"When a state has authorized a municipal corporation to contract, and to exercise the power of local taxation to the extent necessary to meet its engagements, the power thus given cannot be withdrawn until the contract is satisfied The state and the corporation in such cases are equally bound." Von Hoffman v Quincy, 4 Wall. 535

175. Where a law requires of a municipal corporation the levy of an annual tax to be paid on the debt of the corporation, and while such act is in force a debt is contracted and bonds issued therefor, it is beyond the power of the legislature to repeal such taxing law so far as it concerns such bonds. Galena v Amy, 5 Wall. 705

176. When a municipal corporation, acting under legal authority, creates a debt and issues bonds as evidence thereof, it is not within the power of the legislature to so alter the charter of such municipal corporation as to take away its power to levy and collect taxes to pay such debt Such contract is protected by this clause of the constitution. United States ex rel. Wolf v New Orleans, 103 U S 358

177. Where a state by law has authorized a city to contract a debt and levy a tax to pay the same, and the power thus conferred has been exercised, this forms a contract in which the city and state are equally bound The power given becomes a trust which the state cannot annul by subsequent legislation. Von Hoffman v Quincy, 4 Wall. 535

178 In the above case the following cases are cited and commented upon. Fletcher v Peck, 6 Cranch, 87, New Jersey v Wilson, 7 Cranch, 164, Terrett v. Taylor, 9 Cranch, 43, Green v Biddle, 8 Wheat 92, Bronson v Kinzie, 1 How 319, McCracken v Hayward, 2 How 612, People v. Bond, 10 Cal 570, Ogden v Saunders, 12 Wheat 231, Sturges v. Crowninshield, 4 Wheat. 122, Planters Bank v Sharp, 6 How 327, Beers v. Haughton, 9 Pet 359, Mason v Hale, 12 Wheat. 373, Dodge v Woolsey, 18 How. 331, Piqua Bank v Knoop, 16 How 369 Dominick v Sayre, 3 Sandf. 555

179 In Meriwether v Garrett, 102 U S 472, Mr Justice Field, speaking for himself and Mr Justice Miller and Mr Justice Bradley, in a concurring opinion, says 'Municipal corporations are the mere instrumentalities of the state for the more convenient administration of local government. Their powers are such as the legislature may confer, and these may be enlarged, abridged or entirely withdrawn at pleasure This is common learning . . There is no contract between the state and the public that the charter of a city shall not be at all times subject to legislative control All persons who deal with such bodies are conclusively presumed to act upon knowledge of the power of the legislature There is no such thing as a vested right held by an individual in the grant of legislative power to them Citing United States v Railroad Co, 17 Wall 322, Commissioners v Lucas, 93 U S 108; People v. Morris, 13 Wend 325, Philadelphia v Fox, 64 Pa. St. 169, Montpelier v East Montpelier, 29 Vt. 12

180 Provisions of municipal charter subject to amendment, when — A state legislature may at any time restrict or revoke the powers conferred on municipal corporations, provided in doing so it does not place it beyond the reach of such municipality to raise money and pay debts theretofore legally contracted by it. Such debts are protected by this clause of the constitution Wolff v New Orleans, 103 U. S 358

181. Water-works belonging to a city, like the public parks and buildings, are not subject to judicial sale for the ordinary debts of the city Therefore an act of the legislature authorizing a city to convert its ownership in such works into the shares of a joint-stock corporation, which shares shall be exempt from judicial sale for the debts of the city, does not impair the obligation of contract with respect to any of the existing debts of such city New Orleans v Morris, 105 U S 600

182 Torts — Judgments for not protected.— A judgment against a city for damages done by a mob is not a contract within the meaning of this clause, and is no more subject to it than was the tort before being merged into the judgment. A state law which so limits the taxing power of a city as to prevent the collection of such judgment is not a violation of this clause Louisiana v. Mayor of New Orleans, 109 U S 285; Louisiana v. Police Jury, 111 U. S. 716

183. Authority to contract debt implies authority to tax for payment thereof.— When the legislature authorizes a municipality to contract an extraordinary debt and to issue bonds therefor, it impliedly authorizes such municipality to levy and collect the taxes necessary to meet said debt as it matures, and any law or provision of the constitution of the state passed after such debt had been contracted under such authority, which so limits the power of taxation as to defeat or delay the payment of such debts, impairs the obligation of the contract so entered into, and to the extent of such limitation is invalid Quincy v Jackson, 113 U S 332

184. Authority of creditor to apply debts of city on taxes does not impair contract with other creditors — A state law which authorized the tax-payer within a city to use, under certain regulations, the debts of the city in his hands as creditor in the payment of back taxes due to the city, does not divest any vested rights or impair the obligation of contracts between such city and other creditors Amy v Shelby Taxing District, 114 U. S 387.

185. Ordinances of municipal corporation, effect of.— A by-law or ordinance of a municipal corporation may be such an exercise of legislative power delegated by the legislature to the corporation as a political subdivision of the state, having all the force of law within the limits of the municipality, that it may properly be considered as a law within the meaning of this clause. N O Water-works v. La. Sugar Co, 125 U S 18–32.

186. Rule of property, law as expounded constitutes — By an act of the general assembly of Iowa, approved January 28, 1857, the city of Dubuque was authorized to aid in the construction of certain railroads by issuing to such railroad corporations the bonds of the city, and the law authorized and required the city to levy a special tax to meet the interest and pay the principal of such bonds when due Similar laws giving like authority to other municipalities of the state had been declared constitutional by the supreme court of Iowa. In a suit on the coupons of bonds issued by Dubuque under the act of January, 1857, the supreme court overruled its former decisions and held the law under which they were issued to be in violation of the constitution of Iowa. On error to the supreme court of the United States it is held that "the sound and true rule is that if the contract when made was valid by the laws of the state as then expounded by all departments of the government, and administered by its courts of justice, its validity and obligation cannot be impaired by any subsequent action of legislation, or decision of its courts altering the construction of the law" Citing and quoting from Ohio Life & Trust Co. v. Debolt, 16 How 432 and adding · 'The same principle applies where there is a change of judicial decisions as to the constitutional power of the legislature to enact the law.' Gelpcke v Dubuque, 1 Wall 175, affirmed in Meyer v Muscatine, 1 Wall 384, Thomson v Lee Co, 3 Wall 327, Mitchell v. Burlington, 4 Wall. 270, Larned v Burlington, 4 Wall. 275

187. Where state courts have at different times given different constructions to the same state statute, the supreme court of the United States will not follow the latest construction if contract rights have accrued by reason of or upon the faith of the first decision which would be impaired by following such later decision Such change of construction will be regarded in the same light as a legislative act impairing the obligation of a contract, if such be the effect thereof. Douglass v Pike County 101 U. S 677, Darlington v Jackson County, 101 U. S 688, note; Foote v Pike County, 101 U S 688, note

188 Where a contract is valid under the laws of a state in force at the time it is made, the legislature cannot impair its obligation, nor can any decision of the state courts be permitted to have that effect. Chicago v Sheldon, 9 Wall 50

189. The laws which subsist at the time and place of the making of a contract and where it is to be performed enter into and form a part of it as if they were expressly referred to or incorporated in its terms. Von Hoffman v. Quincy, 4 Wall. 535

190. When the highest court of a state has construed a statute of the state such construction must be taken as correct, in so far as it affects contracts made under such statute. Such construction becomes as to such contracts a part of the law, and cannot be changed so as to affect contracts made subsequently thereto and before such change in such construction. Louisiana v Pilsbury, 105 U. S. 278.

191 Constitutional provision.—A state can no more impair an existing contract by a constitutional provision than by a legislative act, nor can congress, by ratification, give effect to a constitution or law of a state affected with such infirmity A provision in a state constitution which increases the amount of property exempt from execution is, as to debts contracted prior thereto, inoperative and void Gunn v Barry, 15 Wall 610

192 Where a contract was valid when made, any subsequent constitutional provision rendering it void impairs the obligation of such contract and is in violation of the federal constitution. Delmas v Merchants' Mut Ins Co, 14 Wall 661.

193. The federal supreme court has jurisdiction to pass upon and determine whether an amendment to a state constitution, as construed by the state courts, has the effect to impair the obligation of contracts existing prior to its adoption. Williams v Louisiana, 103 U S 637. Followed in Durkee v Board of Liquidation, 103 U S 646

194. The constitution of the state of Illinois, adopted in 1870, declares "No county, city, township or other municipality shall ever become subscriber to the capital stock of any railroad or private corporation, or make any donation to, or loan its credit in aid of, such corporation" *Held*, that where, prior to the adoption of this constitution, a county had contracted that in consideration of the construction of a railroad therein it would deliver its bonds, etc, to said railroad company, and the railroad company had partially complied therewith, that this section of the constitution could not be held to interfere with said contract. Clay County v. Society for Savings, 104 U S 579

195 A contract to subscribe to the stock of a railroad company made by a municipal corporation or county when it was legal to so do, cannot be annulled or impaired by a subsequent amendment to the constitution of the state forbidding such subscription on the part of the municipality Moultrie County v Savings Bank, 92 U S 631

196 Where a county issues securities valid when issued, a law subsequently passed, taking from such county the power to levy a tax to pay the same is in conflict with this clause and void. Ralls County v. United States, 105 U S 733

197. A state can no more impair the obligation of a contract by constitutional changes than by legislative or judicial action. New Orleans Gas Light Co. v. Louisiana Light Co, 115 U S 650.

198. Police power.—A company was incorporated as expressed in its charter "for the purpose of manufacturing malt liquors in all their varieties," and this right was granted in its most unqualified form *Held*, that it cannot be construed as conferring any greater or more sacred right than any citizen had to manufacture the same kind of liquor, nor as exempting the corporation from any control therein to which a citizen would be subject if the interest of the community required it. And a law prohibiting the manufacture and sale of such liquors in the future does not impair any contract obligation Beer Company v Massachusetts, 97 U S 25

199. In respect to the exercise of the police powers of a state, one legislature cannot curtail the power of its successor. This police power extends to all matters affecting the public health or public morals. One legislature cannot by a charter to a lottery prevent the people from abating the same by law when their will in respect thereto is properly expressed. The constitution protects such contracts as affect property rights, not such as are governmental. The right to suppress lotteries is governmental and may be exercised at the will of the legislature. Stone v. Mississippi, 101 U. S. 814.

200. The preservation of the public health and the public morals is so necessary to the best interests of social organizations that a wise policy forbids a legislative body to divest itself of the power to enact laws for the preservation of health and the repression of crime. Butchers' Union v. Crescent City, etc. Co., 111 U. S. 746.

201. Laws enacted for the control of corporations which have for their object the protection of the public in the matters pertaining to corporate action, and which provide for such reasonable regulations as the legislature may deem wise, and which are not inconsistent with the objects for which the corporation was created, do not, when applied to corporations theretofore in existence, impair the obligation of contracts. Chicago Life Ins. Co. v. Needles, 113 U. S. 574.

202. This clause does not restrict the state in matters of protection of the public health, public morals or public safety, as the one or the other of these may be involved in the execution of contracts. New Orleans Gas Light Co. v. Louisiana Light Co., 115 U. S. 650; New Orleans Water-works Co. v. Rivers, 115 U. S. 674.

203. Where upon an indictment for setting up and carrying on a lottery the defendant justified by pleading the provisions of a statute authorizing the act, it was admitted that the statute authorized the act, but the constitutionality of the act was denied by the prosecution. Under a prior indictment against the same defendant for a similar offense, the supreme court of the state had held that the statute under which the defendant justified constituted a contract. But the court did not pass upon the constitutionality of the act. On the trial upon the second indictment, the defendant further relied on this decision of the supreme court, but the trial court held the act unconstitutional, and the defendant was convicted. The supreme court of the state sustained the conviction. *Held*, that the previous adjudication that the statute constituted a contract did not estop the state from denying its constitutionality in the subsequent case, nor conclude the court upon that question, although the point might have been raised by the state and determined in the first case. The following are the concluding remarks of the court, speaking by Mr. Justice Field: "We are not prepared to admit that it is competent for one legislature, by any contract with an individual, to restrain the power of a subsequent legislature to legislate for the public welfare, and to that end to suppress any and all practices tending to corrupt the public morals." Citing Moore v. State, 48 Miss. 147, and Board of Excise v. Barrie, 34 N. Y. 663. Boyd v. Alabama, 94 U. S. 645.

204. Exercise of eminent domain. — A bridge belonging to a corporation chartered by state law may be condemned and taken for a public highway the same as other private property may be condemned and taken for public uses. It stands upon the same footing, and the franchise of the corporation cannot be distinguished from other property. The constitution intended to prohibit such laws by the states as interpolate into a contract some new terms or conditions foreign to the original agreement. West River Bridge v. Dix, Same v Town of Brattleboro, 6 How 507

205. The obligation of the contract between the state and a railroad company is not impaired by reason of another railroad company being authorized to cross the track of the first. The franchise may be condemned the same as individual property R F & P R R v L R R Co, 13 How 71

206 Miscellaneous — Office no contract — The office of canal commissioner, to which a person was under the law of a state appointed for a year, may be abolished at the pleasure of the state The appointment to the office and acceptance thereof constitutes no contract within the meaning of this clause Butler v Pennsylvania, 10 How 402

207. The appointment to and the tenure of an office created for public use, and the regulation of the salary thereof, is not a "contract" within the meaning of this section Whatever the form of the statute creating the office and regulating the salary, the incumbent does not hold by contract It is a privilege, and is revocable by the sovereignty at will One legislature cannot deprive its successor of the power of revocation. Crenshaw v United States, 134 U S 99.

208 Where a statute for the pay of police officers provided that $2 per month be retained from the pay of each officer for a fund, a certain portion of which should, on the death of each officer, be paid to his representatives, there was no contract by the state that the disposition of such fund should continue as originally provided And a subsequent statute making a different disposition thereof did not impair the obligation of a contract Pennie v. Reis, 132 U. S 464

209 When a person is elected or appointed to an office for a definite term, for which there is a fixed salary or compensation, there is no contract which forbids the legislature or other proper authority to change the rate of compensation or salary for services to be rendered after the change is made, though this may include a part of the unexpired term of the officer Butler v Pennsylvania, 10 How 402.

210 But after the services have been rendered under a law, resolution or ordinance which fixes the rate of compensation, there arises an implied contract to pay for such services at that rate. This contract is a completed contract, and any statute or constitutional provision thereafter, fixing another and less compensation, impairs the obligation of such contract. Fisk v. Police Jury, 116 U S 131

211. The legislature of California in 1878 enacted a statute which provided for the payment of the police force of San Francisco, at a rate "which should not exceed $102 per month for each one," subject to the condition that the treasurer of the city and county "should retain from the pay of each police officer the sum of $2 per month to be paid into a fund known as the police life and insurance fund" The act further provided that upon the death of any member of the police force after June 1, 1878 there should be paid by said treasurer out of said life and health insurance fund to his legal representatives the sum of $1,000 On March 1, 1889, the legislature repealed this law, and in lieu thereof enacted a statute creating "a police relief and pension fund," and transferred to it the money then accumulated in the "life and health insurance fund," and made new and different

provision for the distribution of the said fund W was a police officer of the city for twenty years prior to his death, which occurred March 13, 1889, one week after the new law was enacted and had gone into operation His administrator sued to recover the $1 000 from the police life and health fund, which at the time it was transferred to the "relief and pension fund" amounted to $40 000 *Held* that this was a public fund subject to legislative control, and that W had no vested interest in it which could not be divested by law during his life-time That while the $2 per month was called a part of his compensation for services he never received it or controlled it, and was powerless during his life to prevent its appropriation to the fund in question That, if in fact it had been paid to him and thus passed under his absolute control, and after such payment he had been induced to contribute it to such fund on the conditions named, a different question would have been raised, at least so far as applied to the sum actually contributed by him Pennie v Reis, 132 U S 464-471

212. The act of the legislature of Kentucky of February 27, 1797, concerning occupying claimants of land, was repugnant to the constitution of the United States. So, also, was the act of January 31, 1812, which repealed the act of February 27, 1797, in that it was in violation of the compact between the states of Virginia and Kentucky contained in the act of the legislature of Virginia of December 18, 1789, and which is incorporated into the constitution of Kentucky. Green v Biddle, 8 Wheat 1

213 Extent of impairment not material — The invalidity of a state law as impairing the obligation of contracts does not depend on the extent of the change which the law effects Any deviation from its terms by postponing or accelerating the period of its performance, imposing conditions not expressed in the contract, or dispensing with those which are expressed, however minute or immaterial in their effect upon the contract, impairs its obligation Id., Von Hoffman v Quincy, 4 Wall 535, Farrington v Tennessee, 95 U. S. 679.

214 Nuisance — License to tolerate not a contract — Where a mill was erected on the Jersey shore of the Delaware river prior to 1781, and a dam extended from the shore to an island in the river, whereby water-power was furnished to the said mill, and thereafter, in 1781, by the concurrent legislation of the provinces of New Jersey and Pennsylvania, the River Delaware was declared a common highway for the purpose of navigation, and provision was made for the removal of obstructions in the river, saving, however, the dam to said mill, which was not to be obstructed, or the river so diverted as to destroy its use, *held*, that this amounted only to a license to tolerate what was otherwise a nuisance That it did not amount to a contract with Hoops, the owner of the mill, and that legislation by the state of New Jersey after the formation of the Union, whereby the use of the dam was interfered with, was not unconstitutional Rundle v Canal Co, 14 How. 80

215 Laws to correct mistakes — Laws of a state enacted to obviate mistakes and irregularities in the proceeding of municipal corporations which do not have the effect to impair the obligation of a contract are within the scope of legislative authority. Bissell v. City of Jeffersonville, 24 How. 287.

216 **Case stated** — Where the legislature of a state provided by law for canal commissioners to borrow money to be used in the construction of a canal, and pledged the canal and its lands granted by the government for the payment of the loan, said loan became a lien on such property, and the law amounted to a contract which could not be impaired by subsequent legislation. Wabash & Erie Canal Co v Beers, 2 Black, 418

217. **Bank law diverting assets impairs contract with bill-holder.**— The bills of a bank being payable on demand there was a contract with the holder to so pay them, and a law which diverted the assets of the bank to other purposes impaired the obligation of such contract, notwithstanding the state was the sole stockholder and owner of such assets Curran v. Arkansas, 15 How 304

218 **Competition.**— Where there is no contract in the charter of a turnpike company that prohibits the legislature from chartering a rival railroad company, the construction and operation of such rival railroad is not a subject of legal remedy. W. & B Turnpike Co v Maryland, 3 Wall 210

219 **Liability of stockholder — Repeal of.**— A law which repeals the liability of stockholders for corporate debts is, as to such debts as were contracted during the existence of such liability, a law impairing the obligation of contracts. Hawthorne v. Calef, 2 Wall 10

220. **Future acquisitions** are liable for contracts, and to release them from liability impairs the obligations of contracts Sturges v Crowninshield, 4 Wheat 198

221. **Discharge of debtor.**— An act of a state legislature which discharges a debtor from all liability for debts contracted previous to his discharge, on his surrendering his property for the benefit of his creditors, is unconstitutional, and it makes no difference that both parties to the contract were citizens of the same state and so continued to be Bank v Smith, 6 Wheat 131

222 **Release of state's interest in lands.**— An act of the legislature of Kentucky releasing the state's interest to certain lands does not impair the obligation of a contract made with the auditor whereby he concedes a moiety of the lands to an attorney for their recovery Mulligan v. Corbins, 7 Wall 487

223. **Requiring money to be withheld from non-resident bond-holders to pay tax on bonds** — A law of Pennsylvania, passed May 1, 1868, which requires the treasurer of a company incorporated and doing business in that state to retain five per cent. of all interest due on bonds of the company made and payable out of the state to non-residents of the state is not a legitimate exercise of the taxing power of the state Under pretense of levying a tax it impairs the obligation of the contract between the parties State Tax on Foreign-held Bonds, 15 Wall 300

224 **Virginia coupon cases** —Act of 1876 of Virginia in respect to tax on coupons and bonds issued under funding act of 1871, *held* invalid as applied to coupons separated from the bonds and held by different owners. Hartman v Greenhow, 102 U.S 672. Poindexter v Greenhow, 114 U. S. 270; Chaffin v Taylor, 114 U S 309, White v Greenhow, 114 U S 307 Allen v. Railroad Co, 114 U S 311, Royall v Virginia, 116 U S 572, Sands v. Edmunds, 116 U S 585

225 The state of Virginia, by an act refunding its debt, provided, *inter alia*, that the interest coupons on the bonds should be "receivable at and after maturity for all taxes, dues, debts and demands due the state," and further provided that when a collector, etc, refused so to accept the coupons the courts could compel him so to do by *mandamus*. Thereafter, by an act of the legislature, it was provided generally that when such coupons were presented to the tax collector, the tax-payer should pay his taxes in legal money and surrender his coupon, which the collector would indorse, and deliver the same to the judge of the county court, etc, and the owner could then make a case before the court and prove the genuineness of his coupons It in such case he succeeded in so proving them the treasurer was to refund the money so paid to the amount of such coupon "out of the first money in the treasury in preference to all other claims." *Held*, that the latter law did not impair the obligation of the contract requiring the coupons to be received in payment of taxes, etc , that it only affected the remedy; and that the reasonableness of such change in remedy is primarily with the legislature. Antoni v. Greenhow, 107 U. S. 769, Moore v Greenhow, 114 U S 338.

226. The cases of Hartman v. Greenhow, 102 U S 672, Antoni v Greenhow, 107 U S. 769, Virginia Coupon Cases, 114 U. S 269, Barry v Edmunds, 116 U S 550, Chaffin v. Taylor, 116 U S 567, Royall v Virginia, 116 U. S 572, Sands v. Edmunds, 116 U S 585, Royall v Virginia, 121 U S 102 In re Ayers et al, 123 U S 443, are reviewed, and without committing the court to all that has been adjudged in those cases on the subject of the act of the legislature of Virginia of March 30, 1871, to provide for the funding and payment of the public debt and the issue of coupon bonds of the state under its provisions, *held*, (1) that the provisions of the act constitute a contract between the state and the lawful holders of such bonds and coupons (2) That the subsequent acts passed for the purpose of restraining the use of said coupons for the payment of taxes, and the obstructions interposed to such use, etc, materially impair the obligation of the contract (3) That while the holder of such coupons cannot sue the state, either directly or indirectly, by proceeding against the executive officers to control them in the exercise of their official functions as agents of the state, neither can such holder who tenders such coupons in payment of taxes, etc, and continues to hold himself ready to make such tender good, be molested in person or goods on account of such taxes, dues, etc , and if his property is so disturbed or taken he may recover it, or by injunction prevent its being taken when it would be attended with irreparable injury, by suit against the officer so taking or threatening to take such property McGahey v Virginia, and seven other cases, where the whole subject is reviewed, 135 U S 662

227. Contracts of states included — The prohibition of the constitution against the passage of laws impairing the obligation of contracts applies to the contracts of states and to those of its agents under its authority as well as to contracts between individuals United States ex rel. Wolff v New Orleans, 103 U S 358

228. Contract with state — Case stated.— Where, by a law of Wisconsin, commissioners were appointed to make a geological survey, and their duties were defined in the law, and wherein it was provided that the governor should contract with such commissioners to perform said duties and also stipulate as to the amount of compensation therefor; and where, under said law the governor did so contract, and the commissioners entered upon their duties in accord therewith,—*held*, that this was a contract protected by the constitution, and that a subsequent act repealing the law under which the contract was made, and proposing to annul said contract, is void The case of abolishing an office created by the legislature considered, and distinguished from the law abolishing such commission Hall v. Wisconsin, 103 U S 5

229. Repealing act, when invalid —A repeal by the legislature of the charter of a street railroad, and the transfer of its franchises to another corporation, impairs the obligation of its contract, unless the power so to do was reserved to the legislature, either by the constitution or law in force when the charter was granted, or by the terms of the charter itself Greenwood v Union Freight R. R Co, 105 U S 13

230. Issuance of municipal bonds prevented.— Where a town, acting under legal authority, agrees to issue bonds to a railroad company, upon conditions to be complied with by the company, and the company relying thereon has fully complied with such conditions, any attempt by the legislature to prevent the issue of such bonds is invalid. Red Rock v Henry, 106 U S 596

231 Municipal corporation; change of not permitted at expense of creditors.— When the legislature has by designated boundaries incorporated or permitted the incorporation of a municipal organization, and thereafter repeals its charter and dissolves the corporation and incorporates substantially the same people as a municipal body under a new name, for the same purpose, and the great mass of the property of the old is included in the new corporation, and the property of the old used for public purposes is transferred without consideration to the new for the same purposes, the latter will be held the successor of the former and liable for its debts Girard v Philadelphia, 7 Wall 1; Broughton v. Pensacola, 93 U S 266, O'Connor v. Memphis, 6 Lea, 730, Mt. Pleasant v Beckwith, 100 U S. 514, Colchester v Seaber, 3 Burr 1866; Cuddon v Eastwick, 1 Salk 192, People v Morris, 13 Wend 325, New Orleans R R v New Orleans 26 La Ann 478

232 Any legislation which withdraws or limits the ability of the corporation to discharge its obligations is forbidden by this clause of the constitution Port of Mobile v Watson, 116 U S 289

233. The so-called Confederate congress enacted a law sequestrating the lands, tenements, goods, chattels, rights and credits within the Confederate States held by or for any alien enemy since May 21, 1861 The plaintiffs, residents of Pennsylvania, were creditors of Geo N Bruffy, of Virginia, and the defendant was his administrator The debt sued on was for goods sold in March, 1861 The defendant pleaded specially the act of the Confederate States sequestrating said credit, and that he had, under the provisions of said act, paid the same to the Confederate States. *Held* (1) That under the second and third clauses of section 2 of the amendatory judiciary act of 1867 the supreme court of the United States had jurisdiction to review a judgment sustaining the validity of said act of sequestration (2) That the said enact-

ment of the confederation which, by the consent of Virginia, was enforced as a law in that commonwealth, brought the same within this clause of the constitution. That the said clause prohibits a state from *enforcing* as a law an enactment of that character, from whatever source originating. That this law, as enforced in Virginia, became a law of that state, and was a law impairing — and in fact, if enforced, destroying — the obligations of the contract, and was void. Williams v. Bruffy, 96 U. S. 176; Dewing v. Perdicaries, 96 U. S. 193; New Orleans Water-works v. La. Sugar Co., 125 U. S. 31.

234. Texas, laws of, prior to annexation.— Laws passed in Texas before its annexation to and admission as a state in the Union cannot be in conflict with the constitution of the United States. League v. De Young, 11 How. 185; Herman v. Phalen, 14 How. 79.

235. Divorces.— This clause does not restrict the general right of the legislatures to legislate upon the subject of divorces. Those acts enable some tribunal, not to impair the obligation of a marriage contract, but to release one of the parties because the contract has been broken by the other. Hunt v. Hunt, Book 24, Lawyers' Co-operative Ed. United States Supreme Court Reports, 1109.

236. County seat, removal of.— By an act of the legislature of Ohio the county seat of Mahoning county was located at Canfield upon certain terms which were prescribed in the act and complied with. Twenty-eight years later the legislature by an act changed the location to Youngstown. *Held*, that the first act and the location under it was not a contract within the meaning of this clause. Both acts were public laws on a public subject, with respect to which a former legislature could not bind a subsequent one. Newton v. Mahoning Commissioners, 100 U. S. 548.

237. Notice of reserved rights to lessee.— The board of public works of Ohio leased the surplus water in a canal, reserving the right to resume the privilege when necessary to navigation. A subsequent lease of the canal as a highway amounted to a rescission of the water leases. *Held* not invalid. The water lessees took with notice of the reserved right. Fox v. Cincinnati, 104 U. S. 783.

238. Confederate money — Payment in.— Where notes were executed in Alabama in 1860, between citizens thereof, and falling due in 1862 were paid in Confederate money, which the payee was forced to accept, *held*, that an averment of such fact in a state court and a decision therein that the contract was discharged by such payment does not raise a federal question under this clause. Dugger v. Bocock, 104 U. S. 596, citing Delmas v. Insurance Co., 14 Wall. 666; Tarver v. Keach, 15 Wall. 68; Rockhold v. Rockhold, 92 U. S. 129; Insurance Co. v. Hendren, 92 U. S. 286; Bank v. McVeigh, 98 U. S. 332; Thorington v. Smith, 8 Wall. 1; Railroad Co. v. King, 91 U. S. 3; Stewart v. Salamon, 94 U. S. 435.

239. Railroad station vacated and required to be reopened.— Where the railroad commissioners of a state consented that a railroad operated therein might discontinue a station in use on its road, and by act of the legislature thereafter enacted the same railroad was required to stop its trains at that station, *held*, that no obligation of contract was impaired by such legislative act. Railroad Co. v. Hamersley, 104 U. S. 1.

240. Compromise of a part of state debt does not impair the obligation of the contract as to remainder.—A statute of Louisiana provided for refunding certain of its bonded indebtedness at sixty cents on the dollar, and further provided that when any holder of valid bonds of the state desired so to refund, and the board of liquidation refused, he could have his writ of *mandamus* to compel them so to do. A subsequent act prohibited the board of liquidation from funding under said former act any bonds of questionable and doubtful obligation until the supreme court had declared such bonds valid. *Held*, that said latter act did not impair any obligation of contract between the state and the holders of any bonds so refused to be refunded; that in proposing a scheme for compromise the state may choose what debts shall be included in the compromise without violating the obligation of its contract with other creditors not so included; that such creditors had all the remedies left that they had when the contract was made. Guaranty Co. v. Board of Liquidation, 105 U. S. 622.

241. Removal of state capital after contract for erection.—Where a state has made a contract to erect a capital in a certain place, and thereafter the constitution removes the capital to another place, this is not a law impairing the obligation of a contract. It is simply a breach of contract. Brown v. Colorado, 106 U. S. 95.

242. Provision for compromise of canal bonds.—Where a canal company had issued over $2,000,000 of mortgage bonds which had been sold to various parties, a plan for settlement of the affairs of the debtor corporation was devised by parties in interest, and a statute was enacted to give authority for such settlement, and provided, *inter alia*, that the agreement, if entered into, should only be binding on such bondholders "as shall signify their assent in writing thereto, and in case any such bondholder shall fail to file with the president of such corporation his or her refusal in writing to concur in such agreement within three months, etc., shall be taken to have assented thereto." *Held* not in conflict with this clause; that while a majority cannot compel a minority to enter into such agreement against their will, it may require a minority to act when such arrangement is proposed for the general good. It is analogous to the provisions of a statute of limitations. Gilfillan v. Canal Co., 109 U. S. 401.

243. Bonds of townships, act requiring registration of.—A township in Missouri voted to subscribe to the stock of a railroad company, and to issue bonds in payment of such subscription, and the railroad company accepted the same. Thereafter the legislature by an act required all such bonds to be registered with the state auditor before they should have any validity. *Held*, that such law applied to the bonds issued in payment of such subscription, and that the said requirement did not impair any obligation of such contract of subscription. Hoff v. Jasper County, 110 U. S. 53.

244. Same.—Such law was not void under article 1, section 28, constitution of 1870 of Missouri, forbidding the passage of retrospective laws. Id.

245. United States supreme court will decide independently when a contract exists.—Whether an alleged contract arises from state legislation, or by agreement with agents of a state, by its authority, or by stipulations between individuals exclusively, the supreme court of the United States will form its own judgment, and, independently of the adjudications of the state, decide whether there exists a contract within the protection of the federal constitution Jefferson Branch Bank v Skelly, 1 Black, 436; Wright v Nagle, 101 U S 794; Railroad Co v Palmes 109 U S 257.

246. A statute of Kentucky examined and held to constitute a contract with the Louisville Gas Company, the obligation of which was impaired by a subsequent grant to another company Louisville Gas Co. v Citizens' Gas L. Co, 115 U S 683

247. In reaching a conclusion upon the question as to whether or not given legislation impairs the obligation of a contract, the United States courts decide for themselves independently of any decision of the state courts on that question And if the decision requires a construction of a state constitution and laws the federal court is not governed by previous decisions of the state courts on the same or similar questions, except where they have been so firmly established as to become a rule of property Louisville, etc. R. R. v Palmes, 109 U. S 241

248 Impairment must be by law of a state.—In order to come within the provisions of this clause, not only must the obligation of a contract have been impaired, but it must have been impaired by a law of the state. The prohibition is aimed at the legislative power of the state and not at the decisions of its courts, or the acts of administrative or executive boards or officers, or the doings of corporations or individuals. The supreme court has, therefore, no jurisdiction to review a judgment of the highest court of a state on the grounds that the obligation of a contract has been impaired, unless some legislative act of the state has been upheld by the judgment sought to be reviewed. New Orleans Water-works v Louisiana Sugar Co, 125 U. S 18

249. Extent of provision—The supreme court has authority to declare a state law unconstitutional, upon the ground of its impairing the obligation of contracts between different states Green v Biddle, 8 Wheat 1

250. The prohibition of the constitution embraces all contracts, executed or executory, between private individuals, or a state and individuals, or corporations, or between the states themselves. Id

251. It applies to contracts between a state and the United States. Achison v Huddleson, 12 How 293

252 This clause necessarily refers to a law enacted after the date of the contract in suit. Lehigh Water Co. v Easton, 121 U S 388

253 A state constitution is not a contract within the meaning of this clause Church v Kelsey, 121 U S 282.

254 This clause does not refer to national legislation No provision of the constitution prohibits congress from doing this as it does the states Mitchell v Clark, 110 U S 633

255 Congressional grant a contract—A congressional grant to a state on conditions named therein becomes a contract when the conditions are agreed to by the state, and the grant accepted subject thereto Such contract is binding upon the state and cannot be violated without infringement of the constitution. McGee v Mathis, 4 Wall 143

256 State constitution—A state constitution is a law within the meaning of this clause, and a state can no more do what is here forbidden by the one than by the other M & M R. R. Co. v. McClure, 10 Wall 511

257. Fourth article, ordinance of 1787, no contract—The fourth article of the ordinance of 1787, "for the government of the territory of the

United States northwest of the River Ohio," declares that "the navigable waters leading into the Mississippi and St. Lawrence, and the carrying places between the same, shall be common highways and forever free, as well to the inhabitants of the said territory as to the citizens of the United States, and those of any other states that may be admitted into the confederacy, without any tax, impost or duty therefor." The state of Michigan was formed out of a part of the territory embraced in the provisions of said ordinance. The Manistee river is wholly within the state of Michigan and is a tributary of the St. Lawrence river. A corporation of the state of Michigan under authority of the laws of that state improved the navigation of the Manistee river and exacted tolls for the use thereof by parties using it in the transactions of commerce. *Held*, that there was no contract in the said fourth article of the ordinance of 1787, respecting the navigable waters of the territory northwest of the Ohio river emptying into the St Lawrence, which bound the people of the territory, or of any portion of it, when subsequently formed into a state and admitted into the Union. Sands v. Manistee River Imp. Co., 123 U. S. 288.

258. Taxation of debts due from citizens of other states.— There is nothing in the federal constitution which prohibits a state from taxing in the hands of one of its resident citizens a debt due to such citizen from a citizen of another state, such debt being evidenced by the bond of the debtor and secured by mortgage on real estate situated in the state in which the debtor resides. Kirtland v. Hotchkiss, 100 U. S. 491.

259. Intent of provision.— The provision of the federal constitution prohibiting states from enacting laws impairing the obligation of contracts was intended to secure the observance of good faith in the stipulations of parties against any state action. When a transaction is not based upon any assent of the parties it cannot be said that any faith is pledged with respect to it and no case arises for the operation of the prohibition. Garrison v. New York City, 21 Wall. 203. Quoted and approved in Freeland v. Williams, 131 U. S. 405-414.

260. Law of West Virginia forbidding sale of property on execution founded on judgment for acts of war.— The provision of the constitution of West Virginia of 1872 that the property of a citizen of the state should not 'be seized or sold under final process issued upon judgments or decrees *heretofore* rendered, or otherwise because of any act done according to the usages of civilized warfare in the prosecution of 'the war of the rebellion' by either of the parties thereto," does not impair the obligation of a contract within the meaning of the federal constitution when applied to a judgment previously rendered and founded upon tort. A judgment for the recovery of damages in tort does not convert a transaction wanting the assent of the parties into one which necessarily implies assent. Freeland v. Williams, 131 U. S. 405, citing and approving Louisiana v. Mayor of New Orleans, 109 U. S. 285, Garrison v. New York City, 21 Wall. 196, Satterlee v. Matthewson, 2 Pet. 380.

261. Withdrawal of Texas lands from sale.— The statute of Texas, July 14, 1879, and March 11, 1881, providing for the sale of a portion of the vacant and unappropriated public lands of the state did not confer upon a person making an application for a survey of a part of said lands, and paying the fees for filing and recording the same, a vested interest in such lands which could not be impaired by a withdrawal of them from sale under the provisions of a subsequent statute Such application is in the nature of a pre-emption of government lands under the federal statutes. It has always been held that occupation under pre-emption does not confer upon the pre-emptor such right as prevents the United States from withdrawing the lands from sale. So held in Frisbie v. Whitney, 9 Wall. 187 Yosemite Valley Case, 15 Wall 77, 87 Until the applicant had done everything required by law to secure the right no contract could arise Campbell v Wade, 132 U S. 34.

262. Marriage contract.—The contract of marriage is not a contract within the meaning of the provision which prohibits states from impairing the obligation of contracts Hunt v. Hunt, appendix to 131 U. S. Reports (cases omitted in reports), CLXV.

2 No State shall, without the consent of the Congress, lay any imposts or duties on imports or exports, except what may be absolutely necessary for executing its inspection laws, and the net produce of all duties and imposts laid by any State on imports or exports shall be for the use of the treasury of the United States, and all such laws shall be subject to the revision and control of the Congress

1 Imposts—Imports—Duties—Definition.—An impost or duty on imports is a custom or tax levied on articles brought into the country, and it is no less an impost or duty when levied on the goods after they are landed. Imports are the articles themselves which are brought into the country. A duty on imports, then, is not merely a duty on the act of importation, but is a duty on the thing imported, and extends to a duty levied after the import has entered the country Brown v Maryland, 12 Wheat. 419-438, Low v Austin, 13 Wall 29, Woodruff v Parham, 8 Wall 123, Hinson v Lott, 8 Wall 148, License Cases, 5 How. 504, Leisy v. Hardin, 135 U S 100, Murray v Charleston, 96 U S 447

2. A branch of the taxing power.—This power to lay duties or imposts on imports is considered in the constitution as a branch of the taxing power of the government. It is so treated in the first clause of the eighth section "Congress shall have power to lay and collect taxes, duties, imposts and excises" The power of imposing duties on imports, then, is classed with the power to levy taxes, and that seems to be its natural place. The states might have exercised this power had the constitution contained no prohibition on this subject This is an exception to the acknowledged power of the states to levy taxes Gibbons v Ogden, 9 Wheat. 1, 201, 202, Hamilton Co v. Massachusetts, 6 Wall. 639, State Tonnage Tax Cases, 12 Wall 204-215

3. Case stated.—An act of Maryland required all importers of foreign goods by the bale or package, and other persons selling the same by wholesale bale or package, to take out a license, for which they were charged a license fee. *Held*, that it amounted to laying a duty on imports as prohibited in this section, and was void Brown v Maryland, 12 Wheat. 419

4. Stamp tax on bills of lading — A law of California which imposed a stamp tax on bills of lading for transportation of gold or silver coin, gold dust, or gold or silver in bars or other form, when the same was to be transported from points within to points without the state, is a duty on exports, and so in violation of the constitution Almy v California, 24 How 169

5. The case of Pace v Burgess, 92 U. S 372, wherein a stamp is required to be placed on snuff intended for importation, is distinguished from the case of Almy v. California. In the case of the stamp upon the snuff it was held that it was simply a stamp to distinguish between snuff intended for export, on which no tax was levied, and that designed for domestic use and commerce, and which was subject to internal revenue tax

6. Auction sales — A tax levied under state law upon the amount of sales by an auctioneer, when applied to the sale of goods imported and sold for the importer in the original packages, is a duty on imports, and the law authorizing such tax is invalid Cook v. Pennsylvania, 97 U S 566

7. Money used for investment in exports — Where capital was uniformly and continuously employed in the business of purchasing cotton for exportation out of the United States to foreign countries through the customs department, but was in fact in money on the 1st day of January, the same being the date fixed by law at which property, including money, became liable to taxation, such money could not escape a subsequent assessment upon the ground that at the time such assessment was made the money was invested in cotton purchased for such exportation. People ex rel. Hanneman v Com'rs of Taxes, 104 U S 466

8. Articles transported from a sister state.— This provision does not extend to articles brought from another state of the Union, and an ordinance of a city taxing auction sales is valid when applied to goods, the products of other states, in original packages. Woodruff v. Parham, 8 Wall. 123.

9. Same — And a tax on spirituous liquors brought into a state, where the same tax is laid on liquors manufactured in the state, is a legitimate exercise of the taxing powers of the states Hinson v. Lott, 8 Wall. 148 But see Leisy v Hardin, 135 U S 100

10. Duty on exports, what constitutes.— A duty on exports must either be a duty levied on goods as a condition, or by reason of their exportation, or, at least, a direct tax or duty on goods which are intended for exportation. Where a general tax is laid on all property alike it cannot be construed as a duty on exports when falling on goods not then intended for exportation, though they should happen to be exported afterwards Brown v. Houston, 114 U. S. 622.

11. Exportation, when begun — Exportation is not begun until the goods are committed to the carrier for transportation out of the state, and until then they are taxable as a part of the general mass of property of the state, and such tax is not an export duty. Carrying goods by any means of transportation to the place from whence they are to be shipped out of the state is no part of the exportation shipment. Coe v. Town of Errol, 116 U. S. 517.

12. The prohibition in this clause does not mean goods carried from one state of the Union to another It applies exclusively to articles imported from foreign countries Brown v Houston, 114 U. S 622, Woodruff v Parham, 8 Wall 123. But see Leisy v. Hardin, 135 U. S. 100

13. Original package.— Goods imported from a foreign country are not subject to taxation by the state or municipal governments while they remain unbroken in the original packages in which they are imported and in the hands of the importer unsold. Brown v. Maryland, 12 Wheat. 419, Waring v Mobile, 8 Wall. 110, Low v Austin, 13 Wall 229

14. But when once sold by the importer, or when the packages are broken or the goods are mixed with other goods for sale, they are taxable as other property Waring v. Mobile, 8 Wall. 110, Pervear v Massachusetts, 5 Wall. 475.

15 Tobacco inspection law.— A law of Maryland requiring tobacco to be brought to a state warehouse to be there inspected and branded, etc, and to pay charges for outage and storage, examined, and held not to be in violation of the restrictions contained in this clause. Turner v Maryland, 107 U. S 38

16 Inspection laws — In interest of commerce and security of navigation.— Taxes in aid of the inspection laws of a state, under special circumstances, have been upheld as necessary to promote the interests of commerce and the security of navigation. They are so upheld as contemplating benefits and advantages to commerce and navigation, and as altogether distinct from imposts and excise duties, and duties on tonnage State Tonnage Tax Cases, 12 Wall 204-219

17. When the right of inspection exists and is properly exercised, it applies alike to imports and exports Neilson v Garza 2 Woods, 287.

18. What the exception consists of — Inspection laws, so far as they act upon articles of exportation, are generally executed on land, before the article is put on board the vessel, so far as they act on importation they are generally executed on articles which are landed. The tax or duty of inspection, then, is a tax paid for the performance of the services and while the article inspected is in the bosom of the country This is an exception to the prohibition on the states to lay duties on imports or exports, and was made because the tax would otherwise have been within the prohibition. Brown v Maryland, 12 Wheat. 419-438.

19. This inspection does not apply to human beings — This clause has reference to the inspection of property, and cannot be made to apply to free human beings The methods of determining whether such persons are criminals, paupers, lunatics, etc., are not to be determined by inspection laws alone People v Compagnie Gen. Transatlantique, 107 U. S 59

20 Minnesota meat inspection laws.— The statute of Minnesota approved April 16, 1889, entitled "An act for the protection of the public health, by providing for inspection, before slaughtering, of cattle, sheep and swine designed for slaughter for human food," is unconstitutional and void in so far as it requires, as a condition of sales in Minnesota of fresh beef, veal, mutton, lamb or pork for human food, that the animals from which such meats are taken shall have been inspected in that state before being slaughtered. The inspection thus provided for is of such character, or is burdened with such conditions, as will prevent the introduction into the state of sound meats, the product of animals slaughtered in other states Minnesota v. Barber, 136 U S. 314.

3 No State shall, without the consent of Congress, lay any duty of tonnage, keep troops or ships of war in time of peace, enter into any agreement or compact with another State or with a foreign power, or engage in war unless actually invaded, or in such imminent danger as will not admit of delays

1. **Definition.**— "Duty on tonnage" is a charge on vessels according to their tonnage, as instruments of commerce, charged for entering or leaving a port or for navigating public waters of the nation Huse v. Glover 119 U S 543

2 Tonnage, in our law, is a vessel s internal cubical capacity in tons of one hundred cubic feet each, to be ascertained in the manner prescribed by congress. Tonnage duties are duties upon vessels in proportion to their capacity An act of the legislature of a state which requires vessels landing in the harbors of such state to pay three cents per ton, to be computed on the capacity of the vessel, for the privileges of the harbor, wharf, etc, is a tonnage duty, and when so levied without the consent of congress is void Inman Steamship Co. v. Tinker, 94 U. S 238; State Tonnage Tax Cases, 12 Wall. 204–212

3. **Wharfage.**—Where a municipal corporation of a state has by the law of its organization an exclusive right to make wharves, collect wharfage and regulate wharfage rates, it can consistently with the constitution charge and collect such wharfage, proportioned to the tonnage of the vessels, from the owners of enrolled and licensed steamboats landing and mooring at its wharves constructed on the banks of a navigable river Keokuk N. L. Packet Co. v Keokuk, 95 U S. 80; N. W. Union Packet Co v St. Louis, 100 U S 423; Vicksburg v Tobin, 100 U S 430.

4. A municipal ordinance which provides for rates of wharfage, to be measured by the tonnage of the vessels landing thereat and using such wharf, is not in conflict with the constitution. Ouachita Packet Co v Aiken, 121 U. S. 444, citing and approving Transportation Co v Parkersburg, 107 U. S. 691, Morgan Steamship Co v Louisiana, 118 U. S. 455, Huse v. Glover, 119 U S 543

5. Where a town has the right, under its charter or the laws of the state, to demand compensation for the use of an improved landing wharf which it has made, it is no objection to the ordinance fixing the amount of this compensation that it is measured by the size of the vessel, and that this size was ascertained by the tonnage of each vessel. Cincinnati, etc Packet Co v Catlettsburg, 105 U. S 559, citing Cannon v. New Orleans, 20 Wall 577, Packet Co v. St. Louis, 100 U. S 423, Packet Co. v Keokuk, 95 U. S. 80, Guy v. Baltimore, 100 U. S 442

6. This clause interposes no hindrance to the recovery from a vessel landing at a wharf or pier owned by an individual, or municipal or other cor-

poration, of a just compensation for the use of such property, and it is within the power of the state to regulate this compensation so as to prevent extortion, and the same authority may be delegated to municipalities. In doing so however, the constitution must not be infringed. Cannon v. New Orleans, 20 Wall 577

7. **Quarantine tax.**— A state cannot, for the purpose of defraying the expenses of quarantine regulations, levy a tax on vessels entering her harbors in pursuit of commerce, and owned in foreign ports. Peete v. Morgan, 19 Wall 581.

8 **Tonnage duties are taxes,** as much so as duties on imports or exports, and the prohibition of the constitution extends as fully to such duties, if levied by the states, as to duties on imports or exports. State Tonnage Cases, 12 Wall. 204-215.

9. **Vessels may be taxed on property value.**— A state may levy taxes on vessels owned by its citizens as property, and based upon a property valuation, without being in conflict with this clause. The enrollment does not exempt the owner from taxation on his interest as property. W. P. & Cin Trans. Co v. Wheeling, 99 U S. 273.

10. An act of a state legislature which levys a tax on all steamboats, etc., plying in the navigable waters of the state, at the rate of $1 per ton of the registered tonnage of the vessel, is in direct contravention of this clause. The prohibition applies to all ships and vessels employed in the coasting trade, whether employed in commerce between ports in different states or between ports in the same state This does not, however, prevent a state from taxing ships and vessels owned by its citizens as property based on a valuation the same as other property within the state is taxed. State Tonnage Tax Cases, 12 Wall. 204.

11. A duty, or tax or burden imposed upon vessels under the authority of the state, which is by the law imposing it to be measured by the capacity of the vessel, and is in its essence a contribution claimed for the privilege of arriving and departing from a port of the United States, is within the prohibition of this clause. Cannon v. New Orleans, 20 Wall. 577.

12 **Pilotage — Forfeiture.**— A law of Pennsylvania providing that vessels neglecting or refusing to take a pilot shall forfeit a certain sum for the use of the society for relief of distressed and decayed pilots, etc , is not in conflict with clauses 2 and 3 of this section Cooley v. Board of Wardens, 12 How. 299.

13. **Compacts between states.**— A compact between two states of the Union, assented to by congress, whereby the boundary line is fixed between such states, becomes conclusive upon all the citizens thereof and binds their rights, and is to be treated to all intents and purposes as the real boundary. Poole v. Lessee of Fleeger, 11 Pet. 185, Rhode Island v. Massachusetts, 12 Pet. 657.

14. **Same.**— There can be but two tribunals that can act on the boundaries of states, the legislative or judicial power. The former is limited to assent or dissent where a compact or agreement in reference thereto is referred to them by the compacting states, and as the latter can be exercised only by the supreme court when a state is a party, it is there or it does not exist. *Held,* that the power does exist in the supreme court. Id.

15. The compact of 1789 between Virginia and Kentucky was valid under this provision. Congress impliedly assented thereto by the admission of Kentucky upon the condition mentioned in said compact. Green v. Biddle, 8 Wheat. 1.

16. The agreement between Virginia and West Virginia in respect to jurisdiction over the counties of Berkley, Jefferson and Fredrick can only be made valid and effective by consent of congress. This consent is contained by implication in the act of December 31, 1862, admitting West Virginia as a state in the Union. Virginia v. West Virginia, 11 Wall. 39.

ARTICLE II.

EXECUTIVE DEPARTMENT.

Section I.

PRESIDENT AND VICE-PRESIDENT.

1 The executive power shall be vested in a President of the United States of America. He shall hold his office during the term of four years, and, together with the Vice-President, chosen for the same term, be elected as follows —

1. Authority when beyond the reach of other departments.—The executive power is vested in a president, and as far as his powers are derived from the constitution, he is beyond the reach of any other department, except in the mode prescribed in the constitution through the impeaching power It does not follow from this that every officer in every branch of that department is under the exclusive direction of the president. As to their political duties they are under his direction But the congress may impose on such officers any duty they may think proper, which is not repugnant to any rights secured and protected by the constitution, and in such cases the duties grow out of and are subject to the control of the law and not to the discretion of the president. Kendall v United States, 12 Pet. 524, 610.

2 Where S & S. held claims against the government for postal services which had been allowed and credited to them by one postmaster-general, and by a succeeding postmaster-general had been disallowed and the credit so made had been charged back against the account of said S. & S , and thereupon the congress, by an act thereof, submitted the matter in dispute to the solicitor of the treasury, with authority and direction to settle and adjust the claims of said S. & S., . . . and directing by said act that the postmaster-general credit the relators with whatever sum or sums of money the solicitor should so decide was due them on such claim , and where upon such finding by the solicitor, stating the amount to be due to the claimants. the postmaster-general refused to make the credit,— *held* that the duty required of the postmaster-general was not an executive or political act under his office as head of a department in the executive office, but was a ministerial duty constitutionally devolved on him by the law of congress, and as such was examined by the court as a question of law, and that *mandamus* would lie to compel its performance, and that the matter was not subject to the control of the president, and that to so hold would (in the language of the court) "be vesting in the president a dispensing power, which has no countenance for its support in any part of the constitution, and is asserting a principle which, if carried out in its results to all cases falling within it, would be

clothing the president with power entirely to control the legislation of congress and paralyze the administration of justice." Id. 524, 613.

NOTE to Kendall v United States, 12 Pet 524 Taney, C J, in his dissenting opinion in the above cause, very tersely disposes of all the learned reasoning of the court in its opinion relative to the powers of the postmaster-general and the control which congress and the courts may exercise over that officer He agrees with the court in the conclusions as to the right of congress to control the office, and states his conclusions in the following language "I can hardly understand how so many grave questions of constitutional power have been introduced into the discussion of a case like this, and so earnestly debated on both sides The office of postmaster-general is not created by the constitution, nor are its powers or duties marked out by that instrument. The office was created by an act of congress, and whenever congress creates such an office by law, it may unquestionably by law limit its powers and regulate its proceedings, and may subject it to any submission or control, executive or judicial, which the wisdom of the legislature may deem right. There can, therefore, be *no* controversy about the constitutional powers of the executive or judiciary in this case." 12 Pet. at p. 626

3 **Appointment to office.**— The appointment to office is the sole act of the president, the transmission of the certificate is the sole act of the officer to whom that duty is assigned, and may be accelerated or retarded by circumstances which can have no influence on the appointment Marbury v Madison, 1 Cranch, 137

4. **Appointment to office dates from signing of commission.**— A commission bears date, and the salary of the officer commences, from his appointment, not from the transmission or acceptance of his commission. When a commission has been signed by the president, the appointment is made, and the commission is complete when the seal of the United States has been affixed to it by the secretary of state Id

5. **Discretion of president as to officer — When it ceases** — The discretion of the executive is to be exercised until the appointment has been made But having once made the appointment his power over the office is terminated in all cases where by law the officer is not removable by him. Id

6. **Political powers.**— By the constitution of the United States the president is invested with certain important political powers, in the exercise of which he is to use his own discretion, and is accountable only to his country in his political character and to his own conscience To aid him in the performance of those duties he is authorized to appoint certain officers who act by his authority and in conformity with his orders. In such cases their acts are his acts, and whatever opinion may be entertained of the manner in which executive discretion may be used there exists no power to control that discretion And in all cases where the executive possesses a constitutional or legal discretion, to be exercised by him through the heads of departments, their acts are only politically examinable. But where a specific duty is assigned by law, and individual rights depend upon the performance of that duty, it seems equally clear that the individual who con-

siders himself injured has a right to resort to the laws of his country for a remedy. Id.

7. **Heads of departments — Acts, how construed** — The heads of departments, when acting in their political capacity and in the discharge of the executive or political duties of their offices, are simply the aids of the president. In the exercise of such duties their acts are his acts They respect the nation, not individual rights, and being intrusted to the executive are executive acts and as such conclusive. But as to other duties imposed by law on such officers, and which are purely ministerial in their character, and do not partake of executive functions, and where individual rights depend upon the performance of such acts, such officer is the officer of the law, and amenable to the law for his acts, and cannot, at discretion, sport away the rights of others. Id , Kendall v United States, 12 Pet. 524.

8. **Habeas corpus.**— The president has no authority to suspend the privilege of the writ of *habeas corpus*, except as authorized and directed by congress McCall v McDowell, Deady, 233, S C 1 Abb (U S) 212

9. The president is the only officer known to the government that is not liable to answer to the writ of *habeas corpus* In Matter of Keeler, Hemp. 306

10. **Distilled spirits — Order excluding from territories.**— The act of congress authorizing the president to forbid the introduction of distilled spirits into the territory of Alaska is constitutional, and the executive order of the president based upon said act is a valid exercise of the executive authority The Louisa Simpson, 2 Sawy 57, United States v The Francis Hatch, 13 Am. Law Reg. 289.

2 Each State shall appoint, in such manner as the Legislature thereof may direct, a number of electors, equal to the whole number of senators and representatives to which the State may be entitled in the Congress, but no senator or representative, or person holding an office of trust or profit under the United States, shall be appointed an elector

The only rights and duties expressly vested by the constitution in the national government with regard to the appointment or the votes of presidential electors are by those provisions which authorize congress to determine the time of choosing the electors, and the day on which they shall give their votes, and which direct that the certificate of their votes shall be opened by the president of the senate in the presence of the two houses of congress, and the votes shall be then counted. In re Green, 134 U. S. 377.

3. [The electors shall meet in their respective States, and vote by ballot for two persons, of whom one at least shall not be an inhabitant of the same State with themselves And they shall make a list of all the persons voted for, and of the number of votes for each, which list they shall sign and cer-

tify, and transmit, sealed, to the seat of the government of the United States, directed to the President of the Senate The President of the Senate shall, in the presence of the Senate and House of Representatives, open all the certificates, and the votes shall then be counted. The person having the greatest number of votes shall be the President, if such number be a majority of the whole number of electors appointed. and if there be more than one who have such majority, and have an equal number of votes, then the House of Representatives shall immediately choose by ballot one of them for President, and if no person have a majority, then, from the five highest on the list, the said House shall in like manner choose the President. But in choosing the President, the votes shall be taken by States, the representation from each State having one vote, a quorum for this purpose shall consist of a member or members from two-thirds of the States, and a majority of all the States shall be necessary to a choice. In every case, after the choice of the President, the person having the greatest number of votes of the electors shall be the Vice-President But if there should remain two or more who have equal votes, the Senate shall choose from them by ballot the Vice-President.][1]

4 The Congress may determine the time of choosing the electors, and the day on which they shall give their votes, which day shall be the same throughout the United States

5. No person except a natural-born citizen, or a citizen of the United States at the time of the adoption of this Constitution, shall be eligible to the office of President; neither shall any person be eligible to that office who shall not have attained to the age of thirty-five years, and been fourteen years a resident within the United States.

6. In case of the removal of the President from office, or of his death, resignation, or inability to discharge the powers and duties of the said office, the same shall devolve on the Vice-President; and the Congress may by law provide for the case of removal, death, resignation, or inability, both of the President and Vice-President, declaring what officer shall then act as President; and such officer shall act accordingly, until the disability be removed or a President shall be elected.

[1] Altered by the XIIth Amendment.

7. The President shall, at stated times, receive for his services a compensation, which shall neither be increased nor diminished during the period for which he shall have been elected, and he shall not receive within that period any other emolument from the United States, or any of them.

8 Before he enter on the execution of his office, he shall take the following oath or affirmation:

"I do solemnly swear (or affirm) that I will faithfully execute the office of President of the United States, and will, to the best of my ability, preserve, protect, and defend the Constitution of the United States"

Section II.

POWERS OF THE PRESIDENT.

1. The President shall be commander-in-chief of the army and navy of the United States, and of the militia of the several States when called into the actual service of the United States; he may require the opinion in writing of the principal officer in each of the executive departments upon any subject relating to the duties of their respective offices, and he shall have power to grant reprieves and pardons for offenses against the United States, except in cases of impeachment.

1. **Calling out the militia** — The authority to do this is vested in congress (art 1, sec. 8, clause 15), and the congress may so provide by directing the president to call the militia into service and vest him with the discretion to decide when the necessity for such call exists Martin v. Mott, 12 Wheat. 19-29

2 And the decision of the president upon this question of necessity or exigency is conclusive upon all other persons and all other departments of the government Martin v Mott, 12 Wheat. 19-30, Luther v Borden, 7 How 43, United States v Cruikshank, 92 U. S 556.

3 **Commander-in-chief.**— In issuing his commands to the army and navy the president must not exceed the laws as established by the usages of nations, and as prescribed by the legislative department, otherwise his orders will afford no protection to those acting under them Little v Barreme, 2 Cranch 170, Otis v. Bacon, 7 Cranch, 589, Tracy v Swartwout, 10 Pet. 80

4 **Establish rules and regulations.**— The power of the executive to establish rules and regulations for the government of the army is undoubted; this necessarily implies the power to modify or repeal or to create anew. When promulgated by the secretary of war they must be received as the acts of the president, and, as such, are binding on all within the sphere of

his legal and constitutional authority United States v Eliason, 16 Pet. 291; The Confiscation Cases, 20 Wall 109

5. **May direct the movements of forces.**— As commander-in-chief the president is authorized to direct the movements of the naval and military forces placed by law at his command, and to employ them in the manner he may deem most effectual to harass and subdue the enemy. Fleming v. Page 9 How 603-615

6 **May subjugate enemy's country** — As commander-in-chief the president may cause the army and navy to invade the hostile country and subjugate it to the sovereignty and authority of the United States But his conquests do not enlarge the boundaries of the Union, nor extend the operation of our institutions and laws beyond the limits before assigned to them by the legislative power. Id.

7. **May employ secret agents.**— During the war the president, as commander-in-chief of the armies, was authorized to employ secret agents to enter the rebel lines and obtain information respecting the strength, resources and movements of the enemy, and to contract to pay for the services out of his contingent fund. Totten v United States, 92 U. S. 105.

8 **May form military government** — The president of the United States had authority in the exercise of belligerent rights to authorize the formation of a military and civil government in the territory of the enemy held by the armies of the nation Such government being valid in its inception would continue to be a valid government after a treaty of peace had been concluded whereby the territory thus occupied had been ceded to the government. Until congress by appropriate legislation had provided for the formation of, and another government in conformity to such provision had been actually formed Cross v Harrison, 16 How 164

9. **May allow added rations** — The president has the discretionary power to allow such additional number of rations to officers commanding at separate posts as he may think just having respect to the special circumstances of such post. Parker v United States, 1 Pet. 293.

10 **May declare blockade** — The president of the United States has the right *jure belli* to declare a blockade of ports in possession of insurgent states which neutrals are bound to regard. Prize Cases, 2 Black, 635

11 **Cannot establish prize court.**— The president of the United States cannot establish a prize court or confer power to condemn prizes upon any inferior officer of the government, civil or military. Jecker v Montgomery, 13 How 498

12. **May establish provisional courts** — It was within the power of the president under this section to establish provisional courts in states in rebellion and occupied by federal forces, for the hearing of all causes under the state or federal laws The Grapeshot, 9 Wall 129

13 **Pardon; meaning of word as used in constitution.**— To understand the extent to which the power to pardon may be exercised, we must look to the extent of this prerogative, rightfully belonging to the executive of that nation whose language we speak, and whose principles of jurisprudence the people of the United States brought with them as colonists and established here If it had a well known meaning in that language and in that jurisprudence, the conclusion is that the convention which framed the

constitution, and the people who adopted it, used and understood the word as being used in the instrument with that defined and settled meaning. United States v. Harris, 1 Abb (U S) 110–114; Calder v Bull 3 Dall 390, Watson v Mercer 8 Pet. 110, Carpenter v Commonwealth, 17 How 493, United States v Wilson, 7 Pet. 160 Ex parte Wells, 18 How 316; United States v. Athens Armory, 2 Abb (U S) 150

14. Pardons, effect of — The proclamation of pardon issued by the president December 25, 1868, blots out the offense of treason and restores all those to whom it applies to all the rights, privileges and immunities of citizens under the constitution Armstrong v. United States, 13 Wall. 154, Pargoud v United States, id 156

15. It is unnecessary for persons to whom the pardon applies to prove adhesion to the United States in order to sustain a claim for captured or abandoned property. Pargoud v United States, *supra*

16 The proclamation of pardon issued by the president under date of December 25 1868, includes aliens domiciled in the country who gave aid and comfort to the rebellion Carlisle v United States, 16 Wall 147

17 Pardons — The president could annex to his offer of pardon any condition or qualification he sees fit, but after those conditions and qualifications had been complied with, the pardon, with its promises, took full effect. United States v Klein, 13 Wall 128

18 The president can grant a conditional pardon, or can commute a sentence from death to imprisonment for life. Ex parte Wells, 18 How. 307.

19. Pardon to be available in a given case must be pleaded and proved as any other fact — Delivery and acceptance are essential. The power to pardon in criminal cases is an ancient, immemorial prerogative of the executive power in a state, and our national constitution has adopted this as a part of the fundamental law of the nation The pardon is a private, though official act It is official in that it is the act of the executive, it is private in that it is delivered to the individual, and not to the court It must be pleaded or brought officially to the knowledge of the court in order that the court may give it effect in any given case There is nothing peculiar in it to distinguish it from other acts It is a deed to the validity of which delivery is essential, and the delivery is not complete without acceptance It may be rejected by the person to whom it is tendered, and if rejected there is no power in the court to force it upon the individual United States v Wilson, 7 Pet. 150

20. Not subject to injunction — The supreme court of the United States has no jurisdiction to enjoin the president of the United States in the performance of official acts, and no bill seeking to so enjoin him will be entertained by that court against the president as such or against him as an individual citizen in relation to any public act. Mississippi v Johnson, 4 Wall 475

21. Amnesty. — The term "to grant reprieves and pardons" as here used includes the right to grant amnesty United States v Klein, 13 Wall 128

22. Amnesty act, effect of, on confiscated property. — The proclamation of amnesty of 1868 did not have the effect to repeal the confiscation act United States v. Clarke, The Confiscation Cases, 20 Wall 92

23 For further authority as to the effect of amnesty upon property and confiscation, see Wallach v. Van Riswick, 92 U S 203, where Day v. Micou, 18 Wall 156, and Bigelow v. Forrest, 9 Wall 339, are cited and explained See, also, United States v Thomasson, 4 Biss 340, Armstrong v. United States, 13 Wall. 154, Pargoud v. United States, id 156

24. Exclusive power.—The power as here granted is exclusively in the president, and cannot be controlled or restricted by congress United States v Klein, 13 Wall. 128· Ex parte Garland, 4 Wall 380

2 He shall have power, by and with the advice and consent of the Senate, to make treaties, provided two-thirds of the senators present concur, and he shall nominate, and by and with the advice and consent of the Senate, shall appoint ambassadors, other public ministers and consuls, judges of the Supreme Court, and all other officers of the United States, whose appointments are not herein otherwise provided for and which shall be established by law, but the Congress may by law vest the appointment of such inferior officers as they think proper in the President alone, in the courts of law, or in the heads of departments.

3 The President shall have power to fill up all vacancies that may happen during the recess of the Senate, by granting commissions, which shall expire at the end of their next session

1. Treaties, manner of giving effect to.—When a treaty stipulates for anything of a legislative nature the manner of giving effect to the stipulation is by that power which possessed the legislative authority, and which consequently is authorized to prescribe laws to the people Ware v Hylton, 3 Dall 272

2. A law of the land—Under our constitution a treaty is a law of the land, and is to be regarded by the courts as equivalent to an act of the legislature whenever it operates of itself without the aid of legislation But when the terms of the stipulation import a contract—when either of the parties engages to perform a particular act—the treaty addresses itself to the political, not the judicial department, and the legislature must execute the contract before it can become a rule of court Foster & Elam v. Neilson 2 Pet 314, Ware v Hylton, 3 Dall 272

3 **May be with Indians.**—Indian tribes are states in a certain sense, and treaties may be made with them as such, although they are neither foreign states nor states of the Union within the meaning of the constitution of the United States Holden v Joy 17 Wall 211

4 **Made citizens.**—Indians may be admitted to citizenship of the United States by treaty. United States v Rhodes, 1 Abb (U S) 43.

5 The treaty with Spain by which Florida was ceded to the United States is the law of the land. It admitted the inhabitants of Florida to the enjoyment of the privileges, rights and immunities of citizens of the United States

except the right to participate in the government, which right was in abeyance until Florida became a state. While it continued a territory it was, pursuant to the constitution, under the government of congress. American Ins. Co. v. Canter, 1 Pet. 511.

6. **Appointment of officers.**— The nomination is the sole act of the president. He sends in the name for the designated office to the senate, and it is in this manner that the "advice of the senate" is asked. Marbury v. Madison, 1 Cranch, 137.

7. **Appointment not complete until commission is signed.**— When the nomination has been made to the senate and concurred in, the appointment is not complete until the commission is signed by the president. When this is done the appointment is complete, and the right to the office vests in the appointee even before the commission is delivered. Such was the holding in Marbury v. Madison, 1 Cranch, 137.

NOTE — But Mr. Jefferson refused to be bound by this decision and to deliver the commission, claiming that the act was an executive or political act over which the courts had no control. See Jefferson's Correspondence, pp. 75, 317, 372.

8. **The power to appoint includes the power to remove** when the constitution has not otherwise provided, and when the laws of congress have not fixed a tenure of office. Ex parte Hennen, 13 Pet. 259; United States v. Avery, Deady, 204.

NOTE — The controversy over this power resulted in the passage of tenure of office act during the administration of President Johnson, which was passed over his veto, March 2, 1867.

9. **Has power to supersede, when.**— The president has power to supersede or remove an officer of the army by appointing another in his place, with the advice and consent of the senate. Keyes v. United States, 109 U. S. 336.

10. **Navy agents appointed by president.**— The power to appoint navy agents is vested in the president, by and with the advice and consent of the senate. Such agents cannot be appointed in any other way. Strong v. United States, 6 Wall. 788.

11. **Ambassadors and other public ministers and consuls.** — These words, as used in this section, and as used in section 3 of article II, and section 2 of article III, are descriptive of a class existing by the law of nations, and apply to diplomatic agents, whether accredited by the United States to a foreign power or by a foreign power to the United States. In re Baiz, 135 U. S. 403–419.

12. **"Congress may by law vest the appointment of such inferior officers as they think proper in the president alone, in the courts of law, or in the heads of departments."**— Under this clause congress had the power to vest in the circuit courts the appointment of supervisors of election, as provided for in relation to elections where representatives in congress are chosen. Ex parte Siebold, 100 U. S. 371; Ex parte Clarke, id. 399.

13. **Extradition.**— The power to surrender to a foreign government, upon demand therefor, any person found within the limits of the United

States, whether within a state or the territories of the United States, is a power undoubtedly belonging to the government of the United States It is clearly included in the treaty-making power and the corresponding power of appointing and receiving ambassadors and other public ministers. Holmes v Jennison, 14 Pet. 540-569

14. What the power includes and how conferred — The power to make treaties is given by the constitution in general terms, without any description of the objects intended to be embraced by it, and consequently is designed to include all those subjects which, in the ordinary intercourse of nations, had usually been the subject of negotiation and treaty, and which are consistent with the nature of our institutions and the distribution of power between the national and state governments Id.

Section III.

DUTIES OF THE PRESIDENT.

He shall, from time to time, give to the Congress information of the state of the Union, and recommend to their consideration such measures as he shall judge necessary and expedient, he may, on extraordinary occasions, convene both houses, or either of them; and in case of disagreement between them, with respect to the time of adjournment, he may adjourn them to such time as he shall think proper, he shall receive ambassadors and other public ministers; he shall take care that the laws be faithfully executed, and shall commission all the officers of the United States.

1. Extraordinary occasion — The decision of whether the occasion is extraordinary rests wholly with the president — While there is no case in which this clause receives direct construction, the general doctrine is that, when a discretion is reposed in the executive neither the legislative nor judicial departments can control the executive in the exercise of such discretion Probably the case most nearly in point here is Martin v Mott, 12 Wheat. 19. It is there decided that "the authority to decide whether the exigency contemplated in the constitution of the United States and the act of congress of 28th February, 1795, chapter 101, in which the president has authority to call forth the militia 'to execute the laws of the Union suppress insurrection and repel invasion,' have arisen, is exclusively vested in the president, and his decision is conclusive on all other persons."

2. Power to adjourn congress — This power has never been exercised by the president, and there are no decisions of the supreme court of the United States bearing directly on the power, or its exercise It has been held in Illinois to the effect that when the executive of the state assumes that there is a disagreement between the two houses in respect to the question of adjournment, and acting upon such assumption, adjourns the general assembly to a day certain, and both bodies acquiesce therein by failing to hold sessions for eleven days, the legislature will be held in law to have adjourned. People v Hatch, 33 Ill. 9.

3. **Power to receive ambassadors — Recognition of foreign government exclusively a political act.**— The courts have no power or authority to recognize a foreign government. That belongs exclusively to the political department. In case of civil war in a foreign state, the courts of the Union must recognize the contending powers as the legislative and executive departments of the government of the United States recognize them. United States v. Palmer, 3 Wheat. 610, Gelston v Hoyt, 3 Wheat. 246, The Divina Pastora, 4 Wheat. 52, The Neustra Senora de la Caridad, 4 Wheat. 497

4. **President shall take care that the laws be faithfully executed** — A civil war is never publicly proclaimed *eo nomine* against insurgents The president is bound to accept the challenge of such war without waiting for any special legislation therefor The constitution confers on him the whole executive power and he is bound to see that the laws be faithfully executed Prize Cases, 2 Black, 667.

5. **Not subject to injunction.**— In the exercise of his executive duties the president cannot be enjoined by the courts, or required to act by *mandamus* Mississippi v Johnson, 4 Wall. 498

6 **Execute the laws — Commission officers — The discretion of executive is not subject to control.**— By the constitution the president is intrusted with certain important political powers, in the exercise of which he is to use his own discretion, and is accountable only to his country in his political character, and to his own conscience, and whatever opinion may be entertained as to the manner in which such discretion is exercised, there is no power and can be none, to control that discretion Marbury v. Madison, 1 Cranch, 137 See pp 165, 166

7 **Justices of supreme court — Protection of** — While there is no express statute authorizing the appointment of a deputy marshal or any other officer to attend a judge of the supreme court when traveling in his circuit, and to protect him against assaults or other injury, the general obligation imposed upon the president of the United States by the constitution to see that the laws be faithfully executed, and the means placed in his hands, both by the constitution and the laws of the United States, to enable him to do this, impose upon the executive department the duty of protecting a justice or judge of any of the courts of the United States when there is just reason to believe that he will be in personal danger while executing the duties of his office. In re Neagle, 135 U. S. 1.

SECTION IV.

IMPEACHMENT OF THE PRESIDENT.

The President, Vice-President, and all civil officers of the United States shall be removed from office on impeachment for and conviction of treason, bribery, or other high crimes and misdemeanors.

ARTICLE III.

JUDICIAL DEPARTMENT.

SECTION I.

UNITED STATES COURTS.

The judicial power of the United States shall be vested in one Supreme Court, and in such inferior courts as Congress may from time to time ordain and establish The judges, both of the supreme and inferior courts, shall hold their offices during good behavior, and shall, at stated times, receive for their services a compensation, which shall not be diminished during their continuance in office

1. **Justices of supreme court as judges of circuit courts** — The judges of the supreme court have the right, by virtue of their office as such, without other or further commission, to sit as circuit judges in the respective circuits Practice and acquiescence in it for several years, commencing with the organization of the judicial system, have fixed the construction. Stuart v Laird, 1 Cranch, 299

2. **Circuit courts — Source of jurisdiction** — The circuit courts of the United States do not derive their judicial powers immediately from the constitution Their jurisdiction in every case must depend on congressional legislation, as the constitution provides the judicial powers of the United States shall be vested in one supreme court and such inferior courts as the congress may from time to time ordain and establish. Grover & Baker S M Co. v. Florence S M Co., Case of the Sewing Machine Companies, 18 Wall 553

3. **Number and character of courts in discretion of congress** The discretion of congress as to the number, the character and the territorial limits of the courts among which it shall distribute the judicial power is unrestricted except as to the supreme court. United States v Union Pac R R. Co, 98 U. S 569

4 **Authority to bring parties before court** — There is no prohibition in the constitution against declaring by an act of congress that, as to a class of cases of a special character, any circuit court in which such suit may be brought shall have power to bring before it all the parties necessary to its decision, by process served anywhere in the United States, nor is there anything in the constitution that prohibits congress from providing, as a rule of practice, that bills may be filed which otherwise would, under the rules of practice as adopted by the courts, be subject to objection as multifarious United States v U P. R R Co, 98 U S 569

5. **Territorial courts.**— These are not constitutional courts in which the judicial power conferred by the constitution on the general government

can be vested They are created by virtue of the general right of sovereignty which exists in the government; or in virtue of that clause which enables congress to make all needful rules and regulations respecting the territories The jurisdiction with which they are invested is not a part of the judicial power defined in this article of the constitution American Insurance Co v. Canter, 1 Pet 511

6 Territorial courts are not courts of the United States within the meaning of this section American Ins Co. v. Canter, 1 Pet 511 Benner v Porter, 9 How 235, Clinton v. Englebrecht, 13 Wall 434; Hornbuckle v. Toombs, 18 Wall 648, Good v. Martin, 95 U. S. 90, Reynolds v United States, 98 U S 145.

7. **They are legislative courts** —The courts of a territory are legislative courts. Congress in organizing territories and legislating for them combines the powers of both state and federal authorities With respect to the jurisdiction or subjects committed to such courts the distinction between federal and state jurisdiction, under the constitution of the United States, does not exist. Benner v Porter, 9 How. 235, Forsyth v. United States, id 571

8. **Judicial powers of — How derived.**—The powers of the general government are made up of concessions from the several states; whatever is not expressly given to the former the latter expressly reserves. The judicial power of the United States is a constituent part of these concessions United States v Hudson & Goodwin, 7 Cranch, 32

9. **Jurisdiction derived from constitution — What courts have.** Of all the courts which the United States may, under their general powers constitute, one only — the supreme court — possesses jurisdiction derived immediately from the constitution, and of which the legislative power cannot deprive it. All other courts created by the general government possess no jurisdiction but what is given them by the power that creates them Id

10. **Implied powers — Crimes against a state not such** —Certain implied powers must necessarily result to our courts But jurisdiction of crimes against the state is not among those powers. Id.

11. **Common-law jurisdiction.**— The courts of the United States have no common-law jurisdiction in cases of libel against the government of the United States Id.

NOTE —This decision is questioned by the court in United States v. Coolidge, 1 Wheat 415, but adhered to. There was no argument in either the leading case of United States v Hudson & Goodwin or in the later case

SECTION II.

JURISDICTION OF THE UNITED STATES COURTS.

1. The judicial power shall extend to all cases in law and equity arising under this Constitution, the laws of the United States, and treaties made or which shall be made, under their authority; to all cases affecting ambassadors, other public ministers, and consuls, to all cases of admiralty and maritime

jurisdiction; to controversies to which the United States shall be a party, to controversies between two or more States, between a State and citizens of another State, between citizens of different States, between citizens of the same State claiming lands under grants of different States, and between a State, or the citizens thereof, and foreign states, citizens, or subjects

1. **Departmental powers not interchangeable.**— Neither the legislative nor the executive branches of the government can constitutionally assign to the judiciary any duties but such as are properly judicial, and to be performed in a judicial manner. Nor can the executive or legislative departments review or sit as a court of errors on the judicial acts or opinions of the courts of the United States Per Jay, chief justice, Cushing, justice, and Duane, district judge, in circuit court of United States for district of New York, passing upon an act of congress See note to Hayburn's Case, 2 Dall. 410, 1 Lawyers' Co-operative Ed U S Sup Ct. Rep 436

2 **As to subject-matter — Cases arising under the constitution, the laws of the United States and treaties** — The act incorporating the Bank of the United States, giving the circuit courts of the United States jurisdiction of suits against them, *held* constitutional. Osborn v Bank of United States, 9 Wheat 739

3 The circuit courts of the United States have jurisdiction under the constitution and acts of congress in suits by the postmaster-general on bonds given to him by his deputy to pay all money that shall come into his hands, etc Postmaster-General v Early, 12 Wheat 136

4. The twenty-fifth section of the judiciary act is limited by the constitution and must be so construed as to be confined within such limits, but to construe this section so that a case can only arise under the constitution or treaty — when such right is created by the constitution or a treaty — would defeat the obvious purpose of the constitution as well as the act of congress. The language of both instruments extends the jurisdiction of the supreme court to rights protected by the constitution, treaties or laws of the United States from whatever source these rights may spring New Orleans v Armas, 9 Pet. 224.

5. This provision embraces alike civil and criminal cases arising under the constitution and laws Cohens v Virginia, 6 Wheat. 399 Both are equally within the domain of the judicial power of the United States, and there is nothing in the grant to justify the doctrine that whatever power may be exerted over a civil case may not be exerted as fully over a criminal one. Tennessee v Davis, 100 U S 257

6. Where it appears from the questions raised that some title right, privilege or immunity, on which the recovery depends will be defeated by one construction of the constitution or laws of the United States or sustained by the opposite construction, the case will be one arising under the constitution or laws of the United States. Starin v New York, 115 U. S. 248

7 The courts of the United States have exclusive jurisdiction of all seizures made on land or water for breach of the laws of the United States,

and any intervention of a state authority which, by taking the thing seized out of the hands of the United States officer, might obstruct the exercise of this jurisdiction is unlawful. Slocum v Mayberry, 2 Wheat. 1, Gelston v. Hoyt, 3 Wheat. 246.

8 Where a party claiming title to lands under an act of congress brought a bill for conveyance, and stated equities other than those arising under said act of congress, *held*, on appeal to United States supreme court, that no distinct equities arising out of the contract or transactions of the parties would be considered. The examination was confined to equities arising under the act of congress Matthews v Zane, 7 Wheat 164

9. The federal supreme court has jurisdiction on writ of error to examine the judgment of a state court, where the laws of congress and the acts of officers executing them in perfecting titles to public lands have been drawn in question and construed by the state court and the decision is against the validity of the title so set up. Cousin v Labatut, 19 How 202, Fulton v. McAfee, 16 Pet 149, affirmed, Burke v Gaines, 19 How 328

10. A judgment of the highest court of a state, sustaining the validity of an assessment upon lands under a statute of the state which was alleged to be unconstitutional and void because it afforded to the owners no opportunity to be heard upon the whole amount of the assessment, involves a decision against a right claimed under the provisions of this section, and may be reviewed in the United States supreme court notwithstanding the constitution of the state contains a similar provision, and no constitutional provision is specifically mentioned in the record of the state court Spencer v. Merchant, 125 U. S 345.

11. In an action of ejectment between two citizens of Maryland for a tract of land in Maryland, if the defendant set up an outstanding title in a British subject which he contends is protected by the treaty, and therefore the title is out of the plaintiff, and the highest state court in Maryland decides against the title thus set up, it is not a case in which a writ of error can lie to the supreme court of the United States It is not a case 'arising under a treaty" The judiciary act must be restrained by the constitution. Owings v Norwood s Lessee, 5 Cranch, 344.

12 The supreme court of the United States has no jurisdiction of a bill to enjoin the president in the performance of his official duties, and no such bill will be received by that court whether presented against the president as such or against him as an individual citizen. Mississippi v. Johnson, 4 Wall 475

13. A court of the United States cannot enjoin proceedings in a state court. Diggs & Keith v Wolcott, 4 Cranch, 179

14. The constitution vests in the supreme court a jurisdiction for its final interpretation and for the laws passed by congress, to give them an equal operation in all of the states Also to determine when the laws of the states conflict with the federal constitution and with the laws of congress Dodge v Woolsey, 18 How 331

15. **Mandamus** — The courts of the United States have no jurisdiction to entertain a *mandamus* on the secretary of the treasury commanding him to pay out the money in the treasury on a disputed claim The power of these courts to command the heads of departments to perform any duty of

their offices has been strongly contested in the supreme court, in these contests it would seem that the power is limited to acts or proceedings by the officer not implied in the several and inherent functions or duties of his office — acts required of the individual rather than of the functionary United States ex rel. v. Guthrie, Secretary of the Treasury, 17 How 284

16. Political questions not cognizable by courts — The question as to whether or not the constitution of a state of the Union has been ratified by a majority of those entitled to suffrage is not such a question as can be settled by judicial proceedings This subject is political in its nature, and is so treated in the constitution of the United States, the power of recognizing a state government is in congress Luther v. Borden, 7 How 1

17. A bill to restrain the secretary of war of the United States, and the generals acting under him and under the command of the president as commander-in-chief, from carrying into execution certain acts of congress, and claiming that such execution would subvert state governments, does not present a case within the judicial cognizance of the federal supreme court. It calls for the judgment of the court upon political questions which do not involve personal or property rights and over such questions the court has no jurisdiction Georgia v Stanton, 6 Wall 50.

NOTE.— In this case the court review and distinguish. Rhode Island v. Massachusetts, 12 Pet 669, Florida v Georgia 17 How 478, Cherokee Nation v Georgia, 5 Pet. 1, and cite in support of decision, New York v Connecticut 4 Dall 3, Nabob of Carnatic v East Ind Co, 1 Ves Jr. 375, S C. 2 Ves Jr 56, Penn v Lord Baltimore, 1 Ves. Sr 446.

18. The power of the courts of the United States to punish for contempts of their authority is not merely incidental to their general power to exercise judicial functions, but is expressly recognized and provided for by laws of congress. Ex parte Terry. 128 U S 289-304; Ex parte Savin, 131 U S. 267.

19 As to parties — Cases affecting ambassadors, etc, and consuls.— Where the record discloses that a foreign consul is defendant, the state has no jurisdiction except for certain offenses enumerated in the judiciary act. The jurisdiction of the United States courts in cases against ambassadors, other public ministers and consuls is exclusive Davis v. Packard, 7 Pet. 276.

20. These words as here used apply to and are descriptive of a class existing by the law of nations, and apply to diplomatic agents, whether accredited by the United States to a foreign power or by a foreign power to the United States. In re Baiz, 135 U S. 403-419

21. An indictment for infracting the law of nations by offering violence to the person of a foreign minister is not a case "affecting ambassadors, other public ministers and consuls" The United States v Ortega, 11 Wheat. 467

22. Same.— *Quære*, whether the jurisdiction of the supreme court is not only original but exclusive in cases affecting ambassadors, etc Id.

23. Admiralty — There are three classes of cases enumerated in this section to which the judicial power extends 1st. All cases in law or equity arising under this constitution, the laws of the United States, and treaties made or to be made under their authority 2d To all cases affecting ambassadors or other public ministers and consuls 3d To all cases of admiralty and maritime jurisdiction A grant of jurisdiction over one of these classes does not confer jurisdiction over either of the other two A case in admiralty does not arise under the constitution or laws of the United States. The law of admiralty and maritime, as they have existed for ages, is applied by the courts to these cases as they arise American Ins Co v Canter, 1 Pet. 511

24. The constitution and laws of the United States give jurisdiction to the district courts over all cases in admiralty. Id

25 But jurisdiction over the case does not constitute the case itself. The constitution declares that "the judicial power shall extend to all cases in law and equity *arising under this constitution*, the law of the United States, and treaties made or which shall be made under their authority, to all cases affecting ambassadors or other public ministers and consuls, *to all cases of admiralty and maritime jurisdiction*" This comprises three distinct classes of cases, and jurisdiction over one does not confer jurisdiction over either of the other classes A case in admiralty does not, in fact, arise under the constitution or laws of the United States. These cases are as old as navigation itself, and the law of admiralty and maritime, as it existed for ages, is applied by the courts to the cases as they arise. Id.

26 The admiralty courts possess a general jurisdiction in cases of suits by material-men *in personam* and *in rem.* (Instance court) The General Smith, 4 Wheat 438

27. The grant to the United States in the constitution of all cases of admiralty and maritime jurisdiction does not extend to a cession of the waters in which those cases may arise or of general jurisdiction over the same Congress may pass all laws which are necessary for giving the most complete effect to the exercise of the admiralty and maritime jurisdiction granted to the government of the Union, but the general jurisdiction over the place, subject to this grant, adheres to the territory as a portion of territory not yet given away; and the residuary power of legislation will still remain in the state United States v. Bevans, 3 Wheat 336

28. Admitting that the third article of the constitution, which declares "the judicial power shall extend to all cases of admiralty and maritime jurisdiction" vests in the United States courts exclusive jurisdiction of all such cases, and that a murder committed in the waters of a state where the tide ebbs and flows is a case of admiralty and maritime jurisdiction, congress has not by the eighth section of the act of 1790, chapter 9, 'for the punishment of certain offenses against the United States," so exercised this power as to confer on the courts of the United States jurisdiction over such murder United States v Bevans, 3 Wheat 336

29 Although admiralty jurisdiction can be exercised in the states in those courts only which are established by congress, in pursuance of the powers conferred in the third article of the constitution, the same limitation does not extend to the territories In legislating for them congress exercises the combined powers of the general and state governments American Ins. Co v Canter, 1 Pet. 511.

30 The act of the territorial legislature of Florida erecting a court with power to decree for salvage, the sale of a cargo of a vessel stranded and brought within the territorial limits is not inconsistent with the constitution and laws of the United States, and is valid Id

31 The grant in the constitution extending the judicial power "to all cases of admiralty and maritime jurisdiction" is neither to be limited to or interpreted by what were cases of admiralty jurisdiction in England at the date of the adoption of our constitution Such jurisdiction is not taken from the United States courts because the common-law courts may have concurrent jurisdiction Waring v Clarke, 5 How 441

32 All the navigable waters of the Atlantic coast which empty into the sea, or into bays and gulfs that form a part of the sea, are as much within the admiralty and maritime jurisdiction of the United States as is the sea itself Transportation Co. v Fitzhugh, 1 Black, 574.

33. The act of congress of February 26, 1845, extending the jurisdiction of the district courts so as to include certain cases arising upon the lakes and navigable waters connecting them, is constitutional, and rests upon the ground that the lakes and navigable waters connecting them are a part of the admiralty and maritime jurisdiction as it existed when the constitution was adopted Propeller Gennesee Chief v Fitzhugh, 12 How 443

34 This jurisdiction is not confined to tide waters. It extends to all public navigable lakes and rivers where commerce is carried on between states or with foreign nations Id.

35. All previous decisions limiting the admiralty jurisdiction to tide-waters is overruled, and the broad doctrine announced that jurisdiction as conferred by the federal constitution extends wherever ships float and navigation successfully aids commerce whether internal or external. Such is the scope of the decision in Gennesee Chief v Fitzhugh, 12 How 457, Hine v Trevor, 4 Wall 555

36 The general system of maritime law which was familiar to the lawyers and statesmen of this country when the constitution was adopted was intended and referred to when it was declared in that instrument that the judicial power of the United States should "extend to all cases of admiralty and maritime jurisdiction," and the question of its true limits is exclusively a judicial question, and no state law or act of congress can make it broader or narrower than the judicial power may determine those limits to be But what the law within the limits may be depends on what has been received as maritime law in the usages of this country and on such legislation as may have been competent to affect it And it is the settled adjudication of the supreme court that material-men furnishing repairs and supplies to a vessel in her home port do not acquire thereby any lien upon the vessel by the general maritime law as received in the United States It cannot be supposed that the framers of the constitution contemplated that the maritime law should remain unchanged, but the courts cannot change it they can only declare it If within its proper scope any change is desired in its rules, other than of procedure it must be made by the legislative department. *Semble*, that congress, under the power to regulate commerce, has authority to establish a lien on vessels of the United States, in favor of material-men, uniform throughout the whole country. In particular cases in which congress has not exercised the power of regulating commerce, and

where the subject does not require the exclusive exercise of that power, the states, until congress acts, may continue to legislate *Hence*, liens granted by state law to material-men for furnishing necessaries to a vessel in her home port in said state are valid, although the contract is a maritime one and can only be enforced in United States district courts The Lottawanna, 21 Wall. 558.

37. The admiralty jurisdiction of the United States courts is limited to contracts claims and services which are purely maritime and such as have respect to rights and duties appertaining to navigation A contract to build a vessel or to furnish labor or material therefor is not such a contract as gives jurisdiction to a court of admiralty to enforce, and a law of a state providing a lien for such contractor material-man or laborer is not in conflict with the constitution of the United States Edwards v Elliott, 21 Wall. 532, citing The Jefferson (Ferry Co v Beers), 20 How 400, Morewood v. Enequist, 23 How 491, Cunningham v Hall, 1 Cliff. 45; Young v The Orpheus, 2 Cliff. 35

38 State legislatures have no authority to create a maritime lien nor can they confer any jurisdiction upon a state court to enforce such a lien by suit or proceeding *in rem*, as practiced in the admiralty courts Edwards v. Elliott, 21 Wall 532, citing The Belfast, 7 Wall 644. The Moses Taylor, 4 Wall 411, Hine v Trevor, 4 Wall 555

39 The courts of the United States have admiralty jurisdiction over cases of collision occurring on the high seas between vessels owned by foreigners of different nationalities The Belgenland, 114 U S 355.

40. The courts of the United States have no jurisdiction of the crime of manslaughter committed by the master upon one of the seaman on board a merchant vessel of the United States lying in the river Tigris, in the empire of China thirty-five miles above its mouth, off Wampoa, about one hundred yards from the shore, in about four and a half fathoms of water, and below low-water mark United States v Wiltberger, 5 Wheat. 76

41. A vessel navigating the Chicago river by means of being towed by a steam tug struck a building on land with its jib-boom and damaged it and its contents, a statute of Illinois gave a lien in such cases on the tug, enforceable in the courts of the state In an action *in personam* against her owner and surety in a bond for her release *held* 1 That such cause of action was not a maritime tort cognizable in a court of admiralty 2 That the lien created by the state law did not conflict with the constitution of the United States Johnson v. Chicago Elevator Co, 119 U S 388

42 Controversies to which the United States shall be a party — Where persons hold claims against the United States, suit cannot be brought by such claimants to enforce the claim, except consent therefor is obtained through an act of congress Kendall v. United States, 12 Pet 524, and at 611

43. The government of the United States is not liable to be sued except on its own consent given by law. Hill v. United States, 9 How 386.

44. A money judgment cannot be rendered against the United States except by the court of claims If the government is liable on a contract, the court of claims alone has jurisdiction to try the question. Case v. Terrell, 11 Wall 199

45. The doctrine that the United States cannot be sued in any court except provision therefor is made by congress is limited to suits against the United States directly and by name This exemption cannot be pleaded by officers or agents of the government when sued by private persons for property in their hands as such officers or agents. United States v Lee, 106 U S 196

46 **Controversies between two or more states.**— Although the constitution does not in terms, extend the judicial power to all controversies between two or more states, yet it, in terms, excludes none, whatever may be their nature or subject Rhode Island v Massachusetts, 12 Pet. 657

47. A state which is indebted to a citizen of another state cannot be sued upon such demand by the state whereof the creditor is a citizen. One state cannot in this manner create a controversy with another state Nor is a state an independent nation, clothed with authority and power to make an imperative demand upon a sister state for the payment of debts due to the citizens of the former from the latter New Hampshire v Louisiana, New York v Louisiana, 108 U S. 76

48. **"Between a state and citizens of another state."**— Under this clause, and prior to the adoption of the eleventh amendment, it was held that a state could be sued in *assumpsit* by a citizen of another state, and that service of process on the governor and attorney-general of the defendant state was sufficient to confer jurisdiction upon the United States court, and that the state failing to appear after such summons judgment by default could be rendered against it Chisholm v Georgia, 2 Dall 419

49 **"Between citizens of different states"— Corporations** —A corporation aggregate cannot be a citizen, and cannot litigate in the courts of the United States unless in consequence of the character of the individuals who compose the body politic, which character must appear by proper averments upon the record Hope Insurance Co v Boardman, 5 Cranch, 57.

50. A corporation aggregate composed of citizens of one state may sue a citizen of another state in the United States courts Bank of U S v Deveaux, 5 Cranch, 61

51. An act of congress incorporating a bank with power to sue and be sued, plead and be impleaded, does not confer upon such corporation a right to sue in the courts of the United States because of such incorporation. It only gives it capacity to appear as a corporation in any court which would by law have cognizance of the cause if brought by individuals Id.

52 The complainants are stated in the bill to be citizens of the state of South Carolina. The defendant, the Bank of Georgia is a body corporate existing under the laws of Georgia There is no averment that the members composing the corporation are citizens of Georgia *Held*, that the record does not show that the defendants are citizens of Georgia, and that the United States court has no jurisdiction Breithaupt v Bank of the State of Georgia 1 Pet 238

53. Bank of United States v Deveaux, 5 Cranch 61, cited and affirmed to the extent, viz That in a question of jurisdiction the court will look to the character of the persons composing the corporation and, if it appear that they are citizens of another state than that in which the defendant resides, and that fact is made to appear by proper averment, the corporation may sue in its corporate name in the courts of the United States. Bank of Augusta v. Earle 13 Pet 519.

54. A citizen of one state can sue a corporation which has been created by and transacts business in another state in the United States courts of the state in which the corporation is organized, although some of the members of the corporation are not citizens of such state, and although the state itself may be a member of the corporation Railroad Co v Letson, 2 How 497

55 A corporation created by and transacting business in a state is an inhabitant of the state, capable of being treated as a citizen for all purposes of suing and being sued, and an averment of the fact of its creation and the place of transacting business is sufficient to give the circuit courts jurisdiction Id

56. The right of a citizen of one state to sue a citizen of another state in the federal courts cannot be taken away by the latter being formed into a corporation by the laws of the state of which he is a citizen The corporation itself may then be sued as such. Marshall v B & O R. R Co, 16 How 314

57. In a suit against a corporation in its corporate name, an averment that it was a citizen of a particular state is sufficient to give the United States courts jurisdiction Where the law creating the corporation is a public law of which courts are bound to take notice it is sufficient to aver the citizenship of its members Covington Drawbridge v Shepherd, 20 How 227

58 An averment that the plaintiff is a citizen of Ohio and "complains of the Lafayette Insurance Company, a citizen of the state of Indiana," is not sufficient to show jurisdiction The supreme court does not hold that a voluntary association of persons, or an association into a body politic created by law is a citizen of a state within the meaning of this clause. The allegation, however, that the defendants are "a corporation created under the laws of the state of Indiana having its principal place of business in that state,' when confessed by demurrer, is sufficient to give jurisdiction It brings the case within the decision in Marshall v B & O R. R Co, 16 How 314, and the previous decisions therein referred to. Lafayette Ins Co. v French, 18 How 404

59 A bill which avers that "the Covington Bridge Company is a corporation and citizen of the state of Indiana" is sufficient for jurisdictional purposes Covington Drawbridge Co v Shepherd, 21 How 112.

60. A suit by or against a corporation of a state must be presumed to be by or against the citizens of the state which created the corporation, and no averment or evidence is admissible to prove the contrary for the purpose of withdrawing the jurisdiction of the court. Ohio & Miss R. R Co v Wheeler, 1 Black, 286

61 For the purposes of federal jurisdiction a corporation is regarded as if it were a citizen of the state where it was created, and no averment or proof as to citizenship of its members elsewhere will be permitted B & O R R. Co v Harris, 12 Wall 65, citing L C & C R R v Letson, 2 How. 497, Marshall v B. & O R R. Co, 16 How 329, O & M R. R. Co. v Wheeler, 1 Black, 297

62 Where a corporation is created by the laws of a state it is, in suits brought in the federal courts in that state, regarded as a citizen of such state, whatever the *status* of its citizenship may be elsewhere by the legislation of other states Therefore, where a citizen of Illinois sued the Chicago & Northwestern Railway Company in Wisconsin, and on his petition the

case was removed to the United States court, on the ground that the railroad company was a citizen of Wisconsin, the jurisdiction of the federal court was sustained notwithstanding the fact that the railroad company had a corporate existence in Illinois as well as in Wisconsin C & N W R'y Co. v Whitton, 13 Wall 270

63 The individual members of a corporation are, for the purposes of this section, conclusively presumed to be citizens of the state creating the corporation Steamship Co v Tugman, 106 U S 118

64 Where a statute of Wisconsin required that certain classes of actions against railroad corporations in that state should be brought "in some court established by the constitution and laws of that state," *held*, that such provision does not prevent a non-resident plaintiff from removing the action, under the act of congress of March 2, 1867, to the federal court, and maintaining it there C & N W R y Co v Whitton, 13 Wall 270

65. The constitution of the United States secures to citizens of another state than that in which suit is brought an absolute right to remove their cases into the federal court, upon compliance with the terms of the act of 1789 A statute of Wisconsin which obstructed this right, by providing that foreign insurance companies desiring to do business in that state, as a condition on which the state would permit them to do business therein, should file with the secretary of state an agreement not so to remove any case, is repugnant to the constitution and the law of congress The agreement of the insurance company derives no support from an unconstitutional statute, and is void. Home Ins Co v Morse, 20 Wall 445

66. The decision in Home Ins Co v Morse, 20 Wall. 445, re-affirmed, that an agreement to abstain in all cases from resorting to the United States courts is void as against public policy, and that a statute of a state requiring such an agreement is in conflict with this section of the constitution Doyle v. Continental Ins Co 94 U. S 535

67 *Held farther*, that a state may compel a foreign insurance company to abstain from litigating in the federal courts or to cease to do business in the state, and that this is justifiable because such foreign company has no constitutional right to do business in such state Id

68 Chapter 76, Laws of the Twenty-first General Assembly of Iowa, which requires a foreign corporation to obtain a permit to do business in the state, and further, as a prerequisite to obtaining such permit, requires the corporation to stipulate that it will be subject to all the provisions of the act, one of which provisions is as follows "Any foreign corporation sued or impleaded in any of the courts of this state upon any contract made or executed in this state, or to be performed in this state or for any act or omission, public or private arising originating or happening in the state, who shall remove any such cause from such state court into any of the federal courts, etc. shall forfeit such permit,—*held*, that the provision quoted is void because it denies to such corporation the right secured by this section. Home Insurance Co v. Morse 20 Wall 445, approved and the decision in Doyle v Continental Ins Co, 94 U S 535, explained and modified Barron v Burnside, 121 U S 186

69. Courts of equity have jurisdiction over corporations at the instance of one or more of their members to apply preventive remedies by injunction,

to restrain those who administer them from doing acts which would amount to a violation of the charters, or to prevent any misapplication of their capital or profits which might result in lessening the dividends or the value of shares, if the acts contemplated to be done create in law what is denominated a breach of trust. And such suit may be brought and maintained in the United States courts when the member of the corporation who is plaintiff is a citizen of a state other than the state under the laws of which the corporation exists and has its principal offices Dodge v. Woolsey, 18 How 331, Piqua Bank v Knoop, 16 How 369, Mechanics, etc Bank v Debolt, 18 How 380; Mechanics' Bank v Thomas, 18 How 384.

70. African race — The provisions of this section do not embrace the negro African race It does not put it in the power of a state to make a citizen out of one of that race so as to endue him with the full rights of citizenship in another state without the consent of such state It does not so act on the negro race as to raise him to citizenship when made free Dred Scott v Sandford, 19 How 393

71. Held that the plaintiff in error, being a negro African, was not a citizen of the state of Missouri within the meaning of this section, and was not entitled to sue in the courts of the United States Id.

72. Territory, citizen of — A citizen of a territory cannot sue a citizen of a state in the courts of the United States, nor can those courts take jurisdiction by other parties being joined who are capable of suing All the parties on each side must be subject to the jurisdiction or the suit will be dismissed Corporation of New Orleans v. Winter, 1 Wheat 91

73. The constitution does not restrain congress from giving the courts of a territory jurisdiction over a case brought by or against a citizen of the territory and the citizens of a territory may sue and be sued in the courts of such territory in such manner as may be regulated by act of congress defining and limiting the jurisdiction of such territorial courts Sere & Laralde v Pitot, 6 Cranch, 332.

74. District of Columbia, citizen of.— A citizen of the District of Columbia cannot maintain an action against a citizen of Virginia in the circuit court for the Virginia district A citizen of the District of Columbia is not a citizen of a state, in the meaning of the constitution Hepburn v Ellzey, 2 Cranch, 445

75 Miscellaneous — State laws cannot impair jurisdiction.— The jurisdiction of the United States courts over controversies between citizens of different states cannot be impaired or abridged by the laws of the states prescribing modes of redress in state courts, or regulating the distribution of judicial power The federal courts cannot abdicate their authority or duty in any case in favor of another jurisdiction Hyde v Stone, 20 How 170, citing Suydam v Broadnax, 14 Pet 67 Union Bank v Jolly, 18 How 503

76 Nor can laws of states prescribing regulations for state courts have any influence on the practice in federal courts unless adopted as a rule by such courts United States v Breitling, 20 How 252

77. A sovereign state, and one of the states of the Union when not restrained by constitutional prohibition might, in virtue of its sovereignty, act upon the contracts of its citizens wherever made, and discharge them by denying the right of action in its own courts, but the validity of such contracts as were made outside the jurisdiction of the sovereignty would exist and continue everywhere else according to the *lex loci contractus* Suydam v Broadnax, 14 Pet 67.

78. State laws cannot affect the jurisdiction of the courts of the United States They can neither enlarge nor diminish such jurisdiction Neither can they destroy nor control the rights of parties litigant therein under the general commercial law Watson v Tarpley, 18 How 517

79 Neither a state constitution nor a state statute can prohibit the judges of the courts of the United States from charging juries with reference to matters of fact Vicksburg, etc R. R Co v Putnam, 118 U S 545, Nudd v Burrows, 91 U S 426, 441, Indianapolis, etc R. R v Horst, 93 U S 291, St Louis, etc R y v Vickers, 122 U. S 360

80 Assignees under state insolvent laws —The assignee of an insolvent estate or corporation, appointed by a state court under the insolvent laws of such state, cannot be sued in the United States court for debts claimed to be due by such insolvent estate or corporation. Such assignee is but the officer of the court, and must account to the court appointing him Peale v Phipps, 14 How 368, Vaughan v Northrup, 15 Pet 1, Williams v Benedict, 8 How 107, Wiswall v Sampson, 14 How 52, Bank v Horn, 17 How 157

81. Formal parties, or nominal parties, or parties without interest, united with real parties to the litigation, cannot oust the federal courts of jurisdiction, if the citizenship or character of the real parties be such as to confer jurisdiction within the eleventh section of the judiciary act. Wood v Davis, 18 How 467, citing 7 Cranch, 98, 3 Cranch, 267, 8 Wheat 421, 5 Cranch, 303

82 The courts of the United States have jurisdiction in a case between citizens of the same state if the plaintiffs are only nominal plaintiffs for the use of an alien Browne v Strode, 5 Cranch, 303

83 The act of congress which restrains the assignee of a chose in action from bringing a suit in the United States courts, where the original holder could not have sued there, is constitutional Sheldon v Sill, 8 How 441

84. Suit in name of governor of a state on sheriff's bond.—A citizen of one state has the right to sue upon the bond of the sheriff of another state in the United States courts, notwithstanding the bond runs to the state in which the defendant is sheriff, and the suit is brought in the name of the governor of such state The citizenship of the person for whose use the suit is brought governs the jurisdictional right McNutt v Bland, 2 How. 9

85 Citizen of one state having title to land in another.— It cannot be alleged that a citizen of one state having title to lands in another is disabled from suing for those lands in the United States courts by the fact that he derives his title from a citizen of the state in which the lands lie, and the motives which induced the contract cannot be inquired into when deciding on the jurisdiction of the court. McDonald v Smalley, 1 Pet. 620

86. County supervisors sued by a citizen of another state — The board of supervisors of an organized county of a state can be sued in the United States courts by a citizen of another state, and no limitation upon the suability of such county enacted by state legislation can oust the jurisdiction conferred by the constitution on United States courts Cowles v. Mercer Co 7 Wall. 118.

87. Non-interference —State and national courts are as independent as they are separate Neither can impede or arrest the action of the other within the limits of its jurisdiction, nor interfere with its process for satisfaction of its judgments and decrees Amy v Supervisors, 11 Wall. 136.

88. A state court cannot, by injunction, prevent the execution of process issued from a court of the United States to give effect to its judgment The Mayor v Lord, 9 Wall 409

89 And it matters not whether the injunction was granted before or after judgment in the federal court, or before or after suit brought Supervisors v. Durant, 9 Wall. 415.

90. When case arises under constitution or laws of United States —A case arises under the constitution of the United States or the laws passed in pursuance thereto, not only where one party comes into court to demand something conferred upon him by the constitution or by a law or treaty, but whenever its correct decision depends in whole or in part, upon the construction of either Cases arising under the laws of the United States are such as grow out of the legislation of congress, whether they constitute the right or privilege, or claim or protection, or defense of the party, in whole or in part, by whom they are asserted. Tennessee v. Davis, 100 U S 257.

91. Removal of causes no invasion of state domain —When the constitution was adopted a portion of the judicial power became vested in the new government created, and so far as thus vested it was withdrawn from the sovereignty of the state; therefore the removal of cases arising under the constitution and laws of the United States, from the state to the federal courts, is no invasion of state domain, on the contrary, the refusal of this right is a denial of the conceded sovereignty of the federal government over the subjects expressly committed to it. The court holds the act of July 13, 1866, relative to the removal of suits or prosecutions in state courts against internal revenue officers. the provisions whereof are re-enacted in section 643, Revised Statutes, is constitutional Tennessee v Davis, 100 U S. 257 Same holding as to section 641, Revised Statutes Strauder v. West Virginia, 100 U S 303

92. Proceedings under exclusive control of congress — Congress has the exclusive authority to regulate proceedings in the courts of the United States, and the states have no authority to control those proceedings, except so far as the state's process acts are adopted by congress, or by the courts of the United States under authority of congress Wayman v Southard, 10 Wheat 1, Bank of U S v. Halstead, 10 Wheat. 51

93 Laws of state may be made applicable by congress.— It is no violation of the provisions of this section for congress to adopt and make applicable to a court of the United States the laws of the state wherein such court is held, either as to the nature or form of writs of execution for the enforcement of its judgments Ex parte Boyd, 105 U S 647

94. The laws of a state regulating proceedings in its own courts cannot authorize district courts sitting in the state to depart from the modes of proceeding and rules prescribed by act of congress. Kelsey v Forsyth 21 How 85, affirming Guild v Frontin, 18 How 135

95 **Congress may make jurisdiction exclusive** — In all cases to which the judicial power of the United States extends, congress may make the jurisdiction of the federal courts exclusive The Moses Taylor, 4 Wall 411

96 **Practice — Pleading** — If a constitutional question is in a case it is not necessary for the pleadings to set out specially what article or section of the constitution is involved If the parties in their pleadings make a case which necessarily comes within some of the provisions of that instrument, the court will notice and consider it Bridge Proprietors v Hoboken L. & T. Co, 1 Wall 116, citing Crowell v. Randell, 10 Pet 368, Armstrong v Treas. of Athens, 16 Pet. 281

97 **Jurisdiction over property, how obtained** — The jurisdiction of a court of the United States once obtained over property by its being brought within its custody, continues until the purpose of the seizure is accomplished, and cannot be impaired or affected by any legislation of the state, or by any proceeding subsequently commenced in a state court Rio Grande R R Co v. Gomila, 132 U S 478, citing and affirming Freeman v Howe 24 How. 450, Buck v Colbath, 3 Wall 334, Covell v Heyman 111 U. S 176, Riggs v Johnson Co, 6 Wall 176, distinguishing Yonley v Lavender, 21 Wall 276, Payne v Hook, 7 Wall 425, Hyde v Stone 20 How 170

98 **The province of the courts** is to pass upon the validity of laws, not to make them, and, when their validity is established to declare their meaning and apply their provisions. All else lies beyond their domain. The Chinese Exclusion Case, 130 U. S. 581-603

99 **Violation of treaty not a judicial question.**— Whether a treaty with a foreign sovereign has been violated, whether the consideration of a particular stipulation of a treaty has been voluntarily withdrawn by one party so as to no longer be obligatory on the other, and whether the views and acts of a foreign sovereign manifested through his representative, has given just occasion to the political departments of our government to withhold the execution of a promise contained in a treaty, or to act in direct contravention of such promise, are not judicial questions The power to determine such questions has not been confided to the judiciary It has no suitable means to execute its determinations upon such questions. Their determination and execution belong to the executive and legislative departments The Chinese Exclusion Case, 130 U S 581-602, citing and approving Taylor v Morton, 2 Curtis 454-459

100 **Suits in rem** — Where a suit is brought in a state court and jurisdiction is obtained over property of the defendant in such state, but the defendant, being a non-resident, is not served with process within such state, but is served with notice of the pending suit against his property such notice can have no binding effect upon the defendant personally, and no personal judgment can be rendered against him based on such notice. but, if the suit or proceeding is intended to affect his property found within the jurisdiction of the state court, the notice may be very proper to apprise him of it, and give him an opportunity to look after his property if he chooses. Sugg v Thornton, 132 U S 524-530

101. If it is denied that a state statute impairs a contract exempting a railroad company from taxation and such exemption is pleaded in the state court and its existence denied, the federal supreme court has jurisdiction to review such decision. Yazoo & Miss Val. R. R. Co. v. Thomas, 132 U. S. 174

102 Concurrent jurisdiction of state and federal courts.—Courts of the United States and courts of the states have concurrent jurisdiction in all cases between the citizens of different states, whatever may be the matter in controversy, if it be one for judicial cognizance Dodge v. Woolsey, 18 How. 331, Piqua Bank v. Knoop, 16 How. 369, Mechanics' Bank v Debolt, 18 How 380

103. State and federal courts cannot enjoin each other—Federal courts and state courts act separately and independently, and in their respective spheres of action the processes of one cannot be enjoined by the other Riggs v Johnson County, 6 Wall. 166

104 Process subsequent to judgment is as essential as process antecedent, else the judicial power is incomplete and inadequate to the purposes for which it was conferred by the constitution Id.

105. Chancery jurisdiction.—Chancery jurisdiction is conferred on the United States courts by the constitution of the United States In exercising it the courts of the United States, under the limitations imposed by the constitution, adopt the rules of the high court of chancery of England This chancery jurisdiction is exercised in conformity to these rules in all the states of the Union, whether such states have a chancery system or not. Pennsylvania v Wheeling Bridge, 13 How 519, Neves v Scott, 13 How 268

106. The equity jurisdiction conferred by the constitution on federal courts is not subject to limitation or restraint by state legislation, and is uniform throughout the different states Payne v Hook, 7 Wall. 425

107 The equity jurisdiction of the United States courts is independent of the local law of any of the states, and is the same in nature and extent as the equity jurisdiction of England, from which it is derived, and it is no objection to this jurisdiction that there is a remedy under the local law. United States v Howland, 4 Wheat 108, Neves v Scott, 13 How. 268

108 Circuit courts.—The circuit courts of the Union have chancery jurisdiction in every state, they have the same chancery powers and the same rules of decision in all the states United States v Howland, 4 Wheat. 108.

109. Trespass in foreign country—Where a trespass was committed in a foreign country an action therefor may be maintained in the circuit court of the United States in any district in which the defendant may be found, upon process against him, where the citizenship of the respective parties gives jurisdiction to the court Mitchell v. Harmony, 13 How 115

110 Claiming lands under grants of different states.—If two citizens of the same state, in a suit in a court of their state claim title under the same act of congress, the supreme court of the United States has appellate jurisdiction to revise and correct the judgment of the state court in such case. Matthews v Zane, 4 Cranch, 382.

111 The supreme court has jurisdiction where one party claims land under a grant from New Hampshire and the other under a grant from the state of Vermont, although at the time of the first grant Vermont was a part of New Hampshire. Town of Pawlet v. Clark, 9 Cranch, 292.

112 The jurisdiction of the circuit courts of the United States extends to a case between citizens of Kentucky, claiming lands exceeding in value $500, under different grants, the one issued by the state of Kentucky and the other by the state of Virginia, but upon warrants issued by Virginia and locations founded thereon prior to the separation of Kentucky from Virginia. Colson v. Lewis, 2 Wheat. 377.

113 Where both parties claim title to real estate under grant from the state, and the state court decides between them, there is no jurisdiction in the federal supreme court to review the decision. Shaffer v. Scudday, 19 How. 16.

114. And between a state, or the citizens thereof, and foreign states, citizens or subjects — Foreign creditors — Jurisdiction — State powers.— The supreme court refused to express an opinion on the power of a state to compel foreign creditors to seek their remedy against the estates of decedents in the state courts alone. Williams v. Benedict, 8 How. 107.

115. The courts of the United States have jurisdiction where all the parties to suits are aliens. Mason v. Ship Blaneau, 2 Cranch, 240. Marshall, C. J. "It is the opinion of this court that whatever doubts may exist in a case where jurisdiction may be objected to, there ought to be none where the parties assent to it." Id. 264. This case is referred to, but neither affirmed nor overruled, in Bailiff v. Tipping, 2 Cranch, 406.

116 When both parties are aliens the courts of the United States have not jurisdiction. Montalet v. Murray, 4 Cranch, 46.

117 The plaintiffs were aliens resident in Louisiana. The defendants were citizens of Louisiana. *Held*, that the residence of the aliens within the state constituted no objection to the jurisdiction of the federal court. Breedlove v. Nicolet, 7 Pet. 413.

118. Although the plaintiff may be described as an alien, yet the defendant must be expressly stated to be a citizen of some one of the states of the United States. Otherwise the courts of the United States will not have jurisdiction. Hodgson & Thompson v. Bowerbank, 5 Cranch, 303.

119 Section 11 of act of 1789 must be construed in connection with and in conformity to the constitution of the United States. By this latter the judicial power does not extend to private suits in which an alien is a party unless a citizen be the adverse party, and it is indispensable to aver such citizenship, so that the jurisdiction may appear of record. Jackson v. Twentyman, 2 Pet. 136.

120. A foreign sovereign may as such bring a civil suit in the federal courts upon a public claim arising by virtue of his being such sovereign, and a change in the ruler of the country or a deposition of such sovereign does not abate the suit. The Ship Sapphire, 11 Wall. 164.

121 Foreign state.— The Cherokee nation is not a "foreign state" in the sense in which that term is used in the constitution, consequently as such it cannot maintain a suit in the United States courts against a state of the Union. Cherokee Nation v. Georgia, 5 Pet. 1.

122. When a defendant in a criminal trial offers himself as a witness in his own behalf, he is subject to cross-examination as provided by the law of the jurisdiction wherein he is tried, and the question of the extent of such cross-examination presents no federal question. Spies v. Illinois, 123 U S 131

2. In all cases affecting ambassadors, other public ministers, and consuls, and those in which a State shall be party, the Supreme Court shall have original jurisdiction In all the other cases before mentioned, the Supreme Court shall have appellate jurisdiction, both as to law and fact, with such exceptions and under such regulations as the Congress shall make.

1 **Original jurisdiction.**—Although the constitution vests in the supreme court an original jurisdiction in cases affecting consuls, it does not preclude the legislature from exercising the power of vesting a concurrent jurisdiction in such inferior courts as might by law be established United States v Ravara, 2 Dall 297

2 It is within the power of congress to grant to the inferior courts of the United States jurisdiction in cases where the supreme court has been vested with original jurisdiction. It rests with the legislative department of the government to say to what extent such grant shall be made The act of March 3, 1875 (ch 137, 18 Stat at Large), defining the jurisdiction of the United States courts, is constitutional, and under it suits brought by a state against a citizen thereof, and which suit involves a federal question, may be removed to the United States circuit court, and such removal involves no breach of this section of the constitution. Ames v Kansas 111 U S 449, citing and approving Cohens v Virginia, 6 Wheat. 399, Gittings v. Crawford, Taney s Dec 1 St Luke's Hospital v Barclay, 3 Blatch 265, Bors v Preston, 111 U S 252

3 **Mandamus**—The plain import of the words of the section seems to be, that in one class of cases the jurisdiction is original and not appellate in the other it is appellate and not original The authority, therefore, given to the supreme court, by act of congress establishing the judicial system of the United States, to issue writs of *mandamus* to public officers appears not to be warranted by the constitution Marbury v Madison, 1 Cranch 137

4. The supreme court has *not* jurisdiction to issue a writ of *mandamus* to the register of a land office of the United States commanding him to enter the application of a party for certain tracts of land according to the seventh section of the act of May 10 1800, ' providing for the sale of lands of the United States northwest of the Ohio and above the mouth of the Kentucky river ' which *mandamus* had been refused by the supreme court of the state of Ohio upon a submission by the register to the jurisdiction of that court, being the highest court of law or equity in the state McCluny v Silliman, 2 Wheat 369

5. A *mandamus* will not lie to the secretary of the navy at the instance of an officer to enforce the payment of his salary Brashear v Mason, 6 How. 92

6 **Jurisdiction**—An objection to the validity of a statute founded on the ground that the legislature which enacted it was not a legal body duly

organized under the acts of congress and the constitution cannot be considered by the United States supreme court In order to give jurisdiction, the statute, the validity of which is drawn in question, must be passed by a state of the Union and by a public body owing obedience to the constitution and laws thereof Scott v Jones, 5 How 343

7. Original jurisdiction over "cases in equity" between a state and a citizen of another state is conferred on the supreme court by the constitution And this jurisdiction imposes the duty to adjudicate according to the rules and principles which governed the court of chancery of England at the time of the emigration of our ancestors and down to the period when our constitution was formed Accordingly this court in such cases can award or refuse costs as in its judgment the right of the case requires Pennsylvania v Wheeling, etc Bridge Co, 18 How 460

8. The supreme court has original jurisdiction of a suit brought by a state against citizens of another state as well as controversies between two states Wisconsin v Pelican Ins. Co 127 U S 265

9 Municipal tax — No jurisdiction to cause to be levied — The supreme court of the United States has no power to cause a tax to be levied on a municipality to pay a judgment rendered against such municipality in the circuit court The remedy is by *mandamus* to compel the authorities to levy the tax It that is unavailing the court has no power to appoint its own officer to make the levy. Rees v Watertown, 19 Wall 107, Heine v Levee Commissioners, 19 Wall 655 But it has been held where a judgment was rendered in favor of the holders of county bonds and the county supervisors refused to levy a tax to pay the same, that the circuit court could appoint the marshal to levy such tax and collect the same, in payment of such judgment Lee County v United States ex rel. Rogers, 7 Wall. 175

10. Original jurisdiction may be exercised without enabling act. The supreme court of the United States may exercise its original jurisdiction in suits against a state, under the authority conferred by the constitution, without any further act of congress to regulate its process The court may regulate and mould the process it uses in such manner and form as in its judgment is promotive of justice Kentucky v Dennison, Governor of Ohio 24 How 66

11. Consuls — The original jurisdiction of the supreme court in cases where a consul of a foreign government is a party is not exclusive Subordinate courts of the Union may be invested with jurisdiction affecting such representatives of foreign governments Bors v Preston, 111 U S 252, citing United States v Ravara 2 Dall 297, Cohens v Virginia, 6 Wheat. 399, Ames v Kansas, 111 U S 449, Gittings v. Crawford, Taney's Dec 1, St Luke's Hospital v Barclay, 3 Blatch 259

12 Suits in which a state is a party. — Congress has passed no law prescribing the mode of proceeding in suits against a state or in any case in which the supreme court is to exercise the original jurisdiction conferred by the constitution It has, however, been settled that that court can exercise original jurisdiction in suits against a state In such suits process may be served on the governor and attorney-general of the state sued sixty days before return day This rule applies where one state sues another state. State of New Jersey v. State of New York, 5 Pet. 284

13 It is no objection to the exercise of this original jurisdiction that one of the parties is a state and the other a citizen of that state. Cohens v. Virginia, 6 Wheat. 264

14. The grant in this section is of "judicial power," and was not intended to confer upon the courts of the United States jurisdiction of a suit or prosecution by the one state, of such a nature that it could not, on settled principles of public and international law, be entertained by the judiciary of the other state Wisconsin v Pelican Ins Co, 127 U S 265-289

15 **Removal of obstructions from Ohio river** — The state of Pennsylvania has sufficient interest to sustain an application to the supreme court of the United States in the exercise of its original jurisdiction to maintain a bill in chancery to compel by injunction the removal of obstructions from the Ohio river Pennsylvania v Wheeling Bridge Co, 13 How. 518.

16 **Boundary between states** — The supreme court has jurisdiction to determine questions of boundary between states of the Union and that jurisdiction is not defeated because of the fact that in deciding the question the court must examine and construe compacts between states or because its decision affects the territorial limits of the political jurisdiction and sovereignty of the states Virginia v. West Virginia, 11 Wall 39

17 In the following cases jurisdiction was entertained between states in controversies over boundary lines, to wit New Jersey v New York, 3 Pet. 461, 5 Pet. 284, 6 Pet. 323. Rhode Island v. Massachusetts, 12 Pet 657, 724, 13 Pet 23, 14 Pet. 210; 15 Pet 233, 4 How 591 Missouri v Iowa 7 How. 660, 10 How 1 Florida v Georgia, 17 How 478 Alabama v Georgia, 23 How 505 Virginia v West Virginia, 11 Wall. 39. Missouri v Kentucky, 11 Wall 395

18 A case which belongs to the jurisdiction of the supreme court on account of the interest a state has in the controversy must be one in which the state is either nominally or substantially the party It is not sufficient if the state be but consequentially affected, for in such case the circuit court has jurisdiction Fowler v Lindsey and Fowler v. Miller, 3 Dall. 411, New York v Connecticut, 4 Dall. 3, New York v Louisiana, New Hampshire v. Louisiana, 108 U. S 76

19. **Penal laws of state will not be enforced by United States supreme court** — Notwithstanding the comprehensive words of the constitution, the mere fact that a state is a plaintiff is not a conclusive test that the controversy is one in which the supreme court is authorized to grant relief against another state or the citizens thereof Such jurisdiction will not be entertained when the object is to enforce the penal laws of the state "The courts of no country execute the penal laws of another" The Antelope, 10 Wheat. 123 And this will not be changed even though the demand for the penalty may have been reduced to judgment in favor of the state in its own courts, and the suit is then sought to be maintained by the state in whose favor it was rendered by original process in the supreme court. Wisconsin v Pelican Ins Co, 127 U. S 265, 289, 290 291

20 **Reasons for** — The object of vesting in the courts of the United States jurisdiction of suits by one state against citizens of another was to enable such controversies to be determined by a national tribunal and thereby avoid the partiality, or seeming partiality, or suspicion of partiality,

which might exist if the plaintiff state were compelled to resort to the courts of the state of which the defendants were citizens Id

21 **Citizenship** — A corporation created by a state is a citizen of the state within the meaning of this section Id See, also, as to this last point, Kansas Pac R. R v Atchison, etc R R 112 U S 414 · Paul v Virginia, 8 Wall. 168–178, Pennsylvania v Wheeling Bridge, 13 How 518, St Louis v Wiggins Ferry Co, 11 Wall 423

22. **Appellate jurisdiction.**— The appellate jurisdiction of the supreme court of the United States is given by the constitution, but it is limited and regulated by the act of congress on the subject. Durousseau v. United States, 6 Cranch, 307

23 The appellate jurisdiction of the supreme court in cases brought from state courts, arising under the constitution, laws and treaties of the United States, is not limited by the value of the matter in dispute Buel v Van Ness, 8 Wheat. 312 Compare with Adams v Crittenden, 106 U S 576

24 **From Northwest territory** — Under the constitution a writ of error does not lie from the supreme court to the general court for the territory northwest of the Ohio, congress having made no provision of law therefor Clarke v Bazadone, 1 Cranch 212

25. **Congress may limit appellate jurisdiction.**— Congress has power to limit the jurisdiction of the supreme court upon appeals in admiralty to questions of law arising on the record. Duncan v. The Francis Wright, 105 U S 381

26. The mere fact that the matter in dispute arises under the constitution and laws of the United States, or treaties made, does not give to the supreme court jurisdiction to review the judgments or decrees of the circuit or district courts If the value of the matter in dispute in such cases does not exceed $5 000 it cannot consider them any more than it can consider other causes where the amount involved is below the jurisdiction Adams v Crittenden, 106 U. S 576 Compare with Buel v. Van Ness, 8 Wheat 312

27. **Error to state court, when it lies** — The appellate jurisdiction of the supreme court of the United States extends to a final judgment or decree in any suit in the highest court of law or equity of a state where is drawn in question the validity of a treaty or statute of, or an authority exercised under, the United States, and the decision is against their validity, or where is drawn in question the validity of a statute of, or an authority exercised under, any state on the ground of their being repugnant to the constitution, treaties or laws of the United States, and the decision is in favor of their validity, or the construction of a treaty or statute of, or commission held under, the United States, and the decision is against the title, right, privilege or exemption specially set up or claimed by either party, under such clause of the constitution, treaty statute or commission. Martin v Hunter's Lessee, 1 Wheat 304, Crowell v Randell, 10 Pet. 368

28 Such judgment or decree may be re-examined by writ of error in the same manner as if rendered in a circuit court. Martin v Hunter's Lessee, *supra*

29. If the cause has been once remanded, and the state court refuses or declines to carry into effect the mandate of the supreme court thereon, this court will proceed to final decision of the same and award execution thereon. Id

30. If the validity or construction of a treaty of the United States is drawn in question and the decision is against its validity or the title specially set up by either party under the treaty this court has jurisdiction to ascertain that title and determine its legal validity and is not confined to the abstract construction of the treaty itself Id See, also, Crowell v Randell, 10 Pet 368

31 Propositions which govern case coming upon writs of error from state courts.—The following propositions govern the examination of judgments and decrees by the supreme court of the United States, in cases coming to it on error to the courts of last resort of the states of the Union: It is essential to the jurisdiction of that court over the judgment or decree of the state court that it shall appear that one of the questions mentioned in the statute must have been raised and presented to the state court, that it must have been decided by the state court against the right claimed or asserted by plaintiff in error under the constitution, treaties, laws or authority of the United States or that such a decision was necessary to the judgment or decree rendered in the case These things appearing (or any one of them) that court has jurisdiction, and must examine the judgment so far as to enable it to decide whether this claim of right was correctly adjudicated by the state court If it finds that it was rightly decided the judgment must be affirmed If it was erroneously decided, then the court must further inquire whether there is any other matter or issue adjudged by the state court sufficiently broad to maintain the judgment, notwithstanding the error in the decision of the federal question If this be found to be the case, the judgment must be affirmed without examination into the soundness of the decision of such other matter or issue But if it be found that the issue raised by the federal law must control the whole case, or that there has been no decision by the state court of any other matter which is sufficient of itself to maintain the judgment then the supreme court will reverse that judgment and will either render such judgment as the state court should have rendered, or will remand the case to such court for further proceedings, as the circumstances of the case may require Murdock v Mayor of Memphis, 20 Wall. 590

32. To support the appellate jurisdiction of the supreme court it is not sufficient that the construction of a statute of the United States was drawn in question and the decision was against the party claiming title, etc thereunder It must further appear that the title depended upon the statute. And where in such a case the validity of a state statute is drawn in question upon the ground of its being repugnant to the constitution of the United States and the decision has been in favor of its validity, it must further appear that the title or right of the party depended upon the statute Williams v Norris, 12 Wheat 117

33. Some title, right or privilege must be set up—The supreme court has no appellate jurisdiction from the final judgment of the highest court of a state, in a suit where is drawn in question the construction of a statute of, or commission held under, the United States, unless some title, right, privilege, etc under such statute be specially set up by the party and the decision be against the claim so made by him. Montgomery v Hernandez, 12 Wheat. 129, Hicks v Starke, 1 Pet. 94

34 Cases stated.—Both parties to suit claimed land under the provisions of the same act of congress, and the decision of the supreme court of the state was upon the construction given to the act by the commissioners acting under its authority *Held*, to be a case which draws into question the construction of an act of congress, and that the supreme court of the United States had jurisdiction to review the same on writ of error Ross v *Doe*, 1 Pet. 655

35 The question presented in the case before the court of Pennsylvania was, whether the office of captain of a revenue cutter of the United States was liable to be assessed for taxes under the laws of Pennsylvania The validity of the law imposing such tax was affirmed by the state courts *Held* (1) That the supreme court of the United States had jurisdiction in such case on writ of error (2) That the statute of Pennsylvania was unconstitutional Dobbins v Com'rs of Erie Co, 16 Pet 435

36. Where the title to land under confirmation by United States commissioners was directly drawn in question, and the decision below rejected the title, the supreme court of the United States has authority to re-examine the decision of the state court Berthold v McDonald 22 How 334

37 What must be relied on —It must be the constitution or some law of a state which impairs the obligation of a contract, or which is otherwise in conflict with the constitution of the United States, and the state court must sustain the constitution or law in the matter in which the conflict is supposed to exist, and this must appear on the face of the record before it will be re-examined by the supreme court of the United States M & M R. R. Co v Rock, 4 Wall. 177

38. Pleading —The particular section of the constitution relied upon as being involved need not be stated in pleadings, to entitle the supreme court of the United States to review the judgment of a state court. Furman v Nichol, 8 Wall. 44

39 State laws—Construction by state courts conclusive —The construction given by state courts to their own laws and constitutions are conclusive upon the supreme court of the United States, except when that court is called upon to interpret the contracts of states And whenever the highest court of a state shall adjudge that not to be a contract which is alleged in legal proceedings to be one, within the meaning of this clause, then the supreme court of the United States may review such decision on error to the state court Jefferson Branch Bank v Skelly, 1 Black 436

40 Where the judgment of a state court might have been based, either on a state law repugnant to the federal constitution or laws, or upon some other independent ground, and it appears that the court did in fact base it upon the latter ground, the supreme court of the United States will not take jurisdiction, even though it should think the decision of the state court erroneous. So, also, where it does not appear on which of the two grounds the decision was based, if the independent ground is in the opinion of the supreme court a good and valid one, it will not take jurisdiction, but if in the latter case the independent ground is not a good and valid one the supreme court will take jurisdiction Klinger v Missouri, 13 Wall 257 But see B & O R R v Maryland, 20 Wall 643

41. As to Confederate money when question arises.—A decision of a state court that a contract, the consideration whereof was Confederate money, was void does not, within itself, raise such federal question as belongs to the supreme court to settle, when such decision is made upon grounds of public policy, but when it is based upon the provision of a state constitution which makes all contracts, the consideration whereof was Confederate money, void, and on no other ground, such decision raises a question whether such provision of the state constitution is not in conflict with the federal constitution, and thereby presents a question reviewable on error by the supreme court. Delmas v. Ins Co, 14 Wall 661

42 **Case stated** — Where the record shows that in the state court the plaintiff in error claimed that the contract sued on had been rendered void and of no force by provisions of the federal constitution and of certain acts of congress, and that the decision of the supreme court of Iowa denied this claim, *held*, that the federal supreme court had jurisdiction to re-examine the case on error Railroad Companies v Richmond, 15 Wall 3

43. **Bankrupt act.**— The supreme court has jurisdiction to review a state judgment, in which the only claim set up by the plaintiff in error was founded on the act of congress known as the bankrupt act, and when the decision of the state court was against the claim Mays v Fritton, Book 21, Lawyers Co-operative Pub Co s U S Reports, p 127

44 **State and federal questions combined.**— Where, in a suit in a state court a federal question is raised, and has been decided against the plaintiff in error by the court of last resort in the state the jurisdiction of the supreme court of the United States has attached and the case must then be heard on its merits notwithstanding the fact that the state court also based its judgment on another question which arose in the case, and did not present a federal question Under former decisions the rule was different, but it has been varied in Murdock v Memphis 20 Wall 590, wherein the act of 1867 was held to repeal section 25 of the act of 1789, and to embody in itself the entire rule of law on that subject The present *status* of the law thereon is embodied in the opinion of the court in Murdock v Memphis, 20 Wall 590 Baltimore & Ohio R R. Co v Maryland, 20 Wall. 643

45 Where the only question raised and decided in a case in a state court was whether the acts of the president to inaugurate a war rendered invalid the contract in suit, and the decision was against its validity, the supreme court has jurisdiction in error Mathews v McStea, 20 Wall 646

46. For the rules governing the jurisdiction of the supreme court of the United States upon error to the highest court of a state, see Sevier v. Haskell 14 Wall 12, Weston v Charleston, 2 Pet 449 McGuire v. Commonwealth, 3 Wall 385, note to Matthews v. Zane, 4 Cranch, 382, note to Martin v Hunter, 1 Wheat. 304, note to Williams v Norris, 12 Wheat 117, Home Ins Co v Augusta, 93 U S 116 (The notes referred to are in the Lawyers' Co-op edition United States Supreme Court Reports)

47 In order to give the United States supreme court jurisdiction to review the judgment of a state court it must appear that the decision of a federal question was *necessary* to the determination of the cause, and that such question was *actually* decided or that the judgment rendered could *not* have been given without deciding it Brown v Atwell 92 U S 327.

48 Where, in a state court, a right is claimed under an act of congress, any matter of law found in the record decided by the highest court of the state, bearing on the right so set up under the act, is reviewable in the

United States supreme court Republican River Bridge Co. v. Kansas Pacific R R Co, 92 U S 315

49. When upon a trial in a state court a right or immunity is claimed as arising to a party therein under a judgment of a federal court, and the judgment of the state court is against such claim of right or immunity, the supreme court of the United States has jurisdiction under the constitution and law of congress of February 5, 1867, to review such judgment on error to the state court Dupasseur v. Rochereau, 21 Wall 130

50 Where in a suit in a state court a right of exemption is claimed under the constitution and the decision is against the right so claimed, the United States supreme court has jurisdiction on error to review the decision of the court of last resort of the state Daniels v Tearney, 102 U S 415

51. Where a state court of last resort, as appears from its judgment of affirmance, determined among other things the following propositions (1) That the lien law of the state is not in any respect repugnant to the constitution of the United States, as contended by the original defendants (2) The contract for building the vessel in question is not a maritime contract, and that the remedy given by the lien law of the state does not conflict with the constitution or laws of the United States (3) That the said lien law does not violate the right of trial by jury, nor conflict with the constitution of the state,— *held*, that the first and second propositions, considered in connection, amounted to a determination by the state court that the contract in question for the building of the schooner was not a maritime contract, and that the law of the state giving the remedy which was pursued by the plaintiffs does not conflict with the federal constitution or with federal laws, is sufficient to give the supreme court jurisdiction under writ of error to examine that question Edwards v Elliott, 21 Wall 532

52. In a suit wherein title to real estate under patent from the government was called in question, *held* (1) The supreme court has jurisdiction to review on error a case wherein the claims of a party asserted under a patent from the United States is denied by a state court (2) The land department is a tribunal created by congress to determine contested questions as to priority of right under conflicting pre-emptions, and findings of fact by such department in such cases are not reviewable elsewhere Baldwin v. Stark, 107 U S 463

53 **State courts — Right of supreme court to review denied —** The supreme court of the United States has no authority, on a writ of error from a state court, to declare a state law void on account of its being in collision with the state constitution. Jackson v Lamphire, 3 Pet. 280, Withers v Buckley, 20 How 84.

54. Where slaves from Kentucky were permitted by their master to go to Ohio temporarily, they returning again to Kentucky in custody of the person in charge of them, *held*, that the question of their freedom or servitude depended upon the laws of Kentucky and not of Ohio There is nothing in the constitution of the United States that can control the law of Kentucky on the subject The supreme court of the United States has no jurisdiction to review the decision of the court of appeals of Kentucky on this subject Strader v Graham, 10 How 82

55 Where the supreme court of a state certified there was "drawn in question the validity of a statute of the state," without designating which of the statutes of the state was so called in question and declared valid it is not sufficient to give the supreme court jurisdiction Lawler v Walker, 14 How 149, Bank v Buckingham's Executors, 5 How 317

56 Where complainant has no interest in land, but a naked possession not protected by an act of congress, the supreme court has no jurisdiction of an appeal from a state court deciding adversely to such title No statute of the United States is drawn in question Wynn v. Morris, 20 How 3

57 The supreme court has no jurisdiction to revise the decisions of a state court where there is no complaint that the obligation of a contract has been impaired, nor that any right has been claimed and refused under the constitution of the United States or a treaty or law of congress. White v Wright, 22 How 19

58. The supreme court of the United States will not review a case from a state court where the only question is whether the legislature had exceeded its authority under the state constitution. Medberry v. Ohio, 24 How. 413, Porter v Foley id. 415

59 A controversy wherein no right is claimed under the constitution or laws of the United States, but which depends wholly upon state laws and proceedings, is not subject to review by the supreme court of the United States on error to state court. Congdon v Goodman, 2 Black 574

60. The supreme court cannot go out of the record to examine any question under a writ of error to the state court. It is not sufficient that it is claimed that the state court improperly decided a lien law to be constitutional, when it is nowhere alleged that the law is repugnant to any particular provision of the constitution of the United States or that the court of original jurisdiction rendered any decision on that subject Citing Messenger v Mason, 10 Wall 507 Bridge Prop'rs v Hoboken Co, 1 Wall. 116, Furman v Nichol, 8 Wall 44, Edwards v Elliott, 21 Wall 538

61 Something more must be set forth in such a pleading, to raise a federal question, than the mere allegation that it is invalid and unconstitutional Such assignment is satisfied if held to refer to the state constitution and that question cannot be examined by the United States supreme court on error to a state court Citing Farney v Towle 1 Black 351. Hoyt v Shelden, 1 Black, 521, Railroad Co v Rock, 4 Wall 180

62 Where the right of a plaintiff under the constitution of the United States is not set up and specially claimed in the state court, the federal supreme court has no jurisdiction to review the judgment of the state court Worthy v. Commissioners, 9 Wall 611

63. The supreme court has no jurisdiction to review a judgment of a state court which upholds the validity of a statute of a territory in contravention of the constitution It applies only where is drawn in question the validity of a statute or authority exercised under a state Messenger v. Mason, 10 Wall 507

64 The supreme court of the United States is not authorized to review the judgments of state courts because such judgments refuse to give effect to contracts, or because those judgments in their effect, impair the obligation of contracts Palmer v Marston, 14 Wall 10, West Tennessee Bank v Citizens Bank, 13 Wall. 432, Bethell v. Demaret, 10 Wall. 537, New Orleans Water-works v Louisiana Sugar Co., 125 U S 18

65. A decision of a state court to the effect that an act increasing the debt of the state did not exceed the limit fixed in the state constitution raises no federal question, and is not subject to review by the United States supreme court Salomons v Graham, 15 Wall 208

66 When the United States court will not review a state judgment because no question arose under the constitution of the United States or act of congress, or where there were other questions on which the decision of the state court could be sustained See Kennebec & Port R R Co v Port. & Kennebec R R. Co, 14 Wall 23, Steines v Franklin Co, 14 Wall 15 Palmer v Marston, 14 Wall 10, Sevier v Haskell, 14 Wall 12, Holmes v Sevier, Lawyers' Co-operative Ed U S Sup Ct Rep, B 20, p 877, Capeiton v Ballard, 14 Wall 238

67. The supreme court is not required to examine the judgment of a state court simply because a federal question may have been decided, unless it appears that such question was *necessarily* involved, and where the record on its face shows that such question was not necessarily involved, and is silent as to its being raised, the supreme court will not go outside the record and search for the question in the opinion of the court or elsewhere. Moore v Mississippi, 21 Wall 636

68. Judgments rendered in the state courts against the United States cannot be reviewed in the United States supreme court upon writ of error, except in cases where the same relief would be afforded to private parties. That court has no power to review the decisions of the state court on questions of general law United States v Thompson, 93 U S 586.

69 The decision of a state court declaring its own statutes unconstitutional are not subject to review by the supreme court of the United States. Walker v Taylor, 5 How 64.

70 In a suit of ejectment brought by the state of Colorado, the state relied upon a deed by the defendant to the *Territory of Colorado* To the introduction of this in evidence the defendant (plaintiff in error in supreme court) objected, *inter alia*, "that the territory of Colorado had no right to take a conveyance of real estate at the time of making the deed without the consent of the government of the United States" The objection was overruled and the evidence received, and judgment for plaintiff affirmed on appeal to state supreme court. *Held*, that the objection and ruling thereon constituted no federal question Brown v. Colorado, 106 U S 95

71 The supreme court of the United States has no jurisdiction to review the judgment of the highest court of a state on the ground that the obligation of a contract has been impaired, unless some legislative act of the state has been upheld by the judgment sought to be reviewed New Orleans Water-works v Louisiana Sugar Co., 125 U S 18.

72 **Review by habeas corpus** — The supreme court has authority to issue a *habeas corpus* where a person is imprisoned under the warrant or order of any court of the United States Ex parte Kearney, 7 Wheat 38

73 But the supreme court has no appellate jurisdiction in criminal cases confided to it by law *Hence* the court will not grant a *habeas corpus* where a party has been committed for a contempt adjudged by a court of competent jurisdiction Id.

74 The supreme court has power to issue the writ of *habeas corpus ad subjiciendum*. Ex parte Bollman, Ex parte Swartwout, 4 Cranch, 75

75. There is no jurisdiction in the supreme court of the United States on either *habeas corpus* or *certiorari* to revise the proceedings of a military commission Ex parte Vallandigham 1 Wall 243

76. While the supreme court of the United States has jurisdiction to hear and determine an application for *habeas corpus*, and to discharge the petitioner where he is held in custody under a state law repugnant to the constitution such power ought not to be exercised in advance of his trial by the state courts Ex parte Royall, 117 U. S 241, 254

77 Under this section the supreme court has jurisdiction to hear and determine an application in *habeas corpus* upon conviction and sentence of an inferior court of the United States based on an unconstitutional law, whether it would have jurisdiction to review such judgment upon writ of error or not But where the conviction is based upon a valid law, this court cannot examine errors of the inferior court except on writ of error Ex parte Siebold, 100 U S 371, Ex parte Clarke, id 399, 402, 404

78 **Habeas corpus** —A defendant was sentenced to imprisonment on three separate indictments, for three months each, and also fined for each offense, and there was an order of commitment until fine be paid Before the expiration of the term of imprisonment *fieri facias* was sued, and was returned *nulla bona* After sentence on all the commitments had expired *capias ad satisfaciendum* issued. The defendant was held under this, without being brought before the circuit court. *Held*, that on this state of facts the supreme court had jurisdiction to issue the writ of *habeas corpus* That it did not fall within the rule of Marbury v Madison, 1 Cranch, 137, because it was not an original jurisdiction. Ex parte Watkins, 7 Pet 568 It was appellate in its character, and was supported by the cases of United States v Hamilton 3 Dall 17, Ex parte Bollman, 4 Cranch, 75, and Ex parte Kearney, 7 Wheat 38

79 There can be no such thing as judicial authority unless it is conferred by a government or sovereignty Nor can one sovereign state authorize its courts or judges to exercise judicial powers by *habeas corpus* or otherwise in another and independent government, and although a state of the Union is to a certain extent sovereign within its limits, that sovereignty is limited and restricted by the constitution of the United States Ableman v Booth, 21 How 506

80 While a state court or judge may, by *habeas corpus* inquire by what authority and for what purpose a prisoner is confined within its limits and it is the duty of the marshal having custody of a prisoner to make known to the state court the cause of detention, it is the duty of the state court or judge, when informed that such prisoner is held by virtue of an order of the federal courts to make no further interference If there is any informality or error in the proceedings it is for the federal courts to revise it, and not the state courts Id

81 Irregularities and errors in enforcing a law in the courts can only be corrected by the state courts. The supreme court of the United States can only examine the question of the power of the state courts to proceed

at all Kennard v. Louisiana, 92 U S 480 Case held not to present a federal question Rockhold v Rockhold, 92 U S 129

82. Where the state court does not deny the validity of a statute of the United States but holds that the facts necessary to give the United States courts jurisdiction do not exist, the judgment is not reviewable in the United States supreme court. Craig v. Devlin, Lawyers' Co-operative Ed U S Sup. Ct. Rep B 23, p 510; Boggs v Mining Co, 3 Wall 301

83. When the state court, in its decisions, proceeds upon the general principles of the jurisprudence of the state, the supreme court of the United States will not review its decisions Sevier v Haskell, 14 Wall 12, Holmes v. Sevier, Lawyers' Co-operative Ed U S Sup Ct Rep, B 20, p. 876

84 When a state court decides a contract void for want of consideration, such consideration being Confederate money, if such decision is based upon the general principles by which courts determine whether a consideration is good or bad, on principles of public policy, it is not subject to review by the supreme court of the United States Bethell v Demaret, 10 Wall 537, Delmas v Insurance Co, 14 Wall 661

3 The trial of all crimes, except in cases of impeachment, shall be by jury, and such trial shall be held in the State where the said crimes shall have been committed; but when not committed within any State, the trial shall be at such place or places as the Congress may by law have directed.

1. **This guaranty extends to protection in time of war.**—This guaranty was intended for a state of war as well as a state of peace, and is equally binding upon rulers and people at all times and under all circumstances. Military commissions organized during the civil war, in a state not invaded nor in rebellion, and in which the federal courts were open to the unobstructed transaction of business, had no jurisdiction to try convict or sentence for any criminal offense a citizen who was neither a resident of a rebellious state nor a prisoner of war, nor a person in the military or naval service, and congress could not invest them with such powers Ex parte Milligan, 4 Wall 2

2. **Case arising in land or naval forces not within this provision** —Cases arising in the land and naval forces and in the militia, in time of war or public danger, are excepted from the necessity of presentment or indictment by a grand jury, and the right to a trial by jury in such cases is subject to the same exception Id.

3. But a citizen not connected with the military service, and a resident in a state where the courts are open and in the proper exercise of their jurisdiction, cannot, even where the privilege of the writ of *habeas corpus* is suspended, be tried, convicted or sentenced otherwise than by the ordinary courts of law. Id.

4 **Plea of not guilty, effect of**—The plea of not guilty puts the prisoner upon the country by a sufficient issue without any further express words, and the prisoner is then entitled to a trial by jury. United States v Gibert, 2 Sum. 19 The same is true where the prisoner fails to plead and

the court enters the plea of not guilty United States v. Borger, 19 Blatchf 250, Ex parte Wall, 107 U S 265

5 **The trial — Meaning of words.**— The word "trial means the trying the cause by the jury and not the arraignment and pleading preparatory to such trial United States v. Curtis, 4 Mason, 232

6. **Common-law jurisdiction** — The courts of the United States have no jurisdiction over common-law offenses The crime must be defined by congress, and the mode of punishment and jurisdiction defined, before the court can entertain it. United States v Hudson, 7 Cranch 32 This is doubted, but not overthrown, in United States v Coolidge, 1 Wheat. 415

7 **Crime — Definition of, and how interpreted** — The word crime" in its more extended sense comprehends every violation of public law In a limited sense it embraces offenses of a serious or atrocious character. This provision of the constitution is to be interpreted in the light of the principles which at common law determined whether the accused, in a given class of cases, was entitled to a trial by jury It embraces some classes of misdemeanors the punishment of which involves or may involve, the deprivation of the liberty of the citizen Callan v Wilson, 127 U S 540-549, note, Story on Const. § 1791, Dillon on Municipal Corp, vol 1, § 433, McGear v Woodruff, 4 Vroom, 213, State v Conlin, 27 Vt. 318, Williams v Augusta, 4 Ga. 509, Emporia v Volmer, 12 Kas 622, Jones v. Robbins, 8 Gray, 329, In re Dana, 7 Bene 1

8. **Intent of provision** — 'This article is intended to define the judicial power of the United States, and it is in regard to that power that the declaration is made that the trial of all crimes, except in cases of impeachment, shall be by jury It is impossible to examine the accompanying provisions of the constitution without seeing very clearly that this provision was not intended to be applied to trials in the state courts." Miller, J, in Eilenbacker v Dist. Court of Plymouth Co, Iowa, 134 U S 31.

SECTION III.

TREASON.

1. Treason against the United States shall consist only in levying war against them, or in adhering to their enemies, giving them aid and comfort. No person shall be convicted of treason unless on the testimony of two witnesses to the same overt act, or on confession in open court

1. **Levying war** — An insurrection of armed men, the object of which is to suppress the excise offices and to prevent by force and intimidation the execution of an act of congress, is high treason by levying of war. United States v Mitchell, 2 Dall 348; United States v Vigol, 2 Dall. 346

2 To constitute levying war there must be an assemblage of people with force and arms to overthrow the government or resist the laws. United States v Greathouse, 2 Abb. (U. S) 364.

3 Aid rendered to a rebellion may sustain a conviction under a charge of *levying war* Id

4. There must be an actual assemblage of men with treasonable purpose to constitute levying war. Mere conspiracy is insufficient. The meeting of bodies of men who march from places of partial to places of general rendezvous would be such an assemblage Ex parte Bollman, 4 Cranch, 75

5 To revolutionize by force the government of any territory under the United States would be treason by levying war Id

6 To constitute a levying of war there must be an assemblage of persons for the purpose of effecting by force a treasonable purpose Enlistment of men to serve against the government is not sufficient Id

7 Any assemblage of men for the purpose of revolutionizing by force the government established by the United States in any of its territories, although as a step to or means of executing some greater projects, amounts to levying war The traveling of individuals to the place of rendezvous is not sufficient, but the meeting of particular bodies of men, and their marching from places of partial to places of general rendezvous, is such an assemblage as constitutes a levying of war Id

8. Joining the enemy and arraying one's self with his forces is an overt act of levying war Respublica v Carlisle, 1 Dall 35

9. To levy war is to raise, create, make or carry on war. The term is used in the constitution in the same sense in which it was understood in England and in this country to have been used in 25th Edward III, from which it was borrowed United States v Burr, 4 Cranch, 470.

10 **Assemblage** — Where a body of men are assembled for the purpose of making war against the government, and are in a condition to make war, the assemblage is an act of levying war Id. 470–476

11. The assemblage must be a "warlike assemblage," carrying the appearance of force and in a situation to practice hostility. Id. 480

12 An assemblage of men with a treasonable design, but not in force, nor in condition to attempt the design, nor attended with warlike appearances, does not constitute the fact of levying war Id 482

13. **Actual force required.**— War can only be levied by the employment of actual force Troops must be embodied, men must be openly assembled Id 487

14 **Arms and application of force not required** —Arms are not an indispensable requisite, nor the actual application of force to the object. Id. 488

15. **Who are guilty of** —All those who perform the various essential military parts of prosecuting the war, which must be assigned to different persons, may be said to levy war, as well as those who perform any other part in the prosecution of the war United States v. Burr, 4 Cranch 470

16. War having been levied, all who aid in its prosecution by performing any part in the furtherance of the common object, however minute, or however remote from the scene of action, are guilty of treason United States v Greathouse, 2 Abb (U. S.) 364

17 When war is levied all those who perform any part however minute, or however remote from the scene of action, and who are actually leagued in the general conspiracy, are traitors. Ex parte Bollman, 4 Cranch, 75.

18. Persuading men to enlist is treason only when consummated by actual enlistment, but attempts to enlist men into the service of the enemy may be proved to show, *quo animo*, the accused had joined the enemy's forces, and to show aid to enemy Respublica v Roberts, 1 Dall. 39

19 Overt act —The *overt act* must be specially charged and proved as laid in the indictment One cannot be convicted of other overt acts not so laid If the particular *overt act* as charged be advised, procured or commanded by the accused, he is guilty accessorily, and not directly as principal. United States v. Burr, 4 Cranch, 470, 491, 493, 494

20. Cannot be constructively present at overt act —A person in one part of the United States cannot be considered as constructively present at an *overt act* committed in a remote part of the United States Id

21. The part which a person takes in the war constitutes the *overt act* on which alone he can be convicted. Id 501

22. Procuring provisions.— The going from a British vessel to the shore for the purpose of peaceably procuring provisions for the enemy is not an *overt act*, the conduct resting only in intention. It would be different, however, if the intent had been to procure the provisions by uniting with the enemy in hostilities against the citizens of the United States This would be an *overt act* of "adhering to the enemy." United States v. Pryor, 3 Wash. 234

23. Enlisting or procuring enlistment in the enemy's service is an overt act of treason Nothing will excuse joining the enemy but the fear of immediate death Respublica v. McCarty, 2 Dall. 86

24 Offense consists of what —To constitute the offense of treason against the United States there must be a conspiracy to resist generally and by public force, and an actual resistance by force or by intimidation of numbers, to a law of the United States A conspiracy to resist by force the execution of such law in particular instances only — a conspiracy for a personal or private as distinguished from a public and national purpose, is not treason, however great the violence or force or numbers of the conspirators may be United States v. Hanway, 2 Wall Jr 139, United States v Hoxie, 1 Paine, 265

25 Adhering to their enemies, giving aid and comfort —Rebels, being citizens, are not enemies within the meaning of this clause, and a conviction for treason, in promoting a rebellion, cannot be sustained under it. United States v. Greathouse, 2 Abb. (U. S) 364

26 Confession proved by two witnesses is not sufficient to convict of treason, but is competent as corroborating circumstances, although of another species of treason Id

27 None but a citizen of the United States can be guilty of high treason. United States v Villato, 2 Dall 370

28 Aliens domiciled in the United States in 1862, and who were engaged in the manufacture of saltpeter in an insurgent state, and in selling it to the Confederate States, knowing that it was to be used in the manufacture of gunpowder for the prosecution of the rebellion, were giving aid and comfort to the rebellion *Held*, that such aliens owe a temporary allegiance to the government of the United States and are bound to obey the laws of the country not immediately relating to citizenship, and are equally amenable with citizens for the infraction of the laws And such aliens, therefore, giving such aid and comfort to the rebellion, were subject to be prosecuted for treason and for giving aid and comfort to the rebellion Carlisle v United States, 16 Wall 147

29. The doctrine in Hanauer v Doane, 12 Wall 342, that "he who, being bound by his allegiance, sells goods to the agent of an armed combination to overthrow that government, knowing that the purchaser buys them for that treasonable purpose, is himself guilty of treason or misprision of treason," repeated and re-affirmed. Carlisle v. United States, 16 Wall 147.

2. The Congress shall have power to declare the punishment of treason, but no attainder of treason shall work corruption of blood, or forfeiture, except during the life of the person attainted

1 Where lands are declared by law forfeited to the owner because of conviction of treason the estate is neither annihilated, confiscated nor appropriated to any third party. The owner, as a punishment for his offenses, is disabled from exercising any acts of ownership over it, and no power to exercise any such rights is given to any other person At his death, if not before, the period of suspension comes to an end, and the estate revives and devolves on his heirs at law. Illinois Cent. R. R. Co. v Bosworth, 133 U S 92–101

2 The heirs of the offender at his death take by descent from him and not by gift or grant from the government Avegno v Schmidt, 113 U S 293, Shields v Schiff, 124 U S 351, Bigelow v. Forrest, 9 Wall 339, Wallach v. Van Riswick, 92 U. S. 202.

3. This provision was placed in the constitution for the benefit of the children and heirs alone, it is a declaration that the children should not bear the iniquities of the fathers Mr Justice Strong in Wallach v. Van Riswick, *supra*

4 **Pardon — Effect of on forfeiture** — Where estates forfeited under conviction of treason have been sold to third persons, or vested rights have been acquired, a pardon subsequently granted does not restore the estate to the person pardoned, nor divest the acquired interest during the life-time of the person attainted Ex parte Garland, 4 Wall 333–380, Semmes v United States, 91 U S 21; Confiscation Cases, 20 Wall. 92 112, 113, Knote v United States, 95 U. S. 149, Illinois Cent. R R. Co v Bosworth, 133 U S 92

5 **Allegiance to both state and nation — National paramount** — Every citizen of a state owes a double allegiance, he enjoys the protection and participates in the government of both the state and the United States In those cases in which the United States may exercise the right of exclusive legislation, it will rest with congress to determine whether the general government shall exercise the right of punishing exclusively, or leave the states at liberty to exercise their own discretion Houston v Moore, 5 Wheat. 1–34

ARTICLE IV.

THE STATES AND THE FEDERAL GOVERNMENT.

Section I

STATE RECORDS

Full faith and credit shall be given in each State to the public acts, records, and judicial proceedings of every other State And the Congress may, by general laws, prescribe the manner in which such acts, records, and proceedings shall be proved, and the effect thereof

1. **Record of judgment, conclusive when—Attachment.**—The record of a judgment in one state is conclusive evidence in another, although it appears that the suit in which it was rendered was commenced by an attachment of property, the defendant having afterward appeared and taken defense Mayhew v Thatcher, 6 Wheat 129

2 **In a case stated,** *held* not to embrace an alleged error in a decree of a state court asserted to be in collision with a prior decision of the same court in the same case Mitchell v Lenox, 14 Pet 49.

3 **Judgment of one state, how enforced in another.**—A judgment rendered in one state does not carry with it into another state the efficacy of a judgment upon property or persons to be enforced by execution. To give it such force in another state it must be made a judgment there, and can only be executed in the latter state as its laws may permit McElmoyle v Cohen, 13 Pet. 312-325.

4 **Nil debet will not lie to the record.**—The act of congress passed to carry this section into execution makes the exemplification of the record equivalent to the original record in its proper shape, and communicates to it the same effect as evidence, thereby making it sustain the same averments in pleading and of abiding the same tests as the original record It cannot be denied or controverted by any plea such as *nil debet.* Mills v Duryee, 7 Cranch, 481

5 **What pleas are good**—Any plea that would be good in the state where the judgment was rendered would be good against the exemplified record and none other Hampton v McConnel, 3 Wheat 234

6 **In suits against partners to bind all, all must be served.**—In a suit against partners, one was served with process and the other not so served but judgment was rendered against both Upon a suit brought in a sister state on said judgment, against the party not so served, *held,* that the judgment so rendered in the former state was not conclusive against the defendant. Hortsman v Henshaw, 11 How 177

7. **No new powers are conferred on states by this clause.**—By this provision "the Constitution did not mean to confer any new powers upon the states, but simply to regulate the effect of their acknowledged

jurisdiction over persons and things within their territory It did not make the judgments of other states domestic judgments to all intents and purposes, but only gave a general validity, faith and credit to them as evidence." Story's Conflict of Laws, § 609 quoted and approved by Mr Justice Bradley in delivering the opinion of the court in Thompson v. Whitman, 18 Wall. 457 462, 463

8 **Service on agent of corporation.**— Where process was served in Ohio on an agent of a corporation of Indiana doing business in the former state by permission of the laws thereof and who was qualified by such laws to represent such corporation there in respect to service of process and notice and judgment was thereupon rendered in the case against the corporation by a court of the state of Ohio, *held*, that a judgment so recovered is as valid as if the corporation had its *habitat* in Ohio, that a record of such judgment properly certified is entitled to full faith and credit in the courts of Indiana Lafayette Insurance Co. v French 18 How 404

9. **Conclusiveness of** — Where a judgment is conclusive between the parties in the state where rendered it is equally so in every other state, and is not open to review in a suit upon it in another state Christmas v Russell 5 Wall 290

10 **Effect of judgment on nature of action.**— The essential nature and real foundation of a cause of action are not changed by recovering judgment on it. And the technical rules which regard the original claim as merged in the judgment, and the judgment as implying a promise to pay it, do not preclude a court, to which such judgment is presented for affirmative action (while it cannot go behind the judgment for the purpose of examining into the validity of the claim), from ascertaining whether the claim is really one of such a nature that the court is authorized to enforce it Louisiana v. New Orleans, 109 U S 285-288, Louisiana v Police Jury, 111 id 716, Chase v Curtis, 113 id 452-464, Boynton v Ball, 121 id 457-466; Wisconsin v Pelican Ins Co, 127 id 265-293

11 The title acquired under the attachment laws of a state, and which is valid there, is to be held valid in every other state Green v Van Buskirk, 7 Wall 139

12 **Semble.**— Where a contract is made to pay a certain number of dollars in gold and silver coin, it cannot be satisfied by payment of that number of dollars in legal tender notes Express contracts to pay coin can only be satisfied by payment of coined dollars. Bronson v Rodes, 7 Wall. 229, Butler v Horwitz, 7 Wall 258, Bronson v Kimpton, 8 Wall 444

13 The same legal effect must be given to a New York judgment in New Jersey as would be given to it in New York Chew v Brumagen, 13 Wall 497

14 **Conclusive as matter of evidence** — A final judgment of a court of competent jurisdiction both as to parties and subject-matter in one state, determining the rights of the parties thereto, is admissible as evidence in another suit between the same parties and for the same causes of action, and it has the same force and effect when pleaded or offered in evidence in another state as it would have in the state wherein it was rendered Mutual Life Ins. Co v. Harris, 97 U. S 331.

15. **Case stated** and held not to interfere with the provisions of this section. Boyer v. Chapman 119 U S 587

16 **Effect to be given to laws** — This provision implies that the public acts of every state shall be given the same effect by the courts of other states that is given to them by the law and usage of the state which enacted them C & A R R. Co. v Wiggins Ferry Co., 119 U. S 615

17. **Laws of state must be proved.**— To ascertain what effect such act has in the state where enacted the law of such state must be proved Id

18 **This section establishes a rule of evidence rather than of jurisdiction** — This provision and the laws of congress in relation thereto establish a rule of evidence rather than of jurisdiction While they make the record of a judgment rendered in one state, after due notice, conclusive evidence in the courts of another state or of the United States of the matter adjudged they do not affect the jurisdiction either of the court in which the judgment is rendered or of the court in which it is offered in evidence. They differ from judgments recovered in a foreign country in no other respect than in not being re-examinable on their merits nor impeachable for fraud in obtaining them, if rendered by a court having jurisdiction of the cause and of the parties. Wisconsin v Pelican Ins Co, 127 U S. 265-291, 292

19 **Statute restricting operation of section unconstitutional** — A state statute to the effect that a judgment recovered against one of its citizens in a sister state shall not be enforced in its tribunals if the cause of action which was the foundation of such judgment would have been barred in that state by its statute of limitations, is unconstitutional Christmas v. Russell 5 Wall 290

20 **Effect of taxation.**— No state can legislate except with reference to its own jurisdiction One state cannot exempt property from taxation in another So where one state owes a debt and issues registered bonds therefor, such bonds, when holden by a resident of another state, may be taxed in such other state, under the laws thereof, without violating this section of the constitution. Bonaparte v Appeal Tax Court, 104 U S 592

21 **Statute of limitations held valid as applied to judgments of other states** — A state has power to regulate the remedies by which contracts may be enforced in its courts, unless such regulation is repugnant to the constitution of the United States or the laws of congress. And a law of one state limiting the time in which suits should be brought on a judgment of another state is valid Bank of Alabama v Dalton, 9 How 522

22 **Question of jurisdiction** — Under the constitution and acts of congress the question of jurisdiction remains open as at common law It may, therefore, be shown by proper evidence that the court rendering the judgment had no jurisdiction and the pleadings may be so shaped as to admit such evidence. Warren Manufacturing Co v Ætna Ins Co, 2 Paine, 501

23 In order to sustain the judgment the court rendering it must have jurisdiction of the parties as well as of the subject-matter Id

24 When an action is brought in one state on a judgment recovered in another, it is not enough to show it to be valid in the state where rendered, it must also appear that the defendant was either personally within the ju-

risdiction of the state or had legal notice of the suit, and was in some way subject to its laws, so as to be bound to appear in the suit or suffer a judgment by default. Lafayette Ins Co v French, 18 How. 404

25 The laws of the United States, passed in pursuance to the authority conferred in this section, after providing the mode of authenticating the acts, records and judicial proceedings of the states, declares "And the said records and judicial proceedings, authenticated as aforesaid, shall have such faith and credit given to them in every court within the United States as they have by law or usage in the courts of the state from whence the said records are or shall be taken" This does not prevent an inquiry into the jurisdiction of the court in which a judgment is rendered to pronounce the judgment, nor into the right of the state to exercise authority over the parties or subject-matter, nor whether the judgment is founded in and impeachable for manifest fraud The constitution did not mean to confer any new power on the states, but simply to regulate the effect of their acknowledged jurisdiction over persons and things within their territory It did not make the judgments of the states domestic judgments, but only gave a general validity, faith and credit to them as evidence Cole v Cunningham, 133 U. S 107

26 Judgment against foreign corporation not personal, when.— A judgment rendered in one state against a corporation of another state founded upon service of process on an agent of such corporation found within the state wherein the suit is brought does not authorize a personal judgment against the corporation when such foreign corporation was not doing business in the state wherein the suit was brought A personal judgment rendered on such service, when offered in evidence in the courts of another state, is not such record as this clause applies to St. Clair v Cox, 106 U S 350

27. Judgment against non-residents founded on service by publication not entitled to faith and credit.—Where a personal judgment is rendered in one state against a defendant served alone by publication, and who did not appear in the case, the record thereof is not entitled to faith and credit in a suit thereon in a sister state This clause applies only to records and proceedings of courts in so far as they have jurisdiction Board of Pub Works v Columbia College, 17 Wall 521

28. Record as to jurisdictional facts may be contradicted.— Neither this clause of the constitution nor the act of congress passed to carry it into effect precludes an inquiry into the jurisdiction of the court by which a judgment offered in evidence was rendered The record as to jurisdictional facts may be contradicted Thompson v Whitman, 18 Wall 457

29 Intent of section —This section was intended to vest in congress the full power to declare the judgments of one state conclusive in every other Congress has not gone this far, but has declared that they shall have such effect in every other state as they possessed in the state whence they were taken Green v Sarmiento 3 Wash. C C. 17

30 Conclusiveness of judgment —Under the constitution and acts of congress the judgment of a court in any state is conclusive, and the same effect is given to it in every other state as it had in the state where rendered The record when duly authenticated, contains absolute verity and is conclusive Westerwelt v Lewis, 2 McLean, 511

31. Process or appearance must be shown.—Where no process was served on the defendant, and there has been no appearance, the judgment is a nullity. Id

32 But where the record shows such process or appearance it is conclusive Id

33 Intent of provision—Illustration—The intention of this section was to confer on citizens of the several states a general citizenship, and to communicate all the privileges and immunities which the citizens of the same state would be entitled to under the like circumstances· and this includes the right to institute actions. But where a firm in Massachusetts was about to make an insolvent assignment, and, that fact becoming known to one of the creditors, a citizen of Massachusetts. it (the creditor) caused suit by attachment to be brought in New York and the credits of the insolvent there to be levied upon, it was held that the assignee of the insolvent in Massachusetts might enjoin the attaching creditor from continuing to have and maintain his said action in New York, without violating the provisions of section 1 of this article Cole v Cunningham, 133 U S 107

34 Will, probate of—Where the will of a citizen of South Carolina was executed in that state, and directed that a power of appointment be executed by the person therein named "by her last will and testament duly executed,' this meant that the will of the person designated to execute the power must be duly executed according to the laws of South Carolina And where such will of the person designated in the first will was executed in North Carolina and there probated and declared to be executed according to the laws of that state, but was rejected in South Carolina by the courts of that state because of not being executed according to the laws of South Carolina, this was not refusing to give faith and credit to the laws of North Carolina within the meaning of this section. Blount v. Walker, 134 U S. 607

Section II

PRIVILEGES OF CITIZENS, ETC.

1. The citizens of each State shall be entitled to all privileges and immunities of citizens in the several States

1. Who are citizens of a state.—A citizen of the United States residing in any state of the Union is a citizen of that state Gassies v. Ballon, 6 Pet 761

2 Capitation tax on persons leaving state.—A law of Nevada levying a capitation tax on persons leaving the state by stage-coach or railroad is in conflict with this clause of the constitution, also with the prohibition against laying imposts by a state also against the right of congress to regulate commerce Crandall v Nevada, 6 Wall 35

3. These privileges and immunities are such as are common to all the people.—The privileges and immunities secured to citizens of each state in the several states by this provision are those privileges and immunities which are common to the citizens in the latter states under their constitutions and laws by virtue of their being citizens Paul v. Virginia, 8 Wall. 180.

4. Marital rights, rights of contract, and not of citizenship — No privileges are secured by it except those which belong to citizenship. Rights attached by law to contracts, by reason of the place where such contracts are made or executed wholly irrespective of citizenship of the parties to those contracts, cannot be deemed privileges of citizens within the meaning of the constitution. Therefore it is no abridgment of the "privileges of citizens" to deny to a widow whose marriage was not contracted in Louisiana, nor executed there by matrimonial domicile, the same rights of property in the estate of a deceased husband as is given to a widow whose marriage was there contracted, or where the spouses live in the state. Conner v. Elliott, 18 How. 591.

5. Goods from other states — Sale cannot be prohibited. — A statute of Maryland prohibiting in certain districts the sale of goods other than the agricultural products and articles manufactured in the state by persons not residents of the state until license therefor has been obtained, as in the act directed, is unconstitutional. Ward v. Maryland, 12 Wall. 418.

6. Right of woman to practice law not included in provision. — The supreme court of Illinois, having refused to grant a license to a woman to practice law in the courts of that state on the ground that, under the laws of the state, females are not eligible to be so admitted such decision violates no provision of the federal constitution. It does not violate this clause for the reason that it only guaranties privileges and immunities to citizens of *other* states in that state. Bradwell v. State, 16 Wall. 130.

7. The citizens of one state are not invested by this clause of the constitution with any interest in the common property of another state — Application of rule — It was held that each state owns the tide-waters and beds of all tide-waters within its jurisdiction, that a right of fishery is a property right, and not a mere privilege or immunity of citizenship. Therefore a state may grant to its own citizens the exclusive privilege of using the lands covered by water on its borders for the purpose of maintaining oyster-beds, and may with penalties prohibit such use by citizens of other states. McCready v. Virginia, 94 U. S. 391.

8. Act of sequestration by Confederate government — An act of the Confederate government sequestrating credits due to citizens of the loyal states denies to the citizens of such states the privileges and immunities of citizens in the several states, and is void. Williams v. Bruffy, 96 U. S. 176. In delivering the opinion of the court in this case Mr. Justice Field used the following language in reference to this subject: "A constitutional provision securing to the citizens of each state the privileges and immunities of citizens in the several states could not have a more fitting application than in condemning as utterly void the act under consideration here, which Virginia enforced as a law of that commonwealth, treating the plaintiffs as alien enemies because of their loyalty to the Union, and decreeing for that reason a sequestration of the debts due to them by its citizens."

9. Secession did not sever the union of states — A state does not cease to be a state of the Union, nor the citizens thereof cease to be citizens of the United States, by reason of any ordinance of secession and laws enacted thereunder passed by such state. Texas v. White, 7 Wall. 700.

10 A contract made by an insurgent military board in aid of the rebellion is void Id.

11 An act of an insurgent state legislature in aid of rebellion cannot be enforced or have effect given to it by a federal court. Id.

12. **Statute of limitations.**— A state statute which, in effect, provides that where a defendant is out of the state the statute of limitations shall not run against the plaintiff if the latter resides in the state, but shall if he resides out of the state, is not repugnant to this clause Ryan v Carter, 93 U S 78

13 **Texas cattle** —Section 4059 of the code of Iowa, which provides that a person having in his possession "Texas cattle" which have not been wintered north of the northern boundary line of Missouri and Kansas shall be liable for all damages caused by allowing such cattle to run at large and thereby spread the Texas cattle fever, is not such denial to the citizens of other states of the rights, privileges and immunities accorded to citizens of Iowa as is contemplated by this clause of the constitution. Kimmish v Ball, 129 U. S 217

14 **Purpose and extent of provision.**—This clause does not create those rights called privileges and immunities of citizens of the state, nor does it throw around them any security for the citizen of the state in which they are claimed or exercised, nor does it profess to control the power of the state governments over the rights of their own citizens. Its sole purpose is to declare to the several states that whatever those rights are, as you grant or establish them to your own citizens, or as you limit or qualify, or impose restrictions on their exercise, the same, neither more nor less, shall be the measure of the rights of citizens of other states within your jurisdiction. Slaughter-House Cases, 16 Wall 36

15 **What privileges and immunities are meant** — The privileges and immunities here meant are those privileges and immunities which are fundamental They may all be comprehended under the following general heads Protection by the government, with the right to acquire and possess property of every kind, and to pursue and obtain happiness and safety, subject, nevertheless, to such restraints as the government may prescribe for the general good of the whole By Mr. Justice Washington in Corfield v. Coryell, 4 Wash C C 371. Cited and approved by Justice Miller in Slaughter-House Cases, 16 Wall 36

16 **Object of section** —This section, like the fourteenth amendment, is directed against state action Its object is to place the citizens of each state on the same footing with citizens of other states, and inhibit discriminating legislation against them by other states There is no authority in this section for the enactment of section 5519 of the Revised Statutes United States v Harris, 106 U S 629

17 **Corporation a citizen of the state creating it and cannot emigrate** — A corporation is regarded in effect a citizen of the state which creates it. It has no faculty to emigrate, it can exercise its franchises extraterritorially only so far as may be permitted by the policy or comity of other sovereignties St Louis v Wiggins Ferry Co, 11 Wall. 423

18 **Corporations are not citizens within the meaning of this clause.**— They are creatures of local law and have not even an absolute

right of recognition in other states, but depend for that, and for the enforcement of their contracts, upon the assent of those states, which may be given accordingly on such terms as they please Paul v. Virginia, 8 Wall 168; Insurance Co v Massachusetts, 10 Wall 566, Ducat v. Chicago, 10 Wall 410, Pembina Mining Co v Pennsylvania 125 U S. 181, Doyle v Continental Ins Co, 94 U S 535, Lafayette Ins Co v French, 18 How 404; Bank of Augusta v Earle, 13 Pet. 519, Warren Manufacturing Co v Ætna Ins. Co, 2 Paine, 501

19. A state has power to discriminate between its own corporations and those of other states, and the nature and degree of such discrimination belongs to the state to determine, subject only to such limitations as are found in the federal constitution The case of Paul v. Virginia cited and followed. Ducat v Chicago, 10 Wall. 410

20. The terms imposed must be consistent with the constitution. While the states may regulate the conditions upon which corporations of other states may be permitted to do business within the state granting it, they cannot impose conditions which are repugnant to the constitution of the United States A restriction which has for its purpose a restraint upon the right of the corporation to sue in or remove cases to the United States courts, where such right exists under the constitution and laws of congress, is void. Barron v. Burnside, 121 U S. 186–200, and cases cited.

NOTE — The doctrine seems now also to be settled by a thread of reservation running through all the cases upon the subject, that corporations engaged in commerce among the states or with foreign countries cannot be restrained in the transactions of such commerce by the legislation of the several states, wherein such commerce is being transacted Barron v. Burnside, *supra*, Lafayette Ins Co v French, 18 How 404, Ducat v Chicago, 10 Wall. 410, Ins. Co v. Morse, 20 Wall 455, St Clair v Cox, 106 U. S 350, Fire Association v New York, 119 U S 110

21. Women as citizens — The word ' citizen ' is often used to convey the idea of membership in a nation In that sense women born of citizen parents within the United States have always been considered citizens, as much so before the adoption of the fourteenth amendment as since Minor v Happersett, 21 Wall. 162

22 Suffrage not a privilege or immunity of citizenship — The right of suffrage was not necessarily one of the privileges or immunities of citizenship before the adoption of the fourteenth amendment, and that amendment does not add to these privileges and immunities It simply furnishes additional guaranty for the protection of such as the citizen already had. Neither at the time of the adoption of the amendment, nor at the time of the adoption of the constitution, was suffrage co-extensive with the citizenship of the state. Id

2 A person charged in any State with treason, felony, or other crime, who shall flee from justice and be found in another State, shall, on demand of the executive authority of

the State from which he fled, be delivered up, to be removed to the State having jurisdiction of the crime.

1 **What acts are included in this article.**— The words of this article embrace every act forbidden and made punishable by a law of the state, whether treason, felony or misdemeanor, and gives the right to the state where any such crime is committed to demand the fugitive from the executive of the state to which he has fled. Kentucky v Dennison, 24 How 66

2 **Party demanded must be charged with crime.**— This demand is only authorized to be made when the party is charged in the regular course of judicial proceedings Id

3. **General government cannot coerce submission** — If the governor on whom demand is made refuses to discharge his duty, there is no power in the general government through any of its departments, judicial or otherwise, to use any coercive means to compel action. Kentucky v. Dennison 24 How 66, Taylor v. Taintor, 16 Wall 366–370.

4 **Habeas corpus will lie to inquire into the legality of arrest.** The state courts have power by writ of *habeas corpus* to inquire into the legality of the arrest of persons charged with crime in another state, and who are arrested upon requisition from such other state. Robb v Connolly, 111 U. S 624

5. **Federal courts have not exclusive jurisdiction in such cases.** Congress has not attempted to confer upon the federal courts exclusive jurisdiction in matters of *habeas corpus* growing out of such arrests The cases of Ableman v Booth, United States v Booth, 21 How 506, and Tarble's Case, 13 Wall 397, reviewed and distinguished Id

6 **Duties and powers of executive on whom demand is made.**— Each state has the right to prescribe the forms of pleading to be used in its courts of justice, and where a fugitive from justice is demanded by the executive of one state from the executive of another, wherein the fugitive is found, it is the duty of the latter to surrender the fugitive notwithstanding the information or indictment may not be framed according to the technical forms of criminal pleading, if it is in substantial compliance with the laws of the state making the demand The act of congress does not require the surrender of the person demanded unless it is made to appear that he is in fact a fugitive from justice The determination of that question rests with the executive of the state on whom the demand is made. Ex parte Reggel, 114 U S 642

7. **Case stated and rule applied.**— M. was indicted in Kentucky for murder charged to have been committed in said state Subsequently he was found in the state of West Virginia, and requisition was made by the governor of Kentucky to the governor of West Virginia for his surrender Pending the settlement of some questions which arose between the respective governors as to the form of the requisition, etc, M was forcibly seized by a mob headed by the agent appointed by the governor of Kentucky to receive him from the authorities of West Virginia upon the requisition, and was forcibly carried to Louisville, Ky After he was taken there, and while still forcibly held by the agent and his posse, M. was arrested by the sheriff

of the county upon a warrant issued upon an indictment for murder and was lodged in the jail of the county. The governor of West Virginia thereafter made requisition upon the governor of Kentucky, "that Plyant Mahon be released from confinement, set at large and returned in safety to the state of West Virginia." This requisition was refused by the governor of Kentucky. The governor of West Virginia then petitioned the United States district court for the district of Kentucky to grant a *habeas corpus* and to set M. at liberty. M. also petitioned for like relief. Upon trial the writ was refused. Upon appeal to the supreme court, *held*: (1) That states of the Union are not absolutely sovereign. Their sovereignty is qualified and limited by the conditions of the federal constitution. They cannot declare war or authorize reprisals on other states. Their ability to prevent the forcible abduction of persons from their territory consists solely in their power to punish violations of their criminal laws committed within the state, whether by their own citizens or citizens of other states. That to so punish the violators of their criminal laws they may demand the surrender of the person charged with the crime when found in another state. (2) That although M. had the right, while in West Virginia, to insist that he should not be surrendered to the authorities from Kentucky except in pursuance of the acts of congress, nevertheless, having been subsequently arrested in Kentucky under writs issued by the courts of that state founded upon indictments against him, the question is not as to the validity of the proceeding in West Virginia, but as to the legality of his detention in Kentucky. There is no comity between the states by which a person held upon an indictment for a criminal offense in one state can be turned over to the authorities of another, even though abducted from the latter. (3) The laws of the United States do not recognize that a fugitive from justice in one state has the right of asylum in another, unless removed in conformity with the laws for the surrender of such fugitives; and there is no authority in the courts of the United States to act upon any such alleged right. (4) That a person indicted for a felony in one state, forcibly abducted from another state and brought to trial in the state where he is indicted by parties acting without warrant or authority of law, is not entitled under the constitution or laws of the United States to release from detention, when arrested under the indictment, by reason of such forcible and unlawful abduction. Mahon v. Justice, 127 U. S. 700. Bradley and Harlan, JJ., dissenting.

8. Legality of arrest upon a requisition may be tested in state court.—A person arrested upon a requisition warrant may have the legality of his arrest tested by the courts, and to this end the state courts have jurisdiction in *habeas corpus*. Two things should be made to appear to the executive on whom the demand is made: 1st. That the person demanded is substantially charged with a crime against the laws of the state from which the demand comes. 2d. That he is a fugitive from the justice of the state making the demand. The first of these is a question of law, to be determined by inspection of the papers, and may be a subject of judicial investigation. The second is a question of fact, to be determined by the governor on whom the demand is made, and such a determination is sufficient to justify a removal until the presumption is overcome by contrary proof. Roberts v. Reilly, 116 U. S. 80.

9. **Laws of congress upon subject are valid** — There is no express grant to congress of legislative power to execute this provision, and it is not self-executing, but the contemporaneous construction embodied in the act of 1793 (1 Stat. at L. p 302), and now embodied in sections 5278 and 5279, Revised Statutes, has established the validity of the legislation of congress on the subject. Id.

10 **Authorities not harmonious.**— Whether or not the determination by the governor on whom demand is made of the questions of fact in relation to an alleged fugitive from justice is conclusive, or how far they may be reviewed judicially on *habeas corpus*, are questions not settled by harmonious judicial authority Id.

11 **The crime must be charged to have been committed in the state from which the demand for surrender comes** — It must be made to appear to the governor upon whom the demand is made for the surrender of a fugitive from justice — 1st, that the crime with which the fugitive stands charged was committed within the state making the demand, 2d, that the fugitive demanded has *fled* from the state wherein he stands charged with the crime. Ex parte Joseph Smith (the Mormon Prophet), 3 McLean, 121

12 **Duty to surrender not absolute.**— Where a demand is properly made by the governor of one state upon the governor of another, the duty to surrender is not absolute and unqualified It depends upon the circumstances of the case If the laws of the latter state have been put in force against the fugitive and he is imprisoned there, the demands of those laws may be first satisfied The duty of obedience then arises, and not before. Taylor v. Taintor, 16 Wall 366, 370.

13 **Extradition on demand of foreign governments — Exercise of, by state, not an exercise of police power.**— Where the government of Canada demanded from the governor of Vermont the extradition of a person accused of the crime of murder committed in Canada, the state, in acting upon such a requisition, does not thereby exercise its police powers These operate only on the internal concerns of the state, and require no intercourse with a foreign state in order to carry them into execution The power thus exercised is a part of the foreign intercourse of this country which has undoubtedly been conferred on the federal government. It is clearly included in the treaty-making power and the power to appoint and receive ambassadors and other public ministers This power has been denied to the states, and its exercise by them is inconsistent with the powers conferred upon the general government, and, therefore, a state cannot legally surrender a fugitive upon demand made by a foreign country. Per Taney, J, for himself and Justices Story, McLean and Wayne, in Holmes v Jennison, 14 Pet. 540, 569–574.

14. **Does not apply to foreign nations** — This provision by the obvious import of its terms has no relation whatsoever to foreign nations, but is confined in its operation to the states of the Union. Per Mr Justice Barbour, in Holmes v. Jennings, 14 Pet. at p. 587

3 No person held to service or labor in one State, under the laws thereof, escaping into another, shall, in consequence of

any law or regulation therein, be discharged from such service or labor, but shall be delivered up on claim of the party to whom such service or labor may be due.

1 The act of the Pennsylvania legislature of March 25, 1826, in reference to carrying negroes out of the state, and the penalties for so doing, is unconstitutional and void. It purports to punish as a public offense the act of seizing and removing a slave by his master, which act the constitution of the United States was designed to justify and uphold. Prigg v Pennsylvania, 16 Pet 539

2. The "persons" here referred to were African slaves. Dred Scott v Sandford, 19 How. 393.

3. The act of congress commonly called the Missouri Compromise, and which prohibited slavery north of 36° 30', declared unconstitutional. Id.

4 The right of slavery is distinctly affirmed in the constitution Id

5. **Object of the clause was to secure to slaveholders their property.**—It is historically well known that the object of this clause was to secure to the citizens of the slave-holding states the complete right and title of ownership to their slaves as property in every state of the Union into which they might escape. Per Story, J, in Prigg v Pennsylvania, 16 Pet. 539

6. **States cannot control the subject.**—This clause contemplates the existence of a positive, unqualified right on the part of the owner of the slave, which no state law or regulation can in any way qualify regulate, control or restrain Id.

7. **Nor interfere with the regulations made by congress.**—Where congress have a constitutional power to regulate a particular subject, and they do actually regulate it in a given way, state legislatures have no right to interfere therewith. Id. See, also, Houston v. Moore, 5 Wheat 1 21, 22.

8. **Act of congress constitutional.**—The act of congress February 12, 1793, relative to fugitive slaves in the northwestern territory, is constitutional, and the power of legislation upon the subject is exclusive in the national legislature Prigg v Pennsylvania 16 Pet. 539, Jones v. Van Zandt 5 How. 215

9 **Same**—Nor is it repugnant to the ordinance of 1787, entitled "An ordinance for the government of the territory of the United States northwest of the River Ohio" Jones v Van Zandt, 5 How. 215

10. Where a master voluntarily carried his slaves into a free state, they could not be deemed *fugitives* from labor, and were not subject to be delivered up under this provision. The owner thereby forfeited his right to them as slaves Strader v Graham, 10 How 82, Butler v Hopper, 1 Wash. C C 499; Vaughan v Williams, 3 McLean, 530, Miller v. McQuerry 5 McLean, 469

Section III

NEW STATES AND TERRITORIES.

1. New States may be admitted by the Congress into this Union; but no new State shall be formed or erected within the jurisdiction of any other State; nor any State be formed by the junction of two or more States, or parts of States, without the consent of the Legislatures of the States concerned, as well as of the Congress.

1. **Acquisition of territory by war.** — A war declared by congress can never be presumed to be waged for conquest or the acquisition of territory, nor does the law declaring war imply an authority to the president to enlarge the limits of the United States by subjugating the enemy's country. The boundaries of the United States may be extended by conquest or treaty, and the government may demand the cession of territory as a condition of peace in order to indemnify its citizens for the injuries they have received, or to reimburse the government for the expense of the war. Fleming v. Page, 9 How. 603-614.

2. **Compact by government upon admission of a state.** — That part of the compact admitting Alabama as a state respecting the public lands is nothing more than the exercise of a constitutional power vested in congress, and would have been binding on the people of the new state whether they consented to be bound or not. Pollard v. Hagan, 3 How. 212.

3. **Rights of new states in navigable waters.** — The shores of navigable waters and the soils under them, were not granted by the constitution to the United States, but were reserved to the states respectively, and the new states have the same rights, sovereignty and jurisdiction over this subject as the original states. Pollard v. Hagan, 3 How. 212; Withers v. Buckley, 20 How. 93; McCready v. Virginia, 94 U. S. 391; Bridge Co. v. United States, 105 U. S. 491.

4. **Eminent domain.** — Upon the admission of a new state the right of eminent domain passes from the general government to the new state. Nothing remains in the United States but the public lands. Pollard v. Hagan, 3 How. 212.

5. **Prior laws of congress** in relation to the territories and their government have no force in the new state after its admission and adoption of a constitution unless they are adopted by the state constitution. Permoli v. First Municipality, 3 How. 589; Strader v. Graham, 10 How. 94; Scott v. Sandford, 19 How. 491; Woodman v. Kilbourn Manuf. Co., 1 Abb. (U. S.) 158; S. C. 1 Biss. 546.

2. The Congress shall have power to dispose of, and make all needful rules and regulations respecting, the territory or other property belonging to the United States; and nothing

in this Constitution shall be so construed as to prejudice any claims of the United States or of any particular State

1 **Power of congress over territories, how derived** — The government of the Union may acquire territory either by treaty or by conquest, and when such territory is acquired it continues to be a territory of the United States until admitted as a state, and is governed by congress by virtue of this clause of the constitution This power to govern such acquired territory may result necessarily from the fact that it is not within the jurisdiction of any particular state and is within the power and jurisdiction of the United States Or the right to govern may be the inevitable consequence of the right to acquire territory Whichever may be the source whence the power is derived, the possession of it is unquestioned. American Ins Co v Canter, 1 Pet. 511, Sere v. Pitot, 6 Cranch, 336, Worcester v Georgia, 6 Pet 515

2 By the treaty with Spain Florida became a territory of the United States, and must, while such be governed by virtue of that clause of the constitution which empowers congress to make all needful rules and regulations respecting the territory or other property belonging to the United States" American Ins. Co v Canter, 1 Pet. 510

3 The power of congress to govern territories arises from its power to declare war and make treaties of peace, and the incidental power, in connection therewith, of acquiring territory It is also conferred in the clause which gives to congress ' the power to dispose of and make all needful rules and regulations respecting the territory and other property belonging to the United States" Mormon Church v. United States, 136 U S 1

4. **Territories — Powers of congress to amend acts of, and to enact laws for** — In the organic act of Dakota there was not an express reservation of power in congress to amend the acts of the territorial legislature Nor was it necessary Such a power is incident to sovereignty, and continues until granted away. Congress may not only abrogate laws of the territorial legislatures, but may itself legislate directly for the local government. It may make a void act of the territorial legislature valid and a valid act void In other words, it has full and complete legislative authority over the people of the territories and all departments of the territorial governments. It may do for the territories what the people under the constitution of the United States may do for the states ' National Bank v County of Yankton, 101 U S. 129, cited and approved in Mormon Church v United States, 136 U S 1-43

5. The constitutional power of congress to enact laws for the government of the territories has passed beyond the stage of controversy to final judgment The people of the United States as sovereign owners of the national territories have supreme power over them and their inhabitants. Murray v Ramsey, 114 U S 15-44.

6. **May regulate suffrage.**— It may prescribe the qualification of voters within a territory, and may exclude from such privilege persons guilty of bigamy Murphy v Ramsey, 114 U S 15

7. **Territories — Power of congress over.**— The power of congress over territories is general and plenary, arising under the powers granted in this section, as well as being derived from the power to acquire territory,

which latter right arises from the power to declare war and make treaties of peace. Under these powers congress had authority to repeal the act of the territory of Utah incorporating the Church of Jesus Christ of Latter-day Saints Mormon Church v. United States, 136 U S. 1.

8. Territorial legislatures — Powers of.— The powers of territorial legislatures extend to all rightful objects of legislation not inconsistent with the laws and the constitution of the United States. Id., at p. 543

9. Congressional legislation for territories — In legislating for territories congress possesses the combined powers of the federal and state governments American Ins. Co v Canter, 1 Pet. 511, Benner v Porter, 9 How 235, Forsyth v. United States, id 571

10. Territories — Extent of national sovereignty in.— The United States never had any municipal sovereignty, jurisdiction or right of soil in and to the territory of which any of the new states were formed, except for the temporary purpose of executing the trust created by the deeds of cession and the treaties by which such territory was acquired When the cession was accepted the United States took upon itself the trust to hold the municipal eminent domain for the new states, and to invest them with it to the same extent in all respects that it was held by the states ceding the territories. When the territory is admitted as a state nothing remains in the United States except the public lands This right of eminent domain over the shores and the soils under the navigable waters, for all municipal purposes, belongs exclusively to the states within their respective territorial jurisdiction, and they and they only have the constitutional right to exercise it. Pollard v Hagan, 3 How. 212, Goodtitle v Kibbe, 9 How 471, Doe ex dem. Hallett v. Beebe, 13 How. 25

11 Powers of congress cannot be interfered with — The power of congress in the disposal of the public domain cannot be interfered with nor its exercise embarrassed by state legislation Nor can such legislation deprive the grantee of the government of the possession and enjoyment of the property granted, by reason of any delay in the transfer of the title after the initiation of proceedings for its acquisition. Gibson v Chouteau, 13 Wall. 92.

12. A territorial legislature has no power to pass a law in contravention of the constitutional authority of congress over the territory of the United States or which will have the effect to deprive the supreme and district courts of the territory of chancery as well as common-law jurisdiction Dunphy v Kleinsmith, 11 Wall 610

13 This provision applies only to territory within the chartered limits of some one of the states when they were colonies of Great Britain, and which was surrendered by the British government to the old confederation of the states in the treaty of peace. It does not apply to territory acquired by the present federal government by treaty or conquest from a foreign nation Dred Scott v. Sandford, 19 How 393 What was said in American & Ocean Ins Co v Canter, 1 Pet 511, here held to be *obiter dictum,* and not authority

14. Railroad in — Power of congress to grant.— Congress can grant to a corporation existing under the laws of an individual state the right to construct a railroad within any of the territories of the United States, and the state afterward created out of the territory could not put any impediment on the enjoyment of the right thus conferred except upon the same terms that it could do when applied to its own previously granted right. In such matters the state only succeeds to the authority of congress over the territory. Van Wyck v. Knevals, 106 U. S. 360; Railroad Co. v. Baldwin, 103 U. S. 426.

15. Territories — Relation of to United States. — All territory within the jurisdiction of the United States not included in any state must, necessarily, be governed by or under authority of congress. The territories bear much the same relation to the general government that counties do to the states, and congress may legislate for them as states do for their respective municipal subdivisions. National Bank v. County of Yankton, 101 U. S. 129.

16. Indian reservations — Crimes committed in. — Congress has the authority to provide for the punishment of crimes committed by Indians against each other, upon an Indian reservation, whether this reservation be within a territory or a state. If in the former, such crimes may be tried in the United States courts; if in the latter, the congress may authorize their trial by the territorial courts. The states have no such power over the Indians so long as they maintain their tribal relations; the state gives them no protection and they owe it no allegiance. United States v. Kagama, 118 U. S. 375.

17. Territorial legislation — Power to annul marriage contract. A clause in the organic act of the territory of Oregon provided that the legislative power of the territory should "extend to all rightful subjects of legislation not inconsistent with the constitution of the United States." *Held*, that under the power so conferred the territorial legislature had power to enact a law annulling the marriage of one of its citizens, even though the wife from whom he was so divorced had never resided within the territory. Maynard v. Hill, 125 U. S. 190. The law upon the subject is fully discussed and authorities cited by Mr. Justice Field, citing Cooley on Const. Lim. § 664; 2 Kent's Com. 97; Cronise v. Cronise, 54 Penn. St. 255-261; Crane v. Meginnis, 1 G. & J. 463, 464 (Maryland); Starr v. Pease, 8 Conn. 541; Sparhawk v. Sparhawk, 116 Mass. 315; State v. Fry, 4 Mo. 120-138; Dartmouth College Case, 4 Wheat. 629; Butler v. Pennsylvania, 10 How. 402; Adams v. Palmer, 51 Me. 480-483, 484, 485; Maguire v. Maguire, 7 Dana, 181, 183; Ditson v. Ditson, 4 R. I. 87; Wade v. Kalbfleisch, 58 N. Y. 282-284; Noel v. Ewing, 9 Ind. 37.

18. Laws of acquired territory remain in force until congress forms a new government. — The formation of the civil government of California, under authority of the president as commander-in-chief of the army and navy, made while the war with Mexico was in progress, was the lawful exercise of a belligerent right over a conquered territory. This continued to be the existing government when the territory was ceded to the United States as a conquest, and did not cease as a matter of course or as a consequence of the restoration of peace, but was rightfully continued until congress legislated otherwise under its constitutional power to dispose of and make needful rules and regulations respecting the territory. Cross v. Harrison, 16 How. 164.

19. Effect of non-recognition by congress of a law of a territory. Under the powers of congress, reserved in the organic acts of the territories, to annul the acts of their legislatures, the absence of congressional action annulling a law that is in conflict with the organic act cannot be construed as recognition by congress that such law is valid. Clayton v. Utah, 132 U S. 632.

Section IV.

GUARANTEE TO THE STATES.

The United States shall guarantee to every State in this Union a republican form of government, and shall protect each of them against invasion, and, on application of the Legislature, or of the executive (when the Legislature cannot be convened), against domestic violence.

1 **Congress is to decide what state government is legal** — Under this section it rests with congress to decide what government is the established one in a state For as the United States guaranties to each state a republican government, congress must necessarily decide what government is established in the state before it can determine whether it is republican or not. When the senators and representatives of a state are admitted to seats in congress, both the authority of the government under which they are appointed as well as its republican character, is recognized by the proper constitutional authority Luther v Borden, 7 How 1-42 · Texas v White 7 Wall. 700-730, United States v Rhodes, 1 Abb (U. S) 47, White v Hart. 13 Wall 646

2 **Congress may delegate this power to the president** — By the act of February 28, 1795, it is provided that ' in case of an insurrection in any state against the government thereof it shall be lawful for the president of the United States, on application of the legislature of such state, or of the executive when the legislature is not in session, to call forth such number of the militia of any other state or states as may be applied for, as he may judge sufficient to suppress such insurrection " This confers on the president the authority to determine in case of conflicting governments which is the real government, and whether it is republican, and the congress had authority to so confer the power upon the president. Luther v. Borden, 7 How. 1-42, 43.

3 **Decision conclusive.**— The decision of congress, or of the president when made under the authority of congress, is final upon the subject. Luther v Borden, 7 How 44; Martin v Mott, 12 Wheat 29

4. **Unauthorized bodies assuming to legislate** — If public bodies not duly organized or admitted into the Union undertake, as states, to pass laws which might encroach on the Union or its granted powers, such conduct would have to be reached either by the power of the Union to put down insurrection, or by the ordinary penal laws of the states or territories within which these bodies are situated and acting. Scott v. Jones, 5 How. 343

5 **States in rebellion were not out of the Union** — At no time during the rebellion were the rebellious states out of the pale of the Union. Their constitutional duties and obligations remained unaffected by the rebellion They could not then pass a law impairing the obligation of contracts any more than before or since the rebellion. White v Hart, 13 Wall. 646.

ARTICLE V.

POWER OF AMENDMENT

The Congress, whenever two-thirds of both Houses shall deem it necessary, shall propose amendments to this Constitution, or, on the application of the Legislatures of two-thirds of the several States, shall call a convention for proposing amendments, which, in either case, shall be valid to all intents and purposes as part of this constitution, when ratified by the Legislatures of three-fourths of the several States, or by conventions in three-fourths thereof, as the one or the other mode of ratification may be proposed by Congress, provided that no amendment which may be made prior to the year one thousand eight hundred and eight shall in any manner affect the first and fourth clauses in the ninth section of the first Article, and that no State, without its consent, shall be deprived of its equal suffrage in the Senate

An amendment to the constitution need not be presented to the president for his approval. Hollingsworth v Virginia, 3 Dall 378

ARTICLE VI.

PUBLIC DEBT, SUPREMACY OF THE CONSTITUTION, OATH OF OFFICE, RELIGIOUS TEST.

1. All debts contracted and engagements entered into before the adoption of this Constitution shall be as valid against the United States under this Constitution as under the Confederation.

2 This Constitution, and the laws of the United States which shall be made in pursuance thereof, and all treaties made, or which shall be made, under the authority of the United States, shall be the supreme law of the land, and the judges in every State shall be bound thereby, anything in the Constitution or laws of any State to the contrary notwithstanding.

1. Supremacy of general government.—The government of the United States though limited in its powers is supreme, and its laws, when made within the constitution, form the supreme law of the land, "anything in the constitution or laws of any state to the contrary notwithstanding" McCulloch v. Maryland, 4 Wheat 316, Gibbons v Ogden, 9 Wheat. 1, Sinnot v. Davenport, 22 How 227, Bank of Commerce v. New York, 2 Black, 620

2. Necessary to existence of national government.—"The general government must cease to exist whenever it loses the power of protecting itself in the exercise of its constitutional powers" Mr. Justice Johnson in Martin v Hunter's Lessee, 1 Wheat. 363 "The national government can act only through its officers and agents, and they must act within the states If, when thus acting, and within the scope of their authority, those officers can be arrested and brought to trial in a state court for an alleged offense against the law of the state, yet warranted by the federal authority they possess, and if the general government is powerless to interfere at once for their protection, if their protection must be left to the action of the state court; the operations of the general government may at any time be arrested. . . We do not think such an element of weakness is to be found in the constitution The United States is a government with authority extending over the whole territory of the Union, acting upon the states and upon the people of the states While it is limited in the *number* of its powers, so far as its sovereignty extends it is supreme" Tennessee v Davis, 100 U S. 257–263

3 Power to enforce—'We hold it to be an incontrovertible principle that the government of the United States may, by means of physical force exercised through its official agents, execute on every foot of American soil the powers and functions that belong to it. This necessarily involves the power to command obedience to its laws, and hence the power to keep the peace to that extent. This power to enforce its laws and to execute its functions in all places does not derogate from the power of the state to execute its laws at the same time and in the same places. The one does not exclude the other except where they both cannot be executed at the same time. In that case the words of the constitution itself show which is to yield. Without the concurrent sovereignty referred to the national government would be nothing but an advisory government. Its executive power would be absolutely nullified." Mr. Justice Bradley in Ex parte Siebold, 100 U. S. 371-394, quoted and approved by Mr. Justice Miller in In re Neagle, 135 U. S. 1, 60, 61.

4. Relation of national and state governments compared.—The governments of the United States and of the states are distinct and independent of each other. Each has its separate departments and distinct laws, and its own tribunals for their enforcement. Neither government can intrude within the jurisdiction of the other, or authorize any interference therein by its judicial officers. The two governments in each state stand in their respective spheres of action in the same independent relation to each other, except when any conflict arises between the two governments the supremacy of the federal government must prevail until its courts shall have settled and determined the conflict. Tarble's Case, 13 Wall. 397.

5. State laws must yield to laws of congress.—When the powers remaining in the states are so exercised as to come in conflict with those vested in congress, that which is not supreme must yield to that which is supreme. The laws of congress must prevail. Brown v. Maryland, 12 Wheat. 419-448; Sinnot v. Davenport, 22 How. 227; Bank of Commerce v. New York, 2 Black, 620; Gibbons v. Ogden, 9 Wheat. 1.

6. The government of the United States is supreme within its sphere of action; the means necessary and proper to carry into effect the powers of the constitution are in congress. United States v. Rhodes, 1 Abb. (U. S.) 28-44; Dobbins v. Erie County, 16 Pet. 435.

7. "The line which divides what is occupied exclusively by any legislation of congress from what is left open for the action of the states is not always well defined, and is often distinguished by such nice shades of difference on each side as to require the closest scrutiny when the principle is invoked. We have more than once held in this court that the national banks organized under the acts of congress are subject to state legislation, except where such legislation is in conflict with some act of congress, or where it tends to impair or destroy the utility of such banks as agents or instrumentalities of the United States, or interferes with the purposes of their creation." Waite v. Dowley, 94 U. S. 527.

8. State assessment for taxation.—The states have the sole right to decide by legislation as to how property shall be appraised for taxation; as to who shall appraise it and what method shall be pursued by such appraisers in certifying their action, and also to fix the time and place, etc., when parties may be heard for correction of errors. And further, the legislature of a state may by act cure errors and omissions of local assessment boards. And such legislation, when applied to the valuation and assessment of shares of stock in national banks, is not in conflict with the law of congress respecting the taxation of such shares. Williams v. Supervisors of Albany, 122 U. S. 159, affirming Stanley v. Supervisors, 121 U. S. 535.

9. Act of congress operates by its own force upon the subject-matter in all states.—Every constitutional act of congress is passed by the will of the people of the United States expressed through their representatives. It is the supreme law of the land, and operates by its own force on the subject-matter in whatever state or territory it may happen to be Pollard v Hagan, 3 How 212

10 State tribunals must conform to this supreme law.—The constitution of the United States is the supreme law of the land and binds every forum, whether it derives its authority from a state or from the United States When the supreme court has declared state legislation to be in conflict with the constitution of the United States and therefore void, the state tribunals are bound to conform to such decision Cook v Moffat, 5 How 295.

11 The unity of the state and national governments is consistent with the supremacy of the latter.—The United States form for many and for most important purposes a single nation In war we are one people In making peace we are one people In all commercial regulations we are one and the same people In many other respects the American people are one, and the government which alone is capable of controlling and managing their interests in all these respects is the government of the Union. It is their government, and in that character they have no other America has chosen to be in many respects, and to many purposes a nation, and for all these purposes her government is complete, to all these objects it is competent In the exercise of all powers given for these objects it is supreme, and in effecting them it can legitimately control all individuals or governments within the American territory The constitution and laws of a state, so far as they are repugnant to the constitution and laws of the United States, are absolutely void These states are constituent parts of the United States, members of one great empire—for some purposes sovereign, for some purposes subordinate Cohens v Virginia, 6 Wheat 264, 413, 414

12 Acts in violation of constitution not supreme law—It is only such acts of congress as are within the scope of their powers as conferred by the constitution that become the supreme law of the land. Where such acts are in violation of the constitution, it is the province of the courts of the United States to declare the law void and refuse to execute it The final appellate power upon all such questions is in the supreme court of the United States Ableman v. Booth, 21 How. 506-520, Marbury v Madison, 1 Cranch, 137, McCulloch v. Maryland, 4 Wheat 316, Cohens v Virginia, 6 Wheat. 264-412

13 National bank legislation—Supremacy of—The national banks having been brought into existence by laws of congress, and with the design to aid the government in the public service, the several states can exercise no control over them nor in any wise affect their operation, except in so far as congress may see proper to permit Congress having declared what rate of interest such banks may receive, and fixed the penalty for taking a greater rate, the states cannot subject them to any other penalties for usury, nor are they liable under the usury laws of the state wherein they are located. Farmers', etc Nat Bank v. Dearing, 91 U. S 29.

14. The statute of a state which requires national banks within the state to transmit to the clerks of the several towns in the state in which any stockholder of such bank may reside a true list of such stockholders with the number of their shares etc., held to be valid, at least in so far as the town in which the bank is located is concerned That being the only question properly involved in the case, the court refused to decide further Waite v. Dowley, 94 U S 527

15 The rate of taxation upon the shares of national banks imposed by a state cannot be greater than that imposed upon moneyed capital of the individual citizen Adams v Nashville, 95 U. S 19

16. A statute of a state which values the shares of stock in national banks for taxation upon a valuation higher in proportion to their real value than other moneyed capital is void although the percentage of taxes on the ascertained value is no greater than the percentage on the valuation of other moneyed capital People v Weaver, 100 U. S 539

17. Where in a state, large amounts of securities were exempted from local taxation, *held* that this constituted a discrimination in favor of other moneyed capital against capital invested in shares of national banks, and was inconsistent with section 5219, Revised Statutes of the United States Boyer v. Boyer, 113 U. S 689

18 The law of New York in relation to the taxing of personal property allows to be deducted from the assessed valuation any debts which the owner owes The law providing for the taxing of bank stock as construed by the court of appeals does not permit such deduction of debts to be made. *Held*, (1) that in so far as the said law applies to a tax assessed against national bank stock in the hands of one who owes debts not so deducted, it is invalid as being in contravention of the laws of congress in relation to the right of a state to tax national bank stock (2) That it is not so invalid when applied to holders of such stock who have no debts to be deducted. (3) That it is not invalid as to the taxation of holders of stock in any banks other than national banks. Supervisors of Albany Co v. Stanley, 105 U S 306, People v Weaver, 100 U S 539, Hills v Exchange Bank, 105 U S 319; Britton v National Bank, 105 U. S. 322.

19 Under the laws of congress a state is not permitted, while imposing the same taxation upon national bank shares as upon shares in state banks, to discriminate against national bank shares in favor of moneyed capital not invested in state bank stock Boyer v Boyer, 113 U. S 689

20. Treaty power — Extent of — The treaty power extends to all proper subjects of negotiation between the government of the United States and the governments of other countries By the words 'states of the Union ' in the treaty with France, February 23, 1853, is meant all political communities exercising legislative power, and includes territories and the District of Columbia. Treaties should be liberally construed so as to carry out the apparent intention of the parties to secure equality and reciprocity between them Geofroy v. Riggs, 133 U S 258.

21. Treaties are supreme law — A treaty is the supreme law of the land, and courts cannot go behind it for the purpose of annulling its effect and operation Fellows v. Blacksmith 19 How 366.

22. Chinese subjects — Treaties made by the United States and in force are part of the supreme law of the land, and are as binding within the territorial limits of the states as elsewhere And the United States have power, under the constitution, *to provide for the punishment of those who are guilty* of depriving Chinese subjects of the rights privileges, immunities and exemptions guaranteed to them by the treaty with the emperor of China. Baldwin v Franks, 120 U S. 678

23. An act of congress is supreme when in conflict with a treaty. If an act of congress is in conflict with a treaty of the United States with a foreign power, the supreme court is bound to follow the statutory enactments of its own government The court in such cases has no power to set itself up as the instrumentality for enforcing the provisions of a treaty with a foreign nation which the government of the United States as a sovereign power chooses to disregard Botiller v Dominguez, 130 U S 238–247, citing The Cherokee Tobacco, 11 Wall 616, Taylor v. Morton, 2 Curtis, 454, Head-Money Cases, 112 U S 580, 598 Whitney v Robertson, 124 U S 190–195

24 Extradition — A person was charged with murder on board an American vessel on the high seas. He fled to England, and upon charge of murder which was an extraditable offense, he was claimed by the United States and delivered up by the British government. When returned to the authorities the court did not proceed against him for murder, but for a lesser and non-extraditable offense *Held* 1 That the treaty under which he was demanded was a law of the land of which all courts, state or federal, were bound to take notice, and be governed. 2 That under such treaty the defendant could not be lawfully tried for any other offense than that of murder United States v Rauscher, 119 U. S 407

25. With Indian tribes — The laws of Kansas taxing real estate cannot apply to the property of the Wea Indians within its limits The treaty leaves them under the protection of the general government and withdraws their property from the taxing power of the state The Kansas Indians, 5 Wall. 737

26. The constitution, by declaring treaties made, as well as those to be made, to be the supreme law of the land, has adopted and sanctioned the previous treaties with the Indian nations, and, consequently, admits their rank among those powers who are capable of making treaties. Worcester v Georgia, 6 Pet. 515.

27. British corporations — Title to property in Vermont protected by treaty. — The property of British corporations in this country is protected by the sixth article of the treaty of peace of 1783, and their title thus protected, is confirmed by the ninth article of the treaty of 1794, so that it could not be forfeited by an intermediate legislative act or other proceeding for the defect of alienage The termination of a treaty by war does *not divest the rights of property already vested under it.* The Society for the Propagation of the Gospel, etc. v The Town of New Haven, 8 Wheat 464.

28. Same — Rule applied. — The act of Vermont of October 30, 1794, granting the lands in that state belonging to "The Society for Propagating the Gospel in Foreign Parts" to the respective towns in which the lands lie, is void, and conveys no title. Id.

29 Laws of congress and treaties have same force — Both are part of supreme law — By this clause the laws of congress and treaties are of the same binding force, neither having precedence of the other.

Therefore, when a statute and a treaty are found to be inconsistent in their provisions, the one of later date will control, *provided*, the stipulations of the treaty (it being of later date) are self-executing. Whitney v Robertson, 124 U S 190

30. State laws enacted with assent of congress become supreme law, and not subject to state control — An act was passed by the state of Maryland, and assent thereto given by congress, whereby it was agreed by the state of Maryland that no toll should be charged for passing over the Cumberland road upon coaches carrying United States mail This, by the act of congress, became the supreme law. And an act of the legislature of Maryland passed thereafter, imposing a toll upon all passengers traveling in mail-coaches, was inconsistent with the compact and void Achison v Huddleson, 12 How. 293

31. Congress having sanctioned the compact between Virginia and Kentucky whereby "the use and navigation of the River Ohio, so far as the territory of Virginia and Kentucky are concerned, shall be free and common to the United States" it (said compact) becomes supreme law and can be carried out by the supreme court of the United States Pennsylvania v Wheeling Bridge Co, 13 How 518

32. Right of way over public domain.— Where congress has granted a right of way over the public domain in a territory to a railroad, such right cannot be interfered with by the state created from such territory and subsequently admitted into the Union St Jo & Den R. R Co v. Baldwin, 103 U. S. 426

33 Patents — How subject to state control — The laws of congress regulating the granting of patents to inventors cannot be so construed as to deprive the states of their admitted police powers The rights secured to inventors must be enjoyed in subordination to the general authority of the state over all property within its limits Webber v Virginia, 103 U S 344, Patterson v Kentucky, 97 U. S 501

34. Government license to sell liquors subject to state laws — A license from the United States to deal in liquor gives the licensee no right to sell liquor in violation of state law. McGuire v. Massachusetts, 3 Wall. 387 License Cases, 5 How. 504

35. Laws affecting telegraph companies invalid, when.— A statute of the state of Massachusetts provided, *inter alia*, that where a corporation, organized in another state and doing business in Massachusetts, was in arrears of taxes assessed against it under the laws of the latter state. the courts, upon application, might by injunction restrain such corporation so in arrears of taxes from doing business therein until such arrears of taxes were paid *Held*, that in so far as it attempted to restrain the Western Union Telegraph Company (which had accepted the provisions of the Revised Statutes of the United States, section 5263) from operating its lines over military and post roads of the United States it was invalid. Western Union Tel. Co v Massachusetts, 125 U S 530

36. Agencies of federal government.— The agencies of the federal government are only exempted from state legislation so far as that legislation may interfere with or impair their efficiency in performing the functions by which they are designed to serve the government. So as applied to national banks, they are subject to the laws of the state, and are governed in their daily course of business far more by the laws of the state than of the nation It is only when the state law incapacitates the banks from discharging their duties to the government that it becomes unconstitutional National Bank v Commonwealth, 9 Wall. 353.

37. **Chapter 4, title 10, of the code of Iowa,** is not in conflict with section 5254, Revised Statutes of United States Under this chapter a railroad company cannot take and use a dyke or pier which a riparian owner has erected in front of his property on a navigable river, to be used by him in connection with the river, without compensation, even though the owner has not complied with the act of congress prescribing the conditions on which such pier may be erected. Railway Co v. Renwick, 102 U S 180

38 **State cannot tax government officers' salaries** — The compensation of an officer of the United States is fixed by the laws thereof, and a state law seeking to tax such compensation is unconstitutional because it conflicts with the law of congress made in pursuance to the powers conferred by the constitution Dobbins v Erie County, 16 Pet. 435

39. **The legal tender act of congress** does not apply to the payment of involuntary contributions exacted by a state, in matters of local assessments and taxes and as to such payments the state may require them to be made in coin Hagar v Reclamation Dist No 108, 111 U S 701

40. **Franchises conferred by act of congress** cannot without permission of that body be taxed by the states California v Pac. R R Co., 127 U S 1.

41. **Supremacy of constitution** — The departments of the government are legislative, executive and judicial. They are co-ordinate in degree to the extent of the powers delegated to each of them Each in the exercise of its powers, is independent of the other, but all, rightfully done by either is binding on the others And the constitution is supreme over all. Dodge v Woolsey 18 How 331

42. **Protection to poll books.**— Congress has full power to protect by law the poll books which contain the vote for a member of congress from any danger that might arise from exposure, loss, change, falsification or tampering This is so notwithstanding state officers are voted for at the same time and the results kept in the same poll books or tally sheets In re Coy 127 U S 731

43 **Provision applied to case stated** — An inhabitant of Louisiana died in 1848 intestate and without issue, leaving property By the laws of the state as then existing the property so left vested in a French subject residing in France — subject, however to a tax of ten per cent payable to the state *Held* that the state had a vested right in such tax, and that the same could not thereafter be divested by treaty stipulations between the United States and France Prevost v Greneaux, 19 How 1

44 **Provision applied to case stated** —Iowa was admitted into the Union March 3, 1845 A supplemental act passed the same day extended over the state all laws of the United States not locally inapplicable Under this law the process act of congress of May, 1828, became applicable in the federal courts in Iowa at the date of their organization. Wherefore *mandamus* may issue to a municipal corporation in that state to enforce levy

and collection of tax to pay judgment rendered against such municipality by United States courts. United States v. Keokuk, 6 Wall 514

45. A railroad constructed in part by subsidies from the United States and under a charter granted by congress, on condition that it should perform certain services for the general government, is not exempt from state taxation in absence of legislation by congress to that effect. Thomson v. Union Pacific Ry Co., 9 Wall 579, Union Pacific Ry Co v. Peniston 18 Wall. 5.

3 The senators and representatives before mentioned, and the members of the several State Legislatures, and all executive and judicial officers, both of the United States and of the several States, shall be bound by oath or affirmation to support this Constitution, but no religious test shall ever be required as a qualification to any office or public trust under the United States

The legislature may superadd to the oath here required such other oath of office as its wisdom may suggest. McCulloch v. Maryland, 4 Wheat. 316-416

ARTICLE VII.

RATIFICATION OF THE CONSTITUTION.

The ratifications of the Conventions of nine States shall be sufficient for the establishment of this Constitution between the States so ratifying the same.

Done in Convention, by the unanimous consent of the States present, the seventeenth day of September, in the year of our Lord one thousand seven hundred and eighty-seven, and of the Independence of the United States of America the twelfth.

The following is the order in which the thirteen states ratified the constitution Delaware, December 7, 1787, Pennsylvania December 12, 1787, New Jersey December 18 1787 Georgia, January 2 1788 Connecticut, January 9, 1787, Massachusetts, February 6, 1788, Maryland April 28, 1788, South Carolina May 23, 1788 New Hampshire, June 21, 1788· Virginia June 26, 1788, New York, July 26, 1788, North Carolina, November 21, 1789, Rhode Island, May 29, 1790.

AMENDMENTS TO THE CONSTITUTION.

ARTICLE I.

Congress shall make no law respecting an establishment of religion, or prohibiting the free exercise thereof, or abridging the freedom of speech, or of the press; or the right of the people peaceably to assemble, and to petition the government for a redress of grievances

1. This section does not limit the powers of the state governments over their citizens It was intended to operate on the national government alone. Fox v Ohio, 5 How 410, United States v Cruikshank, 92 U S 542

2. This right of assembly and petition existed prior to and at the adoption of the constitution, and, as an attribute of national citizenship, is under the protection of and guarantied by the United States. Id.

3. **Establishment and exercise of religion** — While this section forbids congress from interfering with the free exercise of religion, neither it nor any other clause of the constitution makes any provision for protecting the citizens of the respective states in their religious worship or religious liberties, this is left entirely to the state constitutions and laws, and there is no inhibition in regard to the subject imposed upon the states. Permoli v First Municipality, 3 How. 589-606, Ex parte Garland, 4 Wall. 398.

4. **Polygamy not protected.**— This amendment was not intended to prohibit legislation forbidding and punishing polygamy Reynolds v United States, 98 U S 145.

5. Bigamy and polygamy are crimes by the laws of all civilized and christian countries and this section cannot be invoked as a protection against legislation for their punishment. Davis v. Beason, 133 U. S. 333.

6. The statutes of Idaho territory forbidding bigamists or polygamists to vote, and requiring the voter to make oath that he is not a member of an order that teaches the commission of these crimes, are valid Id.

7. **Freedom of press** — Liberty of circulation is essential to the "freedom of the press" And while congress may exclude any printed or other matter from the mail, its power over the methods of circulation ends there. It cannot forbid the transportation of any kind of printed matter by any other means than through the mail. In the Matter of Jackson, 96 U S. 727.

8. **Right of assembly and petition.**— The right of the people peaceably to assemble for lawful purposes existed long before the adoption of the constitution. This amendment was not intended to limit the action of the state governments in respect to their own citizens, but to operate upon the national government alone It left the authority of the states unimpaired, added nothing to the already existing powers of the United States, and guarantied the continuance of the right only against congressional interference. The people, therefore, for protection in the enjoyment of it must look to the states, where the power for that purpose was originally placed United States v. Cruikshank, 92 U S 542

9. The right of the people peaceably to assemble, and petition congress for a redress of grievances, or for anything else connected with the powers and duties of national government, is an attribute of national citizenship, and as such, under the protection of and guaranteed by the United States. The very idea of a government republican in form implies that right, and an invasion of it presents a case within the sovereignty of the United States. United States v Cruikshank, 92 U. S. 542.

10. **Applies only to the United States.**—The first ten amendments are in the nature of a bill of rights, and apply only to the national government They were not intended to restrict the powers of the states. Barron v Mayor, etc., 7 Pet 247, Withers v. Buckley, 20 How. 84, United States v. Rhodes, 1 Abb (U. S.) 28–48

ARTICLE II.

A well regulated militia being necessary to the security of a free state, the right of the people to keep and bear arms shall not be infringed.

1 This right is neither granted by the constitution nor dependent upon that instrument for its existence. It simply means that this inherent right shall not be infringed by congress. United States v Cruikshank, 92 U S. 542

2 A law which only forbids bodies of men to associate together as military organizations, or to drill or parade with arms in cities and towns unless authorized by law, does not infringe on the prohibitions of this article. This amendment is a limitation on the power of congress and not upon the states Presser v. Illinois, 116 U. S 252, citing United States v. Cruikshank, 92 U S 542, Fox v. Ohio, 5 How. 410

ARTICLE III.

No soldier shall, in time of peace, be quartered in any house, without the consent of the owner, nor in time of war, but in a manner to be prescribed by law

ARTICLE IV

The right of the people to be secure in their persons, houses, papers, and effects, against unreasonable searches and seizures shall not be violated, and no warrants shall issue but upon probable cause, supported by oath or affirmation, and particularly describing the place to be searched, and the persons or things to be seized

1 **Probable cause.**—All the facts necessary to constitute this probable cause must appear upon oath or affirmation. Ex parte Bollman and Ex parte Swartwout. 4 Cranch, 75

2. **Letters and sealed packages** subject to letter postage in the mail can be opened and examined only under like warrant issued upon similar

oath or affirmation particularly describing the thing to be seized, as is required when papers are subjected to search in one's own household The constitutional guaranty contained in the fourth amendment extends to papers sealed and deposited in the mail against inspection. In the Matter of Jackson, 96 U S. 727

3 **Amendment applies only to proceedings in federal courts** — This amendment is applicable only to proceedings in the federal courts It is a limitation on the federal and not on the state governments. Fox v Ohio, 5 How. 410

4. **Persons subject to penalties cannot be compelled to produce private books** — It is a violation of this amendment to compel persons to produce their private books and papers to be used in evidence against them upon a trial of a case involving a penalty or forfeiture, or on a criminal charge It does not require actual entry and search and seizure to constitute unreasonable search and seizure within the meaning of this amendment. Therefore a law of congress which requires a person to produce such books and papers in such cases, and which in default of such production provides that the matters charged to be contained therein shall be taken as confessed, is unconstitutional and void. Boyd v. United States, 116 U S 616.

5. **Purpose of provision.**— The genius of our liberties holds in abhorrence all irregular inroads upon the dwelling-houses and persons of citizens, and with wise jealousy guards them as sacred except when assailed in the established and allowed forms of law. This amendment, with others, was adopted to guard against abuses of power in those modes by the general government, and was designed to restrict even modified "martial law' to cases happening among military men, or militia when in actual service Luther v Borden, 7 How 1-66

6. **Revenue officers.**— The statute of the United States authorizing and requiring revenue officers in certain cases to compel the production of books and papers relating to or which are supposed to relate to, matters connected with the internal revenue, is not in violation of this section. Matter of Meador, 1 Abb, (U S.), 317.

7. **Distress warrant by solicitor of treasury.**— A distress warrant issued by the solicitor of the treasury under the act of congress passed on the 15th day of May, 1820 (3 Stats at Large, 592), is not inconsistent with this amendment. Murray v Hoboken Land, etc Co., 18 How 272

8 **Oath or affirmation.**— This has no application to proceedings for the recovery of debts where no search-warrant is used. Id., Ex parte Burford, 3 Cranch, 448, Ex parte Milligan, 4 Wall 119.

ARTICLE V.

No person shall be held to answer for a capital, or otherwise infamous crime, unless on a presentment or indictment of a grand jury, except in cases arising in the land or naval forces, or in the militia when in active service in time of war or public danger, nor shall any person be subject for the same offense to be twice put in jeopardy of life or limb, nor shall be compelled, in any criminal case, to be a witness against himself, nor be deprived of life liberty, or property, without due process of law, nor shall private property be taken for public use without just compensation

1 **This section has reference to restraints on the general government and its courts only.**—The constitution was ordained and established by the people of the United States for themselves, for their own government and not for the government of the individual states . . . The powers conferred upon this government were to be exercised by itself; and the limitations on powers, if expressed in general terms, are naturally, and we think necessarily, applicable to the government created by the instrument. The fifth amendment must be understood as restraining the power of the general government, not as applicable to the states. The provision in the fifth amendment, declaring that private property shall not be taken for public use without just compensation, is intended solely as a limitation on the exercise of power by the government of the United States, and is not applicable to the legislation of the states. Barron v Mayor of Baltimore, 7 Pet. 243, Withers v. Buckley, 20 How 84; Pumpelly v Canal Co, 13 Wall 166, Eilenbecker v. District Court of Plymouth County, 134 U S 31

2. **Habeas corpus will lie to protect persons under this provision.**—This amendment is intended as a limitation on the powers of the government in its dealings with private persons, and is applicable to those powers which are peculiarly within the cognizance of the judicial department, and the right of the courts of the nation to exercise the powers of *habeas corpus* in protecting these rights is now firmly established United States v Lee, 106 U S 196

3 This clause is not applicable to or restrictive of the legislation of the states. Withers v Buckley, 20 How. 84. See, also, Barron v. Mayor of Baltimore, 7 Pet. 247, Fox v. Ohio, 5 How 411, West River Bridge Co v Dix, 6 How. 507.

4. **Nor shall private property be taken for public use without just compensation — Eminent domain — Exercise of by railroad companies.**—A railroad, although constructed and owned by a private corporation, is for a public use, and the power of eminent domain may be exercised to condemn its right of way Olcott v Supervisors, 16 Wall. 678.

5. **Territories — Government may authorize railroad companies to exercise right of eminent domain in** —The United States may exercise the right of eminent domain in the territories, as well as in the states, for purposes necessary to the execution of the powers of the government. All lands held by private persons within the limits of the United States are subject to this authority A railway being primarily a public highway, may exercise this power when so authorized by proper legislative sanction. Cherokee Nation v Railway Co, 135 U S 641

6. **Navigable waters — Government may remove bridges over without compensation.**— When in the judgment of congress the public

good requires a bridge over the navigable waters of the nation to be removed or altered, the United States is not bound to make compensation for damages incurred, although the bridge was constructed so as to comply substantially with the provisions of law relating thereto Newport, etc. Bridge Co v United States, 105 U. S 470

7. **Eminent domain an incident to sovereignty.**—The power of eminent domain is an incident of sovereignty and requires no constitutional provision to call it into existence The fifth amendment to the constitution is a limitation upon the exercise of this inherent power United States v Jones, 109 U. S 513

8 **Proceedings to ascertain compensation may be under state laws** —While this right in the federal government cannot be transferred to a state, the proceedings to ascertain the compensation to be paid for private property taken may be made to conform to the laws of the state in which such property is situate Id

9. **Property of the general government not subject to power of eminent domain in states.**—A city has no right to open streets through property belonging to the United States adjacent to the city, although the grounds have been laid out in lots and streets by the government. United States v Chicago, 7 How. 185

10. **State laws cannot interfere with exercise of this right by the general government** —The right of eminent domain exists in the government of the United States and may be exercised by it within the states so far as is necessary to the enjoyment of the powers conferred upon it by the constitution, and the right cannot be affected either by the unwillingness of the property holders to sell or by the action of a state prohibiting a sale to the federal government Kohl v United States, 91 U S 367

11. **Property of an incorporated company may be condemned.** A bridge held by an incorporated company under a charter from a state may be condemned and taken as part of a public road under the laws of the state Notwithstanding the charter is a contract with the state, yet like all private rights it is subject to the right of eminent domain All property is held by tenure from the state and all contracts are made subject to the right of eminent domain The West River Bridge Co. v Dix, 6 How 507

12. **Franchises are property within the meaning of this clause.** Property held by incorporated companies stands upon the same footing with that held by individuals, and a franchise cannot be distinguished from other property Id., Wilkinson v Leland, 2 Pet. 658, Charles River Bridge v. Warren Bridge, 11 Pet. 645

13. **Where only the use of the property is impaired no compensation can be enforced.**—Acts done in the exercise of governmental powers, and not directly encroaching on private property, although their consequences may impair its use, are not a taking within the meaning of this clause. Transportation Co. v. Chicago, 99 U S 635

14 **When property is taken because it is obnoxious to public health, morals or policy, compensation must be made** —Whenever any business, occupation rights, franchises or privileges become obnoxious to the public health, manners or morals they may be regulated by the police power of the state even to suppression, individual rights being compelled to

give way for the benefit of the whole body politic But when, in the exercise of this police power, private property or private vested rights must be taken for public use, in order to carry out or allow to be carried out improvements or regulations, or to carry on business or occupations, or schemes of public works, looking to the amelioration and benefit of the public health, manners or morals, compensation must be made for the property taken. N O Water-works Co v. St. Tammany Water-works Co, 14 Fed. Rep. 194

15 Compensation for government appropriations of property may be sued for in court of claims — Where the United States, by its officers or agents, acting under provisions of law, appropriates private property, the government is under an implied obligation to make just compensation therefor, and, upon failure to do so, the owner may bring suit upon such obligation, in the court of claims, although there may have been no formal act looking toward such compensation. United States v Great Falls Manuf g Co., 112 U S. 645

16 Compensation need not be in advance of taking.— The constitution does not require that compensation shall be made in advance of the appropriation of lands for railroad right of way It is sufficient if adequate provision be made for just compensation, but the title does not pass from the owner until the compensation is actually made. Cherokee Nation v. Railway Co, 135 U S 641.

17. Common-law principles were intended to be established by this provision.— By the general law of European nations and the common law of England private property cannot be taken by the government for public use without compensation, and the provisions in the federal and state constitutions on this question were intended to establish this principle beyond legislative control. Pumpelly v. Canal Co, 13 Wall 166

18 The taking need not be actual and literal to entitle owner to recover — It is not necessary that the property should be absolutely taken to entitle the owner to the protection of this clause. If there is such serious interruption with the common and necessary use as to practically destroy its value, it would be a taking within the meaning of this provision Id.

19 When taken by government during war, compensation must be made.— Where private property is taken by the government in time of war or public danger and converted to public use, the government is bound to pay for the same United States v Russell, 13 Wall 623

20 Military seizures — Private property may be taken by a military commander to prevent its falling into the hands of the enemy, or, where necessary, it may be taken for the use of the public. In such case the government is bound to make full compensation but the officer is not a trespasser, provided the danger is imminent or the necessity urgent, and such as will not admit of delay Mitchell v Harmony, 13 How 115

21. Due process of law — Plenary suit and trial by jury not required — Cases where this is not required enumerated — A rule on an attorney to show cause why he shall not be disbarred from practicing in a court because of the commission of crime or for official misconduct is a regular and lawful method practiced from time immemorial. It is a mistaken idea that due process of law requires a plenary suit and trial by jury in all cases where property or personal rights are involved The important right of personal liberty is often determined by a single judge on *habeas corpus*, using affidavits or depositions for proofs. Assessments for damages and benefits occasioned by public improvements are usually made by commissioners in a summary way Conflicting claims of creditors amounting to thousands of dollars are often settled by the court on affidavits or depositions alone, and courts of chancery, admiralty, bankruptcy and probate administer immense fields of jurisdiction without trial by jury In all cases, that kind of procedure is "due process of law," suitable and proper to the nature of the case and sanctioned by the established customs and usages of courts Ex parte Wall 107 U S. 265, citing Cooley's Const Lim, 353 Davidson v New Orleans, 96 U. S 97, Murray v Hoboken Land, etc Co, 18 How 272

22 **"Due process of law"—Meaning of the term**—The words "due process of law" were undoubtedly intended to convey the same meaning as the words "by the law of the land" in *Magna Charta*. Lord Coke, in his commentaries on those words (2 Inst 50), classes them as of the same meaning Murray v Hoboken Land & Improvement Co, 18 How 272-276.

23. **Rules for construing phrase**—We must first examine the constitution itself to see whether the process under consideration be in conflict with any of its provisions If not found to be so, we must look to those settled usages and modes of proceeding existing in the common and statute law of England before the emigration of our ancestors, and which are shown not to have been unsuited to their civil and political condition by having been acted upon after their settlement in this country Id.

24. **Prohibition extends to the government**—The United States cannot, any more than a state, interfere with private rights except for legitimate governmental purposes They are not included within the constitutional prohibition which prevents states from passing laws impairing the obligation of contracts, but equally with the states the United States is forbidden to deprive any person of life, liberty or property without due process of law Union Pacific R. R. v United States 99 U S 700

25 **Power to distrain for taxes**—The power to distrain personal property for the payment of taxes is due process of law Springer v United States, 102 U S 586

26 **An act of congress authorizing a warrant to issue without oath**, against a public debtor, for the seizure of his property, is valid, and the warrant is conclusive evidence of the facts recited in it and the proceeding thereunder is "due process of law" Murray v Hoboken Land Co, 18 How. 274 See, also De Treville v Smalls, 98 U S 517; Sherry v McKinley, 99 U S 496, Miller v United States, 11 Wall. 268, Tyler v. Defrees, 11 Wall. 331 · Springer v United States, 102 U S 586

27 **A distress warrant** issued by the solicitor of the treasury against a delinquent collector is not in violation of this clause Such warrant is "due process of law." Murray v Hoboken Land & Improvement Co, 18 How 272

28 **Restraining importers from suing to recover excessive duties.**—A law denying to importers the right to bring an action at law to

recover duties claimed to have been paid upon an excessive valuation does not deprive such person of his property without due process of law. Hilton v Merritt, 110 U S 97

29 **Change of sentence cannot be made, when.**—While the rule is that during the term the judgments, orders and decrees of the court are under its control, and may be set aside and modified as law and justice may require, nevertheless this power cannot be so used as to violate rights guaranteed to parties by the federal or state constitutions Hence when a court has imposed a fine *and* imprisonment, when under the statute it was authorized only to fine *or* imprison, and the fine has been paid, the court cannot, during the term, alter the sentence by imposing imprisonment alone The judgment of the court having been executed by a satisfaction of one of the alternatives, the other cannot be imposed Ex parte Lange, 18 Wall 163

30. **Infamous crime.**—The offenses defined in sections 5511 and 5512, Revised Statutes in relation to illegal registration and illegal voting for members of congress are "infamous" crimes, within the meaning of this amendment, and must be prosecuted by indictment, and not by information. Parkinson v United States, 121 U S 281

31. A crime which is punished by imprisonment at hard labor for a term of years is an infamous crime and a person convicted of such crime without presentment or indictment by a grand jury may be discharged by the supreme court upon *habeas corpus* Ex parte Wilson 114 U S 417, United States v. Petit, 114 U S 429.

32. The words "infamous crime" have a fixed and settled meaning. In a legal sense they are descriptive of an offense that subjects a person to infamous punishment or prevents his being a witness The fact that it may be or must be imprisonment in the penitentiary does not necessarily make it in law infamous. United States v Maxwell, 3 Dill 275 citing Rex v Hickman 1 Moody, 34, Commonwealth v. Shaver, 3 W. & S 338, Russell on Crimes 126, 1 Greenleaf on Ev, secs 372, 373, People v. Whipple, 9 Cow 707, United States v Shepard, 1 Abb (U S) 431–439

33. **What changes in law the clause produced**—This provision produced no change in the practice of law except perhaps as regards a class of misdemeanors regarded as infamous crimes and which might before the amendment, be prosecuted by information It recognizes the right to pursue the common-law course by criminal information in all but capital and infamous crimes United States v. Shepard, 1 Abb. (U. S) 431, United States v Maxwell, 3 Dill 275, United States v. Waller, 1 Sawyer, 701, United States v Wynn, 3 McCrary, 266

34 **What is not an infamous crime**—A conspiracy to make counterfeit coin is not an infamous crime within the meaning of this article and may be prosecuted by information United States v Burgess, 3 McCrary, 278.

35 No crime is infamous within the meaning of this act unless expressly made infamous or declared a felony by an act of congress Stealing from the mail is not an infamous crime United States v. Wynn, 3 McCrary, 266

36. Passing counterfeit money is not an infamous crime within the meaning of this article, and may be prosecuted by information. There is no statute of the United States in force making it an infamous crime. The punishment is severe, but the extent of the punishment does not alter the nature

of the offense United States v Field, 16 Fed Rep. 778, United States v. Coppersmith, 4 Fed Rep 198, United States v Yates, 6 Fed Rep 861, United States v. Petit, 11 Fed Rep 58

37 **Indictment by grand jury — Proceeding to disbar an attorney not included in** — This does not apply to prevent the courts from punishing its officers for contempt, or from removing them in proper cases And an attorney may be disbarred upon a hearing before the court upon a charge involving a crime, without previous indictment, trial and conviction therefor The proceeding is in its nature civil, and collateral to any criminal prosecution by indictment. It is not for the purpose of punishment, but for the purpose of preserving the courts from official ministrations of persons unfit to practice in them. Ex parte Wall, 107 U S. 265

38. **"Nor be compelled in any criminal case to be a witness against himself" — Cross-examination** — When a defendant in a criminal trial offers himself as a witness in his own behalf he is subject to cross-examination as provided by the law of the jurisdiction where he is being tried, and the question of the extent of such cross-examination presents no federal question Spies v. Illinois, 123 U. S 131.

39. **Indictment** — This requirement is jurisdictional, and no court of the United States has authority to try a prisoner without indictment or presentment in such cases as are therein enumerated This means an indictment as presented by the grand jury, and a trial upon an indictment which has been changed either on the motion of the court or at the request of the district attorney, by striking out redundant words, is void. Ex parte Bain, 121 U S. 1

40. **Civil in form and criminal in nature.**— An action which has for its object the forfeiture of a person's property, even though in the form of a civil suit, whether *in rem* or *in personam*, is a criminal case, within the meaning of this amendment. Boyd v. United States, 116 U S 616

41. **Retroactive laws** — An act passed after an event which in effect ratifies what has been done, and declares in effect that no suit shall be sustained against the party acting under color of authority, is valid so far as congress could have conferred such authority before They are ordinary acts of indemnity passed by all governments when occasion requires it. Mitchell v. Clark, 110 U. S 633

42 **Twice in jeopardy — Object of provision** — The provisions of the common law and of the federal constitution that no man shall be twice placed in jeopardy of life or limb are mainly designed to prevent a second punishment for the same crime or misdemeanor Ex parte Lange, 18 Wall. 163.

43. **Recovery of penalty in civil suit no bar to prosecution for crime for same acts.**— Where a statute provides for a penalty for an offense and also for a fine and imprisonment for same offense, the recovery of the penalty in a civil suit in the name of the United States is no bar to the prosecution criminally for the misdemeanor The person so prosecuted is not twice put in jeopardy within the meaning of this clause. In re Leszynsky 16 Bla ch. 9

44. **Unlawful cohabitation and adultery — Conviction for one bars the other.**— A conviction for the crime of unlawful cohabitation is

a bar to a subsequent prosecution for the crime of adultery, committed during the same period, where the adultery charged in the second indictment was an incident and a part of the unlawful cohabitation for which there had been a conviction. Ex parte Nielsen, 131 U. S. 179, In re Snow, 120 U S 274

45. **Mistrial or failure of jury to agree is not a bar to second trial.**— The discharge of the jury from giving a verdict in a capital case without the consent of the prisoner the jury being unable to agree, is not a bar to a subsequent trial for the same offense The court has discretionary power to discharge a jury in such a case without verdict whenever, in their opinion, there is a manifest necessity for such an act, or the ends of public justice would otherwise be defeated. United States v. Perez, 9 Wheat. 579.

46 **Insanity of juror and discharge of jury no bar to future prosecution.**— In a capital case insanity of one of the jurors is a good cause for discharging the jury without consent of the prisoner or his counsel. Such discharge is in the discretion of the court, and cannot form the subject of a plea in bar to the further trial of the prisoner. United States v Haskell, 4 Wash. C. C 402

47. **Want of jurisdiction — Defective indictment — Mistrial.**— Where the court has no jurisdiction, or where the indictment is defective, or there was a mistrial, the court may discharge the jury or set aside its verdict, and it will be no bar to further trial. United States v. Keen, 1 McLean, 429–434, United States v. Morris, 1 Curt. 23

48. **Jury sworn and discharged before arraignment** —Where the jury was impaneled and sworn to try an indictment before the defendant had been arraigned or had pleaded to the indictment, and the jury so sworn was then discharged and the prisoner arraigned and plea of not guilty entered, when a new jury was impaneled and sworn, *held*, that he had not been put in jeopardy by the impaneling of the first jury United States v Riley, 5 Blatchf. 204.

49. **Sudden and uncontrollable emergency.**— A jury sworn in a criminal case may be discharged by the court under any sudden and uncontrollable emergency, and such discharge is no bar, even in a capital case, to another trial. United States v. Shoemaker, 2 McLean, 114.

50. **Nolle prosequi after jury impaneled and witness sworn.**— Where after the jury are impaneled and sworn and witnesses sworn, the prosecuting attorney enters a *nolle prosequi* because the evidence is not sufficient to convict, it is a bar to a future trial for the same offense. Id.

51. **Punishments cannot be added one after another.**— In a case where the penalty fixed by statute was either fine or imprisonment, and the court has imposed both a fine and imprisonment, and the defendant has paid the fine, the court cannot thereafter, even during the term, modify its judgment by changing it into a sentence for imprisonment only. The judgment as to one of the alternative penalties having been executed, the power of the court as to that offense is at an end. Ex parte Lange, 18 Wall 163

52. **Applies only to general government and courts of the United States** — This is not a limitation on the states It is exclusively a restriction on federal power, intended to prevent interference with the rights

of the states, and of their citizens Affirming Barron v. Mayor of Baltimore, 7 Pet. 243 Fox v State of Ohio, 5 How 410

53. The law as declared in Prigg v Commonwealth, 16 Pet. 539, examined and re-affirmed. Moore v. People, 11 How 13

54 **Case stated where restriction held to apply.**—Where a defendant was indicted for robbing the mail and putting the life of the driver in jeopardy, and the conviction and judgment pronounced upon him extended to both offenses, *held*, after this judgment no prosecution could be maintained for the same offense, or for any part of it, provided the former conviction was pleaded United States v Wilson, 7 Pet. 150

55 **When in actual service in time of war or public danger—Refers only to militia**—This clause has no reference to the regular army or the navy, but refers only to the militia. In re Bogart, 2 Sawyer, 396

56 **Arising in the naval forces.**—An offense committed by a party while actually in the naval service is a "case arising in the naval forces," within the meaning of this clause, and congress has power to authorize the trial of a person for such an offense by a court-martial, upon proceedings commenced after the connection with service by the party charged has been severed. Id.

57. Every one connected with the military or naval branches of the public service is amenable to the jurisdiction which congress has created for their government, and while thus serving, surrenders his right to be tried by the civil courts. Ex parte Milligan, 4 Wall. 2-123.

ARTICLE VI.

In all criminal prosecutions, the accused shall enjoy the right to a speedy and public trial, by an impartial jury of the State and district wherein the crime shall have been committed, which district shall have been previously ascertained by law, and to be informed of the nature and cause of the accusation, to be confronted with the witnesses against him; to have compulsory process for obtaining witnesses in his favor, and to have the assistance of counsel for his defense.

1. This clause has reference only to trials in courts of the United States. It has no reference to trials in state courts Edwards v Elliott, 21 Wall. 532.

2. It is not applicable to state governments, but was designed exclusively as a limitation upon federal powers Twitchell v. Pennsylvania, 7 Wall. 321; Fox v Ohio, 5 How 410, Eilenbecker v. Dist. Court of Plymouth Co., 134 U. S 31.

3. **Of the state and district wherein the crime shall have been committed, which district shall have been previously ascertained by law**—This clause applies only to the case of offenses committed within the limits of a state It has no reference to crimes committed upon the high seas, or in any place out of the jurisdiction of any state, provision for which

has been made by the crimes act, passed April 30, 1790, § 8 (1 Stat. at L. p 114) United States v. Dawson, 15 How. 467–488.

4. **Speedy and public trial.**—The statute of Illinois provides, "In the trial of any criminal cause, the fact that a person called as a juror has formed an opinion or impression based upon rumor or upon newspaper statements (about the truth of which he has expressed no opinion) shall not disqualify him to serve as a juror in such case, if he shall upon oath state that he believes he can fairly and impartially render a verdict therein in accordance with the law and the evidence, and the court shall be satisfied of the truth of such statement." In passing upon a challenge to a juror under this law, the state court ruled that under the statute "it is not a test question whether the juror will have the opinion which he has formed from the newspapers changed by the evidence, but whether his verdict will be based only upon the account which may here be given by witnesses under oath" The statute as thus interpreted did not deprive the accused of the right to a trial by an impartial jury. Spies v. Illinois, 123 U. S. 131.

5. **To be confronted with the witnesses against him.**—Notwithstanding this provision of the constitution, if the witnesses are absent by the procurement of the accused, or where this fact sufficiently appears to cast upon him the burden of showing, and he, having opportunity to do so, fails to show, that he has not been instrumental in concealing them or in keeping them away he is in no condition to assert that his constitutional right has been violated by allowing competent evidence of the testimony which they gave on a previous trial between the same parties and upon the same issues Such evidence is admissible Reynolds v. United States, 98 U S 145

6. **To be informed of the nature and cause of accusation.**—This requires the indictment to set forth the offense with clearness and all necessary certainty to apprise the accused of the crime with which he stands charged and every ingredient of which the crime is composed must be accurately and clearly alleged It will not do to merely state the crime in the generic terms used in its definition, it must state the species, it must descend to particulars. United States v. Cruikshank, 92 U S 542, In re Coleman, 15 Blatchf. 415

7. **Right of trial by jury—Military commission—Habeas corpus**—The circuit court has authority to certify questions in proceedings in *habeas corpus* to inquire into a sentence of a military commission, and the supreme court of the United States has jurisdiction to hear and determine them In a state where federal authority has always prevailed and where the federal courts have been at all times open to hear and determine legal questions, congress has no authority to authorize trials by military commission for offenses in civil life, in no way connected with the military service Ex parte Milligan, 4 Wall 2

8 **Jury trial.**—The right of trial by jury is preserved to every one accused of crime who is not in the naval or military service Id

9 **This amendment is in force in the District of Columbia.**—Callan v Wilson, 127 U. S. 540.

NOTE—This applies also to the fifth and seventh amendments, and to that clause in section 3 of the original constitution which provides "that the trial of all crimes, except in cases of impeachment, shall be by jury."

10 Confiscation of the property of public enemies not restrained by this amendment.— The confiscation acts of August 6, 1861, and July 17, 1862 are constitutional. Excepting the first four sections of the latter act they are an exercise of the war powers of the government, and not an exercise of its sovereign municipal power Consequently they are not in conflict with the restrictions of the fifth and sixth amendments Miller v. United States, 11 Wall 268.

ARTICLE VII.

In suits at common law, where the value in controversy shall exceed twenty dollars, the right of trial by jury shall be preserved, and no fact tried by a jury shall be otherwise re-examined in any court of the United States than according to the rules of the common law.

1. Common law — What the term includes.— This amendment may in a just sense be construed to embrace all suits which are not of equity or admiralty jurisdiction, whatever may be the peculiar form which they assume to settle legal rights. By "common law" is meant the same as in the third article denominated "law," not merely suits which the common law recognized among its old and settled proceedings, but suits in which legal rights were to be ascertained and determined, in contradistinction to equitable rights Parsons v Bedford 3 Pet 433

2. Embraces all suits except in admiralty or equity—This amendment embraces all suits for the settlement of legal rights, whatever the form may be, except suits of equity or admiralty jurisdiction Parsons v Bedford, 3 Pet. 433, Shields v Thomas, 18 How 253, Barton v Barbour, 104 U. S. 126, Ins Co v. Comstock, 16 Wall 258, United States v. La Vengeance, 3 Dall 297; Webster v. Reid, 11 How. 437.

3. Does not apply to admiralty.— Admiralty jurisdiction in the courts of the United States is not taken away because the courts of common law may have concurrent jurisdiction in a case with admiralty, nor is a trial by jury any test of admiralty jurisdiction. Waring v Clarke, 5 How. 441

4. Does not invade the jurisdiction of equity.— This provision, correctly interpreted, cannot be made to embrace the established, exclusive jurisdiction of courts of equity, nor that which they have exercised as concurrent courts of law, but should be understood as limited to rights and remedies peculiarly legal in their nature, and such as it was proper to assert in courts of law and by the appropriate modes and proceedings of courts of law Shields v Thomas, 18 How 253

5. Does not apply to fugitive slave law—The provisions of this amendment do not apply to an examination as to the claim for services under the provisions of the statute commonly known as the fugitive slave law. Such an examination is not a proceeding at common law, but a statutory one, slavery being a municipal regulation not existing at common law. Miller v. McQueny, 5 McLean, 469, In the Matter of Martin, 2 Paine, 348

6 **Cannot be deprived of right by reference to referees** — The constitution and laws of the United States having secured to parties the trial of issues of fact by a jury, the United States courts cannot deprive them of that right by referring such issues to referees United States v. Rathbone, 2 Paine, 578

7. **Where complete remedy at law exists.**— In all cases wherein there exists a complete remedy in a court of law without the aid of chancery the plaintiff must proceed at law, for the reason that the defendant has a constitutional right to trial by jury Killian v. Ebbinghaus, 110 U. S 568

8 **A trial by the court** without a waiver of jury is simply error, and cannot be attacked collaterally Maxwell v. Stewart, 21 Wall 71; 22 Wall 77

9. **All the facts must go to the jury.**— In a trial at law the court cannot submit part of the facts to the jury and determine the remainder itself To do so violates this amendment, and is error. Hodges v Easton, 106 U S 408.

10 **Statute of Iowa in regard to half-breeds invalid.**— A law of the territory of Iowa which provided that suits against the half-breeds, to whom were ceded certain lands in said territory by treaty with the Sac and Fox Indians, should be determined by the court without the intervention of a jury, was in violation of this amendment, where the value in controversy exceeded $20 Webster v. Reid, 11 How 437.

11. **Does not apply to trials in state courts.**— The provisions of this amendment do not apply to trials in state courts. It is a limitation upon the powers of congress and the federal courts only Edwards v Elliott, 21 Wall 532, Walker v. Sauvinet, 92 U. S. 90, Pearson v. Yewdall, 95 U. S. 294, Fox v Ohio, 5 How 410

12. **Rule is applied in United States courts notwithstanding state statutes providing otherwise.**— A statute of Ohio which provides that in actions of ejectment the occupying claimant may have commissioners appointed to value improvements was held in a suit at common law in the United States courts to be unconstitutional *as applied to that court* The court held that, it being a suit at common law, the question must, if passed upon at all, be submitted to a jury, the value being in excess of $20 Held, further, that the United States court could, in an action in equity, appoint such commissioners. Bank of Hamilton v Dudley, 2 Pet 492.

13 **Interest may be computed without jury, when** — Where suit was brought in United States circuit court for Louisiana on record of a judgment in Massachusetts, it was held "that as by the local laws and practice of Louisiana questions of fact in civil cases were tried by the court, unless either of the parties demanded a jury, the interest upon the original judgment in Massachusetts might be computed and made a part of the judgment in Louisiana, without a writ of inquiry and the intervention of a jury" Mahew v Thatcher, 6 Wheat 129, Renner v Marshall, 1 Wheat. 215.

14 **Statute of Maryland held not to violate provision** — The act of assembly of Maryland of 1793, chapter 30, incorporating the Bank of Co-

lumbia, and giving to the corporation summary process by execution, in the nature of an attachment, against its debtors who have, by an express consent, in writing, made the bonds, bills or notes by them drawn or indorsed negotiable at banks, is not repugnant to the constitution of the United States nor of Maryland Bank of Columbia v. Okely, 4 Wheat 235

15 Statute of Pennsylvania held not to violate provision — The acts of the legislature of Pennsylvania providing for the sale of the estate of John Nicholson do not contravene this article of the constitution of the United States Livingstone's Lessee v. Moore, 7 Pet 469

16 Otherwise examined — Removal after judgment — The limitation on the power of the supreme court to re-examine facts tried by a jury extends to cases tried in state courts and to writs of error to such courts as well as to inferior federal tribunals Therefore so much of the act of congress of March 3, 1863, as provided for the removal of a cause after judgment by a state court, and in which the cause was tried by a jury, to the circuit court of the United States for retrial on the facts and law, is not in pursuance of the constitution and is void. Justices v Murray, 9 Wall 274.

17. Otherwise re-examined — When judgment vacated — After a trial by a jury in a state court if the judgment thereon is vacated, and a new trial granted (in a case proper for removal), the cause may then be removed to the United States court. This article of the constitution does not apply to such case by reason of the first judgment having been vacated by the state court. So the act allowing such removal is constitutional Home Life Ins Co. v Dunn, 19 Wall. 214

18 Trial of seizures by land must be by jury. — In the trial of cases of seizure made upon land as contradistinguished from marine seizures the court proceeds as at common law, and the trial by jury in such cases is preserved by this amendment The Sarah, 8 Wheat. 391, Morris v United States (Morris' Cotton), 8 Wall 507.

19. Does not apply to contests in court of claims. — The provisions contained in the act of March 3, 1863, whereby the court of claims is empowered to render judgment in favor of the United States and against a claimant without intervention of a jury, is not in violation of this amendment McElrath v United States, 102 U. S 426.

20. Re-examined — Remittitur after verdict held not to be a re-examination — Upon a trial at common law in the United States circuit court in a suit for damages the jury returned a verdict for plaintiff in the sum of $39 958 33 On defendant's motion for a new trial, and in arrest of judgment, the court decided that if the plaintiff would remit $22,833 33 the motion for a new trial should be overruled The sum was remitted, whereupon the court entered judgment for $17,125 and overruled the motion *Held*, that this was not a re-examination by the court of facts tried by a jury in a mode not known at the common law, and is no violation of the seventh amendment Arkansas Cattle Co v Mann. 130 U S. 69

ARTICLE VIII

Excessive bail shall not be required, nor excessive fines imposed, nor cruel and unusual punishment inflicted.

1 **Cruel and unusual punishment.**— This clause is not applicable to a state It applies exclusively to national legislation Pervear v Commonwealth, 5 Wall 475, Fox v Ohio, 5 How 410, Barron v Baltimore, 7 Pet. 243, Eilenbecker v District Court of Plymouth County, 134 U S 31; In re Kemmler, 136 U S 436

2. **Appeal in criminal cases** — This section is addressed to courts of the United States having criminal jurisdiction and is doubtless mandatory to and in limitation of their discretion. But the supreme court has no appellate jurisdiction to revise the sentences of inferior courts in criminal cases, and cannot even if the excess of the fine was apparent on the record, reverse the sentence Ex parte Watkins, 7 Pet. 568.

ARTICLE IX.

The enumeration in the Constitution of certain rights shall not be construed to deny or disparage others retained by the people.

ARTICLE X.

The powers not granted to the United States by the Constitution, nor prohibited by it to the States, are reserved to the States respectively or to the people

1. **Powers of state not limited by this amendment.**— "That the first ten articles of amendment were not intended to limit the powers of the state governments in respect to their own people, but to operate on the national government alone, was decided more than half a century ago, and that decision has been steadily adhered to since" Waite, C J., in Spies v. Illinois, 123 U S at p 166 The following cases are cited by the chief justice: Barron v Baltimore, 7 Pet. 243, Livingston v Moore, id 469, 552, Fox v Ohio, 5 How 410-434, Smith v Maryland, 18 How 71, Withers v Buckley, 20 How 84, Pervear v Commonwealth, 5 Wall 475, Twitchell v Commonwealth, 7 Wall 321, The Justices v. Murray, 9 Wall. 274, Edwards v Elliott, 21 Wall 532, Walker v Sauvinet, 92 U S 90, United States v Cruikshank, id 542, Pearson v. Yewdall, 95 U S 294, Davidson v New Orleans, 96 U. S. 97, Kelly v Pittsburgh, 104 U S 78, Presser v Illinois, 116 U S 252

2 **Taxation — Railroad used as post-road may be taxed by state** — A railroad constructed under the direction and by authority of congress for uses and purposes of the United States as a post-road and military road the stock whereof, however, is owned by private parties, is not exempt from taxation by the states through which it runs, in absence of any legislation by congress declaring such exemption. Thomson v U P R. R Co, 9 Wall 579.

3 **Private corporations and all trades** are subject to be taxed by the state for support of state government. Such authority resides in the states

primarily, and has not been surrendered. Society for Savings v Coite, 6 Wall 594, Hamilton Manuf Co v Massachusetts, 6 Wall. 632; Prov Sav. Inst v Massachusetts, 6 Wall 611

4 **Treasury notes not legal tender for state taxes** — The clause in the act of congress making United States treasury notes legal tender for debts has no reference to taxes imposed by state authority Lane County v Oregon, 7 Wall 71

5. It is competent for the state to require such taxes to be paid in coin Id

6 **State may exempt from taxes** — A state may, by contract based on consideration, exempt the property of an individual or corporation from taxation either for a specified period or permanently. Home of the Friendless v Rouse, 8 Wall 430.

7. **Power to tax an incident to sovereignty.**— The power to tax resides in the government as a part of itself, and need not be reserved when property of any description is granted to individuals and corporate bodies. And unless exempted in terms which amount to a contract not to tax, the property, privileges and franchises of a corporation are as much the legitimate subject of taxation as any other property of the citizens within the sovereign power of the state Per Clifford, J, in North Missouri R. R. Co v. McGuire, 20 Wall 46

8. **Same** — The taxing power of a state is an attribute of sovereignty and exists independently of the constitution of the United States, and is not derived from that instrument. It may be exercised to an unlimited extent on all property, trades, business and avocations carried on within the territorial boundaries of the state, except so far as surrendered to the federal government. The extent to which it shall be exercised, the subjects on which it shall be exercised, and the mode in which it shall be exercised, are equally within the discretion of the legislatures of the states Union Pacific R. R. Co v Penniston, 18 Wall. 5

9 The property of the Union Pacific Railroad Company, although the corporation was created by congress, and the company is an agent of the government, both military and postal, is nevertheless subject to state taxation Id.

10. **Taxation a sovereign right — It may be waived by the state — The intent to do so must be clear, when by contract it is binding on state** — The right of taxation is a sovereign right, and presumptively belongs to the state, in regard to every species of property, and to an unlimited extent The right may be waived in particular instances, but this can only be done by a clear expression of legislative will (Citing Tomlinson v Branch, 15 Wall 469, Tomlinson v. Jessup, 15 Wall 454) When a contract of exemption is thus established it is binding upon the state, and laws violating its terms will not be sustained (Citing Osborne v. Mobile, 16 Wall. 481, Humphrey v Pegues, 16 Wall 247.) This is a settled principle of law Pacific R R. v McGuire, 20 Wall 36, Charleston v Branch, 15 Wall. 470.

11. The power of taxation by a state is a part of all governmental sovereignty, and is inseparable from it It is for the legislature to decide what persons and property shall be taxed and how There can be no limit to the degree of its exercise except what is found in the wisdom of the law-making power St. Louis v Wiggins Ferry Co, 11 Wall. 423.

12. How subject to control by the United States.—While the power of taxation is one of vital importance retained by the states, not abridged by the grant of similar powers to the government of the Union, but to be concurrently exercised by the two governments yet even this power of a state is subordinate to and may be controlled by the constitution of the United States The constitution and laws made in pursuance thereof are supreme, they control the constitution and laws of the respective states and cannot be controlled by them The sovereign power of a state does not extend to those means employed by congress to carry into execution the powers conferred on that body by the people of the United States and the states cannot, by taxation, impede or control or otherwise retard the exercise of those powers The states cannot tax real estate purchased by the United States in payment of direct taxes Van Brocken v Anderson, 117 U. S 151 For further limitation upon the power of the state, see Savings & Loan Assoc v Topeka, 20 Wall 655

13 National bank—State may tax shareholders—The state in which a national bank is situated may tax all the shareholders of the bank, both resident and non-resident, and all of its shares of stock, and may enact suitable legislation therefor Tappan v Merchants' Nat. Bank, 19 Wall. 490

14. National bank shares may be taxed by state, when.—A state has power to tax the shares in national banks in the hands of the stockholders whose capital is invested wholly in bonds of the United States, under act of congress, June 3, 1864. The tax on the shares is not a tax on the capital of the bank, but upon the property of the stockholders as such. Bank Tax Cases, 3 Wall. 573; People v Commissioner of Taxes (eleven cases), 4 Wall. 244.

15 Right of state to exempt property from taxation.—The legislature of a state may exempt particular parcels of property or the property of particular persons or corporations from taxation for a limited period or in perpetuity Minot v. Philadelphia, Wil. & Balt. R R. Co. (The Delaware R. R. Tax), 18 Wall 206, Tomlinson v Branch, 15 Wall 460, Charleston v Branch, 15 Wall 470

16 Railroad extending interstate may be taxed in one and exempt in the other.—Where two railroads are consolidated, and one of the constituent lines is exempted from taxation by legislation, and the other not, the two united lines will be held, in the respective states, with the respective privileges and burdens attached thereto. Tomlinson v Branch, 15 Wall 460, Scotland Co v Thomas, 94 U S 682, Philadelphia, Wil. & Balt. R. R v Maryland, 10 How 376

17. Limitations of power on cities to tax for private improvements—There is no such thing in the theory of our governments—state and national—as unlimited power in any of their branches The executive, the legislative and the judicial departments are all of limited and defined powers There are limitations of such powers which arise out of the essential nature of all free governments, implied reservations of individual rights, without which the social compact could not exist, and which are respected by all governments entitled to the name Among these is the limitation of the right of taxation, that it can only be used in aid of a public object—an object which is within the purpose for which governments are established It cannot therefore, be exercised in aid of enterprises strictly private, for the benefit of individuals, though in a remote or collateral way the *local* public may be benefited thereby A statute which authorizes a town to issue its bonds in aid of manufacturing enterprises of individuals is void, because the taxes necessary to pay the bonds would, if collected, be a transfer of the property of individuals to aid in the projects of gain and profit of others, and not for a public use, in the proper sense of that term. Syllabus by Mr Justice Miller in Savings & Loan Assoc v Topeka, 20 Wall. 655

18. Same.—The numerous cases wherein it has been held that the state legislature, in the absence of restrictions in the state constitution, may authorize counties and municipalities to subscribe to the stock of railroad corporations and provide for the payment thereof by taxation, have never based this right upon the ground of the unlimited power of the state legislature to tax the people, but concede that, where the purpose for which the tax was to be levied could no longer be claimed to be for a public use, a purpose and object which it was the right and duty of the state government to assist by money raised from the people by taxation, but was purely in aid of private or personal objects, the law authorizing it was held to be beyond the legislative power, and an unauthorized invasion of private rights Savings & Loan Association v Topeka, *supra*, citing Olcott v Supervisors, 16 Wall 689, People v Salem, 20 Mich. 452, Jenkins v Andover, 103 Mass 94, Dill Mun Corp sec 587, 2 Redf on R'ys, 398, rule 2

19. Limited to persons and property within state.—The power of the state over taxation is limited to persons and property and business within her jurisdiction. All taxation must relate to one of these subjects Railroad Co v Pennsylvania State Tax on Foreign-held Bonds, 15 Wall. 300

20 To tax carrying companies—The states have authority to tax the estate, real and personal, of all their corporations, including carrying companies, precisely as they may tax similar property when belonging to natural persons and to the same extent. State Tax on Railroad Gross Receipts, 15 Wall. 282–284

21 Imported merchandise in original packages in the hands of persons other than the importer, or which have been once sold after importation, is subject to taxation by the state the same as other property. Perveau v Commonwealth, 5 Wall 475.

22 Powers of state legislatures.—The states of the Union retain for the purpose of government all the powers of the British parliament except such as have been delegated to the United States or reserved to the people. Munn v Illinois, 94 U S 113

23 Police powers.—Under the reserved powers of the state which are designated under the somewhat ambiguous term of police powers regulations may be prescribed by the state for the good order, peace and protection of the community. The subjects upon which the state may act are almost infinite, with the limitation, however, that in the exercise of the power the state does not encroach upon the free exercise of the power vested in congress by the constitution of the United States Western Union Tel. Co. v Pendleton, 122 U S 347

24. Local improvements — The states have power over the subject of local improvements designed to promote the health or prosperity of the community, and to this end may provide by law for a system of drainage by canals, ditches, etc, and of levees to prevent inundation And the expense of such works may be charged against the persons directly benefited thereby and made a lien upon their lands. Hagar v Reclamation District No 108, 111 U S 701.

25 Inspection and gauging of oils.— A state statute regulating the inspection and gauging of oils and fluids used for illuminating, etc, is a valid police regulation within the power of the state and does not contravene the constitution The right of a patentee to use and vend an oil for illuminating purposes must be exercised in subordination to such police regulations as the states may establish Patterson v Kentucky, 97 U S. 501.

26. Protection of lives, health, etc — The police power of the state extends to the protection of the lives, health and property of the citizen and to the preservation of good order and public morals. The legislature cannot by contract divest itself of the power to provide for these objects. They are to be attained and provided for by such appropriate means as the legislative discretion may devise. Neither this discretion nor the power can be bargained away Beer Company v Massachusetts 97 U. S 25

27. Preservation of health and morals — The power of a state to make municipal regulations for the restraint and punishment of crime, for the preservation of the health and morals of her citizens, and of the public peace, has never been surrendered by the states or restrained by the constitution of the United States Moore v People, 14 How 13

28 Government license — Effect of — The license granted by the United States to sell liquor is but a mode of levying and enforcing the collection of a tax, and does not confer on the licensee the right to carry on the licensed business in a state where prohibited by state law License Tax Cases 5 Wall 462, Pervear v Massachusetts, 5 Wall 475, License Cases, 5 How 504 Mugler v Kansas, 123 U S 658

29 Over the internal commerce of the state congress has no control. That is reserved to the states exclusively, and a congressional license to engage in such trade is but an internal tax, and while congress may tax such business it cannot authorize a trade or business within a state in order to tax it. License Tax Cases (Mass), 5 Wall. 463, Same from Iowa, seven cases, 5 Wall 480

30 Control of sale of intoxicating liquors — A law of a state taxing or prohibiting a business already taxed by congress is not unconstitutional The sale of home-made liquors or imported liquors in second hands, as also the mode of prohibiting the sale thereof, is subject exclusively to state control, and the laws of Massachusetts on this subject are not unconstitutional Pervear v Massachusetts, 5 Wall 475

31. Miscellaneous — Limitations and prescription — There is no clause in the constitution which restrains the right in each state to legislate on limitation and rights by prescription in suits on judgments of other states exclusive of interference with their merits Bacon v. Howard, 20 How. 22

32. **Administration.**—The several states of the Union have full control over the subject of administration and over estates of decedents within their respective states. Yonley v. Lavender, 21 Wall 276

33. **Power over corporations** —A state has power to enact laws subjecting the land of a corporation whose charter has expired to the debts of her citizens McGoon v. Scales, 9 Wall 23

34. **Invasion on Indian lands** —The New York statute respecting intrusions on Indian lands, authorizing the removal of persons (other than Indians) by summary process who have settled on lands belonging to or occupied by the Indians, is not in violation of the constitution or of any treaty or act of congress New York v. Dibble, 21 How 366.

35 **Aliens—Limitations as to holding property** —A state of the Union may refuse to allow an alien to take either real or personal property situated in the state by descent or devise, and may direct that such property escheat to the state, or it may annex conditions to such devise or distribution of estates It may tax an alien on such estate as a condition on which he may inherit or take it by devise. Mager v. Grima, 8 How 490

36 **Ferries—Power to establish and regulate, reserved to the state** —The power to establish and regulate ferries is reserved to the states respectively Conway v. Taylor, 1 Black, 603

37 **Same** —The power to license, regulate and tax ferries is one of the powers reserved to the states by this article and this is true when applied to a ferry plying between landings in different states. Wiggins Ferry Co v East St Louis, 107 U S 365, Fanning v Gregoire, 16 How 534

38 **Powers of legislation** —The state legislatures retain all the powers of legislation delegated to them by the state constitution which are not expressly taken away by the constitution of the United States Calder v Bull, 3 Dall 386

39. **Exclude foreign corporations** —A state has the right to exclude foreign insurance corporations from doing business within its territory, or it may admit such companies to transact business within the state on such conditions as it sees fit to impose Doyle v Continental Ins Co 94 U S 535.

40 Such company has no constitutional right to transact business in a state other than that under whose laws it is chartered, and hence its exclusion therefrom, for whatever cause, violates no constitutional right Id.

41. **Construction of state statutes.**—The ruling of a state court that a state law is in conformity to the state constitution is binding on the federal courts. Gut v. State, 9 Wall. 35

42. **Charges by railroads** —It is the settled law that a state has the power to limit the amount of charges by railroad companies for the transportation of persons and property within its own jurisdiction, unless restrained by some contract in the charter, or unless what is done amounts to a regulation of foreign or interstate commerce This power of regulation is a power of government continuing in its nature, and if it can be bargained away at all it can only be done by words of positive grant or their equivalent. Railroad Commission Cases, 116 U S 307

43. **Bankrupt laws** —State legislatures have authority to pass bankrupt or insolvent laws. Baldwin v. Hale, 1 Wall. 223

44. But a discharge of a debtor under a state bankrupt law is not valid against a creditor or citizen of another state who has not subjected himself to the state laws other than by the original contract out of which the indebtedness accrued Id

45 **Use of military force.**—Although a state cannot establish a military government, it may use its military force to quell domestic insurrection when too strong to be overcome by the ordinary processes of law, and the state has the right to determine when the necessity exists Luther v Borden, 7 How. 1

46 **Corporations—Power of state over.**—One state may make a corporation of another state, as there organized and conducted, a corporation of its own *quoad hoc* any property within its territorial jurisdiction That this may be done was distinctly held in O & M R R. Co v Wheeler 1 Black, 297, B & O. R. R Co v Harris, 12 Wall 65, 82

47. The question is always one of legislative intent, and not of legislative power or legal possibility B. & O. R R. Co. v. Harris, 12 Wall 65.

48 **Implied powers not excluded** —There is no phrase in the constitution which excludes incidental or implied powers—as was the case in the articles of confederation The tenth amendment does not exclude such powers McCulloch v Maryland, 4 Wheat. 316

49. **Corporations—Government may create.**—The government of the United States has power to create a corporation. Id

50. **Sovereign power of states unaltered.**—The constitution was not necessarily carved out of existing state sovereignties, nor a surrender of powers already existing in state institutions. The powers of the states depend upon their own constitutions. and the people of the state had the right to modify and restrain them according to their own views of policy or principle. The sovereign powers vested in the states by their respective constitutions remained unaltered and unimpaired by the adoption of the constitution of the United States, except so far as they were granted to the government of the United States Whatever of doubt as to this doctrine might have existed under the constitution as originally adopted has been removed by this amendment. Martin v Hunter's Lessee 1 Wheat 304-325.

51. **Powers retained not necessary to be defined.**—When the American people created a national legislature, with certain enumerated powers, it was neither necessary nor proper to define the powers retained by the states These powers proceed, not from the people of America, but from the people of the several states, and remain, after the adoption of the constitution, what they were before, except so far as they may be abridged by that instrument Sturges v. Crowninshield, 4 Wheat. 122, 193

ARTICLE XI.

The judicial power of the United States shall not be construed to extend to any suit in law or equity, commenced or prosecuted against one of the United States by citizens of another State, or by citizens or subjects of any foreign State

1. **Under the constitution prior to the eleventh amendment a state could be sued in assumpsit by a citizen of another state.**

Service on the governor and attorney-general was sufficient, and unless the state appeared after summons judgment by default could be rendered Chisholm v Georgia, 2 Dall. 419

2 **The amendment is retroactive** —The eleventh amendment to the constitution of the United States having been adopted, there cannot be exercised any jurisdiction in any case, past or future, in which a state was sued by a citizen or citizens of another state, or by citizens or subjects of any foreign state Hollingsworth v. Virginia, 3 Dall 378, Cohens v Virginia, 6 Wheat 294, Georgia v. Brailsford, 2 Dall 401, 415

3 **Controversies between states not inhibited** —The prohibition of this amendment does not extend to controversies between two or more states or between a state and a foreign state The jurisdiction of the United States courts still extends to such cases, and in these a state may still be sued Cohens v. Virginia, 6 Wheat. 405 et seq

NOTE —The causes which led to the adoption of the amendment are fully discussed by Mr. Chief Justice Marshall in delivering the opinion of the court in the above case

4. **Bonds of state; suit upon will not lie in United States court** Those who deal in bonds and obligations of a state must rely on the sense of justice of the state The state courts cannot enforce the contract, and the federal courts are expressly prohibited from exercising such jurisdiction Bank of Washington v Arkansas, 20 How 530

5. **Officers of state—In what cases suits may be maintained against them as such.**—A circuit court of the United States, in a proper case in equity, may enjoin a state officer from executing a state law in conflict with the constitution or a statute of the United States, when such execution will violate the rights of the complainant. Where the state is concerned the state should be made a party, if it can be done That it cannot be done is a sufficient reason for the omission to do so, and the court may proceed to a decree against the officer of the state in all respects as if the state were a party to the record. In deciding who are parties to the suit the court will not look beyond the record Making a state officer a party does not make the state a party, although her law may have prompted his action and the state may stand behind him as the real party in interest A state can be made a party only by shaping the bill expressly with that view as where individuals or corporations are intended to be put in that relation to the case Dodge v Woolsey, 18 How 331, Bank v Knoop, 16 How 369, Bank v Skelly, 1 Black, 436, Ohio L & T Co v Debolt, 16 How 432, and Bank v Debolt, 18 How 380, proceeded upon the same principles and were controlled by that authority with respect to the jurisdictional questions arising in each of those cases as to the defendant. Davis v Gray, 16 Wall 203.

6 **Same** —Neither a state nor the United States can be sued as defendant in any court in this country without its consent, except in the limited class of cases in which a state may be made a party in the supreme court of the United States by virtue of the original jurisdiction conferred on that court by the constitution Whenever it can be clearly seen that the state is an indispensable party to enable the court, according to the rules which govern its procedure, to grant the relief sought, it will refuse to take juris-

diction The cases wherein the officers of the state may or may not be made parties defendant fully analyzed, compared and distinguished by Mr Justice Miller in Cunningham v Macon, etc R. R., 109 U S 446 United States v. Lee, 106 U. S. 196, belongs to this class of cases

7 **Same.**—The vital principle in all the cases wherein the United States supreme court has held that an injunction will lie to restrain the collection of taxes, sought to be collected by seizure of property, imposed in the name of the state, but contrary to the constitution of the United States,—the defendants being officers of the state,—is that such officers, though professing to act in their official capacity, are threatening a violation of the personal or property rights of the complainant, for which they are personally and individually liable. In re Ayers, 123 U S at 500; McGahey v Virginia, 135 U S 662

8. **Same** —Suits may be maintained against state officers as individual defendants who, under color of authority of unconstitutional legislation by the state, are guilty of personal trespasses and wrongs Also against officers in their official capacity, to arrest or direct their official action by injunction or *mandamus* where such suits are authorized by law, and the act to be done or omitted is purely ministerial, in the performance or omission of which the plaintiff has a legal interest. In re Ayers, 123 U S at 506

9 **Same.**—Where an individual is sued in tort for some act injurious to another in regard to person or property, to which his defense is that he has acted under the orders of the government, he is so sued, not as or because he is the officer of the government, but as an individual, and the court is not ousted of its jurisdiction because he *asserts* authority as such officer Mitchell v Harmony, 13 How 115, Bates v Clark, 95 U S. 204, Meigs v McClung, 9 Cranch, 11, Wilcox v Jackson, 13 Pet. 498, Brown v Huger 21 How 305 Grisar v. McDowell, 6 Wall 363, cited and approved by Mr. Justice Miller in Cunningham v Macon & C. R R. Co, 109 U S 446

10 **Same** —Where, under the provisions of a law of Virginia, the coupons on the state bonds were allowed to be detached and pass from hand to hand by delivery, and were expressly made receivable for taxes by the tax collector, and where the tax collector refused to receive such coupons for taxes when duly tendered, and, acting under a statute held to be unconstitutional and void, proceeded to levy upon the property of such tax-payer to enforce payment of the taxes for which such coupon was tendered the tax-payer is entitled to maintain a suit against him personally, as a wrong-doer, and such suit will not be against the state within the meaning of this amendment. Poindexter v Greenhow, 114 U S. 270

11 **Same.**—The circuit courts of the United States have jurisdiction of a bill brought by the Bank of the United States for the purpose of protecting the bank in the exercise of its franchises, which are threatened to be invaded under the unconstitutional laws of a state, and as the state itself cannot be made a party because of the provisions of the eleventh amendment to the constitution, it may be maintained against the officers and agents of the state who are intrusted with the execution of such laws Osborn v Bank of United States, 9 Wheat 738

12. **Same — Where suit may not be maintained against the officer.**—Where the defendants who are sued as officers of the state, have not

a real, but merely a nominal, interest in the controversy, the state appearing to be the real defendant, and therefore an indispensable party, if the jurisdiction does not fail for want of power over the parties, it does fail as to the nominal defendants, for want of suitable subject-matter Mr Justice Matthews in In re Ayers, 123 U S at p. 488

13 **Mandamus against state officers, when maintainable**—"A state without its consent cannot be sued by an individual, and a court cannot substitute its own discretion for that of executive officers in matters belonging to the proper jurisdiction of the latter But it has been well settled that when a plain official duty, requiring no exercise of discretion, is to be performed and performance is refused, any person who will sustain personal injury by such refusal may have a *mandamus* to compel its performance, and when such duty is threatened to be violated by some positive official act any person who will sustain personal injury thereby, for which adequate compensation cannot be had at law, may have an injunction to prevent it In such cases the writs of *mandamus* and injunction are somewhat correlative to each other In either case if the officer plead the authority of an unconstitutional law for the non-performance or violation of his duty, it will not prevent the issuing of the writ. An unconstitutional law will be treated by the courts as null and void" Board of Liquidation v McComb, 92 U. S 531 cited and approved in Allen v Balt & Ohio R R Co, 114 U S 311 See, also Marbury v Madison, 1 Cranch, 137, Kendall v Stokes 3 How 87, United States v Schurz, 102 U S 378, United States v Boutwell, 17 Wall 604 This doctrine is fully considered, criticised and distinguished by Mr. Justice Miller in Cunningham v Macon etc R. R. Co 109 U S 446

14. **When not maintainable against state officer**—Where a state cannot be sued and does not voluntarily submit itself to the jurisdiction of the courts, the courts will not be permitted to set up jurisdiction over the officers in charge of the public money so as to control them as against the political power in their administration of state affairs. Therefore where under an admitted debt the state, as provided in the contract creating the debt, had levied a tax and collected into the treasury money to pay the interest thereon, and then by an amended constitution the state had changed the contract and reduced the interest, and prohibited the auditor and treasurer from paying out the money upon the original contract, it was held that while such later provision impaired the obligation of the contract yet the courts had no power to control the officers of the state, and to compel them to pay the money out of the state treasury in liquidation of interest coupons on the original debt, that the money in the treasury was the property of the state, in the manual possession of the state officers that the bondholders never owned it, that the most they could claim was that the state ought to use it to pay their coupons, but until so paid it was in no sense theirs and as the state could not be sued therefor, and the officers of the state have no contract relations with the state, they (the officers) could only act as the state directed and were not subject to be sued by the bondholders This case and United States v Lee, 106 U S. 196, compared and distinguished Louisiana v Jumel, 107 U S 711

15 **Same.**—When a suit is brought in a court of the United States against officers of a state to enforce performance of a contract made by the state, and the controversy is as to the validity of the obligation of the contract, and the only remedy sought is the performance of the contract by the state, and the nominal defendants have no personal interest in the subject-matter of the suit, but defend only as representing the state, the state is the real party against whom the relief is sought, and the suit is substantially within the prohibition of this amendment. Hagood v Southern, 117 U S 53

16 The jurisdictional difference between cases in which the relief sought is the performance of a plain official duty requiring no exercise of discretion or where state officers, under color of a state authority which is unconstitutional, have invaded and violated personal and property rights, and cases like the one above, in which the relief sought is affirmative official action by state officers in performing an obligation which attaches to the state in its political capacity, pointed out Id.

17 **How to determine whether the state is a party**—Whether the state is the actual party defendant in a suit within the meaning of this section is not in all cases to be determined by a reference to the nominal parties to the record The whole record and the nature of the case as therein presented should be considered and the amendment will be held to cover not only suits brought against a state by name, but those against its officers agents, etc where it is apparent that the state is the real party against which the relief is demanded and upon which the judgment will operate Osborn v Bank, 9 Wheat 738, explained and limited In re Ayers, 123 U S 443

18 **Same.**—A suit against the auditor of state to compel the raising a tax to pay interest on state bonds is virtually a suit against the state State of North Carolina v Temple, 134 U S 22, State of Louisiana ex rel v Steele, id. 230

19 **State may waive the exemption.**—A state may waive the right to exemption under this section, and by appearing in a court of the United States in a suit in which it has an interest it does waive it. Clark v Barnard, 108 U S 436

20 **State may consent to suit.**—A state cannot without its consent be sued in a circuit court of the United States by one of its own citizens upon the ground that the case is one that arises under the constitution and laws of the United States, nor can a state be sued by the citizens of another state or foreign state without its consent. Hans v State of Louisiana, 134 U S 1

21. **Consent of state may be upon terms such as it sees fit to impose**—A state cannot be sued in its own courts or in any other without its consent When the consent is given it may be on such conditions as the state may see fit to impose This consent may be withdrawn and no contract will be thereby violated It merely regulates the proceedings in its own courts Beers v. Arkansas, 20 How 527

22 **When consent is given jurisdiction is complete for all purposes.**—"When a state submits itself without reservation to the jurisdiction

of a court in a particular case, the jurisdiction may be used to give full effect to what the state has, by its act of submission, allowed to be done, and if the law permits coercion of the public officers to enforce any judgment that may be rendered, then such coercion may be employed for that purpose. But this is very far from authorizing the courts, when a state cannot be sued, to set up their jurisdiction over the officers in charge of the public money so as to control them as against the political power in their administration of the finances of the state" Waite, C J, in Louisiana v Jumel, and Elliott v. Wiltz, 107 U S 711

23 **Consent given may be withdrawn.**— While in contracts between individuals the remedies for their enforcement or breach, in existence at the time the contract is entered into, become a part of the agreement and constitute a substantial part of their obligation, it is not so with contracts between individuals and states In respect to these, there being no remedy by suit against the state, the contract is substantially without sanction, except that which arises out of the honor and good faith of the state itself Although the state may, at the inception of the contract, have consented as one of its conditions to subject itself to suit it may subsequently withdraw that consent and resume its original immunity without any violation of the obligation of its contract in the constitutional sense In re Ayers, 123 U S at p 505, citing Beers v Arkansas, 20 How 527, Railroad Company v Tennessee, 101 U S 337

24 **Creditors cannot use the name of the state whereof they are citizens to maintain suit against another state** — Owners of the obligations of a state who by reason of this amendment are precluded from maintaining a suit against such state cannot sue it in the name of the state whereof they are citizens by getting consent of the latter to use its name as plaintiff in such suit A state of the Union is not an independent nation, clothed with the right to make demands upon a sister state which the latter may owe to a citizen of the former New Hampshire v Louisiana, 108 U. S. 76, New York v Louisiana, 108 U S 76

25 A contract with a citizen of Texas to furnish money in aid of equipping armies to carry on war with Mexico, before the United States had acknowledged Texas as a nation, could not be enforced in the United States courts after Texas became a state of the Union Kennett v Chambers, 14 How 38

26 **Counties not within the inhibition.**— The restriction contained in this article is limited to suits in which the state is the real party, or a party on the record Counties are corporations created by the state with such powers as are conferred upon them, and are not within the constitutional restriction, and may be sued in the United States circuit courts County of Lincoln v Luning, 133 U S 529

27. **Exception — Cases of original jurisdiction in the United States supreme court.**— Neither a state nor the United States can be sued as defendant in any court in this country without its consent, except in the limited class of cases in which a state may be made a party in the supreme court of the United States by virtue of the original jurisdiction conferred on that court by the constitution And whenever it can be clearly seen that the state is an indispensable party to enable the court, according

to the rules which govern its procedure, to grant the relief sought, it will refuse to take jurisdiction Cunningham v Macon etc R. R, 109 U S 446.

28 **Object and purpose of amendment.**— "The very object and purpose of the eleventh amendment were to prevent the indignity of subjecting a state to the coercive process of judicial tribunals at the instance of private parties. It was thought to be neither becoming nor convenient that the several states of the Union invested with that large residuum of sovereignty which had not been delegated to the United States, should be summoned as defendants to answer the complaints of private persons, whether citizens of other states or aliens, or that the course of their public policy and the administration of their public affairs should be subject to and controlled by the mandates of judicial tribunals without their consent, and in favor of individual interests" Mr Justice Matthews in In re Ayers, 123 U S. at 505

29 Juan Madrazo, a subject of the king of Spain, filed a libel praying admiralty process against the state of Georgia, alleging that the state was in possession of a certain sum of money, the proceeds of the sale of certain slaves which had been seized as illegally brought into the state of Georgia, and which seizure had been subsequently, under admiralty proceedings, adjudged to have been illegal, and the right of Madrazo to the slaves and the money arising from the sale thereof established by the decision of the United States circuit court for the district of Georgia. The libel was presented to the supreme court with a prayer to award admiralty process against the state of Georgia, to be issued and served as the court might direct, citing said state, as well as others concerned to show cause why the proceeds of said slaves, paid into the treasury of the state, should not be paid out to the libelant, the slaves remaining in the possession of the state were restored to him, a just and reasonable compensation decreed to him for the slaves converted to her own use, or otherwise taken by the state, and for other damages, etc. It was claimed by counsel for libelant that, notwithstanding the eleventh amendment, the supreme court had jurisdiction of the case, that the amendment did not take away the jurisdiction of the courts of the United States in suits in admiralty against a state Mr Chief Justice Marshall delivered the opinion of the court briefly as follows "The case is not a case where property is in the custody of a court of admiralty or brought within its jurisdiction It is a mere personal suit against a state to recover proceeds in its possession, and in such case no private person has a right to commence an original suit in this court against a state" Governor of Georgia v Madrazo 1 Pet 123

30 **The interest of the state must be direct** —Although the claims of a state may be ultimately affected by the decision of a cause yet if the state be not necessarily a defendant, the courts of the United States are bound to exercise the jurisdiction United States v Peters 5 Cranch, 115; Louisville etc R. R Co v. Letson, 2 How 550

31 Where the state was a member of a banking corporation existing under its laws which corporation under the laws creating it had the right to sue and be sued *held*, that in a suit against such bank the fact that the state was a member of the corporation did not oust the jurisdiction of the court Bank of United States v. Planters Bank of Georgia, 9 Wheat. 907

32 By becoming a member of the corporation the state, in so far as this inhibition is concerned and in respect to the concerns of the corporation, abdicates its sovereignty in respect to this amendment. Briscoe v. Bank of Kentucky, 11 Pet 324, Darrington v Bank of Alabama, 13 How. 12, Curran v Arkansas, 15 How 304.

33. The fact that land which is the subject of legal controversy was granted by a state, and is claimed under such grant, does not make the state a party to the suit, nor does the issue whether such lands be within the limits of a state. Fowler v. Lindsey, 3 Dall 411.

ARTICLE XII

1. The electors shall meet in their respective States, and vote by ballot for President and Vice-President, one of whom, at least, shall not be an inhabitant of the same State with themselves, they shall name in their ballots the person voted for as President, and in distinct ballots the person voted for as Vice-President, and they shall make distinct lists of all persons voted for as President, and of all persons voted for as Vice-President, and of the number of votes for each, which lists they shall sign and certify, and transmit sealed to the seat of government of the United States, directed to the President of the Senate, the President of the Senate shall, in the presence of the Senate and House of Representatives, open all the certificates, and the votes shall then be counted, the person having the greatest number of votes for President shall be the President, if such number be a majority of the whole number of electors appointed, and if no person have such majority, then from the persons having the highest numbers, not exceeding three, on the list of those voted for as President, the House of Representatives shall choose immediately by ballot the President But in choosing the President the votes shall be taken by States, the representation from each State having one vote, a quorum for this purpose shall consist of a member or members from two-thirds of the States, and a majority of all the States shall be necessary to a choice And if the House of Representatives shall not choose a President, whenever the right of choice shall devolve upon them, before the fourth day of March next following, then the Vice-President shall act as President, as in the case of death or other constitutional disability of the President.

2. The person having the greatest number of votes as Vice-

President shall be the Vice-President, if such number be a majority of the whole number of electors appointed, and if no person have a majority, then from the two highest numbers on the list the Senate shall choose the Vice-President; a quorum for the purpose shall consist of two-thirds of the whole number of senators, and a majority of the whole number shall be necessary to a choice.

3 But no person constitutionally ineligible to the office of President shall be eligible to that of Vice-President of the United States

1 The sole function of the presidential electors is to cast, certify and transmit the vote of the state for president and vice-president. They are no more officers or agents of the United States than are the members of the state legislatures when acting as electors of federal senators, or the people of the states when acting as electors of representatives in congress In re Green, 134 U. S. 377.

2. Fraudulent voting for electors of president and vice-president is punishable by the state under the laws thereof wherein such fraudulent voting was done Id.

ARTICLE XIII

1. Neither slavery nor involuntary servitude, except as a punishment for crime whereof the party shall have been duly convicted, shall exist within the United States, or any place subject to their jurisdiction.

2 Congress shall have power to enforce this article by appropriate legislation.

1. **Scope and object of the amendment** — This amendment simply and only abolishes slavery or involuntary servitude, except as a punishment for crime But it has a reflex character also establishing and decreeing universal civil and political freedom throughout the United States, and it invests congress with the requisite power to pass laws necessary and proper, abolishing all badges and incidents of slavery But the provisions of the first and second sections of the act of March 1, 1875, commonly known as the civil rights act, is not such law as is included in this power Civil Rights Cases, 109 U S 3

2 **The main purpose of the amendment was to free the African slaves, but the letter and spirit apply to all cases coming within their purview** — The power of granting exclusive rights, when necessary and proper to effectuate a purpose having in view the public good, is not in contravention of the provisions of the thirteenth and fourteenth amendments to the federal constitution The main purpose of the thirteenth, fourteenth and fifteenth amendments was to effectuate the freedom of the African race — to perpetuate that freedom and protect the freedmen from the oppres-

sion of the white men who had formerly held them in slavery. While, in construing these amendments, it is necessary to keep these main objects in view, nevertheless the letter and spirit of the amendments apply to all cases coming within their purview whether the party concerned be of African descent or not. The thirteenth article equally with the abolishment of slavery, forbids Mexican peonage or the Chinese cooly trade, when they amount to slavery or involuntary servitude. Slaughter-House Cases, 16 Wall. 36.

3. All forms of involuntary slavery included.—The word servitude, as used in this section, covers and is intended to prohibit all forms of involuntary slavery, of whatever class or name. It is a word of broader meaning than the word slavery. Id., Matter of Turner, 1 Abb. (U. S.) 84.

4. An indenture of apprenticeship made in violation of law, and sought to be enforced by compulsory submission, creates "involuntary servitude" within the meaning of this amendment. Matter of Turner, 1 Abb. (U. S.) 84.

5. Under the amendment congress has power to protect all persons within its jurisdiction from all forms of slavery.—"It is clear that this amendment, besides abolishing forever slavery and involuntary servitude within the United States, gives power to the congress to protect all persons within the jurisdiction of the United States from being in any way subjected to slavery or involuntary servitude, except as a punishment for crime, and in the enjoyment of that freedom which it was the object of the amendment to secure." Mr. Justice Wood in delivering opinion in United States v. Harris, 106 U. S. 629, citing United States v. Rhodes, 1 Abb. (U. S.) 28, United States v. Cruikshank, 1 Woods 308.

6. A law under which two or more free white citizens could be punished for conspiring or going in disguise for the purpose of depriving another free white citizen of a right accorded by the law of the state to all classes of persons as for instance, the right to make a contract, bring a suit or give evidence, clearly cannot be authorized by the thirteenth amendment, which simply prohibits slavery and involuntary servitude. Section 5519 of the Revised Statutes has such scope. Its provisions are broader than the amendment, and are, therefore, not warranted by it. United States v. Harris, 106 U. S. 629.

7. Consideration for sale of slaves prior to passage of amendment can be enforced.—Where a slave was sold in 1861 before the rebellion, and was warranted to be a slave for life and suit was brought on the note given for the purchase-money after the adoption of this amendment, *held*, that negro slavery having been recognized as lawful at the time and the place where the contract was made, the right to sue upon it was not taken away by the adoption of this amendment, destruction of vested rights by implication never being presumed. Osborn v. Nicholson, 13 Wall. 654. Boyce v. Tabb, 18 Wall. 546.

8. Same.—Contracts made to pay money for slaves which were valid when made, are not affected by this amendment. Boyce v. Tabb, 18 Wall. 546.

ARTICLE XIV

1. All persons born or naturalized in the United States, and subject to the jurisdiction thereof, are citizens of the United States and of the State wherein they reside No State shall make or enforce any law which shall abridge the privileges or immunities of citizens of the United States, nor shall any State deprive any person of life, liberty, or property, without due process of law, nor deny to any person within its jurisdiction the equal protection of the laws

1. **Object of amendment** — This amendment is a guaranty of protection against the act of the state government itself It is a guaranty against the exertion of arbitrary and tyrannical power on the part of the government and legislature of the state not a guaranty against the commission of individual offenses, and the power of congress, whether express or implied to legislate for the enforcement of such guaranty does not extend to the passage of laws for the suppression of crime within the state It does not extend to or warrant such legislation by congress as is contained in section 5519 of the Revised Statutes United States v Harris, 106 U S 629, citing and affirming United States v Cruikshank, 92 U S 542 Virginia v Rives, 100 U S 313 followed and affirmed in Baldwin v. Franks, 120 U. S. 678

2. **Gives citizenship, and denies to state the power to withhold the privileges thereof.**— This amendment is one of a series, having a common purpose viz, to secure to a recently emancipated race which had been held in slavery for many generations all the civil rights enjoyed by the superior race and to place such enjoyment under the protection of the general government It not only gives citizenship and its privileges to persons of color, but denies to any state the power to withhold from them the equal protection of the law, and invests congress with power to enforce its provisions by appropriate legislation. Strauder v. West Virginia, 100 U. S 303

3. **The first clause of this section was primarily intended to confer citizenship on the negro race, and secondly to give definitions of citizenship of the United States and of the states** —It recognizes the distinction between citizenship of a state and citizenship of the United States The second clause protects the privileges and immunities of citizens of the United States from hostile legislation of the states as distinguished from the privileges and immunities of citizens of the states. The privileges and immunities of citizens of the United States are those which arise out of the nature and essential character of the national government, the provisions of the constitution and treaties made in pursuance thereof; and it is these which are placed under the protection of congress by this clause of the fourteenth amendment. Slaughter-House Cases, 16 Wall 36

4. **Non-interference with police power** — This amendment was not designed to interfere with the police powers of the states These may still be exercised for the protection of health, the prevention of fraud and the

preservation of the public morals. The laws of Pennsylvania prohibiting the manufacture, sale or keeping for sale within said state of any compound or oleaginous substance to be used as butter or cheese, except that produced from unadulterated milk or cream from unadulterated milk, that is to say, the prohibition of the manufacture, sale or keeping for sale of the compound known to commerce as oleomargarine, are not unconstitutional. Powell v Pennsylvania, 127 U. S. 678

5 **Prohibition on state.**— It is state action of a particular character that is prohibited by this section Individual invasion of individual rights is not the subject-matter of the amendment It does not invest congress with power to legislate upon subjects which are in the domain of state legislation, but to provide modes of relief against state legislation or state actions which would have the effect to injure persons in life, liberty or property, or which denies to any of them the equal protection of the laws There is no warrant in the amendment for the enactment of the first and second sections of the act known as the civil rights act of March 1, 1875. Civil Rights Cases, 109 U S. 3.

6 **Citizens, who are — "All persons born or naturalized in the United States and subject to the jurisdiction thereof are citizens of the United States, and of the state wherein they reside "** — The above phrase, "subject to the jurisdiction thereof," was intended to exclude from the operation of the amendment children of foreign ministers and consuls and citizens or subjects of foreign states born within the United States. This phrase overturns the Dred Scott decision, by making all persons born within the United States and *subject to its jurisdiction* citizens of the United States Slaughter-House Cases, 16 Wall. 36

7. **Corporations.**— An incorporated company is not a citizen of the United States within the meaning of this section. Insurance Co. v. New Orleans, 1 Woods, 85

8. **Must reside in the state** — Under the first clause of this amendment a person must reside within a state to make him a citizen of it, but it is only necessary that he should be born or naturalized in the United States to be a citizen of the Union So it is quite clear that there is a citizenship of the United States and a citizenship of a state which are distinct from each other, and which depend upon different characteristics or circumstances in the individual Slaughter-House Cases 16 Wall 36

9. **Citizen — Definition of word** — In its broad sense the word is synonymous with the words "subject" and 'inhabitant,' and is understood as conveying the idea of membership of a nation, and nothing more. Minor v Happersett, 21 Wall 162

10 **Suffrage not necessary.**— The right of suffrage is not one of the necessary privileges of a citizen of the United States Id

11. The fourteenth amendment did not add to the privileges and immunities of a citizen It simply furnished an additional guaranty for the protection of such as he already had. No new voters were necessarily made by it, except as it may have increased the number of citizens entitled to suffrage under the constitution and laws of the states; but it operates for this purpose, if at all, through the states and state laws, and not directly on the citizen. Id.

12. Indians with tribal relations not citizens.—An Indian born within the United States, and belonging to a tribe recognized as such by the government, cannot become a citizen of the United States by severing his tribal relations and residing in a state and submitting himself to the jurisdiction and laws of such state, when it is not shown that he has been naturalized or taxed, or in any way been recognized as a citizen by the state or by the United States, or by some treaty with his tribe. Elk v Wilkins, 112 U S. 94.

13. Two sources of citizenship — This section contemplates two sources of citizenship and two sources only. 1 Birth. 2 Naturalization. The words "subject to the jurisdiction thereof" mean completely subject to the political jurisdiction and owing it direct and immediate allegiance. They further relate to the time of birth in the one case, and to the date of naturalization in the other. Id

14 When word used in its political sense — In describing offenses against citizens of the United States for which punishment is provided in section 5508 the word citizen is used in its political sense as it is in the fourteenth amendment, and is not synonymous with "resident," "inhabitant," or "person. Baldwin v Frank, 120 U S 678

15 Privileges and immunities of citizens — What are such privileges — The supreme court upon one occasion deemed it wise not to attempt to define or declare what were the essential privileges which belong to a citizen of the United States as such Conner v. Elliott, 18 How. 591

16 So far as they relate to this amendment, it may be safely said that it is one of the privileges of every American citizen to adopt and follow such lawful industrial pursuits — not injurious to the community — as he may see fit, without unreasonable regulation or molestation, and without being restricted by those unjust, oppressive and odious monopolies or exclusive privileges which have been condemned by all free governments; it is also his privilege to be protected in the possession and enjoyment of his property so long as such possession and enjoyment are not injurious to the community, and not to be deprived thereof without due process of law It is also his privilege to have, with all other citizens, the equal protection of the laws. Live Stock Association v. Crescent City. etc Co., 1 Abb (U S) 398

17. Citizens of a state, as distinguished from citizens of United States, not protected by amendment.—The act of congress of March 1, 1875, entitled "An act to protect citizens in their civil and legal rights," so far as it seeks to inflict penalties for the violation of the rights which belong to citizens of a state, as distinguished from citizens of the United States, is unconstitutional The right to use a public conveyance for local travel is in general a right which belongs to a person as the citizen of a state, and not as a citizen of the United States, and the denial of that privilege (except where it is charged in the pleadings and proved in evidence to have been on account of race, color, etc.) does not subject one to the penalties of said act. Cully v Baltimore & Ohio R. R Co, 1 Hughes, 536.

18. Refers to citizens of United States only.—These rights are those of citizens of the United States only, that is, the rights existing or belonging to that capacity The amendment does not refer to the rights of citizens of the states These are guarded by a different provision. The two are separate and distinct. Slaughter-House Cases, 16 Wall 36, United States v Anthony, 11 Blatchf 203, 204.

19 **Privilege of voting not protected by this clause** — The privilege of voting is a privilege arising under the constitution of the state, and not of the United States, and is not protected by this clause United States v Anthony, 11 Blatchf 204, Minor v Happersett, 21 Wall 162

20 **The right to drill and parade with arms not an immunity of citizenship.**— This clause has reference only to the privileges and immunities of citizens of the United States. A state may pass laws to regulate the privileges and immunities of its own citizens, provided in so doing it does not abridge their privileges and immunities as citizens of the United States. The right voluntarily to associate together as a military company or organization to drill or parade with arms, without and independent of an act of congress or law of the state authorizing the same, is not an attribute of national citizenship and cannot properly be said to be a privilege or immunity of such citizenship Presser v Illinois, 116 U S 252

21. **Citizens of state and United States — Privileges and immunities of, distinguished** — This amendment has not radically changed the whole theory of the relations of the state and federal governments to each other, and both governments to the people The same persons may at the same time be citizens of the state and of the United States Protection to life, liberty and property rests primarily with the states, and the amendment furnishes an additional guaranty against any encroachments by the states upon those fundamental rights which belong to citizenship and which the state governments were created to secure The privileges and immunities of citizens of the United States, as distinguished from the privileges and immunities of the citizens of the states, are protected by this amendment, but those are privileges and immunities arising out of the nature and essential character of the national government, and granted or secured by the constitution of the United States It forbids any arbitrary deprivation of life, liberty or property, and secures equal protection to all under like circumstances The legislature of New York having decided that the statute providing for the infliction of the death penalty is not cruel and unusual punishment, and the courts of the state having sustained that determination, *held*, that the statute does not deprive the condemned of the equal protection of the laws or of life without due process of law In re Kemmler, 136 U S 436.

22. **Privileges and immunities of citizens — Laws prohibiting sale of intoxicating liquors.**— The usual and ordinary laws of a state prohibiting the sale of intoxicating liquors raises no question under the constitution of the United States prior to the fourteenth amendment. The right to sell intoxicating liquors is not one of the privileges and immunities of the citizens of the United States which by that amendment the states were forbidden to abridge. But if a case were presented in which a person owning liquor or other property at the time a law was passed by the state absolutely prohibiting any sale of it, it would be a very grave question whether such a law would not be inconsistent with the provisions of that amendment. Bartemeyer v Iowa, 18 Wall. 129

23 **Prohibition of sale of liquors no infringement of privilege or immunity of citizen.**— The prohibitory law of Kansas, which pro-

hibits the manufacture within the state of intoxicating liquors to be there sold or bartered for use as a beverage, does not infringe any right, privilege or immunity of the citizen secured by the constitution of the United States. The fact that it prohibits such manufacture in buildings which were erected, equipped with machinery and used for that purpose prior to the enactment of the prohibitory law, and at a time when under the laws of the state it was legal so to do, does not alter the case, nor does such prohibition deprive the owner of such buildings and machinery of his property without due process of law. Mugler v Kansas, 123 U S 623.

24 That part of the statute of Iowa concerning the sale of liquors which declares that no person shall own or keep, or be in any way concerned, engaged or employed in owning or keeping, any intoxicating liquors, with intent to sell the same within the state, and all the prohibitory clauses of the statute, are within the constitutional powers of the state legislature Eilenbecker v District Court of Plymouth County, 134 U S 31

25. A state has the right to prohibit or restrict the manufacture of intoxicating liquors within her limits, to prohibit all sale and traffic in them therein, to inflict penalties and provide for abatement of the places where sold as a nuisance Such legislation is a clear exercise of the police power, and does not violate this clause of the constitution Kidd v. Pearson, 128 U S 1-16

26 A law of a state prohibiting the manufacture and sale of intoxicating liquors is constitutional Affirming Bartemeyer v. Iowa, 18 Wall. 129. Beer Co v Massachusetts, 97 U S 25

27. The right to practice law in the courts of a state is not a privilege or immunity of a citizen of the United States within the meaning of this section. The power to prescribe the qualifications of admission to the bar rests solely with the states Bradwell v State, 16 Wall 130

28 Jury trial.—A trial by a jury in the state courts in suits at common law is not a privilege or immunity of national citizenship which the states are by this amendment forbidden to abridge. Walker v. Sauvinet, 92 U. S 90.

29. Jurors to be white male citizens.—A law of West Virginia which provided that jurors should be drawn from the white male citizens, *held*, when applied to a case where a man of color was on trial upon criminal indictment, to be such discrimination as this amendment was intended to prohibit and that upon such trial a case for removal legitimately arose under the provisions of section 641, Revised Statutes Strauder v West Virginia, 100 U. S 303, Virginia v Rives, 100 U S 313

30. Some of the privileges and immunities of citizens of the United States as contemplated in this clause may be described as follows. The right of the citizen of this great country, protected by the implied guaranties of its constitution, to come to the seat of government to assert any claim he may have upon that government, to transact any business he may have with it, to seek its protection, to share its offices, to engage in administering its functions, free access to its sea-ports, through which all operations of foreign commerce are conducted, also to the sub-treasuries, land-offices and courts of justice of the several states. Another privilege of a citizen of the United States is to demand the care and protection of the federal government over his life, liberty and property when on the high seas or within the jurisdiction of a foreign government, the right to peaceably assemble and petition for redress of grievances, the privilege of the writ of *habeas corpus*, the right to use the navigable waters of the United States, however they may penetrate the territory of the several states, and all rights secured to our citizens by treaties with foreign nations, and the right of a citizen of the United States of his own volition to become a citizen of any state of the Union by *bona fide* residence therein Slaughter-House Cases, 16 Wall. 36, Crandall v Nevada, 6 Wall 35–44

31 **No state shall make or enforce any law which shall abridge the privileges or immunities of citizens of the United States** — It is only citizens of the United States that are placed by this clause under the protection of the federal constitution, citizens of the state, whatever they may be are not intended to have any additional protection by this paragraph of the amendment. Slaughter-House Cases, 16 Wall 36

32 **Marriage between white and black races not a privilege of a citizen of the United States.**— Marriage laws are under the control of the states, and a state law prohibiting the marriage relation between the white and black races is not in conflict with the civil rights bill of congress, nor with this amendment. Ex parte Hobbs and Johnson 1 Woods, 537

33. **Nor deprive any person of life, liberty or property without due process of law; nor any person within its jurisdiction the equal protection of the law — Due process of law, what is** — The due course of legal proceedings, according to those rules and forms which have been established for the protection of private rights, is 'due process of law " The question is not whether the court having jurisdiction of the subject-matter and the parties has proceeded as by the law required to do, but whether the law, if followed, would have furnished the protection guarantied by the constitution Kennard v. Louisiana, 92 U S 480

34 **Eminent domain.**— When private property is taken for public use and ample provision is made for inquiry as to damages before a competent court, and for review upon appeal to the highest court of the state, this is due process of law Pearson v. Yewdall, 95 U. S. 295.

35. **This implies the same exemptions as well as the same affirmative relief.**— The equality of protection guarantied in this amendment implies not only equal accessibility to the courts for the prevention or redress of wrongs and enforcement of rights, but also equal exemption with others of the same class from all charges and burdens of every kind Within these limits the power of the state exists, as it did previously to the adoption of the amendment, over all matters of internal police In re Ah Fong, 3 Sawyer, 144

36. **Due process of law** does not imply that all trials in the state courts affecting the property of persons must be by jury The requirement is met if the trial is in accordance with the settled course of judicial proceedings and this is regulated by the law of the state. Id

37 **By due process of law** is meant one which, following the forms of law, is appropriate to the case and just to the parties to be affected It must be pursued in the ordinary mode prescribed by law it must be adapted to the end to be attained, and, whenever it is necessary to the protection of the parties, it must give them an opportunity to be heard respecting the jus-

tice of the judgment sought. But where the taking of property is in the enforcement of a tax, the proceeding is necessarily less formal, and, whether notice to the party is at all necessary, may depend upon the character of the tax and the manner in which its amount is determinable. Hagar v. Reclamation Dist No 108 111 U S 701

38. In respect to taxation — This phrase remains to-day without that satisfactory precision of definition which judicial decisions have given to nearly all the other guaranties of personal rights found in the constitutions of the several states and of the United States. When, however, the constitution declares that "no state shall deprive any person of life, liberty or property without due process of law, it does not mean that a state can make anything due process of law which by its own legislation it chooses to declare such Neither do they necessarily imply a regular proceeding in a court of justice or after the manner of such courts See Murray v Hoboken Land Co, 18 How 272 It is therefore held in the case at bar "that whenever by the laws of a state or by state authority, a state tax, assessment, servitude or other burden is imposed upon property for the public use, whether it be of the whole or of some limited portion of the community, and those laws provide for a mode of confirming or contesting the charge thus imposed in the ordinary courts of justice, with such notice to the person or such proceeding in regard to the property as is appropriate to the nature of the case the judgment in such proceedings cannot be said to deprive the owner of his property without due process of law." Davidson v. New Orleans 96 U S 97

39 Same — The federal constitution imposes no restraint upon a state in regard to unequal taxation which may be in violation of the provisions of the state constitution Id.

40 Same — There is no provision of the federal constitution which forbids a state to tax or assess property twice for the same purpose, or which forbids unequal taxation by a state Id

41. Methods adopted for the summary collection of taxes by seizure and sale, etc, although they differ from proceedings in courts, are nevertheless ' due process of law ' Kelly v. Pittsburgh, 104 U S 78.

42 The taxing of lands in a municipal corporation by the municipality and for municipal purposes, where such land is farm land within the city, is due process of law Id

43 It does not require that persons taxed by law of a state shall be present or have opportunity of being present when the tax is assessed, nor that the tax shall be collected by judicial proceeding A right to enjoin the proceeding whereby the validity of the tax may be adjudicated is due process of law, and the fact that the plaintiff is required to give bonds as in other injunction proceedings does not affect the constitutionality of the law. McMillen v Anderson, 95 U S 37

44. Proceedings to raise revenue by levying and collecting taxes are not necessarily judicial, and "due process of law," as applied to that subject, does not imply or require the right to such notice and hearing as are considered to be essential to the validity of the proceedings and judgments of judicial tribunals Notice by statute is generally the only notice given, and that has been held sufficient. Kentucky Railroad Tax Cases, 115 U. S. 321, citing, quoting from and approving Davidson v. New Orleans, 96 U S 97, McMillen v Anderson, 95 U S 37, State Railroad Tax Cases, 92 U S 575, Neal v. Delaware, 103 U. S 370, Cooper v Board of Works, 14 C. B (N S) 180

45. Where an existing law makes water rents a lien upon land paramount to all other incumbrances to the same extent and with the same effect as are taxes, such lien is paramount to a mortgage executed after the law was enacted and prior to the introduction of the water on the land, and the law is not for that reason unconstitutional It does not deprive the mortgagee of his property without due process of law, nor deny him the equal protection of the law. Provident Institution v Jersey City, 113 U S 506

46. A law which directs that the expense of laying out, grading or repairing a street shall be assessed upon the owners of the lands benefited thereby, and determines the whole amount of tax to be levied and what lands are benefited thereby, and provides for notice to and hearing of each owner at some stage of the proceedings upon the question as to what proportion of the tax shall be assessed upon his land, is not in violation of this clause Spencer v. Merchant, 125 U S 345.

47. Chapter 230, Laws of New York of 1813, does not deprive persons of liberty or property without due process of law, nor of the equal protection of the laws. The phrase "due process of law" does not necessarily mean a judicial proceeding and when assessment laws provide for a mode of confirming or contesting the assessment upon notice to the person assessed, and for review, the assessment does not deprive the owner of his property without due process of law Palmer v McMahon, 133 U S 660

48. An act of the legislature of New Jersey, providing for the drainage of certain low lands, upon proceedings instituted by five persons owning separate lots within such district, and not objected to by a majority of the owners of the tract sought to be drained, the assessment to be made by commissioners upon notice and hearing, does not deprive the non-consenting owners of their property without due process of law Wurts v Hoagland, 114 U S 606

49. A statute of Kentucky which authorizes the city of Louisville to open and improve streets and assess the cost thereof to the owners of adjoining lots does not deprive such owners of their property without due process of law nor deny to them the equal protection of the laws Walston v Nevin, 128 U. S 578

50. A law of a state which so limits the taxing power of a city as to prevent the raising of revenue to pay a judgment for damages caused by a mob is not in violation of this amendment, because the owner is not deprived of his property in the judgment. Louisiana v New Orleans, 109 U S 285

51 Notice by publication, held due process of law when no personal judgment taken — Under section 1230, Revised Statutes of Texas, which provides for service of notice upon non-resident defendants, and in a case wherein the court of that state had acquired jurisdiction of the property of such non-resident and notice of the pendency of suit was served on him in a sister state *held,* that such notice was not repugnant to the provision of the constitution respecting *due process of law,* no personal judgment having been rendered thereon It was proper to apprise the defendant of the proceeding intended to affect his property only Sugg v Thornton, 132 U S 524.

52. Physicians' examination and regulation — A state statute which requires every practitioner of medicine to obtain a certificate from the state board of health that he is a graduate of a reputable medical college in the school of medicine to which he belongs, or that he has practiced medicine for ten years continuously in the state prior to March 8, 1881, or that he has been found upon examination to be qualified to practice medicine in all its departments, and which subjects any person practicing without such certificate to prosecution and punishment for a misdemeanor, does not when enforced against a person who had practiced medicine in such state for five years before the named date without diploma, etc, deprive him of his estate or interest in the profession without due process of law The state may exact as a qualification to practice medicine a degree of skill and learning on which the community employing such services may confidently rely and a board of examiners is a proper method of determining such qualification. Dent v. West Virginia, 129 U. S 114

53. Railroads — Examination of locomotive engineers.— A state statute which requires locomotive engineers engaged in running locomotive engines on railroads to be examined as to their ability to distinguish and discriminate between the colors used on such railroads as signals, and which exacts a fee from the respective railroad companies for such examination, does not deprive the company of its property without due process of law Nashville & Chattanooga R R Co v Alabama, 128 U. S 96

54 Railroads' liability for injury to employees.— Section 1, chapter 93 Laws 1874 of state of Kansas is as follows "Every railroad company organized or doing business in this state shall be liable to all damage done to any employee of such company in consequence of any negligence of its agents or by any mismanagement of its engineers or other employees to any person sustaining such damage" *Held,* that this does not deprive any such railroad company of its property without due process of law nor deny to it the equal protection of the laws Mo. Pac R R v Mackey, 127 U S 205, Minneapolis & St Louis R R. v Herrick, 127 U S 210

55. Fixing rates for railroads — A law which allows a railroad commission to establish rates for railroads, which are final, without issue made or inquiry had as to their reasonableness and forbids the courts to stay the hands of the commission if the rates established by it are unequal and unreasonable, deprives the company of its right to judicial investigation by due process of law, in violation of this section. Chicago, Mil. & St. Paul R y Co v State of Minnesota, 134 U S 418

56. It is no violation of the provisions of this clause of the constitution for the legislature to fix by statute a maximum of charges to be made by public warehouses for storage of grain therein Munn v Illinois 94 U S 113 Nor to fix the maximum rates of fare and freight on railroads. C, B. & Q R. R Co v Iowa, 94 U S 155

57. A statute of a state which fixes the maximum rates for fare and freight on railroads, and for other common carriers, is not repugnant to this amendment. Railroad Co. v. Iowa, 94 U S 155, Peik v. C. & N. W. R. R. Co., 94 U S 164

58. A railroad was sold under foreclosure of mortgage, and was reorganized as a corporation by the purchasers. A state statute fixed the maximum of fare that any railroad company within the state should charge at three cents per mile. *Held*, that such statute was not in violation of this section as taking property without due process of law, notwithstanding evidence that, with such compensation with its other existing traffic, its net yearly income will pay less than one and one-half per cent. on the original cost of the road and only a little more than three per cent. of the bonded indebtedness, or the amount of the capital stock of the reorganized corporation, or the price paid by the corporation for the road. Dow v. Beidelman, 125 U. S. 680.

59. Condemnation of right of way.—As a mode of appropriating land for a railroad by the exercise of the right of eminent domain, for the use of railroads, it was provided that the railroad company might apply to the judge of the district court of the county through which the railroad is built, who shall appoint commissioners to make the location, appraisement and assessment of damages. The application for and appointment of the commissioners is to be in writing and recorded in the office of the register of deeds. Notice of the appointment, etc., is given to non-residents by publication, and specifies the section, township and range in which the location is proposed to be made. There is a right of appeal from the decision of the commissioners. *Held*, that such condemnation constitutes due process of law; that a non-resident cannot hold his property exempt from the liabilities, duties and obligations which the state has a right to impose upon such property; that it is his duty to take measures that in some way he shall be represented when his property shall be called into requisition. Huling v. Kaw Valley R'y, 130 U. S. 559, citing Harvey v. Tyler, 2 Wall. 328; Secombe v. Railroad, 23 Wall. 108; Pennoyer v. Neff, 95 U. S. 714, 722, 743, 744; Hagar v. Reclamation Dist., 111 U. S. 701; McMillen v. Anderson, 95 U. S. 37; Davidson v. New Orleans, 96 U. S. 97, 105; Boom Co. v. Patterson, 98 U. S. 403, 406.

60. Right of city to prohibit use of engines on streets.—The ordinance of the city of Richmond prohibiting the use of the engines of the R. F. & P. R. R. Co. on Broad street does not impair the vested rights of the company under its charter, nor deprive the company of its property without due process of law, nor deny to the company the equal protection of the laws. Such prohibitions rest on the maxim, *Sic utere tuo ut alienum non lædas*, which lies at the foundation of the police power of the state. Richmond, Fredericksburg & Potomac Railway Co. v. City of Richmond, 96 U. S. 521.

61. Fencing of track.—A statute of Missouri requiring railroad companies to fence and maintain gates and cattle-guards, etc., where the track runs through inclosed fields and providing that in cases where such fences, etc., are not maintained the company shall be liable to double damages for stock killed, is not in violation of either of the two restrictions contained in this clause of the fourteenth amendment. The additional damages are by way of punishment for failure to comply with the law. Mo. Pac. R'y Co. v. Humes, 115 U. S. 512.

62. Corporations are persons within the state of their creation. A corporation is a person within the meaning of this amendment and is included in the phrase, ' Nor shall any state deprive any person of life liberty or property without due process of law, nor deny to any person within its jurisdiction the equal protection of the laws.' Santa Clara County v South Pac R R., California v. Same and Same v Cent. Pac. R. R, 118 U S 394

63. Corporation of one state not a "person" within another state — A corporation of one state cannot claim to be a person of another state so as to come within the protection of the clause of this section which forbids a state to deny to any person within its jurisdiction the equal protection of the laws" It is the right of a state to decide upon what terms foreign corporations may be permitted to do business therein And this will apply to foreign corporations doing business within such state upon license from year to year The privilege only extends to the expiration of the term for which the license is granted. Philadelphia Fire Association v New York, 119 U S 110

64. Power of state over corporations as persons.— A corporation is a "person" within the meaning of the word as used in this section, but the provision does not prohibit a state from requiring such conditions as it chooses for admission of foreign corporations to do business within the state. The only limitation upon such power in the state arises in respect to such corporations as are in the employ of the federal government, or such as are engaged strictly in commerce, foreign or interstate Pembina Mining Co v Pennsylvania, 125 U. S. 181, Minneapolis R'y Co. v Beckwith, 129 U S. 26 Santa Clara County v Railroad Co., 118 U. S. 394

65 Corporation — Right to improve water-ways and take tolls. It is not a violation of this clause for the state to authorize a corporation or individual to charge and collect tolls for the use of an improved natural water-way wholly within such state nor does the enforcement of the payment of such toll deprive the party of his property without due process of law Sands v Manistee River Improvement Company, 123 U S 288

66 Chinese are persons.— Where the ordinances of the county and city of San Francisco devolved upon the supervisors the power arbitrarily to grant or withhold a license to conduct laundries within certain limits and as to certain persons and it is shown that the right to maintain and conduct such laundries is universally granted to Caucasians and as universally denied to Mongolians, under similar conditions, *held* to be in contravention of the constitution and void. The fourteenth amendment is not confined to the protection of citizens. It is applicable alike to all "persons" within the territory without regard to differences of race, color or nationality, and the equal protection of the laws" is a pledge of the protection of equal laws Though the law itself be fair on its face, and impartial in appearance, yet if it is applied and administered by public authority with an evil eye and an unequal hand so as to practically make unjust and illegal discriminations between persons in similar circumstances, material to their rights the denial of equal justice is still within the prohibition of the constitution Yick Wo v Hopkins, 118 U S 356, citing Henderson v Mayor, 92 U. S 259; Chy Lung v Freeman 92 U S 275, Ex parte Virginia, 100 U S. 339 Neal v Delaware, 103 U S 370, Soon Hing v Crowley, 113 U. S. 703

67 Police regulation.— An ordinance prescribing the hours when laundries shall be closed, and prohibiting work therein on Sunday, is a police regulation wholly within the powers of state legislation, and the federal tribunals cannot supervise such regulations They do not deprive persons of property without due process of law nor deny them the equal protection of the law Barbier v. Connolly, 113 U S 27, Soon Hing v. Crowley, 113 U. S 703

68 Proceeding may be adapted to the nature of the case — Legislation is not open to the charge of depriving one of his rights without due process of law if it be general in its operation upon the subjects to which it relates, and is enforceable in the usual modes established in the administration of government with respect to kindred matters; that is by process or proceedings adapted to the nature of the case Ex parte Garland, 4 Wall. 333, and Cummings v Missouri, id 277 examined and distinguished. Dent v West Virginia, 129 U S 114.

69 Punishment for contempt is due process of law.— The right to punish for contempt is a power that resided in courts at the time of the adoption of this amendment, and the exercise of this power without the intervention of a trial by jury was then and is now "due process of law" Eilenbecker v District Court of Plymouth County, 134 U S 31

70 Does not refer to errors in decision by courts of law — Where the laws of a state if followed will insure to persons the enjoyment of life, liberty and property, the state has fulfilled its duty under the constitution If one of its courts, acting within its jurisdiction, makes erroneous decisions in the application of such laws, it cannot be said that the state has deprived such person of life, liberty or property without due process of law Arrowsmith v Harmoning, 118 U S 194

71 Statute of limitations — Repeal of — To remove the bar which the statute of limitations enables a debtor to interpose to prevent the payment of his debt does not deprive such debtor of his property without due process of law" There is a distinction between such cases and that affecting title to real estate After the statute has run in favor of the party in possession his claim has ripened into ownership, and a subsequent repeal of the statute, if applied to such possessor, would deprive him of his property without due process of law. Campbell v Holt 115 U S 620.

72 Partnership — Service on one member of firm — The provision in the laws of Texas that, when service is made in an action against a partnership upon one of the firm, the judgment may be rendered against the partnership and the member thereof so served, a judgment upon such service against the partnership does not deprive a non-resident partner of his property without due process of law Sugg v Thornton 132 U S 524

73 Law forbidding armed assemblies and drills, valid — This section does not guaranty to citizens of the United States the right to associate together, drill or parade, independent of any act of congress or state law. A statute of Illinois forbidding such assembly or drill, except as therein provided, held valid Presser v Illinois. 116 U. S. 252

74. Equitable suits to determine title to real estate, due process of law — A state statute which gives to its courts jurisdiction in equity of a suit brought by an equitable owner of land to establish his rights against the holder of the legal title is not void because it deprives the holder of the legal title of the right of trial by jury, which he would have if the case were tried by suit at law Church v. Kelsey, 121 U. S. 282.

75 **Right of state to tax bonds of United States.**— Where a state tax of one per cent. was laid upon the stock of corporations of the state, and it was claimed by one of such corporations that its capital, being invested in United States bonds, was exempt from such tax, which claim of exemption was denied by the state court, on error in the federal supreme court the judgment was affirmed by a divided court, Justice Wood not sitting Home Ins Co v New York, 119 U. S. 129.

76 **In respect to crimes and criminal trials — Effect of irregular verdict** — If in a trial in a state court of a person accused of crime the jury is brought into court, and on being polled it is disclosed that they were agreed upon a verdict of guilty under two counts in the indictment, but not agreed as to the other counts; and in the presence of the jury the prosecuting attorney proposes to enter a *nolle prosequi* as to those counts, and the jury having retired the court permits this to be done, and the jury being then instructed to pass upon the remaining counts return a verdict of guilty as charged in the indictment,— all this, however irregular, does not amount to a deprivation of the defendant's liberty without due process of law. Cross v North Carolina, 132 U S 131.

77. **Trial for felony on information is due process of law.**— The mode of procedure in California whereby persons are tried for felonies, including murder upon information and without indictment, is a trial by due process of law and is not in conflict with the provisions of the fourteenth amendment. Hurtado v People of California, 110 U S 516.

78. **Grand jury to exclude persons on account of race, etc, prohibited** — This section prohibits the formation and selection of a grand jury by excluding therefrom persons on account of race, color or previous condition of servitude, and a grand jury so selected and impaneled is invalid, and an indictment by it will, upon removal of the cause to a United States court, be quashed. Bush v. Kentucky, 107 U S 110, Neal v. Delaware, 103 U. S 398

79. **Adultery between whites and negroes punished more severely than between persons of the same race, valid** — A statute which punishes fornication or adultery committed between a white person and a negro more severely than when the like offense is committed between persons of the same color, but which in the former case visits the same measure of punishment on both parties whether white or black, is not in violation of this amendment The discrimination is as to the offense and not against a person of any particular race, etc. Pace v Alabama, 106 U. S 583

80. **Amendment adds nothing to fundamental rights of citizens** It is neither the duty nor within the power of the United States to punish for a conspiracy to falsely imprison or murder within a state. The provision of this amendment does not add anything to the fundamental rights of citizens That duty was originally assumed by the states and still remains there The amendment simply confers on the United States the power and duty to see that the states do not deny the right, and the power of the general government is limited to the enforcement of this guaranty. United States v Cruikshank, 92 U S. 542

81. **Not deny any person within its jurisdiction the equal protection of the laws.**— This restriction is not violated by any diversity in

the jurisdiction of the several courts as to subject-matter, amount or finality of decision, if all persons within the territorial limits of their respective jurisdictions have an equal right in like cases and circumstances to resort to them for redress. Missouri v Lewis, 101 U S. 22, quoted and approved in Kentucky Railroad Tax Cases, 115 U. S 321

82 Juries — Right of challenge — Greater number allowed in city — Equal protection of law — A statute of Missouri which provides that in trials in capital cases the state shall be allowed fifteen peremptory challenges where such trial is in a city having one hundred thousand or more inhabitants, while in other parts of the state there are but eight such challenges allowed, does not deprive the defendant in such trial of the equal protection of the laws Hayes v Missouri, 120 U S 68.

83. Insurance companies — Examination of by auditor — Due process of law — A statute which authorizes the auditor to institute proceedings in court to inquire into the financial standing of an insurance company, and to have a receiver appointed if after full opportunity for defense it is found to be financially unsound, or to have exceeded its corporate powers or violated the rules of its conduct as prescribed by law, does not deny to such corporation the equal protection of the law nor deprive it of property without due process of law. Chicago Life Ins Co. v Needles, 113 U S 574

84. Court of appeals for St. Louis valid — The provision in the constitution of the state of Missouri creating a court of appeals for the county of St. Louis and eight other counties, and giving to such court final jurisdiction in certain classes of cases, while as to the same class of cases in the remaining counties of the state the supreme court has final jurisdiction, is not in conflict with any of the provisions of this section. This amendment extends to and contemplates persons and classes of persons It has no respect to local and municipal regulations that do not injuriously affect or discriminate between persons or classes of persons within the places or municipalities for which such regulations were made Missouri v Lewis, 101 U S 22

85. Same.— It never was intended to prevent a state from arranging and parceling out the jurisdiction of its courts at its discretion Id

86. Corporate securities — Assessment of, on face value, valid.— An assessment of a three-mill tax on the face value of corporate securities, instead of on their actual value, is not a discrimination which the state is not competent to make, when all corporate securities are subject to the same rule. This amendment does not prevent a state from adjusting its system of taxation in all proper and reasonable ways, nor compel it to adopt an iron rule of equal taxation. The amendment intended only that equal protection and security should be given to all under like circumstances and that no greater burdens should be laid upon one than are laid upon others in the same calling and condition Bell's Gap R R. Co v. Pennsylvania, 134 U S 232, Chester v Pennsylvania, id 240.

87 Classification of property for taxation.— The classification of property for taxation, subjecting one kind of property to one rate of taxation and another kind of property to a different rate distinguishing between franchises, licenses and privileges, and visible and tangible property, and between real and personal property, is not such distinction as is contemplated by the constitution when it declares that no state shall "deny to any person within its jurisdiction the equal protection of the laws." Home Ins Co of N Y v People of the State of N Y, 134 U S 594

88 **New trials — Number limited, valid.**— The statute of Tennessee forbidding the granting of more than two new trials in the same cause on the facts is not in conflict with this amendment. Louisville & Nashville R R. Co. v Woodson, 134 U S 614

89. **Railroad's double liability for stock killed, valid.**— The provision of section 1289 code of Iowa which declares that railroad companies shall, under certain circumstances, be liable to double damages for stock killed when the company has the right to fence and has not so fenced, etc, is not in conflict with this clause of the constitution Minneapolis R y Co. v Beckwith 129 U S 26.

90 The fourteenth amendment does not limit the subjects over which the police power of the state may be exercised for the protection of its citizens Id, and Barbier v Connolly, 113 U S 27, Soon Hing v Crowley, id 703, Mo Pac Ry Co v Humes, 115 id 512

91. **Railroads — Classification and rates** — A statute of a state which classifies its railroad corporations on the basis of the length of their lines and which fixes different limits of the rate of passenger fare for each class is not in violation of this section because of denying to any corporation affected thereby equal protection of the laws Dow v Beidelman, 125 U. S 680

92. **Miscellaneous — Arrest by militia in time of insurrection.**— When the governor has declared a particular locality to be in a state of insurrection, and sent troops to suppress it, an arrest made by order of the commander, while engaged in suppression of the insurrection, is not made without due process of law In re Bergen, 2 Hughes. 517

93. **Laws validating contracts** — Where corporations of another state had made loans in Illinois under doubtful authority or without authority of law, *held* that an act of the legislature subsequently validating such contracts did not deprive the debtors of property without due process of law. Gross v United States Mortgage Co, 108 U S 477

94 **Kidnaping fugitives from justice** — Where a fugitive from justice in one state is found in another, or in a foreign state, and from there kidnaped and taken to the state wherein the crime was committed, his trial in the courts of such state cannot be said to be without due process of law The "due process of law" here guaranteed is complied with when the party is regularly indicted and tried, according to the forms and modes for such trials as prescribed by the laws of the state Ker v Illinois 119 U. S 436, approving State v Brewster, 7 Vt 118, State v Smith, 1 Bailey (S C Law), 283, Dow s Case, 18 Penn St. 37, State v Ross & Mann, 21 Iowa, 467, The Richmond, 9 Cranch, 102

95 **Back-water — Ad quod damnum proceeding** — A law authorizing a person to erect a mill upon his own land and a dam across a non-navigable stream and which provides for payment of damages to the owner of lands flowed by such dam, and for judicial proceedings to ascertain and fix such damages, does not deprive such owner of property without due process of law Head v Amoskeag Manuf Co., 113 U S 9

96. Judgment for torts—Military authority—Bill to vacate.—A bill in equity to vacate a judgment obtained against a defendant for a tort committed under military authority, according to the usages of civilized warfare, and as an act of public war, and also to enjoin its enforcement, is "due process of law," and is not in conflict with the fourteenth amendment. Freeland v Williams, 131 U S 405

97 Prior to the adoption of the fourteenth amendment the power to provide such remedies, although they might have interfered with what are called vested rights, seems to have been fully conceded Freeland v Williams, 131 U S. 405, citing Calder v Bull, 3 Dall 386, Satterlee v Matthewson 2 Pet. 380, Sampeyreac v United States, 7 Pet. 222, Watson v. Mercer, 8 Pet. 88; Frieborn v Smith, 2 Wall 160

98 Discrimination in selecting jurors—The act of March 1, 1875 (18 Stat. at Large, 336), which provides against discrimination in the selection of jurors on account of race, color or previous condition of servitude, is a proper exercise of the powers of congress as conferred by the thirteenth and fourteenth amendments The inhibition in the fourteenth amendment applies to all agencies of the state, and is enforceable against the individual officers and agents by whom the duties are discharged Ex parte Virginia, 100 U. S. 339.

99 Proceeding for removal of officer—A state statute regulating proceedings for the removal of a person from a state office is not repugnant to this section if it provide for bringing such officer into court and notifying him of the case he had to meet, and giving him an opportunity to be heard in his defense, and for the deliberation and judgment of a court. Affirming Kennard v Louisiana, 92 U S 480 Foster v. Kansas, 112 U. S 205

100. Limitation on state action only.—The prohibitions of this section have reference to state action exclusively, and not to any action of private individuals Virginia v. Rives, 100 U S 313

101. Prohibitions apply to all the agencies of the state.—The state may act through different agencies, either legislative, executive or judicial, and the prohibitions of the amendment apply to all such agencies which may deny the equal protection of the laws, and by virtue of the fifth section of the amendment congress may enforce the prohibitions whenever they are disregarded by any of the state agencies The mode of this enforcement is wholly within the discretion of congress. Id.

102. The constitution is broader than the statute (sec 641 R S), and authorizes the interference of the supreme court under its revisory power over judgments of the courts of last resort of the states Id

103 The doctrine announced in the Slaughter-House Cases that this amendment was designed primarily to apply to the freedmen is re-announced and adhered to Whether it had any other purpose is not decided but doubt is expressed whether any action of a state not directed by way of discrimination against the negroes as a class will ever be held to come within the purview of this provision.' Strauder v. West Virginia, 100 U. S. 303

104. Doctrine as it existed prior to this amendment.—Down to the time of the adoption of the fourteenth amendment, it was not supposed that statutes regulating the use, or even the price of the use, of private property, necessarily deprived the owner of his property without due process of law Under some circumstances they may but not under all The amendment does not change the law in this particular, it simply prevents the state from doing that which will operate as such deprivation Munn v Illinois, 94 U S. 113

2 Representatives shall be apportioned among the several States according to their respective numbers, counting the whole number of persons in each State, excluding Indians not taxed But when the right to vote at any election for the choice of electors for President and Vice-President of the United States, representatives in Congress, the executive and judicial officers of a State, or the members of the Legislature thereof, is denied to any of the male members of such State, being twenty-one years of age, and citizens of the United States, or in any way abridged, except for participation in rebellion or other crime, the basis of representation therein shall be reduced in the proportion which the number of such male citizens shall bear to the whole number of male citizens twenty-one years of age in such State.

3. No person shall be a senator or representative in Congress, or elector of President and Vice-President, or hold any office, civil or military, under the United States, or under any State, who, having previously taken an oath, as a member of Congress, or as an officer of the United States, or as a member of any State Legislature, or as an executive or judicial officer of any State, to support the Constitution of the United States, shall have engaged in insurrection or rebellion against the same, or given aid and comfort to the enemies thereof. But Congress may, by a vote of two-thirds of each House, remove such disability.

4. The validity of the public debt of the United States, authorized by law, including debts incurred for payment of pensions and bounties for services in suppressing insurrection or rebellion, shall not be questioned But neither the United States nor any State shall assume or pay any debt or obligation incurred in aid of insurrection or rebellion against the United States, or any claim for the loss or emancipation of any slave, but all such debts, obligations, and claims shall be held illegal and void

5. The Congress shall have power to enforce by appropriate legislation the provisions of this article

1 Persons in office by lawful appointment or election before the promulgation of this amendment (to wit, July 28, 1868) were not removed therefrom by the direct and immediate effect of the prohibition to hold office as contained in the third section Congressional legislation was necessary to give effect to the prohibition, by providing for such removal, and until such removal the exercise of the functions of office by such persons was not unlawful Cæsar Griffin's Case, Chase's Decisions, 364

2. **The congress shall have power to enforce by appropriate legislation the provisions of this article** — The "civil rights bill is constitutional, and applies to all conditions prohibited by it, whether originating before or since its enactment. Ex parte Turner, Chase's Decisions, 157

3. This does not confer upon congress the authority to enact laws for the suppression of crime within the state, and section 5519, Revised Statutes, which is supposed to have been enacted in obedience to this section, is not warranted by the provisions of the amendment. It (sec 5519, R S) is directed exclusively against the action of private persons, without reference to the laws of the state or their enforcement by her officers, whereas the provisions of the first section of this amendment have reference to state action exclusively, and not to any action of private individuals United States v Harris, 106 U. S 629; United States v Cruikshank, 92 U S 542, Virginia v Reeves, 100 U S 313. Civil Rights Cases, 109 U. S 3

ARTICLE XV.

1. The right of citizens of the United States to vote shall not be denied or abridged by the United States or any State on account of race, color, or previous condition of servitude.

2. The Congress shall have power to enforce by appropriate legislation the provisions of this article

1 This amendment relates to the right of citizens of the United States to vote It does not confer the right of suffrage on any one. It merely invests the citizens of the United States with the constitutional right of exemption from discrimination in the enjoyment of the elective franchise on account of race, color or previous condition of servitude. United States v Reese, 92 U S 214, United States v Cruikshank, 92 U S 542, United States v Harris, 106 U. S. 629–637, Minor v Happersett, 21 Wall. 178.

2 The power of congress to legislate at all upon the subject of voting at state elections rests upon this amendment. United States v. Reese, 92 U S 214.

NOTE — The power of the states over the subject is not otherwise limited except as to discrimination on account of race, color or previous condition of servitude It does not relate to discrimination on account of sex Van Valkenburg v Brown, 43 Cal 43, S C 13 Am Rep 136

3 This amendment has invested the citizens of the United States with a new constitutional right, which is exemption from discrimination in the exercise of the elective franchise on account of race, color or previous con-

dition of servitude. From this it appears that the right of suffrage is not a necessary attribute of national citizenship, but that discrimination in the exercise of that right on account of race, etc, is. The right to vote in the states comes from the state, the right of exemption from this prohibited discrimination comes from the United States The first has not been granted or conferred by the constitution, but the last has been. United States v Cruikshank, 92 U. S 542

4 Section 5519 of the Revised Statutes, providing a punishment for any two or more persons who may conspire to deprive any other person in any state or territory of the equal protection of the laws, is not authorized by anything contained in this amendment United States v Harris, 106 U S. 629

5. Colored persons, equally with whites, are citizens of the United States In re Turner, 1 Abb (U S) 88

6. Persons who have merely declared their intentions to become citizens are not citizens of the United States. McKay v. Campbell, 2 Sawy. 129.

7. This amendment had the effect, in law, to remove from a state constitution or render inoperative, a provision restricting the right of suffrage to the white race Therefore, where a constitution of a state in force before the adoption of this amendment so restricted suffrage, and the law in relation to jurors provided that all qualified to vote at the general election, being sober and judicious persons, should be liable to serve as jurors, *held*, (1) that after the adoption of this amendment colored men were included in those qualified to serve as jurors, (2) that such being the law it was not competent to remove a case from the state to the federal court under section 641 of the Revised Statutes, because citizens of the African race, otherwise qualified, were not by reason of the constitution and laws of such state excluded from service on juries, because of their race, color or previous condition of servitude. Neal v Delaware, 103 U. S 370.

8 **Right of congress to legislate as to state elections.**—The authority of congress to legislate upon the right of voting at state elections, under this amendment, is limited to prohibitions against discriminations on account of race, color, or previous condition of servitude, by the United States the states and their officers, or others claiming to act under color of laws which come within the prohibition of the amendment It does not extend to individuals acting upon their own responsibility and not under color of law United States v Amsden, 10 Biss. 283

9. The act of May 31, 1870, known as the "enforcement act," is not authorized by this amendment, and is unconstitutional and void Id.

10 Under article I, section 4, of constitution, congress has general powers of legislation concerning federal elections, but under the fifteenth amendment can legislate concerning state and municipal elections solely for the purpose of preventing discrimination on account of race, color, or previous condition of servitude. United States v. Munford, 16 Fed. Rep 223.

RULES OF CONSTRUCTION

1. **Nature and objects of power.**—The safest rule is to look to the nature and objects of the particular powers, duties and rights, with all the lights and aids of contemporary history, and to give to the words of each

such operation and force consistent with their legitimate meaning as to fairly secure and attain the ends proposed Prigg v Pennsylvania, 16 Pet. 539.

2 **Presumption is in favor of validity of acts of congress.**— Proper respect for a co-ordinate branch of the government requires the courts of the United States to give effect to the presumption that congress will pass no act not within its constitutional power This presumption should prevail unless the lack of constitutional authority to pass the act in question is clearly demonstrated United States v Harris, 106 U S 629

3. **Construction of state laws by state court, when binding on United States courts** —The construction of a statute or constitution of a state by the courts of such state is binding on the supreme court of the United States as a question of state statutory and constitutional law Stone v. Wisconsin, 94 U S 181

4. The courts of the United States follow the construction of the state courts in respect to questions arising merely under the constitution or laws of the state Luther v Borden, 7 How 1

5. **Statutes valid in part, upheld as to such part when** — It is a settled rule that statutes that are constitutional in part only will be upheld so far as they are not in conflict with the constitution, provided the allowed and prohibited parts are separable Packet Co v Keokuk, 95 U S 80, Unity v Burrage, 103 U S 447, Penniman's Case, 103 U S 717, Trade-Mark Cases, 100 U S 82. This rule held applicable to the case of Presser v Illinois, 116 U S 252

6 In a statute which contains unconstitutional provisions, that which is unaffected by such provisions, or which can stand without them, must remain If the valid and the invalid are capable of separation, only the latter are to be disregarded. Supervisors v Stanley, 105 U S 305, Railroad Companies v Schutte, 103 U S 118, State Freight Tax Cases, 15 Wall 232, Austin v Aldermen of Boston, 7 Wall. 694, People v Cassity, 46 N Y 46, Gordon v. Cornes, 47 N Y 608; Village of Middleton, Ex parte, 82 N Y 196

7. **Same.**— To give effect to the rule that a statute may be unconstitutional in part and in part constitutional, and that the part which is constitutional will be enforced, and only that part which is unconstitutional rejected, the parts must be capable of separation so that each may be read by itself. Elimination by construction only is not sufficient. Baldwin v Franks, 120 U S 678, United States v Reese, 92 U. S. 214; Trade-Mark Cases, 100 U S. 82, United States v Harris, 106 U S 629, Virginia Coupon Cases, 114 U. S 269 These cases are distinguishable from Packet Co v. Keokuk, 95 U S. 80, Presser v Illinois, 116 U S 252 See Baldwin v Franks, *supra*.

8. **Held entirely void, when** —If a clause in a statute of a state violates the constitution of the United States, and cannot be so separated from the remainder of the statute as to leave the residue in force the whole statute will be declared void And if the clause which violates the constitution cannot be rejected without giving to the remainder a meaning different from what was intended by the legislature, the whole statute must fall. Sprague v Thompson, 118 U S 90

9 **Exceptions of particular things presupposes that those not excepted are embraced** —The supreme court, in construing the constitution as to grants of powers to the United States, and the restrictions upon

the states, has ever held that an exception of any particular case presupposes that those which are not excepted are embraced within the grant or prohibition, and have laid it down as a general rule that where no exception is made in terms none will be made by mere implication or construction. Rhode Island v Massachusetts, 12 Pet. 657

10 **Same** —It is a rule of construction that the exception from a power marks its extent Gibbons v Ogden, 9 Wheat, at page 191

11 **History of the times considered.**— In construing the constitution the court must look to the history of the times, and examine the state of things existing when it was framed and adopted, to ascertain the old law, the mischief and the remedy Id

12 **Exemption from future general legislation,** either by a constitutional provision or legislative enactment, to be effective must be expressly given, or follow by an implication equally as clear as express words Pennsylvania R R. Co v Miller, 132 U. S 75.

13 **Construction not imposed in constitution, strict.**— There is no provision of the constitution limiting the courts to a strict construction of the powers conferred upon congress by that instrument. It should not have such an enlarged construction as to extend the words beyond their natural and obvious import It must, however, be so construed as not to deny to the government those powers which the words of the grant, as usually understood, import, and which are consistent with the general views and objects of the instrument Gibbons v Ogden, 9 Wheat 1-188

GENERAL PROVISIONS

1 **Extradition.**— An executive order of surrender to a foreign government is purely a national act. It is an executive act which must be performed through the secretary of state by order of the president. It does not follow from this that congress has no power to vest authority in judicial magistrates to arrest and commit preparatory to surrender The treaty also confers this power, and it is equally binding with an act of congress. In re Kaine, 14 How 103

2. **Sovereignty of colonial states.**— When the Revolution took place the people of each state became sovereign, and in that character held the absolute right to all their navigable waters, and the soils under them, for their own common use, subject only to the rights since surrendered by the adoption of the constitution Martin v Waddell, 16 Pet. 410

3 **Territories acquired by cession** —It cannot be admitted that the king of Spain, by treaty or otherwise, could impart to the United States any of his royal prerogatives, much less have they the capacity to receive or power to execute, them. Every nation acquiring territory, by treaty or otherwise, must hold it subject to the constitution and laws of its own government and not according to those of the government ceding it. Pollard v Hagan, 3 How 212

4. **Power to make legal tender.**— A contract entered into before the law making treasury notes a legal tender was enacted must be paid in coin. Willard v Tayloe, 8 Wall 557

5 And to give a contrary construction will render that part of the law unconstitutional Hepburn v. Griswold, 8 Wall 603.

6. The legal-tender act fully examined by Chase, C J, and in its essential features declared unconstitutional Miller, Swayne and Davis, JJ, dissenting Id, McGlynn v Magraw, 8 Wall 639

7. Suppress insurrection — Liability of persons engaged in such suppression.— An officer of the federal army while in service during the late war in insurgent states did not become liable to civil action in the courts of such insurgent states for any acts of war ordered by him in his military capacity The question of the necessity of such military orders was not subject to be called in review by the courts upon complaint of injured parties. He was responsible only to his government, and could be called upon to answer for his acts in no other manner Dow v Johnson, 100 U. S. 158.

8 Civil war — Hostile acts of insurgents not criminal — When a civil war is in progress in a nation, one party to such war having separated itself from the old established government, and erected for itself an independent and separate government, the courts of the United States must view the newly established government as it is viewed by the legislative and executive departments of the government of the United States If that government remains neutral, but recognizes the existence of civil war, the courts of the Union cannot consider as criminal those acts of hostility which are authorized by the laws of war and which the new government may direct against the old as its enemy United States v Palmer, 3 Wheat. 610.

9. Civil war — Military power in conquered states.— Although the city of New Orleans was conquered and taken possession of in a civil war waged on the part of the United States to put down an insurrection and restore the supremacy of the national government in the Confederate States, that government had the same rights in territory held by conquest as if the territory had belonged to a foreign country and had been subjugated in a foreign war. The Prize Cases, 2 Black, 635, Mrs Alexander's Cotton, 2 Wall 417; Mauran v. Insurance Co, 6 Wall 1.

10 In such cases the conquering power has a right to displace the pre-existing authority, and to assume, to such extent as it may deem proper, the exercise by itself of all the powers and functions of government. It may appoint all the necessary officers and clothe them with designated powers, larger or smaller, according to its pleasure It may prescribe revenues to be paid and apply them to its own use or otherwise It may do anything necessary to strengthen itself and weaken the enemy There is no limit to the powers which may be exerted in such cases save those which are found in the laws and usages of war In such cases the laws of war take the place of the constitution and laws of the United States as applied in times of peace, and contracts made by such authority, which are a fair and reasonable exercise thereof, do not necessarily terminate with the military jurisdiction New Orleans v The New York Steamship Co, 20 Wall 387.

11. Territorial courts not continued under state — The constitution under which Florida was admitted as a state provided that all officers, civil and military, then holding office under the United States should continue to hold them until superseded under the state constitution *Held*, that this did not continue the existence of courts which had been created by congress as part of the territorial government Benner v. Porter, 9 How.

235 Proceedings before such courts were *coram non judice.* Forsyth v. United States, 9 How 571

12 **National banks — State laws for taxing** — If a state statute providing for taxation does not on its face discriminate against national banks, and there is neither evidence of legislative intent to discriminate nor proof of actual and material discrimination, the law cannot be said to be unconstitutional Davenport Bank v Davenport, 123 U. S 83

13. **Mandamus by state court.**— A state court cannot issue a *mandamus* to an officer of the United States McClung v Silliman, 6 Wheat. 598 McIntire v. Wood, 7 Cranch, 504, referred to and explained

14 **Land grants from Indians.**— A title to lands under grants to private individuals made by Indian tribes or nations northwest of the Ohio river in 1773 and 1775 cannot be recognized in the courts of the United States Johnson & Graham's Lessees v McIntosh, 8 Wheat 543

15. **Distribution of power** — The powers of the government are divided into three departments, viz, legislative, executive and judicial, and the lines which separate these departments are clearly and broadly defined. The powers confided to one department cannot be exercised by the other Kilbourn v Thompson, 103 U. S. 168

16 **Congress can exercise no authority over pending suits** — Where a suit is pending in a court of competent jurisdiction the congress nor either house thereof has no right to declare that justice cannot be done in such suit to either party, and has no power to investigate the subject-matter of such suit and to compel the attendance of witnesses upon such investigation. Id.

17. **Conflicting state governments.**— When there are two opposing governments the question as to which is the legal government has been considered more a political than judicial question The political department in power has always determined whether a proposed constitution or amendment had been ratified, and the courts have followed the political determination so made Luther v Borden, 7 How. 1.

18 **Powers of states before adoption of articles of confederation.**— "The legislative power of every nation can only be restrained by its own constitution" In June, 1776, the convention of Virginia formally declared that Virginia was a free, sovereign and independent state; and on the 4th of July, 1776, the United States in congress assembled declared the thirteen united colonies free and independent states, and as such they had full power to levy war, conclude peace, etc This is a declaration, not that the united colonies jointly, in a collective capacity, were independent states, but that each of them was a sovereign and independent state, that each of them had a right to govern itself by its own authority and its own laws without any control from any other power upon earth All laws made by the legislatures of the several states after the declaration of independence were the laws of sovereign and independent governments Chase, J, in Ware v Hylton, 3 Dall 199.

19 **Co-ordinate jurisdiction of state courts, when.**— The laws of the United States are, within the limits of the states, as much the law of the land as are the laws of the particular state Exclusive jurisdiction for the enforcement of such federal laws may be conferred on the federal courts.

But, in the absence of a law conferring such jurisdiction on the federal courts, the said laws may be enforced by the state courts In such case the jurisdiction in the state courts is derived from the constitution and laws of the state Claflin v Houseman, 93 U S 130

20 **Power of president to waive the exemption of the United States from suit** — Where the president of the United States, when negotiating with a foreign government, waived the right of this government to be exempt from suit, and asked a prize court having rightful jurisdiction to complete the adjudication of a cause before it, the government is bound by such waiver The Nuestra Senora de Regla, 108 U. S 92

21 **State constitutions** — Clauses in state constitutions providing that taxes shall be uniform in respect to persons and property do not prevent the legislature from commuting, with individuals or corporate bodies, the burden of general or specific taxes or assessments Chicago v Sheldon, 9 Wall. 50

22 **Judgment in United States court, enforcement of** — A marshal may be appointed a commissioner to levy a tax in satisfaction of a judgment upon the taxable property of a county Lee County v United States ex rel Rogers, 7 Wall 175 But see Rees v Watertown, 19 How 107; Heine v. Levy Comm'rs, 19 Wall 655

23. **King can do no wrong, not recognized.**— The maxim that the king can do no wrong has no place under our form of constitutional government, and is not to be applied to the acts of any of the officers of government. Langford v. United States, 101 U S 341

24. **Confederate currency — Contracts payable in** — Contracts made during the war in one of the Confederate States, and payable in Confederate currency, are not necessarily void as between the parties They are not so invalid where they were not designed to aid in insurrection. Wilmington, etc R R v. King, 91 U. S. 3, citing Thorington v Smith, 8 Wall. 1, Hanauer v Woodruff, 15 Wall. 448, Confederate Note Case, 19 Wall. 556

25. Contracts made in the seceded states during the insurrection were not invalid because of the fact that they were made payable in the notes called Confederate notes, where such contracts were not made in aid of the insurrectionary government. And if a contract was entered into during said insurrection, in said insurrectionary states, payable in dollars, without specifying the kind of currency in which it was to be paid, it may be shown by the nature of the transaction and the attendant circumstances, as well as by the words of the contract, to have contemplated payment in Confederate currency; and if that fact is shown in a suit on such contract, no more can be recovered than the value of that currency in lawful money of the United States Effinger v Kenney, 115 U S 566.

26 **Unconstitutional law no law** — An unconstitutional law is no law It confers no right, it imposes no duties, it affords no protection, it creates no office,— it is wholly inoperative Norton v. Shelby County, 118 U S 425

27 **Power of congress to impair the obligation of a contract** — Where, under authority of congress, the postmaster-general made a contract with a railroad company to carry mails for four years at a stipulated price,

it is not within the power of congress thereafter to change the contract to a lesser price without the consent of the company. The government cannot retain the obligation of the contract as against the company, and at the same time vary its own, unless it has reserved the right to do so in the contract itself C. & N W. R'y Co v United States, 104 U S 680, C, M & St. P. R'y Co v United States, 104 U S 687

28 **Decision of state court** —The decision of a state court is not unconstitutional which holds that certain promissory notes and the mortgage securing them are nullities, on the ground that the Confederate currency which constituted the consideration was illegal by the law of the state at the date of the contract. Bethell v. Demaret, 10 Wall 537

29. **Rebellion; debts in aid of, unconstitutional** —Treasury notes issued under the provisions of the act of Mississippi of December 19, 1861, are invalid because issued by the state while in insurrection against the government of the United States, and were so issued in aid and support of such insurrection, and because the act, in its purpose and mode of enforcement is hostile to the authority of the national government and impairs the rights of citizens under the constitution. Taylor v. Thomas, 22 Wall 479

30. **Laws of insurgent states—How far valid** —All acts of *de facto* legislatures of insurgent states, which in their terms or operation were not hostile to the national government or the state constitution, have the same validity as if enacted by a legitimate legislature United States v. Insurance Companies, 22 Wall. 99.

31 **Taxation by state.**—Where bonds were issued by a consolidated railroad company, the line of which extends into two different states, neither state can tax the bonds in the hands of non-resident holders. To do so would in effect be permitting the state to tax that part of the road lying in another state, and if one state could so tax the bonds the other could do so also, and this would be double taxation Railway Co v Jackson, 7 Wall. 262

32 **Ordinance of secession, effect of** —By the ordinance of secession of the state of Texas, and the acts of the legislature of that state designed to give effect to such ordinance, the state did not cease to be a state of the Union, nor its citizens cease to be citizens of the United States Texas v White, 7 Wall 700

33 **States have no extraterritorial jurisdiction** —No state can authorize its judges or courts to exercise judicial power by *habeas corpus* or otherwise within the jurisdiction of another and independent government The jurisdiction and sovereignty of the United States courts represent a government separate from and independent of, the state, although acting and exercising jurisdiction and sovereignty within the territorial limits of the state. United States v Booth, 21 How 506

34 **National and state sovereignty.**—The powers of the federal government and of the states are those of distinct and separate sovereignties, notwithstanding both exist and are exercised within the same territorial limits United States v. Booth, 21 How 506

35 **State and federal governments distinct—Federal supreme.** The federal and state governments are distinct and independent of each other within their respective spheres Neither government can intrude

within the jurisdiction of the other by judicial process, or judicial officers. When a contest arises between the enactments or processes of the two governments, the federal authority will be regarded as supreme until the question of supremacy of the enactments or tribunals is settled by the courts of the United States. Tarble's Case, 13 Wall 397; United States v Booth, 21 How 506

36. **Non-liability of state for acts of its officers.**—It is a general principle applicable to all governments, which forbids, on a policy imposed by necessity, that they should hold themselves liable for unauthorized wrongs inflicted by their officers on the citizen, though occurring while in the discharge of official duties Gibbons v United States, 8 Wall 269-275. This is cited and approved in United States v Cumming, 130 U. S 452-454 In this last case, congress had enacted that A B and C D ' be permitted to sue in the court of claims, which court shall pass upon the law and facts as to the liability of the United States for the acts of its officer, E F, collector of internal revenue, etc, ' and this suit may be maintained, any statute of limitation to the contrary notwithstanding ' *Held*, that the only right waived was the statute of limitations, and not the general principle stated in Gibbons v. United States, *supra*

37. **General maritime law** — While the general maritime law, with slight modifications, is accepted as law in the United States, it is subject, under the constitution, to such modification as congress may see fit to enact. The constitution has not placed the power to change or modify this general maritime law in the state legislatures Whether a law of a state can have force to create a liability in a maritime jurisdiction, where neither the general maritime law nor act of congress has created such liability, is not decided Butler v Boston Steam Ship Company, 130 U S 527

38. **Limitation laws — Retrospective.**— There is no limitation on the power of congress which prohibits the enactment of limitation laws that may be retrospective in their operation. Stewart v. Kahn, 11 Wall 493-504

39. **Religious liberties.**— The constitution of the United States makes no provision for protecting the citizens of the respective states in their religious liberties, this is left to the state constitutions and laws Permoli v. First Municipality, 3 How 588.

40. **The powers of congress subject to judicial inquiry** — The power of congress to pass a statute under which a prisoner is held in custody may be inquired into under a writ of *habeas corpus* as affecting the jurisdiction of the court which ordered his imprisonment, and if the want of power appears on the face of the record of his condemnation, whether in the indictment or elsewhere, the court which has authority to issue the writ is bound to release him Ex parte Siebold, 100 U S 371, Ex parte Hans Nielsen, 131 U S 176-183

41. **Same.**— It is well established that if, in a criminal prosecution, the court which renders a judgment has not jurisdiction to render it, either because the proceedings, or the law under which they are taken, are unconstitutional, or for any other reason, the judgment is void and may be questioned collaterally, and a defendant who is imprisoned under and by virtue of it may be discharged from custody on *habeas corpus* Ex parte Hans Nielsen, 131 U S 176-183, approving Ex parte Lange, 18 Wall. 163, Ex parte Siebold 100 U S 371

42. Territorial charters — Rights to be preserved by the succeeding state.— A railroad was chartered by an act of the territorial legislature of Wisconsin When Wisconsin became a state the constitution provided that all charters to corporations should be subject to alteration and repeal. *Held*, that the territorial law, being continued in force under the state jurisdiction, became a state statute and subject to the provisions of the constitution Stone v Wisconsin, 94 U S 181

43. Sovereign powers.— While under our constitution and form of government the great mass of local matters is controlled by local authorities, the United States, in their relation to foreign countries and their subjects or citizens, are one nation, invested with powers which belong to independent nations, the exercise of which can be invoked for the maintenance of its absolute independence and security throughout its entire territory The powers to declare war, make treaties, suppress insurrection, repel invasion, regulate commerce, secure republican governments to the states, and admit subjects of other nations to citizenship, are all sovereign powers, restricted in their exercise only by the constitution itself and considerations of public policy and justice, which control, more or less, the conduct of all civilized nations The Chinese Exclusion Case, 130 U S 581–604, Cohens v Virginia, 6 Wheat. 264–411.

44. Powers of congress, when exclusive.— Whenever the terms in which a power is granted to congress or the nature of the power require that it should be exercised exclusively by congress, the subject is as completely taken from the state legislatures as if they had been expressly forbidden to act upon it. Sturges v. Crowninshield, 4 Wheat 122–193

INDEX.

[The black figures refer to paragraphs, the other figures are to pages]

ACTIONS —
may be civil in form and criminal in nature, **40**, 187.

ADMINISTRATION —
states have full control over subject, **32**, 199.

ADMIRALTY —
case in does not arise under constitution or laws of United States, **23**, **25**, 123, 124
murder committed on waters of a state not a case in, **28**, 124.
territorial legislatures legislate upon, **30**, 125.
navigable waters which empty into the sea are within its jurisdiction, **32**, 125
same applies to navigable lakes, **33**, 125
is not confined to tide waters, **34**, **35**, 125.
what was referred to in constitution by declaring that the judicial power should extend to cases of, **36**, 125.
jurisdiction in suits by material-men, **26**, 124.
jurisdiction over, is in district court, **24**, 124
jurisdiction extends to cases of collision between vessels owned by foreigners of different nationalities, **39**, 126
jurisdiction in cases of, does not extend to manslaughter committed on a merchant vessel of United States in river of foreign nation, **40**, 126
jurisdiction in courts limited to what class of cases, **37**, 126
jurisdiction, how interpreted, **31**, 125
jurisdiction in does not extend to cession of waters in which cases arise; the power of legislation over remains in state, **27**, 124.
as to jurisdiction of courts of, 253 See COURTS (UNITED STATES)

ALIENS —
United States court has jurisdiction where all parties are, **115**, 135
when both parties are, the United States courts have *not* jurisdiction, **116**, **119**, 135
residing in a state, may sue citizen of same state in United States court, **117**, **118**, 135
section 11, act of 1789, does not extend jurisdiction to United States court in suits wherein alien is a party, unless a citizen be the adverse party, **119**, 135
state may refuse to allow to take by descent, **35**, 199.
congress may exclude, **16**, 17.

ALLEGIANCE—
that to nation paramount 4, 151.
faith and credit to records of, etc, to be given in each state (art. IV, sec. 1, clause 1), 152
conclusive when 1, 152, 9, 14, 153
judgment of one state, how enforced in another, 3, 152
pleas, *nil debet* will not lie to the record, 4, 152
what will lie, 5, 152.
partners, to bind all, all must be served, 6, 152
effect to be given to judgment, 8, 152, 13, 153
service, on agent of corporation of another state, effect of, 8, 153; 10, 155
effect of judgment on nature of action 10, 153.

ALLIANCE—
treaties of by states (art. I, sec 10, clause 1), 63.

AMBASSADORS, CONSULS, ETC.—
words apply to diplomatic agents whether to or from a foreign power, 20, 123
indictment for violence to, not a case affecting ambassadors, etc, 21, 123

AMENDMENTS—
ARTICLE I—
does not limit power of state, 1, 179; 10, 180.
ARTICLE II—
militia, 180
is a limitation on congress only, 2, 180.
ARTICLE III—
quartering soldiers, 180
is a restriction on congress only, 10, 180.
ARTICLE IV—
security of person, houses, papers and effects, 180.
applies only to proceeding in federal courts, 10, 181
purpose of provision, 5, 181
ARTICLE V—
applies only to general government and United States courts, 1, 3, 182, 52, 188

AMENDMENT OF CONSTITUTION—
resolution for, need not be approved by president, 169.

AMNESTY—
included in pardoning power, 21, 114.
effect of on confiscated property, 22, 114, 23, 115.

APPROPRIATIONS—
no money shall be drawn without (art. I. sec 9, clause 7), 62.

ARKANSAS—
law making notes of state bank receivable for taxes held valid, 11, 64.

ARMIES —
to raise and support (art. I, sec. 8, clause 12), 52
power of government on subject plenary 1, 52.
power includes power to make laws to carry on, 2, 52
power to enlist minors, 3, 53.
state courts cannot discharge on *habeas corpus*, 4, 53

ASSEMBLY —
right to, 2, 179; 8, 179, 9, 180

ATTAINDER, BILL OF —
forbidden (art. I, sec 9, clause 3), 61
object of provision, 22, 66
constitution of Missouri held to contain, 23, 66.
as used in constitution embraces bills of pains and penalties, 17, 65
defined, 16, 19, 65
sense in which term is used, 18, 65
clause in constitution requiring priests, etc, to subscribe an oath, held void, 20, 66
same as to oaths required by congress, 21, 66

BAIL —
"excessive bail shall not be required nor excessive fines imposed, nor cruel and unusual punishment inflicted" (art VIII, Amendments), 194
this amendment is not applicable to states, 1, 2, 194.

BANKRUPTCY —
cases in which states may legislate on, 14, 44. 15, 19, 45
valid though enacted while national law in force, effect of, 18, 45
powers of congress over, 22, 45.
insolvent laws distinguished from, 24, 45
"uniform laws," meaning of term, 25, 46
discharge from imprisonment under state laws does not affect imprisonment under execution from United States court, 16, 45
cannot discharge from contracts with citizens of other states, 17, 45
discharge under state law no bar to, in United States courts, 21, 45
national law may relieve against existing debts, 23, 45
uniformity of national law incompatible with state legislation on same subject, 25, 46.
state laws have no extraterritorial effect, do not act on non-residents, 19, 45
persons in custody under national law cannot be discharged by state, 20, 45
exercise of power is optional in congress, 26, 46

BILLS OF CREDIT —
state forbidden to emit (art. I, sec. 10, clause 1), 63
definition of, 2, 3, 4, 63.
how construed by courts, 5, 64.
state may authorize corporations to emit, 6, 64.

CITIZENS OF UNITED STATES—
all persons born or naturalized in the United States and subject to the jurisdiction thereof (14th Amend.), 210
what the phrase "subject to the jurisdiction thereof" was intended for, 6, 211, 13, 212.
sources of citizenship are two—1 birth, 2, naturalization, 13, 212
corporations are not, 7, 211
privileges and immunities, what are, 15, 16, 212, 30, 214
distinction between the privileges and immunities of citizens of state and United States, 21, 213
right to sell intoxicating liquors not a privilege or immunity, 22, 213
suffrage is not a necessary privilege or immunity of a citizen, 10, 211
fourteenth amendment did not add to the privileges or immunities It simply furnished an additional guaranty, 11, 211, 80, 222
right to drill and parade with arms not an immunity 20, 213, 73, 221
marriage between white and black races not an immunity, 32, 215
right to practice law is not, 27, 214
trial by jury in state courts is not, 28, 214
distinction between citizen of United States and of a state, 8, 17, 211
definition of word, 9, 211
when word is used in its political sense, 14, 212
alone are placed under the clause of fourteenth amendment, prohibiting the making or enforcing of laws which abridge privileges and immunities, 31, 215.

CIVIL WAR—
hostile acts of insurgents not criminal, 8, 231.
military power in conquered states, 9, 231
right of conquering power to displace pre-existing authority, 10, 231
when it exists, 2, 49.
courts bound to take notice of, 2, 49

COIN MONEY—.
congress may restrain circulation of notes as money not issued by its authority, 5, 46.

COLONIAL STATES—
sovereignty of over navigable waters, 2, 130

COLORADO—
constitution and statute respecting foreign corporations reviewed, 171, 41

COMMERCE—
power to regulate (art. I, sec 8, clause 3), 19.
why vested in congress, 68, 27
object of clause for regulating, 167, 40
what constitutes, see pages 19, 20
freights carried interstate is commerce among the states, 7, 20.
includes manufactures and growth, 4, 20
sale is an ingredient of, 2, 20
intercourse is, 3, 20
extends to persons as well as instruments, 5, 20.

COMMERCE — continued.
insurance is not, **8**, **9**, 20
regulation of, includes control of telegraph. **110**, 33.
regulation, what is not, **11**, **12**, 20.
embraces navigation, **51**, 26.
includes free navigation, **31**, 23; **13**, 20
includes improvements of harbors, bays, etc, **51**, 26.
control of navigation incidental to power to regulate, **18**, 21.
includes vessels as well as articles carried, **14**, 20.
a bill providing for recording hypothecation is regulation, **16**, 20
as including navigation, see, also, pp. 20, 21, 22, 23, 24, 25
power to regulate navigation in, exclusive in congress, **15**, 20.
bridge which obstructs navigation a nuisance, **23**, 21.
wharfage relating to commerce, **147**, **148**, 37.
corporations may be instruments of, **146**, 37.
among the states means with the states, **6**, 20
telegraph is instrument of, **94**, **96**, **99**, 30, 31.
power to regulate defined, **104**, 32.
regulation defined. **10**, 20.
state and interstate defined and distinguished, **108**, 33.
laws regulating interpreted, **70**, 27
powers of congress over foreign and interstate is supreme when exercised, **103**, 32
over marine is supreme, **49**, 25.
when power of congress over is exclusive, **101**, 31, **115**, **118**, 34, **50**, 25.
when not exclusive, **102**, 32 **115**, 34
power to regulate navigation is exclusively in congress, **15**, 20.
on rivers between states is under control of congress, **29**, 22
navigable streams, what power of congress over comprehends, **24**, 21.
railroad bridges over navigable waters within control of congress, **37**, 23
must be given by sovereign power, **40**, 23
congress, under this authority, may construct or authorize the construction of railroad in state, **172**, 41.
under the power conferred congress may prescribe punishment for bringing in counterfeit coin, **151**, 37.
congress may prescribe conditions for commerce in all its forms between states and foreign countries **51**, 26
congress has power to punish offenses committed on navigable waters, **38**, 23
this power does not stop at state boundary, nor is it confined to acts done on the water if the act obstructs navigation, **38**, 23.
state regulation of interstate, when invalid —
non-legislation by congress means commerce shall be free, **69**, 27; **127**, **129**, **130**, 35, **135**, 36
state legislation may affect but not regulate, **124**, 35
state law regulating telegraphic messages held invalid, **166**, 40.
state statute to impose license on railroad agent invalid, **176**, 42.
state laws for suppression of intemperance must not regulate interstate commerce, **131**, 36.

COMMERCE — continued.
state regulation of interstate, when invalid (continued) —
state discrimination against non-residents invalid, **164**, 39
state regulation respecting passage on steamboats navigating Mississippi river, held invalid, **163**, 39
state cannot prohibit sale of intoxicating liquor imported and sold by importer in original packages, **177**, 42
state tax on telegraph company, when invalid, **94**, 30.
on railroad franchises granted by congress, invalid **90**, 30.
on persons taking orders for sale of goods of another state, invalid, **92**, 30
on passengers, **52**, 26, **75**, 28.
on money or exchange engaged in, **53**, 26
on products of agriculture, **54**, 26.
on vessels plying between states, **55**, 26.
on citizens of state, **56**, 26
on license for selling beer, **57**, 26.
on vessel engaged in, void when, **61**, 26
on stipulation in charter of railroad company to pay *bonus*, valid, **64**, 27
on peddlers, when void, **65**, 27; **71**, 28.
on auctioneers, when void, **66**, 27
on wine and beer manufactured out of the state, when void, **67**, 28
on peddlers, when valid **73**, 28.
on products of other states, **72**, 28
on tobacco, charge for storage of when shipped out of state valid, **74**, 28
on vessels engaged in, when valid, **82**, 29
on sleeping-cars, when invalid, **83**, 29
on money earned in commerce, after so earned is valid, **85**, 29.
on gross earnings of railroad held invalid **85**, 28
on receiving and landing passengers and freight, void when, **79**, 28.
on goods coming from other states, when void, **80**, 28
on persons engaged in selling liquors, when invalid, **81**, 29.
on commercial travelers, when invalid, **84**, 29
on transportation company, when invalid, **86**, 29.
taxing is a form of regulation, **87**, 30
taxing transportation interstate, invalid, **87**, 30
wholly within state, not subject to congressional regulation, **107**, **108**, **112**, **113**, 33.
subjects of local nature intended only as aids may be exercised by states, **51**, 26.
state law making persons engaged in commerce liable for torts not repugnant to this clause, when, **121**, 34.
power of congress over does not prohibit state legislation relating to health, etc., **122**, 34, **123**, 35.
state statute relative to examination of locomotive engineers held not invalid, **133**, 36.
when states may act in absence of congressional action, **114**, **115**, 34.

COMMERCE—continued
on streams entirely within a state, until congress acts state has plenary powers, **33, 34,** 23
on streams wholly within a state may be regulated by state, when and how, **26,** 22 **28,** 22, **32,** 23, **33,** 23.
when state may authorize dam over navigable stream, **17,** 21; **22,** 21
state may authorize dam on navigable waters until congress acts. **125,** 35
but when congress acts it is supreme **126,** 35
exclusive power of congress over, does not extend to *intra*-state commerce, **50,** 25
states may legislate as to rates etc., on railroads, when and how, **155,** 38
state may fix rates for railroads when, **159,** 39
state may tax gross receipts of railroad company, **58,** 26
state cannot tax freight transported interstate **60,** 26
ordinance of city may require license, when **62,** 26
a state may tax corporations of other states, when, **88,** 30
contract between railroad and elevator held not a regulation of, **156,** 38
upon lakes wholly within state, not subject to this power, **149,** 38
act of congress taxing passengers held valid, **78,** 28
when states may act concurrently with congress **115, 117,** 34, **134,** 36.
state cannot obstruct navigable streams, when **40,** 24.
rights of steamboats enrolled and licensed under act of congress, **42,** 24.
when act of congress for enrolling vessels does not apply, **26,** 22.
lien on vessels in favor of material-men, congress may establish, **117,** 34.
compact between states cannot affect powers of congress over, **150,** 38
how affected on River Savannah by compact between South Carolina and Georgia, **27,** 22
legislative acts of District of Columbia taxing commercial agents held invalid, **93,** 30
Texas cattle, transportation of, 39.
possession of, **158,** 40
Pierce v. New Hampshire (License Cases) overruled, **135a,** 36
railroad grant, congressional grant of right of way to railroad an exercise of this power, **145,** 37.
with Indian tribes, power of congress over, extends to tribes and the individual members of tribes wholly within limits of a state, **143,** 37
congress regulates, although the tribe is within the limits of a state, **136,** 36, **142,** 37
congress may license or prohibit trade with, **137,** 36
congress may prohibit or license traffic with, **137,** 36
congress may prescribe punishment for crimes committed by Indians, **139,** 36
under the authority of this clause congress may exclude spirituous liquors from Indian country, **109,** 33.
foreign, has been fully regulated by congress, **128,** 35

COMMON LAW—
in suits at, where the value exceeds $20, the right of trial by jury is preserved (art. VII, Amendments), 191.

COMMON-LAW SUITS —
what the term includes, 1, 191
embraces all suits not of equity or admiralty, 1, 2, 3, 4, 191, 7, 192
does not apply to fugitive slave law, 5, 191
provision cannot be evaded by referring case to referees, 6, 192
trial by court without waiver of jury is error, 8, 192
all the facts must go to the jury. 9, 192
when interest may be computed without jury, 13, 192.

COMMON-LAW TRIALS —
trial of seizures by land must be by jury. 18, 193
state courts are not governed by this provision, 11, 192.
but it will be applied in federal courts irrespective of state laws, 12, 192
court of claims, the provision does not apply to, 19, 193
otherwise re-examined, limitation of supreme court extends to facts tried by state court, 16, 193.
when not applied to removal of causes. 17, 193.
remittitur after verdict held not a re-examination, 20, 193.

COMPACT —
between states, forbidden (art. I, sec 9, clause 3), 105.
boundaries of states, how regulated by, 13, 14, 106
implied assent of congress held to have been given in two cases, 15, 16, 107
between states, cannot abridge power of congress, 150, 38.

CONFEDERATE CURRENCY —
contracts payable in, not necessarily void, 24, 25, 233.

CONFISCATION —
the confiscation of the property of public enemies is not restrained by the fifth and sixth amendments, 10, 191.

CONNECTICUT —
law of, held not to be *ex post facto*, 35, 67.

CONGRESS —
shall have power (art I, sec. 8), 15.
powers classified, 4, 15.
powers implied, 1, 9.
powers, rules for construing, 7, 8, 9, 15.
cannot confer its powers on state, 6, 15.
extent of power granted, 2, 15
power to incorporate Bank of United States 20, 59.
may make laws to carry into effect judgments 21, 59
power to legislate in respect to form and effect of processes of United States courts uncontrolled, 17, 58.
powers of, when exclusive, 44, 236
powers of, subject to judicial inquiry in relation to crimes; inquiry may be by *habeas corpus*, 40, 41, 235
when may and when may not enact retrospective laws, 10, 57.
may name commission to determine indemnity under treaty, 13, 58.
may exempt from liability for acts of war. 16, 58
right to legislate as to state elections, 2, 227; 8, 9, 10, 228.

CONGRESS — continued.
exclusive legislation, where and how (art. I, sec. 8, clause 17), 54
over District of Columbia; all powers of government are united, national and municipal, 1, 54
may constitute District of Columbia a body corporate for municipal purposes, 2, 54.
may authorize Washington city to assess for repairs of streets, 3, 54
to make laws for carrying powers into execution (art. I, sec. 8, clause 18), 56
implied powers, 1, 2, 3, 4, 56, 5, 6, 7, 57.
the cause is direct authority for exercise of implied powers, 2, 56
implied powers are requisite from nature of constitution, 4, 56.
members of privileged from arrest, 1, 13.
the privilege is personal 2, 13
postponement of suit not a matter of right, 3, 13.
when privilege commences, 4, 13
right in contested election, 5, 13.
disorderly conduct of members, how punished, 6, 12
expulsion of members, 9, 12.
may compel attendance, 7, 12
bill passed by, becomes a law when, 1, 14.
date of approved not required, 1, 14
act of, operates by its own force upon the subject-matter in all states, 9, 172
members of, not permitted to hold other office, when, (art. I, sec. 6, clause 2), 13
necessity; under article 1, section 8 clause 18, congress to determine what is ' necessity," 11, 58.
power of president to adjourn, 2, 117

CONSTITUTION —
power of, to be carried into effect by congress, 8, 171.
deals in general language, minute specifications not provided for, 3, 15.

CONSTITUTION AND LAWS OF UNITED STATES —
case arises under, when, 90, 132

CONSTITUTIONAL QUESTIONS —
pleadings need not set out specific article involved, 96, 133.

CONSTRUCTION, RULES OF —
to look to nature and object of power, 1, 228
presumption in favor of validity of act, 2, 229.
history of the times considered, 11, 230.
strict construction is not imposed by constitution, 13, 230.
the construction of state laws by state court binding on United States court, 3, 229
when valid in part must be upheld as to such part if separable, 5, 6, 7, 229
when not separable all will be held void, 8, 229
exception of particular thing presupposes that those not excepted are embraced, 9, 229, 10, 230

CONTEMPTS —
right to punish for, exists at common law, 4, 12
court's power to punish for, 18, 123
house of representatives may punish its members for, 1, 11.
may punish other persons for, when, 1, 11
punishment for, when terminates, 2, 11
contumacious witnessess before may be punished and how, 5, 12.
CONTRACTS —
obligation; states forbidden to impair (art. I, sec. 10, clause 1), 63
"law impairing obligation of," defined, 38, 69
test, is diminished value, 39, 68.
impairment must arise under a state law. The prohibition is aimed at state legislation, 248, 100.
contracts between states may be thus impaired, 249, 250, 100
or between state and United States, 251, 100.
law in force when made, enters into and becomes part of, 189, 90.
prohibition against impairment extends to contracts of states, 227, 228, 98.
impairment of, extent not material, 212, 94.
states cannot impair by change of constitution, 191, 192, 193, 194, 195, 197, 91; 256, 100.
WHAT ARE —
exclusive right to streets by water company held to be. 119, 79.
agreement in bank charter to accept its notes for taxes is, 117, 79, 140, 82
charters of corporations held to constitute, 102, 103, 104, 105, 106, 77.
the remedy in existence at date of contract becomes part of contract, 76, 77, 80, 81, 73.
a congressional grant is a contract, 255, 100.
law exempting certain lands owned by Indians from taxes, held to be, 124, 80
a provision in charter of railroad company exempting from taxes is, 125, 80
a stipulation in a charter for a fixed sum in lieu of taxes is a contract, 137, 82.
municipal corporations, laws giving authority to incur debts is a contract with creditors, 174, 175, 176, 177, 178, 88, 180, 183.
exemption from taxation may be, 123, 80.
WHAT ARE HELD NOT TO BE —
bridge charter held not to be, 86, 74.
ferry franchise to a town held not to be, 108, 74.
rights conferred on corporation subsequent to charter are not, 120, 79.
provision in railroad charter authorizing the fixing of rates is not, 121, 122, 79
law authorizing municipal aid to railroad no contract, 89, 74; 90, 75.
law authorizing lottery for benefit of turnpike company not a contract, 91, 75.
license to tolerate a nuisance is not a contract, 214, 94.

CONTRACTS — continued.
WHAT ARE HELD NOT TO BE — continued.
an office is not, **206, 207, 208, 209, 211,** 93
after service of officers is rendered under a fixed compensation, it cannot be changed, **210,** 93
a state constitution is not a contract, **253,** 100.
taxes levied in aid of corporations ordinarily form no contract preventing repeal of charter, **96,** 76
marriage is not, within meaning of constitution, **262,** 102
LAWS HELD TO IMPAIR —
city ordinance may have effect of a statute, and so impair a contract, **185,** 89
liability of stockholders; repeal of, impairs contracts, when, **219, 220,** 95
legislative discharge of debtor invalid, **221,** 95.
diverting assets of bank impairs contract with bill-holders, **217,** 95
law reducing taxes for payment of municipal bonds invalid, **78,** 73
law requiring money to be withheld from non-resident bondholders to pay tax on bonds held invalid, **223,** 95
authority for municipality to contract debt implies power to levy tax to pay same, a statute afterward denying this right is void, **183,** 89
same rule applied to county, **196,** 91
a law annulling conveyances is unconstitutional, **98,** 76
a law which attempts to discharge a debtor is unconstitutional, **99,** 76
and this applies whether law was passed before or after debt is contracted, **100,** 77.
repealing act when invalid, **229,** 97
law to prevent issuance of municipal bonds, when invalid, **230,** 97.
municipal corporations cannot be changed at expense of creditors, **231, 232,** 97.
Confederate sequestration laws held to impair, **233,** 97.
LAWS HELD NOT TO IMPAIR —
authority to creditor of city to apply debts due him on taxes under certain regulations does not impair contract of other creditors, **184,** 89.
a law prohibiting an existing corporation from manufacturing beer does not impair contract, **198,** 91.
constitution protects such contracts as affect private rights, not such as are governmental, **199,** 91
divorce laws do not come within the restriction, **234,** 98.
county seat removed does not impair contract, **236,** 98
reserved rights, effect of, **237,** 98.
railroad station vacated and required to be reopened does not impair contract, **239,** 98
removal of state capitol after contract for erection does not impair the contract, **241,** 99
not impaired by curative acts, **95,** 76
statute requiring a minority of bondholders to declare their dissent to a refunding scheme or be taken to have assented, held valid, **242,** 99

CONTRACTS — continued
LAWS HELD NOT TO IMPAIR — continued.
act requiring registration of township bonds held to apply to bonds previously issued and to be valid, 243, 244, 99
where judgment is for torts, subsequent legislation affecting will not be invalid, 68, 71, 69, 72, 182, 89
laws regulating and changing security for preservation of estates of minors do not impair contracts 92, 75
a law changing liability of stockholders held not to impair the contract of creditors of corporation, 93, 75
condemnation proceedings have nothing of contract in them between owner and state or corporation, 94, 76
held not impaired by law authorizing bank-notes to be offset against judgment of bank, 109, 78.
law to correct mistake in municipal proceedings, valid when, 215, 94
rehearing, state has right to grant, 87, 88, 74.
EFFECT OF CHANGE OF REMEDY ON OBLIGATION —
statute of frauds impairs contract, when, 57, 70
stay and appraisement law held to impair, 59, 70
redemption law held to impair, 60, 71
change in rules of evidence held to impair, 61, 62, 71.
effects of recording acts on, 70, 71
laws affecting remedy held void, 72, 73, 74, 75, 72, 76, 77, 78, 79, 80, 81, 73, 82, 74.
distinction between obligation and remedy, 40, 68.
cases enumerated in which change of remedy may be made, 41, 68.
change in mode of service on railroad held valid, 42, 68
remedy, state may so act upon the contract of one of its citizens as to deny the right of action in its own courts, results of such action, 77, 130, 131
law providing name in which suit shall be brought, valid, 64, 71.
action, form of may be changed, 65, 71.
usury laws held not to impair, 67, 71.
state law giving its creditors right to sue in its courts may be repealed, 63, 71.
exemption laws, if reasonable, do not impair, 58, 70
statute for recording mortgages held valid, 56, 70
remedy, change of, 40, 41, 42, 68, 43, 44, 47, 48, 69
as to imprisonment for debt, 43, 44, 69.
discharge in bankruptcy, 45, 69
change of mode of proceeding. 48, 69
limitation laws, 50, 51, 69, 52, 53, 54, 70
limitation laws do not impair obligation of contract, when, 50, 51, 69 52, 53, 70.
statute of, limiting time for collection of bonds, held void, 54, 70; 79, 73.
EXEMPTION FROM TAXES —
effect of consolidation of railroad corporations on exemption, 127, 128, 80

CONTRACTS — continued.
EXEMPTION FROM TAXES — continued.
exemption of property of railroad includes franchise and rolling stock, **131, 132**, 81.
general words of exemption held not to include municipal tax, **153, 159**, 84
exemption from taxes by law will not be implied, **135**, 81, **144**, 82; **145, 148**, 83; **149, 150, 151**, 84
charitable institution, implied consideration in charter, **130**, 81.
state ordinance of Missouri held invalid, **134**, 81.
exemption of franchise held not to exempt corporate property, **126**, 80.
exemption of bank held to exempt stock, **129**, 80
held not to pass to purchaser, **155**, 85.
when it begins and how long it runs, case stated, **156, 157**, 85.
not transferable, **172, 173**, 88.
exemption held void for want of power in legislature, **152**, 84.
exemption by state of Missouri of Iron Mountain Railroad held invalid, **145**, 83.
act of Missouri legislature in *Re* N. M. R. R. no contract of exemption, **147**, 83
lack of consideration for exemption authorizes repeal, **141, 142**, 82.
rule applied to state university of Illinois, **138**, 82.
IMPAIRMENT OF OBLIGATION — MISCELLANEOUS PROVISIONS —
intent of provision against impairment, **259**, 101.
construction, supreme court of United States will decide independently of state court whether under a given statute a contract exists, **245**, 99, **247**, 100
a law as expounded by the courts of a state becomes a rule of property and cannot be changed so as to impair contracts made while rule was in force, **186, 187, 188, 190**, 90.
a law in force when constitution took effect which impaired the obligation of contract was not void, **101**, 97
a grant of land to a corporation not in existence becomes vested when corporation capable of taking is formed, **111, 112, 113**, 78.
a state may tax its citizens on debts due them from citizens of other states, **258**, 101.
exclusive right to maintain a bridge, held not to include a railroad bridge, **114**, 78.
charter of state bank held to include branches, **115**, 79.
rights of one corporation conferred by law upon another, effect of, **116**, 79
case in which legislative reservation as to chartered privileges was held to exist, **110**, 78.
consolidation of railroad companies, effect of on chartered rights, **169**, 87.
when a law is in its nature a contract, its repeal cannot divest vested rights, **97**, 76.
compromise of state debt, effect of, **240**, 99

CONTRACTS — continued
IMPAIRMENT OF OBLIGATION — MISCELLANEOUS PROVISIONS — continued
charter of corporation, legislative reservation of alteration or repeal, effect of, **159**, 85, **160**, **161**, **162**, **164**, **165**, **166**, **167**, 86, **169**, 87.
taxation, a city cannot tax its own stock in hands of the holders, **136**, 81.
retrospective laws, valid when, **36**, 68.
Virginia Coupon Cases considered, **224**, 95, **225**, **226**, 96
there is no prohibition on national legislation as to impairment of contracts **254**, 100

CORPORATIONS —
aggregate, cannot be citizens of a state, **49**, 127.
are citizens within article III, section 2, clause 2, **21**, 139
are not citizens within meaning of section 2, article IV, **18**, 158.
nor within meaning of fourteenth amendment, **7**, 211.
states may discriminate in favor of their own, **19**, 159
the terms imposed must be consistent with the constitution, **20**, 159
cannot emigrate **17**, 158.
cannot be denied the right to sue in United States courts by state laws, **64**, 129
nor the right to remove case to United States court, **65**, **66**, **68**, 129.
state may exclude foreign, **39**, 199
may domesticate them, how far, **46**, 200
federal government may create, **49**, 200
are "persons" within the state creating them, **62**, 219.
but not in other states, **63**, 220
powers of state over as "persons," **64**, 220.
right to improve water-ways and take tolls, **65**, 220.
state may subject lands of to pay debts of citizens after charter expires, **33**, 199
carrying companies may be taxed by state, **20**, 197
of one state may sue a citizen of another state in United States courts, when, **50**, **51**, **53**, 127, **54**, **55**, **56**, **57**, **58**, **59**, **60**, **61**, **62**, 128, **63**, **64**, 129.
may be enjoined by a member of, when, **69**, 129
charters held to be contracts, **102**, **103**, **104**, **105**, **106**, 77; **133**, 81
municipal, ferry franchise held not a contract, **108**, 77.

CORPORATE PRIVILEGES —
legislature may charge for, **16**, 19
stockholders' liability, law changing held not to impair contract of creditors, **93**, 75.

COUNTERFEITING —
to provide punishment for (art. I, sec. 8, clause 6), 46.
bringing counterfeit money from other countries may be punished, **1**, 46, **4**, 47
counterfeiting notes of foreign banks may be punished, **2**, 46.
language of constitution, how limited, **3**, 47.
power of state over, **5**, 47.

COUNTERFEIT COIN —
congress may prescribe punishment for bringing in, 151, 38.

COURTS (UNITED STATES) —
jurisdiction of (art. III, sec 2, clause 1), 120
jurisdiction, source of, 2, 19

JURISDICTION, EXTENT OF —
extends only to judicial questions, 1, 121
as to subject-matter, it extends to cases arising under the constitution and laws of the United States and to treaties, 2, 121
extends to suits by postmaster-general on bonds given by deputy, 3, 121
to cases involving the question of the constitutionality of laws of congress, 2, 4, 121, 14, 122

JURISDICTION —
as to parties, public ministers and consuls, 19, 123
have none in suits against United States, 42, 43, 44, 45, 126
controversies between states 46, 47, 127
controversies between a state and a citizen of another state, 48, 127.
controversies between a state and citizen thereof, foreign states, citizens and subjects, 114, 115, 116, 117, 118, 119, 120, 121, 135
controversies between citizens of different states 49, 127, 69, 129
the citizenship of person for whose use suit is brought governs the jurisdictional right 84, 131
formal parties cannot oust if real parties give 81, 82, 131
a citizen of a territory cannot sue a citizen of a state in United States courts, 72, 130
citizens of District of Columbia cannot sue a citizen of a state in United States courts, 74, 130
citizenship of corporations for purpose of suit in United States courts, 49, 50, 51, 52, 53, 127, 54, 55, 56, 57, 58, 59, 60, 61, 62, 128; 63, 64, 65, 68, 129
supervisors of county can be sued in United States court by citizen of another state, 86, 131
circuit, jurisdiction between citizens claiming land, etc, 112, 135.
citizen of one state having title to lands in another, 85, 131
state laws cannot impair jurisdiction of United States courts, 75, 76, 130, 78, 79, 131; 95, 132
proceedings in, under exclusive control of congress, 93, 132
may make jurisdiction exclusive, 95, 133.
jurisdiction over trespass committed in foreign country, when and where, 109, 134.
jurisdiction over property once obtained continues, 97, 133
federal and state, concurrent jurisdiction, when, 102, 134.
cannot enjoin each other, 103, 134.
have no jurisdiction in common-law offenses. 6, 148.
exclusive in seizures on land and water, 7, 121
same, in respect to ministers, consuls, etc., 19, 123.
none to entertain *mandamus* on secretary of treasury, where, 15, 122
contempts, have power to punish for, 18, 123

COURTS (UNITED STATES) — continued
JURISDICTION — continued.
implied powers of, 10, 120
common-law jurisdiction of, 11, 120
number and character of in discretion of congress, 3, 119
authority to bring parties before, 4, 119
province of is to construe laws and not to make them, 98, 133
territorial, not constitutional courts, 5, 119.
not courts of United States, 6, 120
are legislative courts, 7, 120
process subsequent to judgment essential, 104, 134
state; jurisdiction where title to real estate is claimed under grant of state, 113, 135
state court cannot enjoin process from United States court, 88, 89, 132
CHANCERY JURISDICTION —
conferred by constitution, 105, 134.
rules of high court of chancery of England adopted in, 105, 134.
not subject to limitation or restraint by state, 106, 134.
has chancery jurisdiction in every state, and it is the same in each, 108, 134.
state and national, are as independent as separate, 87, 132
none to enjoin proceedings in state court, 13, 122
JURISDICTION IN ADMIRALTY —
jurisdiction in admiralty does not extend to murder committed on waters of a state, 28, 124.
has jurisdiction in suits by material-men, when, 36, 124
limited to contracts of what class, 37, 126.
over cases of collision on high sea between vessels owned by foreigners of different nationalities, 39, 126.
no jurisdiction of manslaughter on board a merchant vessel of United States in rivers of foreign nation, 40, 126
UNITED STATES SUPREME COURT —
jurisdiction on appeal, when examination confined to equities arising under act of congress, 8, 122
jurisdiction under twenty-fifth section of judiciary act, 4, 5, 6, 121.
embraces civil and criminal cases, 5, 121

CRIMINAL LAW —
effect of irregular verdict, 76, 222
trial for felony on information is due process of law, 77, 222
exclusion of persons from grand jury is in violation of the fourteenth amendment, 78, 222.
adultery between whites and negroes may be punished more severely than between persons of same race, 79, 222

CRIMINAL PROSECUTIONS —
right of accused to a speedy and public trial (art. VI, Amendments), 189
refers only to trials in United States courts, and as limitation on federal power, 1, 2, 189.

CRIMINAL PROSECUTIONS — continued
state and district wherein crime was committed; refers only to cases of crimes committed within limit of state, 3, 189.
speedy trial by impartial jury; rule in Spies' case, 4, 190.
congress has no power to authorize trial by military commission for offenses in civil life, 7, 190
confronted with witnesses against him, does not apply where witnesses are absent by procurement of accused, 5, 190
informed of nature and cause of accusation, what indictment may contain, 6, 190.

DAY —
no fraction computed in taking effect of law, 4, 114.

DEPARTMENTS OF GOVERNMENT —
co-ordinate in power; independent of each other; acts rightly done by one binding on all, 41, 176.

DIRECT TAX (see TAXATION) —
what is, 1, 2, 3, 61
what is not, 4, 61; 5, 62.

DISTRICT OF COLUMBIA —
sovereign power over is in the government, and not in the corporation of the District, 13, 56
government may levy direct tax in, 9, 55
process of courts in, 10, 55
local municipal assessments, 11, 55.
citizenship, permanent inhabitant in is not a citizen of a state, 12, 55.
legislative regulation of persons engaged in business held regulation of commerce, 93, 30
words "states of the Union" held to include, 20, 173.
sovereign power over, is in congress, 1, 2, 54.
article 6 of amendments is in force and binding upon courts in, 9, 190.

DUE PROCESS OF LAW —
meaning of term same as law of the land, 22, 185.
rules for construing phrase, 23, 185
what is, 33, 37, 215, 38, 216.
arrest by militia in time of insurrection is, 92, 224.
distraint for taxes is due process of law, 25, 185
distress warrant issued by solicitor of treasury is, 26, 185
ordinary rule on attorney in disbarment proceeding is, 21, 184.
notice by publication is, when no personal judgment is taken, 51, 217.
to require physicians to be examined before they can practice medicine, or to cease to practice until examined, etc., is due process of law, 52, 218.
proceeding to remove officer upon hearing is, 99, 225
a bill in equity to vacate judgment for tort committed under military authority is, 96, 97, 225.
ad quod damnum proceeding is, 95, 224.
a law validating contracts is, 93, 224.

DUE PROCESS OF LAW — continued
service on one member of firm to bind firm and member served is, 72, 221
control of insurance company by state auditor held to be, 83, 223.
law requiring railroads to be fenced is, 61, 219
proceedings adapted to the nature of the case and enforced in the usual methods are, 68, 221
punishment for contempt is, 69, 221
authority to corporation to improve water-way and take tolls does not deprive persons of property without due process of law, 65, 220.
exercise of eminent domain when properly guarded is, 34, 215; 59, 219
law forbidding use of engines on streets is. 60, 219
equitable proceeding to determine title to real estate is, 74, 221.
effect of irregular verdict in criminal trial, 76, 222
trial for felony on information is, 77, 222
law requiring locomotive engineers to be examined, and requiring railroad company to pay, held valid, 53, 218.
railroad's liability for injury to employees held valid, 54, 218.
a law fixing rates on railroads held invalid, 55, 218
other laws on same subject sustained, 57, 218, 58, 219.
a law fixing charges for warehouses sustained, 56, 218.
plenary suit and trial by jury not necessary, 21, 184
does not imply that all trials in state court be by jury, 36, 215
in respect to taxation, what is, 38, 39, 40, 41, 42, 43, 44, 216, 45, 46, 47, 48, 49, 50, 217
prohibition does not refer to erroneous decisions of courts, 70, 221.
nor to prohibit passage of statute of limitations, 71, 221
change of sentence cannot be made by court, when, 29, 186.
a fugitive from justice who is kidnaped and taken back for trial is not deprived of liberty without due process of law if trial is in other respects regular, 94, 224
restraining importers from suing to recover excessive duties does not violate this clause, 28, 185, 186
prohibition extends to the government, 24, 185.

DUTIES —
synonymous with imposts, 3, 16.
a state law requiring importers to take out license held to be a duty on imports, 3, 102.
stamp tax on bills of lading of interstate commerce held to be a duty, 4, 103
tax on auction-sales of imported goods a duty, 6, 103
definition of, 1, 102
power to lay is a branch of the taxing power, 2, 102.

DUTY ON EXPORTS —
what constitutes, 10, 103.

ELECTIONS FOR SENATORS AND REPRESENTATIVES
time, place and manner of holding (art. I, sec. 4, clause 1), 9.

ELECTORS —
not uniform in different states, **2**, 4
for president and vice-president, how appointed (art. II, sec 1, clause 2), 110.
clause 3 altered by twelfth amendment
time of choosing, how determined clause 3, 111.

ELEVATORS AND WAREHOUSES —
state may fix rates for, **157**, 39.

EMINENT DOMAIN —
the power is an incident of sovereignty the fifth amendment is a limitation on the power, **7**, 183
proceedings to ascertain compensation may be made to conform to state laws, **8**, 183
right of, exists in general government, **18**, **19**, 59
state laws cannot interfere with exercise of, by general government, **10**, 183
state cannot exercise over property of general government, **9**, 183.
railroads may be authorized to exercise right, **4**, 182.
United States may authorize a railroad company to exercise in territory **5**, 182.
general government may exercise by requiring removal of bridges over navigable waters without compensation, **6**, 182 183
when taken by government during war, compensation must be made, **19**, **20**, 184.
taking need not be actual and literal to entitle the owner to compensation, **18**, 184
property of incorporated company may be condemned, **11**, 183.
franchises are property, and stand on same footing as the property of individuals, **12**, 183.
where use only is impaired no compensation can be enforced, **13**, 183
when taken because obnoxious to public health, morals or policy, compensation must be made, **14**, 183.
common-law principles were intended to be established beyond legislative control by fifth amendment **17**, 183
compensation against government may be enforced in court of claims, **15**, 184
compensation need not be made in advance, **16**, 184.
corporate property subject to, **204**, **205**, 92
there is nothing in nature of contract between owner and state in condemnation proceedings, **94**, 76.
when ample provision is made for inquiry as to damages, etc., held due process of law, **34**, 215, **59**, 219.

EQUAL PROTECTION OF LAWS —
what term implies, **35**, 215
a statute which authorizes greater number of challenges to juror in city than country is not in violation of this provision, **82**, 223.
see further on subject, **79**, **81**, 222, **82**, **83**, **84**, **85**, **86**, **87**, 223, **89**, **91**, 224.

ESTATES OF MINORS —
laws relating to may be amended without impairing obligation of contract, **92**, 75

EXCISE —
what is, **4**, 16.
income tax is, **2**, 6

EXPORTATION —
when it begins, **100**, 31, **11**, 103.

EXPORTS —
money used in business of, when subject to taxation, **7**, 103.
when prohibition to tax begins, **11**, 103
stamp on snuff, etc, intended for exportation held not export duty, **7**, 62

EX POST FACTO LAW —
defined, **24**, **25**, **26**, **27**, 66
does not apply to civil proceedings, **29**, 66.
relates to criminal cases only, **30**, **31**, 67
act of Colorado held to be, **32**, 67
a statute increasing punishment held to be, when **33**, **34**, 67.
a statute changing place of trial held not to be, **35**, 67

EXTRADITION —
included in treaty-making power **14**, 116
courts must take notice of treaty in respect to, **24**, 174.
person extradited cannot be tried for an offense different from, **24**, 174.
purely a national act, **1**, 130
on demand of foreign government a state has no right to surrender fugitive under, **13**, 162.

FAITH AND CREDIT —
to be given to records of other states, intent of section, **29**, 155, **33**, 156
record when duly authenticated imports absolute verity **30**, 155
process or appearance must be shown or judgment is a nullity, **31**, 156
but where it is shown record is conclusive, **32**, 156
wills, probate of, **34**, 156
attachment laws, effect of title acquired under, **16**, 153.
laws of states, effect to be given in other states, **16**, 154.
must be proved **17**, 154.
this section establishes a rule of evidence rather than of jurisdiction, **18**, 154
statutes which restrict this clause are unconstitutional, **19**, 154
statute of limitations held valid as applied to judgments of other states **21**, 154
jurisdiction must be shown to have attached to the court rendering the judgment, **22**, **23**, **24**, 154, **25**, **27**, 155
record as to jurisdictional facts may be contradicted, **28**, 155.

FEDERAL COURT—
processes of authority of congress to regulate, **17**, 58.

FEDERAL GOVERNMENT—
agencies of, how far exempt from state control, **36**, 175.

FELONIES ON HIGH SEAS—
define and punish (art. I, sec. 8, clause 10), 48.

FERRIES—
states have power to establish and regulate, **36**, **37**, 199.

FLORIDA—
statute regulating telegraph, invalid, **111**, 38

FORCES—
land and naval: to make rules for (art. I, sec 8, clause 14), 53.

FOREIGN GOVERNMENTS—
recognition exclusively a political act, **3**, 118.

FOREIGN SOVEREIGN—
as such, may sue in federal court, **120**, 135.

FOREIGN STATE—
Cherokee Nation is not, **121**, 135

FOURTEENTH AMENDMENT—
object of, **1**, 210.
gives citizenship, and denies to state power to withhold, **2**, 210.
first clause, intent of, **3**, 210
not designed to interfere with police power of state, **4**, 210.
second clause is a prohibition on states, **5**, 211
refers to citizenship of United States only, **18**, 212.
voting privilege of not protected by this amendment, **19**, 213.
is a limitation on state action only, and does not apply to acts of individuals, **100**, 225
applies to all agencies of state, legislative, executive or judicial, **101**, 225
constitution is broader than the statute, **102**, 225.
doctrine of Slaughter-House Cases, that amendment applied primarily to the freedmen adhered to, **103**, 225.
whether to any other purpose, *quære* **103**, 225
doctrine as it existed prior to amendment, stated, **104**, 225
"civil rights bill held valid **2**, 227
does not confer on congress the power to enact laws for suppression of crime within a state, **3**, 227

FREEDOM OF PRESS—
congress cannot limit circulation of printed matter except through mails, **7**, 179.

FUGITIVES FROM JUSTICE, **2**, 159, 160.
what acts are included in clause, **1**, 160
party demanded must be charged with crime within the state, **2**, 160; **11**, 162
and must have fled from state, **11**, 162.

FUGITIVES FROM JUSTICE — continued
general government cannot coerce submission, 3, 160
habeas corpus will lie to inquire as to legality of arrest, 4, 160
federal courts have not exclusive jurisdiction in such case, 5, 160, 8, 161.
duties and powers of executive on whom demand is made, 6, 7, 160
duty to surrender not absolute, 12, 162
authorities on subject not harmonious, 10, 162
state cannot surrender fugitive upon demand of foreign government 13, 162.

FUGITIVES FROM LABOR, 3, 162, 163.
persons referred to were African slaves, 3, 163.
object of clause was to secure to slaveholders their property, 5, 163.
states cannot control subject, 6, 7, 163.

GENERAL GOVERNMENT —
supremacy of, 1, 170.
right to protect this supremacy, 2, 170.
powers may be exercised through physical force, 3, 170.
when conflict, state laws must yield, 4, 171
relation of state and nation compared, 4, 171.
their unity consistent with national supremacy, 11, 172

GOVERNMENT BONDS —
capital of bank invested in, not subject to state tax, 13, 19
a tax on, is a tax on the power of the government to borrow money, 15, 19

GOVERNMENT SECURITIES —
state cannot tax, 1, 17, 12, 19.

GUARANTY TO THE STATES —
1 Republican form of government 2 Protection from invasion. 3. Against domestic violence (art. IV, sec 4), 168
congress is to decide what government is legal, 1, 168.
may delegate this power to president, 2, 168.
decision when made is conclusive, 3, 168
unauthorized bodies assuming to legislate, how reached, 4, 168.

HABEAS CORPUS —
a generic term, 10, 60
the writ here referred to is *ad subjiciendum* 9, 60
suspension of privilege does not suspend the writ. 1, 59
suspension, congress alone can authorize, 11, 60.
president cannot suspend. 11, 60.
president cannot authorize suspension, 11, 60.
congress sole judge of necessity of suspension, 12, 61
congress may authorize president to suspend 13, 61
will lie to protect persons under provisions of fifth amendment, 2, 182.

HABEAS CORPUS — continued.
state court has no jurisdiction in, when person held under authority of United States, **6**, 60
power of congress to pass statute may be inquired into, **7**, 60
constitutionality of law may be inquired into under proceedings, **8**, 60.
writ lies to inquire into sentence by military commission, **7**, 190.
legality of arrest upon requisition may be tested by, **8**, 161, **10**, 162
when supreme court of United States may issue, **4**, 60, **72**, **73**, 145, **74**, **75**, **76**, **77**, **78**, 146
state courts cannot extend writ beyond limits of state, **79**, 146
how term is understood **5**, 60
no law of congress prescribes cases in which it shall issue, **5**, 60.
when usages of war cannot sanction suspension of, **2**, **3**, 60.

HIGH SEAS —
crimes committed on, defined, **1**, 48, 49
words do not include navigable rivers, **2**, 49.
robbery on, is piracy, **3**, **6**, 49
words defined, **7**, 49

HOMESTEAD ON PUBLIC LANDS —
protection to settlers on, **12**, 58

HOUSE OF REPRESENTATIVES —
how composed (art. I, sec. 11, clause 1), 4
who may vote for members of, **1**, 4
when not the final judge of its own powers and privileges, **8**, 12.
vacancies in, how filled, **1**, 6
speaker of, how chosen (sec 11, clause 5), 6.

IMMUNITIES —
protection of, **9**, 57.

IMPOSTS —
definition of, **1**, 102.
synonymous with duties, **3**, 16.
state forbidden to levy (art I, sec 10, clause 2), 102
this clause is an exception to the acknowledged power of states to levy taxes, **2**, 102.

INDIANS —
land-grants from not recognized, **14**, 232

INDIAN TRIBE —
tribal relation and rights, **141**, 37
when tribal or other relations exist, is wholly a political question, **144**, 37

INDICTMENT —
the requirement is jurisdictional, **39**, 187.

INDICTMENT BY GRAND JURY —
does not prevent courts from punishing for contempt, or disbarring an attorney, **37**, 187

INFAMOUS CRIME—
offense constituting, defined, **30, 31**, 32, 34, 186.
what changes in law this clause of fifth amendment produced, **33**, 186
what is not, **35, 36**, 186, 187.

INHABITANT—
meaning of term, **1, 2**, 5

INJUNCTION—
will not lie to restrain president in performance of official duties, **5**, 118, **12**, 122
will not lie from federal to state court, **13**, 122.

INSOLVENT LAWS OF STATE—
assignees under of insolvent corporation cannot be sued in United States court, when, **80**, 131

INSPECTION, **15, 16, 17, 18, 19, 20**, 104.

INSURRECTION—
liability of persons engaged in suppression of, **7**, 231.

INTEMPERANCE—
laws to promote must not regulate interstate commerce, **131**, 36.

INTOXICATING LIQUOR—
congress may exclude from Indian country, **109**, 33–37.
congress may prohibit sales of to Indians, **143**, 37.
tax on wine and beer manufactured out of state, when void, **67**, 27
a state tax on persons selling liquors not manufactured in state, when invalid, **81**, 29
brought from a sister state may be taxed, **9**, 103
right to sell not an immunity of citizenship, **22, 23**, 213
right of state to prohibit manufacture and sale of, **24, 25, 26**, 214.
manufacture for export may be prohibited by state, **169**, 40
sale by importers in original package not subject to state laws, **177**, 42
government license to sell does not confer right to sell in violation of state laws, **28, 30**, 198.
excise tax on, no bar to state laws, **5**, 16
government license to sell subject to state laws, **34**, 175.

IOWA—
mandamus may issue in to compel levy of tax by municipal corporation, when, **44**, 176

JUDGMENTS—
congress may annul when, **20**, 21.
in United States courts, marshal appointed to levy tax in satisfaction of **22**, 233.

JUDICIAL POWERS—
how derived, **8**, 120

JUDICIAL QUESTION—
violation of treaty is not, **99**, 133.

JURORS, SELECTION OF —
law of congress prohibiting discrimination on account of color, etc., is authorized by thirteenth and fourteenth amendments, **98**, 225

KENTUCKY AND VIRGINIA
compact between, **31**, 175

KING CAN DO NO HARM —
is a maxim not recognized in this country, **23**, 233

LANDS —
government, within state, when not ceded by state government, holds as ordinary proprietor, **4**, 54
government can only obtain control under article I, section 8, clause 17, by cession from or ratification of state, and acceptance of congress, **5**, **6**, 55

LEGAL TENDER —
state forbidden to make (art. I, sec. 10, clause 1), 63
making bank-notes legal tender does not affect the validity of bank, **8**, 64
power of congress to declare what is is considered settled, **1**, 46
constitution only recognizes gold and silver coin as such, **6**, 46

LEGAL TENDER ACTS (**17**, 19) —
unconstitutional as to prior debts, **3**, 46.
above overruled, **4**, 46.
decisions on, **3**, **4**, 46, **4**, **5**, 230; **18**, 19, **6**, 231
act making treasury notes such, not applied to payment of state taxes, **4**, 195; **39**, 176.

LICENSE —
tax on tow-boats held void **77**, 28
cities may demand for sale of beer, **57**, 26
government, to sell intoxicating liquors, does not confer on licensee power to sell in violation of state law, **28**, **30**, 198.

LIMITATION —
statutes of held valid as applied to judgments of other states, **21**, 154.

LIMITATION LAWS —
no clause in constitution restrains state from enacting, **31**, 198
retrospective, congress may enact, **38**, 235

LOTTERY —
law authorizing may be repealed without violating contract, **91**, 75
charter held a contract, cases distinguished, **118**, 79

MAINE —
law of, respecting navigation of Penobscot river, valid **22**, 21.

MANDAMUS —
president is not subject to in relation to official duties, **5**, 18
United States court cannot issue to compel secretary of treasury to pay out money, when **15**, 122
will not lie from state court to United States officer, **13**, 232.

MARITIME LAW—
subject to modification by congress, 37, 235.
MARITIME LIEN—
state legislatures cannot create, 38, 126
MARTIAL LAW—
cannot be declared in anticipation of threatened invasion, 3, 60.
MARYLAND—
law of, regulating storage of tobacco, held valid, 74, 28.
MASSACHUSETTS—
law of, when applied to telegraphs, held invalid, 35, 175
MIGRATION OR IMPORTATION OF PERSONS—
this refers to African slaves, 2, 3, 59
MILITARY TRIAL—
usage of war cannot sanction, where federal authority is unopposed, 2, 60
MILITIA—
article II, Amendments, the right here secured is inherent, 1, 180.
to provide for calling (art. I, sec. 8, clause 15), 53.
congress may authorize president to call, 1, 3, 53
power conferred to be exercised in emergency 2, 53.
decision of president as to emergency final, 1, 2, 53
order for calling, given to chief executive of state, 5, 54.
refusal to obey call may be punished, how, 6, 54
MINNESOTA—
statute to regulate inspection of cattle held invalid, 175, 41
MISSISSIPPI—
statute respecting colored passengers on railroad valid, 178, 42
MISSOURI—
constitutional provision held a bill of attainder 23, 66.
law to establish a loan office held to authorize emission of bills of credit and invalid, 10, 64

NATIONAL BANKS—
shares subject to state tax, 7, 18
conditions on which shares may be taxed, 8, 18
limitation on state in taxing, 14, 15, 16, 17, 173
shareholders may be taxed by state, 13, 14, 196
tax on shares, bank may be required to pay, 9, 18.
state laws for taxing, when valid, 12, 232
taxation of, state cannot discriminate against, 19, 173.
assessment of by state held valid, 7, 171
not subject to state usury laws, when, 13, 172
subject to state legislation, how and to what extent, 6, 171; 36, 175, 176
NATIONAL CURRENCY—
power of congress to provide for, 18, 19.

NATURALIZATION—
alien thereby becomes a citizen of United States and of any state in which he resides, **10**, 44
only foreign-born are subjects of, **8**, 44
state has concurrent authority on subject to what extent, **1**, **5**, 43, **6**, 44.
state laws on subject cannot contravene laws of congress, **1**, 43.
power of held to be exclusive in congress, **3**, 43, **7**, 44.
above commented on and explained, **4**, 43.
evidence of, **12**, 44.
effect of, **13**, 44
of Indians, **11**, 44
state cannot make subject of foreign government a citizen of United States, **9**, 44.

NAVIGABLE RIVERS—
wholly within a state, subject to state laws, **26**, 22.

NAVIGABLE WATERS—
state may authorize dam across until congress acts, **125**, 35
also may authorize a bridge over, **126**, 35
regulation of commerce on, see pages 20, 21, 22, 23, 24, 25.

NAVIGATION—
steamboat, state legislation regulating rights of passengers on, held void, **163**, 39
state cannot obstruct streams when, **41**, 24
on high seas, national in character, **39**, 24.
bridge obstructing, **20**, 21.

NAVY—
to provide and maintain (art. I, sec 8, clause 13), 53.
what government is authorized to do, **1**, 53
jurisdiction, extent of, **2**, 53

NEGROES—
not included in the term "We, the people," **2**, 1.

NEW STATES—
rights of in navigable waters, **3**, 164
right of eminent domain passes to, **4**, 164.
prior laws of congress for territory have no force in, **5**, 164.

NEW TRIALS—
number may be limited, **88**, 224.

NEW YORK—
statute concerning masters of vessels, etc, held valid, **173**, 41.
statute imposing tax on passengers from foreign state void, **75**, 28
act granting exclusive right to navigate Hudson river invalid, **36**, 23.

NUISANCE—
bridge that obstructs navigation is, **23**, 21
if constructed in accordance with laws of the state and of congress, is not, **30**, 22

OATH OF OFFICE—
state officers may prescribe further oath, 177.
OBLIGATION OF CONTRACTS—
congress cannot impair when made under its authority, **27**, 233.
ORDINANCE OF SECESSION—
effect of, **32**, 234
OREGON—
provisions respecting navigable waters in act admitting state, **34**, 23
ORIGINAL PACKAGE—
goods in, when not subject to tax, **13**, 104.
when may be taxed, **14**, 104.

PARDONS—
meaning of word, how determined, **13**, 113
effect of, **14**, 114
proclamation of, includes aliens, **16**, 114
conditions may be annexed, **17**, **18**, 114
issuance of cannot be enjoined, **20**, 114
president cannot be enjoined from issuing, **20**, 114
exclusive power in president, and cannot be controlled by congress, **24**, 115
effect of proclamation of December 25, 1868, **14**, 114.
includes aliens, **16**, 114
unnecessary to prove adhesion to the United States, when, **15**, 114
may be conditional, **17**, **18**, 114
must be pleaded and proved to be of avail in any given case, **19**, 114.
PARTNERSHIP—
service on one member of firm is sufficient to bind firm and the member served, **72**, 221
PATENTS—
how subject to state control, **33**, 175.
PENNSYLVANIA—
law respecting trials by court-martial in militia valid, **3**, 53
PENSION MONEY—
embezzlement of by guardian may be punished under law of congress, **15**, 58
PEOPLE—
we the, **1**, 1
government emanates from, **3**, 1
of the United States, synonymous with citizen, **4**, 1.
constitution ordained and established by, **5**, 2.
competent to vest power in congress, **1**, 15
PERSONS—
corporations are, **62**, 219
corporations of one state are not persons within another state, **63**, 220
power of state over corporations as such, **64**, 220.
Chinese are, **66**, 220.

PETITION—
right of **2**, 179, **8**, 179, **9**, 180.

PILOTAGE—
state law regulating, **14**, 17
states may legislate on, **43**, 24, **44**, 24, **45**, 24, **47**, 25.
law of state held not to be a tonnage tax, **12**, 106
law of Louisiana regulating, held void, **46**, 24
law of Georgia regulating held void, **48**, 25.

PIRACY—
robbery on high seas is, **3**, **6**, 49

PLEADINGS—
need not set out specific article of constitution involved, **96**, 133

POLICE POWER—
limit of, **105**, 32.
extent of power **106**, 32
legislature cannot barter it away **199**, 91; **200**, **203**, 92.
laws for control of corporations how far police power, **201**, 92
what is **202**, 92.
in exercise of the manufacture of intoxicating liquors may be prohibited by state, **198**, 91
right to legislate as to health, life and safety of citizens, **122**, 34; **123**, 35
law respecting vessels and passengers valid **173**, 41
inspection of cattle designed for meat law relating to held invalid, **175**, 41.
regulations may be made for good order, peace and protection of community, **23**, 197
local improvements for health or prosperity of community, **24**, 198.
protection of lives, health and morals, **26**, **27**, 198
oils, inspection and gauging of, **25**, 198.
over internal commerce **29**, 198
prohibiting use of engines on streets is a valid exercise of, **60**, 219.
ordinance fixing time for closing laundries and forbidding work on Sunday is **67**, 220.
not limited by fourteenth amendment, **90**, 224.

POLITICAL DEPARTMENTS OF GOVERNMENT—
relation of Indian tribes to government a question for, **142**, 37.

POLITICAL POWERS—
decisions in regard to, when made, are conclusive, **3**, 168

POLITICAL QUESTIONS—
when there are two opposing governments, which is legal is a political and not a judicial question, **17**, 232
not cognizable by courts, **16**, **17**, 123.

POLYGAMY—
may be punished, **4**, 179
article I of amendments does not protect **5**, 179.
Idaho statute concerning, valid **6**, 179

PORTS OF DIFFERENT STATES—
no preference (art. I, sec. 9, clause 6), 62
POST-OFFICES AND POST-ROADS—
article I, section 8, clause 7, 47
congress may designate what shall be carried in mails and what excluded, 4, 17, 5, 6, 48
congress cannot forbid transportation by other methods, 6, 48
implied powers under this clause, 2, 47
powers conferred not confined to instrumentalities used when constitution was adopted, 3, 47
POWERS OF GOVERNMENT—
how distributed, legislative, executive and judicial, 15, 232.
PRACTICE—
evidence in criminal case witness in his own behalf subject to cross-examination as other witnesses, 122, 136
PRESIDENT AND VICE-PRESIDENT—
election of (article XII, Amendments), 207 208
presidential electors' functions 1, 208.
fraudulent voting for, punishable by state, 2, 208
PRESIDENT OF UNITED STATES—
executive power vested in (art II, sec 1 clause 1), 108
authority of, when beyond the reach of other departments, 1.
as commander-in-chief (art. II, sec 2, clause 1) 112
may form military government, 8, 114
and establish provisional courts, 12, 113
may allow added rations, 9, 113
may declare blockade, 10, 113
cannot establish prize courts, 11, 113.
must observe laws of nations, 3, 112.
establish rules etc 4, 112.
call out militia, 1, 112
decision of, conclusive when, 2, 112
may direct movements of forces, 5, 113.
subjugate enemy, 6, 113
employ secret agents 7, 113.
political powers of, 6, 109
suspension of *habeas corpus* when power may be exercised by, 8, 110
not liable to answer to writ of *habeas corpus*, 9, 110
power to adjourn congress 2, 117.
power to waive exemption of United States from suit, 20, 233.
pardoning power of, cannot be controlled by congress 23, 115
appointment of officers, nomination is the sole act of the president, 6, 116; 3, 109.
dates from when, 4, 109
when complete, 7, 116
power to appoint includes power to remove 8, 116.
when discretion of president as to ceases, 5, 109
appointment to office, has power to supersede, when, 9, 116.

PRESIDENT OF UNITED STATES—continued.
appointment of ambassadors, etc., in what sense the words are used, **11**, 116.
discretion of, when not subject to control, **6**, 118
not subject to injunction or *mandamus*, **5**, 18, **12**, 122.
when acts of heads of all departments may be controlled by courts, **2**, 108.
how acts of departments are construed, **7**, 110
decision of, conclusive when, **1**, 117
cannot suspend writ of *habeas corpus* except as authorized by congress, **17**, 60
has authority to protect justices of supreme court, **7**, 118

PRIVATE BOOKS—
persons subject to penalties cannot be compelled to produce, **4**, 181.

PRIVILEGE OF CITIZENS—
the citizens of each state are entitled to all the privileges and immunities of citizens in the several states (art. IV, sec. 2, clause 1), 156
statute of limitations discriminating against non-residents, held not to violate clause, **12**, 158.
Texas cattle; laws restraining not in violation of clause, **13**, 158.
what privileges and immunities are meant; such as are common to all, **3**, 156
those which are fundamental, **15**, 158
what are not privileges within meaning of clause—
marital rights are not, **4**, 157.
right of women to practice law is not, **5**, 157.
citizens of one state are not invested by this clause with any interest in common property of another state, **7**, 157.
right of suffrage is not, **22**, 159
citizens of a state, who are, **1**, 156.
women are, **21**, 159
corporations are not within meaning of this clause, **18**, 158.
corporation cannot emigrate, **17**, 158
state may discriminate in favor of its own, **19**, 159
but the terms imposed must be consistent with the constitution, **20**, 159
object of section, is directed against state action, **16**, 158
it secures rights but does not create them, **14**, 158
secession, did not sever the Union of the states, **9**, 157.

PUNISHMENT—
one cannot be added after the other, **51**, 188

QUARANTINE—
states may regulate, **165**, 40

RAILROAD—
right of way over public domain in territory must be respected by state, **32**, 175.

RAILROAD — continued.
effect of consolidation on chartered rights, **127, 128**, 80, **169, 170, 171**, 87
contract with elevator held valid, **156**, 38.
state may fix rates for, **159, 160, 161, 162**, 39.
state cannot control rates on commerce interstate, note to **159**, 39; **162**, 39
power of state over rates, **155**, 38
double liability for stock killed held valid, **61**, 219 **89**, 224.
classification of for fixing rates held valid, **91**, 224
chartered by territory, rights to be preserved by succeeding state, **42**, 236

RAILROAD ENGINEERS —
examination of, **168**, 40.

REBELLION —
states in, were not out of Union, **5**, 168
debts in aid of, unconstitutional, **29**, 234.
how far laws of states in, were valid, **30**, 234.
power of congress to suppress, **1**, 44.

RELIGION —
protection in worship not guarantied by constitution, **3**, 179.

RELIGIOUS LIBERTIES —
not protected by constitution, this is left to the state, **39**, 235.

REMITTITUR —
after verdict, held not to be a re-examination, **20**, 193.

REVIVAL OF CAUSES —
after trial by jury in state court and vacating of verdict the cause may be removed, **17**, 193
no invasion of state domain, **91**, 132

REPRESENTATIVE IN CONGRESS —
qualification of (sec 11, clause 1), 5.
state can fix no additional qualification, **3**, 5.

REPRESENTATIVES AND DIRECT TAXES —
apportioned (art. I, sec 11, clause 3), 5

RETROSPECTIVE LAWS —
when may and when may not be enacted, **10**, 57.

REVENUE —
bills for raising, must originate in house (art. I, sec. 7, clause 1), 13
bills for senate may amend (clause 2), 13
internal, law valid, **9**, 16.

REVENUE OFFICERS —
right of, to compel production of bonds and papers, **9**, 181.
distress warrants issued by solicitor of treasury valid, **7**, 181.

RIGHTS —
protected by congress, **9**, 57.

SALARIES—
of government officers, not subject to state taxation, 38, 176.
SEARCH-WARRANTS—
probable cause, 1, 180
oath or affirmation does not apply, when, 8, 181.
SECESSION—
did not sever the union of states, 9, 157.
SEIZURES—
United States courts have exclusive jurisdiction in cases of, 7, 121.
SENATE—
vice-president to preside (art I sec 111, clause 4), 8.
sole power to try impeachment, 8.
SENATORS—
classification of, 3, 7.
seat of, how vacated, 1, 7
SLAVERY—
abolished (art XIII, Amendments) 208
scope and objects of the amendment, 1, 208; 3, 4, 5, 209
main purpose of, 2, 208
letter and spirit of, applies to all cases within its purview, 2, 208
section 5519 Revised Statutes not within scope of amendment 6, 209
sale of slaves prior to adoption of amendment, consideration for may be enforced 7, 209
SOVEREIGN POWERS—
the federal government possesses, 43, 236
SOVEREIGNTY—
of state and nation. distinct that of nation will be regarded as supreme until question is settled, 35, 234.
SPIRITS—
distilled, tax on, valid, 12, 17
STATE—
not subject to be sued in United States courts (art. XI, Amendments), 200
cases in which officers of state may be sued, 5, 6, 201, 7, 8, 9, 10, 11, 12, 202 13, 203
when not maintainable against state officers, 14, 203. 15, 16, 18, 204
how to determine when state is a party within meaning of the eleventh amendment 17, 18, 204.
may waive exemption, 19, 20, 204.
to prevent suit the interest of state must be divested, 30, 206.
where state is a member of a corporation, the corporation may be sued, 31, 206. 32, 207
Juan Madrazo's Case, 29, 206.
object of provision, 28, 206
counties are not within the prohibition, 26, 205.
not liable for acts of its officers 36, 235
consent may be upon such terms as the state sees fit to impose, 21, 204.

STATE — continued
may be withdrawn, 21, 204, 23, 205
consent given makes jurisdiction complete, 22, 204
creditors cannot use the name of the state whereof they are citizens to maintain a suit against another state, 24, 205
original jurisdiction of supreme court is the only exception to the prohibition 27, 205.
powers of, before adoption of articles of confederation, 18, 232.
STATE CONSTITUTIONS —
adoption of, a political question not cognizable by courts, 16, 123.
STATE COURTS —
may enforce laws of congress when, 19, 232.
STATE GOVERNMENTS CONFLICTING —
which is legal is a political and not a judicial question, 17, 232.
STATE LAWS —
construction of, by state court, conclusive, 39, 141.
STATE LEGISLATION —
must be with regard to its own jurisdiction, 20, 154
STATE, POWERS OF —
state has all the power of British parliament when not restrained by constitution, 22, 197.
retain all powers of legislation not taken away by constitution of state or United States, 38, 199
the sovereign powers of remain unaltered except so far as they were granted to the United States by the constitution, 50, 200
the powers thus retained were not necessary to be defined, 51, 200.
are not limited by tenth amendment, 1, 194
over property of corporation after charter expires, 33, 199.
state may refuse to allow aliens to take by descent, 35, 199.
to establish and regulate ferries, 36, 37, 199
may exclude foreign corporations, 39, 40, 199
or may make them corporations of state, 46, 200.
may limit charges by railroads, 42, 199.
may enact bankrupt laws, 43, 199
restricted as to discharge of bankrupt, 44, 200
may use military force to quell domestic insurrection, 45, 200.
may tax a railroad used as a post-road, 2, 194, 9, 195.
private corporations and all trades may be taxed by state, 3, 194.
right of taxation is a part of the sovereignty of a state, 7, 8, 10, 11, 195
may tax shareholders in national bank, 13, 14, 196
may exclude foreign corporations, 39, 199
may exempt property from taxation, 6, 10, 11, 195
may punish fraudulent voting for presidential electors, 2, 208.
STATE SOVEREIGNTY —
limited by constitution of United States, 79, 146
cannot extend beyond limits of state, 79, 146.
cannot interfere by *habeas corpus* where person is held by United States court, 80, 146.

STATE STATUTES—
construction of by state court conclusive, 41, 199.

STATE TRIBUNAL—
must conform to supreme law, 10, 172.

STATUTE—
when it takes effect, 1, 2, 3, 14.

SUFFRAGE—
each state regulates, 3, 4.

SUITS PENDING—
congress can exercise no power over, 16, 232.

SUITS IN REM—
effect of; no personal judgment can be rendered in, when, 100, 134.

SUPREME COURT—
original jurisdiction (art. III, sec. 2, clause 2). 136
this is not exclusive, 1, 2, 136
jurisdiction conferred by this clause does not authorize the issuance of *mandamus*, 3, 4, 136.
in cases in equity, 7, 137
by a state against a citizen of another state, 8, 137
none to cause levy of municipal tax to pay judgment, 9, 137.
in case of consuls, not exclusive 11, 137
may be exercised without enabling act and how, 10, 12, 137
may be between state and one of its citizens, 13, 138
extends to removal of obstructions from navigable river running between states, 15, 138
to determine boundary between states 16, 17, 138
when state has interest it must be substantially affected, 18, 138.
penal laws of state will not be enforced 19, 138.
appellate jurisdiction (art. III, sec 2, clause 2), 122, 22, 23, 24, 25, 26, 139
jurisdiction is regulated by congress, 22, 139
appellate jurisdiction from state court not limited by amount in controversy, 23, 25, 139
Northwest Territory, writ of error does not lie to courts of, 24, 139
mere fact that constitution is involved gives no right to review judgment of district or circuit court, the amount involved controls, 26, 139
error to state court· pleading· particular section of constitution relied on need not be pleaded, 38, 141.
not sufficient to aver that law of state is unconstitutional, it must refer to United States constitution, 61, 144
right under constitution of United States must be specially set up and claimed in state court, 62, 144
state and federal questions combined, rule in, 40, 141, 44, 142.
rules governing question of writ of error 46, 142
federal question must be necessary to determination, 47, 142
state constitution, laws in violation cannot be reviewed by United States supreme court on writ of error to state court, 53, 143, 58, 144.

SUPREME COURT — continued
jurisdiction on writ of error to state court, does not lie when law of a territory is called in question, 43, 144
cannot review because judgment of state court refuses to give effect to contracts; a law of the state must be called in question, 64, 144
where no right is claimed under constitution or laws of United States proceedings are not subject to review by United States court, 59, 144
supreme court cannot go out of record to examine questions under writ of error, 60, 144.
decisions by state courts declaring its own statutes unconstitutional, not subject to review, 69, 145
when it will examine on writ of error the judgments of state court, 6, 121 9, 10, 122, 101, 110, 134, 111, 135 6, 136, 137, 23, 27, 28, 29, 139, 30, 31, 32, 33, 140, 34, 35, 36, 37, 38, 39, 40, 41, 141, 42, 43, 44, 45, 46, 47, 48, 142, 49, 50, 51, 52, 143
cases in which a writ of error will not lie to state court, 11, 122, 53, 54, 55, 143, 56, 57, 58, 59, 60, 61, 62, 63, 64, 144, 65, 66, 67, 68, 69, 70, 71, 145, 82, 83, 84, 147
cases in which *habeas corpus* will lie from, 72, 73, 145, 74, 76, 77, 78, 81, 146
no appellate jurisdiction in cases confided to it by law, 73, 145
has no jurisdiction to enjoin president as to official duties, 12, 122.
jurisdiction of, derived immediately from constitution, 9, 120.
final appellate tribunal 12, 172
justices of, are judges of circuit courts, 1, 119
justices are entitled to protection against assault, and the president may authorize persons to so protect them, 7, 118.

SUPREME LAW —
state tribunals must conform to, 10, 172
treaties are, 21, 173
state laws, when enacted with assent of congress become, 30, 175
when acts of congress are not, 12, 172
when act of congress and treaty conflict, the act is the supreme law, 23, 174.

SUPREMACY —
of general government, 1, 170.

TAX —
direct, how laid, 1, 6.
how limited, 3, 6
how many kinds, 1, 6.
a capitation tax is a direct tax, 1, 61.
direct taxes, limited how, 2, 61
tax on bank circulation not a direct tax, 4, 61.
tax on alien is not a direct tax 5, 62
income, not a direct tax but a duty or excise, 2, 6.
on bank circulation, not a direct tax, 3, 6
succession tax, not direct, 4, 6
direct on District of Columbia valid, 7, 16, 9, 55.

TAX — continued.
succession, valid, **13**, 17
on employments, valid, **15**, 17.
on state banks, held valid, **6**, 16
on government securities by state, invalid, **1**, 17
United States stocks as capital of state banks, not subject to state tax **2**, 17, **3**, 18.
franchise of bank may be taxed, **4**, 18.
state may tax United States bonds, when, **11**, 18
shares in national bank may be taxed by state, **6**, 18.
extent of power of congress to lay and collect, **1**, 16
power not exclusive in congress. **2**, 16.
exemption from, see CONTRACTS.
lands purchased from United States under statutory exemption are protected by constitution, **158**, 85

TAXATION —
power in congress, how limited, **10**, 17.
power to lay imposts and duties is a branch of taxing power, **2**, 102.
occupation cannot be taxed where business itself could not, **98**, 31.
limitation of power in states **8**, 16.
state cannot tax passengers from foreign ports, **52**, 26; **75**, **76**, 28.
state cannot tax vessels plying between states, **55**, 26.
capitation tax on persons leaving a state unconstitutional, **2**, 156.
state tax on railroad gross receipts held invalid, **85**, 29.
franchises conferred by congress not subject to state taxes, **90**, 30; **40**, 176
a state law taxing persons taking orders for sale of goods of other states held void, **92**, 30
state tax on transportation company, when invalid, **86**, 29.
on peddlers, when void, **65**, 27
auctioneers, when void, **66**, 27.
on wine and beer manufactured out of state, when void, **67**, 27
on vessel engaged in commerce, when void, **61**, 26
on transportation interstate in any form, invalid, **87**, 30
on salaries of United States officers is invalid, **38**, 176
upon receiving and landing passengers and freight. void. **79**, 28
on goods coming from another state because of such fact, is invalid **80**, 28.
on persons selling liquors not manufactured in state, when invalid, **81**, 29.
state may tax money or exchange used in commerce, **53**, 26.
products of agriculture, **54**, 26
its own citizens on business, **56**, 26
sale of beer, **57**, 26
shareholders in national bank, **13**, **14**, 196.
railroad used as a post-road, **2**, 194.
private corporations and all trades, **3**, 194
imported merchandise, when not in hands of importer, **21**, 197.

TAXATION — continued
a railroad chartered by congress and built in part by subsidies from United States, 45, 177
money earned in commerce after it is so earned, 85, 29.
auction sales of products of other states, 8, 103
money used for investment in exports, when subject to tax, 7, 103
tax on spirituous liquors brought from a sister state, valid, when, 9, 103
when vessels may be taxed by state, 9, 106
state tax on vessels engaged in commerce, valid, when, 82, 29
state may tax its citizens on debts due to them from citizens of other states, 258, 101
gross receipts of railroad may be taxed by state, when, 58, 26.
right of state to exercise, 7, 171
to regulate appraisement of property for, 7, 171.
to regulate correction of errors, 7, 171.
to tax carrying companies, 20, 197
state laws in relation to, have no extraterritorial effect, 20, 151
power to impose is incident to sovereignty, 7, 8, 9, 10, 11, 195
right of states in regard to, how subject to federal control, 12, 196.
on exports, when prohibition begins, 11, 103
by state, limited to property within its jurisdiction, 19, 197.
original package, when goods in not subject to, 13, 104.
when made subject, 14, 104
how imposed by state on national bank, 14, 15, 16, 17, 173
limitations on power of cities to tax private improvements, 17, 195; 18, 196
state may exempt property from, 6, 10, 11, 195, 15, 196.
when legislature may commute taxes, 21, 233.
stipulation in charter of railroad to pay *bonus* on earnings valid, 64, 27
when state cannot tax bonds of a consolidated railroad, 31, 234
what methods constitute due process of law, 38, 39, 40, 41, 42, 43, 44, 216.
unequal taxation not restrained by federal constitution, 39, 216.
nor double taxation, 40, 216
a form of regulating commerce, 87, 30
land of Wea Indians in Kansas not subject to, 25, 171.
TELEGRAPH COMPANIES —
congress may control, 110, 33.
communications are both postal and commercial, 96, 31.
may be taxed by states, 89, 30, 97, 31.
where messages are sent interstate, state cannot regulate delivery, 166, 40
cannot be taxed by state on messages sent interstate, 95, 31
may be taxed on messages wholly within state, 95, 31.
when state laws concerning, invalid, 18, 175.
TENNESSEE —
law taxing sleeping-cars held invalid, 83, 29
law taxing "drummers" held invalid, 83, 29

TEXAS CATTLE —
transportation of, **158**, 39.
possession of, **170**, 40

TERRITORY —
power to acquire, **6**, 30
power of congress to dispose of and make all needful rules and regulations for (art. IV, sec 3 clause 2). 164
power of congress, how derived, **1, 2, 3**, 165
to make and amend laws for, **4, 5**, 165
may regulate suffrage **6**, 165
is general and plenary, and arises under this clause **7**, 165
over the territory is the combined power of state and federal governments, **29**, 121, **9**, 166
cannot be interfered with, **11**, 166.
to grant franchise for railroad in, **14**, 166.
may be acquired by war, **1**, 164
admission as a state the compact is binding upon the people without their consent **2**, 164
acquired by cession, must be held subject to constitution and laws of government to which it is ceded, **3**, 230
relation to United States **15**, 167.
laws of when acquired remain in force until congress forms a new government, **18**, 167
words "states of the Union" held to include, **20**, 173.

TERRITORIAL LEGISLATURES —
power of, **8, 12, 13**, 166
to annul marriage contract, **17**, 167.

TERRITORIAL COURTS —
suits in, regulated by congress, **73**, 130.
not continued under state, **11**, 231

TONNAGE DUTIES —
state forbidden to lay (art. I, sec 9, clause 3), 105
definition of. **1, 2**, 105
when not held to apply to wharfage regulations **3, 4, 5, 6**, 105.
when applied to quarantine laws and effect of, **7**, 106
tax on vessels held to be a tonnage tax **10, 11**, 106
vessels may be taxed by state how **9**, 106
when pilot laws held not to be a tonnage tax **12**, 106

TRANSPORTATION —
what it implies, **79**, 28

TREASON —
against United States (art. III, sec 3, clause 1), 148.
levying war, what constitutes **1, 2**, 148, **3, 4, 5, 6, 7, 8, 9, 10, 11**, 149
assemblage with treasonable design is not enough; it must be in force, **12, 13**, 149.
but arms are not indispensable, **14**, 149.

TREASON — continued
WHO ARE GUILTY OF —
all who perform essential military parts or perform any part, however minute, **15**, **16**, **17**, 149
persuading men to enlist is not, unless there is actual enlistment, **18**, **23**, 150
OVERT ACT — PRACTICE —
must be specially charged and proved, **19**, 150
cannot be by constructive presence, **20**, 150.
the part taken in war constitutes the overt act, **21**, 150
procuring provisions, when an overt act and when not, **22**, 150
consists of what, **24**, **25**, 150.
who can be guilty of, **27**, 150; **29**, 151
alien can be, when, **28**, 150
confession out of court, effect of proof, **26**, 150
congress to declare punishment of (art. III, sec. 3, clause 2) 151
forfeiture of land effect of, **1**, **2**, 151
no attainder to work corruption of blood, intent of provision, **3**, 151
pardon effect of, on forfeiture, **4**, 151

TREATIES —
manner of giving effect to, **1**, 115.
are laws of the land **2**, 115
are supreme law, **21**, 173
may be made with Indians, **3**, 115, **25**, 174.
power to make extends to extradition, **13**, 116.
what it includes and how conferred, **14**, 117

TREATIES AND LAWS OF CONGRESS —
have same force, **29**, 174
not suspended when in conflict with law of congress, **23**, 174
when treaty conflicts with act of congress, the congressional act is the supreme law, **23**, 174

TREATY —
indemnity under, congress may name commission to determine, **13**, 58
violation of, not a judicial question, **99**, 133.

TREATY POWER —
extent of, **20**, 173

TRESPASS IN FOREIGN COUNTRY —
action for, may be maintained in United States courts, when and where, **109**, 134

TRIAL OF CRIMES BY JURY —
article III, section 2, clause 3, 147.
this guaranty extends to prosecution in time of war **1**, 147.
cases arising in land and naval forces are not within it **2**, 147
a citizen not connected with the army or navy is within the protection of the clause, **3**, 147
trial, meaning of word, **5**, 148
plea of not guilty, effect of, **4**, 147
crime, definition of and how interpreted, **7**, 148.
extent of provision, **8**, 148.

TWICE IN JEOPARDY—
object of provision forbidding, **42**, 187.
recovery of penalty in a civil suit no bar to prosecution criminally for same act, **43**, 187.
a *nol. pros* after jury impaneled and witness sworn is a bar, **50**, 188
case stated where restriction applies, **54**, 189
want of jurisdiction, or defective indictment or mistrial, no bar to subsequent trial, **47**, 188
nor does a jury sworn and discharged before arraignment, **48**, 188.
nor discharge of jury because of sudden or uncontrollable emergency, **49**, 188
mistrial or failure of jury to agree does not bar subsequent prosecution, **45**, 188
nor does discharge of jury because of the insanity of a juror, **46**, 188
unlawful cohabitation and adultery, conviction for one bars the other, **44**, 187.

UNCONSTITUTIONAL LAW—
is no law, **26**, 233.

UNION PACIFIC R. R. CO.—
act of congress to establish sinking fund to pay debts of, valid, **14**, 58

UNITED STATES—
'of the United States' meaning of term, **7**, 2.
a government of the people, **9**, 3
corporate powers, **10**, 3.
not a league, **11**, 3
constitution of, supreme over all, **11**, 3.
government is supreme, **8**, 57
its nationality and powers, **12**, 3.
a new political body, **13**, 3
a firm union is essential to liberty, **8**, 2.
implied powers are not excluded, **48**, 200.
may create corporation **49**, 200.
cannot be sued, **42, 43, 44, 45**, 126
judicial power of, does not extend to any suit in law or equity, commenced or prosecuted against one of the United States by citizens of another state or by citizens or subjects of any foreign state (art. XI, Amendments), 200
prior to adoption of this amendment a state could be sued by citizen of another state, **1**, 200
this amendment is retrospective, **2**, 201
does not apply to controversies between states, **2**, 201
states cannot be sued in United States courts by holders of its bonds, **4**, 201.
stock of, not subject to state tax, **10**, 18.
state law impairing the rights of persons to litigate in courts of, held void, **179**, 42

USURY—
as applied to existing contracts see **67, 71**
national banks are not subject to state usury laws, **13**, 172.

VESSELS, ENROLLMENT OF—
law held not to apply to rivers wholly within a state, 26, 22

VESTED RIGHTS—
nothing in constitution of United States to prohibit a state from divesting vested rights, 95, 76
may be divested by state if no contract is impaired, 83, 84, 85, 87, 71

VIRGINIA—
law making coupons legal tender for taxes sustained, 9, 64.

VIRGINIA AND KENTUCKY—
compact between, 31, 175

VOTERS—
protection of, 1, 9

VOTING—
privilege of not protected by fourteenth amendment, 19, 213
the fifteenth amendment does not confer the right to vote upon any one, 1, 227.
the fifteenth amendment simply prevents discrimination in the right to vote, based on "race, color or previous condition of servitude," 1, 3, 227

WAR—
power to declare (art. I, sec 8, clause 11), 49.
is exclusively in congress, 3, 4, 50
what constitutes, 5, 50
civil, exists when, 2, 49.
property of citizen taken must be paid for, 8, 50.
declaration of, what is, 9, 51.
effect of, does not confiscate property, 10, 51.
what is public war, 11, 51
what is solemn war, 12, 51
rules for capture on land and water, 21, 22, 23, 52.
effect of capture, 24, 52
liability of captors, 25, 52.
rights of members of nation declaring it, 13, 51.
implied powers in, 15, 51
to acquire territory is, 16, 51.
to guard against renewal of conflict, 17, 51
to legislate for prosecuting, 18, 51.
to permit commercial intercourse with enemy, to what extent, 19, 20, 52
acts of exempt from liability, 16, 58

WEIGHTS AND MEASURES—
to fix the standard of (art. I, sec. 8, clause 5), 46.

WHARFAGE—
instrument of commerce, 147, 148, 37.
rights of cities to regulate, 3, 4, 5, 6, 105